Integrating Micro-Credentials With AI in Open Education

Gürhan Durak
Balıkesir University, Balıkesir, Turkey

Serkan Çankaya
İzmir Democracy University, Turkey

IGI Global
Scientific Publishing
Publishing Tomorrow's Research Today

Vice President of Editorial Melissa Wagner
Managing Editor of Acquisitions Mikaela Felty
Managing Editor of Book Development Jocelynn Hessler
Production Manager Mike Brehm
Cover Design Phillip Shickler

Published in the United States of America by
IGI Global Scientific Publishing
701 East Chocolate Avenue
Hershey, PA, 17033, USA
Tel: 717-533-8845
Fax: 717-533-8661
E-mail: cust@igi-global.com
Website: https://www.igi-global.com

Library of Congress Cataloging-in-Publication Data

Names: Durak, Gürhan, 1984- editor. | Cankaya, Serkan, 1979- editor.
Title: Integrating micro-credentials with AI in open education / edited by Gürhan Durak, Serkan Cankaya.
Other titles: Integrating micro-credentials with artificial intelligence in open education
Description: Hershey, PA : IGI Global Scientific Publishing, 2025. | Includes bibliographical references and index. | Summary: "This edited volume is designed to be a pivotal resource for those at the forefront of educational innovation, including technology enthusiasts, online course designers, and institutions actively engaged in the cutting-edge implementation of micro-credentials. Our aim is to offer an extensive exploration of micro-credentials, not only in terms of their design and development but also in their application across various educational and professional contexts"-- Provided by publisher.
Identifiers: LCCN 2024038679 (print) | LCCN 2024038680 (ebook) | ISBN 9798369354889 (hardcover) | ISBN 9798369354896 (paperback) | ISBN 9798369354902 (ebook)
Subjects: LCSH: Artificial intelligence--Educational applications. | Microcredentials. | Open educational resources.
Classification: LCC LB1028.43 .I58634 2024 (print) | LCC LB1028.43 (ebook) | DDC 371.33/43--dc23/eng/20240925
LC record available at https://lccn.loc.gov/2024038679
LC ebook record available at https://lccn.loc.gov/2024038680
ISBN:979-8-3693-5488-9
eISBN:979-8-3693-5490-2

British Cataloguing in Publication Data
A Cataloguing in Publication record for this book is available from the British Library.

Table of Contents

Detailed Table of Contents

Micro-credentials are transforming digital education by offering flexible, targeted, and accessible ways for learners to acquire and demonstrate skills. Micro-Credentials are small, specialized certifications following a short learning experience, which recognize the knowledge or skills someone acquires in specific subjects or fields. Since 2011, when the Mozilla Foundation introduced the Open Badges system, the use of Micro-Credentials has grown and is now widely employed by all digital platforms offering distance education (Coursera, edX, Udacity, etc.) to certify learners' knowledge, and they are recognized as additional qualifications by employers. Micro-Credentials are becoming increasingly popular as an alternative or complementary form of education, particularly in fields where skills evolve rapidly, such as technology and digital skills, and represent a significant advancement in the field of non-formal and lifelong learning.

MOOCs and micro-credentials make high-quality education accessible to people from all backgrounds, leveling the playing field and promoting equitable access to skills and knowledge. These concepts are closely tied to global competitiveness by enabling individuals and economies to rapidly adapt to evolving skill demands, access cutting-edge knowledge, and foster innovation. This chapter aims to incorporate both concepts considering the sections and intersections from a global perspective to shape the future of education and bridge the skills gap. When the term makes it more important than ever to be competitive in a global sense, the chapter emphasizes to be aware of the competencies that the institutions have. Designing the skill-oriented online course contents would be a motivation source within the concept of internationalization. The recommendations for the stakeholders given in the frameworks that triggered the quality assurance, internationalization, and global competitiveness.

This chapter offers a guide to designing and developing microcredentials, highlighting their key characteristics, benefits, and theoretical foundations. It explores core design elements, including the value for higher education providers and learners, assessment methods, partnerships, infrastructure, and financial planning. The development process encompasses market analysis, governance and accreditation, and strategies for integration and transferability. Quality assurance and continuous improvement are emphasized, focusing on delivery methods, technological platforms, assessment strategies, and alignment with labor market needs. The chapter stresses defining specific skills, providing evidence of achievement, and engaging internal and external stakeholders. Implementation strategies cover promotion, marketing, leveraging partnerships, and effective branding. Practical insights are provided through case studies and examples of successful programs. The chapter concludes with a discussion on future trends and challenges, offering a forward-looking perspective on microcredentials.

Distance learning has become more popular during the COVID-19 years and the micro-credentials (MCs) has been accepted widespread as an alternative to traditional degree programs. Higher Education Institutions play a critical role in the creation of MCs, taking into account the needs of learners and industry requirements. Hence, it is important to understand and develop this field due to the complexity and diversity of factors that influence the structuring of MCs in distance learning. Moreover, different stakeholders have various influences and priorities on the design, implementation, and adoption of MCs. Therefore, this chapter aims to explore the factors influencing the structuring of MCs in distance learning, considering multiple stakeholders' perspectives. Using the MICMAC method, factors are categorized into influential, key, dependent, and autonomous groups, offering a comprehensive factor map. The chapter concludes with recommendations for effectively structuring MCs in distance learning, addressing both challenges and opportunities to enhance their impact and integration.

This chapter, according to the authors, explores the transformative potential of Generative Artificial Intelligence (Gen-AI) in the design, development, and delivery of micro-credentials, aimed at enhancing efficiency and accessibility in education. By analyzing research from a pilot study conducted at a private university, the chapter delves into AI-driven approaches that improve learner engagement, course completion rates, and learner satisfaction. It addresses the role of AI in personalizing learning experiences, supporting learner success, and ensuring equitable access to educational opportunities. The chapter further examines how AI-powered learning designs can streamline the creation of micro-credentials and deliver them on demand. Additionally, it offers insights into the ethical considerations of integrating AI in education, providing recommendations for educators, technologists, and policymakers on leveraging AI to democratize education effectively.

The global trends in higher education are moving toward skill-based credentials. Micro-credentials and digital badges are the buzzwords to demonstrate the acquisition of industry-specific skills of the candidates. Integration of AI in open education could enhance the deployment of personalized higher education for everyone and can address several challenges related to retention, assessment, and credibility of micro-credentials in open pedagogy. Timely sharing of these credentials across a wide range of international systems through AI will widen the prospects of continuing education and employment for learners. The Middle East is making timely responses to the digitization of education systems. According to some market forecasts, the market for AI tools in the Middle East region will reach nearly eight billion dollars by the year 2027. There are several ethical dilemmas surrounding use of AI in education and micro-credential programs such as data privacy, biasness and fairness, equity in access, accountability, transparency, cultural sensitivity and the impacts on traditional education models and current review therefore stresses the need for comprehensive ethical guidelines and policies in the Middle East region rather blind adoption. The book chapter offers an analysis of the existing scenario, emerging opportunities and challenges and makes specific recommendations to expand and integrate AI tools in open education in the Middle East region.

AI-enhanced micro-credentials can optimize learning pathways, improve access to education, and boost workforce skills, according to this report. It addresses traditional education delivery model issues and an increasing requirement for lifelong learning. An AI expert system tool called EDMENTUM validates credentials and customizes learning routes in the quasi-experimental study on AI-enhanced micro-credentials and learning efficiency. Discussing micro-credentials history and integration with AI, case examples show their practical use. The document also emphasizes linking education with industrial demands and addressing fairness, access, data privacy, and security issues for policy and practice. AI-enhanced micro-credentials have many benefits, but careful design and execution are needed to maintain data transparency, trust, and management.

Micro-credentials, which signify the attainment of particular skills, have attracted considerable interest due to their adaptability, alignment with industry requirements, and congruence with lifelong learning endeavors. While encompassing various types, micro-credentials are often linked with Massive Open Online Courses (MOOCs). Despite the increasing number of MOOCs and the rising enrollment of students acquiring micro-credentials, there is a challenge regarding the recognition of these micro-credentials within formal educational contexts. At this stage, the Flipped Classroom (FC), which involves both online and in-class phases, could present a suitable approach for integrating micro-credentialing into formal educational contexts under the guidance of course instructors. Accordingly, the aim of this chapter is to advance a conceptual proposal for acknowledging and recognizing MOOCs as a source of micro-credentials within the context of higher education environments while accounting for the intricate interactions among micro-credentialing, MOOCs, and the FC approach.

The mission of this chapter is to provide a comprehensive overview of the importance and potential of microcredentials in advancing education and professional practice in Gerontology, emphasising the need for an adaptable, competency-oriented educational approach in this vital field. The following objectives are proposed: to reiterate the value of microcredentials as a strategic educational resource to meet the specific demands of Gerontology in higher education and to emphasise the need for a continued commitment to educational innovation and interdisciplinary collaboration to prepare trained gerontologists to meet the challenges of the Decade of Healthy Ageing 2021-2030.

In the rapidly evolving landscape of education, the integration of Artificial Intelligence (AI) has emerged as a transformative force, promising to revolutionize the way to teaching and learning. This book chapter presented the applications of AI tools in online education in these online learning environments, the interaction between learners and instructors significantly influences satisfaction and learning outcomes. Therefore, understanding how AI impacts this interaction is crucial for identifying potential challenges and ensuring safe and effective learning environments. Also, this book chapter presented the case studies, success stories, and benefits of AI applications in online education. This chapter will be useful for educational institutions to improve their efficiency with their stakeholders and learners.

Preface

Micro-credentials have emerged as a transformative force in modern education, providing an adaptable, competency-based approach that addresses the limitations of traditional degree structures and the need for skill-specific, lifelong learning pathways (Ward et al., 2023). The integration of artificial intelligence (AI) within micro-credential systems offers an unparalleled opportunity to enhance the flexibility, scalability, and personalization of these credentials, aligning education with rapidly evolving industry demands and learner expectations. Together, micro-credentials and AI are reshaping the educational landscape, opening doors for diverse learning environments and creating pathways to career development, which are adaptable, scalable, and widely accessible across varied socio-economic and cultural contexts (Durak & Çankaya, 2024).

At its core, micro-credentialing allows learners to acquire, validate, and showcase specialized skills and knowledge without committing to long-term degree programs. This approach has been particularly effective in addressing skill gaps in sectors such as technology, healthcare, and education, where evolving demands necessitate ongoing professional development (Gerbaudo et al., 2021). As traditional educational structures struggle to keep up with the need for specific skill acquisition and rapid retraining, micro-credentials offer a more flexible and efficient solution. Studies indicate that professionals benefit from these short, targeted learning experiences as they offer direct application to specific job functions or industry needs (Cheng et al., 2020). For example, micro-credentials support continuous skill development and goal-setting, thereby enhancing motivation and enabling learners to demonstrate their competencies effectively to employers (Gerbaudo et al., 2021).

The incorporation of AI into micro-credentialing frameworks amplifies the adaptability and effectiveness of this approach. AI-powered systems facilitate a personalized learning experience, where adaptive algorithms can tailor learning content to the specific needs, preferences, and progress rates of individual learners (Carter & Youssef-Morgan, 2022; Durak et al., 2024). These adaptive systems enable real-time monitoring of student progress and provide instant feedback, allowing learners to identify and address gaps in their knowledge. In higher education, AI-driven analytics support educators in tracking and analyzing student engagement, which improves learning outcomes and optimizes content delivery methods. Additionally, AI applications, such as chatbots and virtual teaching assistants, have become valuable tools in providing scalable support to learners, making it possible to offer consistent, high-quality educational experiences across various platforms (Ma et al., 2023).

In the context of open education, micro-credentials supported by AI address some of the most persistent challenges in lifelong learning. The growth of Massive Open Online Courses (MOOCs) and micro-learning strategies has created more accessible, modular learning opportunities, but these formats often lack the depth of learner engagement necessary for sustained knowledge retention and practical skill application. Research indicates that AI can fill these gaps by enhancing learning environments with interactive, responsive elements that promote engagement and ensure that learners retain and apply their knowledge effectively (Qian et al., 2021). For example, during the COVID-19 pandemic, educational institutions globally leveraged AI-based micro-learning systems to deliver timely, adaptive learning experiences that helped learners maintain academic continuity despite disruptions (Cheng et al., 2020).

Micro-credentialing also holds significant promise in addressing the skill demands of the workforce by providing credentials that are both industry-recognized and competency-based. In Canada, for instance, government policies have increasingly supported micro-credentials as a strategy to bridge the skill gaps in human capital markets. Employers benefit from this system as it allows them to identify candidates who possess specific skills rather than relying solely on traditional degree qualifications. This shift aligns with global hiring trends, where competencies and hands-on experience are increasingly valued over theoretical knowledge (Ward et al., 2023).

As educational technology continues to evolve, the future of micro-credentials appears increasingly entwined with AI capabilities. The potential of AI to support ongoing skill development, credentialing, and career advancement is evident in areas such as skill profiling, predictive analytics, and automated assessment (Shamir-Inbal & Blau, 2022). Skill profiling enables AI systems to analyze an individual's competencies and provide recommendations for tailored micro-credential pathways. Such profiling aligns educational offerings with career goals, creating a more seamless transition from education to employment (Ward et al., 2023). Furthermore, predictive analytics allow for the early identification of learning challenges and can assist educators in implementing timely interventions, ultimately supporting higher completion rates and more successful learning outcomes (Carter & Youssef-Morgan, 2022).

By aligning education with real-world skill demands and integrating powerful AI tools, micro-credentials provide a pathway to an inclusive, adaptable, and efficient learning system. The shift from traditional, degree-centric models to skill-based learning is a response to the demands of a fast-paced, globalized economy, where adaptability and continuous learning are paramount. The research and applications discussed in this book underscore the transformative potential of micro-credentials and AI, suggesting a future where education is more equitable, accessible, and directly linked to individual career advancement and societal progress.

The primary objective of this edited reference book, Integrating Micro-Credentials with AI in Open Education, is to provide readers with a comprehensive and up-to-date exploration of emerging technologies, methodologies, and applications within the realms of micro-credentials and artificial intelligence in education. Our intention is to serve as a guide for technology enthusiasts, online course designers, and educational institutions aiming to leverage these transformative tools in supporting skill-based learning and professional development. Moreover, this book aspires to be a valuable resource for educators, researchers, instructional designers, workforce development professionals, and anyone with an interest in the growing potential of micro-credentials and AI to create accessible, personalized, and relevant learning experiences.

The target audience for this book is broad, encompassing professionals and researchers from various educational and technological domains with a specific interest in micro-credentials and artificial intelligence. Educators, administrators, and learners seeking to understand the integration of micro-credentials in open education will find this book to be a valuable source of the latest advancements in the field. Readers will gain both theoretical insights and practical applications drawn from the expertise of leading researchers and organizations actively involved in micro-credentials and AI in education.

This book is organized into a series of chapters, each dedicated to a distinct aspect of micro-credentials and AI integration, providing in-depth exploration of essential topics. The chapters include:

Chapter 1: The Rise of Micro-Credentials: A New Certification System for Career Development

Authors: Gürhan Durak, Serkan Cankaya

This chapter provides a foundational exploration of micro-credentials, positioning them as a flexible, skill-focused alternative to traditional certification systems. Durak and Cankaya discuss how micro-credentials allow learners to demonstrate specific competencies relevant to industry needs, facilitating career development without the lengthy commitments of traditional degrees. The chapter also addresses the challenges related to standardization, quality assurance, and international recognition, setting the stage for readers to understand the transformative role of micro-credentials in today's workforce.

Chapter 2: Micro-Credentials Establish New Realities in Digital Education

Authors: Antonios Stamatakis, Ilias Logothetis, Konstantinos Petridis, Michail Kalogiannakis, Nikolas Vidakis

This chapter examines the rise of micro-credentials within digital education environments, highlighting how they create new opportunities for flexible and accessible learning. The authors analyze the growth of digital platforms, such as Coursera and edX, that employ micro-credentials to validate learning outcomes. The chapter provides insights into how these credentials cater to rapidly evolving skill demands, establishing micro-credentials as critical tools for lifelong learning in a digital age.

Chapter 3: Triggering Competitiveness From A Global Perspective: MOOCs and Micro-Credentials

Authors: Nazire Burcin Hamutoglu, Mesut Aydemir, Clifford De Raffaele

Exploring the synergy between MOOCs and micro-credentials, this chapter presents a global perspective on how these models can democratize education. By lowering barriers to high-quality content, MOOCs and micro-credentials empower individuals worldwide, fostering global competitiveness and equitable access to knowledge. The authors offer a framework for understanding how MOOCs and micro-credentials can drive skill acquisition and create a level playing field in a globalized economy.

Chapter 4: Designing and Developing Microcredentials

Authors: Stacey L Rosenberg, Toni Clayton

Rosenberg and Clayton provide a comprehensive guide to designing effective micro-credential programs. They delve into the critical components of micro-credential development, including assessment methods, quality control, and alignment with industry needs. Through case studies, the chapter illustrates best practices for educators and institutions, offering practical insights into creating micro-credentials that are valued by learners and employers alike.

Chapter 5: Exploring Factors Influencing the Structure of Micro-Credentials in Distance Learning from Multiple Stakeholders' Perspective

Authors: Hulya Yilmaz, Seda Yanik

This chapter explores the factors shaping micro-credential structures in distance education, with a focus on various stakeholder perspectives. The authors employ the MICMAC method to categorize these factors, providing a thorough analysis of the complex interactions that influence micro-credential design and implementation. This chapter is invaluable for educational leaders seeking to align micro-credentials with both learner needs and industry standards.

Chapter 6: Exploring the Potential and Future Directions of Micro-Credentials Through the Scenario Archetypes Method

Authors: Şeyda Kır, Hakan Yıldırım, Aras Bozkurt

Using the Four Archetypes Scenario model—continuous growth, collapse, disciplined society, and transformation—this chapter projects future scenarios for micro-credentialing in education. The authors outline potential paths and challenges, emphasizing the transformative potential of micro-credentials. This analysis provides readers with strategic insights into the evolving role of micro-credentials in higher education.

Chapter 7: Leveraging AI-Managed Learning Analytics and Micro-Credentials for Enhanced Student Engagement

Authors: Semiral Öncü, Merve Çolakoğlu, Harun Cigdem

This chapter discusses the role of AI-managed learning analytics in supporting student engagement through micro-credentials. AI-driven insights into student behaviors enable tailored interventions and real-time feedback, which improve retention and motivation. The authors address potential barriers, such as data privacy and standardization, offering recommendations for effective implementation of AI in learning environments.

Chapter 8: AI-Enhanced Micro-Credentials for Efficiency and Accessibility

Authors: Jonathan JS Kovilpillai, Abtar Darshan Singh, Analisa Hamdan, Kelly McKenna, Fahd Ali Raza

This chapter examines how Generative AI can enhance the design, development, and accessibility of micro-credentials. By examining a pilot study on AI-driven instructional design, the authors illustrate how these technologies increase learning accessibility and effectiveness. Ethical considerations are discussed, providing a balanced view of AI's role in democratizing education.

Chapter 9: Harnessing AI and Digital Tools for Micro-Credentialing in Mathematics Education, Enhancing Learning Outcomes for Students with Learning Difficulties

Author: Georgios Vasileios Polydoros

This chapter focuses on the use of AI and digital tools to support students with learning difficulties in mathematics. Through AI-enhanced platforms like Khan Academy, the chapter demonstrates how micro-credentials can validate learning achievements and support individualized learning. This provides valuable insights for educators working with diverse student needs.

Chapter 10: Micro-Credentials in Vocational and Professional Training

Authors: Tendai Charles, Soha Zoelfakar, Suraj Sebastian

This chapter delves into the application of micro-credentials in vocational training, emphasizing their adaptability to professional development. Through AI-assisted learning and assessment, micro-credentials align with the fast-changing demands of the workforce. This chapter offers a practical roadmap for institutions looking to integrate micro-credentials into professional education.

Chapter 11: Integration of Micro-Credentials with Artificial Intelligence in Open Education: Developments and Challenges for Middle East Countries

Author: Sehar un Nisa Hassan

This chapter provides a regional analysis of micro-credentialing trends in the Middle East, highlighting the role of AI in open education. The author examines how AI-powered micro-credentials can address retention, assessment, and skill validation, presenting recommendations tailored to the region's educational landscape.

Chapter 12: Redefining Learning Pathways: The Impact of AI-Enhanced Micro-Credentials on Education Efficiency

Authors: Andi Asrifan, Sadaruddin Sadaruddin, Ashar Ashar, Jusmaniar Nonci, Trisno Setiawan, Erniati Erniati

This chapter examines how AI-enhanced micro-credentials can streamline learning pathways and improve educational outcomes. By using AI to tailor learning experiences, micro-credentials become more effective and accessible. The authors discuss data privacy and equitable access, offering recommendations for the responsible use of AI in education.

Chapter 13: Flipped Classroom Approach to Incorporate MOOCs as Micro-Credentials into Higher Education

Author: Amine Hatun Atas

This chapter proposes using the Flipped Classroom model to integrate MOOCs as recognized micro-credentials within formal education. Atas presents a conceptual framework for embedding MOOCs within academic programs, bridging the gap between informal learning and formal credentialing.

Chapter 14: Artificial Intelligence in Micro-Credentials for Open and Distance Learning: A Technologically Enhanced Systematic Review

Authors: Siti Haslina Md Harizan, Mohamed Ally

This chapter offers a systematic review of AI's role in micro-credentials within open and distance learning (ODL) environments. By analyzing 46 studies, the authors provide a comprehensive overview of the field, identifying research gaps and future directions for AI-integrated micro-credentials.

Chapter 15: Micro-Credentials in Higher Education and the Learning Compass 2030: Intersections and Reflections

Authors: Ana Galvão, Isabel Chumbo, Eugénia Anes

This chapter explores the intersection of micro-credentials with the OECD's Learning Compass 2030 framework, which supports lifelong learning and adaptability. The authors discuss how micro-credentials can be designed to enhance student well-being, skill acquisition, and career readiness.

Chapter 16: Micro-Credentials in Higher Education: A New Path for Gerontology

Authors: Ana Galvão, Isabel Chumbo, Eugénia Anes

Focusing on gerontology, this chapter highlights how micro-credentials can address specialized educational needs in this field. The authors discuss competency-based learning for gerontology students, emphasizing interdisciplinary approaches and practical skill development for healthcare professionals.

Chapter 17: Applications of Artificial Intelligence Techniques in Education

Authors: Soundarya M, Joel Jebadurai Devapitchai, Krishnakumari S, Thirupathi Manickam

The final chapter provides an overview of AI applications in education, including micro-credentials. Through case studies, the authors illustrate how AI enhances learner engagement and supports flexible, scalable education solutions, positioning AI as an essential tool for modern education.

Chapter 18: Micro-Credentials - Not Working as Advertised

Author: Stephen Murgatroyd

In this chapter, Murgatroyd critically examines the effectiveness of micro-credentials in Canada, questioning their ability to meet labor market demands. This thought-provoking analysis challenges readers to consider the limitations of micro-credentials and their implications for workforce development.

CONCLUSION

The book Integrating Micro-Credentials with AI in Open Education makes a significant contribution to the field of educational technology by addressing the rapidly growing domains of micro-credentials and artificial intelligence. By combining research-based insights with practical applications, this book provides a timely resource that aligns with global shifts in workforce development, education, and lifelong learning. Its chapters explore various aspects of micro-credentialing, including its potential to improve educational accessibility, support personalized learning, and foster career-ready skills, all while addressing the dynamic demands of modern industries.

One of the book's primary impacts lies in its comprehensive exploration of the ways micro-credentials can revolutionize traditional education systems. By focusing on their role as agile, skill-focused alternatives to conventional degrees, it underscores the adaptability and specificity that micro-credentials offer to learners and employers alike. For instance, foundational chapters like "The Rise of Micro-Credentials: A New Certification System for Career Development" provide readers with a clear understanding of how these credentials address skill gaps and offer more relevant career paths for learners across industries. Chapters such as "Micro-Credentials in Vocational and Professional Training" further emphasize how this credentialing system meets specialized training needs, particularly in vocational and technical fields, making learning pathways more flexible and responsive to changing job requirements.

Another notable contribution of this book is its examination of how artificial intelligence enhances the delivery and effectiveness of micro-credentials. Chapters like "Leveraging AI-Managed Learning Analytics and Micro-Credentials for Enhanced Student Engagement" and "AI-Enhanced Micro-Credentials for Efficiency and Accessibility" highlight how AI-powered analytics and adaptive learning systems enable educators to personalize learning experiences based on real-time feedback. These chapters showcase AI's potential to not only improve learner engagement but also provide educators with tools to optimize content delivery and enhance skill acquisition.

Furthermore, the book is enriched by its attention to regional and global perspectives, with chapters like "Integration of Micro-Credentials with Artificial Intelligence in Open Education: Developments and Challenges for Middle East Countries" offering insights into how different cultural and economic contexts are approaching micro-credentials and AI. Such chapters make this book invaluable for educators, policymakers, and researchers seeking to understand the broader impact of these technologies across diverse educational landscapes.

In addition to exploring educational frameworks, this book also addresses practical design and development strategies for micro-credential programs, as seen in chapters like "Designing and Developing Microcredentials" and "Exploring Factors Influencing the Structure of Micro-Credentials in Distance Learning from Multiple Stakeholders' Perspective." These chapters provide readers with actionable strategies and best practices, equipping institutions and instructional designers with the tools to create effective, industry-aligned micro-credential programs that are responsive to learner and employer needs.

This book also challenges readers to consider critical perspectives and potential limitations of micro-credentials, as discussed in "Micro-Credentials - Not Working as Advertised." By addressing both the strengths and weaknesses of micro-credentialing, it fosters a nuanced understanding that is essential for those involved in shaping future educational policies and practices. It serves as a valuable resource for a wide range of stakeholders—including educators, researchers, and industry professionals—who are invested in the future of skill-based, AI-enhanced learning. It outlines the transformative potential of micro-credentials and AI while offering a roadmap for implementing these technologies in ways that are equitable, scalable, and aligned with the needs of modern learners and global industries.

We extend our heartfelt gratitude to the 47 authors from 11 different countries for their invaluable contributions to this book. Their diverse perspectives and expertise have enriched our exploration of micro-credentials and AI in education. To our readers, thank you for joining us on this enlightening journey into the future of accessible, skill-focused learning.

Gürhan Durak
Balıkesir University, Turkey & The Open University, UK (Visiting Scholar)

Serkan Cankaya
Izmir Democracy University, Turkey

REFERENCES

Carter, J. W., & Youssef-Morgan, C. (2022). Psychological capital development effectiveness of face-to-face, online, and Micro-learning interventions. *Education and Information Technologies*, 27(5), 6553–6575. DOI: 10.1007/s10639-021-10824-5 PMID: 35068989

Cheng, Z., Richardson, J. C., & Newby, T. J. (2020). Using digital badges as goal-setting facilitators: A multiple case study. *Journal of Computing in Higher Education*, 32(2), 406–428. DOI: 10.1007/s12528-019-09240-z

Durak, G., & Çankaya, S. (2024). Are alarm bells ringing in academia? ChatGPT as a sample of using chatbots in education. *Turkish Online Journal of Distance Education*, 25(3), 1–17. DOI: 10.17718/tojde.1353737

Durak, G., Çankaya, S., Özdemir, D., & Can, S. (2024). Artificial intelligence in education: A bibliometric study on its role in transforming teaching and learning. *International Review of Research in Open and Distance Learning*, 25(3), 219–244. DOI: 10.19173/irrodl.v25i3.7757

Gerbaudo, R., Gaspar, R., & Gonçalves Lins, R. (2021). Novel online video model for learning information technology based on micro learning and multimedia micro content. *Education and Information Technologies*, 26(5), 5637–5665. DOI: 10.1007/s10639-021-10537-9

Ma, N., Zhao, F., Zhou, P. Q., He, J. J., & Du, L. (2023). Knowledge map-based online micro-learning: Impacts on learning engagement, knowledge structure, and learning performance of in-service teachers. *Interactive Learning Environments*, 31(5), 2751–2766. DOI: 10.1080/10494820.2021.1903932

Qian, Q., Yan, Y., Xue, F., Lin, J., Zhang, F., & Zhao, J. (2021). Coronavirus disease 2019 (Covid-19) learning online: A flipped classroom based on micro-learning combined with case-based learning in undergraduate medical students. *Advances in Medical Education and Practice*, 12, 835–842. DOI: 10.2147/AMEP.S294980 PMID: 34349586

Shamir-Inbal, T., & Blau, I. (2022). Micro-learning in designing professional development for ICT teacher leaders: The role of self-regulation and perceived learning. *Professional Development in Education*, 48(5), 734–750. DOI: 10.1080/19415257.2020.1763434

Ward, R., Crick, T., Davenport, J. H., Hanna, P., Hayes, A., Irons, A., Miller, K., Moller, F., Prickett, T., & Walters, J. (2023). Using Skills Profiling to Enable Badges and Micro-Credentials to be Incorporated into Higher Education Courses. *Journal of Interactive Media in Education, 2023*(1). https://doi.org/DOI: 10.5334/jime.807

Chapter 1
The Rise of Micro-Credentials:
A New Certification System for Career Development

Gürhan Durak
https://orcid.org/0000-0003-2944-3713
The Open University, UK

Serkan Cankaya
https://orcid.org/0000-0002-3951-9809
Izmir Democracy University, Turkey

ABSTRACT

Micro-credentials focus on specific skills and competencies, enabling learners to acquire, demonstrate, and validate expertise in a shorter timeframe. Educational institutions, online platforms, and employers increasingly support these certifications, acknowledging their value for career development, workforce adaptability, and lifelong learning. They empower individuals to continuously update their knowledge and skill sets without the need for long-term study commitments, offering cost-effective, modular, and scalable education solutions. Despite their advantages, micro-credentials face challenges, including standardization, quality assurance, and recognition across countries. As educational institutions, employers, and policymakers work to address these barriers, the potential for micro-credentials to reshape education remains significant. Their rise reflects an era where flexible, skills-focused learning pathways are not only desirable but necessary for meeting the demands of a modern workforce and supporting lifelong personal and professional development.

DOI: 10.4018/979-8-3693-5488-9.ch001

INTRODUCTION

In recent years, micro-credentials have become a highly sought-after and rapidly growing certification model within both education and professional domains. This concept allows individuals to acquire a specific skill set or knowledge base through short-term training programs, validated via digital certificates or badges. Typically provided by online platforms, these certifications enable individuals to adapt to the swiftly changing demands of technology and digital skills in the workforce. Unlike traditional degrees, micro-credentials offer more concentrated, skill-focused, and short-duration educational programs (Oliver, 2019). Structured to foster targeted skills and knowledge, these certifications allow individuals to develop competencies in a condensed timeframe.

The importance of micro-credentials in digitalization and adaptation to technology is becoming critical for individuals' career development. By offering flexibility and accessibility, these certifications enable individuals to gain a competitive advantage in the job market. For instance, a software developer seeking to learn a new programming language does not need to return to university; instead, he/she can join a relevant micro-credential program to quickly acquire this skill and present it to the job market. Therefore, it can be said that such certificates have become an important need, especially today, when digital transformation is accelerating (Brown et al., 2023).

Micro-credentials have also introduced new perspectives into educational systems. Higher education institutions, in particular, are adopting the principle of lifelong learning, creating certification programs that enable students and professionals to continuously develop their skills. These certifications help students acquire in-depth knowledge and skills in specific areas, while also enhancing graduates' competitiveness in the job market (Varadarajan et al., 2023). Micro-credentials can support students to continue their studies in a more flexible way, supporting them to achieve both their academic and professional goals.

During the Covid-19 pandemic, the rapid expansion of online learning platforms led to the broader adoption of micro-credentials. Limited access to physical classrooms made it essential for individuals to acquire skills via digital platforms, further highlighting the importance of micro-credentials and boosting demand for online education. These certifications also provided educational institutions to offer students more diverse and accessible learning opportunities (Flynn et al., 2023).

A primary advantage of micro-credentials is that they can be achieved more quickly and at a lower cost than traditional degree programs. Whereas conventional degrees involve long-term, intensive education, micro-credentials can be completed in a shorter period and impart skills that are immediately applicable in the workplace.

Furthermore, these certifications offer individuals the chance to learn at their own pace and gain essential skills within flexible schedules (Oliver, 2019).

Micro-credentials are also in great demand in the business world. Employers are increasingly seeking employees who can meet rapidly shifting technological and skill requirements. Micro-credentials allow employers not only to verify the specific skills possessed by their employees but also to encourage continuous skill development (Brown et al., 2023). For example, an employer who sees that an employee has a certification in a particular area might assign them new roles that leverage this skill. Thus, micro-credentials enable individuals to make their competencies more visible in the workplace, while employers can better evaluate the skills required in a dynamic business environment. These certifications assist employers in assessing new hires efficiently and determining necessary skills (Pichette et al., 2021).

The growing prominence of micro-credentials has led to their rapid expansion worldwide. For instance, the European Union aims to promote lifelong learning by expanding the use of micro-credentials. Within this framework, the European Commission's strategies target enhancing the availability of these certifications in higher education institutions and fostering stronger links between education providers and industry (Orr et al., 2020; OECD, 2021)

With the increasing pace of digitalization in education (Urfa & Durak, 2017), such certifications are also gaining acceptance rapidly across various countries. For example, countries like New Zealand, Canada, and Australia are integrating micro-credentials into their national education systems, helping individuals to more quickly meet evolving job market requirements (Tamoliune et al., 2023). The educational policies of these countries provide opportunities for micro-credentials to gain international recognition and better align with professional needs.

Micro-Credentials and Digital Badges

Micro-credentials are often confused with digital badges and other alternative certifications, though there are clear distinctions among them. Digital badges can generally be described as visual symbols representing shorter learning experiences or the completion of specific tasks. Digital badges are commonly used in informal learning settings and serve as a means to show that individuals have acquired a particular skill or competency. In contrast, micro-credentials document a more comprehensive educational process and the achievement of competencies (Varadarajan et al., 2023). Therefore, while digital badges may be considered a subcategory of micro-credentials, micro-credentials typically possess a more formal and academic structure (Brown et al., 2023).

Digital badges are awarded at the conclusion of informal learning processes, whereas micro-credentials usually formalize competencies attained through a specific educational program or course. For example, a student who successfully completes a software development course may document these skills with a micro-credential, while digital badges may indicate the acquisition of smaller skill components. In the digital badge system developed by IBM, for instance, digital badges are used to acknowledge the acquisition of minor skills and are often recognized in the workplace. These badges can be integrated with micro-credentials to form part of a larger certification framework (Flynn et al., 2023).

Definitions of Micro-Credentials

Micro-credentials have rapidly become a widely accepted certification model on a global scale. However, the definitions and applications of these certifications vary across regions. While the European Union and other international organizations define micro-credentials as certifications documenting a specific learning outcome, in the United States and other regions, this term is more commonly viewed as a bridge between the professional and academic sectors. One of the most comprehensive initiatives in Europe is the MICROBOL project, supported by the Erasmus+ program. This project aims to develop a micro-credential system aligned with the Bologna process and to facilitate the integration of these certifications into the educational framework (MICROBOL, 2022).

The European Union emphasizes the importance of micro-credentials for lifelong learning and employability, stating that these certifications should document a specific learning process and be recognized by both academia and industry. There is an emphasis on structuring these certifications to address particular workforce needs and ensuring that they are transferable, allowing individuals to use them across different job roles.

In the United States, micro-credentials are primarily developed by industry and technology firms and focus more on specific skills training. Major tech companies such as Google, IBM, and Cisco offer micro-credentials to employees and users, aiming to address the skills gap in the labor market (Oliver, 2019). These certifications enable employees to quickly acquire the skills needed to operate particular technologies or software.

In New Zealand, micro-credentials are generally defined as certifications covering up to 40 credits, designed to document skills that address specific industry or community needs (NZQA, 2023). New Zealand has established various standards to promote the widespread acceptance of these certifications within the workforce and their integration into the national education system. For instance, these certifications often require an assessment process and formal approval (NZQA, 2023).

Micro-Credentials and Higher Education

Higher education institutions are increasingly integrating micro-credential programs into their educational strategies. These certifications aim to provide students with specialized learning opportunities and specific skills that are in demand within the job market, offering a shorter alternative to traditional degree programs. The use of micro-credentials in higher education arises from the need to respond to the rapid digital transformation and evolving demands of the workforce. By developing programs that allow students to acquire a specific skill or competency in a short period, universities seek to enhance their graduates' employability prospects (Brown et al., 2023).

Micro-credential programs align particularly well with universities' lifelong learning and professional development strategies. These programs are popular not only among current university students but also among alumni and working professionals. Certifications offered via online platforms especially provide flexible learning options, allowing working professionals to continue their education alongside existing workloads (Pichette et al., 2021). Prestigious institutions like the Massachusetts Institute of Technology (MIT), for instance, offer various micro-credential programs, enabling students to quickly gain access to specialized skills needed in the job market (Coursera, 2023).

In this context, micro-credential programs developed by universities are typically modular, enabling students to gain a specific skill set that can be integrated into a broader academic program. This allows students to build competencies in a particular area of expertise before advancing to a bachelor's or master's program. Universities also facilitate the recognition of these certifications, making it easier for students to integrate their micro-credential achievements into traditional degree programs (FutureLearn, 2020).

The widespread of micro-credentials has largely been made possible through MOOC (Massive Open Online Courses) platforms. MOOCs provide opportunities for students to take courses from prestigious universities and educational providers worldwide, offering cost-effective, flexible, and accessible learning options. The combination of micro-credentials and MOOCs has created a significant structure in education, emerging as an important alternative for individuals aiming to advance their careers (Brown et al., 2023).

MOOCs, which refer to large-scale, open online courses, are educational programs that reach vast audiences via the internet. They allow individuals to participate in online courses from anywhere at any time and are often free or low-cost. These courses typically include a range of learning materials, such as video lectures, reading materials, online discussion forums, and interactive assessments (Pichette et al., 2021). One of the key advantages of MOOCs is their ability to cater to a large audience while allowing learners to progress at their own pace. Micro-credentials are one type of certification obtained upon completing courses offered through MOOCs.

These platforms offer courses that enable individuals to acquire specific skill sets in a short time, outside traditional educational institutions. MOOCs allow individuals to gain in-depth knowledge in a particular area and apply this knowledge within the professional world. Micro-credentials are issued upon successful completion of MOOC courses, providing a formal record of individuals' educational achievements (Oliver, 2021).

The increasing popularity of micro-credentials on MOOC platforms has led to greater recognition of these certifications by employers. For instance, when a student completes a certification program on platforms like Coursera, edX, or Udemy, this certification demonstrates to employers that the individual has acquired a specific skill. Below, some of the leading MOOC platforms are introduced.

Coursera is a MOOC platform founded in 2012 by Stanford University professors Daphne Koller and Andrew Ng. The platform offers a wide range of courses to millions of users worldwide. By collaborating with businesses and universities, Coursera provides courses and micro-credentials aimed at equipping students with specific skills. The courses on Coursera are generally offered by globally recognized universities and educational providers, covering a broad range of fields, particularly in technology, data science, business, and health. One of Coursera's standout features is the digital certificates and badges awarded to individuals upon successful course completion. Additionally, the platform offers a micro-credential program called "Coursera Specializations." This program provides a series of courses for individuals seeking in-depth knowledge in a particular field, culminating in a digital certificate upon completing all courses. Coursera's micro-credentials are widely recognized and valued by employers worldwide (Coursera, 2023).

edX is a MOOC platform established by Harvard University and MIT (Massachusetts Institute of Technology). Founded in 2012, edX offers online education to millions of students worldwide. Like Coursera, edX collaborates with universities and businesses to offer a wide array of courses. Known for its extensive offerings in STEM (Science, Technology, Engineering, and Mathematics) fields, edX is also a prominent platform for micro-credentials (Oliver, 2021). One of the most popular micro-credentials on edX is the "MicroMasters" program. MicroMasters programs are short, graduate-level courses providing in-depth learning in specific fields. These certifications allow students to advance both academically and professionally. For instance, a student could earn a MicroMasters certificate in data science or artificial intelligence through edX, a credential that is recognized in the job market as a qualification and can also facilitate entry into an academic program (Durak & Çankaya, 2024). edX also offers "Professional Certificate" programs, which are particularly popular among professionals seeking career advancement.

Udemy is another popular MOOC platform where users come together to access and share knowledge. Founded in 2010, Udemy differs from other MOOC platforms in that it allows any instructor to create courses and make them available to students worldwide. Udemy is especially known for its practical and hands-on skill-building courses, offering courses in various fields such as technology, business, marketing, language learning, and personal development. Unlike platforms like Coursera and edX, Udemy is generally not academic or university-focused. However, Udemy courses are designed to help individuals acquire specific skills and are particularly suitable for students looking to gain competency quickly (Oliver, 2021). At the end of Udemy courses, students typically receive a completion certificate. These certificates can be used to document specific skills in the professional world, though they may not be as widely recognized as the formal academic certifications on other MOOC platforms.

As MOOCs continue to play a vital role in enhancing flexibility and accessibility in education, micro-credentials lie at the heart of this process. The micro-credential programs offered by MOOC platforms enable individuals to specialize in specific areas while rapidly acquiring skills needed in the workforce (Chandler & Perryman, 2023). Platforms like Coursera, edX, and Udemy help broaden the reach of these certifications, creating potential for greater educational equity.

The importance of MOOCs and micro-credentials is expected to grow in the future. With the rapidly changing demands of the professional world, individuals need to continuously update their skills, and MOOC platforms provide a quick and effective solution to this need (Pichette et al., 2021). Additionally, universities can use these platforms to reach wider audiences, playing an essential role in promoting educational equity.

The Impact of Covid-19 on Micro-Credentials

The Covid-19 pandemic has driven significant transformations across various sectors, including a major shift in education. With the closure of physical classrooms and the enforcement of social distancing measures, traditional educational methods were rapidly shifted to online platforms (Durak et al., 2020). This transition increased the demand for online learning among both students and professionals, positioning flexible learning models such as micro-credentials as valuable alternatives (Brown et al., 2023).

During the pandemic, universities and other educational institutions were compelled to quickly develop remote learning strategies as physical classrooms became inaccessible (Durak & Çankay, 2020). In this context, micro-credential programs provided an ideal solution, enabling students and professionals to acquire specific skills in a short timeframe. Platforms like Coursera, edX, and FutureLearn expanded their micro-credential offerings, reaching millions of users globally. There was a notable increase in demand for digital skills, data analytics, healthcare, and related fields during this period (Coursera, 2023; FutureLearn, 2020).

Another factor that heightened the importance of micro-credentials during the pandemic was the rapid digitalization within the professional world. At the start of the pandemic, millions of students and workers turned to online education to enhance their skills and gain a competitive edge in the job market. The swift shift towards digitalization in the workplace created a heightened demand for new skills among employees. For instance, remote work models quickly became widespread across many industries. Micro-credentials provided a rapid solution to these needs, enabling individuals to develop competencies in digital skills, data analysis, and remote work management. In particular, micro-credentials have played a critical role for those working in or aspiring to enter the technology sector (Oliver, 2021).

Platforms like Coursera, edX, and Udemy collaborated with universities and educational providers throughout the pandemic, offering digital learning opportunities to individuals worldwide. In 2020, at the onset of the pandemic, Coursera provided free access globally, offering millions the opportunity to engage in online education, with many of these courses transforming into micro-credential programs. Platforms like FutureLearn and edX similarly offered extensive micro-credential programs to students and professionals worldwide. Courses structured to address specific needs saw high demand, particularly in areas such as AI, data science, digital marketing, leadership, and remote work management. These platforms responded to the rapidly changing demands of the professional world, helping individuals acquire new skills to meet these needs (FutureLearn, 2020).

The significance of micro-credential programs is expected to continue post-pandemic. The growing demand for digital skills since the start of the pandemic has led to greater acceptance of these certifications within the workforce. Additionally, individuals' increased experiences with online learning (Durak, 2013) have made short-term, focused learning programs like micro-credentials more appealing. Universities and educational institutions have continued to expand their micro-credential offerings, providing students with opportunities for both academic and professional development (Brown et al., 2023). The professional landscape has also undergone significant changes post-pandemic, with remote work, digital skills, and flexible work models becoming more valued. In response, employers have offered micro-credential programs to help employees quickly adapt to this new work environment and enhance their competencies (Oliver, 2021).

The Impact of Micro-Credentials on the Workforce

Micro-credentials have rapidly become a widely accepted certification model in the labor market. Many employers are increasingly valuing these certifications, which recognize specific skills and competencies, alongside traditional degrees. Particularly in response to the swiftly evolving workforce demands in digitalization and technology, micro-credentials serve as a tool for employers to verify that candidates possess specific skills (International Labour Organization, 2024).

For employers, micro-credentials are valuable as they demonstrate that employees have specialized expertise in a particular field and possess skills they can immediately apply. In today's landscape, where technology and digital skills are gaining importance, employers prefer candidates with micro-credentials in areas like digital marketing, data analytics, and software development. These certifications directly showcase the specific skills of candidates, thus streamlining hiring processes (Flynn et al., 2023). Compared to traditional degrees, micro-credentials document targeted skill sets that can be acquired more quickly, allowing employers to view them as an asset that enables candidates to adapt swiftly to the job market (Brown et al., 2023). For example, major tech companies like Google and IBM offer micro-credential programs to help employees acquire specific programming languages or digital skill sets.

Micro-credentials also stand out as a tool for employers to support the continuous professional development of their employees. Particularly in fast-paced technological and digitalization contexts, it is essential for employees to stay current and acquire new skills. Micro-credentials enable employers to see which areas their employees are developing in and what new skills they have acquired. This presents a significant advantage in enhancing productivity and achieving a competitive edge in the business world (Varadarajan et al., 2023).

Impact on Students' Career Development

Micro-credentials play a crucial role in students' career development. The long-term structure of traditional university programs can sometimes make it challenging for students to keep up with the rapidly changing demands of the job market. However, micro-credentials offer students the opportunity to quickly learn a specific skill and apply it in the professional world. For this reason, many students are integrating micro-credential programs into their education, allowing them to progress faster in their careers (Selvaratnam & Sankey, 2020).

One of the most significant advantages of micro-credentials for students is the competitive edge they provide in the job market. Employers prefer candidates with specialized expertise in certain areas, and micro-credentials serve as a certification of this expertise. Particularly for recent graduates and those looking to change careers, micro-credentials enable them to acquire job-recognized competencies in a short time (Pichette et al., 2021).

In conclusion, micro-credentials present valuable opportunities for both employers and students. Employers can quickly assess the skills of their employees and candidates through these certifications, while students and professionals can advance more rapidly in their careers. As digital skills and technology-based competencies continue to grow in importance, micro-credentials will play a critical role in the workforce.

Challenges of Micro-Credentials

Micro-credentials have gained widespread acceptance as an innovative certification model within both higher education and the professional sector in the fast-evolving field of educational technology. However, various challenges need to be addressed for this new model to reach its full potential. This section focuses on the primary obstacles faced during the implementation of micro-credentials in higher education, especially in terms of technological and bureaucratic barriers.

Challenges in Definition and Recognition: One of the key challenges in implementing micro-credentials is the lack of a clear definition of their relationship with traditional degrees. Some universities and educational institutions struggle to fully recognize micro-credential programs or integrate these certifications into degree programs. This ambiguity creates difficulties regarding how these certifications are perceived within the academic and professional sectors. For example, many employers do not fully understand the value of micro-credentials, limiting their broader acceptance in the workforce (Oliver, 2021).

Technological and Digital Access Challenges: Another significant issue is the limited access to micro-credential programs, especially for students in low-income regions. Although these programs are generally offered online, technological infrastructure deficiencies can prevent some students from fully benefiting from them (Omona & O'dama, 2024). This raises inclusivity concerns and highlights the need for additional investments to expand the reach of these programs.

Bureaucratic Barriers: Bureaucratic obstacles also pose a considerable challenge to the expansion of micro-credentials. There is no standardized approach to the recognition of micro-credentials at international level (Selvaratnam & Sankey, 2020).

This uncertainty complicates the acceptance of these certifications in the workforce and their validity across different countries. For employees holding micro-credentials from other countries, it can be challenging to ensure their acceptance in the local or global job market (Brown et al., 2023). The lack of international recognition may restrict the effective use of these certifications in professional contexts.

Quality Assurance and Accreditation: The success of micro-credentials depends on the presence of quality assurance processes. Ambiguity in quality assurance and accreditation procedures can lead to a lack of confidence among students and employers. When these processes lack transparency, it becomes difficult for the true value of micro-credentials to be understood (Cowie & Sakui, 2022). Differences in quality standards among providers of micro-credentials can also lead to issues with the transferability of these certifications.

In higher education, quality assurance and accreditation processes are generally well-established. For example, the European Credit Transfer and Accumulation System (ECTS) in the European Union allows students to transfer credits gained in exchange programs, enabling them to continue their academic progression without disruption (European Commission, 2015). The ECTS system supports the recognition of courses taken in various institutions and promotes the standardization of education programs internationally. Additionally, it contributes to the assurance of program quality and transparency in accreditation processes.

However, such established systems have not yet been fully developed for micro-credentials. Since micro-credentials typically offer short-term training focused on specific skills, their accreditation and quality assurance processes are more challenging than those of traditional programs. Differences in quality across micro-credential programs provided by various institutions complicate the transferability and stackability of these certifications from one institution to another. Therefore, creating accreditation systems is crucial for micro-credentials to gain wider acceptance and effective utilization.

Standardizing accreditation processes will also enhance the credibility of these certifications among employers. Employers need to be assured of the reliability and validity of the skills that employees or potential hires acquire through micro-credentials. Adapting systems like ECTS to micro-credentials could support their broader acceptance within both educational institutions and the professional world (European Commission, 2020). Thus, improving quality assurance and accreditation processes will further strengthen the future role of micro-credentials.

To extend the reach and acceptance of micro-credentials in the workforce, more collaboration between educational institutions and employers is needed. Additionally, governments and international organizations are working on the recognition and standardization of micro-credentials (European Commission, 2020). Enhancing technological infrastructure will facilitate students' access to these programs and support broader acceptance in the professional sector. While micro-credentials present significant opportunities for higher education and the workforce, overcoming various technological and bureaucratic barriers is essential. Addressing these challenges will allow these certifications to reach wider audiences and gain greater acceptance in the job market.

Lifelong Learning and Micro-Credentials

Lifelong learning refers to the continuous process of self-improvement that individuals undertake throughout their lives. In this process, micro-credentials emerge as a powerful tool, enabling individuals to quickly and effectively acquire the new skills needed over the course of their careers. While traditional degree programs can be lengthy and cover extensive curricula that may delay the acquisition of specific skills, micro-credentials offer focused training on particular skills in a shorter time (Brown et al., 2023). This allows individuals to gain a competitive advantage by acquiring the essential skills required for their careers.

When considered as a support for career development, micro-credentials facilitate individuals' adaptation to the changing demands of the professional world. In an era where digital skills are increasingly prioritized, employees must continually update themselves to adapt to new technologies and digital tools. At this point, micro-credentials enable employees to respond quickly to these changes (Flynn et al., 2023).

One of the greatest advantages of micro-credentials in lifelong learning is their modular structure. This flexibility allows individuals to gain specific skills as needed and continue their learning journey by stacking these certificates. This modular setup is especially beneficial for individuals with demanding work schedules, helping them balance professional and educational responsibilities. Additionally, this structure provides individuals with the opportunity to progress at a personal pace, supporting their advancement toward career goals (Oliver, 2021).

From the perspective of employers and organizational development, micro-credentials offer benefits not only for individual growth but also for employers. Employers increasingly rely on micro-credential programs to enhance organizational efficiency by equipping their workforce with the necessary skills. Recognizing that these certifications reliably verify employees' competencies in specific areas, employers are placing greater importance on these certifications during the hiring process (Galindo et al., 2024).

Future Developments

Micro-credentials are expected to be further supported by increased collaboration in the future. Partnerships, particularly between universities and the professional sector, will drive greater acceptance of these certifications across both academic and professional spheres. Universities can offer micro-credentials as supplements to degree programs or integrate them within these programs, allowing individuals to launch their careers more swiftly. Employers, in turn, can offer these programs to employees as part of continuous professional development, helping them gain a competitive advantage in the job market (Brown et al., 2023). Such collaborations allow universities to tailor programs that align with the skills employers need.

The international recognition and standardization of micro-credentials stand out as critical factors for the future growth of this system. Currently, a lack of international standardization in micro-credential recognition exists. However, this is expected to change in the coming years. In particular, global companies can foster wider acceptance of these skills in the international workforce by recognizing micro-credentials acquired in various countries (European Commission, 2020). This trend would position micro-credentials as a tool to enhance global workforce mobility.

Technological advancements offer significant potential for the verification and reliability of micro-credentials. Innovative digital tools, such as blockchain technology, can safeguard micro-credentials against fraud, increasing employers' confidence in the authenticity of these certifications. The use of such technologies is likely to boost the acceptance of micro-credentials in the job market (Flynn et al., 2023). Blockchain's verification mechanism can establish a trusted bridge between educational institutions and the professional sector, facilitating broader acceptance of this system (Galindo et al., 2024).

CONCLUSION

Micro-credentials hold a significant place as a transformative certification model in education and the workforce. With their short-term and flexible structure, these certifications accelerate the acquisition of new skills, allowing educational systems to meet the evolving demands of the labor market. However, to unlock the full potential of this innovative model, certain structural and strategic steps are necessary.

Collaboration between industry and educational institutions is a key factor in enhancing the effectiveness of micro-credentials. Stronger dialogue and partnership between educational institutions and employers are essential for better addressing the rapidly changing demands of the professional world. Employers' acceptance of skills gained through micro-credentials will encourage wider adoption of these certifications in the workforce. Similarly, educational institutions that work with employers to develop programs targeting in-demand skills will contribute to the success of this process (Flynn et al., 2023).

The international recognition and standardization of micro-credentials are also critical areas to address. Currently, there are significant differences in how micro-credentials are recognized across various countries, complicating their use and limiting their validity in the global job market. Increased collaboration and policy development efforts are needed to enhance the acceptance of these certifications in the international workforce. While initiatives like the European Union's MICROBOL project offer a promising start, accelerating the creation of a unified global framework remains essential (MICROBOL, 2022).

Strengthening technological infrastructure is another important requirement for broader adoption of micro-credentials. With the rise of online learning platforms, further advancements in educational technology are needed. However, the technical infrastructure of these platforms may not always be adequate. Improving digital access for individuals in low-income regions is crucial for creating an inclusive learning environment (Brown et al., 2023). Additionally, secure digital tools like blockchain technology can increase the verifiability of micro-credentials, enhancing employers' confidence in these certifications (Flynn et al., 2023). Technology can create new opportunities in education and increase system reliability through such solutions.

Integrating micro-credentials into lifelong learning strategies is a valuable step to support individuals' career development. The rapid changes in education and the professional world make continuous self-improvement essential. The modular structure of these certifications allows individuals to learn flexibly and progress toward their career goals. By incorporating these programs into lifelong learning strategies, educational institutions can foster continuous development among individuals (Selvaratnam & Sankey, 2020).

One of the main challenges in the adoption of micro-credentials is the yet unclear relationship between these certifications and traditional degrees. Some educational institutions face difficulties in determining how to integrate micro-credentials into degree programs, while uncertainty remains about their value and validity in the professional world. Employers may not fully understand the level of competence these certifications represent or their relevance in the workforce (Oliver, 2021). This uncertainty slows the adoption of micro-credentials among both educational institutions and employers. Clarifying recognition and acceptance processes will aid the broader integration of these certifications into educational systems and improve their acceptance in the professional sector.

Overcoming bureaucratic barriers is crucial for broader acceptance of micro-credential programs. Educational institutions and governments must work toward developing regulations to formally recognize these certifications. Addressing uncertainties surrounding their integration with traditional degree programs will speed up their acceptance. Moreover, increased collaboration between the professional world and educational institutions will facilitate this process (Selvaratnam & Sankey, 2020).

It is clear that micro-credentials will play an increasingly prominent role in the future. With the rapid advancement of technology and growing demand for digital skills, these certifications will see wider use in the job market. Expanding micro-credential programs, especially in fields like artificial intelligence, data science, and digital marketing, is expected (Pichette et al., 2021, Durak et al., 2024).

In this context, innovative approaches and broad collaboration efforts are needed to ensure the sustainability of micro-credential programs and to support individuals' professional growth. These certifications are expected to complement traditional educational models and even assume a leading role in the future. In an era where education needs to become more modular, personalized, and responsive to the demands of the professional world, micro-credentials offer strong support for individuals aiming to achieve their career goals. Developing technological infrastructure, increasing international recognition, and integrating these programs into lifelong learning strategies are essential elements that will enhance the future potential of micro-credentials. Investments from educational systems and the professional sector in these areas will broaden the reach of the opportunities offered by micro-credentials, contributing to individuals' career advancement and professional success.

REFERENCES

Brown, M., McGreal, R., & Peters, M. (2023). A strategic institutional response to micro-credentials: Key questions for educational leaders. *Journal of Interactive Media in Education*, 2023(1), 7. DOI: 10.5334/jime.801

Chandler, K., & Perryman, L. A. (2023). 'People have started calling me an expert': The impact of Open University microcredential courses. *Journal of Interactive Media in Education*, 2023(1), 8. DOI: 10.5334/jime.804

Coursera (2023). How industry micro-credentials are transforming higher education. Coursera Blog. https://blog.coursera.org/how-industry-micro-credentials-are-transforming-higher-education/

Cowie, N., & Sakui, K. (2022). Micro-credentials: Surveying the landscape. In T. D. Cooper & J. York, *Remote Teaching and Beyond: Selected papers from the JALTCALL2021 Conference*. https://jaltcall.org/wp-content/uploads/2022/02/Proceedings-2021.pdf

Durak, G. (2013). *The online teaching of programming languages: Examining learner's attitudes, satisfaction and success.* Unpublished doctoral dissertation. Anadolu University, Institude of Social Sciences.

Durak, G., & Çankaya, S. (2020). Undergraduate students ' views about emergency distance education during the COVID-19 pandemic. *European Journal of Open Education and E-Learning Studies*, 5(1), 122–147. https://doi.org/https://doi.org/10.46827/ejoe.v5i1.3441. DOI: 10.46827/ejoe.v5i1.3441

Durak, G., & Çankaya, S. (2024). Are alarm bells ringing in academia? Chatgpt as a sample of using chatbots in education. *Turkish Online Journal of Distance Education*, 25(3), 1–17. DOI: 10.17718/tojde.1353737

Durak, G., Çankaya, S., & İzmirli, S. (2020). COVID-19 pandemi döneminde türkiye'deki üniversitelerin uzaktan eğitim sistemlerinin incelenmesi. *Necatibey Eğitim Fakültesi Elektronik Fen Ve Matematik Eğitimi Dergisi*, 14(1), 787–809. DOI: 10.17522/balikesirnef.743080

Durak, G., Çankaya, S., Özdemir, D., & Can, S. (2024). Artificial intelligence in education: A bibliometric study on its role in transforming teaching and learning. *International Review of Research in Open and Distance Learning*, 25(3), 219–244. DOI: 10.19173/irrodl.v25i3.7757

European Commission. (2015). ECTS users' guide 2015. https://op.europa.eu/en/publication-detail/-/publication/da7467e6-8450-11e5-b8b7-01aa75ed71a1

European Commission. (2020). A European approach to micro-credentials: Output of the micro-credentials higher education consultation group. https://education.ec.europa.eu/sites/default/files/document-library-docs/european-approach-micro-credentials-higher-education-consultation-group-output-final-report.pdf

Flynn, S., Cullinane, E., Murphy, H., & Wylie, N. (2023). Micro-credentials and digital badges: Definitions, affordances, and design considerations for application in higher education institutions. *All Ireland Journal of Teaching and Learning in Higher Education*, 15(1), 1–19.

FutureLearn. (2020). FutureLearn launches microcredentials with six global partners. https://www.futurelearn.com/info/press-releases/futurelearn-launches-microcredentials-with-six-global-partners

Galindo, M., Fennelly-Atkinson, R., Franklin, K., & Luna, C. (2024). The role of micro-credentials in lifelong learning and development: Empowering learners, empowering organizations. Digital Promise. https://digitalpromise.dspacedirect.org/bitstreams/a0742249-256a-479c-92dd-fd9d0784f4f5/download#:~:text=Micro%2Dcredentials%20disrupt%20postsecondary%20pathways,proving%20their%20competence%20through%20assessments

International Labour Organization. (2024). Micro-credentialing: Powerful new learning tool, or just "pouring old wine into new bottles"? ILO Employment Podcast Episode 38. https://www.ilo.org/media/543076/download

MICROBOL. (2022). Common framework for micro-credentials in the EHEA. https://microcredentials.eu/wp-content/uploads/sites/20/2022/03/Micro-credentials_Framework_final-1.pdf

NZQA. (2023). Guidelines for micro-credential listing, approval and accreditation. Wellington: New Zealand Qualifications Authority. https://www2.nzqa.govt.nz/tertiary/approval-accreditation-and-registration/micro-credentials/guidelines/

OECD. (2021). Quality and value of micro-credentials in higher education: Preparing for the future. https://www.oecd.org/en/publications/quality-and-value-of-micro-credentials-in-higher-education_9c4ad26d-en.html

Oliver, B. (2019). *Making micro-credentials work for learners, employers, and providers*. Deakin University., https://dteach.deakin.edu.au/wp-content/uploads/sites/103/2019/08/Making-micro-credentials-work-Oliver-Deakin-2019-full-report.pdf

Oliver, B. (2021). Micro-credentials: A learner value framework. *Journal of Teaching and Learning for Graduate Employability*, 12(1), 48–51. DOI: 10.21153/jtlge2021vol12no1art1456

Omona, K., & O'dama, M. K. (Eds.). (2024). *Global perspectives on micro-learning and micro-credentials in higher education*. IGI Global., DOI: 10.4018/979-8-3693-0343-6

Orr, D., Pupinis, M., & Kirdulytė, G. (2020). Towards a European approach to micro-credentials: A study of practices and commonalities in offering micro-credentials in European higher education: Analytical report. Publications Office of the European Union. https://op.europa.eu/en/publication-detail/-/publication/033a7af4-40e3-11eb-b27b-01aa75ed71a1/language-en

Pichette, J., Brumwell, S., Rizk, J., & Han, S. (2021). Making sense of microcredentials. Higher Education Quality Council of Ontario. https://heqco.ca/pub/making-sense-of-microcredentials

Selvaratnam, R., & Sankey, M. (2020). Survey of micro-credentialing Practice in Australasian Universities 2020. ACODE Whitepaper. https://publications.ascilite.org/index.php/APUB/article/view/695/424

Tamoliune, G., Greenspon, R., Tereseviciene, M., Volungeviciene, A., Trepule, E., & Dauksiene, E. (2023). Exploring the potential of micro-credentials: A systematic literature review. *Frontiers in Education*, 7, 1006811. DOI: 10.3389/feduc.2022.1006811

Urfa, M., & Durak, G. (2017). Implementation of the flipped classroom model in the Scientific Ethics course. *Journal of Education and e-learning Research*, 4(3), 108–117. DOI: 10.20448/journal.509.2017.43.108.117

Varadarajan, S., Koh, J. H. L., & Daniel, B. K. (2023). A systematic review of the opportunities and challenges of micro-credentials for multiple stakeholders. *International Journal of Educational Technology in Higher Education*, 20(1), 13. DOI: 10.1186/s41239-023-00381-x PMID: 36874535

Chapter 2
Micro-Credentials Establish New Realities in Digital Education

Antonios Stamatakis
https://orcid.org/0009-0008-0429-5906
Hellenic Mediterranean University, Greece

Ilias Logothetis
https://orcid.org/0000-0002-6660-1891
Hellenic Mediterranean University, Greece

Konstantinos Petridis
Hellenic Mediterranean University, Greece

Michail Kalogiannakis
https://orcid.org/0000-0002-9124-2245
Univeristy of Thesssaly, Greece

Nikolas Vidakis
https://orcid.org/0000-0003-0726-8627
Hellenic Mediterranean University, Greece

ABSTRACT

Micro-credentials are transforming digital education by offering flexible, targeted, and accessible ways for learners to acquire and demonstrate skills. Micro-Credentials are small, specialized certifications following a short learning experience, which recognize the knowledge or skills someone acquires in specific subjects or fields. Since 2011, when the Mozilla Foundation introduced the Open Badges system, the use of Micro-Credentials has grown and is now widely employed by all digital

DOI: 10.4018/979-8-3693-5488-9.ch002

platforms offering distance education (Coursera, edX, Udacity, etc.) to certify learners' knowledge, and they are recognized as additional qualifications by employers. Micro-Credentials are becoming increasingly popular as an alternative or complementary form of education, particularly in fields where skills evolve rapidly, such as technology and digital skills, and represent a significant advancement in the field of non-formal and lifelong learning.

INTRODUCTION

In recent decades, the demand for distance education and training has been continuously increasing, peaking during the period of the COVID-19 pandemic, where the demand for upgrading skills and expertise exceeded forecasts. It is worth noting that the European Association of Distance Education Universities (EADTU) currently has 28 members, including 11 open, online and distance learning universities, 14 national university associations and individual universities and 3 associate members. In total, EADTU represents over 150 European universities and 3 million students. Additionally, the global e-learning market was valued at around $165 million by the end of 2015 and is projected to grow by 5% between 2016 and 2023(ELEARNING MARKET TRENDS AND FORECAST 2017-2021, 2016). Researchers also estimate, before pandemic, that between 2020 and 2024, the corporate e-learning market will expand by more than $35 million.

The rising demand has provided the necessary momentum for significant advancements in digital education methods and tools, aimed at improving knowledge delivery and encouraging students to complete their education. Key e-learning trends that have emerged and evolved include:

- **Gamification** refers to the integration of game design elements into non-game contexts (Deterding et al., 2011). It is used to increase learners' engagement by encouraging them to achieve goals, collect reward points, and more during learning activities. The biggest advantage of this method is that fun activities motivate students to try new things and increase the time they spend on the learning process (Lee & Hammer, 2011). Additionally, gamification offers the benefit of incorporating game-like elements into educational content at a low cost.

-**Personalized learning** is made possible by technological advancements, enabling tailored solutions for individuals. Modern learning systems must provide personalized experiences, offering learning processes that best match each learner's needs. These recommendations should be based on individual preferences, behaviors, and needs, with the ability to adapt to each user's current learning stage(Jeng & Huang, 2019; Stamatakis et al., 2020).

- **Microlearning** means providing easily accessible, bite-sized learning content. The bite-size of content allows for the delivery of highly relevant material at the most optimal time. Microlearning is relying on AI-algorithms to more valuable content, precisely tailored to the learner's specific circumstances.

- **Learning analytics** involves the measurement, collection(A. Papadakis et al., 2022; S. Papadakis et al., 2018a), analysis, and reporting of data related to the learning process and its context, with the goal of understanding and optimizing learning(S. Papadakis et al., 2018b). Data such as time to completion, time spent on tasks, and the duration and frequency of resource usage are analyzed to continuously enhance the learning experience and outcomes. xAPI is a technology that plays a key role in the learning analytics process(Panagiotakis et al., 2019; Vidakis et al., 2018, 2019).

- **Serious games** are defined as games designed for educational purposes, aimed at enhancing users' skills by combining entertainment with learning (Zyda, 2005). A key advantage of serious games is their suitability for all age groups, including children, adolescents, adults, and the elderly. They can be used for various learning objectives, such as teaching, training, education, or even therapy. Additionally, serious games can be applied across numerous fields, including education, vocational training, health, defense, politics, advertising, business, the hiring process and more (Mouaheb et al., 2012).

- **Badges** are digital signs that certify the successful completion of an educational process by learners. The badges are collected by learners to demonstrate the acquisition of knowledge or the attainment of additional skills or expertise. The importance of signals is linked to the specific weight of the organization that issues them.

- **Micro-credentials** are concise certifications that verifies expertise or competence in a specific skill or subject area. These credentials are typically awarded after the completion of a short course, workshop, or training module and are designed to offer learners flexible, targeted learning experiences. Micro-credentials are often used to validate specialized skills that may not be covered by traditional degree programs, and they are increasingly recognized by employers as evidence of relevant expertise in fields like technology, education, and business.

-**Artificial Intelligence (AI)** offers a wide range of tools to support and enhance the educational process, primarily in the following areas: a) assisting course creators by enriching content and adapting it to the needs of each learner (e.g., LLM, ChatGPT)(İpek et al., 2023), b) supporting and monitoring learners during the educational process and adjusting it according to their needs, and c) automating the evaluation and grading of learners.

- **Extended Reality (XR)** offers the ability to use ideal simulation environments that meet the needs of learners, providing realistic educational scenarios, increasing engagement, and encouraging learners. The technology allows for adaptation to users' individual preferences and needs, enabling practice without risks or consequences in the real world. Additionally, it eliminates geographical limitations, supporting virtual collaboration and enabling transportation to distant locations.

Of all the above tools or methods, micro-credentialing is the one that has had the greatest impact on the evolution of e-learning, to the extent that even traditional educational institutions are trying to integrate micro-credentials into their operations. But what are micro-credentials? Where are they used? What is their reach in different countries? How are they evolving? These are some of the questions we will try to answer below.

MICRO-CREDENTIAL

Micro-credentials validate the learning outcomes of brief educational experiences, such as a short course or training program. They provide a flexible, focused approach to helping individuals build the knowledge, skills, and competencies essential for their personal and professional growth.

In contrast to traditional degrees or certificates awarded by conventional educational institutions, which serve as evidence of a person's skills and knowledge across a broad academic field, micro-credentials are compact certifications that validate an individual's skills and knowledge in a specific subject or competency(Ponte & Saray, 2022).

The main characteristics of micro-credentials are that they certify the successful completion of a learning process that has:

a) **Short duration**: typically, a few hours or days,
b) **Focused topic**: covers a specialized topic or the development of a specific skill
c) **Flexibility**: offered remotely, allowing learners to complete them at their own pace and schedule
d) **Recognition in the job market**: many employers view them as valid proof of an individual's skills and knowledge(Tan et al., 2024; Yılık, 2021).

Major educational platforms offering online learning (Coursera, edX, Udacity, etc.) use micro-credentials to certify learners, and these certificates are recognized by companies such as Google, Microsoft, Amazon, etc.

There are various definitions for micro-credentials, with the most widely used being: "Micro-credentials are small, focused certifications that validate specific skills, knowledge, or competencies acquired by an individual in a particular subject or field". The European Commission has defined micro-credentials as follows: "A micro-credential means the record of the learning outcomes that a learner has acquired following a small volume of learning. These learning outcomes have been assessed against transparent and clearly defined standards".

The need for employees to adapt to technological advancements and demonstrate specialized knowledge in a specific field, which may have been acquired through work experience or a short educational process, supports the expansion of micro-credentials. The demand for micro-credentials is also supported by the rapid pace of change in the job market, making retraining essential for a large number of adults with higher education degrees who seek to pursue better job opportunities, update outdated qualifications, change career paths, or meet the demands of a new role. The COVID-19 crisis has driven a rapid surge in demand for brief, specialized learning opportunities(Cedefop, 2020; Köse et al., 2022; Kuloglu & Yıldız, 2022). Additionally, the rise of flexible learning methods, such as micro-learning, which meet the needs and demands of learners (limited time, changing schedules, interest in focused knowledge, etc.), supports the expanded use of micro-credentials as proof of completing targeted education.

HISTORY

Micro-credentials are the evolution of digital badges, which validate the acquisition of specific skills or achievements by a user in an educational or professional setting. Each badge typically includes information such as the skill name, competency level, issuing organization, and acquisition date.

Badges are characterized by:

- **Skill Recognition**: They certify specific knowledge or skills acquired by an individual.
- **Flexibility**: They can be issued for various achievements, from course completion to the development of specialized skills.
- **Sharing**: Users can share them on professional networks, such as LinkedIn, to enhance their professional profile.
- **Transparency**: They include detailed information about the acquisition criteria and the issuer, increasing their credibility in the job market.

However, badges carry the credibility provided by their issuer and have never been a primary choice for certifying knowledge and skills. This may be because users have become accustomed to seeing them as rewards in gamified activities aimed at encouraging participation.

In 2011, the Mozilla Foundation, in collaboration primarily with the MacArthur Foundation, created the first badge management system called Open Badges. This system allowed learners to acquire and manage digital badges, while educational institutions and organizations could issue skill and achievement certifications in a way that was easily recognizable and trustworthy. The system enabled organizations to create and issue their own badges, customized to meet their specific needs and criteria(Ahn et al., 2014; Gibson et al., 2013).

At the same time, the Mozilla Foundation developed the Backpack platform to provide users with a tool to store, organize, and share the badges they earned from various organizations through the successful completion of educational programs or professional accomplishments, serving as a central repository for their achievements, provided that the organizations use the Open Badge Infrastructure (OBI)(Ahn et al., 2014; Gibson et al., 2013).

The main functions of the Backpack platform include:

1. **Badge Storage**: Each user can store all badges earned from different issuers in one place after completing educational or thematic activities.
2. **Organization and Categorization**: Users can organize their badges according to their own criteria, by thematic category or educational activity.
3. **Sharing**: Users can share their badges on professional and social networks, such as LinkedIn, to highlight their skills and achievements.
4. **Credibility and Transparency**: Each badge contains information about the issuer and the acquisition criteria, lending credibility to its content and the badge holder.

The “Backpack” platform was retired in August 2019, and its functionalities have now been transferred to a new open badge system called “Badgr.” All digital badges from the “Mozilla Backpack” have been migrated and preserved in Badgr. The open badge standard is now maintained by **IMS Global Learning Consortium**, the organization responsible for SCORM standards, ensuring continued support and development of open badge standards.

In 2017, a team of academics and librarians from RMIT University in Australia designed and created the first micro-credential for “Information Literacy”(Ponte & Saray, 2022). The team developed this micro-credential to be integrated into the curriculum, allowing students to build skills in recognizing, locating, evaluating, and effectively using information. Students who received the micro-credentials were awarded a digital badge that detailed their learning achievements, with recognition reflected in their official academic transcript. Furthermore, they shared these badges on social media platforms like LinkedIn, providing a way to showcase their newly acquired skills and engage potential employers.

In 2021, the European Commission issued a recommendation outlining the strategies and actions member states should implement to adopt a unified approach to leveraging micro-credentials for lifelong learning and employability. This Council recommendation aims to establish a harmonized system across Europe, enabling the recognition of skills and knowledge while fostering citizens' professional growth and competitiveness.

The main guidelines provided in the recommendation for designing and developing micro-credentials are:

1. **Enhancing Transparency**: Establishing harmonized standards for micro-credentials with detailed information on learning duration, learning outcomes, and acquisition criteria, making them easily recognizable by educators and employers across the EU.
2. **Promoting Recognition and Integration**: Developing systems for the recognition of micro-credentials within the European Qualifications Framework (EQF), facilitating the transfer and acceptance of qualifications between member states.
3. **Supporting Collaboration between Educators and Employers**: Encouraging partnerships among universities, professional organizations, and employers to create micro-credentials that align with labor market needs, ensuring that the skills acquired are relevant and applicable.
4. **Flexible Learning Options**: Creating flexible learning formats, such as online courses or short training programs, accessible to individuals with different schedules and needs, making micro-credentials adaptable to professional and personal requirements.
5. **Supporting Digital Participation**: Promoting the use of digital technologies for the development and dissemination of micro-credentials, improving access to online learning opportunities, and enhancing the visibility of skills on a European scale.

These strategies aim to enhance mutual recognition of skills and knowledge across Europe, supporting workforce mobility and fostering a European environment for lifelong learning

The European Union has set a target for 2030 to have 60% of all adults participating in training each year and to achieve an employment rate of at least 78%. The EU considers micro-credentials to be a crucial tool in reaching this goal, as they provide flexible and accessible opportunities for skill development, helping to increase employability and participation in lifelong learning.

Standards, Formats, and Characteristics

Although globally accepted standards have been developed to facilitate the recognition, verification, and interoperability of micro-credentials, the International Organization for Standardization (ISO) has not yet created specific standards for digital education and the certification of skills and knowledge. The most widespread standards include:

- **European Qualifications Framework (EQF):** The EQF allows for the recognition of skills and qualifications across various European Union countries. Micro-credentials are integrated into the EQF to link them with recognized education and qualification levels, facilitating their transfer between member states.
- **Common Microcredential Framework (CMF):** The CMF was developed by the European MOOC Consortium and supports the European approach to micro-credentials. It proposes standardized elements for describing micro-credentials, such as learning duration, program level, learning outcomes, and credit points (ECTS).

Notably, platforms like **Blockcerts** and **Credly** have begun utilizing blockchain technology to offer high-security solutions for the storage and sharing of micro-credentials. This protocol, known as Blockchain-Based Standards aims to enhance the integrity, security, and verification of micro-credentials. The main features of this protocol include:

- **Integrity**: Blockchain technology ensures that the data stored regarding a micro-credential cannot be modified or deleted without proper authorization. Each record is encrypted and linked to previous entries, creating a chain (blockchain) that protects data integrity.
- **Verification and Transparency**: Employers, educational institutions, or other stakeholders can easily confirm the authenticity of a micro-credential, as the data is accessible through public or private blockchain networks.
- **Security**: Blockchain technology prevents forgery, duplication, or tampering of data, ensuring the authenticity and reliability of certificates.
- **Decentralized System**: Blockchain technology ensures that there is no central control or administrator, which creates greater transparency and prevents malicious interference, as the data is stored across multiple nodes in the network.

These features make blockchain-based micro-credentials more secure, transparent, and reliable, encouraging wider adoption and trust in digital certification systems.

The structure and forms of micro-credentials vary depending on their purpose and use, and they include specific features and elements that ensure their effectiveness, verifiability, and recognition. Below are the main characteristics of the structure of a micro-credential:

1. Title of the Micro-Credential:
    - A clear and descriptive title that indicates the subject or skill being certified.
2. Description of Learning Outcomes:
    - Explanation of specific skills, knowledge, or competencies acquired through the education or training covered by the micro-credential.
    - Reference to the assessment criteria used for obtaining the credential.
3. Issuer Information:
    - Details about the organization or platform that issued the micro-credential.
    - The name, reputation, and reliability of the issuer are key elements for evaluating and accepting the credential by employers and other organizations.
4. Learning Duration and Completion Time:
    - Description of the time required to complete the micro-credential, such as hours of learning or weeks of training.
    - Indication of the effort or level of engagement needed to complete the program.
5. Metadata and Digital Verifiability:
    - Micro-credentials often include metadata that allow the verification of authenticity and learning outcomes.
    - This metadata may contain information such as the issuance date, awarded credits (e.g., ECTS), and encrypted links that enable easy verification of validity.
6. Compatibility with Qualification Frameworks:
    - Connection, if available, of the micro-credential with national or international qualification frameworks, such as the European Qualifications Framework (EQF). This facilitates cross-border recognition and integration into formal educational pathways.
    - Specification of the education level or specialty that the credential represents.
7. Issuance Date and Validity Period:
    - Record of the date when the micro-credential was obtained, along with information on whether it has a specific validity period or is indefinite.

- This helps verify the relevance of the skills described.

8. Flexibility and Stackability:
   - Description of whether micro-credentials are designed to be flexible and can be "stacked," meaning they can be combined with others to obtain larger certificates or degrees.
9. Shareability:
   - Indication of whether micro-credentials are digital and can be shared on professional networks and personal resumes, allowing holders to showcase their skills easily and quickly.

All these features are important, but stackability stands out because it allows learners to tailor their education according to their professional needs, schedule, and personal goals, and to gradually achieve an upgraded or comprehensive academic qualification.

Forms of Micro-Credentials

Micro-credentials can take various forms depending on their design, issuance, goals, and usage. Each form has its advantages, offering flexibility and covering different educational and professional needs. Over time, these forms have evolved, aiding in the international recognition of micro-credentials and enhancing their use as effective tools for learning and skill development. The main forms of micro-credentials include:

1. **Digital Badges**
   - o Digital badges are one of the most popular forms of micro-credentials. They contain information (metadata) about what the badge represents, such as learning outcomes, the issuer, and acquisition criteria. They can be easily shared on social platforms and digital resumes.
2. **Digital Certificates**
   - o Digital certificates are traditional certificates in electronic form that acknowledge the completion of an educational unit or the acquisition of specific skills. These certificates are often issued by educational institutions and are verifiable through digital services.
3. **Modular Learning Units**
   - o Certificates for small learning units that can be combined and "stacked" to create larger certificates or degrees. This form offers flexibility, allowing learners to progress based on their needs and develop their skills step by step.
4. **Open Badges**

- Open Badges are an open standard for issuing and managing digital badges. Created by the Mozilla Foundation, they enable easy storage, sharing, and verification of skills through an open infrastructure (Open Badge Infrastructure - OBI). These badges are portable and can be integrated into different platforms and systems.

5. **Blockchain-Based Micro-Credentials**
    - Using blockchain technology, this form of micro-credentials offers a high level of security and verification. Blockchain-based micro-credentials ensure that data cannot be altered and can be easily verified by employers and other stakeholders.
6. **Professional Platform-Based Micro-Credentials**
    - Platforms like Coursera, edX, and Udemy offer micro-credentials developed in collaboration with universities and professional organizations. These credentials often incorporate credit points (ECTS) and are linked to more formal academic programs, facilitating their transfer to larger degrees.
7. **Professional Development Certificates**
    - These micro-credentials certify the completion of professional training and skills programs, often designed to enhance employability in specific fields such as IT, marketing, or project management.

Objectives, Advantages, Disadvantages

In a rapidly changing job market, mainly due to technological advances, the **IFF - Institute for the Future** reported in 2017 that "...approximately 85% of the jobs today's students will be doing in 2030 have not been invented yet." This highlights the growing need for retraining and acquiring highly specialized skills. Furthermore, the need for employees to verify knowledge gained in the field has created a growing demand for certification of skills and knowledge. Micro-credentials have been introduced to address modern needs for certifying skills and knowledge in education and professional training. Micro-credentials have numerous features, as outlined above, which help address contemporary demands, specifically in:

1. the need for continuous and lifelong learning

In a world where technology and job markets are constantly evolving, there is an increased need for continuous learning and skill updates. Micro-credentials allow employees to develop new skills or improve existing ones without having to commit to full degree programs.

2. flexibility in Learning and attendance

Unlike traditional programs, micro-credentials offer small and flexible learning modules that allow learners to learn at their own pace. This suits workers with demanding schedules or those who cannot commit to extended periods of study, as well as those who travel frequently.

3. urgent need for upskilling

The rapid technological advancements in various fields and changes in the job market have increased the demand for specialized skills. Micro-credentials facilitate upskilling or reskilling, enabling workers to stay competitive in the job market. By attending highly specialized courses in a short period, they can respond to growing demands.

4. integration of vulnerable groups into the job market

Micro-credentials provide learning opportunities to vulnerable groups, such as the unemployed, migrants, or individuals with disabilities, allowing them to quickly acquire specific professional skills that help integrate them into the job market. The courses can be accessed remotely, with low equipment requirements and minimal cost. This helps reduce social exclusion, provides new opportunities, and strengthens social cohesion.

5. recognition and certification of non-formal and informal learning

Many skills are acquired during work, through solving problems, participating in short training programs, or independent study. Micro-credentials enable the formal recognition of these skills, offering a form of certification that can be utilized by employers and educational institutions, aiding professional advancement.

6. transparency and ease of skill verification

Micro-credentials come with metadata that fully describes all aspects of the educational process, making it easy to verify their authenticity and assess the learning outcomes. This helps employers recognize and appreciate the skills of the holders directly without complexity, providing greater transparency compared to traditional certificates.

The fact that micro-credentials address all these needs makes them a flexible and effective method of education and training in the modern world.

Advantages

From the points mentioned above, it is clear that micro-credentials provide an excellent option for learners, particularly adults, to grow or change their career paths, offering the flexibility to combine learning with other responsibilities. Here are the main advantages of micro-credentials:

- Flexibility: Micro-credentials offer learners the ability to control their learning pace, allowing them to adapt their studies to fit their schedules. This means they can utilize free time at work, during commuting, or while waiting in service areas.
- Personalized Learning: Learners can choose topics that interest them and are relevant to their career development. This customization enables them to focus on specific subjects and acquire specialized knowledge.
- Practical Experience: Micro-credentials allow the combination of theory and practice, helping learners develop more specific, hands-on skills that can be applied to real-world problems.
- Self-Promotion: Engaging in distance learning demonstrates a desire and capability for learning, growth, and development. This can lead to personal satisfaction, increased confidence, and new career advancement opportunities.
- Certification of Knowledge and Skills: Micro-credentials enable employees to receive formal recognition for professional knowledge or skills they have acquired through experience or self-learning (non-formal and informal learning).
- Blended Learning: They can combine different learning methods, such as online courses, hybrid learning, apprenticeships, or in-person classes. This flexibility can make learning easier for adults and reduce the cost of validating and recognizing skills acquired through informal education.
- Speed: Learning can begin immediately through online platforms, and the duration is typically short, ranging from a few hours to days. Educational materials are always available for review and study.
- Low Cost: Learning modules are accessible remotely with minimal equipment requirements, no need for travel, and very low cost. This also reduces the expense of validating and recognizing skills acquired through informal learning pathways.
- Retention of Human Resources: Companies can invest at a low cost in the training of their workforce, providing opportunities for growth and incentives for employees to stay with the organization.

The comprehensive set of advantages makes micro-credentials an excellent strategy for promoting lifelong learning and supporting informal education. Their adaptability to the needs of learners has encouraged traditional educational institutions to incorporate them into their curricula, providing students with additional incentives. By integrating micro-credentials, these institutions can offer more flexible, targeted learning paths that appeal to students seeking to upskill or gain specialized knowledge without committing to a full degree program. This trend not only aligns with modern educational demands but also bridges the gap between formal and informal learning, creating a more inclusive and dynamic approach to skill development.

Disadvantages

Like many aspects of life, micro-credentials, despite their benefits, also face challenges that hinder their growth and expansion. The existence of these drawbacks and gaps is natural for a developing technology, and it takes time for these issues to be addressed and mature. Below is a list of problems that need to be tackled to ensure the continued development of micro-credentials. The main issues include:

- Questionable Program Quality: Many programs are developed rapidly to meet demand and often do not maintain high quality or fail to meet the needs of the learner.
- Lack of Evaluation: Many micro-credential programs are used only once, preventing proper evaluation of the program's structure and content, which limits opportunities for improvement and redesign.
- Lack of Transparency: With a vast array of programs available, there is no clear method for learners to identify the most suitable courses, leading them to choose programs that may not align with their advertised objectives.
- Lack of Recognition: Many micro-credential programs are not compatible with national qualification frameworks, and not all national frameworks accept titles from non-formal education programs or private providers. This affects the recognition and credibility of micro-credentials, which often rely on the reputation of the issuer.
- Limited Universal Recognition: Despite their growing popularity, micro-credentials do not yet have the same level of recognition and credibility as traditional degrees or diplomas. Many employers may not see them as equally reliable or accept them as sufficient proof of skills and knowledge.
- Fragmented Learning: While flexibility is an advantage, micro-credentials can lead to fragmented learning, where learners acquire individual skills without a broader foundation of knowledge. This can make it harder for them

to understand the significance of micro-credentials or to connect new skills with professional growth or further training.

- Limited Opportunity for Deeper Learning: Micro-credentials generally focus on specific skills or topics and have short durations. This means they may not offer opportunities for a deeper understanding of a subject, as would be found in a full educational program or degree. Traditional programs also train students to acquire knowledge both independently and collaboratively, which is difficult to achieve in shorter courses.
- Integration with Traditional Programs: While many educational institutions are trying to integrate micro-credentials into their curricula, linking them with traditional programs can be challenging. Some micro-credentials may not be recognized as part of a larger degree, or they may not easily translate into academic credits, especially when skills and knowledge are acquired through non-formal and informal education.
- 9. Cost: Although the initial cost of obtaining a micro-credential may be low, there is evidence that the need to accumulate multiple micro-credentials to earn a larger title or degree can increase the overall cost, sometimes surpassing that of traditional methods.
- Stackability Issues: According to a study by Cedefop, 88% of VET providers confirmed that at least some of their micro-credentials could be stacked and combined with other certificates or titles(Cedefop, 2022). However, without consistent quality standards and accreditation by formal education and training authorities, recognition and stackability for achieving a full official title remain problematic, especially for those acquired outside formal education systems.
- Lack of Immediate Rewards: Acquiring knowledge and training requires significant effort, but the rewards may not be immediate. This can reduce the motivation of learners, although it is a general disadvantage seen in education overall.
- Limited Communication: Due to the short duration of the training, there are limitations on communication and collaboration with other learners and instructors. This reduces interaction, the ability to learn from others' experiences, and the development of professional partnerships.

Micro-credentials offer an alternative form of education or training, providing opportunities for reskilling or specialization. While they spread quickly due to their unregulated nature, they also create confusion due to their complexity and variety, raising questions about their benefits and leading to the aforementioned issues. To enable micro-credentials to play their intended role, these disadvantages must be addressed and minimized.

Micro-Credentials and AI

Artificial intelligence (AI) has rapidly developed over recent years, permeating all aspects of human activity, including education, and more specifically, micro-credentials. AI has introduced numerous tools to enhance the educational process, facilitating its development. Specifically, AI helps by: a) Assisting course creators in enriching content, tailoring it to the needs of each learner (e.g., using language models like LLMs, ChatGPT), and updating the material; b) Monitoring learners during the educational process, analyzing their behavior, and adjusting the educational approach according to their needs; c) Automating the assessment and grading of students through tests, quizzes, and assignments.

Additionally, artificial intelligence (AI) is used to detect needs in education and professional training, helping to address the demands of the modern job market and adapt educational processes to new trends. The fields of application is:

a) In labor market data analysis, AI is used to identify current and future skills that employers seek, enabling better forecasting and preparation to address these needs. Data is collected from various sources, such as social networks, market statistics, and job postings, to help anticipate trends and adjust training programs accordingly.
b) In understanding students' needs and identifying learning gaps, AI helps pinpoint areas where learners require additional support. This allows educational programs to focus on specific skills or subjects that need more attention, ensuring a more tailored and effective learning experience.
c) in facilitating the development of educational policies and training programs by governments and organizations aimed at reducing skill shortages and boosting employability.
d) in forecasting the necessary infrastructure that governments or organizations need to develop to meet future demands. For example, AI can make predictions about population growth and determine where new schools may need to be built, using data from registries, housing rental ads, and other sources.
e) in reducing operational costs by optimizing student transportation logistics and predicting the timely procurement of supplies.

Specifically, regarding the use of artificial intelligence in micro-credentials, AI is employed to enhance, automate, and accelerate the learning process. It is used in the following ways:

a) in the development of personalized learning paths by analyzing student data and adjusting programs according to each learner's needs, knowledge level, and goals. This allows learners to focus on the specific areas they need, thereby increasing the efficiency and effectiveness of the educational process.
b) in developing micro-credential recommendations based on users' previous selections and the skills they have already acquired.
c) in the automatic assessment of learners' knowledge and skills through questionnaires, quizzes, and assignments. This reduces the time needed for evaluation and certification issuance while enhancing reliability, as the criteria remain consistent for all participants.
d) in verifying the validity of micro-credentials, ensuring in a short period that the certified skills have indeed been acquired by the holder.
e) in enriching content by creating educational materials such as presentations, diagrams, and course summaries.
f) in maintaining the integrity of micro-credentials, in conjunction with blockchain technology. AI helps process large volumes of data and detect any anomalies, while blockchain ensures that information remains secure and verifiable.
g) in providing immediate feedback to learners during the learning process. Through advanced natural language processing (NLP) tools and chatbots, AI can answer questions, explain concepts, and offer support, enhancing the overall learning experience.
h) in adapting educational content in real time based on the learner's performance and progress. If a student encounters difficulties with a particular topic, AI can provide additional material or exercises to help address the gap.
i) in analyzing large volumes of data to identify learning patterns and determine which types of micro-credentials are most effective and which need improvement. This allows educational organizations to refine and enhance their programs.
j) in linking the skills acquired through micro-credentials to workplace performance, monitoring and evaluating how these new skills are applied in practice. This provides employers with a clearer understanding of the effectiveness of the training.
k) in managing VR and AR technologies to create interactive and realistic learning environments, making the educational process more engaging and effective.

From the above, it is clear that artificial intelligence (AI) enhances the effectiveness and reliability of micro-credentials, facilitating skill recognition and supporting a personalized learning experience. AI continuously evolves and improves, and it is almost certain that its integration into the educational process, particularly in micro-credentials, will continue to grow. This ongoing development promises to make micro-credential systems more efficient, adaptable, and accessible, thus reinforcing their value in education and professional development.

Challenges for the Future

The challenges facing the future of micro-credentials are diverse and relate to their technological development, institutional recognition, and social acceptance. Essentially, these challenges are about addressing the disadvantages or issues that micro-credentials currently present, as mentioned earlier.

The most significant challenge is solving the issue of accumulation and combination of micro-credentials from different issuers to achieve larger certifications or degrees. Developing common rules that are followed by all, along with integration aξnd alignment at a central level, is needed. However, achieving consensus among all stakeholders is not easy.

Additionally, ensuring the quality and transparency of micro-credentials requires the development of harmonized standards. These standards will safeguard the quality and validity of learning programs, enhancing trust and acceptance among employers and employees.

CONCLUSION

Micro-credentials represent a method of certifying knowledge and skills that can offer solutions for lifelong learning and the retraining of unemployed individuals, providing them with an opportunity to enter the job market. It is crucial for all stakeholders (governments, educational organizations, workers, unemployed individuals, learners, etc.) to gain a clearer understanding of what micro-credentials are and what they can offer to achieve the best possible outcomes from their use.

The authors aimed to provide a comprehensive overview of micro-credentials to assist in this direction. Initially, a brief presentation of modern trends in digital education was made, highlighting how they influence its evolution. This was followed by a detailed analysis of micro-credentials, their characteristics, forms, and types, along with a brief review of their development. Additionally, an overview was given of the benefits and drawbacks of micro-credentials and how they interact with artificial intelligence. Finally, the main challenges were addressed, identifying the obstacles that need to be overcome for micro-credentials to fulfill their role effectively.

REFERENCES

Ahn, J., Pellicone, A., & Butler, B. (2014). Open badges for education: What are the implications at the intersection of open systems and badging? *Research in Learning Technology*, 22. Advance online publication. DOI: 10.3402/rlt.v22.23563

Cedefop. (2022). *ARE MICROCREDENTIALS BECOMING A BIG DEAL?* Deterding, S., Dixon, D., Khaled, R., & Nacke, L. (2011). From Game Design Elements to Gamefulness: Defining Gamification. *Proceedings of the 15th International Academic MindTrek Conference: Envisioning Future Media Environments, MindTrek 2011, 11*, 9–15. DOI: 10.1145/2181037.2181040

ELEARNING MARKET TRENDS AND FORECAST 2017-2021. (2016). www .docebo.com

Gibson, D., Ostashewski, N., Flintoff, K., Grant, S., & Knight, E. (2013). Digital badges in education. *Education and Information Technologies*, 20(2), 1–8. DOI: 10.1007/s10639-013-9291-7

İpek, Z., Gözüm, A. I. C., Papadakis, S., & Kalogiannakis, M. (2023). Educational Applications of the ChatGPT AI System: A Systematic Review Research. *Educational Process International Journal*, 12(3), 26–55. DOI: 10.22521/edupij.2023.123.2

Jeng, Y. L., & Huang, Y. M. (2019). Dynamic learning paths framework based on collective intelligence from learners. *Computers in Human Behavior*, 100, 242–251. Advance online publication. DOI: 10.1016/j.chb.2018.09.012

Köse, S., Karakurt, P., & Fırat, M. (2022). Relationship of Nursing Students' Anxiety Level in the Covid-19 Pandemic with E-Learning. *Turkish Journal of Science and Health*, 3(3), 168–175. DOI: 10.51972/tfsd.1085398

Kuloglu, M. E., & Yıldız, S. (2022). UNDERGRADUATES' ATTITUDES TOWARDS DISTANCE EDUCATION AND PERCEPTIONS OF READINESS FOR E-LEARNING DURING THE COVID-19 PANDEMIC. *Turkish Online Journal of Distance Education*, 23(4), 121–130. DOI: 10.17718/tojde.1182767

Lee, J., & Hammer, J. (2011). Gamification in Education: What, How, Why Bother? *Academic Exchange Quarterly*, 15, 1–5.

Mouaheb, H., Fahli, A., Moussetad, M., & Eljamali, S. (2012). The Serious Game: What Educational Benefits? *Procedia: Social and Behavioral Sciences*, 46, 5502–5508. https://doi.org/https://doi.org/10.1016/j.sbspro.2012.06.465. DOI: 10.1016/j.sbspro.2012.06.465

Panagiotakis, S., Papadokostaki, K., Kostas, V., & Malamos, A. (2019). *Towards a novel and LMS-free Pervasive Learning System exploiting the Experience API*. 156383. DOI: 10.4108/eai.13-7-2018.156383

Papadakis, A., Barianos, K., Kalogiannakis, M., Papadakis, S., & Vidakis, N. (2022). ARION: A Digital eLearning Educational Tool Library for Synchronization Composition & Orchestration of Learning Session Data. *Applied Sciences (Basel, Switzerland)*, 12(17), 8722. DOI: 10.3390/app12178722

Papadakis, S., Kalogiannakis, M., Sifaki, E., & Vidakis, N. (2018a). *Access Moodle Using Smart Mobile Phones. A Case Study in a Greek University* (pp. 376–385). DOI: 10.1007/978-3-319-76908-0_36

Papadakis, S., Kalogiannakis, M., Sifaki, E., & Vidakis, N. (2018b). Evaluating Moodle use via Smart Mobile Phones. A case study in a Greek University. *EAI Endorsed Transactions on Creative Technologies*, 5(16), 156382. DOI: 10.4108/eai.10-4-2018.156382

Ponte, F., & Saray, V. (2022). The evolution of a micro-credential. *ASCILITE Publications*, 546–551. DOI: 10.14742/apubs.2019.328

Stamatakis, A., Trampas, A. M., Kontoulis, V., Barianos, A. K., Papadakis, A., & Vidakis, N. (2020). *AN OPEN SOURCE TRAINING MANAGEMENT SYSTEM TO SUPPORT THE PERSONAL PHYSICAL AND MENTAL TRAINING*. 5558–5566. DOI: 10.21125/edulearn.2020.1457

Tan, K. T., Chan, J. I. L., Arumugam, P. V., & Lee, H. W. (2024). CLOSING THE TALENT GAP: A PROPOSED MICRO-CREDENTIAL MODEL IN MALAYSIAN FORMAL EDUCATION. *Turkish Online Journal of Distance Education*, 25(4), 67–80. DOI: 10.17718/tojde.1400152

Vidakis, N., Barianos, K., Trampas, A., Papadakis, S., Kalogiannakis, M., & Kostas, V. (2019, October). *Generating Education in-Game Data: The Case of an Ancient Theatre Serious Game*. DOI: 10.5220/0007810800360043

Vidakis, N., Barianos, K. A., Xanthopoulos, G., & Stamatakis, A. (2018). Cultural inheritance educational environment: The ancient theatre game thimeledu. *Proceedings of the European Conference on Games-Based Learning, 2018-Octob*.

Yılık, M. A. (2021). Micro-credentials, Higher Education and Career Development: Perspectives of University Students. *Higher Education Governance and Policy*, 2(2), 126–139.

Zyda, M. (2005). From Visual Simulation to Virtual Reality to Games. *Computer*, 38(9), 25–32. DOI: 10.1109/MC.2005.297

Chapter 3
Triggering Competitiveness From a Global Perspective:
MOOCs and Micro-Credentials

Nazire Burcin Hamutoglu
Eskisehir Osmangazi University, Turkey

Mesut Aydemir
https://orcid.org/0000-0002-2035-1292
Anadolu University, Turkey

Clifford De Raffaele
https://orcid.org/0000-0002-7081-702X
Middlesex University, UK

ABSTRACT

MOOCs and micro-credentials make high-quality education accessible to people from all backgrounds, leveling the playing field and promoting equitable access to skills and knowledge. These concepts are closely tied to global competitiveness by enabling individuals and economies to rapidly adapt to evolving skill demands, access cutting-edge knowledge, and foster innovation. This chapter aims to incorporate both concepts considering the sections and intersections from a global perspective to shape the future of education and bridge the skills gap. When the term makes it more important than ever to be competitive in a global sense, the chapter emphasizes to be aware of the competencies that the institutions have. Designing the skill-oriented online course contents would be a motivation source within the concept of internationalization. The recommendations for the stakeholders given in the frameworks that triggered the quality assurance, internationalization, and

DOI: 10.4018/979-8-3693-5488-9.ch003

global competitiveness.

INTRODUCTION

MOOCs (Massive Open Online Courses) and micro-credentials have the potential to address the skills and upskilling gaps in lifelong learning by making education accessible, flexible, and relevant. Considering the concept and application era of MOOCs and micro-credentials, it is noticeably accessible and typically low-cost or free, and allows individuals across different socioeconomic backgrounds to access high-quality education from reputable institutions. Addition to this, MOOCs offer the flexibility to learn at one's own pace, making them ideal for working professionals who need to balance work, family, and education. The accessibility of MOOCs empowers more people to upskill without the financial burden of traditional education and enables learners to focus on specific skills they need for career advancement, rather than committing to lengthy degree programs. By making education more accessible, industry-aligned, and modular, MOOCs and micro-credentials provide individuals with a practical pathway for continuous skills development, helping bridge the gap in lifelong learning and enhancing workforce readiness.

Micro-credentials focus on specific competencies, enabling learners to gain targeted, job-relevant skills that meet immediate demands in the job market. These "bite-sized" certifications make it easier for individuals to demonstrate proficiency in a niche area without requiring full degrees. Micro-credentials can often be "stacked" into larger qualifications or recognized toward professional development goals. This structure enables learners to build skills incrementally, offering pathways to more formal certifications or degrees if desired.

The educational and skill development ecosystem in the digital era has been completely revolutionized as a result of the introduction of Massive Open Online Courses (MOOCs) and Micro-Credentials. Many MOOCs and micro-credential programs partner with industry leaders to design courses that address real-world skills gaps. This collaboration helps ensure that learners acquire skills aligned with current job market needs, improving employability. In order to close the skills gap and encourage individuals all around the world to pursue their education throughout their lives, these new technologies have proved vital. Within the context of fulfilling the ever-evolving expectations of learners and industry, this chapter investigates the significance of Massive Open Online Courses (MOOCs) and Micro-Credentials as a means of facilitating continuous growth and development. The modular structure of MOOCs and micro-credentials supports lifelong learning by encouraging a continuous approach to education. As industry demands evolve, professionals can return to these platforms to update their skills and stay competitive. The concept of micro-credential is also relevant with international competitiveness and worth taking note of being the subject of quality assurance since learning is occurring anywhere. The importance of quality in terms of national development and global competitiveness is highlighted in the study by Hamutoğlu, Ünveren-Bilgiç, and Özden (2023), which also predicts that awareness will be raised in place of the resistance seen regarding quality assurance in higher education institutions. It has been also concluded that attempting to raise awareness and provide information about the partnerships and articulation strategies that higher education institutions can establish with other international higher education institutions in the context of both their regional mission-oriented differentiation strategies and their competencies by examining the significance of international competitiveness of higher education institutions for national development from the standpoint of internal quality assurance standards in education and training. Hence, the framework of the micro-credential becomes even more meaningful from a quality perspective, especially with the need to recognize prior learning.

Although micro-credentials have been more popular with the MOOCs platform, it is believed that the dynamics and concept of the micro-credentials have not been truly adopted. Buchanan et. al. (2020) suggests that a preoccupation with exciting curriculum reforms such as 21st century skills and micro credentialing, which are promoted to boost employment, may be a distraction from what successful education systems can potentially achieve. Nevertheless, the asserted issue for the future of work could be a huge prejudice that can lead to disappointment when the concept of micro-credentials has not been internalized yet. In fact, the dynamics of the 21st century require us to keep up with the importance of learning in our lives with platforms that will emphasize the importance of gaining skills and competence with technological developments that are so great that learning cannot be limited.

Hence, this chapter aims to (1) incorporate the concepts of MOOCs and micro-credentials from a global perspective to shape the future of education and bridge the skills gap for a sustained lifelong learning. In order to influence education going forward and close the skills gap, this chapter (2) attempts to integrate the ideas of MOOCs and micro-credentials from a global viewpoint and stresses the need of understanding the institutions' competencies at a time when being globally competitive is more crucial than ever in line the paradigms. Within the framework of internationalization, (3) creating and ensuring recognition of the skill-oriented online course materials would serve as a source of inspiration through the MOOCs historical development. The frameworks that sparked (4) quality assurance, internationalization, and global competitiveness provided suggestions for the stakeholders.

A New Paradigm for Lifelong Learning

The growing prevalence of Massive Open Online Courses (MOOCs) and micro-credentials represents a significant shift in higher education, driven by a growing demand for flexibility, accessibility, and relevance in learning possibilities. Iqbal et al. (2016) explain that MOOCs are reshaping education by offering accessible, quality learning opportunities worldwide with just internet access and they challenge traditional education by allowing students to take diverse courses from various institutions, promoting pedagogical research and innovation, although, awareness remains low among some university students and faculty. Ossiannilsson (2021) in her study focused on global initiatives in education as a global common via MOOCs in lifelong learning, equity, and liberation. This invention is particularly important given the gig economy and the evolving demands within the labor market. While MOOCs and micro-credentials are increasingly adopted by educational institutions to address the challenge of providing quality education for various learners, they may be regarded as one of the most promising solutions.

The MOOCs have democratized education by making many learners, from diverse backgrounds, gain access to high-quality content given by world-renowned leading institutions. Accessibility holds the key to addressing the inequality in education as the MOOCs are able to reach populations which cannot afford to attend physically to any university for higher education. For example, research indicates that MOOCs improve learning opportunities for disadvantaged learners and can provide them with increasingly relevant skills and knowledge in today's labor market (Willems & Farley, 2019). However, while MOOCs have such benefits, they equally raise concerns about the privatization of education and the fragmentation of qualifications, among other things (Wheelahan & Moodie, 2021). This unbundling of the curriculum will lead to a lack of coherence in education and hence may undermine the value of a traditional degree.

On the other hand, micro-credentials offer a more granular approach to acquiring skills that allow students to demonstrate specific competencies directly applicable in their desired professions. The flexibility of micro-credentials allows students to study at their own pace, which is a great advantage among students with both work and school obligations. It has also been noted that micro-credentials promote autonomous learning, allowing learners to have a secure pace within which to practice and make mistakes with no pressure from a regular classroom environment (Kumar et al., 2022). Autonomy is an essential feature in today's job market, with great dynamism; it builds up self-confidence and develops lifelong learning.

The relationship between micro-credentials and employability represents a crucial part of this education innovation. Employers are increasingly focused on certain types of skills rather than traditional degrees, which raises demand for micro-credentials to signal that a candidate is ready for a job. Research indicates that micro-credentialing practices can increase the recognition of employability skills in graduates, enhancing employability rate (Maina et al., 2022; Miller & Jorre, 2022). Matching educational and job requirements is of paramount importance, as this addresses the skills gap that most businesses are facing today.

Furthermore, any discussion of MOOCs and micro-credentials must necessarily consider the broader implications of such educational developments. The increasing marketisation of approaches within higher education institutions creates a risk that the focus of employability and skills development overshadows broader higher education goals of critical thinking, creativity, and active citizenship (Ashwin, 2022). The transition does raise critical questions about the role of higher education in society and finding a balance between vocational training and developing a well-rounded individual.

Historical Development and Growth of MOOCs

The origin of Massive Open Online Courses (better known by their acronym: MOOCs) dates back to the early 2000s, although it wasn't until 2012 when those three words became a household name. The term "MOOC" was coined by Stephen Downes and George Siemens back in 2008, during the development of a course entitled Connectivism and Connective Knowledge (Downes, 2012). The rise of MOOCs was significantly influenced by the proliferation of the internet and the availability of digital resources, which democratized access to education. MOOCs emerged to address the constraints of traditional educational structures, especially in higher education, where access was frequently hindered by geographical, financial, and social obstacles. (Wu et al., 2019).

George Siemens and Stephen Downes offered the first MOOC, "Connectivism and Connective Knowledge," in 2008. But 2012 was when the MOOC era began, with Coursera, edX and Udacity launching then. These platforms partnered with universities to provide free online courses for anyone with an internet connection. Despite the initial hype cycle of MOOCs that helped produce tens-of-thousands in student enrollment — even over 100,000 for some courses. The initial enthusiasm for MOOCs stemmed from its promise to provide great educational resources at little or no cost, thereby enhancing access to higher education (Agasisti et al., 2021). However, concerns were raised about the quality of the learning experience and the elevated attrition rates among course participants (Greene et al., 2015).

Figure 1. Evolution and global popularity trends of MOOCs

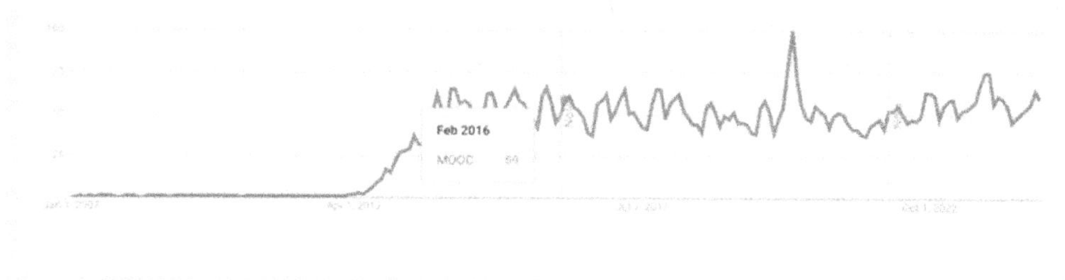

The Figure 1 depicts the evolution of interest in MOOCs over time, as shown by Google Trends data. The data illustrates variations in worldwide search interest, highlighting significant instances of MOOC uptake and proliferation. Peaks on the trend line may indicate noteworthy events or times of increased emphasis on online learning, illustrating the changing significance of MOOCs in educational accessibility and lifelong learning. As MOOCs evolved, they began to include additional instructional strategies, such as gamification and adaptive learning technology, to enhance learner engagement and retention (Rincón-Flores et al., 2019; Li et al., 2021). This approach exemplifies a wider trend towards customized learning experiences designed to address the demands of a really diverse array of learners. The COVID-19 pandemic expedited the adoption of online learning systems, including MOOCs, due to the necessity for educational institutions to sustain learning amid extensive interruptions caused by the pandemic (Hu et al., 2022). The role of MOOCs in higher education is increasingly scrutinized as more institutions investigate their potential for offering recognized programs and professional development opportunities (Wu et al., 2019; Tang & Xing, 2021).

MOOC Variants: Understanding the Distinct Types and their Educational Value

The classification of massive open online courses (MOOCs) is primarily focused on two types: Extensive massive open online courses (xMOOCs) and connectivist Massive Open Online Course (cMOOCs). xMOOCs are designed to be more similar to traditional courses. They include a structured instructor-defined course content and learning pathways, and they frequently rely heavily on video lectures and evaluations to lead students through the subject. cMOOCs, on the other hand, take a collaborative and constructivist approach to learning. This means that the content for learning is created and constructed by the learners themselves. This means that the learners are moving toward a networked learning environment that is interactive and encourages peer-to-peer learning (Alraimi et al., 2015; Geng et al., 2020). These key differences draw attention to the many philosophies that underpin massive open online courses (MOOCs), and as a result, they cater to the various requirements and preferences of students.

The educational value of Massive Open Online Courses (MOOCs), on the other hand, has been a subject of extensive research, reflecting their transformative potential in higher education. According to Walji et al. (2016), MOOCs have been an exceptional force in higher education, serving as a non-formal educational alternative that enhances traditional course offerings. In the study of Ataizi et. al. (2019) the learning theories employed in online educational films were involved research utilizing a selected scale. Accordingly, videos are extensively utilized in MOOC platforms to augment learner engagement and enhance educational settings.

Such flexibility is conducive to part-time students and those with other commitments, as it promotes self-paced learning and revisiting the course contents at any time. Indeed, such convenience as 24/7 access to learning materials has proved to facilitate better learning outcomes because learners could consolidate their knowledge at an appropriate speed. This high-availability of accessing learning materials proved to improve learning outcomes which allows students consolidate their comprehension at their own pace (Ho et al., 2022).

The Emergence and Significance of Micro-Credentials

The Massive Open Online Courses gave rise to Micro Credentials, which is a short-form credential course concerned with specific skills or knowledge domains, and referred to as competency-based certification, recognizing what the learner knows and is able to do.

The emergence of the micro-credential does indeed mark a new frontier in the landscape of education and workforce development, especially considering recent changes in labor market demands and requirements for continuous learning. Micro-credentials are often defined as short qualifications with a focused approach that certifies specific skills or competencies; their usage began to gain significant traction in the past few years, most notably in the higher education and vocational training sectors. This emergence is driven by various factors, including the rapid pace of technological advancement, the increasing complexity of job roles, and the necessity for lifelong learning in a competitive job market (Wheelahan & Moodie, 2021; Ha et al., 2022; Maina et al., 2022).

Figure 2. Micro-credentials impact report 2024

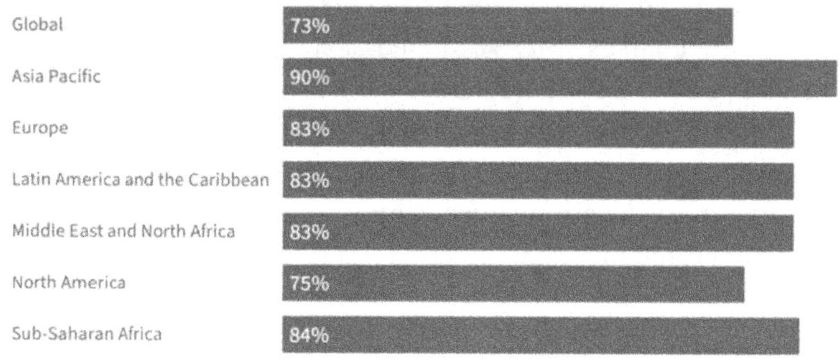

The Figure 2 (Digital Promise, 2024) highlights the expansion of micro-credential offerings in universities following their initial implementation. It reflects the percentage of universities that responded "yes" to questions about scaling up micro-credential programs—either by extending access to more students or by adding new micro-credential options. The data suggests growing institutional interest in micro-credentials as a means to enhance educational flexibility and meet diverse learning needs, underlining the positive impact on program breadth and accessibility. Because micro-credentials have grown in popularity, it is now possible for learners to leverage those small certifications in order to learn new skills and prove skill sets cost-efficiently at any time that suits them. Unlike traditional degrees, micro-credentials are more often recognized by the industry and may be earned within weeks or months. The change in the nature of work itself is one of the key drivers for the emergence of micro-credentials. Indeed, the gig economy-with its very nature of short-term contracting and freelancing-requires a somewhat flexible approach toward education and training (Wheelahan and Moodie (2021). Traditional degree programs often fail to equip individuals with the specific skills required for these roles, and there is a greater demand for more targeted learning experience which should be quickly acquired and easily verified (Ha et al., 2022. Thus, micro-credentials serve as a bridge between formal education and work-relevant competencies that enable learners to demonstrate capability in an accessible and relevant way (Maina et al., 2022).

Moreover, apart from responding to the needs of the labor market, micro-credentials also support the inclusivity and equity of education. They have provided a route for the non-traditional learner-for example, a person coming from a marginalized background or those who do not have access to conventional educational pathways-to gain recognition for their skills and knowledge acquired (Desmarchelier & Cary, 2022). It is the democratization of learning, highly significant in the contemporary world with its growing inequalities in education. Micro-credentials might do much to redress the balance, providing people with an opportunity to improve their employability and career prospects thanks to a more flexible and modular way of learning (Desmarchelier & Cary, 2022; Ha et al., 2022).

From Badges to Certificates: Exploring the Diverse World of Micro-Credentials

The most pervasive form of micro-credential developed to date has been the *digital badge*: a visual marker of skill or competence that is gained from various learning experiences. Additionally, digital badges record professional development activities such as workshops and training programs, allowing them to be shared over social media or professional networking platforms and, in turn, widening access to skills and their recognition (Risquez et al., 2020).

Other key categories include *stackable micro-credentials*, which enables learners to accumulate various credentials over time, leading to a more significant certification, such as a certificate or degree. This modular approach allows learners the ability to personalize their learning routes in accordance with their career goals and personal interests. According to Souto-Otero (2021), stackable micro-credentials are more in tune with lifelong learning due to the flexibility and adaptability this presents to a job market that is increasingly in flux (Kumar et al., 2022).

Professional certifications represent another form of micro-credentials that normally arise from either learning institutions or professional bodies. They generally require more commitment, as compared to digital badges, since they are a series of courses or training with specialization in a particular field or sector (Tang & Xing, 2021). The purpose is making individuals more employable through equipping them with pertinent skills and knowledge to execute their chosen professions (Maina et al., 2022)

Competency-based micro-credentials, on the other hand, focus on the demonstration of specific skills or competencies rather than traditional assessments such as tests or exams. The strategy underlying this approach congruently coincides with the increased need for competency-based hiring practices, a process whereby employers are more concerned with functional skills rather than with credentials such as diplomas (Ha et al., 2022). Competency-based micro-credentials prove particularly helpful in areas such as technology, health, and education, where well-defined competencies are critical to successful performance (Kumar et al., 2022). They provide a clear framework for assessing and approving such talents, hence employers are easily able to identify qualified individuals (Maina et al., 2022)

Finally, MOOC-based micro-credentials have been in the limelight during recent years and especially after the COVID-19 pandemic, which accelerated the adoption of online learning platforms. Many MOOCs offer micro-credentials within their programs and thus allow learners to obtain recognized certificates from highly reputable universities (Ramírez-Montoya et al., 2022; Naidu, 2020). These micro-credentials, ranging from a wide variety of topics, are open to virtually anyone worldwide, and hence make a very attractive option for those individuals interested in enhancing their skills without many of the constraints that come with traditional education (Kumar et al., 2022; Ramírez-Montoya et al., 2022).

Recognition of MOOCs and micro-credentials

The recognition of MOOCs (Massive Open Online Courses) and micro-credentials has become increasingly significant in the landscape of higher education. This recognition process must be seen as a strategic move to enhance employability and lifelong learning opportunities for learners. Recognizing micro-credentials and MOOCs by higher education institutions is, in fact, the linchpin of their effectiveness. Higher Education Institutions are uniquely positioned to lead innovation in this area, having the ability to support students to crystallize learning experiences into formal pathways that enhance employability (Maina et al., 2022). Wheelahan and Moodie (2021) noted that micro-credentials have the potential to better align higher education with the requirements of the workplace. However, unless carefully integrated into existing qualification frameworks, they risk fragmenting education. In addition to employment, micro-credentials can be employed by higher education institutions as components of the curriculum, such as a recognizing mechanism for the completion of a course.

One of the key aspects which most of the recognition approaches is the explicit clarification of the skills and competencies to be developed by means of a micro-credential. Maina et al. (2022) argue that the HEIs are in a privileged position to help students consolidate the learning experiences into structured learning pathways which is recognised also by employers. For this purpose, higher education has to work in close relation with industrial partners in order to guarantee that the competencies taught in higher education correspond to the current needs in the labor market.

For that matter, technology usage would play a major role in the road to recognition for MOOCs and micro-credentials. According to Gribbins (2023), technologies like online proctoring and assessment have the potential to increase the security of assessments while protecting academic integrity in an online learning environment.

Moreover, recognition of prior learning and informal education experiences are another approach to increasing the accreditation of micro-credentials. According to Aydemir (2024), there is a need to recognize non-formal and informal learning within formal education systems, and this validation can be achieved through modularization and the use of stackable credentials. In this context, the diverse ways in which people will gain skills shall enable the educational institutes to establish more inclusive recognition mechanisms that are welcoming of broader spectrums of learners.

From Novice to Expert: Who Benefits from MOOCs and micro-credentials?

Research has shown that learner characteristics and motivation plays a significant role in MOOC engagement and retention. Other contributory factors for this classification include prior experience in online education, self-reported commitment and personal learning goals, all of which are identified to be very important predictors of success in the MOOCs (Greene et al., 2015; Shapiro et al., 2017). Understanding these motivational dynamics will help in the development of MOOCs that engage participants more and ensure continuity in engagement and commitment. Besides, diversity in the MOOC learner population calls for an intentional approach to course design, taking into consideration several levels of prior knowledge and different learning preferences (Knox, 2014).

Participation in MOOCs represents a multi-dimensional engagement that has been avidly researched; different mechanisms have been put forward through which learners are engaged, citing complexity and interplay between personal attributes and the learning environment as the big influencer of engagement (Liu et al., 2022). Deng et al. (2019) highlights a four-dimensional taxonomy of engagement namely behavioral, emotional, cognitive, and social. This holistic approach allows educators to understand how many factors contribute to the level of engagement and achievement of learners in MOOCs. The importance of cognitive presence within the Community of Inquiry paradigm has a strong bearing on learning outcomes, and enhancing cognitive engagement is important if improvement in the education experience within MOOCs is to be achieved (Liu et al., 2022).

Overcoming Challenges and Ensuring Quality: The Future Of Moocs and Micro-Credentials

The implementation of micro-credential faces many challenges. Kumar et al. (2022) stress that harmonization of the frameworks with the prevailing educational system is essential to ensure its value and recognition by interested parties. Specifically, the unvalued badges especially those which are not integrated into an already existing micro-credential framework are bound to fail consistently. Ha et al. (2022) indicate that micro-credentials, on one side, might have the advantages of affordability and accessibility; on the other hand, they may be viewed as insufficient compared to traditionally obtained qualifications. The recent debate about the validity of micro-credentials and their recognition underlines the need for more holistic frameworks that would make it possible to integrate them into existing systems.

International cooperation is, therefore, ever so important not only for developing microcredentials but also for their recognition, especially in the context of vocational education. Borodiyenko (2023) investigates the role of international organizations in the development of qualifications frameworks, enhancing transparency and mobility in vocational training systems. This, in turn, facilitates recognition processes at national and European levels. This study is important for microcredential recognition and valorization at an international level to enhance employability for graduates in the global job market.

Quality assurance of MOOCs and micro-credentials has been a very complex issue. This difficulty was perpetuated by a lack of defined standards against which the quality of MOOCs could be measured. Another big impediment was the issue of accreditation for micro-credentials. Unlike traditional degrees that get accreditation from well-esteemed institutions, they did not get formal recognition. Despite the growing figures of various approaches to education, there is limited awareness among employers concerning their importance. This disconnection can impede graduates' capacity to utilize their micro-credentials in the employment sector.

All the challenges facing MOOCs and micro-credentials, especially those on quality assurance, accreditation, and recognition, require novel solutions. Therefore, the solution calls for a holistic approach entailing the identification and creation of standardized frameworks, foster industry-education linkages, and innovative assessment methods to assure quality and relevance. Each of these methods can significantly enhance the credibility and effectiveness of MOOCs and micro-credentials.

Another urgent need within the MOOC and micro-credential ecosystem is the development of shared frameworks for quality assurance and accreditation. Wu et al., (2019) assert that an increase in numbers of approved MOOCs creates a pressing need for third-party reviews to ensure the quality of courses while protecting the interests of learners. Such frameworks could derive inspiration from established accrediting agencies responsible for quality assurance providing comprehensive standards guiding the evaluation of programs of study. With such methodology being applied, educational institutions will be in a position to give a more standardized and consistent framework toward assessing the qualities of MOOCs and micro-credentials.

Apart from standardization, it is very important to develop collaboration between educational providers and industrial stakeholders. This will allow educational programs to be updated according to the constantly changing demands for employment. Collaborative efforts could facilitate the development of curricula based on labor market demand. This could potentially raise the status and value of micro-credentials within the labor market. Besides this, collaboration with industry can contribute much-needed input regarding competencies and required skills for the framing of suitable educational provisions.

The integration of emergent technologies into MOOCs and micro-credentials brings both opportunities and challenges with regard to considerations for equity and access. MOOCs facilitate swift access to knowledge in advanced domains such as AI, blockchain, and biotechnology, promoting a steady influx of innovative ideas (Durak & Çankaya, 2024; Durak et al., 2024). Emerging technologies such as artificial intelligence and machine learning are anticipated to enhance the personalization of MOOCs and micro-credentials. Adaptive learning systems can analyze learners' progress in real time, providing tailored content and assessments to improve engagement and retention. This degree of personalization may reduce the disparity in educational quality between traditional programs and online alternatives. As industries progress, there is an increasing need for skills that are not consistently included in conventional educational programs. MOOCs and micro-credentials are progressively aligned with industry standards, with numerous platforms collaborating directly with companies to develop skills-based courses. This trend may result in increased specialization of programs, yielding more job-ready graduates and enhanced acceptance of alternative credentials. Institutions are increasingly providing university credits for the completion of MOOCs and micro-credentials, while certain companies are collaborating with online platforms to develop credentialed programs. The increasing recognition of alternative pathways may prompt more students to pursue combinations of micro-credentials and traditional degrees, potentially resulting in hybrid educational models. Stackable micro-credentials, which enable learners to acquire qualifications progressively, are anticipated to rise in prevalence. Learners can systematically receive advanced qualifications, potentially culminating in degrees. This may result in a modular and flexible educational system, enabling individuals to upskill continuously without the necessity of long-term traditional programs. As Naidu (2020) mentioned, the development toward “MOOC 2.0” would come with new economic models and pedagogical scaffolding responsive to diverse student needs. This development may have embedded artificial intelligence and adaptive learning tools that would make the learning personal for each learner; thus, increasing their motivation to persevere in learning.

With the increasing development of higher education, an increasing urgency is felt to embed learning analytics into MOOCs and micro-credentials for enhancing learning experiences. According to Corrin et al. (2020), learning analytics has the potential to provide information on student engagement and performance for educators, enabling them to adapt their methodologies to meet the needs of individual learners. Data-driven insights allow institutions to strengthen course design and delivery for better learning outcomes.

The discourse on quality assurance in higher education will continue to influence the future of both MOOCs and micro-credentials. Grek and Russell (2023) assert that the expanding micro-credentials industry has prompted increasing demands to reevaluate quality assurance frameworks, particularly concerning the Bologna Process. Once these credentials gain prevalence, a definitive standard and regulation must be established to ensure they align with the expectations of learners and businesses.

CONCLUSION

It is a disruptive force in lifelong learning that the combination of massive open online courses (MOOCs) and micro-credentials symbolizes. This combination provides individuals with a flexible, accessible, and effective avenue to bridge the skills gap. Learners have the ability to go on a journey of continuous growth and development by utilizing the educational resources and skill validation mechanisms that are made available by Massive Open Online Courses (MOOCs) and Micro-Credentials. This allows them to equip themselves with the knowledge and skills necessary to succeed in a world that is constantly changing.

MOOC variants allow educational institutions to offer specialized, scalable courses that cater to diverse learner needs across the globe, building pathways for lifelong learning and reskilling. Micro-credentials, often issued upon completion of MOOCs, offer verifiable qualifications that can be used by learners worldwide to demonstrate specific skills or knowledge. This credentialing process enhances global competitiveness by empowering individuals with targeted, employer-recognized skills, thereby addressing workforce gaps and promoting economic growth in multiple countries. From an institutional standpoint, these credentials attract international students, boost enrollment, and extend an institution's global footprint. The variants of MOOCs support internationalization by connecting learners from various backgrounds and cultures within shared learning ecosystems, promoting global knowledge exchange, and fostering collaborations that transcend borders.

The unique intersection of MOOCs and micro-credentials lies in their ability to offer accessible, flexible, and industry-relevant education while providing specific, verified skills. When these two forms of learning intersect, they create a distinctive educational model that stands apart from traditional degrees or certifications. Through MOOCs and micro-credentials, education becomes more agile, accessible, and relevant. This new paradigm not only empowers learners to pursue education on their terms but also aligns learning with the needs of a dynamic workforce, preparing individuals to excel in an evolving global economy. This transformation in education ultimately fosters a culture where knowledge acquisition is a lifelong, flexible journey, equipping learners with the tools to thrive both personally and professionally. Empowering learners through MOOCs and micro-credentials involves creating a new paradigm that is learner-centered, flexible, and relevant to the evolving demands of the workforce. This paradigm shift emphasizes personalized learning, skill validation, and industry alignment, fundamentally transforming how education is accessed and utilized. The concept both combined triggered the competitiveness in line with globalization and internationalization. Considering the universities mission-oriented differentiation strategies of universities, the sharing and recognition of the capabilities at a global level is possible with the harmonious presentation of MOOCs and micro-crediting framework. This sharing and recognition has the potential to provide a capital input to the country in a national context. By providing flexibility in educational environments where the expression "Knowledge is power" finds its most meaningful place; the recognition of the knowledge and skills gained from these environments supports and reinforces the position of England as a service industry country at a global level. Hence, it is important more than ever to redefine higher education in line with a new paradigm to shape the future of workforce development with the concept of MOOCs and micro-credentials framework. Instead of requiring full degree programs, learners can focus on acquiring specific, job-ready skills through micro-credentials that provide direct pathways to employment and advancement. It is also worth noting that embedding project-based assignments in MOOCs allows learners to apply theoretical knowledge to real-world scenarios. This hands-on experience develops practical skills and provides learners with a portfolio of work they can present to employers. Learning centric personalization might be reconsidered via adaptive learning technologies, especially incorporating AI-driven platforms within MOOCs can help provide personalized recommendations, adaptive difficulty levels, and feedback based on individual progress. This also fosters a more engaging, responsive, and personalized learning experience. By collaborating with industry experts, programs ensure skills are immediately applicable in the workforce. Bridging the gap for the skills and upskills in line with the competencies of the institution should be focused in depth for a global competitiveness. By equipping workers with up-to-date competencies in areas like technology, healthcare, and data science, MOOCs help economies address skill shortages that might otherwise hinder their competitiveness. In emerging economies, MOOCs and micro-credentials empower individuals to acquire high-demand skills that might not be available locally. This growth in skilled labor enhances productivity and attracts foreign investment, positioning these countries to compete in high-value sectors globally. As industries evolve, a workforce skilled in the latest technologies and methodologies is crucial for maintaining competitiveness. MOOCs and micro-credentials foster a culture of lifelong learning, enabling employees to update their skills and stay productive, adaptable, and ready to meet emerging industry needs. By providing rapid access to knowledge in cutting-edge fields like AI, blockchain, and biotechnology, MOOCs encourage a continuous inflow of new ideas. This access allows both individuals and companies to adopt innovative practices, enabling countries to lead in technological advancements rather than follow.

Many MOOCs and micro-credential programs are developed with direct input from industry leaders, ensuring that the skills taught align with current market demands. This alignment produces a talent pool that is "job-ready" upon completion, reducing training costs for employers and giving nations a competitive edge by having a skilled workforce that meets industry needs. Micro-credentials offer a faster alternative to traditional degrees, allowing learners to gain verified skills in specific areas. In fields like cybersecurity, data analysis, and digital marketing—where skills quickly become obsolete—micro-credentials enable a rapid upskilling process, ensuring that workers' expertise remains relevant and competitive. MOOCs and micro-credentials provide affordable access to quality education, reducing the need for costly traditional degrees and increasing the return on investment (ROI) for individuals and governments alike. For governments, investing in accessible digital education improves the national talent pool without the significant financial investment required for traditional education infrastructure. For employers, particularly multinational corporations, MOOCs provide a scalable way to upskill employees globally. This scalability enables companies to quickly develop a competitive workforce across regions, contributing to their global efficiency and reducing location-based skill gaps. Recognized micro-credentials enable individuals to validate their skills globally, facilitating cross-border talent mobility. This portability supports countries and companies that need to attract foreign talent, as job candidates can showcase their competencies through widely accepted credentials. With the rise of remote work, employers are looking globally for talent. MOOCs equip individuals with skills that make them competitive in an international job market, increasing their employment opportunities and allowing economies to participate in high-skilled sectors.

As MOOC platforms collaborate with top universities and industry experts, they raise the quality and rigor of educational content available worldwide. Access to this quality education sets a higher standard for local institutions, encouraging countries to improve their own educational offerings to stay competitive. MOOCs help reduce educational disparities between regions by providing access to consistent, high-quality courses globally. This balance enables talent in under-resourced areas to compete with their peers in more developed regions, ultimately contributing to more equitable and robust economic growth. As more people gain high-demand skills, national economies benefit from increased productivity and innovation, which are crucial drivers of economic growth. Skilled workers are more likely to contribute to new business ventures and industries, fostering economic diversity and resilience. Countries with strong adoption of MOOCs and micro-credentials are better positioned to become innovation hubs, as they can provide a pipeline of skilled workers to tech, finance, and creative industries. These hubs attract investment and talent, contributing to economic growth and regional competitiveness. MOOCs often have global student bodies, promoting cross-cultural exchange and fostering networks among learners from different backgrounds. This exposure to diverse perspectives enhances problem-solving skills, creativity, and the ability to collaborate internationally, which are essential qualities in a globally competitive workforce. MOOCs provide knowledge that supports entrepreneurship, especially in developing countries where access to formal business education may be limited. Empowering individuals to start businesses based on current market knowledge fuels innovation and supports local economic independence.

Micro-credentials and MOOCs represent innovative educational formats that have recently gained traction for enhancing the flexibility and accessibility of learning. They differ in relation to professional development, employer acknowledgment, and educational standards. Accessibility, affordability, a diverse array of courses, and reputable instructors are recognized benefits of MOOCs. In contrast, micro-credentials may offer advantages through specialized skills, stackable learning pathways, and enhanced employer recognition. However, MOOCs present several disadvantages, such as limited customization, lower completion rates, and inconsistent recognition by employers. Furthermore, additional drawbacks of micro-credentials encompass their restricted scope, possible expenses, and discrepancies in quality and recognition.

In terms of educational quality MOOCs deliver extensive and cost-effective education with limited customization, whereas micro-credentials provide targeted, skill-oriented training. Micro-credentials are more widely accepted by employers due to their alignment with job requirements, while MOOCs are typically regarded as supplementary and may not significantly enhance a resume. Each format presents distinct advantages based on learners' objectives and the specific professional development requirements.

Considering the potential of MOOCs and micro-credentials in revolutionizing education by making learning more accessible, affordable, and relevant to the workforce, it is important to be aware of the challenges in quality control, recognition, and accessibility they bring and powerful alternatives to traditional education of the adaptability for the rapidly changing skills requirements positions. As technology advances and employers embrace skills-based hiring, MOOCs and micro-credentials may push universities to evolve, possibly leading to a more modular, lifelong-learning-based educational ecosystem that better meets the needs of modern learners.

Another consideration is that credential validation, quality consistency, and access in underprivileged areas represent significant concerns that highlight complex challenges for employers, learners, and providers. For MOOCs and micro-credentials to gain widespread acceptance as educational pathways, it is essential to address the challenges of credential certification, quality consistency, and accessibility. MOOCs and micro-credentials can achieve their full potential as effective and respected alternatives to traditional educational systems by establishing criteria for credential validation, ensuring instructional consistency, and promoting equitable access.

In sum, MOOCs and micro-credentials are reshaping global competitiveness by making skill development affordable, accessible, and aligned with industry needs. By bridging skill gaps, enhancing workforce agility, and promoting economic participation in high-value sectors, they empower individuals and nations alike to thrive in an interconnected, competitive world.

Recommendations

To harness the potential of MOOCs and micro-credentials on a global scale, policy-makers, decision-makers, and practitioners must implement frameworks that prioritize quality assurance, internationalization, and global competitiveness.

Policy-Makers

The integration of MOOCs and micro-credentials into current educational systems poses a number of regulatory and policy challenges, apart from pedagogical issues. The policymakers will have to find their way through details of the current frameworks on accreditation and funding that shall help these innovative educational options. Educational institutions, companies, and government agencies need to come together in laying down a unified ecosystem that recognizes and validates micro-credentials in concert with traditional degrees (Blankenberger & Phillips, 2016). By doing so, such collaboration would ensure that the competencies earned with micro-credentials meet labor market needs and are valuable to both learners and business alike.

Establish Global Quality Assurance Standards: Develop and promote a set of global standards for MOOCs and micro-credentials to ensure consistent quality across providers. This includes benchmarking curriculum rigor, assessment standards, and instructor qualifications, potentially through partnerships with international educational bodies like UNESCO.

Support Accreditation Frameworks for Micro-Credentials: Work with accreditation bodies to establish recognized frameworks for micro-credentials. Such frameworks should define learning outcomes, credit equivalencies, and competencies for each micro-credential, making it easier for employers and educational institutions to recognize and value these qualifications.

Encourage Public-Private Partnerships: Promote collaborations between governments, educational institutions, and private industry to co-design MOOC curricula that align with market needs. This can help to ensure that learning outcomes are relevant to local and global labor markets, enhancing both employability and economic growth.

Incentivize Lifelong Learning and Upskilling: Create funding programs or tax incentives to encourage individuals and businesses to invest in lifelong learning through MOOCs and micro-credentials. Such incentives can motivate continuous upskilling and reskilling, thereby supporting workforce agility.

Promote Digital Infrastructure and Accessibility: Invest in digital infrastructure, especially in underserved regions, to ensure equitable access to MOOCs. This includes improving internet connectivity, providing affordable digital devices, and offering open-access education resources.

Decision-Makers in Educational Institutions

Integrate MOOCs and Micro-Credentials into Formal Programs: Allow students to incorporate MOOCs and micro-credentials as part of degree programs or continuing education credits, creating hybrid learning pathways that support flexible, industry-aligned education. This integration should be mapped to recognized standards, ensuring that credits can transfer across institutions.

Adopt Competency-Based Education Models: Shift towards competency-based education, where learners progress based on skill mastery rather than time spent in class. Decision-makers can create pathways that allow students to advance once they demonstrate proficiency, making micro-credentials more effective for workforce readiness.

Develop Global Collaboration Networks: Form global partnerships with MOOC providers, universities, and employers to co-develop courses that meet international standards. This can create cross-institutional recognition of credentials, expanding opportunities for students to apply their skills in different countries.

Focus on Quality Control and Assessment Rigor: Establish internal quality assurance units to maintain course integrity. Incorporate proctored exams, peer assessments, and project-based evaluations to ensure that MOOC and micro-credential learners meet the institution's academic standards.

Create Learning Pathways for Diverse Learner Needs: Design stackable micro-credential programs to serve different learner profiles, from recent graduates to mid-career professionals. Ensure pathways allow students to build upon their credentials progressively, either leading to advanced qualifications or directly enhancing their employability.

Practitioners (MOOC and Micro-Credential Providers)

Align Content with Industry Standards and Workforce Needs: Regularly update course content to reflect changes in technology, industry practices, and global workforce needs. Engage industry experts to co-develop content and ensure that learning outcomes are closely tied to market demands.

Implement Transparent Assessment and Verification Systems: Adopt rigorous assessment methods that include quizzes, projects, and proctored exams to validate skill acquisition. Provide digital badges or certificates that document verified competencies, allowing employers to see specific skills that learners have mastered.

Focus on Accessibility and Inclusion: Develop MOOCs that consider accessibility features, such as closed captions, multi-language support, and adaptive learning tools for learners with disabilities. Providing diverse language options is crucial for promoting global accessibility and fostering inclusivity.

Create Community and Networking Opportunities: Foster peer interaction and professional networking opportunities within MOOCs through discussion forums, study groups, and virtual events. This approach can create global learning communities and support learners in developing soft skills like collaboration, cross-cultural understanding, and communication.

Monitor and Report Learning Outcomes: Track and analyze learner progress and outcomes to assess the effectiveness of each course. Use this data to continually improve content and to provide learners with personalized feedback, ensuring that they achieve meaningful skill development.

Cross-Sector Recommendations

Encourage Recognition of Micro-Credentials by Employers: All stakeholders should advocate for greater employer recognition of micro-credentials, educating companies about the value of skills-based credentials and collaborating to align educational content with job requirements.

Promote Transparency in Credentialing: Implement a standardized, digital record-keeping system (such as blockchain) for credentials, allowing learners to store and share verified skills easily. This transparency would make it easier for employers and institutions to verify qualifications, supporting global workforce mobility.

Support Research and Innovation in MOOC Pedagogy: Allocate funding for research on best practices in online learning and digital pedagogy to continually refine the effectiveness of MOOCs. This research can guide improvements in instructional design, engagement strategies, and assessment rigor.

The recommendations above, when implemented cohesively, can create a robust global education ecosystem where MOOCs and micro-credentials not only supplement traditional education but also enhance international competitiveness by building a highly skilled, mobile, and adaptable workforce. Through policies, partnerships, and innovative practices, education stakeholders can elevate the role of MOOCs and micro-credentials in preparing learners for a competitive global economy similar to service industries.

REFERENCES

Agasisti, T., Azzone, G., & Soncin, M. (2021). Assessing the effect of massive open online courses as remedial courses in higher education. *Innovations in Education and Teaching International*, 59(4), 462–471. DOI: 10.1080/14703297.2021.1886969

Alraimi, K. M., Zo, H., & Ciganek, A. P. (2015). Understanding the moocs continuance: The role of openness and reputation. Computers &Amp. *Computers & Education*, 80, 28–38. DOI: 10.1016/j.compedu.2014.08.006

Ashwin, P. (2022). The educational purposes of higher education: Changing discussions of the societal outcomes of educating students. *Higher Education*, 84(6), 1227–1244. DOI: 10.1007/s10734-022-00930-9

Ataizi, M., Öztürk, Ö., Demir, M., Kaya, S., İşcan, A., İşkol, S., & Kömür, İ. A. (2019). Examining Mooc Videos in Terms of Learning Theories. *Journal of Educational Technology and Online Learning*, 2(1), 34–55. DOI: 10.31681/jetol.516029

Aydemir, M. (2024). Micro-Credentials and Recognition of prior learning: Offering flexible and relevant learning opportunities for ODL learners. https://www.icetol.com/wp-content/uploads/2024/09/icetol2024_full_paper_proceedings.pdf

Blankenberger, B., & Phillips, A. D. (2016). Performance funding in Illinois higher education. *Educational Policy*, 30(6), 884–915. DOI: 10.1177/0895904814556748

Borodiyenko, O., Melnyk, O., & Nychkalo, N. (2023). The role of international cooperation in the development of vocational education in ukraine. *European Journal of Education*, 58(4), 665–680. DOI: 10.1111/ejed.12586

Buchanan, John vd., (2020) "The Futures of Work: What Education Can and Can't Do", s.2-4, erişim 13 Ekim, 2020. https://unesdoc.unesco.org/ark:/48223/pf0000374435

Corrin, L., Scheffel, M., & Gašević, D. (2020). Learning analytics: Pathways to impact. *Australasian Journal of Educational Technology*, 36(6), 1–6. DOI: 10.14742/ajet.6853

Deng, R., Benckendorff, P., & Gannaway, D. (2019). Learner engagement in moocs: Scale development and validation. *British Journal of Educational Technology*, 51(1), 245–262. DOI: 10.1111/bjet.12810

Desmarchelier, R., & Cary, L. J. (2022). Toward just and equitable micro-credentials: An australian perspective. *International Journal of Educational Technology in Higher Education*, 19(1), 25. Advance online publication. DOI: 10.1186/s41239-022-00332-y PMID: 35669714

Digital Promise. (2024). Micro-credentials impact report 2024. Digital Promise. https://assets.ctfassets.net/2pudprfttvy6/6kCSgjxcL69gh4ziZnlBhr/ff912d112d1af bdf705a893b6e9f99ea/Micro-Credentials_Impact_Report_2024.pdf

Downes, S. (2010). Learning networks and connective knowledge. Collective Intelligence and E-Learning 2.0, 1-26. https://doi.org/DOI: 10.4018/978-1-60566-729-4.ch001

Durak, G., & Çankaya, S. (2024). Are alarm bells ringing in academia? Chatgpt as a sample of using chatbots in education. *Turkish Online Journal of Distance Education*, 25(3), 1–17. DOI: 10.17718/tojde.1353737

Durak, G., Çankaya, S., Özdemir, D., & Can, S. (2024). Artificial intelligence in education: A bibliometric study on its role in transforming teaching and learning. *International Review of Research in Open and Distance Learning*, 25(3), 219–244. DOI: 10.19173/irrodl.v25i3.7757

Geng, S., Niu, B., Feng, Y., & Huang, M. (2020). Understanding the focal points and sentiment of learners in mooc reviews: A machine learning and sc-liwc-based approach. *British Journal of Educational Technology*, 51(5), 1785–1803. DOI: 10.1111/bjet.12999

Greene, J. A., Oswald, C., & Pomerantz, J. (2015). Predictors of retention and achievement in a massive open online course. *American Educational Research Journal*, 52(5), 925–955. DOI: 10.3102/0002831215584621

Grek, S., & Russell, I. (2023). Beyond bologna? infrastructuring quality in european higher education. *European Educational Research Journal*, 23(2), 215–236. DOI: 10.1177/14749041231170518

Gribbins, M., & Bonk, C. J. (2023). An exploration of instructors' perceptions about online proctoring and its value in ensuring academic integrity. *British Journal of Educational Technology*, 54(6), 1693–1714. DOI: 10.1111/bjet.13389

Ha, N. T. N., Spittle, M., Watt, A. P., & Dyke, N. V. (2022). A systematic literature review of micro-credentials in higher education: A non-zero-sum game. Higher Education Research &Amp. *Higher Education Research & Development*, 42(6), 1527–1548. DOI: 10.1080/07294360.2022.2146061

Hamutoğlu. Ünveren-Bilgiç, & Özden, (2023). *The Importance of Internal Quality Assurance Standards in Higher Education for Competitiveness and National Development. Proceeding*, 36th Asian Association of Open Universities Annual Conference (AAOU 2023), 28-30 September, İstanbul, Türkiye.

Ho, N., Pham, H., Sivapalan, S., & Dinh, V. (2022). The adoption of blended learning using coursera moocs: A case study in a vietnamese higher education institution. *Australasian Journal of Educational Technology*, 38(6), 121–138. DOI: 10.14742/ajet.7671

Hu, Y., Donald, C., & Giacaman, N. (2022). A revised application of cognitive presence automatic classifiers for moocs: A new set of indicators revealed? *International Journal of Educational Technology in Higher Education*, 19(1), 48. Advance online publication. DOI: 10.1186/s41239-022-00353-7 PMID: 36118283

Iqbal, S., Naeem, M. A., & Nayyar, A. (2016, November). Status of MOOCs in Pakistan: optimism and concerns. In *2016 European Modelling Symposium (EMS)* (pp. 237-241). IEEE. DOI: 10.1109/EMS.2016.048

Knox, J. (2014). Digital culture clash: "massive" education in thee-learning and digital culturesmooc. *Distance Education*, 35(2), 164–177. DOI: 10.1080/01587919.2014.917704

Kumar, J. A., Richard, R. J., Osman, S., & Lowrence, K. (2022). Micro-credentials in leveraging emergency remote teaching: The relationship between novice users' insights and identity in malaysia. *International Journal of Educational Technology in Higher Education*, 19(1), 18. Advance online publication. DOI: 10.1186/s41239-022-00323-z PMID: 35382441

Li, K., Johnsen, J., & Canelas, D. A. (2021). Persistence, performance, and goal setting in massive open online courses. *British Journal of Educational Technology*, 52(3), 1215–1229. DOI: 10.1111/bjet.13068

Liu, B., Xing, W., Zeng, Y., & Wu, Y. (2022). Linking cognitive processes and learning outcomes: The influence of cognitive presence on learning performance in moocs. *British Journal of Educational Technology*, 53(5), 1459–1477. DOI: 10.1111/bjet.13193

Maina, M. F., Ortiz, L. G., Mancini, F., & Melo, M. M. (2022). A micro-credentialing methodology for improved recognition of he employability skills. *International Journal of Educational Technology in Higher Education*, 19(1), 10. Advance online publication. DOI: 10.1186/s41239-021-00315-5 PMID: 35224180

Miller, K. K., & Jorre, T. J. S. (2022). Digital micro-credentials in environmental science: An employer perspective on valued evidence of skills. *Teaching in Higher Education*, 29(4), 1058–1074. DOI: 10.1080/13562517.2022.2053953

Naidu, S. (2020). The mooc is dead—Long live mooc 2.0! *Distance Education*, 41(1), 1–5. DOI: 10.1080/01587919.2020.1727289

Ossiannilsson, E. (2021). MOOCS for lifelong learning, equity, and liberation. *MOOC (massive open online courses).*

Ramírez-Montoya, M. S., Martínez-Pérez, S., Rodríguez-Abitia, G., & López-Caudana, E. (2022). Digital accreditations in mooc-based training on sustainability: Factors that influence terminal efficiency. *Australasian Journal of Educational Technology*, •••, 164–182. DOI: 10.14742/ajet.7082

Rincón-Flores, E. G., Mena, J., Montoya, M. S. R., & Ramírez-Velarde, R. V. (2019). The use of gamification in xmoocs about energy: Effects and predictive models for participants' learning. *Australasian Journal of Educational Technology*, •••, 43–59. DOI: 10.14742/ajet.4818

Risquez, A., Cassidy, D., & O'Suilleabhain, G. (2020). Badge of honour? an exploration of the use of digital badges to support a partnership approach to faculty development. *Australasian Journal of Educational Technology*, 36(5), 18–29. DOI: 10.14742/ajet.6112

Shapiro, H., Lee, C. H., Roth, N. E. W., & Li, K. (2017). Understanding the massive open online course (mooc) student experience: An examination of attitudes, motivations, and barriers. Computers &Amp. *Computers & Education*, 110, 35–50. DOI: 10.1016/j.compedu.2017.03.003

Souto-Otero, M. (2021). Validation of non-formal and informal learning in formal education: Covert and overt. *European Journal of Education*, 56(3), 365–379. DOI: 10.1111/ejed.12464

Tang, H., & Xing, W. (2021). Massive open online courses for professional certificate programs? perspectives on professional learners' longitudinal participation patterns. *Australasian Journal of Educational Technology*, •••, 136–147. DOI: 10.14742/ajet.5768

Walji, S., Deacon, A., Small, J., & Czerniewicz, L. (2016). Learning through engagement: Moocs as an emergent form of provision. *Distance Education*, 37(2), 208–223. DOI: 10.1080/01587919.2016.1184400

Wheelahan, L., & Moodie, G. (2021). Gig qualifications for the gig economy: Micro-credentials and the 'hungry mile'. *Higher Education*, 83(6), 1279–1295. DOI: 10.1007/s10734-021-00742-3 PMID: 34366441

Willems, J., Farley, H., & Campbell, C. (2019). The increasing significance of digital equity in higher education. *Australasian Journal of Educational Technology*, 35(6), 1–8. DOI: 10.14742/ajet.5996

Wu, X., Hall, A., & Wang, Q. (2019). Investigating the implementation of accredited massive online open courses (moocs) in higher education: The boon and the bane. *Australasian Journal of Educational Technology*, 35(3). Advance online publication. DOI: 10.14742/ajet.3896

Chapter 4
Designing and Developing Microcredentials

Stacey L. Rosenberg
https://orcid.org/0000-0001-9148-5792
Southern New Hampshire University, USA

Toni Clayton
https://orcid.org/0000-0002-2694-4654
Southern New Hampshire University, USA

ABSTRACT

This chapter offers a guide to designing and developing microcredentials, highlighting their key characteristics, benefits, and theoretical foundations. It explores core design elements, including the value for higher education providers and learners, assessment methods, partnerships, infrastructure, and financial planning. The development process encompasses market analysis, governance and accreditation, and strategies for integration and transferability. Quality assurance and continuous improvement are emphasized, focusing on delivery methods, technological platforms, assessment strategies, and alignment with labor market needs. The chapter stresses defining specific skills, providing evidence of achievement, and engaging internal and external stakeholders. Implementation strategies cover promotion, marketing, leveraging partnerships, and effective branding. Practical insights are provided through case studies and examples of successful programs. The chapter concludes with a discussion on future trends and challenges, offering a forward-looking perspective on microcredentials.

DOI: 10.4018/979-8-3693-5488-9.ch004

INTRODUCTION

In recent years, microcredentials have increased in demand, triggering the attention of educators to think about learning outside of the traditional educational pathways. The driving force behind this demand is a shift by industry leaders to better understand what job qualifications and skills are essential to perform a wide variety of jobs (Hancock et al., 2022). Changes in technology and labor shortages have increased the need to find qualified staff while leveraging existing staff through up-skilling strategies. With skills-based hiring on the rise (Fuller et al., 2022), industry leaders are increasing collaboration efforts with members of academia to help them solve a variety of work-related concerns. Some of these concerns include retention, efficiency, productivity, and employee satisfaction where human resource efforts also highlight succession planning and professional development. Educators are cognizant of the challenges and industry demand as they explore learning models that will prepare students, employees, and job seekers with the job-readiness skills they desire.

The Coronavirus Disease 2019 (COVID-19) pandemic and societal challenges have changed the traditional workplace, leading to hybrid models that include remote work and adaptations to processes and procedures. Unsurprisingly, employers have been prompted to be more flexible as they focus on productivity within a technology shift that includes changes in the workplace guided by artificial intelligence (Putnam, 2024). Consequently, there are many possibilities for short-term learning options centered on job readiness and outcome achievement that can appeal to a variety of ages across a variety of industries. Further, creating a career-long learning culture supports skill development that prepares employees to adapt to any organizational change with confidence that they will have the support they need to be effective and succeed.

As the lasting effects of the Great Resignation continue, many organizations are seeking out opportunities to address employee satisfaction, burn-out, recruitment, and retention concerns. Professional development opportunities drive up-skilling of employees, which is needed to align to the changes in technology, policy, and the environment. In a study conducted by Putnam (2024) over 63% of leaders listed "upskilling as a top priority in the next year" (p. 9), and 43% noted having budgeted for reskilling. Unsurprisingly, employees want more options to increase their chances of job advancement with consideration to time, cost, and work-life balance. One strategy some employers are using to attract and retain talent is tuition reimbursement. Financial assistance for learning that aligns with career goals creates a win-win situation for the employer and employee (Sheather & Slattery, 2021). Microcredentials can meet that need as a positive resource for career development that also serves to develop employees in preparation of future career moves (Humphrey et al., 2021).

There are many options for learning, such as a college and trade school education, that can meet educational and personal goals. However, as needs and circumstances change over the course of a lifetime, a college or technical degree is not the answer for everyone seeking skill obtainment. According to the Higher Learning Commission (2022), workers change "...jobs an average of 17 times and career fields an average of 5 times in the course of a lifetime at work (sic), the need for adults to continue pursuing further education is almost inevitable" (p. 8). A Strada 2021 survey indicated if a person was going to seek additional education or training, 24% would seek a certification or license. Twenty-two percent would seek out specific courses for skill obtainment. Venable (2021) found that 81% of business leaders believe alternate credentials will play a vital role in workforce training. Additionally, 85% agree these alternate credentials could help address workforce gaps.

This chapter explores the intricacies of designing and developing microcredentials for use in higher-education institutions. This includes examining their role in addressing skill gaps, enhancing employability, and fostering continuous lifelong learning. These alternate credentials provide learners with specific skills or knowledge in a concise and focused manner, making them ideal for professionals looking to up-skill or reskill in a rapidly changing job market (Educause, 2017).

UNDERSTANDING MICROCREDENTIALS OVERVIEW

Microcredentials represent a paradigm shift in education and professional development, offering "bite sized" learning tailored to meet the dynamic demands of today's workforce. Cedefop (2024) states that "microcredentials hold promise for connecting people's skillsets with labour market demand in a rapidly changing world of work" (p. 1). Benefits extend from affordability and flexibility to a shorter time commitment. Learners are also drawn to multiple learning options that support work-life balance and align with professional needs (Cedefop, 2024). Microcredentials can be offered in many forms, such as certificates, digital badges, and nanodegrees, each designed to meet specific objectives that appeal to a wide variety of end users.

Advancements and proliferation of technology, as well as the widespread availability of online platforms and learning management systems (LMSs), have increased avenues for the delivery of microcredentials. Unsurprisingly, improved learner access to technology has increased demand for knowledge obtainment that meets a wide variety of personal and professional ambitions. Organizations and institutions are capitalizing on this trend by offering an informal education through platforms like massive open online courses (MOOCs). Since the inception of MOOCs, there has been an increase in interest and usage by universities around the world (Voudoukis & Pagiatakis, 2022). Catering to diverse learner goals and objectives continues to be the focus for higher education institutions as they explore educational approaches and models.

Key Characteristics

At their core, microcredentials are designed to recognize and validate individuals' skills, enabling learners to showcase their expertise. Microcredentials are characterized by their modularity and stack-ability, enabling learners to build upon their existing knowledge and credentials incrementally. This modularity allows for personalized learning, where learners can choose microcredentials that align with their interests, career goals, and learning preferences. Microcredentials are being designed by a variety of institutions using a variety of frameworks. However, there is not one standard definition that is being applied (Salman, 2023). Despite the variations in definitions there is a common goal of aligning to the job market to increase employability. According to Salman (2023), there is a clear theme in the literature that courses are being designed and developed with skills and competencies required for employment. Skill obtainment and productivity rests in the theoretical foundations of positional competition theory.

Benefits and Theoretical Foundations

Within the framework of positional competition theories, employees are incentivized to increase their productivity by upgrading their level of skill (Matic, 2019). Up-skilling is one goal of microcredentials because of the ability to conduct a skills assessment to provide just-in-time learning. The labor market and educational attainment have been a guide to the trainability and productivity of employees (Matic, 2019). Consequently, microcredentials can be developed to not only demonstrate skill obtainment, but also provide transferability of those skills, which can be applied towards higher education degree requirements.

Microcredentials can consist of several courses grouped together to align to a curricular requirement, creating a pathway in higher education where credit for prior learning (CPL) or learning experience credit (LEA) can be earned. CPL or LEA have specific requirements and when met can translate to the awarding of credit towards a degree program. This is consistent with the human capital model and the skill-based technological change theory, which predicts increasing economic returns to college education (Goglio et al., 2023). When learners can up-skill further with varied educational options, they increase their investment, which saves on time and cost. Overall, understanding microcredentials rests on recognizing the potential value they hold as flexible, targeted learning experiences that highlight individual achievements, thus supporting lifelong learning efforts.

Designing Microcredentials

Designing microcredentials is a multifaceted process that begins with defining the objectives representing the value of the skills desired in relationship to industry standards. The UNESCO definition of a microcredential contains four elements (Oliver, 2022): it "is a record of focused learning achievement verifying what the learner knows, understands or can do;" it "includes assessment based on clearly defined standards and is awarded by a trusted provider;" it "has standalone value and may also contribute to or complement other micro-credentials or macro-credentials, including through recognition of prior learning;" and it "meets the standards required by relevant quality assurance" (p. 6). This definition, because of its universal application, can be used as an educational guideline for teams working to gain approval for the design and building of microcredentials.

Core Elements

Value as a Higher Education Provider

Reputation and cost-benefit should play a role in determining relevance. According to the European Training Foundation (2022), "by integrating micro-credentials into existing practices, rather than launching them as a separate strand of work, organisations can complement and where relevant widen the organisation's missions and strategies" (p. 28). Alignment to the institutional brand is also needed to minimize resistance and maintain or enhance the external reputation (UPCEA, 2020).

Value Proposition for Learners: Career Advancement and Skill Enhancement

When reflecting on the value proposition of microcredentials, one should consider how these programs can best serve the diverse needs of learners. The debate centers on whether microcredentials should be noncredit-bearing, offering professional development opportunities for working professionals seeking to enhance their skills; or credit-bearing, providing a pathway for academic recognition and advancement. Noncredit options offer flexibility and accessibility, allowing learners to focus solely on acquiring new skills without the constraints of a traditional academic program (Oliver, 2019). On the other hand, credit-bearing microcredentials provide formal recognition of learning achievements, bolstering learners' credentials and opening doors to further academic and career opportunities by constructing a learning pathway (European Training Foundation, 2022; Oliver, 2019). Prioritizing inclusivity is paramount in ensuring equitable access and success for all learners. Generally, "microcredentials in higher education are largely targeted to learners who have already achieved higher education and have greater financial resources" (Golden et al., 2021, para. 3). Institutions should also consider options to facilitate the pathway into higher education and proactively identify and address barriers to access, such as financial constraints and policies; these can help mitigate barriers and foster an inclusive learning environment (Golden et al., 2021). Finally, as industry needs evolve, microcredentials must adapt to ensure relevance and efficacy in addressing current job requirements.

Partnerships

Industry organizations and employers can offer microcredentials internally or in partnership with higher education (Ralston, 2021). When higher education institutions partner with employer organizations, microcredentials can be built to provide educational pathways that can result in CPL or LEA credit towards a college degree. According to a survey from UPCEA (2023, p. 25), 80% of employers reported "a stackable pathway would increase (or greatly increase) their organization's interest in non-degree or alternative credentials." In this way, too, a learner has choices for meeting future educational goals. One approach used by higher education is to design learning experiences that align to course outcomes of existing courses where academic integrity and rigor have been established (Clayton et al., 2024).

These partnerships with employers are essential considerations for the learning institutes, offering mutually beneficial opportunities for both parties. Chapman (2022) emphasizes the importance of dedicating expertise and resources to foster long-term partnerships, ensuring the education and training meets the expectations of the employer partner while remaining relevant to industry needs. This approach allows for the planning of updates to ensure material is reviewed and updated to stay current with industry changes.

Infrastructure

A robust infrastructure is needed to support the microcredential training, including the implementation of an LMS, as well as the assessment of system capability issues and the credentials earned (UPCEA, 2020). Additionally, administrative support may be needed for data analytics. Continuous evaluation and improvement of the learner experience necessitates ongoing assessment and refinement of the microcredential. Finally, an instructional design team and subject matter experts are needed to design and deliver the content, ensuring that the design and delivery are engaging and pedagogically sound (Chapman, 2022). This interdisciplinary collaboration is critical for the development of high-quality microcredentials that empower learners to success in today's dynamic market.

Resource and Financial Planning

Strategic leadership has been identified as one of the gaps in the literature surrounding microcredentials because of the ability of leaders to move forward with planning and delivery of innovative models outside of the existing modes of delivery (Brown et al., 2023). Institutional planning requires communication and commitment from leaders to embrace change and adapt to new ways of delivering learning. Determining key stakeholders and the accompanying roles they will lead is an important element of a microcredential strategy. Bigelow et al. (2022) recommend a core microcredential design team made up of representatives of employer engagement, subject matter experts, pedagogical specialist, learning design and educational technology support. However, the stakeholder team can resemble any curriculum design team where the employer engagement representative is also included.

Cost considerations, funding sources, and financial models must support the sustainability of the microcredential. Identifying the costs associated with developing and delivering the microcredential is vital. This includes technology, faculty, marketing, and administrative expenses (Bigelow et al., 2022). Exploring funding sources or financial models to support the sustainability of the microcredential ensures long-term viability. This might involve institutional funding, grants, partnerships, or revenue-sharing models (UPCEA, 2020). Determining pricing that ensures affordability for learners while maintaining microcredential viability involves analyzing competitor pricing and considering tiered pricing or payment plans. Finally, microcredentials should be priced lower than traditional degrees (Oliver, 2019).

Developing Microcredentials

These credentials, often designed to be more flexible and targeted than traditional degrees, require careful planning and execution to meet the diverse needs of learners. To develop effective microcredential programs, institutions must consider several critical aspects, including market analysis, governance and accreditation, integration and transferability, financial and resource planning, quality assurance, legal and ethical considerations, and promotion and communication. These key considerations provide guidance for institutions aiming to develop effective microcredentials.

Market Analysis and Demand

Conducting a thorough market analysis is a critical step in the development of effective microcredential programs. This process involves understanding the needs and preferences of potential learners and evaluating the competitive landscape to ensure that the microcredentials offered are relevant, attractive, and valuable in the job market. Through comprehensive research, identification of the target audience, and competitive analysis, institutions can design microcredentials that meet the specific demands of the workforce and stand out in the educational marketplace (Prud'homme-Genereux, n.d.; UPCEA, 2020).

To begin, labor market analysis provides essential insights into the skills currently in demand. Regularly reviewing industry reports and publications helps identify emerging trends and critical skills. For example, fields such as data science, cyber-security, and digital marketing often release annual reports detailing the most sought-after competencies. Analyzing job postings on various platforms allows for the identification of frequently requested skills and qualifications, offering a clear picture of current market needs (EMSI, 2021). Additionally, direct feedback from employers, gathered through surveys or interviews, is invaluable. This direct engagement with employers ensures that the microcredential content is precisely tailored to meet market demands (Bigelow et al., 2022).

Simultaneously, an educational needs assessment is conducted to understand the learning preferences and career aspirations of potential learners. Engaging with potential learners through surveys and focus groups provides a wealth of information on their educational needs and preferred learning formats. Current students and alumni also offer valuable feedback, highlighting gaps in existing programs and areas where additional training could be beneficial (Bigelow et al., 2022).

Competitive analysis is another crucial component of market research. By examining the microcredential offerings of other educational institutions and online learning platforms, it is possible to identify both the strengths and weaknesses of their programs. Understanding how existing microcredentials are marketed and priced provides insight into competitor strategies, which can inform the development of one's own unique value propositions and differentiation tactics (Perpetual, n.d.).

Identifying and targeting the intended audience is essential for designing effective microcredential programs. This involves developing a detailed demographic profile of potential learners, including their age range, educational background, and career stages. Understanding whether the target audience consists of recent graduates, mid-career professionals, or individuals seeking career changes helps tailor the program to their specific needs (Kifle, 2023).

Psychographic profiling further refines the understanding of the audience by exploring their motivations and goals. Are they looking to enhance their current job performance, prepare for a career change, or achieve personal growth? Identifying their preferred learning modalities, such as online, hybrid, or in-person formats, is crucial. Behavioral profiling, which examines how and where the target audience consumes information, helps in crafting effective marketing strategies (Webster, n.d.).

By conducting comprehensive market research, identifying and targeting the intended audience, and performing a detailed competitive analysis, institutions can develop microcredentials that are not only relevant and valuable but also positioned for success in a competitive educational landscape. This holistic approach ensures that microcredentials meet the needs of both learners and employers, fostering continuous growth and adaptation in the rapidly evolving world of education and professional development (Prud'homme-Genereux, n.d.).

Governance and Accreditation

The necessary internal governance processes for the approval and implementation of microcredentials need to be explored at the organizational level (UPCEA, 2020). Discussions should revolve around establishing clear protocols for curriculum development, faculty oversight, and quality assurance. Committees may need to be formed to review proposals, ensuring alignment with institutional goals and academic standards (UPCEA, 2020). A thorough audit of any programmatic accreditation standards relevant to the field must be completed, identifying any specific criteria that may be impacted and examining assessment protocols.

Survey data is one of the most common ways to gather information to inform the development of microcredentials. Connecting with employers and partnerships provides industry information, while collaboration with accrediting bodies provides insights for ensuing quality deliverables (Kifle, 2023). The ability to transfer credit rests on a coordinated effort to review the educational requirements of institutions to identify what administrative systems need to be in place in admissions and transfer credit departments. Quality courses and credit transferability are desirable as learners seek value and affordability when selecting microcredential options (Prud'homme-Genereux, n.d.).

Integration and Transferability

Microcredentials should be designed to be stackable towards higher education degree programs, allowing learners to combine them as building blocks to earn credit towards a degree (UPCEA, 2023). Clear pathways need to be established, outlining how microcredentials align with specific degree requirements and transfer seamlessly into academic programs.

In addition to stack-ability, the options for learners to transfer skills and credits earned through microcredentials into more comprehensive educational pathways must be explored (UPCEA, 2023). One should review articulation agreements with partner institutions, credit transfer policies, and pathways for credit for CPL or LEA. Incorporating these opportunities recognizes and validates learners' prior experiences through assessments, portfolio reviews, or competency-based evaluations.

Through these mechanisms, learners can leverage their microcredential achievements to accelerate their progress towards higher degrees or career advancement. By incorporating CPL/LEA opportunities, microcredentials become more accessible and inclusive, catering to learners with diverse backgrounds and experiences (Oliver, 2019).

Quality Assurance and Continuous Improvement

Delivery Methods

An initial consideration in developing microcredentials is the mode of delivery. This involves evaluating whether the credential will be offered online, through a hybrid model, or in-person (Oliver, 2019). Online delivery offers unparalleled flexibility, making it accessible to a global audience and accommodating varying schedules. Conversely, a hybrid model combines the benefits of online convenience with the advantages of face-to-face interaction, which can be crucial for certain disciplines requiring hands-on practice. In-person delivery, while less flexible, may be necessary for microcredentials that involve specialized equipment or direct mentorship. Utilizing research and feedback from employers and learners ensures it will be provided when and where the client needs it (UPCEA, 2020).

Technological Platforms

The selection of an appropriate LMS is pivotal in ensuring a seamless learning experience for the online or hybrid offerings. The LMS serves as the backbone of the microcredential program, supporting various functionalities such as content delivery, interaction, and assessment. Platforms like Moodle, Canvas, and Blackboard are often considered due to their robust features, which include integration of multimedia content, forums for discussion, and tools for real-time feedback. The chosen platform should align with the institution's objectives and the specific needs of the microcredential, providing a cohesive and supportive learning environment

(Clayton et al., 2024). Additionally, it should interact with other digital technologies (UPCEA, 2020).

Assessment Methods

Central to the design process is the selection of appropriate assessment methods. Assessment methods guide the learning experience design to ensure that microcredentials effectively measure and validate mastering skills rather than just fill credit hours, fostering a more authentic and applicable learning experience. Using a competency-based framework, the focus becomes on mastering the skills versus mastery based on the completion of credit hours. A rubric is useful to "determine learning effectiveness by thorough evaluation of the learner deliverables" (Clayton et al., 2024, p. 6).

Assessment methods and criteria must be carefully designed to ensure that learning outcomes are achieved. Traditional assessments such as quizzes and skill tests can provide measurable indicators of learner comprehension. However, incorporating project-based assessments can enhance practical application and critical thinking. These assessments allow learners to demonstrate their skills in real-world contexts, reinforcing their learning. Additionally, peer reviews and reflective essays can provide opportunities for learners to engage in self-assessment and critical analysis, further solidifying their knowledge and skills (Oliver, 2019). According to the European Training Foundation (2022), "Organising fit for purpose assessment and quality assurance of assessment for microcredentials provided in non-formal or informal learning contexts is also expected for the credentials to be recognised for further education and training purposes" (p. 31).

Alignment With Labor Market Needs

Central to the development of microcredentials is ensuring their alignment with current and future labor market needs. Through ongoing research, industry engagement, and collaboration with employers, insight can be made into emerging trends, technological advancements, and evolving skill requirements. By staying attuned to the needs of the job market, microcredentials are designed to equip learners with the practical skills and competencies that employers value most, thereby enhancing their employability and enabling them to thrive in a rapidly changing professional landscape.

Defining Specific Skills and Competencies

The focus is on defining the specific skills and competencies that each microcredential aims to impart. Through an examination of industry trends, labor market analyses, and consultations with subject matter experts, the key areas of knowledge and expertise that are highly sought after in today's workforce are identified (Bigelow et al., 2022). Whether it is proficiency in data analytics, fluency in digital marketing strategies, or mastery of project management principles, each microcredential is carefully crafted to provide learners with practical skills that are immediately applicable in their respective fields (UPCEA, 2020).

Evidence of Achievement

A crucial aspect of microcredentials is providing learners with tangible evidence of their accomplishments. One must explore the various methods of credentialing, including digital badges and certificates. Digital badges, adorned with metadata detailing the skills and competencies acquired, serve as portable credentials that learners can showcase across digital platforms (Proctor, 2021). The awarding of microcredentials can be accomplished using digital badges. Digital badges function as an additional means of documenting skills that can support professional advancement (Carey & Stefanizak, 2018). According to Clayton et al. (2024), "badges…can be displayed on digital resumes as well as on social networking sites that focus on professional networking and career development, such as LinkedIn" (p. 6). What is great about badges is that the competencies and skills achieved are built into the badge; employees can share specifics of what they learned. This contrasts with a certificate, where a name is provided as proof of completion but not much is provided to prove credibility. Verifiable digital certificates, issued by the institution, validate learners' achievements and signify their proficiency in specific areas of study. An example of this would be the "Professional Certificate" programs comprised of a series of courses, offered through edX (n.d.).

Internal and External Stakeholder Involvement

The development of microcredentials is a collaborative effort involving multiple stakeholders, both internal and external. Within the institution's ecosystem, key internal stakeholders play pivotal roles in shaping the development of microcredentials. Institutional champions are essential for advocating and leading initiatives within the university to garner necessary support. They must articulate a vision which is consistent with the organizational strategy (UPCEA, 2020).

Faculty members, with their subject matter expertise and pedagogical insights, are essential partners in defining the curriculum and learning outcomes of each microcredential. Administrators provide crucial support in navigating institutional policies and procedures, ensuring alignment with academic standards and accreditation requirements. Information technology (IT) support staff, adept in the latest technological tools and platforms, lend their expertise in selecting and implementing the digital infrastructure necessary for delivering microcredential programs effectively. Together, these internal stakeholders form a collaborative team, each contributing their unique perspectives and talents to the development process (UPCEA, 2020).

Beyond the institution, external stakeholders play a vital role in enriching the development of microcredentials with real-world relevance and industry insights. Industry partners, representing a diverse array of sectors and professions, provide invaluable input into the identification of skills and competencies most valued in the workforce (Chapman, 2022). Their firsthand knowledge of emerging trends, technological advancements, and evolving job roles help ensure that microcredentials remain responsive to the needs of employers and industry demands. When surveyed, 73% of employers wanted to be active in the microcredential curriculum design (UPCEA, 2023). Additionally, professional associations, with their deep connections to specific sectors and professions, offer valuable guidance on industry standards and best practices, ensuring that microcredentials are aligned with industry benchmarks and certifications. Potential employers, ranging from multinational corporations to local businesses, provide essential feedback on the practical applicability of microcredential programs, helping to tailor them to the needs of the job market (Chapman, 2022).

Incorporating Feedback

Central to the development process is the iterative gathering and incorporation of feedback from these diverse stakeholders. Through a variety of channels—such as surveys, focus groups, advisory committees, and stakeholder meetings— input should be sought at every stage of development, from initial conception to final implementation. Feedback needs to be carefully analyzed and synthesized, informing decisions on curriculum design, content delivery methods, assessment strategies, and programmatic enhancements (Bigelow et al., 2022). This feedback loop ensures that microcredentials remain responsive to the evolving needs of learners, employers, and the broader community, fostering a culture of continuous improvement and innovation. Additionally, learner feedback and success metrics should be analyzed, such as completion rates, learner satisfaction, and career outcomes (Bigelow et al., 2022).

The collaborative involvement of internal and external stakeholders proves instrumental in the successful development of microcredentials that are not only academically rigorous but also relevant and impactful in the real world. By harnessing the collective expertise and insights of a diverse array of stakeholders, the institution is able to create microcredentials that empower learners to thrive in their careers and make meaningful contributions to society (UPCEA, 2020).

By addressing these quality assurance and continuous improvement efforts, institutions can effectively develop and maintain microcredentials that are aligned with learner needs, labor market demands, and educational best practices. This approach ensures that microcredentials remain relevant and valuable, fostering trust and recognition among stakeholders.

Strategies for Implementation

Integration with existing programs and curricula serves as a cornerstone for the successful implementation of microcredentials, enhancing the visibility and accessibility within educational institutions. By seamlessly embedding microcredentials into established educational pathways, institutions can leverage existing infrastructure and resources to support learners' skill development and career advancement opportunities. This approach enhances the visibility and accessibility of microcredentials within educational institutions.

Promotion and Communication

Marketing strategies, communicating benefits, and leveraging partnerships are essential for promoting microcredentials and establishing their credibility. Internally, pertinent policies and procedures should be disseminated to key stakeholders, such as advising and admissions staff, who play a pivotal role in promoting credentials to current students. Developing persuasive communication, such as informational toolkits, ensures that internal stakeholders are well-equipped to support and advocate for microcredentials (UPCEA, 2020).

Externally, marketing and outreach efforts are crucial for raising awareness and attracting prospective learners to the microcredential. Institutions can employ targeted digital marketing strategies, including social media campaigns and partnerships with industry stakeholders, to reach specific demographics. Additionally highlighting the unique value proposition of microcredentials, such as their flexibility, relevance, and potential for career advancement, can incentivize learners to engage with these offerings (UPCEA, 2020).

Marketing Strategies

Using targeted advertising, content marketing, and partnerships with industry associations and professional organizations enhances visibility and credibility. Digital marketing tools help create targeted campaigns to reach specific audiences effectively (UPCEA, 2020). There are online vendors offering a variety of tools and software options that can support microcredential marketing strategies.

Communicating Benefits

Effectively communicating the benefits and features of the microcredential to potential learners and employers involves showcasing outcomes, such as job placement rates, career advancement opportunities, and enhanced skillsets. This clear articulation of benefits helps potential learners and employers understand the value of these programs (UPCEA, 2020).

Leveraging Partnerships

Collaborations with industry associations and professional organizations not only promote microcredentials, but also add credibility. These partnerships can also facilitate the dissemination of information and attract a broader audience, enhancing the overall reach of the programs (UPCEA, 2020).

Targeted Advertising and Content Marketing

Institutions can utilize platforms like Google Ads, Facebook, and LinkedIn for targeted advertising campaigns aimed at specific demographics based on interests and behaviors. Content marketing, such as blog posts and success stories, addresses the pain points and aspirations of the target audience, highlighting the benefits of the microcredentials (Prud'homme-Genereux, n.d.). Partnerships with industry associations and professional organizations can also enhance visibility and credibility (UPCEA, 2020).

Differentiation and Value Articulation

Differentiating a microcredential from others in the market is vital for attracting learners and establishing the program's value. This begins with benchmarking the curriculum against competitors to identify unique content, teaching methods, or assessment strategies. Highlighting unique selling points, such as specialized content, partnerships with industry leaders, and integration with degree programs, can set the microcredential apart (UPCEA, 2020). Articulating the outcomes and benefits of the microcredential, such as job placement rates, career advancement opportunities, or enhanced skillsets, provides clear value to potential learners (Oliver, 2019). Competitive pricing and ensuring accessibility through avenues such as subscriptions, tiered pricing, and payment plans are also critical (Oliver, 2019).

Effective Branding and Messaging

Effective branding and messaging strategies resonate with the target audience and reflect the quality, relevance, and value of the microcredential. Utilizing testimonials and success stories from alumni builds trust and demonstrates the real-world impact of the programs (Bigelow et al., 2022).

Alignment With Learner Goals

Successful implementation involves aligning microcredentials with learner's educational and career goals. Institutions should offer diverse pathways and consider how these credentials can complement and enhance their existing educational offerings, providing learners with flexible pathways to skill development and career advancement. By promoting the value of microcredentials, conducting targeted marketing and outreach, prioritizing inclusivity, and aligning with the learners' goals, institutions can position themselves as leaders in delivering innovative, accessible, and impactful learning experiences in the education and training sector (Prud'homme-Genereux, n.d.).

Case Studies/Examples

Real examples illustrate the effectiveness of alternate credentials, showcasing innovative approaches and best practices. They provide learners with a chance to "stand out" to employers. To help learners attain those skills required in the workplace, an online asynchronous ecosystem, higher education and real-world training (HEaRT), was developed. This was created in conjunction with the university's career services department for students who had limited access to internships. It is a competency-based opportunity offered within the university's LMS for learners to earn a microcredential free of charge (Clayton et al, 2024). According to Clayton et al., (2024) an integral part of the model is that global learners work in groups to collaborate with employer partners to solve current workforce problems needing a solution, including critical thinking, professional communication, and the use of evidence to support a position. This stackable experience is tied to credit for prior learning (CPL), where learners can receive course credit for a minimal fee for their program of study. Learners rate the overall experience as 8.4/10 with 88% willing to recommend the experience to a peer (Clayton et al., 2024). Students who successfully complete all six HEaRT challenges earn the microcredential (Clayton et al., 2023).

Another example of using alternate credentials to address needed workforce skills is a four-part series on 21st century skills, which includes critical thinking, communication, collaboration, and creativity. This experience is free to learners and offered through an online continuing education (CE) platform. Participants can earn CE credit in addition to a digital badge to reflect successful completion of the opportunity, as well as skill attainment (Rosenberg, 2022). A third highlighted microcredential is on trauma informed pedagogy, where educators complete six stackable microcredentials (approximately 15 hours each). This was developed as part of a CE effort by a national educational association to address skill gaps, and they are free to members. Nonmembers must pay a fee (National Education Association, 2024).

A final example is an apprenticeship program where the educational coursework can be aligned to a microcredential. The courses are chosen in collaboration with employer partners to ensure relevancy. The coursework prepares apprentices to complete the nationally recognized journey-worker credential while also providing a stackable pathway to a degree (The State University of New York, n.d.).

Future Trends and Challenges

As the landscape of education continues to evolve, addressing the needs of lifelong learners becomes increasingly imperative. To cater to this demographic, there is a growing demand for opportunities to up-skill outside of traditional higher education structures (Rosenberg, 2022). Microcredentials emerge as a viable solution, offering targeted, flexible learning experiences that empower individuals to enhance their skills and adapt to evolving job market demands. However, there is little research evaluating "theory-based explanations of why microcredentials might be attractive for students' future learning, and what the drivers and challenges of microcredential implementation in higher education are" (Ahsan et al., 2023, sec. 6).

Looking ahead, a pressing challenge in the realm of microcredentials is the need for standardized nomenclature. Currently, there exists a plethora of definitions and interpretations of microcredentials, leading to confusion among stakeholders. According to the European Training Foundation (2022), "this challenge becomes particularly conspicuous when micro-credentials lack standards in describing learning outcomes, skills and competencies as well as/or transparency in assessment methods and criteria which would help individuals understand the quality and value of the micro-learning experience" (p. 8). To foster clarity and coherence in the microcredentialing ecosystem, there is a call for standardized terminology that ensures all parties are speaking the same language and can accurately understand and evaluate microcredential offerings (D'Agostino, 2023).

Moreover, ensuring the verifiability of skills acquired through microcredentials emerges as a critical concern for both learners and employers. Employers increasingly prioritize skills-based requirements tailored to job performance, necessitating mechanisms for verifying the effectiveness and relevance of microcredentials in equipping learners with the requisite skills (D'Agostino, 2023). As LeBlanc (2022) envisions, a future where learners can transparently discern the knowledge and skills required to earn a credential, with faculty guiding them through various learning pathways, underscores the importance of establishing verifiable claims and standards in microcredentialing. Institutional accreditors may consider expanding into quality assurance for "unregulated short-term non-degree credentials" (Higher Learning Commission, 2022, p. 12).

Furthermore, as the emphasis on skills-based education intensifies, there is a growing recognition of the need for microcredentials to align closely with industry demands and job requirements. This entails a shift towards microcredentials that not only impart theoretical knowledge but also emphasize practical, job-specific skills that directly contribute to workplace success (LeBlanc, 2022). Additionally, more research is needed to "link microcredentials with market needs, student engagement, industry support and assessment" (Ahsan et al., 2023, sec. 6).

In summary, future trends in microcredentials point towards a greater emphasis on lifelong learning with the research to support it, standardized nomenclature, verifiability of skills, and alignment with industry needs. Addressing these challenges will be crucial in unlocking the full potential of microcredentials as transformative tools for individual skill development and workforce adaptation in the years to come.

CONCLUSION

In conclusion, the exploration of microcredentials in this chapter illuminates their pivotal role in modern education and professional development. As society navigates the complexities of an ever-evolving job market and the challenges posed by the COVID-19 pandemic, microcredentials emerge as agile solutions, meeting the diverse needs of learners and industries alike.

By embracing a learner-centric approach, institutions can design and develop effective microcredential programs that bridge skill gaps, enhance employability, and foster continuous lifelong learning. Leveraging competency frameworks and industry partnerships, educators can ensure the relevance and efficacy of microcredentials in addressing current job requirements while providing learners with pathways to future educational goals (Braxton, 2023).

The development of microcredentials, underscored by advancements in technology and online platforms, offers learners flexible opportunities to up-skill and reskill in alignment with the demands of the modern workforce. Digital badges, serving as verifiable documentation of skills, empower individuals to showcase their expertise and advance their careers in a competitive job market (Proctor, 2021).

Implementation strategies that integrate microcredentials into existing programs and curricula, prioritize inclusivity, and align with learners' goals are essential for ensuring the accessibility and success of microcredential initiatives. Real-world examples, such as the HEaRT ecosystem (Clayton et al., 2024) and the 21st century skills series (Rosenberg, 2022), demonstrate the effectiveness of alternate credentials in addressing workforce needs and empowering learners.

Looking ahead, future research is needed regarding microcredentials. Emphasis must also be placed on the importance of standardized nomenclature, verifiability of skills, and alignment with industry demands. Addressing these challenges will be crucial in unlocking the full potential of microcredentials as transformative tools for individual skill development and workforce adaptation.

By fostering collaboration among educational institutions and employers, we can harness the power of microcredentials to meet the evolving needs of learners and industries alike. Cultivating a culture of continuous learning and innovation will ensure the quality, relevance, and accessibility of microcredential programs, empowering individuals to succeed in an increasingly dynamic world.

In essence, the journey of microcredentials represents a collective effort towards shaping the future of education and professional development. By working together to navigate the challenges and seize the opportunities presented by microcredentials, the full potential of microcredentials can be unlocked and pave the way for the future.

REFERENCES

Ahsan, K., Akbar, S., Kam, B., & Dan-Asabe Abdulrahman, M. (2023). Implementation of micro-credentials in higher education: A systematic literature review. *Education and Information Technologies*, 28(10), 13505–13540. DOI: 10.1007/s10639-023-11739-z

Bigelow, A., Booth, C., Brockerhoff-Macdonald, B., Cormier, D., Dinsmore, C., Grey, S., Harrison, L., Hobbs, A., Lee, S., Maher, P., McArthur, F., Mitchell-Ashley, T., Mosley, J., Papple, J., Porter, J., Presant, D., Sommer, J., & Zahedi, E. (2022). Ecampusontario's micro-credential toolkit. *Ontario Online Learning Consortium.* https://ecampusontario.pressbooks.pub/microcredentialtoolkit/front-matter/welcome-to-the-toolkit/

Braxton, S. N. (2022). Competency frameworks, alternative credentials and the evolving relationship of higher education and employers in recognizing skills and achievements. *The International Journal of Information and Learning Technology*, 40(5), 373–387. https://doi-org.ezproxy.snhu.edu/10.1108/IJILT-10-2022-0206. DOI: 10.1108/IJILT-10-2022-0206

Brown, M., Mcgreal, R., & Peters, M. (2023). A strategic institutional response to microcredentials: Key questions for educational leaders. *Journal of Interactive Media in Education, 2023*(1). DOI:DOI: 10.5334/jime.801

Carey, K. L., & Stefaniak, J. E. (2018). An exploration of the utility of digital badging in higher education settings. *Educational Technology Research and Development*, 66(5), 1211–1229. DOI: 10.1007/s11423-018-9602-1

Cedefop (2024). *Microcredentials: Striving to combine creditability and agility.* European Centre for the Development of Vocational Training. (Briefing Note).

Chapman, T. (2022, October 13). Microcredentials: Practices for developing employer partnerships. *College Is Education.* https://collegiseducation.com/insights/microcredentials/micro-credentials-practices-for-developing-employer-partnerships/

Clayton, T., Rosenberg, S., & Christman, E. (2023, January 3). Addressing skills gaps. *Educational Technology Insights.* https://distance-and-remote-learning.educationtechnologyinsights.com/cxoinsights/addressing-skills-gaps-nid-2190.html

Clayton, T., Rosenberg, S., Wyatt, J., VanOrsdale, B., & Bisaillon, D. (2024, February 6). Higher education and real-world training (HEaRT) – A new ecosystem for learning. *The Journal of Continuing Higher Education*, 72(3), 392–404. Advance online publication. DOI: 10.1080/07377363.2023.2291592

D'Agostino, S. (2023, March 2). Microcredentials confuse employers, colleges, and learners. *Inside Higher Ed*. https://www.insidehighered.com/news/2023/03/03/microcredentials-confuse-employers-colleges-and-learners

Educause (2017, July 18). 7 things you should read about microcredentialing/digital badging. *Educause*. https://library.educause.edu/resources/2017/7/7-things-you-should-read-about-microcredentialing-digital-badging

edX (n.d.). Professional certificate programs. *edX*. https://www.edx.org/certificates/professional-certificate

EMSI. (2021). A guide to market research for colleges and universities. *EMSI*. https://www.datocms-assets.com/62658/1643839553-emsi-market-research-guide.pdf

European Training Foundation. (2022). Guide to design, issue and recognize micro-credentionals. *European Training Foundation*. www.etf.europa.eu/sites/default/files/2023-05/Micro-Credential%20Guidelines%20Final%20%Delivery.pdf

Fuller, J., Langer, C., & Sigelman, M. (2022). Skills-based hiring is on the rise. *Harvard Business Review*. Hbr.org/2022/02/skills-based-hiring-ison-the-rise

Goglio, V., Bertolini, S., & Parigi, P. (2023). The perceived labour market value of massive open online courses (MOOCs) in Europe and the USA. *Journal of Education and Work*, 36(1), 37–51. DOI: 10.1080/13639080.2022.2162020

Golden, G., Kato, S., & Weko, T. (2021, September 29). Promoting social inclusion through micro-credentials. *OECD Education and Skills Today*. https://oecdedutoday.com/promoting-social-inclusion-through-micro-credentials/

Hancock, B., Higgins, C., Law, J., Olson, S., Patel, N., & Dusen, K. V. (2022, November 15). Taking a skills-based approach to building the future workforce. *McKinsey & Company*. https://www.mckinsey.com/capabilities/people-and-organizational-performance/our-insights/taking-a-skills-based-approach-to-building-the-future-workforce

Higher Learning Commission. (2022). Evolving: Accreditation and the credential landscape. *Higher Learning Commission*. https://download.hlcommission.org/initiatives/2022StakeholdersRoundtablePapers.pdf

Humphrey, W.Jr, Laverie, D., & Muñoz, C. (2021). The use and value of badges: Leveraging salesforce trailhead badges for marketing technology education. *Journal of Marketing Education*, 43(1), 25–42. DOI: 10.1177/0273475320912319

Kifle, T. (2023, September 20). What makes an effective microcredential programme? *The Times Higher Education*. https://www.timeshighereducation.com/campus/what-makes-effective-microcredential-programme

LeBlanc, P. (2022). Microcredentials and skills-based hiring. In *Students first* (pp. 58–64). Harvard Press.

Matic, J. L. (2019). The internationalization of American higher education: A positional competition perspective. *Globalisation, Societies and Education*, 17(3), 274–284. DOI: 10.1080/14767724.2019.1584550

National Education Association. (2024). Trauma informed pedagogy. *National Education Association*. https://nea.certificationbank.com/NEA/CandidatePortal/CategoryDetail.aspx?Stack=TRA

Oliver, B. (2019). Making micro-credentials work for learners, employers and providers. *Research Gate*. https://www.researchgate.net/publication/335109512_Making_micro-credentials_work_for_learners_employers_and_providers

Oliver, B. (2022). Towards a common definition of micro-credentials. *UNESCO*. https://unesdoc.unesco.org/ark:/48223/pf0000381668

Perpetual (n.d.). Suny microcredentials case study: Microcredential website redesign and marketing solutions. *Perpetual*. https://www.perpetualny.com/case-study/suny-microcredentials

Proctor, C. (2021, October 5). Defining the role for high-quality microcredentials in higher education. *Evolllution*. https://evolllution.com/programming/credentials/defining-a-role-for-high-quality-microcredentials-in-higher-education

Prud'homme-Genereux, A. (n.d.). Marketing and launch. *BCcampus Micro-credential Toolkit for B.C.*https://opentextbc.ca/bcmicrocredential/chapter/marketing-and-launch/

Putnam, C. (2024). Upskilling, reskilling become increasingly popular strategies for employers. *Rochester Business Journal*, 39(48), 8–10.

Ralston, S. J. (2021). Higher education's microcredentialing craze: A postdigital-deweyan critique. *Postdigital Science and Education*, 3(1), 83–101. DOI: 10.1007/s42438-020-00121-8

Rosenberg, S. (2022, January 4). Lifelong learning in higher education: Diversifying credentials to engage learners. *Evolllution*. https://evolllution.com/programming/credentials/lifelong-learning-in-higher-education-diversifying-credentials-to-engage-learners/

Salmon, M. (2023). Drivers of the global push for microcredentials in higher education: Flexibility and employability in contemporary university systems. *Perspectives*, 27(4), 179–187. DOI: 10.1080/13603108.2023.2229767

Sheather, J., & Slattery, D. (2021, October 18). The great resignation: How do we support and retain staff already stretched to their limit? [BMJ]. *British Medical Journal*, 375, 2533. DOI: 10.1136/bmj.n2533 PMID: 34663568

Strada (2021). Explore public viewpoint data: Covid-19 work and education survey. *Strada*. https://cci.stradaeducation.org/explore-public-viewpoint-data/

The State University of New York. (n.d.). Microcredentials. *The State University of New York*. https://www.suny.edu/microcredentials/

UPCEA. (2020). Hallmarks of excellence in credential innovation. *UPCEA*. https://upcea.edu/wp-content/uploads/2020/05/UPCEA-Hallmarks-of-Excellence-in-Credential-Innovation-May-20-2020.pdf

UPCEA. (2023). The effect of employer understanding and engagement on non-degree credentials. *UPCEA*. https://upcea.edu/wp-content/uploads/2023/05/The-Effect-of-Employer-Understanding-and-Engagement-on-Non-Degree-Credentials_UPCEA-and-Collegis_February-2023.pdf

Venable, M. A. (2021). 2021 alternative education pathways report. *BestColleges.com*. https://www.bestcolleges.com/research/alternative-education-pathways/

Vodoukis, N., & Pagiatakis, G. (2022). Massive open online courses (MOOCs): Practices, trends, and challenges for the higher education. *European Journal of Education and Pedagogy*, 3(2), 288–295. https://www.ej-edu.org/index.php/ejedu/article/view/365. DOI: 10.24018/ejedu.2022.3.3.365

Webster, W. (n.d.). What is psychogenic segmentation? A beginner's guide. *Qualtrics*. https://www.qualtrics.com/experience-management/brand/psychographic-segmentation/

KEY TERMS AND DEFINITIONS

Alternate Credential: Nontraditional credentials credit and noncredit bearing
Award: Issuing digital credentials/badges to recipients
Badge: Short for digital badge, an award displaying verified skills
Competency: What the learner is demonstrating
Microcredential: A short program to up-skill or re-skill
Re-skill: to acquire new skills to do a different job

Stackable Credential: A sequence of credentials that accumulate over time to help an individual advance on a career or education pathway

Up-skill: to provide advanced skills through education/training

Verifiable: Confirmation that a credential awarded by an institute to a specific learner is authentic and accurate

Chapter 5
Exploring Factors Influencing the Structure of Micro-Credentials in Distance Learning From Multiple Stakeholders' Perspectives

Hulya Yilmaz
https://orcid.org/0000-0002-5415-5708
Kirklareli University, Turkey

Seda Yanik
Istanbul Technical University, Turkey

ABSTRACT

Distance learning has become more popular during the COVID-19 years and the micro-credentials (MCs) has been accepted widespread as an alternative to traditional degree programs. Higher Education Institutions play a critical role in the creation of MCs, taking into account the needs of learners and industry requirements. Hence, it is important to understand and develop this field due to the complexity and diversity of factors that influence the structuring of MCs in distance learning. Moreover, different stakeholders have various influences and priorities on the design, implementation, and adoption of MCs. Therefore, this chapter aims to explore the factors influencing the structuring of MCs in distance learning, considering multiple stakeholders' perspectives. Using the MICMAC method, factors are categorized into influential, key, dependent, and autonomous groups, offering a comprehensive

DOI: 10.4018/979-8-3693-5488-9.ch005

factor map. The chapter concludes with recommendations for effectively structuring MCs in distance learning, addressing both challenges and opportunities to enhance their impact and integration.

INTRODUCTION

In recent years, distance learning has become a popular way of satisfying the learning needs of a growing number of people. In this context, the role of micro-credentials (MCs) is becoming increasingly important as they offer flexible and specialized pathways for skills acquisition and career progression. The MCs, according to the International Standard Classification of Education (ISCED), are defined as a certification of assessed learning that is additional, alternative, complementary, or part of a formal qualification (Oliver, 2019). In the United Nations Educational, Scientific and Cultural Organization (UNESCO) report, the term MCs are defined as a term covering a variety of competencies, including nano-degrees, micro-master competence, certificates, badges, licenses, and approvals (UNESCO, 2018). It can be concluded that MCs are detailed certificates, earned through the completion of short and purposeful skills-based learning experiences and when earned it shows that the person has specialized in the skills or competencies desired and targeted.

The acceptance of MCs as an alternative to traditional degree programs and MCs that offer sector-oriented and competency-based learning are gaining a reputation daily. Providing focused, skills-based learning experiences, MCs have become an important tool in meeting the evolving needs of learners and industry too (Fisher & Leder, 2022). They have started to be a permanent part of HEIs. HEIs play an important role in structuring MCs and designing MCs by identifying the needs of learners and taking into account the requirements of the industry. HEIs are also responsible for ensuring the alignment of MCs with academic standards and aim to maximize the benefits of these programs for learners. However, given the complexity and variety of factors influencing the design of MCs in distance learning, understanding and developing this field is essential (Yilmaz et al., 2024; Yilmaz et al., 2022; Yilmaz & Yanik, 2022).

Understanding the factors influencing the design of MCs in distance learning is important for a variety of reasons. First, by ensuring that MCs are responsive to learners' changing needs and expectations, they provide relevant and valuable learning experiences. This facilitates access to customized educational opportunities in alignment with learners' career goals and supports continuing lifelong learning. Particularly in a dynamic workplace environment, this flexibility and adaptability can enhance an individual's competitive advantage. Secondly, it enables higher educational institutions (HEIs) to effectively design and provide MCs that meet accreditation standards and industry requirements. The content and delivery of MCs should reflect current developments in the sector and equip learners with real-world skills. This will give confidence to employers and other education stakeholders and facilitate the integration of graduates into the workforce. Third, promoting a supportive ecosystem for the development and recognition of MCs facilitates cooperation and alignment between different stakeholders. Consequently, the effective structuring and delivery of MCs in distance learning is essential to meet the needs of learners, and the requirements of industry and to foster collaboration and alignment between stakeholders. This not only contributes to the personal and professional development of individuals but also helps to meet the wider educational and workforce needs of society.

Each stakeholder group has different impacts and priorities on the design, implementation, and adoption of MCs. Learners are among the most important stakeholders in the process of structuring MCs. Their expectations and needs influence the design and delivery of programs. Academic staff play a critical role in determining the content of MCs and delivering them to learners. Their academic expertise and industry experience ensure the effectiveness and relevance of the programs. Employers play a crucial role in determining the acceptance and value of MCs in the business world. Their industry needs and expectations shape the content of MCs and enhance learners' employment opportunities. Policy-makers encourage the wide adoption of MCs by setting education policies and guidelines. Therefore, understanding and classifying the factors that are effective in structuring MCs, taking into account the perspectives of different stakeholders, helps to develop more comprehensive and effective educational policies.

This chapter aims to identify the factors influencing the structuring of MCs in distance learning, taking into account the perspectives of different stakeholders and categorizing these factors. In this scope, the factors affecting the structuring of MCs in distance learning are identified using a literature review and expert opinions, and the factors are categorized using the MICMAC (Matriced' Impacts Croise's Multiplication Appliquee a UN Classement-Cross Impact Matrix Multiplication Applied to Classification) method proposed by Duperrin and Godet (1973). The MICMAC method is used in a wide range of fields, from education to a variety of other fields, to identify the influence of factors on each other. Zhang et al. (2024) analyzed the factors affecting learning burnout of secondary vocational learners in the context of social media and revealed the underlying causes of learning burnout by using the MICMAC method. In another study, Ahmad et al. (2020) proposed a cloud-based mobile learning adoption model to promote sustainable education. They used MICMAC analysis to classify variables as dependent and independent variables. However, the effects of various factors on the structure of MCs and the classification of factors have not yet been addressed. Therefore, in this chapter one aims to fill the gap by using the MICMAC method.

The rest of this chapter is structured as follows: Section 2 provides global perspectives on MCs through case studies and applications. Section 3 reviews the role of MCs in higher education. Section 4 explores the factors influencing the structure of MCs, while Section 5 categorizes these factors using the MICMAC method. Section 6 discusses the opportunities and challenges for effectively structuring MCs in distance learning. Finally, Section 7 presents the conclusions and suggestions for future research.

GLOBAL PERSPECTIVES ON MCs

This section explores the global perspectives on MCs by examining their diverse applications across regions, industries, and educational institutions. The increasing use of MCs reflects their growing significance in addressing specific needs, enhancing professional development, and providing flexible, research-driven learning pathways.

The development and adoption of MCs are not confined to any single region or country. In recent years, major international IT companies have played a crucial role in advancing the use of MCs for professional growth. For example, IBM has pioneered the use of digital badges, offering them to both employees and the public through Coursera. These badges, developed in collaboration with Northwestern University, can be applied to professional master's degree programs, demonstrating the integration of MCs into higher education. Similarly, Google's online IT support certificate, launched in 2018 via Coursera, formed a consortium of over 20 employers committed to hiring certificate holders. More recently, Google introduced Career Certificates, aimed at equipping individuals with job-ready skills without requiring a traditional college education (Brown et al., 2021).

In addition to industry-driven initiatives, educational institutions worldwide are increasingly exploring micro-credentialing as a tool to deliver flexible and high-quality professional development. Universities and schools globally have begun to experiment with MCs, offering educators and academics valuable, relevant learning experiences that enhance their career trajectories. A significant development in Europe is the MicroHE project, part of the Erasmus+ initiative, which supports learning excellence through MCs in higher education. This project aims to measure current trends in MCs, develop models for future impacts, and propose instruments for transparency, such as credit supplements and a European credential repository (Resei et al., 2019).

In another significant development, nine academic institutions announced the establishment of the Digital Credentials Collaboration in 2019. This collaboration, which includes Delft University of Technology, Harvard University, the Hasso Plattner Institute, Massachusetts Institute of Technology, Tecnologico de Monterrey, TU Munich, UC Berkeley, UC Irvine, and the University of Toronto, aims to establish a reliable, distributed infrastructure for the issuance, storage, and verification of academic credentials. The objective is to develop a robust system for the management of digital MCs that can be readily verified and transferred across institutions and borders (Resei et al., 2019).

Overall, the global perspective on MCs reveals a growing trend toward integrating these credentials into various educational and professional contexts, driven by industry leaders and educational institutions alike. The widespread adoption and experimentation with MCs highlight their potential to address diverse educational needs and enhance career development opportunities worldwide. This global momentum suggests that MCs will continue to play a pivotal role in shaping the future of education and workforce development.

IMPLEMENTATION OF MCs IN HIGHER EDUCATION

This section focuses on the crucial role MCs play within higher education, particularly in response to the increasing demand for flexible and skills-oriented learning.

In the evolving landscape of higher education, MCs have become an important tool to meet the growing demand for flexible, skills-based learning. Particularly in the context of distance learning, MCs offer a modular approach that enables learners to acquire specific competencies in a shorter period, making education more adaptable to individual needs and industry demands. HEIs are at the center of this change, playing a key role in developing and structuring MCs in line with labour market trends and technological advances. By offering targeted and industry-relevant certifications, MCs help bridge the gap between formal education and the practical skills required by employers. They also provide an opportunity for lifelong learning, allowing individuals to continually upgrade their skills without committing to full degree programmes. As HEIs continue to integrate MCs into their educational offerings, they are redefining the pathways to academic and career success, particularly in distance learning environments where flexibility and accessibility are paramount (Sharma et al., 2024; Reed et al., 2024; Tee et al., 2024).

The literature addressing the role and applications of MCs in higher education highlights various aspects of this construct and its potential benefits to stakeholders. Varadarajan et al. (2023) aim to develop a framework that analyzes the current concepts and discourses of MCs and identifies their value to learners, HEIs, employers, and government authorities. Thi Ngoc Ha et al. (2023) review the literature published between 2012 and 2022, highlighting the potential benefits of integrating MCs into higher education and the challenges in their implementation. Ahsan et al. (2023) investigate the opportunities and challenges in implementing MCs between 2015 and 2021, suggesting a focus on market needs, learners' engagement, industry support, and assessment. Hunt et al. (2020) identify several benefits that make MCs especially interesting for government leaders and administrators, including personalization, competence, flexibility, cost efficiency, and collaboration. Fisher and Leder (2022) emphasize that MCs are frequently used, especially in technically oriented professions and professional development training. Selvaratnam et al. (2024) aim to guide higher education providers by developing a maturity model for the MCs. The findings revealed that the areas of quality, resources, standards, and strategy exhibited the lowest level of maturity across the sector. Conversely, the technical infrastructure, credentialing system, and platform for delivering MCs demonstrated the highest level of maturity. Fan et al. (2024) examine a MCs program implemented in the United States, noting that the program was beneficial for educators in terms of professional development and faced several challenges. The results determined that the MCs program was beneficial for educators' professional development. Challenges were identified as platform, time, resources, awareness, and mentality. Raj et al. (2024), two ranking methods, Preference Ranking for Organization Method for Enrichment Evaluation (PROMETHEE) and multi-objective optimization based on ratio analysis (MOORA), are used together to rank the major challenges. The results of this study show that lack of clarity of definitions, vague course descriptions, lack of accreditation and quality assurance, lack of clear pricing policies, lack of coordination between learning hours and learning outcomes, insufficient volume of learning, lack of acceptance by individuals and organizations are the top-ranked and most important barriers to the implementation of MCs. Mardisentosa et al. (2021) state the need for evaluation and management systems that assure the confidentiality, permanence, and transparency of student documents in micro-credentialing using blockchain technology. By implementing such systems, students can personalize their education, create permanent documentation, and determine their lifelong learning path.

Previous research has often focused on the challenges and opportunities of MCs. However, these studies have not investigated the interrelationships, strength of influence, and dependencies between factors influencing the structure of MCs in a comprehensive approach. To address this gap, this chapter conducts a thorough investigation of the factors influencing the design of MCs, categorizing them based on the perspectives of multiple stakeholders. These factors are elaborated in detail in the following section.

FACTORS INFLUENCING THE STRUCTURE OF MCs

This section examines the various factors that impact the design and implementation of MCs. Understanding these factors is essential for ensuring their effectiveness and credibility.

The structure of MCs is influenced by many factors that ensure their effectiveness and credibility. Academic standards and quality assurance are fundamental and provide a robust framework for quality maintenance and staff development. This is complemented by the availability of learning resources and the implementation of rigorous program monitoring. Learning outcomes and assessment methods are designed to accurately measure learner achievement, while personalized learning and active learning methods address individual needs and encourage engagement. Policy design and stakeholder involvement play a crucial role in shaping and refining these qualifications. Standardization and recognition of MCs ensure their acceptability and portability across different contexts, while security and technology integration ensure the integrity and accessibility of these learning opportunities. The design and content of the MCs, the expected learning outcomes, the assessment methods, and the degree to which learners achieve these outcomes should be periodically monitored. Risks to quality and changing needs should be identified, and improvements should be planned.

a. **Design of MCs policies:** Policy design in line with the intended objectives is important. These policies should begin with clear objectives and involve stakeholders early in the policy development process (Tooley & Hood, 2021). To ensure academic standards, it is crucial that MCs, designed as credit-bearing pathways to qualifications, adhere to specific guidelines.
b. **Academic staff qualification:** Academic staff with teaching and supervisory roles need to be qualified, including having knowledge of the field and modern teaching practices. They should be able to meet learners' needs and be accessible for individualized support (Oliver, 2019).
c. **Training of academic staff:** By providing comprehensive training to academic staff, institutions can enhance the quality and effectiveness of MCs in distance learning, ultimately leading to improved educational outcomes and greater recognition of the value of MCs in the academic and professional spheres.
d. **Self-assessment of the academic staff:** Regular self-assessment by academic staff is vital to maintaining the quality of the program and ensuring participants have an accurate assessment of their skills. This process encourages the continuous development of staff and supports the long-term success of the program.

e. **Learner-centered design:** The designed program should allow close exchange with other learners, exchange ideas, discuss problems, and help each other (Brown et al., 2021). The program should allow learners to personalize their learning experience, tailoring it to their needs. Emphasis should be placed on active learning methods such as practical applications and project-based learning, which enable learners to develop their problem-solving skills in real-world scenarios (Oliver, 2019).

f. **Learning resources and diversity:** Learning resources should be current, diverse, directly related to learning outcomes, and accessible on an as needed basis (Brown et al., 2021). To ensure that these resources remain relevant and effective, they need to be continually updated to reflect the latest developments and best practices in the field. In addition, incorporating a variety of resources, such as multimedia content, interactive tools, and peer-reviewed materials, can cater to different learning styles and needs, thereby enhancing the overall educational experience and ensuring that all learners have equitable access to quality content.

g. **Collaborative learning methods:** Collaborative learning enhances MCs by promoting peer interaction, teamwork, and active engagement. It fosters critical thinking and communication skills, aligning MCs with real-world work environments where collaboration is essential.

h. **Learning outcomes and assessment:** Assessment methods should align with learning outcomes, validly assess progress, and provide learners with timely feedback to help them achieve the learning outcomes (Oliver, 2019). Expected learning outcomes should be indicated, consistent with the educational level and domain of the target qualification (Tooley & Hood, 2021).

i. **Monitoring and improvement:** Robust monitoring and feedback systems play a critical role in the continuous improvement of MCs in distance learning. By actively engaging stakeholders and using data-driven insights, educational institutions can enhance the value, credibility, and effectiveness of MCs, ensuring they remain responsive to the dynamic needs of the global workforce (Raj et al., 2024; Oliver, 2019).

j. **Accreditation and quality assurance:** To ensure the credibility, transferability, and value of MCs in distance learning, accreditation and quality assurance are essential. By adhering to rigorous standards and continuously improving programmes through stakeholder feedback and technological innovation, institutions can offer MCs that are not only globally recognized but also meet the evolving needs of learners and industries (Raj et al., 2024).

k. **Stakeholder engagement:** Developing a clear understanding of the value and function of MCs requires stakeholder collaboration (McGreal et al., 2022). Support and engagement from a range of stakeholders, including educational institutions, employers, industry associations, and regulatory bodies, are essential for MCs to be widely accepted and recognized (Sharma et al., 2024; Varadarajan et al., 2023; Selvaratnam & Sankey, 2021).

l. **Understandability and comparability of MCs:** For lifelong learners, employers need a way to understand and compare various MCs. A consistent method of comparison and reward is necessary. International organizations such as UNESCO (2018) and the Organisation for Economic Co-Operation and Development (OECD) (Kato et al., 2020) have identified MCs, including the "Common Microcredit Framework" developed by the European Commission and the European MOOC Consortium, as a potential solution. The European MOOC Consortium is engaged in the development of a Common Microcredit Framework (CMF), which is intended for voluntary use by various platforms. This framework may subsequently be translated into a formal qualification or standard for use by a wider group of universities.

m. **Verification of MCs:** One of the major problems with MCs is the issue of security and monitoring. The problem of how to monitor a set of different MCs from different institutions and how to verify their accuracy and quality has not been fully clarified. Blockchain technology-supported digital diplomas can guarantee their originality (Oliver, 2019; Orman et al., 2023). Platforms for securely storing and managing MCs, as well as infrastructure for validating these MCs, are essential. It should also provide the ability to integrate with current learning management systems (LMS), and educational platforms to increase the utility and value of MCs (Shwedeh et al., 2024; Olcott, 2021).

n. **Digital and infrastructure capacity:** By combining distance learning, open educational resources, and MCs into a unified system, institutions can better serve learners, employers, and government agencies. Digitalization enables flexible, scalable learning opportunities, extending the institution's reach (Olcott, 2021).

CATEGORIZATION OF FACTORS USING THE MICMAC METHOD

This section focuses on categorizing the factors that influence the structure of MCs using the MICMAC method. It provides a systematic approach to identifying and analyzing the direct and indirect relationships between various factors affecting MCs.

To understand comprehensively the factors influencing the structure of MCs in distance learning, it is essential to systematically categorize these factors according to their impact and dependence. The MICMAC method provides a robust framework for this purpose by analyzing both direct and indirect relationships between factors

(Godet, 1994). This section outlines the application of the MICMAC method, detailing each step and its relevance to the study. The steps of the MICMAC method can be presented as follows:

Identification of Factors: To identify the factors that play an important role in the field of concern, the factors related to this field are defined. To identify the factors, a detailed literature review can be conducted, industry reports can be consulted or expert opinions can be obtained.

Analyzing direct relationships: Decision makers are identified to assess the existing relationships between the identified factors and the degree of existing relationships. These decision-makers can be selected among relevant stakeholders, industry professionals, or academics. The collected data from the decision-makers is intended to reveal the direct relationships between the factors and is kept in the form of an *nxn* matrix (where *n* is the number of factors).

Analyzing indirect relationships: Direct relationships may not be adequate to represent the complex structure that exists between factors in real life. For this, indirect relationships must also be analyzed. Indirect relationships, which are very difficult to evaluate by decision-makers, are determined by taking the powers of the direct relationship matrix. The powering process is continued until the row and column sums of two consecutive powers are almost the same.

Drawing and evaluating influence-dependency maps: Influence-dependence maps representing both direct and indirect relationships are created. These maps show the degree of dependency. These degrees can be represented in terms of total influence and influence, or in terms of ranks of influence and influence. Factors are divided into four regions: influential factors, key factors, dependent factors, and autonomous factors (Godet, 1994).

- Influential factors have high influence and low dependency, meaning they significantly affect other factors within the system.
- Key factors exhibit high influence and high dependency. They are central to the system, and changes in these factors can impact other factors, making them critical for monitoring and management.
- Dependent factors are characterized by low influence and high dependency, these factors are heavily influenced by other factors and reflect the outcomes of system interactions.
- Autonomous factors show low influence and low dependency, indicating they are relatively disconnected from the system and have minimal impact on or interaction with other factors.

Identification of Factors

A summary of the factors influencing the structure of MCs, examined in detail in Section 4, is presented in Table 1.

Table 1. Factors affecting the structure of MCs.

#	Factor	References
F1	Learning outcomes and assessment	Oliver, 2019
F2	Training of academic staff	Expert opinions
F3	Self-assessment of the academic staff	Expert opinions
F4	Academic staff qualification	Oliver, 2019
F5	Design of MCs policies	Tooley and Hood, 2021
F6	Learner-centered design	Oliver, 2019; Brown et al., 2021
F7	Stakeholder engagement	Tooley and Hood, 2021
F8	Learning resources and diversity	Oliver, 2019; Brown et al., 2021
F9	Monitoring and improvement	Oliver, 2019
F10	Understandability and comparability of MCs	Kato et al., 2020
F11	Verification of MCs	Oliver, 2019; Orman et al., 2023
F12	Collaborative learning methods	Brown et al., 2021
F13	Digital and infrastructure capacity	Olcott, 2021
F14	Accreditation and quality assurance	Raj et al., 2024

Identification of Stakeholders

Stakeholders in the context of MCs in distance learning include various groups, each with different perspectives on how MCs should be structured and implemented. Understanding these different perspectives is essential for developing effective MC programmes that meet the needs of all stakeholders. By understanding and addressing the perspectives of these different stakeholders, the structure and implementation of MCs in distance learning can be better aligned with the needs and expectations of all parties involved, leading to more effective and impactful educational programmes. The stakeholders in the structure of the MCs of the HEIs in this chapter are shown in Figure 1.

Figure 1. Stakeholders in the structure of MCs.

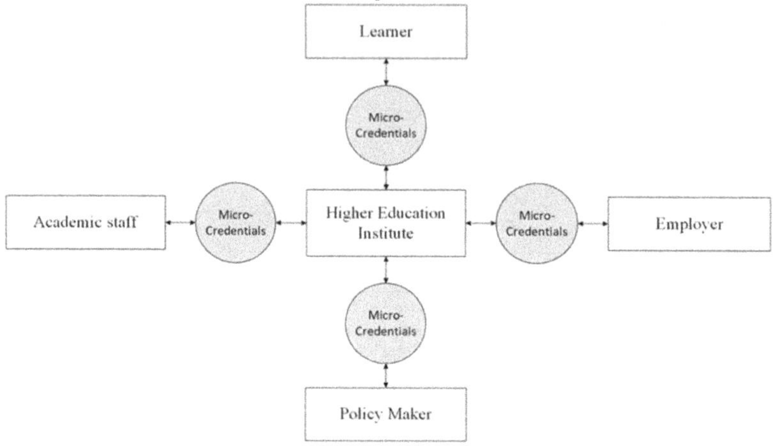

Learners are at the center of the micro-credential system. They may be current learners or working people who want to improve their skills. Their perspective is crucial as they directly experience the benefits and limitations of MCs. Learners are typically motivated by a desire for flexible, relevant, and practical learning opportunities that can advance their careers or facilitate their personal development (Tee et al., 2024; Zou et al., 2024; MicroHE Consortium, 2019). They may seek out MCs for a variety of reasons, such as to gain specialized knowledge, to meet certification requirements, or to improve their employability. Their feedback on the accessibility, content relevance, and value of MCs provides valuable insights into the effectiveness of these programmes.

Academic staff play a key role in the creation and delivery of MCs (Reed et al., 2024). This group includes academic staff, instructional designers, and course developers who are responsible for the design, delivery, and evaluation of MC programmes. They must ensure that the content is academically consistent, in line with industry standards, and meets the educational goals of the programme. Their expertise is essential in transforming educational goals into practical, modular learning experiences that are both engaging and effective. Academic staff also assess learning outcomes and continuously improve MCs based on feedback and evolving educational trends.

Employers are important stakeholders as they represent the needs and expectations of the professional world. They provide insight into the skills and competencies required in the labour market and how MCs can be integrated into recruitment and career development processes. Employers look for MCs that meet industry standards and address specific skills gaps. Their involvement ensures that MCs are relevant and valuable from an employment perspective, making them a critical link between education and the labour market.

Policy makers are responsible for shaping the framework within which MCs are developed and implemented. They establish policies and regulations that influence how MCs fit into broader education and training systems. Policy makers set standards for the accreditation, funding, and recognition of MCs, ensuring that these programmes meet quality benchmarks and serve public and institutional interests (Raj et al., 2024). Their role is essential in creating a supportive environment for MCs, facilitating their integration into national and international education systems, and promoting their adoption across sectors.

Results of the MICMAC Method

Following the identification of factors and stakeholders (Sections 5.1 and 5.2), the results of the MICMAC method offer a comprehensive analysis of the influence and dependencies among these factors.

As shown in Table 1, the factors influencing the structure of MCs were identified from both literature and expert opinions. A questionnaire was designed to gather insights from decision-makers across educational institutions and organizations regarding the pairwise evaluation of these 14 factors. Data collection took place from May to June 2024, involving a total of 12 decision-makers representing different stakeholder groups. Specifically, the group included 2 administrative staff from the distance learning center, 3 academic staff involved in distance learning programs, 1 employer, and 6 learners. To enhance the reliability of the data and ensure the accuracy of the analysis, the data collection was conducted face-to-face. For evaluating the direct relationships between the factors, a scale was used ranging from no influence (0) to very high influence (4) (Bagherian et al., 2024). The results from each input were aggregated by considering the mode of the data, which represents the most frequently occurring value (Rivera & Revilla, 1984). This approach ensures that the analysis accurately reflects the consensus among the decision-makers on the impact and dependencies of the identified factors.

The MICMAC method reveals hidden factors by taking into account the indirect relationships analyzed using matrix multiplications (Godet, 1994). Thus, to examine indirect relationships, the powers of the matrices are taken until equal orders of influence and dependence are obtained in two consecutive powers. In the first iteration, the initial matrix is multiplied by itself to obtain the second matrix, which takes into account first-order indirect relationships, and the influence and dependency levels, which are the row and column sums, are calculated. In the second iteration, the second matrix is again multiplied by the initial matrix to obtain the third matrix, and the influence and dependency values are calculated. According to the procedure, when stability levels are observed to stabilize (stability is achieved with a power of 4), the influence and dependency values are calculated according to the data in the final matrix. The impact and dependency levels of the initial matrix and the matrix obtained after the 4th iteration are given in Table 2.

There are no major differences between direct and indirect influences in Table 2. The influence rankings remain similar for most of the factors. The influence rankings are the same for factors other than F2 (training of academic staff), F3 (self-assessment of the academic staff), and F4 (academic staff qualification). This indicates that these factors have a similar influence in both types of relationships. On the other hand, slightly more significant differences are observed in the dependency rankings. Especially in indirect relationships, the dependency rankings of factors F2 (training of academic staff) and F3 (self-assessment of the academic staff) increase, while the dependency rankings of F7 (stakeholder engagement) decrease. Factor F14 (accreditation and quality assurance) ranks first in both direct and indirect relationships in terms of both influence and dependence. This indicates that F14 (accreditation and quality assurance) is both the most dependent and the most influential factor.

Table 2. Influence and dependency rankings for direct and indirect relationships.

Factors	Direct relationship		Indirect relationship	
	Influence	Dependence	Influence	Dependence
Learning outcomes and assessment	10	7	10	8
Training of academic staff	7	11	8	13
Self-assessment of the academic staff	8	10	6	12
Academic staff qualification	6	14	7	14
Design of MCs policies	4	6	4	7
Learner-centered design	9	4	9	4
Stakeholder engagement	5	13	5	11
Learning resources and diversity	12	5	12	5
Monitoring and improvement	2	2	2	2
Understandability and comparability of MCs	11	8	11	6
Verification of MCs	13	9	13	9
Collaborative learning methods	14	3	14	3
Digital and infrastructure capacity	3	11	3	10
Accreditation and quality assurance	1	1	1	1

The fact that some factors have similar rankings in both types of relationships indicates that these factors generally have a stable level of influence and dependence. On the other hand, the fact that some factors show significant differences in influence and dependence rankings indicates that these factors may play different roles according to the type of relationship. These differences indicate that in complicated systems such as distance learning, the direct and indirect influence of certain factors should be carefully evaluated. Thus, decision-makers can better understand how these factors play a role in both types of relationships and can adapt their strategies accordingly.

Taking into account the influence and dependency levels in this table, the influence-dependency map for direct relationships is shown in Figure 2. As previously described in Section 5, factors are classified into four clusters, including influential, key, dependent, and autonomous factors. The map of indirect relationships is not included as all factors are in the same group according to the effects and dependencies in indirect relationships. Figure 2 shows that there are two factors in the influential factors region, three factors in the key factors region, six factors in the dependent factors region, and three factors in the autonomous factors region.

Figure 2. Influence and dependency map for direct relationships.

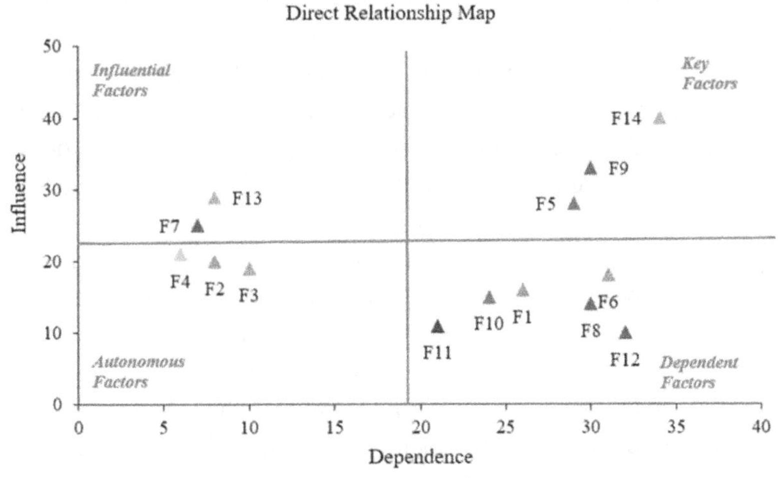

F1 Learning outcomes and assessment
F2 Training of academic staff
F3 Self-assessment of the academic staff
F4 Academic staff qualification
F5 Design of MCs policies
F6 Learner-centered design
F7 Stakeholder engagement
F8 Learning resources and diversity
F9 Monitoring and improvement
F10 Understandability and comparability of MCs
F11 Verification of MCs
F12 Collaborative learning methods
F13 Digital and infrastructure capacity
F14 Accreditation and quality assurance

The upper left region in Figure 2 includes F7 (stakeholder engagement) and F13 (digital and infrastructure capacity). These factors directly influence many other factors and are critical for the successful implementation of MCs. Stakeholder engagement ensures that MCs are designed and adopted according to the needs. Digital and infrastructure capacity increases the viability and accessibility of MCs. These factors can enhance or constrain the effectiveness of other factors. As illustrated in Figure 2, the upper right region contains F5 (design of MCs policies), F9 (monitoring and improvement), and F14 (accreditation and quality assurance). These factors are key to the effective and efficient implementation of MCs. The design of MCs policies establishes the standards for implementation. The implementation of continuous monitoring and improvement strategies serves to enhance the overall effectiveness and quality of MCs. The F9 factor is of critical importance for the dynamic development of MCs. The processes of accreditation and quality assurance serve to ensure validity and reliability. It is thus clear that the F14 factor is of critical importance concerning the acceptance and recognition of MCs.

The region situated to the lower right of Figure 2 includes F1 (learning outcomes and assessment), F6 (learner-centered design), F8 (learning resources and diversity), F10 (understandability and comparability of MCs), F11 (verification of MCs), and F12 (collaborative learning methods). These factors are themselves influenced by other factors, which provide the necessary support. The success of MCs is assessed in terms of learning outcomes and the associated assessment measures. A learner-centered approach to design entails the creation of educational materials that are aligned with the specific needs of the learners in question. The comprehensibility and comparable nature of MCs contribute to their acceptance. The provision of learning resources and diversity allows learners to access a diverse range of high-quality learning materials. This has a direct impact on the achievement and satisfaction of the learners. Verification procedures serve to enhance the credibility of MCs. The implementation of collaborative learning methods has been identified as a strategy that enables learners to optimize their learning outcomes. The autonomous factors region in Figure 2 includes F2 (training of academic staff), F3 (self-assessment of the academic staff), and F4 (academic staff qualification). These factors are components that function independently of other factors and indirectly influence the quality of MCs. In conclusion, the findings from Figure 2 provide insight into the significance and contributions of factors within each region, enabling the identification of critical factors for the successful design, implementation, and evaluation of MCs.

STRUCTURING MCs EFFECTIVELY IN DISTANCE LEARNING

This chapter analyzes the factors affecting the structuring of MCs in distance learning using the MICMAC method. The findings presented in Section 5 highlight the importance of identifying critical factors for the effective design and implementation of MCs, considering the needs and priorities of various stakeholders. It is evident that stakeholder engagement and digital infrastructure capacity significantly impact the feasibility and accessibility of MCs. This underscores the necessity of active stakeholder involvement in the design and adoption of MCs, as also noted in the literature (Raj et al., 2024; Olcott, 2022).

Key factors such as policy design, continuous monitoring and improvement strategies, accreditation, and quality assurance are crucial for the dynamic development and overall effectiveness of MCs. Salmon (2023) suggests that collaborating with higher education accreditation bodies can enhance the validity and reliability of MCs. Additionally, Brown et al. (2021) propose that blockchain technology could play a significant role in maintaining the reliability and currency of MCs. Concerns about the consistency of MCs, as highlighted by Varadarajan et al. (2023), further emphasize the need for robust accreditation and quality assurance processes.

Factors like the diversity of learning resources, validation procedures, and collaborative learning methods contribute to the success of MCs. These findings align with the literature, which asserts that MCs offer opportunities to develop essential 21st-century skills, including digital literacy, communication, collaboration, critical thinking, and problem-solving (El Mawas & Muntean, 2018). The implementation of collaborative learning methods is also shown to enhance learning outcomes (Gauthier, 2020). While independent factors of MCs have an indirect impact on quality, innovative solutions such as blockchain technology can help ensure their reliability (Brown et al., 2021). Nonetheless, employers' concerns about MCs' consistency should be considered (Varadarajan et al., 2024). As Olcott (2021) suggests, preparing for MCs requires careful evaluation of institutional strengths and the competitive environment. Effective management of these factors is crucial for the acceptance and recognition of MCs.

The following sub-sections explore in detail the opportunities and challenges associated with structuring MCs.

OPPORTUNITIES IN STRUCTURING MCs

MCs present a significant opportunity for revolutionizing distance learning and professional development by providing flexible, accessible, and personalized learning pathways. This flexibility enables individuals to tailor their education according to their personal and professional schedules, potentially transforming their approach to higher education (Antoninis et al., 2023; MicroHE, 2019). As MCs promote self-paced learning, learners gain increased control over their professional growth, making these programs particularly appealing to working professionals and non-traditional students who might not otherwise have access to higher education. Furthermore, the online and digital nature of MCs enhances their accessibility by allowing learners from diverse geographic locations to access educational materials anytime and anywhere. Unlike traditional face-to-face education, digital MC programs eliminate the need for physical presence, thus making education more inclusive and broadly accessible (Raj et al., 2024; Hunt et al., 2020). The convenience of earning digital badges upon completing each module serves as a motivational tool, encouraging ongoing engagement and participation (Tooley & Hood, 2021).

In addition to accessibility, MCs address the growing demand for more affordable, shorter, and skill-specific certifications. As traditional university degrees face criticism for their high costs and lengthy duration, MCs offer a dynamic, competitive, and demand-driven alternative that caters to a wide range of learning areas, from specialized technical skills to general non-technical competencies (Raj et al., 2024). The flexibility of MCs makes them particularly advantageous for those balancing part-time or full-time employment, as well as for experienced workers seeking to upskill in specific areas.

Employers benefit from the detailed and granular nature of MCs, which provide valuable insights into the specific skills and competencies of learners. This level of detail supports informed decision-making in recruitment, promotion, and performance evaluations. Additionally, it helps organizations identify skill gaps within their workforce, enabling the design of targeted professional development programs to address these deficiencies (Raj et al., 2024). The transparency offered by MCs enhances their attractiveness to employers, particularly in fast-evolving industries. Nevertheless, the broader recognition and acceptance of MCs by employers are essential for realizing their full potential. While some sectors, particularly technology, have begun to embrace MCs for professional development, wider acceptance across various fields remains a challenge (Garg et al., 2023). Achieving standardized accreditation processes and building employer trust is crucial for the successful integration of MCs into the job market (Antoninis et al., 2023).

In conclusion, MCs offer substantial opportunities for distance learning by providing flexible, accessible, and customized educational experiences. Their ability to cater to diverse learner needs and provide detailed insights into acquired competencies makes them a valuable tool for both learners and employers. However, to fully realize the potential of MCs, continued efforts are necessary to enhance their recognition, scalability, and standardization.

CHALLENGES FOR STRUCTURING MCs

Despite the growing interest in MCs from learners, academic staff, and employers, several notable challenges hinder their broader acceptance and implementation. A key challenge relates to whether MCs receive adequate recognition from employers at both national and international levels. As MCs gain traction, especially in Western countries, questions arise about whether employers value these certifications and recognize the skills and competencies they represent (Ahmat et al., 2021). Although some industries, particularly in the tech sector, have embraced MCs for continuous professional development, broader recognition across various fields and regions remains inconsistent.

One major challenge in the development of MCs is fostering mutual understanding among key stakeholders, including learners, academic staff, universities, policymakers, and employers (MicroHE, 2019). Learners often perceive MCs as an alternative pathway for acquiring new competencies, while academic staff see them as formal and informal credentials that can be completed within a short period. However, employers may regard MCs as similar to traditional professional development certificates, raising concerns about their distinct value in the workforce. This divergence in perceptions can create confusion about the purpose and worth of MCs, making it difficult to establish a common framework for their acceptance. In addition to alignment among stakeholders, the scalability of MC programs, particularly in managing the large number of online learners that MCs often attract. Since many MC programs are fully online, institutions must be prepared to handle a global influx of learners, which can strain their resources for monitoring and assessing learning activities. Institutional readiness is crucial, particularly when scaling MC offerings to a broader market. This requires significant investments in infrastructure, including video production studios, online platforms, and technological tools, to deliver high-quality, interactive learning experiences (Ralston, 2020). Moreover, both academic staff and learners need to possess technological literacy to ensure the smooth implementation of MCs. Without proper infrastructure and support, the expansion of MCs can be severely limited.

Financial investment is another major concern, particularly regarding the development and maintenance of MC programs. Universities and MC providers must allocate sufficient funding to cover the costs of platform development, third-party subscriptions, and technological tools (Chung et al., 2020). Furthermore, reliable internet connectivity is essential, as many learners may face difficulties accessing online courses without it. These logistical challenges must be addressed for MC programs to succeed on a global scale.

Accreditation and quality assurance are also critical challenges. Traditional degree programs follow established accreditation processes, ensuring consistent quality across institutions. However, MCs do not always undergo the same rigorous procedures, raising concerns about their dependability and overall quality (Varadarajan et al., 2023; Ahmat et al., 2021; Fedock et al., 2016). This lack of standardization can impede the acceptance of MCs by employers and other educational institutions, as the breadth and depth of learning outcomes may vary widely. The absence of standardized credit systems and evaluation measures further complicates the transferability and comparability of MCs across different regions and industries (Mashford-Pringle et al., 2023). Moreover, ensuring the security and integrity of digital credentials is vital to maintaining trust in MCs. As these credentials are often issued in the form of digital badges, the risk of fraud or misrepresentation is a significant concern. MC providers must implement robust verification mechanisms to uphold the credibility of these credentials and ensure that they accurately reflect the competencies they represent (Varadarajan et al., 2023; Ahmat et al., 2021). Without proper safeguards, the value of MCs could be undermined, limiting their potential as a viable alternative to traditional qualifications.

The long-term impact and recognition of MCs also remain uncertain. Many systems have not had MCs in place long enough to assess their overall effectiveness or impact on learners' career prospects (Tooley & Hood, 2021). The wide variation in MC offerings, both in terms of assessment methods and content, makes it difficult to measure their success on a broad scale. As a result, questions remain about the sustainability and future scalability of MCs in addressing workforce needs. Lastly, a lack of trust between organizations, including educational institutions and employers, can hinder the adoption of MCs (Pirkkalainen et al., 2023). Building mutual trust is essential for ensuring that MCs are valued and recognized across different sectors. This requires collaboration between stakeholders to establish common standards for MCs, enabling them to be portable and transferable across various industries and regions (MicroHE, 2019). Until this trust is established, the widespread acceptance of MCs may remain limited. In summary, while MCs hold significant promise for the future of education and professional development, their widespread adoption depends on overcoming several challenges. These include achieving recognition at both national and international levels, fostering mutual understanding among key stakeholders, ensuring scalability, establishing standardization, securing financial investment, obtaining accreditation, maintaining quality assurance, and building trust. Addressing these issues is essential to realize the potential of MCs as a flexible, accessible, and globally recognized form of credentialing.

CONCLUSION

MCs have emerged as an alternative approach to career and business development. They offer a fast, flexible, and cost-effective way for learners to develop their skills in designated areas. At this point, the role of HEIs in structuring MCs are very important. However, to manage this process successfully, multi-stakeholder involvement and a clear definition of the factors affecting this process are required. Taking into account the views of learners, employers, academic staff, and other interested stakeholders, the design and implementation of MCs should be optimized to meet the needs of both education and the business world.

This chapter has systematically identified and categorized the factors impacting the structuring of MCs in distance learning. Through a comprehensive literature review and expert consultations, we have pinpointed the critical factors influencing MCs. By utilizing the MICMAC method, we analyzed these factors to determine their influence and dependency, ultimately creating a factor map. The analysis revealed that "stakeholder engagement" and "digital and infrastructure capacity" are influential factors. Meanwhile, "design of MCs policies", "monitoring and improvement", and "digital and infrastructure capacity" emerged as key factors. Additionally, "training of academic staff", "self-assessment of the academic staff", and "academic staff qualification" were categorized as autonomous factors.

In conclusion, this chapter identifies autonomous factors, dependent factors, linkage factors, and independent factors in the structuring of MCs in distance learning. Categorizing these factors is crucial for developing better strategies and offering more effective educational pathways in this field. This chapter considers the perspectives of various stakeholders and provides recommendations for structuring MCs in distance learning more effectively. These recommendations have the potential to impact future educational practice and provide valuable contributions to improving learning experiences. The findings are expected to support strategic planning in distance learning and support progress in the field. The expected contribution of the results of this chapter to the practitioner is the mapping of factors in the structure of MCs. In this way, it will contribute to understanding which factors have what impact on employability, the changing nature of work, and new models of lifelong learning.

Further studies can be conducted to investigate the relationship between the needs of the industry and the demand for MCs and the courses they provide. Additionally, research can be carried out on the roles of the authorities responsible for setting the assessment criteria and the qualification standards.

REFERENCES

Ahmad, N., Hoda, N., & Alahmari, F. (2020). Developing a Cloud-Based Mobile Learning Adoption Model to Promote Sustainable Education. *Sustainability (Basel)*, 12(8), 3126. DOI: 10.3390/su12083126

Ahmat, N. H. C., Bashir, M. A. A., Razali, A. R., & Kasolang, S. (2021). Micro-credentials in higher education institutions: Challenges and opportunities. *Asian Journal of University Education*, 17(3), 281–290. DOI: 10.24191/ajue.v17i3.14505

Ahsan, K., Akbar, S., Kam, B., & Abdulrahman, M. D. A. (2023). Implementation of micro-credentials in higher education: A systematic literature review. *Education and Information Technologies*, 28(10), 13505–13540. DOI: 10.1007/s10639-023-11739-z

Antoninis, M., Alcott, B., Al Hadheri, S., April, D., Fouad Barakat, B., Barrios Rivera, M., ... & Weill, E. (2023). Global Education Monitoring Report 2023: Technology in education: A tool on whose terms?. https://doi.org/10.54676/UZQV8501

Bagherian, A., Gershon, M., Kumar, S., & Mishra, M. K. (2024). Analyzing the relationship between digitalization and energy sustainability: A comprehensive ISM-MICMAC and DEMATEL approach. *Expert Systems with Applications*, 236, 121193. DOI: 10.1016/j.eswa.2023.121193

Brown, M., Giolla Mhichil, M. N., Beirne, E., & Mac Lochlainn, C. (2021). The global micro-credential landscape: Charting a new credential ecology for lifelong learning. *Journal of Learning Development*, 8(2), 228–254. DOI: 10.56059/jl4d.v8i2.525

Chung, E., Subramaniam, G., & Dass, L. C. (2020). Online learning readiness among university students in Malaysia amidst COVID-19. *Asian Journal of University Education*, 16(2), 46–58.

Duperrin, J. C., & Godet, M. (1973). Méthode de hiérarchisation des éléments d'un système: essai de prospective du système de l'énergie nucléaire dans son contexte sociétal, Centre national de l'entrepreneuriat (CNE); hal-02185432.

El Mawas, N., & Muntean, C. (2018). Supporting lifelong learning through development of 21 st century skills 10th International Conference on Education and New Learning Technologies, https://hal.archives-ouvertes.fr/hal-02250150

Fan, X., Wei, X., Lewis, A., & Watts, J. (2024). Micro-credentialing as an approach to educator professional learning: Voices from developers, pursuers, and assessors. *Teaching and Teacher Education*, 148, 104700. DOI: 10.1016/j.tate.2024.104700

Fedock, B., Kebritchi, M., Sanders, R., & Holland, A. (2016). Digital badges and micro-credentials: Digital age classroom practices, design strategies, and issues. Foundation of Digital Badges and Micro-Credentials: Demonstrating and Recognizing Knowledge and Competencies, 273-286. https://doi.org/10.1007/978-3-319-15425-1_15

Fisher, R. M., & Leder, H. (2022). An assessment of micro-credentials in New Zealand vocational education. *International Journal of Training Research*, 20(3), 232–247. DOI: 10.1080/14480220.2021.2018018

Garg, P., Raj, R., Kumar, V., Singh, S., Pahuja, S., & Sehrawat, N. (2023). Elucidating the role of consumer decision making style on consumers' purchase intention: The mediating role of emotional advertising using PLS-SEM. *Journal of Economy and Technology*, 1, 108–118. https://doi.org/10.1016/j.ject.2023.10.001

Gauthier, T. (2020). The value of microcredentials: The employer's perspective. *The Journal of Competency-Based Education*, 5(2), e01209. DOI: 10.1002/cbe2.1209

Godet, M. (1994). *From Anticipation to Action: A handbook of strategic prospective*. UNESCO Publishing.

Hunt, T., Carter, R., Zhang, L., & Yang, S. (2020). Micro-credentials: The potential of personalized professional development. *Development and Learning in Organizations*, 34(2), 33–35. DOI: 10.1108/DLO-09-2019-0215

Kato, S., Galán-Muros, V., & Weko, T. (2020). The emergence of alternative credentials. OECD Education Working Papers, 216. https://doi.org/DOI: 10.1787/19939019

Mardisentosa, B., Rahardja, U., Zelina, K., Oganda, F. P., & Hardini, M. (2021, November). Sustainable learning micro-credential using blockchain for student achievement records. In *2021 Sixth International Conference on Informatics and Computing (ICIC)* (pp. 1-6). IEEE. https://doi.org/10.1109/ICIC54025.2021.9632913

Mashford-Pringle, A., Tan, S., Stutz, S., & Tjong, G. (2023). Designing accountability measures for health professionals: results from a community-based micro-credential: case study on Indigenous cultural safety. *BMC Public Health*, 23(1), 879. https://doi.org/10.1186/s12889-023-15721-9

McGreal, R., Mackintosh, W., Cox, G., & Olcott, D.Jr. (2022). Bridging the gap: micro-credentials for development: UNESCO chairs policy brief form-under the III world higher education conference (WHEC 2021) type: collective X. *International Review of Research in Open and Distributed Learning*, 23(3), 288–302.

MicroHE Consortium. (2019). A briefing paper on the award, recognition, portability and accreditation of micro-credentials: An investigation through interviews with key stakeholders & decision makers. https://microcredentials.eu/wp- content/uploads/sites/20/2019/12/WP3-Interviews-with-Key-Stakeholders-Decision-Makers-Overall-Summary-Report.pdf (accessed 12 September 2024).

Olcott, D.Jr. (2022). Micro-credentials: A catalyst for strategic reset and change in US higher education. *American Journal of Distance Education*, 36(1), 19–35. DOI: 10.1080/08923647.2021.1997537

Oliver, B. (2019). Making micro-credentials work for learners, employers and providers. https://www.assuringgraduatecapabilities.com/uploads/4/5/0/5/45053363/making-micro-credentials-work-oliver-deakin-2019.pdf (accessed 10 May 2024).

Orman, R., Şimşek, E., & Çakır, M. A. K. (2023). Micro-credentials and reflections on higher education. *Higher Education Evaluation and Development*, 17(2), 96–112. DOI: 10.1108/HEED-08-2022-0028

Pirkkalainen, H., Sood, I., Padron Napoles, C., Kukkonen, A., & Camilleri, A. (2023). How might micro-credentials influence institutions and empower learners in higher education? *Educational Research*, 65(1), 40–63. https://doi.org/10.1080/00131881.2022.2157302

Raj, R., Singh, A., Kumar, V., & Verma, P. (2024). Achieving professional qualifications using micro-credentials: A case of small packages and big challenges in higher education. *International Journal of Educational Management*, 38(4), 916–947. DOI: 10.1108/IJEM-01-2023-0028

Ralston, S. J. (2021). Higher education's microcredentialing craze: A postdigital-Deweyan critique. *Postdigital Science and Education*, 3(1), 83–101. https://doi.org/10.1007/s42438-020-00121-8

Reed, A., Kong, Y., & Abramovich, S. (2024). Assessment, credential, or both? Higher education faculty's design principles for micro-credentials. *Discover Education*, 3(1), 16. https://doi.org/10.1007/s44217-024-00100-2

Resei, C., Friedl, C., Staubitz, T., & Rohloff, T. (2019). Micro-credentials in EU and Global. Corship Corporate Edupreneurship. https://openhpi-public.s3.openhpicloud.de/pages/research/27kLG703NBaxDgjuaNjOWe/Corship-R1.1c_micro-credentials.pdf

Rivera, E., & Revilla, M. L. (1984). A cross-impact simulation and analysis of events through time with a micro-computer. Microprocessing and microprogramming, 13(3), 189-198. https://doi.org/DOI: 10.1016/0165-6074(84)90030-9

Salmon, M. (2023). Drivers of the global push for microcredentials in higher education: Flexibility and employability in contemporary university systems. Perspectives. *Perspectives*, 27(4), 179–187. DOI: 10.1080/13603108.2023.2229767

Selvaratnam, R. M., & Sankey, M. D. (2021). An integrative literature review of the implementation of micro-credentials in higher education: Implications for practice in Australasia. *Journal of Teaching and Learning for Graduate Employability*, 12(1), 1–17.

Selvaratnam, R. M., Warburton, S., Parrish, D., & Crew, S. (2024). A maturity model for micro-credentialing and shorter forms of learning practice in Australasian universities. *Journal of Higher Education Policy and Management*, 46(4), 1–16. DOI: 10.1080/1360080X.2023.2299150

Sharma, H., Jain, V., Mogaji, E., & Babbilid, A. S. (2024). Blended learning and augmented employability: A multi-stakeholder perspective of the micro-credentialing ecosystem in higher education. *International Journal of Educational Management*. Advance online publication. https://doi.org/10.1108/IJEM-12-2022-0497

Shwedeh, F., Salloum, S. A., Aburayya, A., Fatin, B., Elbadawi, M. A., Al Ghurabli, Z., & Al Dabbagh, T. (2024). AI Adoption and Educational Sustainability in Higher Education in the UAE. In *Artificial Intelligence in Education: The Power and Dangers of ChatGPT in the Classroom* (pp. 201–229). Springer Nature Switzerland., https://doi.org/10.1007/978-3-031-52280-2_14

Tee, P. K., Cham, T. H., Aw, E. C. X., Khudaykulov, A., & Zhang, X. (2024). Marketing micro-credentials: Understanding learners' engagement and willingness to pay more. *International Journal of Educational Management*, 38(4), 1001–1020. https://doi.org/10.1108/IJEM-03-2023-0096

Thi Ngoc Ha, N., Spittle, M., Watt, A., & Van Dyke, N. (2023). A systematic literature review of micro-credentials in higher education: A non-zero-sum game. *Higher Education Research & Development*, 42(6), 1527–1548. DOI: 10.1080/07294360.2022.2146061

Tooley, M., & Hood, J. (2021). Harnessing Micro-Credentials for Teacher Growth: A National Review of Early Best Practices. New America. https://www.newamerica.org/education-policy/reports/harnessing-micro-credentials-teacher-growth/ (accessed 10 May 2024).

UNESCO. (2018). Digital credentialing: implications for the recognition of learning across borders. UNESCO Education Sector. https://unesdoc.unesco.org/ark:/48223/pf0000264428. (accessed 10 May 2024).

Varadarajan, S., Koh, J. H. L., & Daniel, B. K. (2023). A systematic review of the opportunities and challenges of micro-credentials for multiple stakeholders: Learners, employers, higher education institutions and government. *International Journal of Educational Technology in Higher Education*, 20(1), 13. DOI: 10.1186/s41239-023-00381-x PMID: 36874535

Yilmaz, H., Karadayi-Usta, S., & Yanık, S. (2022). A novel neutrosophic AHP-Copeland approach for distance education: Towards sustainability. *Interactive Learning Environments*, 1–23. DOI: 10.1080/10494820.2022.2141265

Yilmaz, H., Karadayi-Usta, S., Yanik, S., & Kahraman, C. (2024). Decision process: A stakeholder-oriented video conferencing software selection in sustainable distance education. In *Decision-Making Models* (pp. 19–46). Academic Press.

Yilmaz, H., & Yanık, S. (2022). Prioritization of Factors Affecting Sustainability of Distance Education in Higher Education Institutions. International Graduate Research Symposium - IGRS'22, (1-3 June).

Zhang, P., Ma, S., Zhao, Y., Ling, J., & Sun, Y. (2024). Analysing influencing factors and correlation paths of learning burnout among secondary vocational students in the context of social media: An integrated ISM–MICMAC approach. *Heliyon*, 10(7), e28696. Advance online publication. DOI: 10.1016/j.heliyon.2024.e28696 PMID: 38586410

Zou, H., Ullah, A., Qazi, Z., Naeem, A., & Rehan, S. (2024). Impact of micro-credential learning on students' perceived employability: The mediating role of human capital. *International Journal of Educational Management*, 38(4), 897–915. https://doi.org/10.1108/IJEM-01-2023-0002

Chapter 6

Exploring the Potential and Future Directions of Micro-Credentials Through the Scenario Archetypes Method

Şeyda Kır
Yozgat Bozok University, Turkey

Hakan Yıldırım
https://orcid.org/0000-0002-4693-1287
Eskişehir Osmangazi University, Turkey

Aras Bozkurt
https://orcid.org/0000-0002-4520-642X
Anadolu University, Turkey

ABSTRACT

Micro-credentials have emerged as a flexible, skill-based alternative to traditional degrees, meeting the demands of modern education and employment sectors. Using the Four Archetypes Scenario model—continuous growth, collapse, disciplined society, and transformation—this chapter explores their future in higher education. In the continuous growth scenario, micro-credentials integrate with higher education, driving curriculum evolution and industry partnerships. The collapse scenario warns of institutional failures to adapt and employer skepticism, threatening micro-credentials' value. In the transformation scenario, micro-credentials are widely accepted, reshaping higher education by promoting flexibility, upskilling,

DOI: 10.4018/979-8-3693-5488-9.ch006

and lifelong learning. This analysis aims to provide insights into micro-credentials' evolving role in the education landscape, offering a roadmap for their sustainable integration into higher education and industry.

INTRODUCTION

In a time when information is rapidly produced and consumed have ramped up the adoption of skill-based approaches in the workplace. Unemployment rates have risen dramatically following the COVID-19 pandemic, and competency and skill-based professions have become even more popular, providing impetus for this change. In this process, the number of students enrolled in higher education institutions has decreased as a result of the pandemic, and individuals have switched to programs and courses that enable them to easily find work opportunities by obtaining skills and qualifications in a shorter period of time. Micro-credentials, short training programmes, but also bite-sized courses are the leading practices for obtaining employment in an evolving workforce where up-to-date skills are in demand. The increasing interest in skill-based strategies for learning, such as micro-credentials, is an outcome of evolving requirements in professional settings as well as changes to higher education's traditional approaches to teaching. Moreover, the potential of micro-credentials extends beyond individual skill acquisition in that it has the potential to foster inclusivity and personalization in education, whereby learners themselves will be able to tailor their educational pathways toward unique career aspirations. According to Reed (2023) and Bruguera (2023), evidence-based practices imply that micro-credentials could support a more learner-centered approach to equity and access to education by diverse populations. Given the continuing development of the global micro-credential landscape, it becomes important that educational leaders struggle with an informed perspective about the trend at hand and ponder seeking novel approaches to management with great care towards integration into current structures (McGreal & Olcott, 2022; Ha et al., 2022).

Micro-credential programs, which may address the learning needs of many people, particularly those on the path to lifelong learning, enhance individuals' learning processes by providing a prevalent, flexible, and alternative option beyond the employment sector. In the higher education environment, micro-credentials become increasingly more popular as an alternative to traditional degrees, diplomas, and certifications (Pelletier et al., 2021). Consequently, higher education institutions have created structures around institutional or national initiatives that have encouraged micro-credentials programs and frameworks more frequently (Resei et al., 2019). In this regard, the objective of this chapter is to explore the potential and present context of micro-credentials in higher education, and to address their future implications by addressing the Four Archetypes Scenario model.

RELATED LITERATURE

Definition of Micro-credentials

There are many definitions and explanations for micro-credentials in the related literature. The primary reason for explaining this term in different ways can be considered as the fact that it emerges in line with different needs according to the demands of the culture and society in which it is implemented. In addition to this, of course, the fact that it is a fairly new concept and has been re-interpreted by many researchers due to the fact that it is included in current issues can also be seen as another reason.

While there is no universally accepted definition of micro-credentials, they generally represent smaller units of study that are shorter in duration compared to traditional accredited learning programs (Brown et al., 2021; Kır & Bozkurt, 2022). Kiiskilä et al. (2023) defined micro-credentials as short, focused learning experiences that provide learners with specific skills or knowledge, often culminating in a digital credential that can be shared with potential employers or educational institutions. To be discussed in more detail, micro-credentials can be defined as a skill that is smaller in terms of workload than a bachelor's degree or diploma program in the traditional education process, focused on gaining skills in a short time, accepted as an alternative, personalized learning experience in the lifelong learning process and evaluated at the end of the learning process (Bozkurt & Brown, 2022; McGreal & Olcott, 2022; Pelletier et al., 2021; Oliver, 2019). Although there are different definitions and uses of micro-credentials, the EU has pointed out that there are some mandatory features that micro-credentials should have (European Union, 2021). The following image lists (Figure 1) the critical features and is considered significant for all stakeholders using micro-credentials to clearly identify the value and content of micro-credentials.

A Global Overview and Current Trends of Microcredentials

Micro-credentials are a rapidly developing form of education in Europe and around the world, offering shorter learning opportunities than traditional diplomas. They are offered by both public and private institutions and respond to the demand for flexible, student-oriented education and training. Micro-credentials have the potential to offer students the opportunity to gain competence in a specific field, while at the same time providing education and training opportunities to a wider range of learners, including disadvantaged and vulnerable groups. This supports social inclusion by increasing the accessibility of education. However, the lack of common standards to ensure the quality, transparency, cross-border comparability, recognisability and portability of these documents may prevent micro-credentials from reaching their full potential. Therefore, cooperation between higher education institutions, policy makers and other stakeholders is critical for the effective design and implementation of micro-credentials. Standardized approaches will increase the credibility of these documents and ensure international recognition and validation of the competences acquired by students. Thus, micro-credentials will become a powerful tool to support individuals' lifelong learning processes and help them adapt to the labor market.

Figure 1. EU mandatory elements for micro-credentials

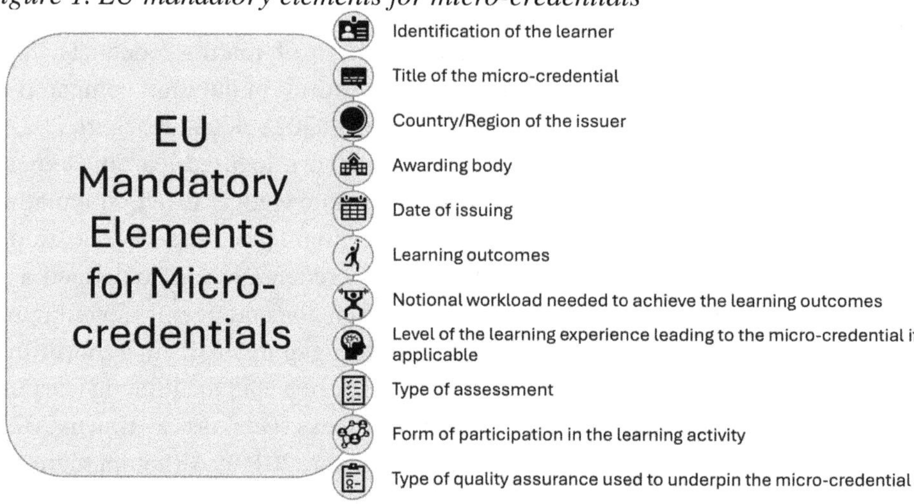

Upon examination of the micro-credentials mandated by the European Union, the initial feature is the identification of the learner who is eligible to receive them. Subsequently, it is mandatory to include concise, unambiguous explanations, including the micro-credential's title, the country/region of issue, the awarding body, and the date of issue. Additional information is anticipated to encompass the learning outcomes that the learner is presumed to have achieved, the workload in ECTS value of the time spent to achieve these these outcomes, the level of the learning experience leading to the micro-credential and the type of assessment used, the manner in which the learner participated in the micro-credential learning activity, and the type of quality assurance used in this process. In addition to these mandatory components, there are certain optional features that are considered appropriate for inclusion in pertinent situations (European Union, 2021). Some of them include prerequisites needed to enroll in the learning activity, grade achieved, Integration/stackability options, and supervision and identity verification during assessment. In addition to these features, the European Union (2021) has identified ten principles that should be taken into account when creating and distributing a micro-credential. These principles reflect the European perspective on micro-credentials and are intended to help build a high-quality micro-credential ecosystem. These principles—quality, transparency, relevance, valid assessment, learning paths, recognition, portability, learner-centeredness, authenticity, and information and guidance—can be used in the development of micro-credentials in any discipline or sector.

Micro-credentials have garnered significant attention as a means to address the evolving demands for specific work competencies and to facilitate professional development among employees (Shay, 2023). They play a crucial role in ensuring the acceptance and stackability of credentials across different institutions, providing employers with a secure and unalterable digital record of applicants' skills relevant to the workplace (McGreal et al., 2022). Additionally, micro-credentials offer short, flexible learning experiences that complement traditional qualifications, supporting learners in achieving their career or life goals (Bruguera, 2023).

Tinsley et al. (2022) indicate that micro-credentials can lead to job promotions, higher wages, and increased self-confidence, particularly benefiting learners in rural postsecondary communities. Furthermore, micro-credentials have been identified as valuable tools for upskilling the workforce and addressing skills shortages in various industries (MacCallum & Brown, 2022). To ensure the success of micro-credentials, it is essential to establish a framework that not only defines them but also ensures their value to key stakeholders, including learners, employers, and providers (Oliver, 2021).

Research on micro-credentials in higher education has made significant progress, particularly in regions like North America, Europe, and Australasia (Bean et al., 2023). However, there are several research gaps that need to be addressed. One key gap is the need to understand how micro-credentials can be effectively integrated into higher education systems to meet the demands of lifelong learning and workforce upskilling (Lang, 2023). While there is a growing interest in micro-credentials, there is still limited evidence of their impact on enhancing employability, widening pathways to higher education, and improving completion rates (OECD, 2023). Another gap in the literature is the need for more clarity on the value and purpose of micro-credentials, which can hinder their adoption in traditional education settings, especially in higher education institutions (Orman et al., 2023). Additionally, there is a need to explore how micro-credentials can influence institutions and empower learners in higher education (Pirkkalainen et al., 2022). Understanding the implications of incorporating micro-credentials into higher education courses, including the role of skills profiling in enabling their integration, is also an area that requires further investigation (Ward et al., 2023). Moreover, the research gap extends to the assessment and credentialing processes associated with micro-credentials. There is a need to explore how evidence-based micro-credentials can support individualized learning, inclusivity, and a more expansive model of assessment and credentialing (Reed, 2023). Furthermore, the potential fragmentation in higher education caused by the introduction of micro-credentials needs to be examined to ensure that they do not detract from fundamental scientific disciplines and professional identity (Kušić et al., 2022).

METHOD

Scenarios can be defined as the ordinary, acceptable, and demanding narratives about how the future might be shaped (Bezold, 2010; Boschetti et al., 2016; Hunt et al., 2012). Scenarios, which are also seen as the alternative future (Fontela & Hingel, 1993), enable the analysis of possible trends against a situation that currently exists or is expected to exist, and thus are especially important for decision makers in formulating strategies for the future (Amer et al., 2013). Scenario archetypes are a classification of views in which the common and similar points in these future prediction stories come together according to a particular purpose (Hunt et al., 2012).

The Four Archetypes Scenario model is a framework that categorizes scenarios into four distinct types to facilitate stakeholder engagement in future thinking. The model is based on predetermined generic alternative futures, including continued growth, collapse, discipline, and transformation, which are the foundation for creating the four archetypal scenarios (Fergnani & Jackson, 2019). By condensing system archetypes into a core set of four generic archetypes, the model simplifies complex feedback loops and aids in understanding the dynamics of different scenarios (Wolstenholme, 2003). The model has been utilized in various fields, such as sustainability research, climate governance, and science-policy processes, demonstrating its versatility and applicability across different domains (Hickmann et al., 2022; Oberlack et al., 2019; Sitas et al., 2019). This model offers a valuable tool for exploring and understanding potential developments by providing a structured framework for scenario analysis and decision-making processes.

Figure 2. The four archetypes scenario model

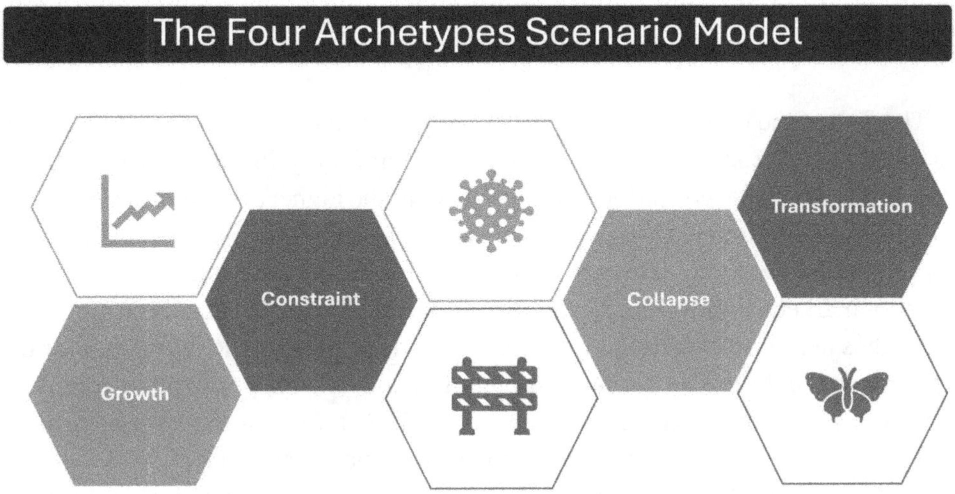

The approach of creating scenarios is able to facilitate researchers to make predictions about the future and generate innovative thoughts regarding many potential outcomes. One of the most effective scenario models for portraying emerging trends and exploring future prospects is the Four Archetypes Scenario model (Fergnani & Jackson, 2019). This model proposes four scenarios—growth, constraint, collapse, transformation—that illustrate potential futuristic possibilities (see Figure 2). Through an understanding of these four different scenarios, every stakeholder concerned may address and evaluate the future context and develop a more comprehensive grasp of exactly what is anticipated to happen in the future. The practice of creating projections for the future through different scenarios facilitates the process of all parties in that context taking actions based on what they have planned for the future. This scenario model has been identified to be a remarkably efficient and advantageous technique for predicting the future, particularly for examining upcoming change processes that are triggered by innovations in science and technology, evolving dynamics in the social, economic, and environmental spheres, as well as making sense of situations in which ambiguity is widespread. Based on the four-archetypes scenario model, the research explores the potential of micro-credentials and how they are going to undergo a disruptive change in the future, taking into account possible challenges alongside their opportunities.

FINDINGS AND DISCUSSION

Growth

The first of the four different scenarios, "growth", takes an optimistic imaginary perspective on the state of micro-credential in the future. In this scenario, micro-credentials and higher education move in harmony and higher education has managed to evolve into a structure that generates resources for the micro-credential needs of learners in line with the demands from the sector. Micro-credentials are based on the labor market, employability, graduate competencies and especially 21st century skills, thus demonstrating that higher education is to prepare the individual for the labor market and this can be done through micro-credentials instead of traditional diploma programs (Wheelahan & Moodie, 2024). Such a scenario assumes a strengthening of cooperation between the sector and higher education, as well as radical changes in the curricula and programmes of higher education towards the successful adaptation of micro-credentials. Blockchain and artificial intelligence tools are anticipated to improve and automate every process in microcredentials ecosystems, as well as higher education and sector alignments (McGreal, 2024). While blockchain technology can guarantee the privacy and security of micro-credential data, artificial intelligence can contribute to expand and improve it. It is further projected that AI will be effective in identifying future labor market skill gaps and recommending personal skill trajectories to learners (Lo, 2023). Artificial intelligence, particularly on the administrative side, provides significant potential for automating micro-credential verification and accreditation processes, and it is considered to be advantageous for testing data accuracy (McGreal, 2024).

This is a growth scenario that is bright and visionary toward the future, where both micro-credentials and higher education develop together in synergy. This probable trend postulates that the emphasis on the labor market demands, employability and 21st-century skills may increasingly push micro-credentials to take their place over traditional diploma programs for preparation of the workforce. The higher education curricula would also see a sea change in this scenario, inspired by far stronger collaboration between academia and industries for the changing requirements of learners. Advanced technologies, like blockchain and artificial intelligence, are very likely to contribute more in such an ecosystem for automating critical processes, ensuring security and privacy concerning micro-credential data, and facilitating easy identification of emerging skills within labor markets. This is particularly true, since AI will have a leading role in ensuring the efficiency, speed, and accuracy of micro-credential verification and accreditation in their accreditation processes.

Constraint

The second scenario in which higher education continues but with a diminished role is "constraint". This scenario refers to the diminishing function of higher education and emphasizes the need for employees with up-to-date knowledge. Higher education institutions are focusing more on learners' employability skills in order to maintain their position in the future and ensure a sustainable working climate (Maina et al., 2022). One of the barriers to the recognition of micro-credentials by employers and the sector is the lack of collaboration and co-design between micro-credential providers such as universities and the sector (Alasmari & Alzahrani, 2024). In the constraint scenario, it is foreseen that the gap in this cooperation may increase in the future and may be one of the major obstacles in the adoption process of micro-credential. To address this gap, higher education, sector representatives and non-academic micro-credential providers may need to come together to work on common quality standards, financing and policy strategies, and certification frameworks. In a systematic review conducted by Ahsan et al. (2023), the barriers to the implementation of micro-credential in higher education were identified, with negative perceptions of learners, lack of readiness on the part of higher education, insufficient technological readiness, lack of awareness and support from the sector, and finally logistical readiness and capabilities cited as the biggest challenges.

The scenario of constraint stresses barriers to wider diffusion in the higher education setting. Core issues concern lack of collaboration between universities and industry, which may increase in the future and narrow employers' recognition of something as low-value as a micro-credential. This gap calls for urgent shared quality standards, financing, and policy within higher education institutions, industry representatives, and non-academic credential providers for a coherent system. What is more, research identifies that, despite these opportunities, further barriers include a lack of technological infrastructure; sectoral support is missing, and negative perceptions of learners add complexity to integrating micro-credentials. Overcoming these challenges will require a collective effort to bridge the gap between academia and the labor market in fully embedding micro-credentials into education and employment systems.

Collapse

In the third scenario, "Collapse", the primary focus is on the failure of micro-credential to have the expected impact, while the second alternative collapse scenario is the devaluation of higher education by rapid breakdowns and forces of change outside its control. The lack of a direct correlation between employers' approaches to recruitment and the learner success of higher education can be seen as a necessity for the emergence of practices such as micro-credentials. On the other hand, employers may have very different recruitment strategies and even if they are aware of micro-credentials, they may have doubts about the value and availability of these skills (Miller & Jorre de St Jorre, 2024). For employers who develop strategies according to different sources in their recruitment processes, micro-credentials may be a reference for assessing skills, qualifications and experience, in short, for measuring employability, but they may not be accepted as evidence to meet this need alone (Miller & Jorre de St Jorre, 2024; Oliver, 2019).

Another alternative scenario could be that higher education institutions such as universities fail to transform to be able to offer micro-credentials and therefore the demand for higher education decreases and traditional diplomas lose their prestige as well as their value. An alternative to this scenario could be that institutions offering micro-credentials create a place for themselves in the higher education ecosystem, resulting in further deterioration of the processes of cooperation and communication between the university, society and the sector.

The collapse scenario does indicate that there is significant, potential risk related to a misalignment of the higher education institutions with the changing employers' needs and thus undermines the value of traditional degrees. Micro-credentials are locating themselves as a way out of this, with their focus on skill sets and employability, though many employers are still dubious about their reliability and value in isolation. This skepticism could dampen the wider enthusiasm for micro-credentials into mainstream recruitment practices. Besides, if the institutions of higher learning do not accept this increasing demand for flexible learning opportunities that are skills-oriented, they are facing a reduction in both enrollment and prestige since traditional degrees may not be valued as much in the job market. It is here that this gap could be filled by non-traditional education providers and further cause fragmentation in the relationship that exists between the universities, the labor market, and society at large.

Transformation

In the last scenario phase "transformation", micro-credentials are accepted as a new paradigm by all stakeholders and partners by creating its own context. In this transformation scenario, the new paradigm of micro-credentials shows that innovations such as increased flexibility, increased mobility, reskilled/upskilled workforce are indispensable building blocks especially in the field of higher education and in the labor market. In particular, these micro-credentials, which can be acquired at a lower cost for learners, provide the ability to move flexibly into higher education and employability contexts. With their characteristic of stackability, micro-credentials support the learner in monitoring their academic progress and career management

(McGreal, 2024). A review of research supporting the transformation scenario highlights implementation research. In a study conducted by Maina et al. (2022), the sector, higher education and learners were involved in the adoption process of micro-credentials and the e-portfolio strategy showed an improvement in developing learners' employability skills that attracted the attention of all stakeholders. They also emphasized the importance of being recognized by a formal institution, the university, for the micro-credentials earned and noted that the recognition process is more transparent and reliable (Ahsan et al., 2023; Varadarajan et al., 2023). Managing micro-credentials, ensuring quality assurance of their processes, creating verification systems to ensure their verifiability and interoperability, and developing micro-credential matrices compatible with the existing education system are crucial for creating a sustainable micro-credential ecosystem (Alasmari & Alzahrani, 2024).

The transformative scenario is one in which micro-credentials become the mainstream paradigm, changing the nature of higher education and the labor market. This said, such a scenario indicates the way micro-credentials would be able to drive innovation by enabling flexibility, mobility, and continuous skill development. To some extent, affordable and stackable micro-credentials would ensure an easier way into higher education and professional growth for learners who then manage both their academic progress and employability more effectively. According to studies, effective implementation of micro-credentials is one that engages all the stakeholders—universities, employers, and learners—while formal university recognition raises the transparency and trust of the system. The development of such a transformation with robust quality assurance mechanisms, verification systems, and alignment with existing educational frameworks will make the ecosystem of micro-credentials reliable and interoperable.

Conclusion and Implications

In conclusion, micro-credentials may offer a promising avenue for professional development, skill acquisition, and lifelong learning, with the potential to enhance employability and address the evolving needs of the workforce. This book chapter provides insights regarding the future use of micro-credentials using the Four Archetypes Scenario model and thus aims to provide a roadmap for educators, higher education institutions, and policymakers. Additionally, they offer a purpose-driven and adaptable support that helps learners of all backgrounds, including those who are beginning their careers in their careers and those wishing to switch industries, acquire new skills and retrain or upskill. Micro-credentials will be accepted by all stakeholders, including higher education and the sector, only if they are tailored to educational systems and the labor market. This is because micro-credentials have an unprecedented impact on how skills are acknowledged in the professional field.

To fully utilize micro-credentials' current potential and ensure their positive representation within the industry, certain initiatives must be created. In particular, higher education and educational institutions need to work with the industry to make sure that micro-credentials can participate in the development of specific training programs to address future skills gaps. At the same time, learners should be informed about micro-credential initiatives and motivated to advance their employability through lifelong learning. Meanwhile, businesses and industry representatives want to figure out how to proactively identify and incorporate micro-credentials into their hiring procedures. Lastly, frameworks that are transparent and confirmed should be created so that representatives from higher education, various industries, and policy makers may collaborate towards sustainability. In future research, micro and macro-level applications of micro-credentials should be examined and the possible results should be evaluated through positive and negative scenarios. Investigating the consequences of micro-credential practices, particularly at the micro level as an institution, will give valuable insights for any stakeholders involved in bigger initiatives and the development of micro-credential ecosystems.

REFERENCES

Ahsan, K., Akbar, S., Kam, B., & Abdulrahman, M. D. A. (2023). Implementation of micro-credentials in higher education: A systematic literature review. *Education and Information Technologies*, 28(10), 13505–13540. Advance online publication. DOI: 10.1007/s10639-023-11739-z

Alasmari, T., & Alzahrani, A. (2024). Leveraging employment with micro-credentials: Policy and practice of the Middle East and North African Universities. *Educational Technology Research and Development*, 72(3), 1869–1891. DOI: 10.1007/s11423-024-10367-9

Amer, M., Daim, T. U., & Jetter, A. (2013). A review of scenario planning. *Futures*, 46, 23–40. DOI: 10.1016/j.futures.2012.10.003

Bean, M., Grant, S., Hardaker, G., & Ward, R. (2023). Signals and noise: Communicating achievement through alternative credentials. *International Journal of Information and Learning Technology*, 40(4), 305–316. DOI: 10.1108/IJILT-02-2023-0020

Bezold, C. (2010). Lessons from using scenarios for strategic foresight. *Technological Forecasting and Social Change*, 77(9), 1513–1518. DOI: 10.1016/j.techfore.2010.06.012

Boschetti, F., Price, J., & Walker, I. (2016). Myths of the future and scenario archetypes. *Technological Forecasting and Social Change*, 111, 76–85. DOI: 10.1016/j.techfore.2016.06.009

Bozkurt, A., & Brown, M. (2022). Microcredentials: Stackable, Combinable, or Transferable Qualifications. *EdTechnica: The Open Encyclopedia of Educational Technology*. DOI: 10.59668/371.8264

Brown, M., Nic Giolla Mhichíl, M., Beirne, E., & Mac Lochlainn, C. (2021). The Global Micro-credential Landscape: Charting a New Credential Ecology for Lifelong Learning. *Journal of Learning for Development*, 8(2), 228–254. DOI: 10.56059/jl4d.v8i2.525

Bruguera, C. (2023). *Exploring learners' motivations and preferences for micro-credentials: a mixed-method study*. Ubiquity Proceedings., DOI: 10.5334/uproc.67

Desmarchelier, R., & Cary, L. J. (2022). Toward just and equitable micro-credentials: An australian perspective. *International Journal of Educational Technology in Higher Education*, 19(1), 25. Advance online publication. DOI: 10.1186/s41239-022-00332-y PMID: 35669714

European Commission. (2021). *A European approach to micro-credentials*. https://education.ec.europa.eu/sites/default/files/2022-01/micro-credentials%20brochure%20updated.pdf Accessed on September 12, 2024.

Fergnani, A., & Jackson, M. (2019). Extracting scenario archetypes: A quantitative text analysis of documents about the future. *Futures & Foresight Science*, 1(2), e17. Advance online publication. DOI: 10.1002/ffo2.17

Fontela, E., & Hingel, A. (1993). Scenarios on economic and social cohesion in Europe. *Futures*, 25(2), 139–154. DOI: 10.1016/0016-3287(93)90160-U

Ha, N. T. N., Spittle, M., Watt, A. P., & Dyke, N. V. (2022). A systematic literature review of micro-credentials in higher education: A non-zero-sum game. Higher Education Research &Amp. *Higher Education Research & Development*, 42(6), 1527–1548. DOI: 10.1080/07294360.2022.2146061

Hickmann, T., Bertram, C., Biermann, F., Brutschin, E., Kriegler, E., Livingston, J. E., Pianta, S., Riahi, K., Van Ruijven, B., & Van Vuuren, D. (2022). Exploring Global Climate Policy Futures and Their Representation in Integrated Assessment Models. *Politics and Governance*, 10(3), 171–185. DOI: 10.17645/pag.v10i3.5328

Hunt, D. V. L., Lombardi, D. R., Atkinson, S., Barber, A. R. G., Barnes, M., Boyko, C. T., Brown, J., Bryson, J., Butler, D., Caputo, S., Caserio, M., Coles, R., Cooper, R. F. D., Farmani, R., Gaterell, M., Hale, J., Hales, C., Hewitt, C. N., Jankovic, L., & Rogers, C. D. F. (2012). Scenario archetypes: Converging rather than diverging themes. *Sustainability (Basel)*, 4(4), 740–772. DOI: 10.3390/su4040740

Kiiskilä, P., Kukkonen, A., & Pirkkalainen, H. (2023). Are micro-credentials valuable for students? perspective on verifiable digital credentials. *SN Computer Science*, 4(4), 366. Advance online publication. DOI: 10.1007/s42979-023-01797-y

Kır, Ş., & Bozkurt, A. (2022). Yükseköğretimde mikro-krediler üzerine kavramsal bir değerlendirme. *Uşak Üniversitesi Eğitim Araştırmaları Dergisi*, 8(1), 12–29. DOI: 10.29065/usakead.1037617

Kušić, S., Vrcelj, S., & Zovko, A. (2022). Micro-credentials – improvement or fragmentation in higher education? *Education and New Developments*, 152–156. Advance online publication. DOI: 10.36315/2022v2end033

Lang, J. (2023). Workforce upskilling: can universities meet the challenges of lifelong learning?. *International Journal of Information and Learning Technology, 40*(5), 388-400. https://doi.org/,Lo, C. K. (2023). What is the impact of ChatGPT on education? A rapid review of the literature. *Education Sciences, 13*(4), 410. https://doi.org/DOI: 10.1108/IJILT-01-2023-0001

MacCallum, K., & Brown, C. (2022). Developing a micro-credential for learning designers: a delphi study. Ascilite Publications, e22198. DOI: 10.14742/apubs.2022.198

Maina, M. F., Guàrdia Ortiz, L., Mancini, F., & Martinez Melo, M. (2022). A micro-credentialing methodology for improved recognition of HE employability skills. *International Journal of Educational Technology in Higher Education*, 19(1), 10. Advance online publication. DOI: 10.1186/s41239-021-00315-5 PMID: 35224180

McGreal, R. (2024). Empowering Micro-Credentials Using Blockchain and Artificial Intelligence. In Omona, K., & O'dama, M. (Eds.), *Global Perspectives on Micro-Learning and Micro-Credentials in Higher Education* (pp. 75–90). IGI Global., DOI: 10.4018/979-8-3693-0343-6.ch006

McGreal, R., Mackintosh, W., Cox, G., & Olcott, D.Jr. (2022). Bridging the gap: Micro-credentials for development. *International Review of Research in Open and Distance Learning*, 23(3), 288–302. DOI: 10.19173/irrodl.v23i3.6696

McGreal, R., & Olcott, D.Jr. (2022). A strategic reset: Micro-credentials for higher education leaders. *Smart Learning Environments*, 9(1), 9. DOI: 10.1186/s40561-022-00190-1

Miller, K. K., & Jorre de St Jorre, T. (2024). Digital micro-credentials in environmental science: An employer perspective on valued evidence of skills. *Teaching in Higher Education*, 29(4), 1058–1074. DOI: 10.1080/13562517.2022.2053953

Oberlack, C., Sietz, D., Bürgi Bonanomi, E., de Bremond, A., Dell'Angelo, J., Eisenack, K., Ellis, E. C., Epstein, G., Giger, M., Heinimann, A., Kimmich, C., Kok, M. T., Manuel-Navarrete, D., Messerli, P., Meyfroidt, P., Václavík, T., & Villamayor-Tomas, S. (2019). Archetype analysis in sustainability research: Meanings, motivations, and evidence-based policy making. *Ecology and Society*, 24(2), art26. Advance online publication. DOI: 10.5751/ES-10747-240226

OECD. (2023). *Micro-credentials for lifelong learning and employability: Uses and possibilities. OECD Education Policy Perspectives, No. 66*. OECD Publishing., DOI: 10.1787/9c4b7b68-

Oliver, B. (2019). *Making micro-credentials work for learners, employers and providers*. DTeach. https://dteach.deakin.edu.au/microcredentials/

Oliver, B. (2021). Micro-credentials: A learner value framework. *Journal of Teaching and Learning for Graduate Employability*, 12(1), 48–51. DOI: 10.21153/jtlge2021vol12no1art1456

Orman, R., Şimşek, E., & Kozak Çakır, M. A. (2023). Micro-credentials and reflections on higher education. *Higher Education Evaluation and Development*, 17(2), 96–112. DOI: 10.1108/HEED-08-2022-0028

Pelletier, K., Brown, M., Brooks, D. C., McCormack, M., Reeves, J., Arbino, N., Bozkurt, A., Crawford, S., Czerniewicz, L., Gibson, R., Linder, K., Mason, J., & Mondelli, V. (2021). *2021 EDUCAUSE Horizon Report Teaching and Learning Edition*. EDUCAUSE. https://www.learntechlib.org/p/219489/

Pirkkalainen, H., Sood, I., Napoles, C., Kukkonen, A., & Camilleri, A. (2022). How might micro-credentials influence institutions and empower learners in higher education? *Educational Research*, 65(1), 40–63. DOI: 10.1080/00131881.2022.2157302

Reed, A. (2023). Micro-credentials and the role of evidence: Increasing the potential for learner-centeredness, inclusivity and an expansive model of assessment and credentialing. *International Journal of Information and Learning Technology*, 40(5), 401–412. DOI: 10.1108/IJILT-12-2022-0228

Resei, C., Friedl, C., Staubitz, T., & Rohloff, T. (2019). *Micro-credentials in EU and global.* Corship Corporate Edupreneurship. https://www.corship.eu/wp-content/uploads/2019/07/Corship-R1.1c_micro-credentials.pdf

Shay, A. (2023). Micro-credentialing. *Clinical Nurse Specialist CNS*, 37(6), 299–300. DOI: 10.1097/NUR.0000000000000780 PMID: 37870516

Sitas, N., Harmáčková, Z. V., Anticamara, J. A., Arneth, A., Badola, R., Biggs, R., Blanchard, R., Brotons, L., Cantele, M., Coetzer, K., DasGupta, R., den Belder, E., Ghosh, S., Guisan, A., Gundimeda, H., Hamann, M., Harrison, P. A., Hashimoto, S., Hauck, J., & Valle, M. (2019). Exploring the usefulness of scenario archetypes in science-policy processes: Experience across IPBES assessments. *Ecology and Society*, 24(3), art35. Advance online publication. DOI: 10.5751/ES-11039-240335

Tinsley, B., Cacicio, S., Shah, Z., Parker, D., Younge, O., & Luke Luna, C. (2022). Micro-credentials for social mobility in rural postsecondary communities: a landscape report. https://doi.org/DOI: 10.51388/20.500.12265/151

Varadarajan, S., Koh, J. H. L., & Daniel, B. K. (2023). A systematic review of the opportunities and challenges of micro-credentials for multiple stakeholders: Learners, employers, higher education institutions and government. *International Journal of Educational Technology in Higher Education*, 20(1), 13. DOI: 10.1186/s41239-023-00381-x PMID: 36874535

Ward, R., Crick, T., Davenport, J. H., Hanna, P., Hayes, A., Irons, A., Miller, K., Moller, F., Prickett, T., & Walters, J. (2023). Using Skills Profiling to Enable Badges and Micro-Credentials to be Incorporated into Higher Education Courses. *Journal of Interactive Media in Education, 2023*(1). DOI: 10.5334/jime.807

Wheelahan, L., & Moodie, G. (2024). Analysing micro-credentials in higher education: a Bernsteinian analysis. In *Towards Powerful Educational Knowledge* (pp. 70–86). Routledge. DOI: 10.4324/9781032712802-6

Wolstenholme, E. F. (2003). Towards the definition and use of a core set of archetypal structures in system dynamics. *System Dynamics Review*, 19(1), 7–26. DOI: 10.1002/sdr.259

KEY TERMS AND DEFINITIONS

Combinability of Microcredentials: It means you are given the chance to pick the different credential programs that would make up a learning journey right for you. Think about putting together an ideal music playlist; instead of songs, you're choosing educational experiences that match up exactly with what you need for your career or personal growth. This way, you can tailor your education to exactly fit your life's goals.

Employability: It includes all the qualities that an individual should possess in order to get recruited, advance in the job, and professional life.

Flexible learning experience: Flexible learning is basically learning on your own schedule. It's about fitting your education around your life, not the other way around. You can study online, mix things up with in-person and virtual classes, or go at your own pace—whatever works best for you. It may be ideal if you've got a busy life with work, family, or other commitments but still want to keep learning and growing.

Four Archetypes Scenario model: The Four Archetypes Scenario Model is a strategic tool that explores potential futures through four scenarios: continuous growth, collapse, disciplined society, and transformation. The model helps researchers and policymakers consider various possibilities, identifying opportunities and challenges.

Micro-credentials: They are small, focused qualifications that award specific skills or competencies after the achievement of learning experiences. These are usually much smaller than traditional learning programs and more flexible in terms of time and requirements for assessment.

Reskilling and upskilling: Reskilling refers to learning new skills to perform a different job, while upskilling involves learning additional skills to enhance performance in the current role. Both are critical in today's rapidly evolving job market, where technological advancements and shifting economic conditions continually redefine skill requirements.

Stackability of Microcredentials: It is all about adding up micro-credentials over time, like building blocks, to work your way toward a bigger qualification, such as a degree or a professional certificate. It gives you the freedom to learn at your own pace, stacking smaller courses that suit your needs and interests, ultimately piecing together a more comprehensive and meaningful qualification.

Traditional learning program: A traditional learning program is the classic school setup—think of college degrees or diplomas where you follow a set curriculum, attend scheduled classes, and learn in a structured environment. It's the usual way of learning, with face-to-face lectures and a broad course load designed to give you a solid, all-around education over several years.

Transferability of Microcredentials: It relates to how your skills move with you and how much they are recognized and valued by other schools, employers, or industries. It's like a passport for your skills, ensuring that the effort you put into earning a micro-credential counts no matter where you go, enhancing its real-world value and usefulness.

Chapter 7 Leveraging AI-Managed Learning Analytics and Micro-Credentials for Enhanced Student Engagement

Semiral Öncü
https://orcid.org/0000-0001-8549-094X
Balikesir University, Turkey

Merve Çolakoğlu
https://orcid.org/0000-0001-5102-0528
Independent Researcher, Turkey

Harun Cigdem
https://orcid.org/0000-0001-5958-5216
National Defense University, Turkey

ABSTRACT

This chapter explores how the integration of Artificial Intelligence (AI)-managed learning analytics and micro-credentials can enhance student engagement and retention in higher education. The authors analyze the growing role of AI in monitoring student learning behaviors, providing real-time feedback, and enabling personalized interventions. They discuss the potential of micro-credentials, particularly digital badges, to motivate learners by recognizing their accomplishments and encouraging skill development. While these technologies present transformative opportunities, challenges such as data privacy, lack of standardization, and accessibility issues

DOI: 10.4018/979-8-3693-5488-9.ch007

are addressed. The chapter emphasizes the importance of collaboration between educators, technologists, and policymakers to implement these tools equitably and effectively, with a focus on fostering lifelong learning and student success.

INTRODUCTION

The integration of learning analytics managed by Artificial Intelligence (AI) and the utilization of micro-credentials, or digital badges, present exciting opportunities to revolutionize student engagement and retention in higher education. This chapter is an attempt to explore how these innovative approaches can transform the higher education landscape by enhancing students' learning experiences and fostering their success.

Overview of Learning Analytics and Micro-Credentials

This section begins by discussing the role of learning analytics and micro-credentials/digital badges in enhancing learner persistence, or retention, in higher education. Learning analytics, driven by AI, involves gathering and analyzing student data to understand their learning behaviors and improve teaching strategies. Digital badges, on the other hand, function as digital representations of earned knowledge, skills, and competencies, encouraging students by recognizing their accomplishments and documenting their educational journeys. For the purposes of this chapter, the terms 'digital badges' and 'micro-credentials' will be used interchangeably to refer to the same concept of skill representation.

Learning analytics has grown as a major research area, particularly within learning supported by technology (Durak & Cankaya, 2023). Brown (2012) describes the process as a systematic approach to gathering and analyzing data from digital platforms with the aim of enhancing learning environments and experiences. By focusing on learner data, learning analytics aims to design systems and make decisions grounded in empirical evidence (Cigdem & Öncü, 2023), ultimately using data insights to inform better instructional methods and educational structures, to enhance student learning experience (Keskin & Yurdugül, 2022).

Learning analytics is becoming more and more important for educational institutions due to the ability of data to transform learning experiences and outcomes. Technology continues to develop day by day, and using data will have a major role in institutions achieving the learning goals they have in mind for their students and gaining and sustaining a competitive advantage over other institutions. Institutions use learning analytics to document (evaluate) their educational strategies and interventions. By using learning analytics, educators can analyze data on student performance and engagement to spot learners at risk and boost retention rates by providing targeted support.

Learning analytics is essential for enlightening educators, students, and administrators in higher education (Long & Siemens, 2011). Using predictive models that provide actionable information, it provides individualized educational opportunities based on student needs and abilities, such as intervention for at-risk students, identifying potential problematic issues (L. Johnson et al., 2011), and providing feedback and learning content (Avella et al., 2016). Students' and educators' awareness of their current situations can be increased through learning analytics, enabling them to perform tasks more effectively (Scheffel et al., 2014). Developing predictive models to identify students who are at danger of failing the class and, as a result, dropping out of college is one of the objectives of learning analytics. By offering individualized feedback as academic support, it assists students in developing their abilities and achieving success in higher education (Mah, 2016).

Digital badges are symbols used on the web in different platforms to validate learner achievements, knowledge, skills, and competencies. James Gee, an academics at an American university, introduced the idea of digital badges in 2007 as credentials or competencies to indicate progress in video games (Gibson et al., 2015; Grant, 2016). It motivates students, improves their general skills, and defines learning methods, encouraging students to persist (EDUCAUSE, 2012; Mah, 2016). Digital badges were addressed by Harvard Business Review in 2012 as a significant development to follow (Ahsan et al., 2023). Digital badges have also been acknowledged by Peer 2 Peer University and the Mozilla Foundation as a useful tool to employ in education (Mah, 2016). Globally, digital badges are being utilized by higher education establishments more and more (Ahsan et al., 2023; Coleman, 2018; Hartnett, 2021). A badge can identify a learning activity, skill, or competency; a set of badges constitutes a micro-credential, and multiple micro-credentials confer an identity.

According to Rieder (2022), past research has shown that micro-credentials and digital badges are highly motivating for students and, when implemented well, support community building, equity, and flexibility. However, many studies have also highlighted the obstacle of establishing the validity and reliability of micro-credentials and badges. But micro-credentials have become a fresh method for self-directed learning that honors students' efforts via digital badges (Farmer & West, 2017; Gish-Lieberman et al., 2021). It supports skill development through digital symbols as a result of learning called badges as proof of success, while offering an alternative to conventional documents such as diplomas, licenses and certificates and (Ellis et al., 2016). The success of such programs depends on the creation of purposeful and rigorous achievement programs when they are designed (Rieder, 2022). In addition, digital badges have begun to be used to indicate success in video games over time (Beattie, 2014; Gish-Lieberman et al., 2021; Ostashewski & Reid, 2015).

Micro-credentials have become a structure that promotes self-directed learning at all educational phases with the development of gamification tools. (Ahn et al., 2014). Badges play a strong role in individuals' self-directed learning and development, and they also create records of where they have mastered and found the appropriate tools among a variety of resources (Gish-Lieberman et al., 2021). Numerous studies have pointed out that micro-credentials and badges promote the demand for self-direction in learners (including, Besser & Newby, 2019; Cheng et al., 2018; Cucchiara et al., 2014; Fastiggi, 2023; Gish-Lieberman et al., 2021; Wills & Xie, 2016). Micro-credentials provide a concrete structure for individuals to organize themselves at each stage in the self-directed learning cycle.

Integration of AI-Managed Learning Analytics

This section of the chapter delves into the integration of AI-managed learning analytics in university settings. Institutions may learn a great deal about students' learning habits and see trends that point to success or dropout risk by using AI algorithms to monitor, trace, and evaluate how students engage with learning materials and activities. These insights can inform personalized interventions and support services to enhance student engagement and retention.

A major global trend in educational settings is the growing use of technology in learning environments. With the advancement of the digital age, technology has increasingly merged with education, creating transformative possibilities, particularly via the implementation of AI in learning analytics (Durak et al., 2024; Vashishth et al., 2024). AI-driven learning analytics has emerged as an effective instrument for enhancing educational outcomes by leveraging data analysis to inform instructional strategies. In higher education, this refers to the application of AI technologies and data analysis techniques to collect, manage, and evaluate education-related data, providing insights that can improve both learning and teaching processes. While learning analytics has traditionally focused on gathering and analyzing data to improve student outcomes, the integration of generative AI significantly broadens its scope. Generative AI enhances learning analytics by enabling more sophisticated profiling, individualized learning experiences, intelligent instructional systems, and more accurate prediction of student performance; this shift allows institutions to create adaptive systems that can respond to diverse student needs, fostering a more engaging and tailored educational environment (Akinwalere & Ivanov, 2022). With the emergence of AI, personalized technology, self-paced learning, adaptable lesson plans, and individualized feedback are offered to students and instructors by leveraging the power of data and complex algorithms (Aithal & Maiya, 2023). The integration of AI into learning environments presents challenges such as high costs, inadequate infrastructure, concerns over data privacy, and biases among decision-makers regarding algorithmic structures; however, it also holds promise for revolutionizing education (Bakar et al., 2024).

As one of the two parts of this cooperation, learning analytics can help administrative decision-making in higher education, identify students at risk and intervene to ensure their success, analyze completed assignments, read messages, and identify learners who are likely to drop out of school. In addition, transparent data and analysis can identify where the institution succeeds and where they experience difficulties and improve institutional throughput by providing rapid response (Long & Siemens, 2011). Learning analytics optimizes educational outcomes and helps collect data about students and learning environments. As the second part of this cooperation, AI improves the data collection process by using algorithms to process large amounts of data, revealing patterns that people may miss during analysis. The idea of lifelong learning globally emphasizes how important it is in terms of adapting to constantly changing conditions and directs individuals to develop their careers through learning paths such as online courses and micro-certifications (Aithal & Maiya, 2023).

The combination of technologies that could transform how students are thought and learn in higher education is known as AI-managed learning analytics (Vashishth et al., 2024). AI-managed learning analytics provide educators with the opportunity to effectively adapt teaching methods with the data-driven tools it provides. Caspari-Sadeghi (2023) stated that learning analytics can be applied at different levels as analytics that use different AI techniques (machine learning, data mining, etc.), such as determining online learning and teaching behaviors (video, simulation, etc.), using various data sources to customize and adapt learning (Student Information System, etc.), or providing a predictive, personalized educational environment.

Compared to traditional learning analytics, learning analytics integrated with AI methods can work faster, identify meaningful or complex patterns that educators may miss, deal better with non-linear information, and allow educators to gain in-depth knowledge about students' learning patterns and behaviors (de Carvalho & Zárate, 2020). In addition, advances in technology allow institutions to create individualized learning environments for learners and augment techniques for learning results by utilizing the power of AI algorithms (Oseremi Onesi-Ozigagun et al., 2024; Shoaib et al., 2024), obtain information about students' learning behaviors and identify patterns that determine their success or dropout factors, help identify at-risk students, understand their learning trajectories, and customize interventions to improve learning outcomes. In other words, AI can help organize and update learning materials, ensuring they remain current and engaging. AI can help students understand their strengths and areas of development by providing instant and personalized feedback. This continuous feedback loop encourages a growth mindset and improves learning outcomes. This approach increases student engagement by making learning more relevant and accessible.

AI can predict future learning behaviors and performances by using past patterns and trends. It can make predictions about student success and learning retention with the modeling feature of machine learning. Machine learning strategies are widely employed to analyze educational data and can provide personalized learning experiences by helping to identify areas that require additional support (Ersozlu et al., 2024). Such applications help improve results by predicting strategies for students by addressing issues such as student selection, student participation in classes, academic performance prediction such as dropping out of school, or group behavior (Bates et al., 2020). It can alert educators in advance about learners who may lag behind. In fact, learning analytics developed with AI can provide a holistic view of previously unthinkable learning insights about student learning. A learning analytics managed by AI can provide notifications and application experiences about students simultaneously. An AI-managed system can monitor student progress and behaviors, identify areas where individuals may have difficulty or lose interest, and provide precautions for these difficulties. Moreover, AI-powered learning analytics enable educators to access data related to curriculum design, instructional strategies, and student resource allocation. By analyzing educational data using AI, educators can recognize patterns, predict future outcomes, and implement preventive measures to increase student success. Integrating AI into learning analytics can transform education by improving learning environments and enhancing student outcomes.

To improve learning and teaching, features of AI such as data processing, big data, statistics or machine learning are used. Although AI-supported learning analytics have high potential, information about students and faculty members contains a large amount of big data, and the privacy of this information may raise data protection issues (Zawacki-Richter et al., 2019). If the problems experienced in the transition to new AI-supported learning methods are overemphasized and the instant benefits are not seen enough, it may negatively affect student participation due to lack of motivation. In this sense, it may be beneficial to support and encourage students by making the fast and comprehensive analytical power of AI more visual. This can be possible by dynamically sharing the results with students. Badges are ideal mediums for this job.

With regard to educational technologies, AI use in education can promote student engagement and agency by creating narrative-centered learning environments with AI-driven functions (Durak & Cankaya, 2024; Lester et al., 2024). Educators can obtain information about learning data by combining AI's algorithms for predicting student performance with learning analytics (Ouyang et al., 2023). Students' learning performance could be enhanced by integrating AI and learning analytics tools (Chango et al., 2021; Darvishi et al., 2022). AI-supported learning analytics can provide data feedback to both researchers or educators and improve students' learning process and performance (Ouyang et al., 2023).

The integration of learning analytics managed by AI in higher education can help educators model how they support students and approach instructional design; by analyzing student data, educators can gain insight into student behaviors, preferences, and challenges, and enable the creation of personalized learning experiences (Abbas, 2024). AI tools can identify at-risk students early and recommend interventions, thereby increasing retention rates and academic achievement. With AI, educational institutions can offer customized curricula, automate administrative tasks, and develop engaging, interactive environments for students.

Learning analytics managed by AI is becoming increasingly common in higher education. AI-powered learning analytics tools can automate instructional elements such as advice, assessment, and feedback to personalize learning experiences and support students in their learning process (Popkhadze, 2021). By offering real-time feedback and adaptable learning routes catered to each student's needs, AI is significantly changing educational processes (Babiak et al., 2024). AI is used as a tool within learning analytics to analyze students' knowledge and learning engagement strategies, enabling the reconstruction of personalized learning paths and the development of supporting strategies throughout all educational stages.

MOTIVATING STUDENT ENGAGEMENT THROUGH MICRO-CREDENTIALS

The central focus of the chapter is on how micro-credentials, or digital badges, can motivate student engagement and success in higher education. By documenting, affirming, and certifying students' competencies, micro-credentials provide tangible recognition of their achievements, incentivizing further learning and skill development. Moreover, the chapter explores how the use of micro-credentials can be integrated with AI-managed learning analytics to personalize feedback and support services, empowering students to navigate their learning pathways effectively.

While there is no universally accepted definition or taxonomy for micro-credentials, they are often understood as a form of competency acquired through structured learning experiences, either online or in-person, outside of traditional degree programs (Messaoud et al., 2022). Various organizations recognize these competencies by awarding digital certificates, such as "digital badges," to individuals upon successful completion of the program (Rossiter & Tynan, 2019). According to Alamri et al. (2021), the concept of micro-credentials is a competency-based instructional approach, typically offered by higher education institutions or businesses, that grant digital badges to learners after they meet the specified learning outcomes.

Micro-credentials provide a flexible way for students to acquire and demonstrate skills. Micro-credentials facilitate learning through the small-scale, steady development of skills (Gish-Lieberman et al., 2021). Micro-credentials are an important factor in career advancement and offer the opportunity to easily adapt to the latest trends and technologies. Micro-credentials help individuals shape their careers by focusing on a specific skill. Offered in the form of online courses or modules, micro-credentials grant individuals the flexibility and opportunity to acquire knowledge and experience at their own pace. Being easily identifiable and tailored to the needs of individuals also provide rapid acquisition of new skills compared to traditional education methods. They are useful in lifelong learning and professional development. Micro-credentials can be clearly aligned with industry needs and integrated into broader educational frameworks.

As illustrated in **Figure 1**, the relationship between AI-powered learning analytics, micro-credentials, and student engagement can be hypothesized to form a cyclical process that continuously reinforces itself. The figure visually represents the interconnected cycle between AI-powered learning analytics, student achievement, micro-credentials, and motivation, with student engagement being the central focus. AI-managed learning analytics act as the foundation of this process by tracking and analyzing student behavior, performance, and engagement data. The insights generated by this system inform educational stakeholders, enabling them to personalize feedback and create tailored instructional interventions aimed at increasing student engagement and retention.

Figure 1. The utilization of AI, learning analytics, micro-credentials in this chapter in relation to student engagement

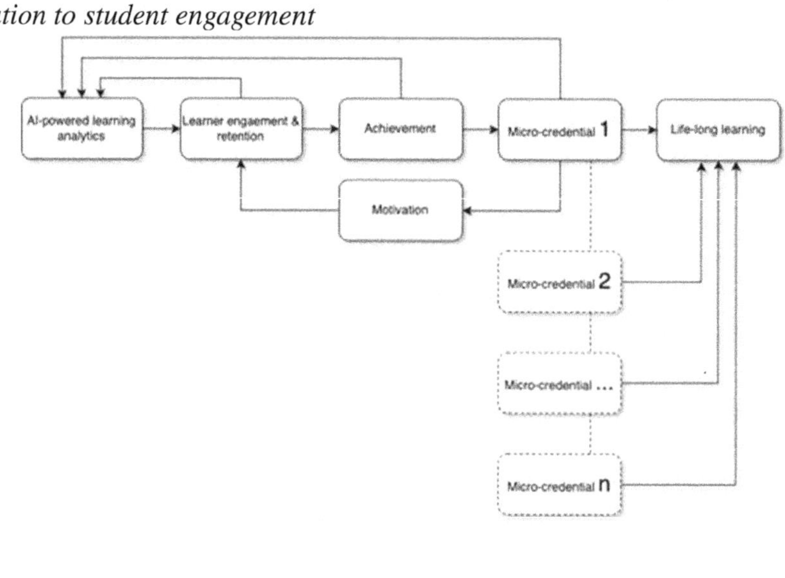

While engagement appears early in the process within the figure, it is actually the driving force and ultimate goal of each step. As learning analytics improve engagement, students demonstrate higher levels of achievement, which are then recognized through micro-credentials. These micro-credentials (e.g., digital badges) are not only proof of the students' competencies but also serve as motivational tools, reinforcing their desire to continue learning. Motivation — recognized in educational research as a key precursor to engagement — grows as students accumulate micro-credentials, leading them to re-engage with their learning in a more meaningful way.

This cyclical process, illustrated in the figure, demonstrates that each stage feeds into the next. AI-powered analytics continuously inform personalized interventions that enhance engagement, while student success and the attainment of micro-credentials further fuel motivation. Over time, students' increasing motivation leads to deeper engagement and higher achievement, thereby restarting the cycle. As students earn more micro-credentials, they accumulate evidence of their growing competencies, which in turn fosters a lifelong learning mindset.

To wrap up, while achievement and motivation are vital components, engagement remains the centerpiece of this cycle. The figure highlights how every element, from AI-managed analytics to micro-credentials, ultimately works to improve student engagement. Research shows that students are more likely to achieve meaningful outcomes, including higher academic success, improved retention, and sustained professional development, when they are deeply engaged in their learning.

Micro-credentials are an approach that supports self-directed learning by gradually revealing students' learning experiences through piecemeal development of skills through digital badges (Bowen & Thomas, 2014; Gish-Lieberman et al., 2021). Students can pursue their passions and interests by using digital badges and micro-credentials to customize their learning experiences. Students find learning more meaningful and pertinent as a result of this customization, which boosts motivation and engagement. In terms of learning and students in the school environment, micro-authentication and digital badging often use gamification to increase student engagement. This helps pave the way for lasting knowledge and lifelong learning.

According to M. A. Johnson (2023), micro-credentials contribute to academic curricula as follows:

- They can enable institutions to remain compliant with ever-changing job market demands and ensure that graduates have the competencies that employers are looking for.
- In addition, the modular structure of micro-credentials allows individuals to explore different interests and provide a unique educational experience for their career goals. Institutions can personalize their learning journeys by offering students a variety of micro-credentials.

- When these credentials are integrated into academic curricula, students adapt to a continuous improvement mindset and are prepared for the demands of a rapidly evolving professional life.
- Institutions can actively involve employers in micro-credential programs by giving students the opportunity to practice their skills and present them in a tangible way, allowing them to stay current and apply them directly in the workplace. It also prepares individuals for the competitive environment in the business world. Therefore, there can be a smooth transition from education to employment.

The rest of this chapter features some case studies and best practices as fit from institutions or publications that have successfully implemented AI-managed learning analytics and micro-credentials to enhance student engagement and retention. These case studies can provide useful guidance for educators and policymakers seeking to adopt similar strategies by highlighting innovative approaches, practical insights, and lessons learned.

The practice of using digital badges in education has become increasingly widespread, appearing in various learning settings and serving a range of objectives. Carey & Stefaniak (2018) explored their use in higher education and found that badges awarded for participation were generally perceived as less valuable compared to those recognizing specific skills. This suggests that skill-based badges may have a greater impact in educational contexts, providing more meaningful recognition of students' competencies.

Several AI-driven initiatives are being introduced in the Malaysian education system (Ahmad & Wan Abdul Ghapar, 2019). For example, an AI-based language learning application utilizing speech recognition instrument has been developed to enhance learners' speaking abilities (Ruan et al., 2021). Additionally, the Malaysian Digital Economy Corporation (MDEC) has introduced the Malaysia Smart Campus Initiative, integrating AI and learning analytics into higher education. This initiative involves a system that uses AI to analyze student data, providing valuable insights for both educators and administrators (Musa et al., 2021). Another significant Malaysian project involves an AI-based assessment platform that employs machine learning algorithms to deliver personalized feedback aimed at improving student performance (Neo, 2022).

According to Parker (2015), digital badges can be used to develop soft skills that correspond to Bloom's emotional domain. Well-designed badges support students' collaboration and participation skills (Carey & Stefaniak, 2018). Purdue University developed a badge system known as Passport, aimed at documenting the acquisition of skills like intercultural openness and curiosity. Passport integrates digital badges with features of learning and content management (Newby et al., 2016). Similarly, the University of Central Oklahoma employs digital badges to assess Bloom's soft skills, defining the specific competencies they expect from their graduates and using the badges to track and certify these skills (Parker, 2015).

Coleman (2018) used a mixed-methods study to examine how digital badges could be optimized on a platform to maximize student engagement in extracurricular education at Maranatha Baptist University. Students were asked to rate the questions asked and students were motivated by opportunities for self-directed learning, but some students indicated that there may be difficulties in using technology.

Nguyen et al. (2024) explore the use of artificial AI applications and chatbots in higher education to enhance student engagement. According to their findings, while these AI technologies provide immersive opportunities for increasing engagement, they also introduce certain challenges. For instance, Nguyen et al. (2024) note that Intelligent Tutoring Systems (ITS), which resemble one-on-one tutoring, can offer students real-time feedback during presentations, helping them identify mistakes and improve their performance. These systems, as pointed out by Nguyen and colleagues, can adapt to a student's understanding level, thereby enhancing engagement and improving learning outcomes. However, they also emphasize the barriers some students face due to limited access to technology and the constraints of under-resourced educational environments.

Nguyen et al. (2024) also highlight the difficulty educators face in aligning advanced AI systems with traditional teaching methods and curriculum objectives. Furthermore, they discuss how the widespread adoption of Generative AI offers a dynamic and responsive learning environment, enabling teachers to create diverse instructional materials—whether visual, textual, or audio-based—and provide feedback on student assignments. In reviewing various studies, Nguyen and colleagues note that while personalized learning has been a focus, many approaches remain static and do not dynamically adapt to student needs.

The authors also underscore the accessibility benefits brought by AI technologies, such as natural language processing and speech recognition, which have made instructional materials more available to learners who have disabilities. For example, Nguyen et al. (2024) point to features like automatic captioning and real-time translation as tools that promote broader access and participation. Despite these advantages, they caution about significant ethical concerns, including risks to data privacy, potential unfair treatment of different student groups, and the increased likelihood of academic dishonesty as reliance on AI-generated content grows.

Challenges and Future Directions

As with any technological advancement, the integration of AI-powered learning analytics and micro-credentials into higher education offers opportunities but also brings challenges. Challenges require attention to be addressed for AI-based learning analytics' widespread and ethical adoption. These challenges primarily revolve around ethical concerns, data privacy, the lack of standardization, and the need for further research and collaboration to ensure equitable and effective implementation.

One of the most pressing challenges involves data privacy and ethical considerations. The deployment of AI in learning analytics necessitates the gathering and analysis of vast amounts of learner data, which raises questions regarding how such data are utilized and who has access to them. For instance, while learning analytics can provide institutions with powerful insights to improve student outcomes, students may not fully understand how their data is being collected or for what purposes it will be used. Research from EDUCAUSE points out that this lack of transparency can undermine trust between students and institutions, particularly when data is used beyond the scope of educational enhancement (A-young Park & Vance, 2021). Institutions must therefore prioritize ethical standards by ensuring students' data rights, including the ability to control or opt-out of data collection, are clearly communicated and upheld.

Another critical issue is the lack of standardization and accreditation for micro-credentials and AI-driven learning analytics systems. Despite their potential to revolutionize higher education, micro-credentials currently suffer from a lack of portability between institutions and even across borders. As (McGreal & Olcott, 2022) emphasize, the absence of a universally accepted framework for accrediting and standardizing micro-credentials limits their value for students seeking to use them across various contexts. Without a structured system of accreditation, micro-credentials risk becoming isolated achievements that do not translate to broader academic or professional recognition.

Moving forward, there is a significant need for further research and collaboration. As AI-driven tools become more embedded in educational practices, collaboration between educators, technologists, and policymakers is essential to ensure that AI is implemented equitably and ethically. Such attemps are discussed in medical research (Hendricks-Sturrup et al., 2023) and are also needed in the educational context. Future research should focus on assessing the long-term impacts of AI-managed learning analytics on diverse student populations, particularly in terms of addressing educational inequities. Moreover, more empirical studies are needed to determine how best to support underrepresented groups in AI-enabled learning environments. The current literature emphasizes that collaboration across disciplines is key to overcoming the challenges posed by AI and to harnessing its full potential for the benefit of students.

CONCLUSION

This chapter has explored the transformative potential of integrating AI-managed learning analytics and micro-credentials to enhance student engagement and retention in higher education. The utilization of AI allows educational institutions to gain deep insights into students' learning behaviors, providing opportunities for personalized interventions that can directly address student needs. At the same time, the awarding of micro-credentials serves as a powerful motivator, offering students tangible recognition for their achievements and skills development.

As discussed, the integration of these technologies creates a positive feedback loop: AI-driven analytics help to improve learner engagement and achievement, which in turn leads to the attainment of micro-credentials. These credentials motivate students to continue their learning journey, further engaging with their education, and reinforcing their sense of accomplishment. Ultimately, this cycle supports life-long learning, an essential goal in today's rapidly evolving knowledge economy.

Looking forward, the potential of these tools will only grow as advancements in AI and data science improve our ability to analyze and respond to complex educational challenges. By continuously enhancing AI-driven learning platforms and improving the standardization and acceptance of micro-credentials, higher education can better equip students for the challenges ahead. Nonetheless, it is essential to address the ethical concerns and implement robust data governance frameworks, as these will be crucial in ensuring that these technological advancements are applied responsibly and fairly.

All in all, by harnessing AI-managed learning analytics and micro-credentials, higher education institutions have the opportunity to establish more engaging, individualized, and meaningful learning experiences. These technologies offer a path toward improved retention, student success, and the development of life-long learning competencies, positioning higher education at the forefront of the digital learning revolution.

REFERENCES

A-young Park. J., & Vance, A. (2021, February 11). *Data privacy in higher education: Yes, students care*. Https://Er.Educause.Edu/Articles/2021/2/Data-Privacy-in-Higher-Education-Yes-Students-Care

Abbas, A. (2024). *Enhancing Student Engagement through AI-driven Analytics in Higher Education Institutions*. DOI: 10.13140/RG.2.2.28982.47682

Ahmad, M. F., & Wan Abdul Ghapar, W. R. G. (2019). The Era of Artificial Intelligence in Malaysian Higher Education: Impact and Challenges in Tangible Mixed-Reality Learning System toward Self Exploration Education (SEE). *Procedia Computer Science*, 163, 2–10. DOI: 10.1016/j.procs.2019.12.079

Ahn, J., Pellicone, A., & Butler, B. S. (2014). Open badges for education: What are the implications at the intersection of open systems and badging? *Research in Learning Technology*, 22. Advance online publication. DOI: 10.3402/rlt.v22.23563

Ahsan, K., Akbar, S., Kam, B., & Abdulrahman, M. D.-A. (2023). Implementation of micro-credentials in higher education: A systematic literature review. *Education and Information Technologies*, 28(10), 13505–13540. DOI: 10.1007/s10639-023-11739-z

Aithal, P. S., & Maiya, A. K. (2023). Innovations in higher education industry – Shaping the future. [IJCSBE]. *International Journal of Case Studies in Business, IT, and Education*, 7(4), 2581–6942. DOI: 10.47992/IJCSBE.2581.6942.0321

Akinwalere, S. N., & Ivanov, V. (2022). Artificial Intelligence in Higher Education: Challenges and Opportunities. *Border Crossing*, 12(1), 1–15. DOI: 10.33182/bc.v12i1.2015

Alamri, H. A., Watson, S., & Watson, W. (2021). Learning Technology Models that Support Personalization within Blended Learning Environments in Higher Education. *TechTrends*, 65(1), 62–78. DOI: 10.1007/s11528-020-00530-3

Avella, J. T., Kebritchi, M., Nunn, S. G., & Kanai, T. (2016). Learning Analytics Methods, Benefits, and Challenges in Higher Education: A Systematic Literature Review. *Journal of Asynchronous Learning Networks*, 20(2), 13–29.

Babiak, Z., Bodnar, O., & Plavutska, I. (2024). Artificial intelligence as a tool for modelling the educational environment. *Humanities Science Current Issues*, 1(73), 269–275. DOI: 10.24919/2308-4863/73-1-41

Bakar, M. H. A., & Ghafar, N. H. Md., & Farid, A. (2024). Exploring the Integration of Artificial Intelligence in Technical and Vocational Education and Training (TVET): Applications, Benefits, Challenges, and Future Prospects Full Paper. In *Borneo Engineering & Advanced Multidisciplinary International Journal (BEAM)* (Vol. 3). https://beam.pmu.edu.my

Bates, T., Cobo, C., Mariño, O., & Wheeler, S. (2020). Can artificial intelligence transform higher education? *International Journal of Educational Technology in Higher Education*, 17(1), 42. DOI: 10.1186/s41239-020-00218-x

Beattie, S. (2014). *Types of digital learning badges: Drawing on the xbox achievement experience*. HASTAC. https://www. hastac. org/blogs/scott-beattie/2014/06/30/types-digital-learning-badges-drawing-xbox-achievement-experience

Ben Messaoud, S., Ilahi, M., & Cheniti-Belcadhi, L. (2022). Towards a personalized micro-credentials approach based on learning analytics for reducing the gap university-industry. *2022 IEEE Global Engineering Education Conference (EDUCON)*, 1448–1454. DOI: 10.1109/EDUCON52537.2022.9766585

Besser, E. D., & Newby, T. J. (2019). Exploring the Role of Feedback and its Impact within a Digital Badge System from Student Perspectives. *TechTrends*, 63(4), 485–495. DOI: 10.1007/s11528-019-00386-2

Bowen, K., & Thomas, A. (2014). Badges: A Common Currency for Learning. *Change*, 46(1), 21–25. DOI: 10.1080/00091383.2014.867206

Brown, M. (2012). Learning Analytics: Moving from Concept to Practice. *EDUCAUSE Learning Initiative*. https://library.educause.edu/-/media/files/library/2012/7/elib1203-pdf.pdf

Carey, K. L., & Stefaniak, J. E. (2018). An exploration of the utility of digital badging in higher education settings. *Educational Technology Research and Development*, 66(5), 1211–1229. DOI: 10.1007/s11423-018-9602-1

Caspari-Sadeghi, S. (2023). Learning assessment in the age of big data: Learning analytics in higher education. *Cogent Education*, 10(1), 2162697. Advance online publication. DOI: 10.1080/2331186X.2022.2162697

Chango, W., Cerezo, R., Sanchez-Santillan, M., Azevedo, R., & Romero, C. (2021). Improving prediction of students' performance in intelligent tutoring systems using attribute selection and ensembles of different multimodal data sources. *Journal of Computing in Higher Education*, 33(3), 614–634. DOI: 10.1007/s12528-021-09298-8

Cheng, Z., Watson, S. L., & Newby, T. J. (2018). Goal Setting and Open Digital Badges in Higher Education. *TechTrends*, 62(2), 190–196. DOI: 10.1007/s11528-018-0249-x

Cigdem, H., & Öncü, S. (2023). *Leveraging Learning Analytics to Improve Student Engagement.*, DOI: 10.4018/978-1-6684-9527-8.ch004

Coleman, J. D. (2018). Engaging undergraduate students in a co-curricular digital badging platform. *Education and Information Technologies*, 23(1), 211–224. DOI: 10.1007/s10639-017-9595-0

Cucchiara, S., Giglio, A., Persico, D., & Raffaghelli, J. E. (2014). *Supporting Self-regulated Learning Through Digital Badges: A Case Study.*, DOI: 10.1007/978-3-319-13296-9_15

Darvishi, A., Khosravi, H., Sadiq, S., & Gašević, D. (2022). Incorporating <scp>AI</scp> and learning analytics to build trustworthy peer assessment systems. *British Journal of Educational Technology*, 53(4), 844–875. DOI: 10.1111/bjet.13233

de Carvalho, W. F., & Zárate, L. E. (2020). A new local causal learning algorithm applied in learning analytics. *The International Journal of Information and Learning Technology*, 38(1), 103–115. DOI: 10.1108/IJILT-04-2020-0046

Durak, G., & Cankaya, S. (2023). *Introduction to Learning Analytics.*, DOI: 10.4018/978-1-6684-9527-8.ch001

Durak, G., & Çankaya, S. (2024). Are alarm bells ringing in academia? Chatgpt as a sample of using chatbots in education. *Turkish Online Journal of Distance Education*, 25(3), 1–17. DOI: 10.17718/tojde.1353737

Durak, G., Çankaya, S., Özdemir, D., & Can, S. (2024). Artificial intelligence in education: A bibliometric study on its role in transforming teaching and learning. *International Review of Research in Open and Distance Learning*, 25(3), 219–244. DOI: 10.19173/irrodl.v25i3.7757

EDUCAUSE. (2012). *7 Things You Should Know About Badges.* https://library.educause.edu/resources/2012/6/7-things-you-should-know-about-badges

Ellis, L. E., Nunn, S. G., & Avella, J. T. (2016). Digital Badges and Micro-credentials: Historical Overview, Motivational Aspects, Issues, and Challenges. In *Foundation of Digital Badges and Micro-Credentials* (pp. 3–21). Springer International Publishing. DOI: 10.1007/978-3-319-15425-1_1

Ersozlu, Z., Taheri, S., & Koch, I. (2024). A review of machine learning methods used for educational data. *Education and Information Technologies*. Advance online publication. DOI: 10.1007/s10639-024-12704-0

Farmer, T., & West, R. E. (2017). Opportunities and challenges with digital open badges. In *Foundations of learning and instructional design technology* (Vol. 56, pp. 45–48). https://lidtfoundations.pressbooks.com/chapter/open-badges/

Fastiggi, W. (2023). *The relationship between STEM education and environmental sustainability*. Technology for Learners. https://technologyforlearners.com/the-relationship-between-stem-education-and-environmental-sustainability/

Gibson, D., Ostashewski, N., Flintoff, K., Grant, S., & Knight, E. (2015). Digital badges in education. *Education and Information Technologies*, 20(2), 403–410. DOI: 10.1007/s10639-013-9291-7

Gish-Lieberman, J. J., Tawfik, A., & Gatewood, J. (2021). Micro-Credentials and Badges in Education: A Historical Overview. *TechTrends*, 65(1), 5–7. DOI: 10.1007/s11528-020-00567-4

Grant, S. (2016). History and Context of Open Digital Badges. In Mullenberg, L. Y., & Berge, Z. L. (Eds.), *Digital Badges in Education* (pp. 3–11). Routledge.

Hartnett, M. K. (2021). How and why are digital badges being used in higher education in New Zealand? *Australasian Journal of Educational Technology*, •••, 104–118. DOI: 10.14742/ajet.6098

Hendricks-Sturrup, R., Simmons, M., Anders, S., Aneni, K., Wright Clayton, E., Coco, J., Collins, B., Heitman, E., Hussain, S., Joshi, K., Lemieux, J., Lovett Novak, L., Rubin, D. J., Shanker, A., Washington, T., Waters, G., Webb Harris, J., Yin, R., Wagner, T., & Malin, B. (2023). Developing Ethics and Equity Principles, Terms, and Engagement Tools to Advance Health Equity and Researcher Diversity in AI and Machine Learning: Modified Delphi Approach. *JMIR AI*, 2, e52888. DOI: 10.2196/52888 PMID: 38875540

Johnson, L., Smith, R., Willis, H., Levine, A., & Haywood, K. (2011). *NMC Horizon Report: 2011 Higher Education Edition*.

Johnson, M. A. (2023, June 27). *Unlocking Student Success: Incorporating Micro-credentials into Academic Curricula*. Linkedin.

Keskin, S., & Yurdugül, H. (2022). E-learning experience: Modeling students' e-learning interactions using log data. *Journal of Educational Technology and Online Learning*, 5(1), 1–13. DOI: 10.31681/jetol.938363

Lester, J., Bansal, M., Biswas, G., Hmelo-Silver, C., Roschelle, J., & Rowe, J. (2024). The AI Institute for Engaged Learning. *AI Magazine*, 45(1), 69–76. DOI: 10.1002/aaai.12161

Long, P. D., & Siemens, G. (2011). Penetrating the Fog: Analytics in Learning and Education. *Creative Education*, 13(9).

Mah, D.-K. (2016). Learning Analytics and Digital Badges: Potential Impact on Student Retention in Higher Education. *Technology. Knowledge and Learning*, 21(3), 285–305. DOI: 10.1007/s10758-016-9286-8

McGreal, R., & Olcott, D.Jr. (2022). A strategic reset: Micro-credentials for higher education leaders. *Smart Learning Environments*, 9(1), 9. DOI: 10.1186/s40561-022-00190-1

Musa, M., Ismail, M. N., & Md Fudzee, M. F. (2021). A Survey on Smart Campus Implementation in Malaysia. *JOIV : International Journal on Informatics Visualization*, 5(1), 51–56. DOI: 10.30630/joiv.5.1.434

Neo, M. (2022). The Merlin Project: Malaysian students' acceptance of an AI chatbot in their learning process. *Turkish Online Journal of Distance Education*, 23(3), 31–48. DOI: 10.17718/tojde.1137122

Newby, T., Wright, C., Besser, E., & Beese, E. (2016). Passport to Designing, Developing and Issuing Digital Instructional Badges. In *Foundation of Digital Badges and Micro-Credentials* (pp. 179–201). Springer International Publishing., DOI: 10.1007/978-3-319-15425-1_10

Nguyen, A., Kremantzis, M., Essien, A., Petrounias, I., & Hosseini, S. (2024). Enhancing Student Engagement Through Artificial Intelligence (AI): Understanding the Basics, Opportunities, and Challenges. In *Journal of University Teaching and Learning Practice* (Issue 6).

Onesi-Ozigagun, O., Ololade, Y. J., Eyo-Udo, N. L., & Ogundipe, D. O. (2024). Revolutionizing education through AI: A comprehensive review of enhancing learning experiences. *International Journal of Applied Research in Social Sciences*, 6(4), 589–607. DOI: 10.51594/ijarss.v6i4.1011

Ostashewski, N., & Reid, D. (2015). A History and Frameworks of Digital Badges in Education. In *Gamification in Education and Business* (pp. 187–200). Springer International Publishing., DOI: 10.1007/978-3-319-10208-5_10

Ouyang, F., Wu, M., Zheng, L., Zhang, L., & Jiao, P. (2023). Integration of artificial intelligence performance prediction and learning analytics to improve student learning in online engineering course. *International Journal of Educational Technology in Higher Education*, 20(1), 4. DOI: 10.1186/s41239-022-00372-4 PMID: 36683653

Parker, H. E. (2015). Digital Badges to Assess Bloom's Affective Domain. *The National Teaching & Learning Forum*, 24(4), 9–11. DOI: 10.1002/ntlf.30031

Popkhadze, N. (2021). The Good, The Bad and The Ugly: AI in the higher education. *Hallinnon Tutkimus*, 40(4), 254–263. DOI: 10.37450/ht.107896

Rieder, A. T. (2022). Using Micro-credentials and Digital Badges in Education and Training: A Literature Review. *Proceedings of Society for Information Technology & Teacher Education International Conference*, 246–251.

Rossiter, D., & Tynan, B. (2019). *Designing and implementing micro-credentials: A guide for practitioners.*

Ruan, S., Jiang, L., Xu, Q., Liu, Z., Davis, G. M., Brunskill, E., & Landay, J. A. (2021). EnglishBot: An AI-Powered Conversational System for Second Language Learning. *26th International Conference on Intelligent User Interfaces*, 434–444. DOI: 10.1145/3397481.3450648

Scheffel, M., Drachsler, H., Stoyanov, S., & Specht, M. (2014). Quality Indicators for Learning Analytics. *Journal of Educational Technology & Society*, 17(4), 117–132.

Shoaib, M., Sayed, N., Singh, J., Shafi, J., Khan, S., & Ali, F. (2024). AI student success predictor: Enhancing personalized learning in campus management systems. *Computers in Human Behavior*, 158, 108301. DOI: 10.1016/j.chb.2024.108301

Vashishth, T. K., Sharma, V., Sharma, K. K., Kumar, B., Panwar, R., & Chaudhary, S. (2024). *AI-Driven Learning Analytics for Personalized Feedback and Assessment in Higher Education.*, DOI: 10.4018/979-8-3693-0639-0.ch009

Wills, C., & Xie, Y. (2016). Toward a Comprehensive Theoretical Framework for Designing Digital Badges. In *Foundation of Digital Badges and Micro-Credentials* (pp. 261–272). Springer International Publishing., DOI: 10.1007/978-3-319-15425-1_14

Zawacki-Richter, O., Marín, V. I., Bond, M., & Gouverneur, F. (2019). Systematic review of research on artificial intelligence applications in higher education – where are the educators? *International Journal of Educational Technology in Higher Education*, 16(1), 39. DOI: 10.1186/s41239-019-0171-0

Chapter 8
AI Enhanced Micro-Credentials for Efficiency and Accessibility:
Using Gen-AI to Improve the Design, Development, and Delivery of Micro-Credentials

Jonathan J. S. Kovilpillai
Asia Pacific University of Technology and Innovation, Malaysia

Abtar Darshan Singh
Asia Pacific University of Technology and Innovation, Malaysia

Analisa Hamdan
https://orcid.org/0000-0003-4225-129X
Asia Pacific University of Technology and Innovation, Malaysia

Kelly McKenna
Colorado State University, USA

Fahd Ali Raza
https://orcid.org/0000-0003-4577-6083
Asia Pacific University of Technology and Innovation, Malaysia

ABSTRACT

This chapter, according to the authors, explores the transformative potential of Generative Artificial Intelligence (Gen-AI) in the design, development, and delivery of micro-credentials, aimed at enhancing efficiency and accessibility in education.

DOI: 10.4018/979-8-3693-5488-9.ch008

By analyzing research from a pilot study conducted at a private university, the chapter delves into AI-driven approaches that improve learner engagement, course completion rates, and learner satisfaction. It addresses the role of AI in personalizing learning experiences, supporting learner success, and ensuring equitable access to educational opportunities. The chapter further examines how AI-powered learning designs can streamline the creation of micro-credentials and deliver them on demand. Additionally, it offers insights into the ethical considerations of integrating AI in education, providing recommendations for educators, technologists, and policymakers on leveraging AI to democratize education effectively.

INTRODUCTION

The rapid evolution of technology continues to reshape numerous sectors, and education is no exception. In particular, artificial intelligence (AI) has emerged as a transformative tool in education, offering innovative solutions to both traditional and emerging challenges. From enhancing personalized learning experiences to driving data-driven instructional design, AI's potential to revolutionize educational systems is now widely recognized (L. Chen et al., 2020; Luckin et al., 2016; van der Vorst & Jelicic, 2019; O'Dea & O'Dea, 2023; Singh & Hiran, 2022). Within the realm of AI, generative AI represents a significant leap forward, capable of creating new content—such as text, assessments, multimedia, and even simulations—tailored to the specific needs of individual learners. This ability to generate real-time, customized educational materials opens new pathways for educators to engage with learners in more meaningful, adaptive ways. As educational institutions around the world explore new modes of delivery, the inclusion of generative AI offers unprecedented opportunities to rethink how learning is designed, delivered, and experienced.

At the same time, the global workforce is undergoing rapid changes, with industries increasingly emphasizing the need for continuous upskilling and reskilling. As a result, there has been a growing demand for flexible and accessible learning options that can accommodate the busy lives of working professionals, career changers, and lifelong learners (Brown et al., 2021). Micro-credentials have emerged as one of the most promising solutions to this need, offering focused, competency-based certifications that allow individuals to acquire specific skills in a relatively short time. Unlike traditional degree programs, which often span multiple years and cover broad subjects, micro-credentials are designed to be short, flexible, and directly applicable to real-world contexts. They are increasingly being used to bridge skills gaps in fields such as technology, healthcare, and education, providing learners with the tools to stay competitive in fast-evolving industries.

However, despite their advantages, micro-credential programs are not without challenges (Pollard & Vincent, 2022). A growing body of research highlights issues related to learner engagement, retention rates, and the scalability of these programs. Learners often struggle to maintain motivation in online and asynchronous formats, which can result in lower completion rates. Additionally, the delivery of micro-credentials across diverse learner populations presents logistical and pedagogical challenges. Programs must balance the need for high-quality content with the demand for flexibility, accessibility, and personalization. In many cases, traditional approaches to instructional design are not sufficient to address these multifaceted challenges. As micro-credentials continue to gain prominence, it is essential to identify new methods and technologies that can overcome these barriers, ensuring that micro-credentials fulfil their potential as a vital component of the education landscape.

Generative AI offers a promising solution to many of the issues faced by micro-credential programs. Through its ability to automate and enhance various aspects of course design, development, and delivery, AI has the potential to revolutionize how educational experiences are structured. One of the key strengths of generative AI is its capacity to personalize learning experiences based on real-time data, adjusting content and assessments according to individual learner performance and preferences (Ruiz-Rojas et al., 2023; Binhammad et al., 2024). This level of personalization helps maintain learner engagement and increases the likelihood of course completion. Moreover, generative AI can significantly reduce the time and resources required to develop high-quality educational materials. AI-powered tools can create learning assets such as lesson plans, assessments, and multimedia content more efficiently than traditional methods, freeing up educators to focus on the more nuanced aspects of teaching and learner support. By integrating AI into micro-credential programs, institutions can offer more engaging, scalable, and flexible learning experiences that meet the diverse needs of today's learners.

The purpose of this chapter is to explore how AI, and specifically generative AI, can fundamentally transform the creation and delivery of micro-credentials. By examining the role of AI in areas such as instructional design, content creation, and learner engagement, this chapter aims to demonstrate how these technologies can make micro-credentials more efficient, accessible, and impactful. Additionally, this chapter draws on practical examples from AI-powered learning design workshops to illustrate how generative AI tools can be used to build effective learning designs that are aligned with educational objectives. By focusing on how AI enhances the development of personalized learning experiences, adaptive assessments, and interactive content, the chapter provides insights for educators, instructional designers, and policymakers interested in leveraging AI to improve the micro-credential ecosystem.

In the sections that follow, the chapter will first provide an overview of instructional design principles, particularly those that are relevant to the development of micro-credentials. It will then delve into the integration of AI tools into the design process, highlighting how generative AI can automate and enhance key components of course creation, including the design of learning outcomes, assessments, and multimedia materials. Finally, the chapter will present case studies and practical applications of AI in educational settings, demonstrating the potential benefits and challenges associated with implementing AI-powered micro-credentials. Through this comprehensive exploration, the chapter aims to offer a clear vision of how AI can be utilized to improve both the efficiency and effectiveness of micro-credential programs in today's dynamic learning landscape.

Background

Consider the case of Maria, a mid-career professional working in the marketing industry. With the rapid digital transformation sweeping through her field, she realized that her current skill set was becoming outdated. Eager to upskill and stay competitive, Maria began exploring various online learning opportunities. She was particularly drawn to micro-credential programs, which promised flexibility, targeted learning, and quick certification in emerging areas such as data analytics and digital marketing. The idea of earning bite-sized credentials without committing to a lengthy degree program seemed like the perfect solution to her needs.

After some research, Maria enrolled in a few micro-credential courses offered by well-known platforms. The promise of advancing her skills in a short period, on her own schedule, was appealing. However, as Maria began working through the content, she quickly found herself struggling to stay engaged. The material, while relevant, lacked interactivity and personalization. Lessons were delivered in a one-size-fits-all format, without adapting to her specific learning pace or offering real-world applications. Additionally, the assessments were generic, often failing to provide meaningful feedback that could help her improve. With no live interactions or support mechanisms to motivate her, Maria's enthusiasm for the course began to wane.

As the weeks passed, the demands of her job and personal life started taking precedence over the course. The flexibility that initially attracted her to the micro-credentials also became a double-edged sword, as it was easy to deprioritize learning when no structured schedule or deadlines were in place. Eventually, Maria stopped logging in altogether, another statistic in the growing issue of low course completion rates in micro-credential programs.

Maria's experience is not unique. Research shows that many learners face similar challenges when enrolling in online micro-credentials. The promise of flexibility and targeted learning often falls short when courses fail to engage learners effectively. According to Tamoliune et al., (2023), learner engagement and motivation are crucial factors in the success of micro-credential programs, yet these elements are frequently neglected. Without personalized content, meaningful interaction, or adaptive learning environments, learners like Maria often struggle to complete their courses. As micro-credential programs continue to grow in popularity, addressing these engagement and retention issues is essential to their long-term success.

Maria's experience with disengagement in a micro-credential course is a common phenomenon, and various established academic theories and research studies provide insight into the factors that contribute to this issue. Her story touches on key concepts in learner motivation, instructional design, and the challenges of self-paced online learning, all of which have been widely studied in educational research. We will now extract some of these key concepts and delve deeper into them in relation to Maria's experience.

Self-Determination Theory (SDT)

One of the most relevant frameworks to explain Maria's experience is Self-Determination Theory (SDT), which posits that individuals are motivated to learn when three psychological needs are fulfilled: autonomy, competence, and relatedness (Sardabi et al., 2023). While Maria initially valued the autonomy offered by the flexible structure of the micro-credential, the course failed to provide sufficient opportunities to build competence or foster relatedness. The material was generic and did not offer tailored feedback or adapt to her learning pace, diminishing her sense of mastery over the subject matter. Additionally, the absence of interaction with instructors or peers meant that Maria lacked the social connections and sense of belonging that could have motivated her to persist. According to SDT, when learners do not feel competent or connected to the learning community, intrinsic motivation declines, leading to disengagement and, ultimately, dropout (Hamilton, 2023). This framework is particularly useful in understanding how online courses, which often lack social elements, can fail to sustain learner motivation over time.

Further research on SDT in online learning contexts supports the idea that creating environments where learners can experience autonomy, competence, and relatedness is essential for retention (Farikah et al., 2023). Many online courses focus heavily on providing autonomy, such as self-paced learning, but neglect the other two needs. Maria's case highlights the importance of a balanced approach, where learners not only have control over their schedule but also feel adequately supported through clear learning pathways, feedback, and opportunities for interaction.

Cognitive Load Theory (CLT)

Another significant factor that may have contributed to Maria's disengagement is the cognitive complexity of the course material and how it was presented. Cognitive Load Theory (CLT) suggests that learners have a limited capacity for processing new information, and when the instructional design does not take this into account, it can overwhelm the learner (Albus, 2023). In Maria's case, the course material was delivered in a way that did not account for her prior knowledge or learning style. Without scaffolding or adaptive elements, Maria had to process a large amount of new information without adequate support, leading to cognitive overload.

CLT distinguishes between three types of cognitive load: intrinsic, extraneous, and germane (Siregar, 2024). In Maria's experience, the extraneous load—the mental effort required to navigate poorly designed content—was likely too high, making it difficult for her to focus on germane cognitive processes, which are essential for deep learning. Research shows that when learners are overloaded with unnecessary information or poorly structured content, they are less likely to engage and more likely to abandon the course (Chen et al., 2023). A more effective course design would have broken down complex concepts into manageable chunks and provided ongoing, adaptive feedback to reduce cognitive load and keep learners like Maria engaged.

Community of Inquiry (CoI) Framework

The absence of social interaction and instructional support in Maria's course is another critical element that can be explained through the Community of Inquiry (CoI) framework. This model, developed by Garrison, Anderson, and Archer (1999), posits that successful online learning environments are built on three key elements: cognitive presence, teaching presence, and social presence. In Maria's case, the lack of teaching presence (e.g., clear guidance or timely, formative feedback) and social presence (e.g., peer interaction or collaborative learning tasks) contributed to her feeling isolated. The CoI framework emphasizes that learners in online environments need structured interactions—not only with the content but also with instructors and fellow learners—to create a sense of community and engagement.

Research supports the idea that social presence is particularly important in online courses, as it reduces feelings of isolation and helps learners stay connected to the material and each other (Garrison et al., 1999). The absence of this social dimension in Maria's course meant that there were fewer opportunities for her to collaborate, discuss, or even troubleshoot with others, which are critical components of engagement. Additionally, the lack of teaching presence meant that Maria did not receive the feedback she needed to feel competent in her progress, further reducing her motivation. Studies by Garrison and colleagues (1999) show that when teaching and social presence are low, learners are more likely to disengage and not complete the course.

The Problem of Attrition in Online Learning

Maria's decision to stop participating in the course is reflective of a broader issue of attrition that has been extensively documented in online education literature. Numerous studies have shown that online courses, particularly those that are self-paced, have significantly higher dropout rates compared to traditional face-to-face programs (Sitar-Tăut et al., 2024; Villar-Aguilés & Muñoz-Rodríguez, 2024; Bosch & Spinath, 2023). This trend can be attributed to several factors, including the lack of interaction, the absence of external accountability, and the overwhelming sense of autonomy without adequate structure or support (Alves et al., 2024). In Maria's case, while the flexibility of the micro-credential initially seemed like an advantage, it eventually became a barrier to completion. Without clear deadlines or ongoing feedback, Maria's engagement with the course waned, and the demands of her personal and professional life took priority.

Attrition in online learning environments is often linked to a lack of support structures that help learners manage their time and stay motivated. Research suggests that learners in online courses are more likely to succeed when there are mechanisms in place that guide their progress and maintain their sense of accountability (Kember et al., 2023; Rueda-Gómez et al., 2024). Strategies such as frequent check-ins, personalized progress tracking, and supportive communication from instructors can help mitigate the effects of isolation and self-directed learning fatigue, which were evident in Maria's experience.

The Role of Engagement and Interaction

Learner engagement is widely recognized as a key predictor of success in online learning environments. Research consistently shows that courses with interactive content and regular feedback result in higher completion rates and learner satisfaction (Rof et al., 2024; Pandita & Kiran, 2023). In Maria's case, the lack of engaging, interactive content—such as personalized assessments, real-world case studies, or gamified learning experiences—led to her declining motivation over time. Moore's Theory of Transactional Distance (1997) is particularly relevant here. The theory posits that as the level of interaction between the learner and the instructor or content decreases, the "transactional distance" increases, leading to a sense of disconnect that often results in disengagement. Maria's course, with its low levels of interaction, is a prime example of this phenomenon.

Increasing the level of interaction and personalization in online courses has been shown to reduce this transactional distance, enhancing both motivation and course completion rates. Studies indicate that incorporating adaptive learning technologies, which tailor content to individual learner preferences and performance, can significantly boost engagement (Zhang & Tobias, 2023). By offering real-time feedback and creating opportunities for meaningful social interaction, online courses can better support learners like Maria, preventing them from feeling disconnected and encouraging them to stay on track.

Addressing the Challenges

Maria's experience is illustrative of broader trends in online learning, where disengagement and attrition rates remain a challenge despite the flexibility that these courses offer. The literature suggests several strategies to address these challenges, including the use of AI-driven tools to enhance personalization and interactivity. Qi et al., (2023) argue that AI has the potential to address many of the issues faced by online learners, such as the lack of adaptive feedback and meaningful engagement. By integrating AI technologies that monitor learner progress and provide timely, personalized interventions, educational institutions can create more engaging and supportive online environments. Additionally, fostering a sense of community through collaborative activities and peer interaction is critical to ensuring that learners feel connected and motivated to complete their courses (Bosch & Spinath, 2023) (Sailer & Homner, 2020).

To effectively address the challenges of learner disengagement, attrition, and cognitive overload that Maria faced in her micro-credential course, several theories offer guidance on designing more effective learning environments.

Universal Design for Learning (UDL)

One potential solution lies in the application of Universal Design for Learning (UDL), a framework that emphasizes the need to create flexible learning environments that accommodate individual learner differences (Hall et al., 2012). UDL promotes providing multiple means of engagement, representation, and action and expression, which would have addressed Maria's need for more personalized and interactive content. By offering various ways to engage with the material—such as interactive videos, discussion forums, and self-assessments—UDL can reduce cognitive overload and increase learner motivation. This approach would have allowed

Maria to access the content in ways that suited her learning preferences, keeping her engaged and motivated to complete the course.

Keller's ARCS Model of Motivation

Another effective framework to consider is Keller's ARCS Model of Motivation, which focuses on four elements—Attention, Relevance, Confidence, and Satisfaction (Keller, 1987). Applying the ARCS model to micro-credential design can help maintain learner interest and engagement throughout the course. For example, Maria's disengagement could have been mitigated by incorporating more attention-grabbing, real-world applications of the course material and ensuring the content was immediately relevant to her professional goals. By offering adaptive feedback and opportunities for success through scaffolded activities, the course could have boosted Maria's confidence and satisfaction, leading to higher levels of persistence and completion.

Self-Regulated Learning (SRL) Theory

Self-Regulated Learning (SRL) Theory also provides a useful lens for addressing the autonomy provided by micro-credential programs. SRL emphasizes the importance of learners being able to set goals, monitor their progress, and reflect on their learning (Puustinen & Pulkkinen, 2001). In Maria's case, implementing SRL strategies could have helped her stay on track with her learning goals. For instance, AI-powered tools that offer personalized learning analytics could support self-regulation by providing real-time insights into her progress, helping her adjust her learning strategies. SRL also promotes the use of prompts and reminders to keep learners focused, which could have been particularly helpful in a self-paced course like the one Maria took.

Cognitive Apprenticeship

Cognitive Apprenticeship theory (Dennen & Burner, 2007) could have been another effective solution for Maria's disengagement. This theory advocates for learning in context and through authentic, situated tasks with the guidance of an expert. Applying this to micro-credential courses means creating more collaborative opportunities where learners can interact with mentors or peers. Integrating real-world case studies and problem-solving tasks, while providing expert guidance, would have allowed Maria to see the practical applications of her learning, thus increasing her engagement and the likelihood of completion. Cognitive apprenticeship supports a more immersive learning experience, which could address the issue of transactional distance by offering opportunities for learners to connect with both the material and other participants.

The Gamification of Learning

Lastly, the gamification of learning has been proven to increase learner motivation and engagement (Sailer & Homner, 2020). Applying gamification elements—such as earning badges, completing levels, or unlocking new content based on performance—can enhance the sense of progress and achievement. For Maria, integrating game-based mechanics could have provided a sense of accomplishment and incentivized her to continue with the course. Gamification also aligns with the principles of personalized learning, as it can offer adaptive challenges that are tailored to individual learner needs and progress.

As can be observed from the above, the design and developments of micro-credentials requires more than just delivering content. Careful consideration of some of the above-mentioned elements can go a long way in ensuring the rich content is accompanied by design principles that keep the learner engaged throughout the course. This is where the power of generative AI really comes into play, as will become evident as we explore further in this chapter.

OVERVIEW OF GENERATIVE AI IN EDUCATION

Generative AI, a subset of artificial intelligence, has rapidly gained traction in various sectors, including education. Unlike traditional AI models that rely on predefined rules or datasets, generative AI systems, such as OpenAI's GPT models, can create new content—whether text, images, videos, or even code—based on a prompt. In the context of education, generative AI has the potential to transform how learning materials are created, tailored, and delivered to students, offering more personalized and dynamic educational experiences.

The adoption of AI in education is not entirely new. Over the past decade, AI-powered tools such as intelligent tutoring systems and adaptive learning platforms have been deployed to enhance student outcomes by tailoring content to individual learning needs (Luckin et al., 2016). However, the emergence of generative AI marks a significant shift. These models can now autonomously generate instructional content, design assessments, create multimedia assets, and even simulate interactive learning environments, reducing the workload for educators while improving the customization of learning experiences (Binhammad et al., 2024). As a result, educators can spend more time focusing on high-level instructional tasks, such as mentoring and addressing individual student challenges.

Generative AI's ability to personalize learning is perhaps its most valuable contribution. By analyzing learner data—such as prior knowledge, learning pace, and engagement levels—AI can generate lesson plans, assessments, and feedback that cater to each learner's unique needs. This personalization is particularly beneficial in online and self-paced learning environments, where learners often struggle with one-size-fits-all content. A report by McKinsey (2018) highlights the growing use of AI in automating lesson design and improving learner engagement, with AI-powered platforms showing improved retention and course completion rates. For instance, adaptive learning technologies, like those employed by platforms such as DreamBox and Knewton, utilize AI to adjust instructional paths based on real-time learner performance data, offering students tailored content that keeps them engaged.

In micro-credential programs, where learners are often juggling professional commitments and time constraints, generative AI can play a critical role in making the learning experience more efficient and engaging. The ability to create on-demand, personalized micro-content allows learners to receive precisely the information they need, at the right time, without overwhelming them with extraneous material. This is especially important given that completion rates in micro-credentials are often lower than in traditional courses, as discussed in several studies (Pollard & Vincent, 2022). By ensuring that the learning experience is closely aligned with each learner's goals and prior knowledge, generative AI has the potential to address this issue by reducing cognitive overload and increasing relevance.

Generative AI's applications are not limited to content generation alone. These systems are increasingly being integrated into learning management systems (LMS) and other educational technologies to provide real-time feedback and support. For example, AI-driven chatbots are now used in several universities to provide 24/7 academic support, answering student queries, guiding them through difficult concepts, and even providing emotional support. In micro-credential programs, this type of AI integration can significantly enhance the learner's experience by offering continuous support, thereby reducing dropout rates and improving satisfaction.

However, the use of generative AI in education also presents challenges. Concerns around the ethical use of AI, particularly issues of bias in AI-generated content and the transparency of AI decision-making processes, are increasingly being discussed in academic and policy circles. These issues will be explored further in later sections, but it is crucial to acknowledge that while generative AI holds immense promise, its implementation must be carefully managed to ensure equitable and fair educational outcomes.

Personalized Learning Experiences

One of the most transformative impacts of generative AI in education is its ability to create personalized learning experiences. Unlike traditional education models, which often rely on standardized content and assessments, generative AI tailors educational materials to meet the specific needs, preferences, and abilities of individual learners. This capacity to customize the learning journey in real time makes AI a powerful tool in addressing one of the most persistent challenges in education: the one-size-fits-all approach.

Personalized learning involves adapting the pace, style, and content of education to match each learner's unique background and learning goals. In micro-credential programs, where learners typically come from diverse professional backgrounds and have varying levels of prior knowledge, personalized learning is especially critical. Generative AI enables this by dynamically generating content, assessments, and feedback that are specific to the learner's progression. For example, an AI system could adjust a learner's path by providing additional resources on topics they find challenging, while streamlining or omitting content in areas where they have already demonstrated proficiency. This ensures that the learning experience is both relevant and efficient, preventing learners from feeling overwhelmed or disengaged.

Research shows that personalized learning significantly enhances engagement and learning outcomes. A study by Kaswan et al., (2024) demonstrated that personalized learning systems improve course completion rates by offering tailored interventions at critical points in a learner's journey. AI's ability to track and analyze data in real-time allows for these interventions to be highly precise. For instance, if a learner struggles with a specific concept, AI can immediately offer supplementary content or rephrase explanations in simpler terms, helping to reinforce understanding. Moreover, AI can personalize assessments by adjusting the difficulty of questions based on the learner's performance, which keeps learners challenged but not frustrated.

In the context of micro-credentials, where time is often a critical factor, this personalized approach can make a significant difference. Many learners pursuing micro-credentials do so alongside full-time jobs or other responsibilities, which means their time for learning is limited. By offering a personalized learning path, AI ensures that learners spend their time efficiently, focusing only on the areas where they need improvement. Studies, such as those by Vashishth et al., (2024), have highlighted that learners who receive personalized feedback and content are more likely to complete online courses compared to those in non-personalized learning environments.

Generative AI tools like ChatGPT and other large language models have also enabled personalized content creation in real time. For example, if a learner is working on a module about leadership in a business context, the AI can generate case studies, scenarios, or questions specific to that topic, all tailored to the learner's professional context. This not only makes the learning experience more relevant but also increases engagement by ensuring that the content resonates with the learner's goals.

The benefits of personalized learning go beyond just content and assessments. AI-powered systems can also offer personalized feedback that is immediate, specific, and constructive. Traditional feedback mechanisms often provide generic comments that may not be particularly helpful to the learner. In contrast, AI can analyze a learner's responses in-depth and generate detailed feedback that not only points out mistakes but also offers suggestions for improvement and additional resources. This kind of timely and actionable feedback is crucial in keeping learners motivated and on track.

Moreover, personalized learning facilitated by AI can help foster greater learner autonomy. As learners receive customized content and feedback, they are empowered to take more control over their learning process. They can make informed decisions about what areas to focus on, how to pace themselves, and when to seek additional help. This aligns with theories of self-regulated learning (Puustinen & Pulkkinen, 2001), where learners who are able to monitor and reflect on their learning progress tend to achieve better outcomes.

However, while the benefits of personalized learning through AI are clear, there are also challenges. One of the primary concerns is ensuring that AI-generated content remains pedagogically sound and free from biases. Since AI systems are trained on large datasets, they may inadvertently reinforce existing biases present in the data, potentially affecting the fairness of the learning experience (Chinta et al., 2024). Additionally, there are concerns about learner privacy, as AI systems rely on collecting and analyzing large amounts of personal data to offer personalization. Ensuring that this data is handled responsibly and securely is paramount to maintaining trust in AI-driven educational systems.

In conclusion, generative AI offers unprecedented opportunities for creating personalized learning experiences in micro-credential programs. By tailoring content, assessments, and feedback to the needs of individual learners, AI can significantly improve engagement, retention, and learning outcomes. However, these benefits must be balanced against the challenges of ensuring fairness, transparency, and privacy in AI-powered learning environments.

Completion Rates and Learner Engagement

While the potential of generative AI in improving learner engagement and personalization is clear, real-world data from micro-credential programs often tells a more complex story. In examining the Microcredential Pilot Report from the first batch of micro-credentials offered at a higher education institute in Malaysia, several key trends emerged that align with broader challenges seen across the online learning ecosystem.

The report revealed that completion rates for the micro-credential programs were lower than anticipated, with only a fraction of enrolled learners completing the courses. The overall completion rate was just 38%, which is consistent with findings from other studies on online learning platforms such as Coursera and edX. The average completion rate for online courses on edX hovered around 15%, while Coursera's rate was slightly higher at 20%. These figures highlight a pervasive issue in online and self-paced learning: learners often struggle to maintain motivation and engagement, leading to higher attrition rates.

In the afore-mentioned report, several factors were identified as contributing to these low completion rates. One of the most significant factors was learner disengagement, particularly in courses that lacked interactive and personalized elements. Many learners reported that the content felt generic and was not sufficiently adapted to their individual learning needs or professional contexts. This aligns with findings from the broader literature on online learning, which consistently points to personalization as a key determinant of learner engagement and success (Rof et al., 2024). Without tailored learning paths or adaptive feedback, learners can easily lose interest, especially when balancing coursework with other responsibilities.

The report also highlighted the importance of timely and meaningful feedback in keeping learners engaged. Participants in the pilot program noted that they often received limited or delayed feedback on their assessments, which led to frustration and decreased motivation to continue. This issue is particularly problematic in self-paced learning environments, where learners lack the structured support typically found in traditional classroom settings. Research by (Iraj et al., 2021) shows that frequent, actionable feedback is crucial for sustaining engagement, as it helps learners track their progress and feel a sense of accomplishment. The absence of this feedback loop can result in learners feeling isolated and disconnected from the learning process.

Another contributing factor to the low completion rates was the absence of peer interaction and collaboration. The Microcredential Pilot Courses Report indicated that learners who participated in courses with no collaborative activities were significantly more likely to drop out compared to those in courses that encouraged discussion and group work. This finding aligns with the Community of Inquiry (CoI) framework, which emphasizes the importance of social presence—interactions with peers and instructors—in fostering a sense of belonging and engagement (Garrison et al., 1999). Without these social elements, learners may struggle to stay motivated, especially in courses that are delivered entirely online.

In addition to these factors, the lack of structured deadlines was identified as a challenge for many learners. While the flexibility of self-paced courses is one of their main advantages, it can also lead to procrastination and reduced accountability. The report noted that learners who had more structured learning schedules—such as weekly goals or periodic assessments—were more likely to complete their courses than those who had complete autonomy over their learning pace. This observation is consistent with findings from studies on massive open online courses (MOOCs), which show that learners with clear deadlines are more likely to stay on track and finish their courses (Wong et al., 2021).

These challenges are not unique to the micro-credential programs at the referenced institution. Similar patterns have been observed in micro-credential and online learning programs at other institutions and platforms. For example, completion rates across various platforms, including Coursera, Udacity, and FutureLearn, remained low, with many learners citing disengagement and a lack of accountability as key reasons for dropping out (Kizito & Kayi, 2024). This suggests that while micro-credentials offer a flexible and accessible way for learners to gain new skills, the absence of effective engagement strategies can severely limit their success.

To address these challenges, there is a growing recognition that micro-credential programs must incorporate more dynamic and personalized learning experiences. The inclusion of AI-powered tools that offer real-time feedback, adaptive learning paths, and personalized content can significantly improve learner engagement and, by extension, completion rates. Studies by Marwan et al., (2020) and Prince et al., (2020) indicate that learners are more likely to persist in courses when the content is tailored to their needs and when they receive regular, meaningful feedback on their progress. By integrating AI technologies that personalize the learning experience, micro-credential programs can overcome some of the most common barriers to learner success.

The findings from the Microcredential Pilot Courses Report provide valuable insights into the challenges and opportunities in this space. While the low completion rates underscore the need for more effective engagement strategies, they also highlight the potential for AI to play a transformative role in improving learner outcomes. By addressing the key factors of engagement, feedback, and collaboration, AI-powered micro-credential programs have the potential to offer a more engaging, personalized, and successful learning experience.

Feedback from Learners

Learner feedback from the Microcredential Pilot Courses Report also provides critical insights into how participants perceived the course content, structure, and overall learning experience. The post-workshop surveys revealed several key areas where learners expressed both satisfaction and concerns, offering valuable guidance for improving future iterations of the micro-credential programs.

One of the most positive aspects highlighted by participants was the flexibility of the courses. Many learners appreciated the ability to work at their own pace and on their own schedules, which allowed them to balance their professional responsibilities with the demands of upskilling. However, this flexibility also posed challenges, as several learners reported difficulty in staying motivated without structured deadlines or consistent guidance.

Another recurring theme in the feedback was the demand for more interactive and engaging content. Learners expressed that while the information presented was relevant, the lack of interactivity—such as discussion forums, collaborative projects, or real-time feedback—limited their overall engagement with the course material. This echoes the findings of earlier research, which emphasizes the importance of social presence and interactive learning elements in online education (Van Wart et al., 2020).

In terms of content delivery, learners praised the use of multimedia elements, such as videos and case studies, but noted that they would have benefited from more personalized feedback on their progress. Many participants suggested that incorporating AI-driven feedback systems could help address this issue, as it would provide timely, individualized guidance throughout the course.

In summary, while learners were satisfied with the flexibility and relevance of the micro-credential courses, their feedback points to a need for more structured support, interactivity, and personalized content. These insights align with broader trends in online learning and will be instrumental in shaping the future design and delivery of micro-credentials.

Engagement and Retention with AI

One of the most promising applications of AI in micro-credential programs is its ability to significantly enhance learner engagement and retention. By leveraging adaptive learning technologies and real-time feedback mechanisms, AI can provide learners with personalized experiences that keep them motivated and on track to complete their courses. These innovations are particularly critical in addressing some of the core challenges identified in micro-credential programs, such as learner disengagement, high dropout rates, and the lack of timely support.

Adaptive Learning Technologies

Adaptive learning systems are designed to adjust the pace and content of instruction based on individual learner performance. These AI-driven systems use real-time data to tailor the learning experience, ensuring that learners are neither overwhelmed nor under-challenged. For example, platforms like Knewton and Smart

Sparrow have successfully implemented adaptive learning models that modify the difficulty of tasks or introduce supplementary content when learners struggle with specific concepts. In some instances, the implementation of Knewton's adaptive learning platform in introductory math courses led to a 25% improvement in pass rates (Tebepah & Ikeremo, 2024). By personalizing the learning experience, adaptive technologies ensure that each learner receives the right level of challenge, improving engagement and persistence.

In micro-credential programs, where learners often have varying levels of prior knowledge, adaptive learning can play a crucial role in ensuring that each participant progresses at a comfortable yet challenging pace. This personalized pacing reduces cognitive overload and frustration, which are key factors contributing to high dropout rates in online education (Taiar, 2023). Additionally, by continuously monitoring learner progress, adaptive systems can identify when a learner is at risk of disengaging and provide targeted interventions, such as additional practice problems or alternative explanations.

Real-time Feedback and AI-driven Support

Another critical factor in boosting retention is the availability of real-time feedback. AI can provide instantaneous, personalized feedback on assessments, assignments, and even forum interactions, ensuring that learners receive the support they need exactly when they need it. This real-time feedback loop is a powerful motivator, as learners are more likely to stay engaged when they feel that their efforts are acknowledged and supported. In contrast, delayed or generic feedback often leaves learners feeling disconnected from the course, leading to disengagement and, ultimately, dropout.

The ability of AI to offer detailed, constructive feedback in real-time helps learners understand their mistakes, learn from them, and make improvements without waiting for instructor input. This is particularly beneficial in self-paced learning environments, where timely instructor feedback may not always be possible.

Predictive Analytics and Early Intervention

AI-powered predictive analytics are also being used to improve learner retention by identifying at-risk students early in the learning process. These systems analyze data from a variety of sources—such as log-in patterns, participation in activities, and assessment performance—to predict which learners are likely to struggle or drop out. Many institutions have implemented predictive analytics systems that flag at-risk students and trigger interventions, such as personalized support emails or tutoring recommendations. These systems have been credited with increasing graduation rates (Sepulveda, 2020).

In micro-credential programs, predictive analytics could be used to monitor learner engagement in real time, alerting instructors when learners show signs of disengagement. Early interventions, such as personalized reminders, additional resources, or one-on-one support, can be deployed to re-engage learners before they fall too far behind. This proactive approach to learner support not only improves retention but also enhances the overall learning experience by making it more responsive to individual needs.

Case Study: AI in edX and Coursera

Major online learning platforms like edX and Coursera have also been incorporating AI to address learner engagement and retention issues. Coursera, for example, uses machine learning algorithms to personalize course recommendations based on learner behavior and performance in previous courses. This ensures that learners are consistently matched with courses that align with their interests and skill levels, increasing their likelihood of success (Pappano, 2018). Similarly, edX has experimented with AI-driven grading and feedback systems that allow learners to receive instant evaluations on their assignments, thus speeding up the learning process and maintaining engagement.

These examples demonstrate that AI's capacity to personalize learning experiences and provide real-time feedback can have a significant impact on engagement and retention. By adopting similar AI-driven strategies, micro-credential programs can address the key challenges identified in earlier sections, such as low completion rates and learner disengagement. The integration of AI into micro-credential programs represents a promising avenue for ensuring that learners remain motivated, supported, and on track to achieve their learning goals.

AI-POWERED LEARNING DESIGNS

The integration of AI tools, such as ChatGPT and other generative AI models, into the design of micro-credentials represents a significant shift in how educational content is created, customized, and delivered. By leveraging these tools, educators and instructional designers can streamline the development of micro-credential courses, enhance learner engagement, and ensure that the content remains relevant and personalized to the needs of diverse learners.

Generative AI in Content Creation

Generative AI models, particularly large language models like ChatGPT, have the ability to autonomously generate lesson plans, assessments, and learning materials tailored to specific instructional objectives. This capability dramatically reduces the time and effort required by educators to develop high-quality content. In micro-credential programs, where the rapid creation and delivery of targeted learning modules is critical, AI can serve as an invaluable resource.

For instance, in the AI: Learning Designs (AILD) workshop, participants used generative AI to create entire lesson plans aligned with their learning objectives. Educators were able to input specific learning outcomes and receive detailed lesson structures, including suggested activities, resources, and assessments, all generated by AI tools like ChatGPT. This not only reduced the workload for the educators but also allowed them to focus on higher-level instructional tasks, such as adapting the AI-generated content to meet the unique needs of their learners.

An example from the AI workshop involved the creation of a lesson plan for a module on "Introduction to Ethical AI in Business." By simply providing the AI with the desired learning outcomes—such as "understand the ethical implications of AI in business settings"—the tool generated a complete lesson plan. This included a breakdown of the topics, suggested case studies, discussion prompts, and even a quiz for assessing the learners' understanding of the material. The flexibility of the AI allowed the educators to tweak the content in real-time, adding or removing elements based on the feedback from learners or the specific requirements of the course. This ability to quickly adapt and iterate on content is particularly valuable in fast-paced learning environments like micro-credentials.

AI for Personalized Assessments and Feedback

One of the most significant contributions of AI in learning design is its ability to personalize not just the content but also the assessments. Traditional assessments in micro-credential courses are often generic and not tailored to individual learner performance or progress. With AI, assessments can be dynamically generated to match each learner's pace, level of understanding, and areas where they need improvement.

For example, in the AI workshop, participants used generative AI to create personalized assessments based on the learner's progress through the course. AI tools like ChatGPT can generate multiple-choice questions, short-answer prompts, and even project-based assignments that align with the learner's current level of understanding. As learners progress through the course, the AI can adjust the difficulty of the questions and tasks, ensuring that learners remain challenged without becoming overwhelmed. This type of adaptive assessment system not only improves engagement but also provides learners with more meaningful feedback.

In addition to generating assessments, AI can provide real-time feedback that is specific, constructive, and actionable. In traditional settings, feedback is often delayed or generic due to time constraints on instructors. However, AI can offer instant feedback on assignments, quizzes, and discussions. This immediate feedback helps learners understand their mistakes and make corrections quickly, thereby improving retention and motivation. For instance, in the AI workshop, AI tools were used to evaluate learner submissions, providing detailed comments on the strengths and areas for improvement, which helped learners adjust their approaches in real-time.

Applications of Generative AI in Other Educational Initiatives

The use of AI in learning design is not limited to the AI workshop. Similar AI-powered initiatives in education have shown promising results. For instance, OpenAI's GPT-3 has been used in platforms like ScribeSense, which automatically grades handwritten assignments and provides personalized feedback (Banerjee et al., 2024). Similarly, Duolingo has incorporated AI-driven feedback mechanisms to enhance language learning, adjusting exercises based on the learner's progress and proficiency levels (Vega et al., 2024).

In higher education, platforms like Coursera and edX are increasingly using AI to enhance their course offerings. Coursera's "CourseMatch" tool, powered by AI, helps learners find the most relevant courses based on their learning history and career goals. Similarly, edX has used AI to personalize learning paths within its MicroMasters programs, enabling learners to focus on the areas where they need the most improvement (Jdidou & Aammou, 2024). These applications parallel the use of generative AI in micro-credentials, where personalization and adaptability are key to addressing the challenges of learner engagement and retention.

Moreover, AI's ability to analyze learner data and provide insights into learning behaviors is helping educators refine their instructional designs. By analyzing patterns in learner performance and engagement, AI tools can suggest adjustments to the course content or structure to improve learning outcomes. This data-driven approach enables continuous improvement in the design and delivery of micro-credentials, ensuring that the content evolves to meet the changing needs of learners.

The Future of AI-Powered Learning Designs

As generative AI continues to evolve, its role in educational design is expected to expand. Future iterations of AI-powered tools may be able to not only create content and assessments but also curate personalized learning experiences across multiple domains. For example, AI could autonomously generate learning pathways that combine micro-credentials from different fields, creating interdisciplinary programs tailored to specific career goals or industry demands. These AI-driven learning pathways could be updated in real-time based on the latest trends and advancements in the industry, ensuring that learners always have access to the most relevant and up-to-date content.

AI-powered learning designs hold immense potential for enhancing micro-credential programs. By automating content creation, personalizing assessments, and providing real-time feedback, AI enables educators to deliver more engaging, efficient, and learner-centered experiences. The examples from the AI workshop, alongside similar AI-powered initiatives, demonstrate that generative AI is not just a tool for automating tasks but a transformative force in reshaping how we think about instructional design and personalized learning.

OVERCOMING SCALABILITY ISSUES

One of the most significant challenges faced by micro-credential programs is scaling effectively while maintaining the quality of the learning experience. As demand for flexible, skill-based learning continues to grow, educational institutions need solutions that can accommodate a large and diverse learner population without overwhelming instructors or compromising the personalization and engagement essential to learner success. AI offers promising solutions to these scalability challenges, providing tools that automate key aspects of course creation, delivery, and support.

AI-Powered Automation for Scalability

Generative AI tools, such as those used in content creation and adaptive assessments, allow educational providers to scale micro-credential programs efficiently. Rather than relying on instructors to manually design each lesson, AI can automate the development of lesson plans, quizzes, and even multimedia resources. This automation not only reduces the workload for faculty but also ensures that content can be produced and updated quickly, making it easier to expand offerings without delays.

For example, platforms like FutureLearn have begun integrating AI to support the rapid scaling of their online courses, allowing them to offer a wide array of micro-credentials across different subject areas. By using AI-driven content generation and automated grading systems, FutureLearn has been able to maintain high-quality learning experiences while significantly expanding their program offerings (Murtaza et al., 2024)

Personalized Learning at Scale

AI technologies also enable the personalization of learning experiences at scale. Adaptive learning platforms, such as those used by the Open University, tailor content to each learner's needs while simultaneously managing thousands of students. By analyzing data on learner performance and engagement, AI can adjust instructional paths in real time, providing a customized learning journey for each student. This ensures that even as programs scale to include more learners, the content remains relevant and engaging for individuals.

There are numerous reports of AI-driven tools significantly improving learner outcomes in large-scale programs by providing personalized feedback and adaptive content (Rane et al., 2023). These technologies reduced the need for individual instructor interventions, allowing for the management of larger cohorts without diminishing the learner experience.

AI-Driven Support Systems

In addition to content creation and personalization, AI can automate learner support services, helping institutions scale without sacrificing learner satisfaction. AI-powered chatbots, for example, are increasingly being used to handle routine learner queries, freeing up instructors and support staff to focus on more complex tasks. This allows institutions to provide 24/7 support, ensuring that learners have access to help when they need it, regardless of time zone or location.

The scalability benefits of AI are clear: by automating content creation, assessments, and support, AI technologies enable institutions to expand their micro-credential offerings while maintaining high levels of learner engagement and satisfaction. As demand for micro-credentials grows, the ability to scale efficiently will be crucial for institutions aiming to stay competitive in the evolving educational landscape.

THE FUTURE OF AI IN MICRO-CREDENTIALING

As artificial intelligence continues to advance, its role in micro-credentialing is expected to grow, transforming how learning experiences are designed, delivered, and supported. Future developments in AI for micro-credentials are likely to focus on further automating course creation, enhancing learner support systems, and enabling more personalized, data-driven learning paths. These advancements will play a crucial role in meeting the increasing demand for flexible, accessible, and targeted education in a rapidly changing job market.

Automation in Course Creation

The automation of course creation is set to become one of the most significant AI-driven innovations in micro-credentialing. While AI tools like ChatGPT are already being used to generate lesson plans and assessments, future developments could take automation even further by creating entire learning modules that are not only content-rich but also pedagogically sound. AI could analyze industry trends, skills gaps, and job market data to develop micro-credential programs that are highly responsive to the evolving needs of employers and learners alike.

In this future scenario, AI could automatically curate learning content from a vast array of online resources, generate tailored assessments, and update course materials in real-time to reflect the latest developments in the field. For instance, as industries shift and new technologies emerge, AI could autonomously create new micro-credentials or update existing ones to ensure learners are always equipped with the most current skills. This would significantly reduce the time required for educators to design and launch new programs, allowing institutions to stay agile in an increasingly competitive education landscape.

Enhanced Learner Support Systems

Another area of future development in AI is the enhancement of learner support systems. AI-driven chatbots and virtual assistants, which are already being deployed to handle routine queries, are expected to become more sophisticated, offering personalized guidance, mentorship, and emotional support. These AI systems could monitor learner progress in real-time, identify when students are struggling, and proactively intervene with suggestions for additional resources or personalized study plans. As AI systems continue to improve their ability to understand and interpret learner emotions and behaviors, they could even provide motivational support, helping learners stay engaged and motivated throughout the course.

A report by the World Economic Forum (2020) predicted that AI will play a critical role in the future of education by enabling 24/7 support and automating many administrative and advisory tasks. This would not only improve learner satisfaction but also reduce the burden on educators, allowing them to focus on higher-value tasks such as mentoring and curriculum development. For micro-credential programs, these enhanced AI-driven support systems could help address some of the most common barriers to completion, such as disengagement and lack of motivation, ensuring that learners remain on track.

Data-Driven Personalization

As AI continues to evolve, its capacity for data-driven personalization will likely expand. Future AI systems could analyze vast amounts of learner data to create hyper-personalized learning experiences that adapt in real-time to each learner's progress, preferences, and goals. This level of personalization would go beyond what is currently possible, offering not only customized content and assessments but also personalized learning pathways that are entirely unique to each learner.

For example, an AI system could track a learner's interactions across multiple micro-credential programs, building a detailed profile of their strengths, weaknesses, and learning preferences. Based on this data, the AI could recommend additional micro-credentials, suggest optimal learning sequences, or even create interdisciplinary learning pathways that align with the learner's career aspirations. This would allow micro-credential programs to offer highly tailored educational experiences that are both efficient and effective, improving learner outcomes and increasing the value of the credentials.

AI and the Future Job Market

The future of AI in micro-credentialing is also closely tied to the future of work. As AI continues to reshape industries and job roles, micro-credential programs will need to stay ahead of these changes by offering timely and relevant skills training. AI's ability to analyze job market trends and predict future skills requirements will be critical in this regard. By continuously monitoring the global job market and identifying emerging skills, AI can help educational institutions design micro-credential programs that are aligned with future employment opportunities.

A report by PwC in 2018 already predicted that AI will have a profound impact on the future job market, with up to 30% of jobs being automated by 2030. In this context, micro-credentials will become an essential tool for individuals seeking to remain competitive in the workforce. AI-driven micro-credentialing systems will be able to adapt rapidly to these changes, offering learners the opportunity to acquire the skills they need to thrive in an AI-dominated job market.

Expert Predictions on AI in Education

Experts in the field of educational technology are optimistic about the potential of AI to revolutionize micro-credentialing. A report by UNESCO (2021) highlights the importance of AI in creating more equitable and accessible education systems, particularly in the context of lifelong learning and upskilling. The report emphasizes that AI has the potential to democratize access to education by providing affordable, scalable, and high-quality learning opportunities to individuals across the globe.

Similarly, a study by the Brookings Institution (2020) suggests that AI will be instrumental in addressing the global skills gap by enabling personalized, on-demand learning experiences that are tailored to the needs of the modern workforce. As AI technologies continue to improve, the ability to offer micro-credentials that are both personalized and scalable will become increasingly important in addressing the diverse educational needs of learners around the world.

ETHICAL USE OF AI IN MICRO-CREDENTIALS

As artificial intelligence becomes increasingly integrated into micro-credentialing programs, it is crucial to consider the ethical implications of using AI to shape learning experiences. While AI holds great promise in terms of scalability, personalization, and efficiency, there are also significant concerns related to bias, transparency, and fairness that must be addressed to ensure ethical use. These issues have the potential to affect both the credibility of micro-credentials and the learning outcomes of participants.

Bias in AI-Generated Content

One of the most pressing ethical concerns in AI-driven learning environments is the potential for bias in the content and assessments generated by AI systems. AI models, such as those used to create personalized learning paths or assessments, are trained on vast datasets that reflect real-world behaviors and decisions. However, these datasets often contain historical biases that can be inadvertently reproduced by the AI, leading to unfair or discriminatory outcomes (Ferrara, 2023). For instance, if an AI system is trained on data from traditional educational settings, it may prioritize learning styles or content that are more suited to certain groups of learners, while neglecting the needs of others.

In the context of micro-credentials, this bias can manifest in the form of unequal access to learning opportunities or misalignment between the content provided and the learner's actual needs. A UNESCO report on AI in education emphasizes the need for developers to actively address bias in AI models to prevent perpetuating inequalities. To ensure fairness, institutions offering AI-powered micro-credentials must rigorously audit their AI systems for potential biases and continuously update their models to reflect more diverse and inclusive data.

Transparency and Explainability

Transparency is another critical issue in the ethical use of AI in micro-credentials. Learners should have a clear understanding of how AI-generated content, assessments, and feedback are produced. However, many AI systems, particularly those based on complex machine learning models, are often described as "black boxes," meaning that the processes by which they arrive at certain decisions or recommendations are not easily understood, even by their developers (Denny et al., 2023). This lack of transparency raises concerns about the validity of AI-driven educational decisions and makes it difficult for learners to trust the feedback they receive or the fairness of the assessments.

For micro-credentials to maintain their credibility, educational institutions must ensure that the AI systems they deploy are explainable and transparent. Learners need to understand how the AI personalizes content, why certain recommendations are made, and how assessments are graded. The European Union's General Data Protection Regulation (GDPR) has also introduced a "right to explanation," which could apply to AI-driven systems in education, requiring institutions to provide clear and accessible explanations of how AI impacts the learner's experience (Habiba et al., 2024).

Fairness in AI-Driven Learning Environments

Fairness is a key ethical consideration when using AI in education. AI systems can inadvertently create disparities by favoring certain learners over others, particularly if the algorithm is optimized for specific types of learners or learning styles. This is particularly concerning in the context of micro-credentials, where learners often come from diverse professional backgrounds and have varying levels of prior knowledge. If AI systems are not designed with inclusivity in mind, they may disproportionately benefit some learners while disadvantaging others, exacerbating existing inequalities in access to education and opportunities for upskilling.

Research from the Brookings Institution (2020) highlights the importance of designing AI systems that promote fairness and inclusivity. In the context of micro-credentials, this could involve ensuring that AI-generated content is accessible to learners with different educational backgrounds, learning preferences, and technological proficiencies. Moreover, developers should consider how AI systems interact with learners from different socioeconomic, cultural, and linguistic backgrounds to avoid reinforcing systemic biases.

Accountability in AI-Driven Education

In addition to bias and fairness, there is the issue of accountability. Who is responsible when an AI system makes a mistake or delivers inaccurate feedback? In traditional education, instructors are accountable for the material they teach and the feedback they provide. However, in AI-driven environments, where much of the learning experience is automated, accountability becomes more ambiguous. Learners may not know who to turn to when they receive inaccurate feedback or feel that the system has misjudged their performance.

To address this, educational institutions must establish clear guidelines on the use of AI in micro-credentials and ensure that there is human oversight at critical points in the learning process. While AI can automate many tasks, human educators should remain involved to ensure that learners receive accurate, context-sensitive feedback and support. A hybrid model where AI handles routine tasks and instructors provide oversight and mentorship may offer the best balance between efficiency and accountability (Fengchun et al., 2021).

Data Privacy and Security

Finally, the ethical use of AI in micro-credentials also involves ensuring the privacy and security of learner data. AI systems rely on vast amounts of personal data to provide personalized learning experiences, including data on learner performance, engagement, and preferences. This raises concerns about how learner data is collected, stored, and used, particularly in light of recent high-profile data breaches in both the educational and technology sectors.

Institutions offering AI-powered micro-credentials must prioritize data privacy and security, cnsuring that learners' personal information is protected and used ethically. This involves complying with data protection regulations, such as GDPR, and implementing robust security measures to prevent unauthorized access to learner data. Additionally, learners should have control over their data, including the ability to access, modify, or delete their information as needed.

ENSURING ACCOUNTABILITY AND TRANSPARENCY

In AI-powered micro-credential programs, ensuring accountability and transparency is crucial to maintaining the integrity of the educational experience. The integration of AI in education introduces new dynamics, where decisions—such as content creation, assessment grading, or feedback provision—are increasingly influenced by algorithms. This shift raises fundamental questions about the role of

AI in decision-making and the responsibility of institutions in ensuring that these systems operate fairly, ethically, and transparently.

Transparency in AI Systems

One of the core ethical concerns surrounding AI in education is the opacity of many AI systems, which are often perceived as "black boxes" that provide little insight into how decisions are made. For learners and educators alike, understanding how an AI system functions and what factors contribute to its decisions is essential. Lack of transparency can undermine trust in AI-generated outcomes, especially in high-stakes environments like credentialing, where learners' progress and qualifications depend on the system's decisions.

UNESCO's competency frameworks emphasize the need for transparency in AI-driven learning environments. Both the **AI Competency Framework for Teachers** and **AI Competency Framework for Students** stress the importance of building AI literacy, helping educators and students understand the principles behind AI algorithms and their potential limitations. These frameworks advocate for clear communication of how AI systems process data and make decisions, ensuring that learners are aware of the factors influencing their assessments and feedback.

Accountability in AI-Driven Education

Accountability refers to the responsibility of educators, institutions, and developers to ensure that AI systems are used ethically, and that errors or biases are addressed promptly. In the context of AI-powered micro-credentials, accountability becomes complex, as AI systems often take over tasks traditionally managed by humans, such as grading assessments or providing personalized content. However, when AI systems fail—either by producing biased content, providing inaccurate feedback, or misinterpreting learner needs—it is essential that there are clear lines of responsibility for rectifying these errors.

The **AI Competency Framework for Teachers** developed by UNESCO highlights the need for institutions to ensure that teachers remain actively involved in overseeing AI systems(391104eng). This framework advocates for maintaining human oversight in key educational decisions and for ensuring that teachers are equipped with the skills to identify and mitigate potential issues arising from AI use. This is critical for preserving human agency and ensuring that AI complements, rather than replaces, the role of educators.

In practical terms, institutions must develop clear policies that define who is accountable for the outcomes produced by AI systems. These policies should include mechanisms for addressing learner grievances and ensuring that errors in AI-generated assessments or content are corrected in a timely manner. As AI becomes more integrated into micro-credential programs, establishing robust accountability frameworks will be essential for maintaining learner trust and ensuring fairness in educational outcomes.

Balancing Automation with Human Oversight

One of the key challenges in using AI for micro-credentials is finding the right balance between automation and human oversight. While AI can efficiently handle many routine tasks, such as grading multiple-choice questions or recommending personalized learning paths, human educators play a vital role in providing context-sensitive guidance and addressing complex learner needs. The UNESCO frameworks emphasize the importance of maintaining this balance, ensuring that AI systems remain tools to support, rather than replace, human educators.

Institutions must therefore establish clear protocols for when and how human intervention is required in AI-driven micro-credential programs. For example, while AI may be capable of providing instant feedback on certain types of assessments, human educators should be involved in reviewing more complex, qualitative assessments, such as written essays or project-based assignments. This hybrid approach not only ensures accountability but also fosters a more nuanced and personalized learning experience for students.

In conclusion, ensuring accountability and transparency in AI-powered micro-credentials is critical to fostering trust and promoting ethical use of AI in education. By implementing transparent AI systems, establishing clear accountability structures, and balancing automation with human oversight, institutions can harness the benefits of AI while safeguarding the integrity of the learning process.

DISCUSSION/ANALYSIS

The integration of artificial intelligence into micro-credentialing holds vast potential, yet it also comes with its own set of challenges. By reflecting on both the successes and limitations observed in practice, particularly through initiatives like the Microcredential Pilot Courses, we can begin to understand how AI can best be leveraged to enhance learning outcomes. This section will explore how AI has influenced learner engagement, scalability, and ethics in micro-credential programs, while discussing the broader implications of these findings for the future of education.

Personalization and Engagement: AI as a Game-Changer

One of the most promising aspects of AI is its ability to personalize the learning experience. In traditional learning environments, content is often static, offering little flexibility to accommodate individual learning styles or paces. The integration of AI into micro-credential programs, however, is a significant step toward providing learners with tailored experiences that adapt in real-time to their needs.

The feedback from learners in the pilot courses underscored the importance of this adaptability. When AI-driven tools, like ChatGPT, were used to generate customized lesson plans or assessments, learners responded positively, noting that the content felt more relevant to their professional goals. This aligns with the growing body of research showing that personalized learning is key to keeping learners engaged, especially in online environments where disengagement is a common hurdle. Yet, while AI-driven personalization can enhance the learning journey, it's not a silver bullet. Many learners also emphasized the need for human touchpoints—mentorship, feedback, and nuanced support that AI cannot always provide.

The lesson here is clear: AI excels at creating efficiency and personalization at scale, but it must be balanced with meaningful human interaction to ensure learners feel connected and supported. For micro-credentials to truly succeed, AI should handle the routine tasks while educators focus on what they do best—providing context, inspiration, and guidance.

Scalability: AI as a Solution to Expanding Access

Scalability has always been a challenge for institutions seeking to expand their micro-credential offerings. Traditional methods of course design and delivery are often too labor-intensive to support rapid scaling, especially when addressing the needs of a growing, diverse learner population. AI offers an elegant solution to this challenge, allowing institutions to create and deliver high-quality content at scale without overburdening educators.

The pilot courses provided a glimpse into how AI can streamline the development and management of micro-credentials. Through the use of generative AI tools, educators were able to produce lesson plans, quizzes, and other instructional materials more quickly than they could manually. This efficiency allowed for faster course iterations, ensuring that the content remained up-to-date and relevant to industry trends. As micro-credential programs continue to expand, this kind of responsiveness will be critical in keeping learners equipped with the latest skills and knowledge.

However, scalability through AI isn't just about creating more courses—it's about ensuring that those courses maintain their quality as they grow. AI can help to manage large cohorts of learners by offering real-time feedback and adaptive learning paths. But just as with engagement, human oversight remains essential. The most successful programs will blend AI's ability to scale with educators' expertise in maintaining course quality and learner satisfaction.

Ethical Considerations: Navigating the Risks of AI

As much as AI can transform micro-credentials, it also brings with it ethical concerns that institutions must carefully navigate. Learner feedback from the pilot programs raised important questions about transparency and fairness, particularly regarding how AI-generated content and assessments were perceived.

AI systems, though powerful, are only as unbiased as the data on which they are trained. In the pilot courses, learners sometimes felt that the content generated by AI did not fully reflect their diverse professional backgrounds or learning preferences. This is a known issue in AI-driven education, where the risk of bias can inadvertently lead to uneven learning experiences. As more institutions adopt AI for micro-credentials, they must remain vigilant in auditing these systems to ensure that they serve all learners equitably.

Moreover, the transparency of AI systems remains a pressing issue. Many learners and educators alike are unaware of how AI algorithms arrive at decisions—whether in grading, feedback, or content delivery. To maintain trust in AI-powered micro-credential programs, it is crucial that institutions demystify these processes, offering clear explanations of how AI tools work and how their outputs are generated. This need for transparency ties into broader conversations about accountability: when an AI system makes an error or produces biased content, who is responsible? These are questions that must be addressed proactively as AI continues to reshape education.

IMPLICATIONS FOR THE FUTURE OF MICRO-CREDENTIALING

Looking forward, the lessons learned from AI integration in micro-credentials are likely to shape the future of these programs. While the technology enables unprecedented levels of personalization and scalability, it must be balanced with the human elements that make education meaningful. Learners still crave connection and support—things that AI, as advanced as it is, cannot fully replace.

The future of micro-credentials will likely involve a hybrid approach where AI handles the back-end logistics—automating content creation, personalizing assessments, and scaling course offerings—while educators focus on providing mentorship and deeper engagement. This dual approach can help institutions overcome the challenges of learner disengagement and low completion rates that were highlighted in the pilot courses, while also ensuring that education remains ethical, transparent, and fair for all.

As AI becomes more integral to education, the need for ongoing dialogue about its ethical use will only intensify. Institutions must develop robust frameworks that prioritize accountability and fairness, ensuring that AI serves as a tool to enhance learning rather than a force that inadvertently exacerbates inequalities. By addressing these challenges head-on, the potential for AI-powered micro-credentials to democratize education and make lifelong learning more accessible to all becomes a more attainable goal.

CONCLUSION AND RECOMMENDATIONS

The integration of artificial intelligence into micro-credentialing programs has opened up new possibilities for personalized learning, scalability, and efficiency. As we have explored throughout this chapter, AI tools like generative models offer institutions the ability to design, deliver, and scale micro-credentials in ways that were previously unimaginable. However, the journey is not without its challenges. The findings from the Microcredential Pilot Courses Report, alongside broader trends in AI-powered education, highlight the need for a balanced approach—one that leverages AI's strengths while maintaining the essential human elements of teaching and mentorship.

Key Insights

The ability of AI to personalize learning is one of its most valuable contributions to micro-credentials. By tailoring content and assessments to the individual learner's needs, AI can keep learners engaged and motivated, helping them complete their courses. However, the feedback from learners in the pilot courses makes it clear that AI alone cannot provide the level of support that many learners require. Personalization through AI is effective, but it needs to be complemented by human oversight and mentorship to ensure learners feel supported and connected throughout their journey.

Scalability is another area where AI has demonstrated great potential. As demand for micro-credentials grows, institutions need to be able to offer high-quality learning experiences to an increasingly diverse and widespread learner base. AI can help by automating content creation, streamlining administrative tasks, and managing large cohorts through adaptive learning technologies. But again, the human element remains critical—educators need to ensure that even as programs scale, the quality of the learning experience is not compromised.

The ethical considerations surrounding AI are perhaps the most complex challenge to navigate. Issues of bias, transparency, and accountability must be addressed to ensure that AI-driven micro-credentials remain fair and accessible to all learners. The concerns raised by learners in the pilot programs reflect broader conversations about the need for transparency in AI processes and the importance of safeguarding against biased or unfair outcomes. Institutions must continue to refine their AI systems, auditing them regularly and maintaining clear lines of accountability to ensure that AI enhances, rather than detracts from, the educational experience.

Recommendations

As institutions continue to explore the potential of AI in micro-credentialing, several key recommendations emerge from this analysis:

1. **Embrace a Hybrid Approach**: While AI excels at automating routine tasks and personalizing content at scale, it cannot replace the need for human interaction in education. Institutions should adopt a hybrid model where AI is used to handle administrative and content creation tasks, while educators focus on providing mentorship, feedback, and support. This balance will ensure that learners receive the personalized attention they need to succeed.
2. **Prioritize Transparency and Accountability**: Learners must understand how AI systems function and how decisions regarding their learning progress are made. Institutions should invest in making AI processes transparent, offering clear explanations of how AI-generated content, assessments, and feedback are created. Additionally, clear accountability structures need to be established to address any issues that arise from AI-driven decisions.
3. **Continuously Audit AI Systems for Bias**: Given the potential for bias in AI-generated content, it is crucial that institutions regularly audit their AI systems to ensure fairness and inclusivity. These audits should assess the diversity of the datasets used to train AI models and examine how well the system adapts to learners from different backgrounds. Any biases identified should be addressed promptly to maintain the integrity of the program.
4. **Enhance Learner Support Systems**: While AI can offer personalized learning paths and instant feedback, learners still require robust support systems to guide them through more complex challenges. Institutions should invest in AI-driven tools that complement, rather than replace, human support. AI-powered chatbots and virtual assistants can handle routine queries, but human educators should be available for deeper, context-sensitive interventions.

5. **Explore Future Applications of AI**: AI's role in micro-credentialing is still evolving, and there are many exciting possibilities on the horizon. Institutions should stay at the forefront of AI innovation, exploring new tools and technologies that can further enhance the learning experience. This might include AI systems capable of creating interdisciplinary learning pathways, curating content based on real-time industry trends, or even offering predictive insights into future job market needs.

Future Research

While much progress has been made in the integration of AI into micro-credential programs, several areas still warrant further exploration. Future research should focus on refining AI's role in personalized learning—particularly in understanding how AI can better anticipate and respond to individual learner needs. Additionally, more work is needed to explore how AI can be effectively used to support underserved or marginalized learner populations, ensuring that AI-driven education is truly accessible to all.

There is also a growing need to examine the long-term impact of AI-powered micro-credentials on learners' career trajectories. How well do AI-generated learning paths align with real-world job market demands? Are learners equipped with the skills they need to thrive in an AI-driven workforce? These are questions that future research must address as the role of AI in education continues to expand.

CONCLUSION

In conclusion, AI has the potential to revolutionize the way micro-credentials are designed, delivered, and scaled. By personalizing learning, automating routine tasks, and enhancing scalability, AI offers institutions a powerful tool for meeting the growing demand for flexible, accessible education. However, this transformation must be managed thoughtfully. Institutions must remain vigilant about the ethical implications of AI, ensuring that transparency, accountability, and fairness are at the forefront of every AI-driven initiative.

As AI continues to evolve, so too must our understanding of how to integrate it responsibly into education. By embracing both the opportunities and challenges of AI, institutions can create micro-credential programs that are not only scalable and efficient but also personalized, equitable, and deeply human.

REFERENCES

Albus, P. (2023). *Virtual reality in education: Impact of instructional design on learning outcomes and cognitive load.* https://oparu.uni-ulm.de/items/bc0bc5f9-464e-45c4-b6c1-811a90e5b852

Alves, P., Lopes, A., Cruz-Correia, R., & Menezes, I. (2024). The interrupted journey: Factors and processes related to withdrawal, re-enrolment and dropout from doctoral education. *Higher Education*, 88(1), 225–242. DOI: 10.1007/s10734-023-01113-w

Banerjee, P. (Dr) M., Sinha, P. (Dr) S., & Pandey, D. P. (2024). *ARTIFICIAL INTELLIGENCE IN EDUCATION: REVOLUTIONIZING LEARNING AND TEACHING.* Red Unicorn Publishing.

Binhammad, M. H. Y., Othman, A., Abuljadayel, L., Mheiri, H. A., Alkaabi, M., & Almarri, M. (2024). Investigating How Generative AI Can Create Personalized Learning Materials Tailored to Individual Student Needs. *Creative Education*, 15(7), 7. Advance online publication. DOI: 10.4236/ce.2024.157091

Bosch, E., & Spinath, B. (2023). Students' Motivation in an Online and a Face-To-Face Semester: A Comparison of Initial Level, Development, and Use of Learning Activities. *Zeitschrift für Psychologie*, 231(2), 93–102. DOI: 10.1027/2151-2604/a000519

Brown, M., Nic Giolla Mhichíl, M., Beirne, E., & Mac Lochlainn, C. (2021). *The Global Micro-credential Landscape: Charting a New Credential Ecology for Lifelong Learning*. http://hdl.handle.net/11599/3894

Bryant, J., Heitz, C., Sanghvi, S., & Wagle, D. (2018). *How artificial intelligence will impact K-12 teachers.*

Chen, A. M. H., Brown, S., Mark, K., & McBane, S. (2023). An overview of Instructional approaches and decision-making strategies to curtail curricular overload. *American Journal of Pharmaceutical Education*, 87(8), 100013. DOI: 10.1016/j.ajpe.2022.12.001 PMID: 37597910

Chen, L., Chen, P., & Lin, Z. (2020). Artificial Intelligence in Education: A Review. *IEEE Access, 8*, 75264–75278. IEEE Access. DOI: 10.1109/ACCESS.2020.2988510

Chinta, S. V., Wang, Z., Yin, Z., Hoang, N., Gonzalez, M., Quy, T. L., & Zhang, W. (2024). *FairAIED: Navigating Fairness, Bias, and Ethics in Educational AI Applications* (arXiv:2407.18745). arXiv. https://doi.org//arXiv.2407.18745DOI: 10.48550

Dennen, V. P., & Burner, K. J. (2007). The Cognitive Apprenticeship Model in Educational Practice. In *Handbook of Research on Educational Communications and Technology* (3rd ed.). Routledge.

Denny, P., Khosravi, H., Hellas, A., Leinonen, J., & Sarsa, S. (2023). *Can We Trust AI-Generated Educational Content? Comparative Analysis of Human and AI-Generated Learning Resources* (arXiv:2306.10509). arXiv. http://arxiv.org/abs/2306.10509

Farikah, F., Astuty, A., Mazid, S., & Mulyani, M. (2023). *Student Engagement in Virtual Learning: The Self-Determination Theory Perspective* (SSRN Scholarly Paper 4593589). Social Science Research Network. https://papers.ssrn.com/sol3/papers.cfm?abstract_id=4593589

Fengchun, M., Wayne, H., Huang, R., Zhang, H., & UNESCO. (2021). *AI and education: A guidance for policymakers*. UNESCO Publishing.

Ferrara, E. (2023). Fairness and Bias in Artificial Intelligence: A Brief Survey of Sources, Impacts, and Mitigation Strategies. *Sci*, 6(1), 1. Advance online publication. DOI: 10.3390/sci6010003

Garrison, D. R., Anderson, T., & Archer, W. (1999). Critical Inquiry in a Text-Based Environment: Computer Conferencing in Higher Education. *The Internet and Higher Education*, 2(2–3), 87–105. DOI: 10.1016/S1096-7516(00)00016-6

Habiba, U.-E. -, Bogner, J., & Wagner, S. (2024). Towards Explainability as a Functional Requirement: A Vision to Integrate the Legal, End-User, and ML Engineer Perspectives. *Proceedings of the 2nd International Workshop on Responsible AI Engineering*, 16–19. DOI: 10.1145/3643691.3648590

Hall, T. E., Meyer, A., & Rose, D. H. (2012). *Universal Design for Learning in the Classroom: Practical Applications*. Guilford Press.

Hamilton, N. (2023). From Dropout to Doctorate: A Phenomenology of the Self-Determination of Individuals who Persisted to Completion. *Doctoral Dissertations and Projects*. https://digitalcommons.liberty.edu/doctoral/4166

Iraj, H., Fudge, A., Khan, H., Faulkner, M., Pardo, A., & Kovanovic, V. (2021). ERIC - EJ1325384 - Narrowing the Feedback Gap: Examining Student Engagement with Personalized and Actionable Feedback Messages. *Journal of Learning Analytics*, 202, •••. https://eric.ed.gov/?id=EJ1325384

Jdidou, Y., & Aammou, S. (2024). TRANSFORMING EDUCATION WITH AI: THE ROLE OF RECOMMENDATION SYSTEMS IN PERSONALIZED LEARNING. *EDULEARN24 Proceedings*, 7662–7669. DOI: 10.21125/edulearn.2024.1801

Kaswan, K. S., Dhatterwal, J. S., & Ojha, R. P. (2024). AI in personalized learning. In *Advances in Technological Innovations in Higher Education*. CRC Press. DOI: 10.1201/9781003376699-9

Keller, J. M. (1987). Development and use of the ARCS model of instructional design. *Journal of Instructional Development : JID*, 10(3), 2–10. DOI: 10.1007/BF02905780

Kember, D., Trimble, A., & Fan, S. (2023). An Investigation of the Forms of Support Needed to Promote the Retention and Success of Online Students. *American Journal of Distance Education*, 37(3), 169–184. DOI: 10.1080/08923647.2022.2061235

Kizito, O., & Kayi, O. Modest. (2024). *Global Perspectives on Micro-Learning and Micro-Credentials in Higher Education*. IGI Global.

Luckin, R., Holmes, W., & Forcier, L. B. (2016). *An argument for AI in Education*.

Marwan, S., Gao, G., Fisk, S., Price, T. W., & Barnes, T. (2020). Adaptive Immediate Feedback Can Improve Novice Programming Engagement and Intention to Persist in Computer Science. *Proceedings of the 2020 ACM Conference on International Computing Education Research*, 194–203. DOI: 10.1145/3372782.3406264

Moore, M. G. (1997). *Theory of transactional distance*. Routledge.

Murtaza, D. A., Fadare, S. A., Mocsir, O. M., Fadare, C., Natividad, L. R., Rafique, T., Akhtar, N., Shaheen, D. J., & Taj, R. (2024). From Theory To Practice: Harnessing Ai For Enhanced Teaching-Learning Dynamics. *Educational Administration: Theory and Practice*, 30(4), 6331–6338.

O'Dea, X., & O'Dea, M. (2023). Is Artificial Intelligence Really the Next Big Thing in Learning and Teaching in Higher Education? A Conceptual Paper. *Journal of University Teaching & Learning Practice*, 20(5), 5. Advance online publication. DOI: 10.53761/1.20.5.06

Pandita, A., & Kiran, R. (2023). The Technology Interface and Student Engagement Are Significant Stimuli in Sustainable Student Satisfaction. *Sustainability (Basel)*, 15(10), 10. Advance online publication. DOI: 10.3390/su15107923

Pollard, V., & Vincent, A. (2022). Micro-credentials: A Postdigital Counternarrative. *Postdigital Science and Education*, 4(3), 843–859. DOI: 10.1007/s42438-022-00311-6

Prince, M., Felder, R., & Brent, R. (2020). ACTIVE STUDENT ENGAGEMENT IN ONLINE STEM CLASSES: APPROACHES AND RECOMMENDATIONS. *Advances in Engineering Education*, •••, 8.

Puustinen, M., & Pulkkinen, L. (2001). Models of Self-regulated Learning: A review. *Scandinavian Journal of Educational Research*, 45(3), 269–286. DOI: 10.1080/00313830120074206

Qi, X., Sun, G., & Yue, L. (2023). Applying Self-Optimised Feedback to a Learning Management System for Facilitating Personalised Learning Activities on Massive Open Online Courses. *Sustainability (Basel)*, 15(16), 12562. DOI: 10.3390/su151612562

Rane, N., Choudhary, S., & Rane, J. (2023). *Education 4.0 and 5.0: Integrating Artificial Intelligence (AI) for Personalized and Adaptive Learning* (SSRN Scholarly Paper 4638365). DOI: 10.2139/ssrn.4638365

Rof, A., Bikfalvi, A., & Marques, P. (2024). Exploring learner satisfaction and the effectiveness of microlearning in higher education. *The Internet and Higher Education*, 62, 100952. DOI: 10.1016/j.iheduc.2024.100952

Rueda-Gómez, K. L., Rodríguez-Muñiz, L. J., & Muñiz-Rodríguez, L. (2024). Factors that mediate the success of the use of online platforms to support learning: The view of university teachers. *Education and Information Technologies*, 29(2), 2459–2482. DOI: 10.1007/s10639-023-11916-0

Ruiz-Rojas, L. I., Acosta-Vargas, P., De-Moreta-Llovet, J., & Gonzalez-Rodriguez, M. (2023). Empowering Education with Generative Artificial Intelligence Tools: Approach with an Instructional Design Matrix. *Sustainability (Basel)*, 15(15), 15. Advance online publication. DOI: 10.3390/su151511524

Sailer, M., & Homner, L. (2020). The Gamification of Learning: A Meta-analysis. *Educational Psychology Review*, 32(1), 77–112. DOI: 10.1007/s10648-019-09498-w

Sardabi, N., Kia, M., & Ghajarieh, A. (2023). *The Role of Motivational Strategies on Young EFL Learners' Basic Psychological Needs: A Self-Determination Theory Perspective*. DOI: 10.30479/jmrels.2022.17055.2042

Sepulveda, T. A. C. (2020). *Development of a System Architecture for the Prediction of Student Success using Machine Learning Techniques—ProQuest* [MISSOURI UNIVERSITY OF SCIENCE AND TECHNOLOGY]. https://www.proquest.com/openview/9f61bd7c4ab8f6b2c90abe399fb21fc3/1?pq-origsite=gscholar&cbl=18750&diss=y

Singh, S. V., & Hiran, K. K. (2022). The Impact of AI on Teaching and Learning in Higher Education Technology. *Journal of Higher Education Theory and Practice*, 22(13), 13. https://articlearchives.co/index.php/JHETP/article/view/3553

Siregar, T. (2024). *Differentiated Instruction from the Perspective of Cognitive Load Theory*.

Sitar-Tăut, D.-A., Mican, D., & Moisescu, O.-I. (2024). To be (online) or not to be? The antecedents of online study propensity and e-learning-dependent dropout intention in higher education. *Technological Forecasting and Social Change*, 207, 123566. DOI: 10.1016/j.techfore.2024.123566

Taiar, T. A. and R. (2023). *Human Interaction & Emerging Technologies (IHIET-AI 2023): Artificial Intelligence & Future Applications*. AHFE Conference.

Tamoliune, G., Greenspon, R., Tereseviciene, M., Volungeviciene, A., Trepule, E., & Dauksiene, E. (2023). *Frontiers | Exploring the potential of micro-credentials: A systematic literature review*. DOI: 10.3389/feduc.2022.1006811

Tebepah, I. R., & Ikeremo, E. S. (2024). *Comparative Review of Selected Adaptive e-Learning Platforms. 10*(5).

van der Vorst, T., & Jelicic, N. (2019). *Artificial Intelligence in Education: Can AI bring the full potential of personalized learning to education?*https://www.econstor.eu/handle/10419/205222

Van Wart, M., Ni, A., Medina, P., Canelon, J., Kordrostami, M., Zhang, J., & Liu, Y. (2020). Integrating students' perspectives about online learning: A hierarchy of factors. *International Journal of Educational Technology in Higher Education*, 17(1), 1. Advance online publication. DOI: 10.1186/s41239-020-00229-8 PMID: 34778515

Vashishth, T. K., Sharma, V., Sharma, K. K., Kumar, B., Panwar, R., & Chaudhary, S. (2024). AI-Driven Learning Analytics for Personalized Feedback and Assessment in Higher Education. In *Using Traditional Design Methods to Enhance AI-Driven Decision Making* (pp. 206–230). IGI Global., DOI: 10.4018/979-8-3693-0639-0.ch009

Vega, J., Rodriguez, M., Check, E., Moran, H., & Loo, L. (2024). Duolingo evolution: From automation to Artificial Intelligence. *2024 IEEE Colombian Conference on Applications of Computational Intelligence (ColCACI)*, 1–6. DOI: 10.1109/ColCACI63187.2024.10666523

Villar-Aguilés, A., & Muñoz-Rodríguez, D. (2024). Complex trajectories in higher education students: Online and face-to-face universities. *Journal of New Approaches in Educational Research*, 13(1), 4. DOI: 10.1007/s44322-023-00006-1

Wong, J., Baars, M., de Koning, B. B., & Paas, F. (2021). Examining the use of prompts to facilitate self-regulated learning in Massive Open Online Courses. *Computers in Human Behavior*, 115, 106596. DOI: 10.1016/j.chb.2020.106596

Zhang, X., & Tobias, T. C. R. (2023). Exploring the Efficacy of Adaptive Learning Technologies in Online Education: A Longitudinal Analysis of Student Engagement and Performance. *International Journal of Science and Engineering Applications*. DOI: 10.7753/IJSEA1212.1007

ADDITIONAL READING

Bryant, J., Heitz, C., Sanghvi, S., & Wagle, D. (2020). *How Artificial Intelligence Will Impact K-12 Teachers*. McKinsey & Company. https://cloudmails-my.sharepoint.com/personal/jonathanj_apu_edu_my/_layouts/15/onedrive.aspx?id=%2Fpersonal%2Fjonathanj%5Fapu%5Fedu%5Fmy%2FDocuments%2FDocuments%2FDLH%2FProjects%2FIGI%2FReading%2FHow%2Dartificial%2Dintelligence%2Dwill%2Dimpact%2DK%2D12%2Dteachers%20%2D%20McKinsey%2Epdf&parent=%2Fpersonal%2Fjonathanj%5Fapu%5Fedu%5Fmy%2FDocuments%2FDocuments%2FDLH%2FProjects%2FIGI%2FReading&ga=1

Manyika, J., Lund, S., Chui, M., Bughin, J., Woetzel, J., Batra, P., Ko, R., Sanghvi, S. (2017) *Jobs Lost, Jobs Gained: Workforce Transitions in a Time of Automation*. McKinsey & Company. https://cloudmails-my.sharepoint.com/personal/jonathanj_apu_edu_my/_layouts/15/onedrive.aspx?id=%2Fpersonal%2Fjonathanj%5Fapu%5Fedu%5Fmy%2FDocuments%2FDocuments%2FDLH%2FProjects%2FIGI%2FReading%2Fmgi%2Djobs%2Dlost%2Djobs%2Dgained%2Dreport%2Ddecember%2D6%2D2017%2Dupdated%2Epdf&parent=%2Fpersonal%2Fjonathanj%5Fapu%5Fedu%5Fmy%2FDocuments%2FDocuments%2FDLH%2FProjects%2FIGI%2FReading&ga=1

Okolo, C.T. (2023). *AI in the Global South: Opportunities & Challenges Towards more Inclusive Governance*. Brookings Report. https://cloudmails-my.sharepoint.com/personal/jonathanj_apu_edu_my/_layouts/15/onedrive.aspx?id=%2Fpersonal%2Fjonathanj%5Fapu%5Fedu%5Fmy%2FDocuments%2FDocuments%2FDLH%2FProjects%2FIGI%2FReading%2FAI%20in%20the%20Global%20South%5F%20Opportunities%20and%20challenges%20towards%20more%20inclusive%20governance%2Epdf&parent=%2Fpersonal%2Fjonathanj%5Fapu%5Fedu%5Fmy%2FDocuments%2FDocuments%2FDLH%2FProjects%2FIGI%2FReading&ga=1

UNESCO (2019). *Beijing Consensus on AI and Education.* https://cloudmails-my.sharepoint.com/personal/jonathanj_apu_edu_my/_layouts/15/onedrive.aspx?id=%2Fpersonal%2Fjonathanj%5Fapu%5Fedu%5Fmy%2FDocuments%2FDocuments%2FDLH%2FProjects%2FIGI%2FReading%2FBeijing%20Concensus%20on%20AI%20for%20Education%2Epdf&parent=%2Fpersonal%2Fjonathanj%5Fapu%5Fedu%5Fmy%2FDocuments%2FDocuments%2FDLH%2FProjects%2FIGI%2FReading&ga=1

UNESCO (2024). *AI Competencies for Students.* https://cloudmails-my.sharepoint.com/personal/jonathanj_apu_edu_my/_layouts/15/onedrive.aspx?id=%2Fpersonal%2Fjonathanj%5Fapu%5Fedu%5Fmy%2FDocuments%2FDocuments%2FDLH%2FProjects%2FIGI%2FReading%2FAI%20Competency%20%2D%20Students%2Epdf&parent=%2Fpersonal%2Fjonathanj%5Fapu%5Fedu%5Fmy%2FDocuments%2FDocuments%2FDLH%2FProjects%2FIGI%2FReading&ga=1

UNESCO (2024). *AI Competencies for Teachers.* https://cloudmails-my.sharepoint.com/personal/jonathanj_apu_edu_my/_layouts/15/onedrive.aspx?id=%2Fpersonal%2Fjonathanj%5Fapu%5Fedu%5Fmy%2FDocuments%2FDocuments%2FDLH%2FProjects%2FIGI%2FReading%2FAI%20Competency%20%2D%20Teachers%2Epdf&parent=%2Fpersonal%2Fjonathanj%5Fapu%5Fedu%5Fmy%2FDocuments%2FDocuments%2FDLH%2FProjects%2FIGI%2FReading&ga=1

World Economic Forum (2023). *Future of Jobs Report 2023.* https://cloudmails-my.sharepoint.com/personal/jonathanj_apu_edu_my/_layouts/15/onedrive.aspx?id=%2Fpersonal%2Fjonathanj%5Fapu%5Fedu%5Fmy%2FDocuments%2FDocuments%2FDLH%2FProjects%2FIGI%2FReading%2FWEF%5FFuture%5Fof%5FJobs%5F2023%2Epdf&parent=%2Fpersonal%2Fjonathanj%5Fapu%5Fedu%5Fmy%2FDocuments%2FDocuments%2FDLH%2FProjects%2FIGI%2FReading&ga=1

KEY TERMS AND DEFINITIONS

Accountability in AI: The responsibility of institutions to ensure that AI-driven educational tools operate fairly, transparently, and ethically, with mechanisms for correcting errors.

Adaptive Learning: An AI-driven educational method that adjusts the difficulty and content in real-time based on the learner's performance, ensuring a balanced and engaging experience.

Autonomy in Learning: Providing learners with control over aspects of their learning journey, such as pacing and content, which can increase motivation but also poses risks of disengagement without structure.

Bias in AI: The unintended yet pervasive tendency of AI models to produce unfair or skewed outputs due to inherent biases in training data, affecting educational outcomes.

Cognitive Load Theory: A principle suggesting that instructional content should be designed to avoid overwhelming learners with information, supporting better understanding and retention.

Community of Inquiry (CoI) Framework: A model for creating engaging online learning experiences by fostering cognitive, teaching, and social presence within a virtual learning environment.

Feedback Mechanism: Systems, often powered by AI, that provide real-time, tailored responses to learners, helping them understand mistakes and stay motivated.

Generative AI: A subset of artificial intelligence that creates new content, such as text, images, or learning materials, based on input prompts, allowing personalized and dynamic educational experiences.

Learner Engagement: The level of attention, motivation, and interaction a learner demonstrates throughout a course, significantly impacting course completion and success.

Micro-credentials: Short, targeted courses that provide focused learning on specific skills or competencies, ideal for flexible, career-oriented upskilling or reskilling.

Personalized Learning: A customized educational approach where learning materials, pace, and assessments are tailored to meet each learner's unique needs and goals.

Scalability: The ability of a program to grow and accommodate more learners without sacrificing quality or requiring extensive additional resources.

Self-Determination Theory (SDT): A theory emphasizing that learning is more effective when individuals feel a sense of autonomy, competence, and connection within the educational environment.

Transparency in AI: The practice of making AI processes understandable to learners and educators, ensuring clarity in how content and assessments are generated.

Universal Design for Learning (UDL): An educational framework promoting the development of flexible learning environments that accommodate diverse learners, supporting engagement and inclusivity.

Chapter 9
Harnessing AI and Digital Tools for Micro-Credentialing in Mathematics Education:
Enhancing Learning Outcomes for Students With Learning Difficulties

Georgiois Vasileios Polydoros
https://orcid.org/0000-0002-0924-5923
University of Thessaly, Greece

ABSTRACT

Understanding decimal place value is a key challenge for students with Learning Difficulties (LD) in mathematics. This study explores the impact of AI-powered ChatGPT, on enhancing learning during the COVID-19 pandemic. Fifty-four sixth-grade students with learning difficulties from six Greek elementary schools engaged with the interactive platforms Khan Academy and DreamBox, with personalized support from ChatGPT. Results revealed significant improvements in decimal place value comprehension post-intervention. Additionally, this research investigated how AI-powered adaptive platforms enhance the effectiveness of micro-credentials in certifying student achievements and upskilling mathematics teachers. The study highlights the potential of micro-credentials to improve pedagogy in technology-driven learning environments. By integrating AI tools and micro-credentials, this study offers insights into how educators can better support students with LD and the importance of micro-credentials in validating learning progress and advancing teachers' skills in the digital age.

DOI: 10.4018/979-8-3693-5488-9.ch009

INTRODUCTION

The rapid evolution of technology, particularly artificial intelligence (AI), has significantly transformed educational practices and approaches, particularly in mathematics education. In the wake of the COVID-19 pandemic, the necessity for adaptive and personalized learning experiences has become increasingly apparent, especially for students with learning disabilities. This demographic faces unique challenges that require tailored instructional methods to foster understanding and engagement in mathematical concepts (Dirani et al., 2020; Walpola & Lucas, 2021).

Effective educators enhance student performance, bridge gaps between advantaged and disadvantaged learners, and boost future earnings (Chetty et al., 2014). Consequently, significant investments have been made in professional development (PD) for teachers. Governments have also allocated billions for research to optimize professional development (Edovald & Nevill, 2021). This increased investment has led to more studies evaluating PD's influence on teaching quality and student learning, revealing modest positive effects. Yet, many schools lack access to evaluated PD programs, creating disparities in available resources. Research highlights significant variability in PD effectiveness based on design (Edovald & Nevill, 2021). Attempts to differentiate effective PD have seen limited progress. Despite abundant data on PD program impacts, clarity on effective PD differentiators remains elusive.

Micro-credentials, as a form of certification, have emerged as a promising strategy to recognize and validate the specific skills acquired by these students in AI-supported learning environments.

Micro-credentials offer a flexible and targeted approach to learning assessment, catering to the diverse needs of students (Gauthier, 2020). They serve as formal recognition of the competencies developed through adaptive learning technologies, enhancing the employability and academic progression of students with learning disabilities (Msweli et al., 2022). The integration of micro-credentials in mathematics education not only supports personalized learning pathways but also promotes self-efficacy and motivation among students, vital components for successful learning outcomes.

Micro-credentials are becoming an increasingly important part of education, particularly in the digital and AI-enhanced learning environments designed to support students with learning difficulties. Micro-credentials offer a way to certify the acquisition of specific skills and knowledge, often through smaller, focused learning modules. In the context of students with learning disabilities, particularly during the COVID-19 pandemic, micro-credentials can be used to recognize the achievements of students who engage with AI-powered educational tools and digital platforms. These tools help personalize learning and offer real-time feedback, enhancing student engagement and learning outcomes.

AI and digital tools like ChatGPT, alongside platforms such as Khan Academy and DreamBox, provide tailored instruction in areas like understanding decimal place values, an essential skill in mathematics. Through these tools, students with learning difficulties can receive structured support, allowing them to progress at their own pace. Integrating micro-credentials in this context would allow educators to formalize the recognition of students' achievements in mastering specific mathematical concepts, thus motivating learners and providing them with tangible proof of their success.

Studies in the field of micro-credentials emphasize their flexibility and scalability, which is especially beneficial for students with learning disabilities. The design of these programs often incorporates backward-design methodology, focusing on learning outcomes and assessment strategies that reflect industry-relevant skills. This can include competency-based assessments that are aligned with real-world applications of knowledge, fostering a deeper understanding of mathematical concepts for students with disabilities (Hughes et al., 2023).

Moreover, micro-credentials offer a structured pathway for personalized learning experiences, where students with learning difficulties can earn recognition for mastering smaller units of learning. This helps break down traditional barriers to academic success, especially during disruptions like the pandemic. The use of AI tools in education thus supports both, enhancing students' ability to learn in ways that align with their unique needs and pace (Freeman-Green et al., 2023).

Research Purpose

The purpose of this study is to examine how AI-powered adaptive learning platforms enhance the effectiveness of micro-credentials in mathematics education. It also aims to explore the role of micro-credentials in certifying the learning achievements of students with learning disabilities during AI-supported mathematics instruction. Additionally, the research investigates whether micro-credentials can be used to upskill or reskill mathematics teachers in the digital age, focusing on their potential to improve pedagogical practices and address the evolving demands of technology-enhanced learning environments.

Research Questions

1. How do AI-powered adaptive learning platforms enhance the effectiveness of micro-credentials in mathematics education?
2. What role do micro-credentials play in certifying the learning achievements of students with learning disabilities during AI-supported mathematics instruction?

3. Can micro-credentials in mathematics be used to upskill or reskill mathematics teachers in the digital age?

By incorporating micro-credentials into educational frameworks for students with learning disabilities, schools can better track progress and provide more targeted support, ensuring that learners are recognized for their incremental achievements. This approach encourages continuous learning and provides students with the skills they need to succeed in both academic and practical contexts.

LITERATURE REVIEW

Micro-credentials are gaining attention in higher education, especially within institutions aiming to offer personalized learning pathways that align with labor market demands (European Commission, 2020; Kato et al., 2020). These credentials cater to students and lifelong learners who may not have access to traditional degrees (Msweli et al., 2022; Ehlers, 2018). They are central to the European HE skills agenda (European Commission, 2021) and are being implemented by pan-European HE alliances (Fischer et al., 2022). Typically, micro-credentials support the concept of "unbundling" education for more flexible learning (MicroHE Consortium, 2019; Oliver, 2019; Rossiter & Tynan, 2019).

Definitions vary, often highlighting "proof-of-learning" via documented skills and competencies (ECIU, 2021; Ellis et al., 2016; European Commission, 2020; Oliver, 2019). Some view them as modular learning programs (Kato et al., 2020), while others emphasize managing digital portfolios of credentials (Kiiskilä et al., 2022). In Europe, the European Council's approach emphasizes learning outcomes under ECTS and the portability of credentials (European Commission, 2022).

Research on micro-credentials is expanding, focusing on employer and professional perspectives, practical barriers, and benefits across the U.S., England, New Zealand, and Europe (Gauthier, 2020; Young et al., 2019; Kato et al., 2020). However, unpredictable technological and policy shifts have impacted widespread adoption (Mac Lochlainn et al., 2022; Fisher & Leder, 2022). This study takes a foresight approach to examine factors enabling adoption of micro-credentials, contributing to strategic planning aligned with international policy and rapid technological advancements.

The World Economic Forum (2020) forecasts that within the next decade, automation will significantly alter half of all jobs following the COVID-19 pandemic. If this projection holds true, the current workforce, irrespective of their existing qualifications, will have to rapidly acquire new skills or enhance their current ones. The report on the European Approach to Micro-credentials (European Commission, 2020) indicates that the need for short learning pathways, alongside their acknowledgment and validation, is expected to rise as a means of achieving sustainable recovery from the COVID-19 crisis within the social and economic spheres, as well as promoting innovations in higher education.

Since the onset of the pandemic, there has been an unprecedented increase in the demand for online education (CEDEFOP, 2020), prompting a significant expansion of online learning options and micro-credentials (Orr et al., 2020). These developments have posed challenges and created new requirements for the higher education sector, as traditional degree programs could no longer adequately address labor market demands (Gauthier, 2020) or meet the needs of individuals seeking professional development. Researchers have confirmed that the pandemic has accelerated the necessity for developing new competencies (Dirani et al., 2020; Reedy et al., 2021; Walpola & Lucas, 2021) and professional development that is "personalized, competency-based, flexible, and collaborative" (Hunt et al., 2020, p. 34). Enhancing skills to adapt to the rapidly changing economic landscape and transitioning to online learning have become essential strategies for global recovery and economic resilience in the post-COVID era (Davidson, 2020). As a result, higher education institutions (HEIs) worldwide face urgent challenges in adapting to these changes.

Micro-credentials offer a targeted means to validate competencies clearly and enhance employability, providing HEIs with opportunities to develop this area as both providers (Porter & Perris, 2021) and innovators. However, recent studies raise concerns that micro-credentials may shift traditional full-course curricula toward more competency-based and work-related structures solely to meet the increasing demand for skilled workers (Ralston, 2021; Desmarchelier and Cary, 2022). Critics warn that such transformations might lead to the commercialization of higher education, potentially resulting in a "moral hazard" (Ralston, 2021, p. 95). While acknowledging the potential risks and challenges associated with micro-credentials in higher education, this paper aims to highlight their potential to drive social, economic, and educational innovations. For the purposes of this discussion, "higher education sector" encompasses universities and universities of applied sciences.

An increasing number of studies have been conducted to explore the emerging impact of micro-credentials from social (Desmarchelier & Cary, 2022; Msweli et al., 2022), economic (Gauthier, 2020; Wheelahan & Moodie, 2021), and professional development perspectives (Hunt et al., 2020; Zhang & West, 2020). It is observed that there is a fine line in the current literature regarding the implications of micro-credentials for social and economic recovery, as these contexts are closely interconnected (Davidson, 2020; Oliver, 2021). This interrelationship indicates that both aspects should be regarded as equally significant. Despite an increasing volume of publications, this paper argues that a more integrative research approach is necessary, one that holistically examines the key drivers and multiple dimensions of micro-credentials. A systematic literature review was selected as an appropriate methodology for summarizing and synthesizing this body of knowledge.

The integration of artificial intelligence (AI) in educational settings has garnered significant attention in recent years, particularly regarding its potential to support students with learning difficulties. Studies show that adaptive learning platforms, such as Khan Academy and DreamBox, are effective in enhancing mathematical comprehension among students who struggle with conventional learning methods (Orr et al., 2020; Walpola & Lucas, 2021). These platforms leverage AI to personalize learning experiences, tailoring instruction to meet individual needs and thereby promoting engagement and achievement in subjects like mathematics, particularly in complex areas such as decimal place value (Gauthier, 2020).

Research indicates that personalized learning, enabled by AI, can positively impact student outcomes. For instance, adaptive learning technologies adjust instructional materials based on real-time student performance data, which helps in addressing specific learning gaps (Dirani et al., 2020; Reedy et al., 2021). This adaptability is especially beneficial for students with learning disabilities, as it allows them to progress at their own pace and receive immediate feedback, fostering a sense of accomplishment and motivation (Gauthier, 2020).

The concept of micro-credentials has emerged as a complementary approach to recognizing the achievements of students in technology-enhanced learning environments. Micro-credentials provide a formal mechanism for certifying specific competencies and skills acquired through these platforms, which is vital for enhancing employability and academic progression (Hunt et al., 2020). The European Approach to Micro-credentials report suggests that these credentials can help validate the personalized learning journeys of students, especially those with learning difficulties, thereby ensuring their achievements are acknowledged (European Commission, 2020).

Moreover, the professional development of educators is crucial in maximizing the benefits of AI and micro-credentials in mathematics education. As the educational landscape shifts towards more technology-driven methods, there is a pressing need for teachers to upskill and reskill to effectively leverage these tools in their instruction (Ralston, 2021; Wheelahan & Moodie, 2021). Micro-credentials offer a flexible framework for ongoing professional development, enabling teachers to gain new competencies relevant to digital pedagogy (Desmarchelier & Cary, 2022). This dual focus on both student and teacher development highlights the potential of integrating technology and innovative credentialing systems in education.

Despite the promising findings, there are concerns regarding the commercialization of education through the proliferation of micro-credentials, which may lead to a focus on competencies at the expense of broader educational values (Oliver, 2021). Critics caution that an overemphasis on employability could undermine the holistic nature of education, emphasizing the need for careful implementation of micro-credentialing frameworks that align with educational goals.

In summary, the literature underscores the transformative potential of AI-powered adaptive platforms and micro-credentials in enhancing the educational experience for students with learning difficulties while simultaneously supporting the professional development of mathematics teachers. This research contributes to the ongoing discourse on leveraging technology to foster inclusive and effective learning environments, suggesting that the strategic integration of these elements can lead to improved educational outcomes. Further investigation into the implications and effectiveness of these technologies in diverse educational contexts is warranted to fully understand their impact on learning and teaching in mathematics.

METHODOLOGY

Research Design

This study employed a convergent mixed-methods design (Creswell & Clark, 2007), a quasi-experimental design with pre-test and post-test measures to assess the impact of digital tools, including AI-powered support like ChatGPT, on improving students' understanding of decimal place value. The intervention was conducted over four weeks during the Covid-19 pandemic, a period when in-person schooling was not possible, thus necessitating a digital approach to teaching. In addition, the study incorporated qualitative interviews with 12 participating mathematics teachers.

Participants

Participants included 54 Greek students from the fourth grade, all identified with LD in mathematics, and were selected based on criteria such as low performance in previous mathematics assessments and teacher recommendations. The sample consisted of both male and female students, ensuring a balanced representation. The students were divided into smaller groups based on their respective schools, and all lessons took place in each school's computer lab under the supervision of trained educators. Each student worked individually at their own computer workstation to ensure focused engagement with the materials. In addition to the student outcomes, the study incorporated qualitative interviews with 12 participating mathematics teachers.

Tools and Digital Resources

The digital tools utilized in this study included:

- Khan Academy Videos: These instructional videos provided foundational knowledge on decimal place value through step-by-step explanations and visual demonstrations.
- DreamBox Applications: An educational platform offering interactive learning modules that reinforce students' understanding of mathematical concepts through adaptive activities.
- ChatGPT: An AI-powered language model was used to provide personalized learning support. ChatGPT assisted students by answering questions, offering hints during exercises, and giving feedback on their progress, allowing for a more tailored learning experience.

These tools were selected to create a comprehensive learning environment, combining interactive content, adaptive learning, and AI-based tutoring.

Procedure

The study was conducted over four weeks, with students participating in three online sessions per week. Each session lasted approximately 60 minutes. During these sessions, students accessed the Khan Academy videos and Dream Box applications through their computers and received additional support through ChatGPT. The lessons were designed to cover key concepts of decimal place value, including understanding tenths, hundredths, and the relationship between decimals and fractions. In addition a parallel four week micro-credential program utilized. In addition 12 teachers participated in this program.

The sessions followed an inquiry-based teaching approach structured in six phases (Grangeat, 2016):

1. Engage: Introduction of decimal concepts through real-life examples and videos.
2. Explore: Hands-on activities with DreamBox applications, where students manipulated digital coins to understand decimals.
3. Explain: Use of ChatGPT to clarify questions and provide explanations on concepts.
4. Elaborate: Practice exercises on the Dream Box platform to deepen understanding.
5. Evaluate: Students took weekly quizzes on their understanding of decimal concepts, with ChatGPT providing immediate feedback.

6. Extend: Activities that connected decimal understanding to everyday contexts, like measuring distances or comparing prices.

Data Collection and Analysis

Data collection included a pre-test administered at the beginning of the intervention and a post-test at the end of the four-week period. The tests were designed to measure students' understanding of decimal place value, including tasks that assessed their ability to identify, compare, and operate with decimal numbers. The tests were administered digitally, allowing for standardized assessment across all participating schools.

Additionally, data from the interactive learning sessions, including students' progress in Dream Box and ChatGPT interaction logs, were collected to provide insights into their engagement and learning patterns. Feedback from the supervising educators was also gathered to evaluate the effectiveness of the digital tools and AI support in fostering student comprehension.

Statistical Analysis

The data were analyzed using paired t-tests to compare pre-test and post-test scores, determining the effectiveness of the intervention in improving students' understanding of decimal place value. Descriptive statistics were used to summarize students' performance and engagement with the digital tools. The significance level was set at $p < 0.05$. Additionally, qualitative data from interaction logs with ChatGPT were analyzed to identify common challenges and areas where AI support was particularly effective in assisting students.

Ethical Considerations

This study adhered to ethical standards, ensuring that all participating students and their guardians provided informed consent. The anonymity and confidentiality of student data were maintained throughout the study. The use of ChatGPT was monitored by educators to ensure appropriate interactions and to prevent over-reliance on the AI for answering exercises.

Table 1 is summarizing the demographic data of the teachers coded A, B, C, D, etc. Table summarizes the age, gender, experience, school type, and area of expertise of the 12 teachers who participated in the thematic analysis.

Table 1. Teachers demographic data

Teacher Code	Age	Gender	Years of Experience	School Type	Area of Expertise
A	34	Female	10	Public Elementary	Mathematics
B	42	Male	15	Private Elementary	Digital Learning
C	29	Female	5	Public Secondary	Mathematics
D	38	Male	12	Public Elementary	Educational Technology
E	45	Female	20	Private Secondary	Special Education
F	32	Male	7	Public Elementary	STEM Education
G	50	Female	25	Private Elementary	Mathematics
H	36	Male	11	Public Secondary	AI in Education
I	40	Female	18	Private Elementary	Mathematics
J	28	Female	6	Public Elementary	Digital Integration
K	39	Male	13	Private Secondary	Mathematics Instruction
L	35	Female	9	Public Secondary	Pedagogy and Curriculum

Thematic analysis based on the interviews of 12 teachers who participated in a micro-credential program. The table outlines the themes, their corresponding codes (Table 2).

Table 2. Thematic analysis, themes and corresponding codes

Theme	Codes
Pedagogical Shift	Innovative teaching methods, lesson design
Confidence with Digital Tools	Enhanced confidence, tool familiarity
Adaptability	Flexibility, curriculum integration
Professional Growth	Continuous learning, reskilling
Challenges Faced	Lack of time, resource limitations
Impact on Students	Improved engagement, better outcomes

This thematic analysis reveals key insights into how micro-credentials impacted teachers' instructional practices, confidence, and adaptability in using digital tools.

RESULTS

Quantitative Research Results

The quantitative research results were based on data collected from pre- and post-tests measuring students' understanding of decimal place value. A paired-sample t-test was conducted to assess whether there was a statistically significant improvement in decimal place value comprehension following the intervention.

Pre- and Post-Test Data Description

The 54 students were initially assessed with a pre-test to establish baseline knowledge in decimal place value. Following the eight-week intervention using Khan Academy, DreamBox, and ChatGPT, a post-test was administered to measure any changes in comprehension.

Statistical Analysis

The paired-sample t-test results indicated a statistically significant improvement in students' scores. The mean score on the pre-test was $M = 58.4$ ($SD = 10.3$), while the mean score on the post-test increased to $M = 74.6$ ($SD = 9.8$). The increase in scores was statistically significant, $t(53) = 8.72$, $p < 0.001$, indicating that the intervention had a positive effect on students' understanding of decimal place value.

Effect Size

An effect size calculation (Cohen's d) revealed a large effect, $d = 1.2$, suggesting that the use of AI-powered tools had a substantial impact on improving students' comprehension of decimal place value.

Subgroup Analysis

To gain deeper insights into how AI-powered tools impacted different types of learners, additional analyses were conducted by dividing students into subgroups based on two main factors: their initial skill level (as measured by pre-test scores) and their engagement levels during the intervention period.

Initial Skill Level Subgroups

Students were grouped into three categories based on their pre-test performance.

-Low Initial Skill Level: Students scoring below 50% on the pre-test.
-Moderate Initial Skill Level: Students scoring between 50% and 70%.
-High Initial Skill Level: Students scoring above 70%.

Analysis revealed that students in the Low Initial Skill Level group demonstrated the most significant improvement, with an average increase of 20 points in their post-test scores, moving from an initial mean score of 42.8 to a post-test mean of 62.3. This improvement was notably higher than that of the Moderate and High Initial Skill Level groups, where the average gains were 12 points and 7 points, respectively. These findings suggest that AI-powered tools like ChatGPT, Khan Academy, and DreamBox may be particularly beneficial for students who initially struggle with mathematical concepts, providing targeted support that helps bridge knowledge gaps.

Engagement Level Subgroups

To assess the role of engagement, students were categorized based on their participation and interaction with the platforms, which was tracked through session logs and task completion rates:

High Engagement: Students who consistently interacted with the tools and completed more than 80% of assigned tasks.

Moderate Engagement: Students who completed between 50% and 80% of tasks.

Low Engagement: Students who completed less than 50% of tasks.

Results showed that students in the High Engagement group had the largest post-test gains, with an average improvement of 18 points. In contrast, the Moderate and Low Engagement groups had gains of 10 points and 5 points, respectively. These results indicate that consistent interaction with AI-powered learning tools may play a critical role in maximizing learning outcomes, reinforcing the importance of sustained engagement in technology-enhanced learning environments.

Conclusion of Subgroup Analysis

This subgroup analysis highlights that AI-powered digital tools are especially effective for students with lower initial skill levels, offering substantial learning gains through personalized and adaptive support. Additionally, the findings underscore the importance of high engagement levels in maximizing the educational benefits of these tools. These insights suggest that AI-powered platforms, when combined with strategies to foster sustained student engagement, can be an effective approach for supporting diverse learners, particularly those with initial learning challenges in mathematics.

Summary of Findings

The quantitative data demonstrates that AI-powered platforms like ChatGPT, when combined with interactive platforms like Khan Academy and DreamBox, can significantly enhance the understanding of decimal place value for students with learning difficulties. This suggests that AI-supported, adaptive learning environments hold promise for addressing specific challenges faced by these students in mathematics.

Results-Thematic Analysis

The thematic analysis of interviews with 12 teachers revealed several key findings regarding their experiences with micro-credentials:

1. Enhanced Instructional Practices
   - Teachers reported that micro-credentials provided targeted training, leading to improved instructional strategies.
   - Quote: "The micro-credential training gave me new strategies that I could implement immediately in my classroom." (Teachers B,C,D, J,K)
2. Increased Confidence in Digital Tools
   - Many teachers expressed greater confidence in integrating digital tools into their teaching after completing micro-credential courses.
   - Quote: "I feel much more capable of using technology effectively now." (Teachers A, B, D, E, F, H, K, L)
3. Adaptability to New Technologies
   - Teachers noted that the training helped them adapt more easily to new educational technologies and methodologies.
   - Quote: "With the skills I gained, adapting to new tools became much less daunting." (Teachers C, D, E, G, H, J, K, L)
4. Professional Growth and Development
   - Participants emphasized the importance of continuous professional development through micro-credentials, which contributed to their overall growth as educators.
   - Quote: "These credentials have been crucial for my development as a teacher." (Teachers A, B, C, G, H, I, J, K)
5. Collaboration and Community Building
   - Several teachers highlighted the collaborative aspect of micro-credential programs, which fostered a sense of community among educators.
   - Quote: "Working with other teachers during the training made the experience even better." (Teachers B, C, E, F, G, H, I, K, L)

Summary of Findings

Overall, the results indicate that micro-credentials play a significant role in upskilling mathematics teachers, enhancing their instructional practices, and improving their confidence and adaptability in a digital learning environment.

DISCUSSION

The results of this study contribute valuable insights into the role of AI-powered adaptive learning platforms and micro-credentials in mathematics education, particularly for students with learning disabilities (LD).

AI-Powered Adaptive Learning Platforms Enhance the Effectiveness of Micro-Credentials in Mathematics Education

AI-powered adaptive learning platforms, such as Khan Academy and DreamBox, personalize the learning experience by tailoring content to individual student needs. This adaptability is particularly crucial for students with learning disabilities, as it allows for differentiated instruction that can adjust based on real-time performance data. The integration of micro-credentials enhances this effect by providing targeted training for educators, ensuring they are equipped to leverage these tools effectively in their teaching (Hunt et al., 2020). Research shows that micro-credential programs foster collaborative learning communities among teachers, promoting the sharing of best practices and innovative strategies that can enhance the use of AI tools in classrooms (Desmarchelier & Cary, 2022).

Role of Micro-Credentials in Certifying the Learning Achievements of Students With Learning Disabilities During AI-Supported Mathematics Instruction

Micro-credentials serve as a formal mechanism to validate the competencies acquired by students, particularly those with learning disabilities, in an AI-supported learning environment. By documenting the specific skills learned through adaptive platforms, these credentials provide evidence of achievement that can enhance employability and academic progression (Gauthier, 2020). Furthermore, micro-credentials can address the personalized learning paths taken by students, ensuring that their unique accomplishments are recognized, which is critical for fostering self-efficacy and motivation (Walpola & Lucas, 2021).

Micro-Credentials in Mathematics Used to Upskill or Reskill Mathematics Teachers in The Digital Age

Yes, micro-credentials are increasingly recognized as effective tools for upskilling and reskilling mathematics teachers in a rapidly evolving digital landscape. These credentials focus on specific competencies and can be tailored to meet the demands of modern educational environments, emphasizing flexibility and adaptability (European Commission, 2020). As the workforce shifts due to technological advancements, micro-credentials provide a means for teachers to acquire new skills relevant to digital teaching methodologies and integrate AI effectively in their instruction (Dirani et al., 2020). This professional development approach aligns with the need for continuous learning and adaptation in response to changing educational needs (Oliver, 2021).

Micro-credentials also offered teachers tangible goals within their professional development journeys, reinforcing findings that these credentials facilitate skill acquisition at an individualized pace (Zamiri & Esmaeili, 2024). By validating competencies in technology-enhanced instruction, micro-credentials enable teachers to build confidence and capacity to use AI tools effectively in the classroom.

Micro-credentials in mathematics can serve as valuable tools for upskilling or reskilling mathematics teachers in the digital age. As the educational landscape evolves, especially in response to rapid technological advancements and shifts in teaching methodologies, there is an increasing need for educators to adapt and acquire new competencies. Micro-credentials offer targeted, flexible learning opportunities that can address specific skill gaps, allowing teachers to enhance their pedagogical approaches, integrate technology effectively, and meet the diverse needs of their students.

According to recent research, micro-credentials can provide a structured pathway for educators to gain recognition for their achievements in various aspects of mathematics instruction, including the integration of digital tools and adaptive learning strategies (Hunt et al., 2020; Gauthier, 2020). They allow teachers to stay current with educational innovations, such as artificial intelligence and online learning platforms, which are becoming essential components of modern mathematics education (Orr et al., 2020).

Furthermore, the push for personalized, competency-based, and collaborative learning environments underscores the importance of micro-credentials as a means to foster professional growth among mathematics teachers (Dirani et al., 2020). This approach not only enhances teachers' skills but also contributes to their ability to provide tailored support to students, particularly those with learning disabilities or other challenges (Desmarchelier & Cary, 2022; Wheelahan & Moodie, 2021).

In conclusion, micro-credentials represent an effective strategy for teachers seeking to adapt to the demands of the digital age, enabling them to improve their teaching practices and enhance student outcomes (Zamiri & Esmaeili, 2024). Therefore, micro-credentials can be an integral part of teacher training programs, providing a structured pathway for teachers to acquire and demonstrate new competencies essential in modern, technology-supported educational contexts.

Limitations and Future Research

Despite the valuable insights gained, this study has some limitations. Firstly, the sample size, consisting of 54 sixth-grade students from six Greek elementary schools, limits the generalizability of the findings. A larger and more diverse sample would provide broader insights and strengthen the applicability of the results to different educational settings and demographic groups. Additionally, the reliance on specific AI-powered platforms, such as Khan Academy, DreamBox, and ChatGPT, may limit the scope, as other platforms could offer unique features and instructional approaches that may yield different outcomes.

The study's duration was also relatively short, focusing on improvements within a single academic term. Future research should consider longer-term studies to assess the sustained impact of AI-powered tools and micro-credentials on student learning outcomes and teacher development. Furthermore, while the study highlighted positive outcomes related to engagement and comprehension, it did not examine the social-emotional aspects of learning with AI support in-depth. Exploring factors such as anxiety reduction, self-efficacy, and motivation in future studies could offer a more holistic view of AI's impact on students with learning disabilities.

Another area for future research is the exploration of different types and formats of micro-credentials for both students and teachers. Research could assess how varied credential structures impact motivation and achievement, especially in adaptive learning environments. Additionally, investigating how micro-credentials influence collaboration among teachers and foster professional learning communities could provide valuable insights into optimizing teacher training in the digital age.

CONCLUSION

The findings of this study underscore the potential of AI-powered adaptive platforms to significantly enhance the effectiveness of micro-credentials in mathematics education, especially for students with LD. Micro-credentials offer incremental validation aligned with individual progress, helping to certify learning achievements in a way that respects each student's learning pathway. Furthermore, micro-credentials show promise in upskilling mathematics teachers, equipping them to adapt to new educational technologies. These insights enrich the growing body of literature supporting the integration of AI-powered learning environments and micro-credentialing in education, suggesting pathways for future research and practice.

REFERENCES

CEDEFOP. (2020). *Coronavirus Boosts Interest in Online Learning*. CEDEFOP.

Chetty, R., Friedman, J., & Rockoff, J. (2014). Measuring the impacts of teachers II: Teacher value-added and student outcomes in adulthood. *The American Economic Review*, 104(9), 2633–2679. DOI: 10.1257/aer.104.9.2633

Cividini-Motta, C., Livingston, C., & Efaw, H. (2024). Systematic review of differential reinforcement in skill acquisition. *Behavior Analysis in Practice*, 17(2), 401–416. DOI: 10.1007/s40617-023-00903-z PMID: 38966267

Creswell, J. W., & Clark, V. L. P. (2007). *Designing and conducting mixed methods research*. Sage Publications, Inc.

Davidson, M. (2020). *The Future of Ontario's Workers: How Micro-Credentials Can be a Vital Part of the Post-pandemic Recovery*. WilsonCenter.

Dawson, A., Yeomans, E., & Brown, E. R. (2018). Methodological challenges in education RCTs: Reflections from England's Education Endowment Foundation. *Educational Research*, 60(3), 292–310. DOI: 10.1080/00131881.2018.1500079

Desmarchelier, R., & Cary, L. J. (2022). Toward just and equitable micro-credentials: An Australian perspective. *International Journal of Educational Technology in Higher Education*, 19(1), 25. DOI: 10.1186/s41239-022-00332-y PMID: 35669714

Desmarchelier, R., & Cary, L. J. (2022). Toward just and equitable micro-credentials: An Australian perspective. *International Journal of Educational Technology in Higher Education*, 19(1), 25. DOI: 10.1186/s41239-022-00332-y PMID: 35669714

Dirani, K. M., Abadi, M., Alizadeh, A., Barhate, B., Garza, R. C., Gunasekara, N., Ibrahim, G., & Majzun, Z. (2020). Leadership competencies and the essential role of human resource development in times of crisis: A response to Covid-19 pandemicm. *Human Resource Development International*, 23(4), 380–394. DOI: 10.1080/13678868.2020.1780078

Edovald, T., & Nevill, C. (2021). Working Out What Works: The Case of the Education Endowment Foundation in England. *ECNU Review of Education*, 4(1), 46–64. DOI: 10.1177/2096531120913039

Ehlers, U. D. (2018). Higher Creduation–Degree or Education? The Rise of Microcredentials and its Consequences for the University of the Future. In *European Distance and E-Learning Network* (EDEN) Conference Proceedings (No. 1, pp. 456-465). European Distance and E-Learning Network.

European Commission. (2020). Achieving the European Education Area by 2025 - Communication. https://ec.europa.eu/education/resources-and-tools/document-library/eea-communication-sept2020_en

European Commission. (2021). European Skills Agenda." Accessed December 6, 2022. https://ec.europa.eu/social/main.jsp?catId=1223

European Commission. (2022). Proposal for a Council Recommendation on a European Approach to Micro-Credentials for Lifelong Learning and Employability - Adoption. https://data.consilium.europa.eu/doc/document/ST-9237-2022-INIT/en/pdf

Fischer, T., Oppl, S., & Stabauer, M. (2022). Micro-Credential Development: Tools, Methods and Concepts Supporting the European Approach. In the 17th *International Conference on Wirtschaftsinformatik*, Nuremberg, Germany, February 2022.

Fisher, R. M., & Leder, H. (2022). An assessment of micro-credentials in New Zealand vocational education. *International Journal of Training Research*, 20(3), 232–247. DOI: 10.1080/14480220.2021.2018018

Freeman-Green, S., Williamson, P., & Cornelius, E., K. (. (2023). Promoting Inclusive Practices in Education: Bridging Gaps and Fostering Independence. *Teaching Exceptional Children*, 56(2), 68–69. DOI: 10.1177/00400599231223785

Gauthier, T. (2020). The value of microcredentials: The employer's perspective. *The Journal of Competency-Based Education*, 5(2), e01209. Advance online publication. DOI: 10.1002/cbe2.1209

Grangeat, M. (2016). Dimensions and Modalities of Inquiry-Based Teaching: Understanding the Variety of Practices. *Education Inquiry*, 7(4), 29863. Advance online publication. DOI: 10.3402/edui.v7.29863

Grangeat, M. (2016). Dimensions and Modalities of Inquiry-Based Teaching: Understanding the Variety of Practices. *Education Inquiry*, 7(4), 29863. Advance online publication. DOI: 10.3402/edui.v7.29863

Hughes, E. M., Witzel, B. S., Myers, J., & Lin, T. H. (2023). Unpacking and Understanding Specific Learning Disabilities in Mathematics. *Teaching Exceptional Children*, 56(1), 26–32. DOI: 10.1177/00400599231175509

Hunt, T., Carter, R., Zhang, L., & Yang, S. (2020). Micro-credentials: The potential of personalized professional development. *Development and Learning in Organizations*, 34(2), 33–35. DOI: 10.1108/DLO-09-2019-0215

Kato, S., Galán-Muros, V., & Weko, T. (2020). The Emergence of Alternative Credentials. www.oecd.org/edu/workingpapers

Mac Lochlainn, C., Nic Giolla Mhichil, M., Wessels, O., Kiiskilä, S., Pirkkalainen, H., & Palvalin, M. (2022). ECIU University Micro-Credentials: A Vision for European Learners, Values, and Priorities. *ECIU White Paper on Micro-Credentials.*

Msweli, N. T., Twinomurinzi, H., & Ismail, M. (2022). The international case for micro-credentials for life-wide and life-long learning: A systematic literature review. *Interdisciplinary Journal of Information, Knowledge, and Management*, 17, 151–190. DOI: 10.28945/4954

Oliver, B. (2019). Making Micro-Credentials Work for Learners, Employers and Providers. https://dteach.deakin.edu.au/2019/08/02/microcredentials/

Orr, D., Pupinis, M., & Kirdulyte, G. (2020). Towards a European Approach to Micro-credentials: A Study of Practices and Commonalities in Offering Micro -credentials in European Higher Education. Luxembourg: Publications of the European Union NESET report. https://www.voced.edu.au/content/ngv:89657

Porter, D., & Perris, K. (2021). *Workforce Development in the Post-COVID World: Digital Micro-credentials as a Lever for Transformation.* https://www.col.org/news/col-blog /workforce-development-post-covid-world-digital-micro-credentials-lever-transformation

Ralston, S. J. (2021). Higher education's microcredentialing craze: A postdigital-Deweyan critique. *Postdigital Science and Education*, 3(1), 83–101. DOI: 10.1007/s42438-020-00121-8

Reedy, A., Pfitzner, D., Rook, L., & Ellis, L. (2021). Responding to the COVID-19 emergency: Student and academic staff perceptions of academic integrity in the transition to online exams at three Australian universities. *International Journal for Educational Integrity*, 17(9), 9. Advance online publication. DOI: 10.1007/s40979-021-00075-9

Rossiter, D., & Tynan, B. (2019). Designing & Implementing Micro-Credentials: A Guide for Practitioners.http://hdl.handle.net/11599/3279

Walpola, R., & Lucas, C. (2021). Reflective practice: The essential competency for health systems and healthcare practitioners during the COVID-19 pandemic. *Reflective Practice*, 22(2), 143–146. DOI: 10.1080/14623943.2020.1860925

Wheelahan, L., & Moodie, G. (2022). Gig qualifications for the gig economy: Micro-credentials and the 'hungry mile'. *Higher Education*, 83(5), 1279–1295. DOI: 10.1007/s10734-021-00742-3 PMID: 34366441

World Economic Forum. (2020). *The Future of Jobs Report 2020.* Switzerland: World Economic Forum.

Young, D., West, R. E., & Nylin, T. A. (2019). Value of Open Microcredentials to Earners and Issuers: A Case Study of National Instruments Open Badges. *International Review of Research in Open and Distance Learning*, 20(5), 104–121. DOI: 10.19173/irrodl.v20i5.4345

Zamiri, M., & Esmaeili, A. (2024). Strategies, methods, and supports for developing skills within learning communities: A systematic review of the literature. *Administrative Sciences*, 14(9), 231. Advance online publication. DOI: 10.3390/admsci14090231

Zhang, J., & West, R. E. (2020). Designing microlearning instruction for professional development through a competency-based approach. *TechTrends*, 64(3), 310–318. DOI: 10.1007/s11528-019-00449-4

Chapter 10
Micro-Credentials in Vocational and Professional Training

Tendai Charles
https://orcid.org/0000-0002-0253-5960
The British University in Dubai, UAE

Soha Zoelfakar
https://orcid.org/0000-0001-8201-8797
Emirates College for Advanced Education, UAE

Suraj Sebastian
https://orcid.org/0000-0002-0249-0475
Gulf Medical University, UAE

ABSTRACT

This chapter explores the integration of micro-credentials within vocational and professional training, emphasising the transformative potential when combined with artificial intelligence (AI). Micro-credentials offer flexible, skill-specific certifications that align closely with the evolving demands of the workforce, providing rapid upskilling and targeted competency development. By leveraging AI, these credentials can be enhanced through personalised learning pathways, efficient assessment methods, and secure validation processes. This synergistic approach not only supports lifelong learning and continuous professional development but also addresses the dynamic needs of the 21st-century job market, fostering a more adaptive and skilled workforce.

DOI: 10.4018/979-8-3693-5488-9.ch010

INTRODUCTION

In recent years, education has been significantly transformed by technological advancements and the evolving needs of the global workforce. One of the most notable developments in this area is the rise of micro-credentials, which are compact, skill-specific certifications designed to provide learners with targeted competencies and knowledge. These credentials have gained considerable traction in vocational and professional training, where flexibility, relevance, and rapid upskilling are paramount. Unlike traditional degrees, which often require years of study, micro-credentials can be completed in a shorter time-frame, making them more accessible, manageable, and cost-effective. Micro-credentials are available in various formats, such as digital badges, nanodegrees, and certificate programmes, and are designed to validate specific skills and competencies that enhance an individual's employability and support lifelong learning pathways (Kohler et al., 2021; Healy, 2021). The demand for micro-credentials has been further accelerated by the COVID-19 pandemic, which has disrupted traditional education and training systems worldwide, highlighting the need for more flexible, accessible, and targeted learning options (Güçlü Aydoğan et al., 2024; Soon & Ismail, 2021). In this context, micro-credentials have emerged as a critical bridge to employment in the post-pandemic world, enabling individuals to quickly acquire the skills needed to remain competitive in the job market.

At the same time, artificial intelligence (AI) has made substantial inroads into education, reshaping traditional teaching and learning processes through personalisation, automation, and data-driven insights (Orak & Turan, 2024). AI technologies have the potential to significantly enhance the value of micro-credentials by enabling personalised learning experiences that are tailored to the individual needs and preferences of each learner (Charles & Charles, 2024). By analysing learner data, AI can provide personalised recommendations for micro-credentials that align with each learner's career goals and learning pace, ensuring that they acquire the skills and knowledge most relevant to their professional development. Moreover, AI-driven systems can play a crucial role in assessing learner competencies, offering real-time feedback and adaptive learning paths that are essential in today's dynamic educational landscape (Azzam & Charles, 2024). This chapter aims to critically examine the integration of micro-credentials with AI in vocational and professional training, exploring how these technologies can enhance the creation, delivery, and validation of micro-credentials, thereby supporting lifelong learning and continuous professional development.

Micro-credentials, which emerged in the early 2010s as a flexible and targeted alternative to traditional educational pathways, have become an essential component of modern education (Soon & Ismail, 2021). Micro-credentials have not only supported immediate skill needs but also emerged as pivotal elements in modern education, offering targeted skill sets and competencies that cater to the specialised needs of various industries. Often developed in collaboration with industry leaders, these concise and directly applicable credentials are designed to ensure relevance to both current and emerging job markets. As digital transformation becomes ubiquitous across sectors, the integration of Industry 4.0 technologies—such as the Internet of Things (IoT), AI, and cyber-physical systems—has become essential. Micro-credentials play a crucial role in this context, providing the necessary digital skills and preparing the workforce to effectively engage with these advanced technologies (Abulibdeh et al., 2024). This adaptability highlights the importance of educational systems that can quickly respond to technological shifts and workforce demands.

The innovative nature of micro-credentials is particularly evident in how they leverage digital platforms and technologies to deliver content. Through online courses and learning modules provided by universities, private companies, and specialised online platforms like Coursera and Udacity, learners can acquire and validate new skills from virtually anywhere in the world. This aspect of micro-credentials not only democratises access to education but also significantly enhances the ability of individuals to adapt to the rapidly changing job market, continuously update their skills, and maintain relevance in their professions (Selvaratnam & Sankey, 2021). Moreover, the appeal of micro-credentials lies in their stackability, which allows learners to accumulate over time a series of credentials that can build upon each other or complement existing qualifications. This flexibility enables both personal and professional growth that is directly tailored to an individual's career path and interests. As the workforce continues to evolve and new industries emerge, micro-credentials offer a dynamic and responsive approach to professional development, aligning educational opportunities more closely with real-world applications and the immediate needs of both learners and employers.

The Integration of AI in Education

AI technologies are increasingly transforming the educational landscape, providing innovative solutions that enhance learning experiences and outcomes. The integration of AI in education encompasses a variety of applications, including adaptive learning systems, personalised learning experiences, and intelligent tutoring systems, which collectively aim to cater to the diverse needs of learners. One of the most significant contributions of AI in education is the development of adaptive learning systems. These systems utilise algorithms to analyse student data and adjust the learning material accordingly, thereby creating personalised learning paths tailored to individual student needs and preferences (Akavova, 2023). For instance, AI can facilitate personalised feedback and learning experiences, which are crucial for effective education. AI enables customised learning paths and adaptive assessments, leading to more efficient learning outcomes (Pendy, 2023). This personalisation is further supported by research indicating that AI-driven systems can optimise learning paths and enhance engagement, ultimately improving academic performance (Gligorea, 2023). Moreover, the COVID-19 pandemic has accelerated the adoption of AI technologies in education, particularly in online and remote learning environments (Öncü et al., 2024). The shift towards digital learning has increased the demand for intelligent and adaptive learning technologies that can provide personalised support to students (Albdrani, 2023).

As noted by various studies, machine learning applications are enhancing teaching and learning processes across various educational contexts, thereby promoting a more engaging and effective learning environment (Yang, 2022). This is echoed by research that discusses how AI empowers ubiquitous and lifelong learning, allowing learners to continuously acquire knowledge in a flexible manner (Masrek, 2024). AI technologies also play a crucial role in supporting educators by providing tools that enhance teaching effectiveness. For instance, AI can assist teachers in evaluating student performance and identifying areas where additional support may be needed (Chen et al., 2020; Sarı et al., 2024). Furthermore, the use of AI in educational settings fosters an interactive learning environment, as highlighted by studies that discuss the impact of AI on learner-instructor interactions in online learning (Seo et al., 2021). This interactivity is essential for maintaining student engagement and motivation, particularly in remote learning scenarios (Hill et al., 2023; Shehzad & Charles, 2023).

Despite the numerous benefits of AI in education, there are challenges and ethical considerations that must be addressed. Issues such as data privacy, algorithmic bias, and the need for educators to develop digital competencies are critical factors that influence the successful implementation of AI technologies in educational settings (Ng et al., 2023). As highlighted by various studies, the integration of AI-driven personalised learning systems must be accompanied by a thorough understanding of these challenges to enhance educational effectiveness and equity (Katiyar, 2024). In conclusion, AI technologies are revolutionising education by providing personalised, adaptive, and engaging learning experiences. The ongoing advancements in AI are set to redefine pedagogical strategies, making education more accessible and tailored to individual learner needs. However, it is imperative to navigate the associated challenges to fully realise the potential of AI in transforming education for the better.

AI and Personalised Learning

The integration of AI in personalised learning is reshaping educational practices by tailoring learning experiences to meet individual student needs. AI technologies facilitate adaptive learning environments that adjust content delivery based on the unique learning styles, preferences, and progress of each student. This approach has been shown to significantly enhance student engagement and academic performance across various educational contexts. AI-driven personalised learning systems allow for the customisation of educational content, enabling students to learn at their own pace. For instance, a study in Vietnam highlighted that AI platforms can adapt learning materials to fit students' individual learning styles, which leads to improved retention rates and academic outcomes (Charles & Hill, 2023).

This adaptability is further supported by research that argues AI-based e-learning systems deliver targeted content to learners, contrasting with traditional systems that provide uniform content to all students (Murtaza et al., 2022). Such personalised content delivery not only enhances the learning experience but also fosters greater student motivation and engagement (Renumol, 2021). The effectiveness of personalised learning is also evident in the development of algorithms designed to recommend learning paths tailored to specific educational goals. For example, research on a personalised learning path recommendation algorithm for English listening skills demonstrates how AI can cater to diverse learner needs, ultimately improving fluency and confidence in language acquisition (Li, 2024).

Similarly, work on optimising vocabulary learning through reinforcement learning illustrates how adaptive algorithms can continuously monitor student progress and adjust learning strategies in real time, thereby enhancing vocabulary acquisition (Zhang, 2024). Moreover, the concept of adaptive personalised federated learning (APFL) has emerged as a promising approach to further enhance personalised learning experiences. This method allows for the development of individualised models that consider the unique data distribution of each learner, thus providing a more tailored educational experience (Deng et al., 2020). The application of such advanced algorithms is crucial in creating effective personalised learning environments that respond dynamically to the evolving needs of students.

Despite the numerous advantages, the implementation of AI in personalised learning is not without challenges. Issues such as data privacy, algorithmic bias, and the need for educators to develop digital competencies are significant barriers that must be addressed to ensure equitable access to personalised learning technologies (Familoni, 2024). Furthermore, the expectations of learners regarding the features of personalised learning analytics systems must be considered to design effective educational tools (Schumacher & Ifenthaler, 2018). In conclusion, AI technologies are pivotal in advancing personalised learning by providing adaptive, individualised educational experiences that cater to the diverse needs of learners. As educational institutions increasingly adopt these technologies, it is essential to navigate the associated challenges to fully leverage the potential of AI in enhancing educational outcomes.

AI-Driven Assessment

The integration of AI in educational assessment and feedback mechanisms is revolutionising how educators evaluate student performance and provide constructive feedback. AI-driven assessment tools leverage advanced algorithms to analyse student responses, offering immediate and personalised feedback that enhances learning outcomes. This shift towards automated assessment not only increases efficiency but also aims to reduce biases and improve the objectivity of evaluations (Charles, 2021). AI systems are capable of analysing various forms of student work, including tests, essays, and assignments, to deliver accurate assessments of learning outcomes. For instance, AI-powered automatic scoring applications utilise natural language processing (NLP) and deep learning techniques to provide real-time feedback to students.

This immediate feedback loop is crucial in helping students understand their strengths and weaknesses, allowing them to adjust their learning strategies accordingly (Akavova, 2023). It is emphasised that such systems can enhance the educational experience by providing personalised feedback tailored to individual learning needs (ibid). Moreover, AI can assist educators in identifying patterns in student performance, thereby informing instructional decisions. AI-based systems analyse learning patterns to offer customised feedback, enabling students to progress at their own pace while addressing specific areas of weakness (Anuyahong, 2023). This data-driven approach not only aids students but also equips teachers with valuable insights that can enhance their teaching strategies and improve overall classroom dynamics.

The use of AI in feedback generation is further exemplified by tools like ChatGPT, which can provide consistent and timely feedback in language learning contexts. Research indicates that such AI-driven platforms can foster a sense of self-efficacy among students by helping them identify common errors and improve their writing skills. However, it is essential to recognise that while AI-generated feedback can be beneficial, some studies suggest that students may respond more positively to human feedback, indicating a need for a balanced approach that combines both AI and human input (Drewery et al., 2022). Despite the advantages of AI in assessment and feedback, challenges remain. For instance, the reliance on historical data can lead to difficulties in predicting the impact of social changes on learning outcomes (Tuomi, 2022).

Furthermore, the implementation of AI-driven feedback systems must consider ethical implications, such as data privacy and the potential for algorithmic bias (Lin et al., 2022). Establishing trustworthy AI systems in education is crucial for ensuring that automated feedback is both effective and equitable (Lin et al., 2022). Ultimately, AI-driven assessment and feedback mechanisms are transforming educational practices by providing personalised, immediate, and data-informed insights into student learning. As educational institutions increasingly adopt these technologies, it is vital to address the associated challenges to maximise their potential and ensure that they complement traditional teaching methods effectively.

Integrating Micro-Credentials with AI: A Synergistic Approach

The integration of AI into the design of micro-credentials is a transformative approach that enhances the personalisation, efficiency, and effectiveness of educational offerings. Micro-credentials, which are short, competency-based recognitions of learning, have gained traction in higher education as institutions seek to provide flexible learning pathways that align with the evolving demands of the workforce (Sharma, 2024). AI technologies can play a pivotal role in this integration by facilitating the development, assessment, and recognition of micro-credentials. AI can enhance the design of micro-credential programmes by enabling personalised learning experiences tailored to individual learner needs. For instance, the use of AI algorithms can analyse learner data to identify skill gaps and recommend specific micro-credential pathways that align with their career goals (Lang, 2023). This personalised approach not only increases learner engagement but also ensures that the micro-credentials offered are relevant and valuable in the context of the job market (Kumar et al., 2022). Understanding the expectations and implementation strategies for micro-credentials is crucial for their success, and AI can provide insights into these areas by analysing feedback and performance data from learners (Halim, 2023).

Moreover, AI can streamline the assessment process associated with micro-credentials. Automated assessment tools can evaluate learner performance in real time, providing immediate feedback that is essential for skill mastery (Reed, 2023). This capability is particularly beneficial in competency-based education, where the focus is on demonstrating specific skills rather than traditional grading systems. By utilising AI for assessments, institutions can ensure that the evaluation process is both efficient and objective, thereby enhancing the credibility of the micro-credentials awarded (Kiiskilä et al., 2023). The role of AI in micro-credentialing also extends to the validation and recognition of these credentials. AI can facilitate the development of verifiable digital credentials that are easily shareable and recognised across various platforms, including professional networks like LinkedIn (Ruddy & Ponte, 2019).

This aspect is critical as it enhances the visibility of learners' achievements and facilitates their employability in a competitive job market (Tammeleht, 2023). Furthermore, the integration of AI can support the creation of a robust framework for micro-credentials that aligns with national qualification frameworks, ensuring that they meet industry standards and expectations (Bruguera, 2023). Despite the numerous advantages, challenges remain in the integration of AI into micro-credential design. Issues such as data privacy, algorithmic bias, and the need for educators to develop digital competencies must be addressed to ensure the ethical implementation of AI technologies (Maina et al., 2022). Additionally, there is a need for ongoing research to explore the long-term impact of AI-driven micro-credentials on learner outcomes and employability (Orman et al., 2023).

AI in Credential Delivery and Management

The integration of AI into the delivery and management of micro-credentials is a significant advancement that enhances the efficiency, personalisation, and effectiveness of these educational offerings. Micro-credentials, which are short, competency-based recognitions of learning, have gained popularity as they provide flexible pathways for learners to acquire specific skills relevant to the job market. AI technologies can facilitate the design, assessment, and recognition of micro-credentials, thereby improving the overall educational experience. One of the primary benefits of AI in micro-credentialing is its ability to personalise learning experiences. AI algorithms can analyse individual learner data to identify skill gaps and recommend tailored micro-credential pathways that align with their career aspirations (Sharma, 2024). This personalised approach not only increases learner engagement but also ensures that the micro-credentials offered are relevant and valuable in the context of the workforce (Tee, 2023). For instance, AI can help in curating content that is industry-relevant and accessible, thereby enhancing the perceived value of micro-credentials among learners (Mir et al., 2021). Moreover, AI can streamline the assessment processes associated with micro-credentials. Automated assessment tools can evaluate learner performance in real time, providing immediate feedback that is essential for skill mastery (Lang, 2023).

This capability is particularly beneficial in competency-based education, where the focus is on demonstrating specific skills rather than traditional grading systems. By utilising AI for assessments, institutions can ensure that the evaluation process is both efficient and objective, thereby enhancing the credibility of the micro-credentials awarded (Kiyasseh et al., 2023). Additionally, the use of AI can facilitate the creation of verifiable digital credentials that are easily shareable and recognised across various platforms, enhancing learners' visibility in the job market (Zou, 2023). AI also plays a crucial role in the management of micro-credential programmes. It can assist educational institutions in tracking learner progress and outcomes, thereby providing valuable insights into the effectiveness of micro-credential offerings (Reed, 2023).

This data-driven approach allows institutions to continuously improve their programmes based on learner feedback and performance metrics, ensuring that the micro-credentials remain relevant and aligned with industry needs (Clausen, 2021). Furthermore, AI can help in automating administrative tasks related to micro-credentialing, such as issuing certificates and managing learner records, thereby reducing the administrative burden on educational institutions (Tammeleht, 2023). Despite the numerous advantages, challenges remain in the integration of AI into micro-credential design and management. Issues such as data privacy, algorithmic bias, and the need for educators to develop digital competencies must be addressed to ensure the ethical implementation of AI technologies (Maina et al., 2022).

Additionally, there is a need for ongoing research to explore the long-term impact of AI-driven micro-credentials on learner outcomes and employability (Orman et al., 2023). In conclusion, the integration of AI into the delivery and management of micro-credentials presents significant opportunities for enhancing personalised learning, streamlining assessments, and improving the recognition of competencies. As educational institutions continue to adopt these technologies, it is essential to navigate the associated challenges to fully leverage the potential of AI in creating effective and meaningful micro-credential programmes.

Validation and Accreditation

The credibility of micro-credentials is essential for their acceptance and recognition by employers and educational institutions. As the demand for flexible and competency-based learning options increases, ensuring that micro-credentials are validated and accredited becomes paramount. AI can significantly enhance the validation and accreditation processes by providing data-driven evidence of learners' competencies, thereby increasing the trustworthiness of these credentials. AI can assist in the validation of micro-credentials by analysing learner performance data to provide objective assessments of competencies. For instance, AI algorithms can evaluate the skills demonstrated by learners in various assessments, ensuring that the awarded micro-credentials accurately reflect their abilities (Eidesen, 2023).

This data-driven approach not only enhances the reliability of the credentials but also allows for real-time feedback, enabling learners to understand their strengths and areas for improvement (Tamoliūnė et al., 2023). The systematic literature review by Tamoliūnė et al. (2023) highlights that micro-credentials provide new opportunities for learners to acquire essential skills while meeting employers' needs for flexible and scalable professional development. Moreover, AI can facilitate the creation of verifiable digital credentials that are easily shareable and recognised across various platforms. This capability is crucial for enhancing the visibility of learners' achievements in the job market (Zou, 2023).

Research indicates that individuals who earn micro-credentials often experience improved employability skills and competencies, which can be further validated through AI-driven assessments (Zou, 2023). By providing a secure and unalterable digital record of competencies, AI helps bridge the gap between educational institutions and employers, fostering greater acceptance of micro-credentials in the workforce (McGreal et al., 2022). In addition to validation, AI can streamline the accreditation process for micro-credentials. By automating the evaluation of educational programmes against established standards, AI can help institutions ensure that their micro-credential offerings meet industry requirements (Sharma, 2024).

This is particularly important as the landscape of micro-credentials continues to evolve, with various stakeholders, including governments and industry leaders, advocating for standardised frameworks (Abdullah, 2023). The integration of AI in accreditation processes can enhance the credibility of micro-credentials, making them more appealing to both learners and employers. Despite the potential benefits, challenges remain in the implementation of AI-driven validation and accreditation processes. Issues such as data privacy, algorithmic bias, and the need for transparency in AI decision-making must be addressed to ensure ethical practices (Lang, 2023; Maina et al., 2022).

Impacts on Vocational and Professional Training

The integration of AI with micro-credentials holds significant potential for bridging the skills gap between traditional education systems and the rapidly evolving requirements of the global economy. By aligning micro-credentials with current industry needs and leveraging AI to deliver personalised learning experiences, vocational and professional training programmes can equip learners with the skills that are most in demand. This alignment not only enhances employability but also supports economic growth by ensuring that the workforce is prepared for the challenges of the 21st century. AI can facilitate the development of micro-credentials that are closely aligned with industry requirements. For instance, micro-credentials have emerged as a crucial response to the volatility of labour markets and the demands of lifelong learners (Miao, 2023). By utilising AI to analyse labour market trends and skill demands, educational institutions can create micro-credential programmes that are relevant and timely, ensuring that learners acquire the competencies needed in the workforce. This dynamic approach helps to ensure that educational offerings remain aligned with the evolving needs of employers, thereby enhancing the relevance of micro-credentials (Clausen, 2021).

Moreover, AI enhances the personalisation of learning experiences associated with micro-credentials. By analysing individual learner data, AI can tailor educational content and assessments to meet the specific needs and preferences of each learner (Reed, 2023). This personalised approach not only improves learner engagement but also increases the likelihood of skill mastery, as learners can progress at their own pace and focus on areas where they need the most improvement (Bruguera, 2023). The ability to provide customised learning pathways is particularly important in vocational and professional training, where practical skills and competencies are paramount. The impact of micro-credentials on employability is further supported by research indicating that these credentials can significantly enhance individuals' perceived employability and increase their chances of securing employment (Zou, 2023). As organisations increasingly recognise the value of micro-credentials, they are more likely to consider them as valid indicators of a candidate's skills and competencies. This recognition is crucial for learners seeking to differentiate themselves in a competitive job market (Wheelahan & Moodie, 2021). Additionally, the alignment of micro-credentials with industry standards and requirements fosters trust among employers, making them more likely to accept these credentials as legitimate qualifications (Surono, 2023).

Despite the numerous advantages, challenges remain in the implementation and recognition of micro-credentials. There is a need for clear standards and frameworks to ensure that micro-credentials are recognised and valued by both educational institutions and employers (Wheelahan & Moodie, 2021). Furthermore, ongoing collaboration between educational institutions, industry stakeholders, and policy-makers is essential to establish robust validation and accreditation processes for micro-credentials (Brown et al., 2023). Addressing these challenges will be critical for maximising the impact of micro-credentials on workforce development and ensuring that they effectively bridge the skills gap in the 21st century.

Supporting Career Transitions and Professional Development

In today's fast-paced job market, individuals frequently find themselves needing to transition between careers or acquire new skills to remain competitive. AI-enhanced micro-credentials provide a flexible and accessible means for learners to upskill or reskill, supporting career transitions and continuous professional development. By offering targeted, competency-based learning opportunities, micro-credentials enable individuals to quickly gain the expertise needed for new roles or industries, thereby reducing the time and cost associated with traditional education pathways. The flexibility of micro-credentials is one of their most significant advantages.

Micro-credentials offer new opportunities for learners to acquire additional skills that are increasingly relevant in the job market, such as digital literacies and critical thinking (Tamoliūnė et al., 2023). This adaptability is crucial as the demand for specific skills can change rapidly, and micro-credentials allow learners to respond to these shifts without committing to lengthy degree programmes. Furthermore, aligning micro-credentials with lifelong learning pathways enables institutions to create smart catalogues that match learners' skill gaps with appropriate learning opportunities (Peters, 2023). This alignment enhances the relevance of the training provided and ensures that learners are equipped with the skills that employers are actively seeking.

AI plays a pivotal role in personalising the learning experience associated with micro-credentials. By leveraging data analytics, AI can assess individual learner needs and preferences, tailoring educational content to optimise skill acquisition (Desmarchelier & Cary, 2022). This personalised approach enhances learner engagement and increases the likelihood of successful career transitions, as individuals can focus on acquiring the specific competencies required for their desired roles. Research supports this notion, indicating that micro-credential learning significantly improves students' employability by equipping them with the qualifications and skills necessary for success in a competitive job market (Zou, 2023). Moreover, the integration of AI with micro-credentials can streamline the process of recognising and validating these credentials. The ability to provide verifiable and industry-recognised micro-credentials is essential for their acceptance among employers (Lang, 2023). By utilising AI to automate the assessment and validation processes, educational institutions can ensure that the micro-credentials awarded are credible and reflective of the skills acquired. This credibility is crucial for fostering trust among employers, who increasingly value skills-based qualifications over traditional degrees. The economic implications of AI-enhanced micro-credentials are significant. By providing accessible and targeted learning opportunities, these credentials support workforce development and economic growth. Micro-credentials are seen as a solution to the rapid changes in job market requirements, enabling individuals to gain industry-relevant skills that are essential for the 21st century (Orman et al., 2023). This adaptability benefits individual learners and contributes to a more agile and responsive workforce, capable of meeting the evolving demands of various industries.

Again, despite the many advantages, challenges remain in the widespread adoption of micro-credentials. Issues such as the need for standardisation, recognition, and the potential for confusion around the term "micro-credential" must be addressed to ensure their effectiveness (Bruguera, 2023). Additionally, there is a need for ongoing research to better understand learners' motivations and preferences regarding micro-credentials, which can inform their design and implementation (Bruguera,

2023). Fundamentally, AI-enhanced micro-credentials represent a powerful tool for individuals seeking to navigate the complexities of today's job market. By providing flexible, personalised, and industry-aligned learning opportunities, these credentials facilitate career transitions and continuous professional development. As educational institutions and employers increasingly recognise the value of micro-credentials, their role in bridging the skills gap and supporting economic growth will become even more pronounced.

Case Studies

The transformative potential of AI-integrated micro-credentials is exemplified through various case studies and examples from vocational and professional training settings. These instances illustrate how the combination of AI and micro-credentials has been successfully implemented to enhance learning outcomes, support workforce development, and foster innovation in education. One notable example is the initiative that focuses on supporting clinical research professionals through educational innovations. The programme incorporates online training that includes shareable, verified micro-credentials, providing validation of the standards met and skills achieved. This approach addresses the challenges faced by clinical research professionals in demonstrating competency and recording completed certifications and trainings (Lee-Chavarria, 2024). By leveraging AI to track and assess competencies, the programme ensures that learners can effectively showcase their skills to potential employers, thereby enhancing their employability.

Similarly, research highlights the impact of micro-credential learning on students' perceived employability. The study indicates that micro-credentials can significantly contribute to students' training and familiarity with the future workplace, helping them develop the required skills and knowledge (Zou, 2023). By aligning micro-credentials with industry needs and utilising AI to deliver personalised learning experiences, educational institutions can better prepare learners for the demands of the job market. In the context of blended learning, research emphasises the multi-stakeholder perspective of micro-credentialing ecosystems in higher education. The study reveals how micro-credentials can be perceived differently across various countries, highlighting the importance of understanding local educational environments and challenges with technology (Sharma, 2024). This global perspective underscores the adaptability of micro-credentials in meeting diverse learner profiles and industry requirements, ultimately fostering a more skilled workforce.

Further arguments for the need to consider knowledge, skills, and values as integral components of the micro-credential curriculum are provided by research. Their work emphasises that a well-rounded educational experience, grounded in good academic practices, can enhance the effectiveness of micro-credentials. By integrating AI to assess and validate these components, institutions can ensure that micro-credentials are not only skill-focused but also promote holistic learner development (Desmarchelier & Cary, 2022). Insights into the relationship between novice users' insights and identity in Malaysia showcase how micro-credentials can leverage emergency remote teaching (Kumar et al., 2022). The study highlights the importance of intrinsic motivation in learning, suggesting that micro-credentials should be designed to encourage learners to demonstrate evidence of their skills and knowledge. This aligns with the broader goal of fostering a culture of continuous learning and adaptability in the workforce.

Moreover, the introduction of a micro-credentialing methodology aimed at improving the recognition of higher education employability skills illustrates how AI can facilitate the development of robust frameworks for micro-credentialing that align with industry expectations (Maina et al., 2022). This approach demonstrates how AI can facilitate the development of robust frameworks for micro-credentialing that align with industry expectations. By integrating various assessment dimensions, the methodology seeks to enhance students' perceptions of their employability opportunities. This approach demonstrates how AI can facilitate the development of robust frameworks for micro-credentialing that align with industry expectations.

The case of engineering practices, as discussed, illustrates the significance of micro-credentials in project management (Surono, 2023). The micro-credential serves as an acknowledgment of an engineer's ability to manage and lead projects effectively. By applying proper project management principles, engineers can enhance their skills and improve efficiency in project execution, showcasing the practical benefits of micro-credentials in vocational training. Finally, insights reinforce the notion that micro-credentials are emerging as a viable alternative for career and professional development (Orman et al., 2023). By offering short courses and certifications, micro-credentials provide learners with the flexibility to acquire new skills without the time and financial commitment associated with traditional degree programmes. This adaptability is crucial in a rapidly changing job market, where the ability to pivot and acquire new competencies is essential for career success.

Essentially, the integration of AI with micro-credentials presents a transformative opportunity for vocational and professional training settings. Through various case studies, it is evident that AI-enhanced micro-credentials can effectively address the skills gap, support workforce development, and foster innovation in education. By providing targeted, competency-based learning opportunities, these credentials enable individuals to quickly gain the expertise needed for new roles or industries, ultimately contributing to a more agile and skilled workforce.

Ethical Considerations

The integration of AI with micro-credentials raises significant concerns regarding data privacy and security. As AI systems collect and analyse vast amounts of learner data, it is essential to ensure that this data is protected and used responsibly. Issues such as data breaches, unauthorised access, and misuse of personal information must be addressed through robust data governance frameworks and ethical guidelines. One of the primary concerns regarding AI in educational settings is the potential for security and privacy risks. The use of AI technology in educational organisations can pose significant security and privacy concerns for students, teachers, and institutions (Sabharwal, 2023). The necessity for specialised skills and knowledge to effectively utilise AI technology further complicates the landscape, as institutions must ensure that personnel are adequately trained to handle sensitive data responsibly.

Moreover, the potential for biases in AI-generated content and the lack of transparency in how AI models arrive at their predictions raise additional privacy concerns. Privacy issues related to data collection and usage are critical, as they can lead to the generation of inappropriate or misleading information (Alrayes, 2024). This highlights the need for transparency in AI decision-making processes, which is essential for building trust among users and stakeholders. The ethical implications of AI in education are further underscored by the argument that AI should be developed to support human intelligence rather than replace it (Kim et al., 2022). This perspective emphasises the importance of maintaining human oversight in AI systems, particularly when it comes to handling sensitive learner data. Ensuring that AI systems are designed with ethical considerations in mind is crucial for mitigating potential risks associated with data privacy and security.

AI's impact on personalised learning necessitates a careful examination of the associated risks (Göçen & Aydemir, 2020). As AI systems become more integrated into educational environments, the need for robust data governance frameworks becomes increasingly apparent. These frameworks should include guidelines for data collection, storage, and usage, ensuring that learners' personal information is protected from unauthorised access and misuse. The implementation of data protection regulations, such as the General Data Protection Regulation (GDPR), is vital for safeguarding learner data in AI systems. Challenges of implementing such regulations within AI systems that are already trained and operational are highlighted (Kamenskih, 2022). This underscores the importance of developing AI systems that prioritise data privacy from the outset, incorporating principles such as data minimisation and user consent.

While patient data privacy concerns in the context of AI in medical imaging are discussed, these concerns can be extrapolated to the educational sector, where the collection and analysis of learner data must be conducted with the utmost care to avoid potential breaches of privacy (Lim et al., 2022). Ensuring that learners are informed about how their data will be used and obtaining their consent is essential for fostering trust in AI systems. The ethical considerations surrounding AI in education are not limited to data privacy; they also encompass broader issues of accountability and transparency. Establishing a community-wide framework for the ethics of AI in education would address the diverse interpretations of ethical issues within the educational community (Holmes et al., 2021).

Such a framework would need to be adaptable to accommodate new knowledge and changing socio-cultural norms, ensuring that ethical considerations remain relevant as AI technology evolves. Crucially, the integration of AI with micro-credentials presents significant challenges related to data privacy and security. As educational institutions increasingly rely on AI systems to collect and analyse learner data, it is imperative to establish robust data governance frameworks and ethical guidelines. By addressing concerns such as data breaches, unauthorised access, and the responsible use of personal information, institutions can foster trust in AI technologies and ensure that they are used to enhance educational outcomes without compromising learner privacy.

Quality Assurance

Maintaining the quality and credibility of micro-credentials is critical to their success in the educational landscape. As AI becomes more involved in the creation and delivery of micro-credentials, establishing rigorous quality assurance processes is essential to ensure the validity and reliability of these credentials. This includes developing clear standards for what constitutes a micro-credential, as well as mechanisms for monitoring and evaluating the effectiveness of AI-driven learning experiences. One of the foundational aspects of ensuring quality in micro-credentials is the establishment of clear definitions and standards. Micro-credentials should be recognised as certified documents issued by an institution, reflecting the learning outcomes achieved through a structured learning experience (Tee, 2023). This definition is crucial as it sets the groundwork for what constitutes a valid micro-credential and ensures that all stakeholders have a shared understanding of its value.

Furthermore, the development of robust quality assurance standards is necessary to maintain the integrity of micro-credentials, as highlighted by the advocacy for the use of registries to track and report micro-credentials earned (Gauthier, 2020). Such systems can help institutions ascertain and protect the validity of the credentials they issue. In addition to establishing standards, ongoing monitoring and evaluation of AI-driven learning experiences are vital.

Micro-credential learning positively impacts students' perceived employability, suggesting that the effectiveness of these credentials should be continuously assessed to ensure they meet industry needs (Zou, 2023). By implementing feedback mechanisms and evaluation frameworks, educational institutions can gather data on the outcomes of micro-credential programmes, allowing for iterative improvements and adaptations based on learner performance and market demands. Moreover, the integration of AI in the assessment and validation processes can enhance the credibility of micro-credentials. AI systems can analyse learner data to provide objective assessments of competencies, ensuring that the awarded micro-credentials accurately reflect the skills acquired. This data-driven approach not only enhances the reliability of the credentials but also allows for real-time feedback, enabling learners to understand their strengths and areas for improvement. The use of AI in this context aligns with the need for transparency and accountability in educational practices, as emphasised by advocating for a community-wide framework for the ethics of AI in education (Holmes et al., 2021). The challenges associated with ensuring the quality and credibility of micro-credentials are multifaceted. There is a risk that the proliferation of micro-credentials could lead to a dilution of their value if not properly managed (Desmarchelier & Cary, 2022). This concern underscores the importance of establishing robust governance frameworks that outline the criteria for issuing micro-credentials and the processes for evaluating their effectiveness.

Such frameworks should include guidelines for data privacy and security, as the collection and analysis of learner data are integral to the functioning of AI systems. Furthermore, the need for collaboration among various stakeholders is crucial for the successful implementation of quality assurance processes. Educational institutions, industry representatives, and policymakers must work together to establish standards and frameworks that reflect the evolving needs of the workforce (Alasmari, 2024). This collaborative approach can help ensure that micro-credentials remain relevant and credible in the eyes of employers and learners alike. In conclusion, the integration of AI with micro-credentials presents both opportunities and challenges in maintaining quality and credibility. By establishing clear standards, implementing rigorous quality assurance processes, and fostering collaboration among stakeholders, educational institutions can ensure that micro-credentials effectively support learners in their career transitions and professional development. As the landscape of education continues to evolve, addressing these issues will be essential for maximising the impact of micro-credentials in the workforce.

Ethical Implications

The integration of AI into education, particularly in the context of micro-credentials, raises a range of ethical considerations that must be carefully addressed to ensure fairness, transparency, and accountability. As AI systems become more prevalent in assessing learner progress and outcomes, it is crucial to ensure that these systems do not reinforce existing biases or create new forms of discrimination. Additionally, transparency in AI algorithms and mechanisms for accountability are essential to foster trust among learners and stakeholders. One of the primary ethical concerns surrounding AI in education is the potential for bias in algorithmic decision-making. "Algorithmovigilance" involves monitoring and understanding the effects of algorithms to prevent adverse outcomes in educational contexts (Klímová et al., 2023). This principle underscores the need for continuous evaluation of AI systems to ensure they operate fairly and do not perpetuate existing inequalities. For instance, if an AI system is trained on biased data, it may inadvertently favour certain groups of learners over others, leading to unequal access to opportunities and resources.

Transparency in AI algorithms is another critical ethical consideration. Establishing a community-wide framework for the ethics of AI in education is essential for addressing diverse interpretations of ethical issues (Holmes et al., 2021). Such a framework should include guidelines for how AI algorithms make decisions about learners' progress and outcomes, ensuring that learners and educators understand the criteria used in these assessments. This transparency is vital for building trust in AI systems and ensuring that learners feel confident in the fairness of the evaluation processes. Moreover, accountability mechanisms must be established to hold AI systems and their developers responsible for their decisions and outcomes. The principles of transparency, fairness, and responsibility are pivotal in the ethical use of AI in education (Arvin, 2023). By implementing accountability measures, educational institutions can ensure that any negative consequences arising from AI-driven decisions are addressed and rectified.

This may involve creating oversight committees or regulatory bodies that monitor the use of AI in educational settings and provide guidance on ethical practices. Equity is another significant concern when integrating AI into micro-credentialing systems. The ethical implications of AI must be considered to ensure that all learners have equitable access to educational opportunities (Kwak et al., 2022). This includes addressing the "digital divide," which can exacerbate existing inequalities in education. Ensuring that AI-driven micro-credentials are accessible to all learners, regardless of their socio-economic background, is essential for fostering an inclusive educational environment. Furthermore, the ethical implications of AI in education extend to the need for comprehensive training for educators and learners alike. Integrating AI into educational practices requires a deep understanding of the ethical challenges associated with its use (Baskara, 2023). Educators must be equipped with the knowledge and skills to navigate these challenges and make informed decisions about the implementation of AI technologies in their teaching practices.

Basically, the integration of AI with micro-credentials presents significant ethical considerations that must be addressed to ensure fairness, transparency, and accountability. By establishing rigorous quality assurance processes, promoting algorithmic transparency, and implementing accountability mechanisms, educational institutions can foster trust in AI systems and ensure that they are used responsibly. As the landscape of education continues to evolve, addressing these ethical challenges will be essential for maximising the benefits of AI in supporting learner success and promoting equitable access to educational opportunities.

Challenges in AI-Enhanced Micro-Credentials

Standardization and Regulatory Frameworks

One of the key challenges in the implementation of micro-credentials is the lack of standardization across regions and industries. Micro-credentials, while flexible and adaptable, often suffer from inconsistent validation processes and a lack of uniform regulatory frameworks. This lack of standardization can lead to confusion among learners, employers, and institutions regarding the value and recognition of these credentials across different contexts (Wheelahan & Moodie, 2021). For example, a micro-credential that is well-regarded in one industry may not carry the same weight in another, particularly when international standards are absent. Governments and accrediting bodies must collaborate to develop standard frameworks that ensure micro-credentials are recognized and valued globally. AI has the potential to streamline these processes by providing tools for the automated validation and verification of micro-credentials. However, without globally recognized standards, the scalability of AI-driven micro-credentials remains limited, particularly when it comes to cross-border recognition.

Data Privacy

The use of AI in micro-credentials raises significant ethical concerns, particularly around the collection, storage, and use of personal data. AI systems rely heavily on learner data to provide personalized recommendations and assessments, which increases the risk of privacy breaches and misuse of personal information (Ng et al., 2023). The General Data Protection Regulation (GDPR) in Europe is a critical step towards protecting individuals' privacy, but challenges remain in enforcing such regulations globally. Institutions leveraging AI must ensure that they implement robust data governance frameworks to safeguard learner data, particularly in the context of micro-credentials where personal and professional information is at stake.

Moreover, there is the risk of algorithmic bias in AI-driven systems, which can reinforce existing inequalities in education. For example, AI models trained on biased data sets may inadvertently disadvantage certain demographic groups, leading to inequitable outcomes. Research suggests that AI-based systems can sometimes perpetuate existing social biases by prioritizing skills or competencies that are more readily accessible to certain privileged groups, thus exacerbating existing access disparities (Familoni, 2024). To mitigate this, AI algorithms must be transparent, and there should be ongoing monitoring (algorithmovigilance) to ensure fairness in decision-making processes.

Data Privacy in AI-Driven Credentialing Systems

Data privacy is a significant concern when integrating AI with micro-credentials. AI systems collect vast amounts of data to personalize learning and validate competencies. However, the potential for data breaches or the misuse of sensitive personal information is a major issue (Alrayes, 2024). Learners are often required to share private details such as their employment history, learning patterns, and even financial data, which, if compromised, could have significant repercussions. Therefore, institutions must not only comply with regulations like the GDPR but also implement state-of-the-art encryption and secure data management practices to ensure the integrity and confidentiality of learner data.

Case Studies Highlighting Challenges

In healthcare, for instance, micro-credentials tailored for clinical research professionals have emerged as a critical tool for upskilling (Lee-Chavarria, 2024). However, the adoption of AI to personalize these credentials has been met with concerns about the ethical use of patient data. Similar issues have arisen in other fields such as engineering, where micro-credentials are designed to validate project management competencies but are constrained by varying levels of technological access and data security concerns (Surono, 2023).

Risks of AI Integration: Algorithmic Bias and Access Disparities

AI-powered systems can inadvertently introduce or amplify biases present in the data used to train them. This bias can manifest in several ways, including unequal access to learning opportunities or preferential treatment of certain learner profiles. Studies have shown that AI models trained on limited or unrepresentative data sets can marginalize underrepresented groups, leading to a widening of access disparities in education (Klímová et al., 2023). For instance, learners from lower socioeconomic backgrounds may lack access to the technology and resources necessary to fully engage with AI-enhanced micro-credentials. Similarly, regional disparities in access to AI-driven education platforms can further exacerbate global inequities in education. Addressing these challenges requires not only improvements in the technology itself but also policy interventions to ensure equitable access to the resources needed to benefit from AI-enhanced micro-credentialing systems.

Recommendations for Mitigating Risks

To mitigate these risks, several measures must be taken. First, AI models used in education must be regularly audited to ensure they are free from bias and that their decision-making processes are transparent. Second, institutions should adopt a participatory approach to the development of AI-driven micro-credential platforms, involving a wide range of stakeholders to ensure diverse perspectives are considered. Finally, there must be sustained efforts to improve access to digital resources, particularly in underserved regions, to ensure that learners from all backgrounds can benefit from AI-enhanced learning experiences.

Future Directions and Recommendations

Looking ahead, several emerging trends are likely to shape the future of AI-integrated micro-credentials. These trends include the increasing use of blockchain technology for credential verification, the growing importance of soft skills and digital competencies, and the expansion of micro-credentialing initiatives in developing countries. By staying abreast of these trends, educators and policymakers can ensure that micro-credentials continue to evolve in ways that meet the needs of learners and employers. One significant trend is the integration of blockchain technology for credential verification. Blockchain offers a decentralised and secure method for storing and verifying educational credentials, which can enhance the credibility of micro-credentials.

Blockchain technology can provide a privacy-enhanced authorisation scheme that protects users' credentials from untrusted nodes in a consensus network (Zhang et al., 2020). This capability is particularly relevant for micro-credentials, as it ensures that learners' achievements are verifiable and tamper-proof, thereby increasing trust among employers and educational institutions. Moreover, the emphasis on soft skills and digital competencies is becoming increasingly important in the context of micro-credentials. As the job market evolves, employers are placing greater value on interpersonal skills, adaptability, and digital literacy. The need for micro-credentials to address these competencies, as they are essential for enhancing employability in a rapidly changing workforce (Sharma, 2024). By integrating assessments that evaluate both technical and soft skills, educational institutions can create more comprehensive micro-credential offerings that align with industry demands.

The expansion of micro-credentialing initiatives in developing countries is another emerging trend. Micro-credentials have the potential to foster post-COVID-19 recovery across various dimensions, including supporting innovation in higher education institutions (Tamoliūnė et al., 2023). In many developing regions, micro-credentials can provide accessible pathways for individuals to acquire skills that are in demand, thereby promoting economic growth and workforce development. By leveraging AI to deliver personalised learning experiences, educational programmes can effectively address local labour market needs and empower learners to enhance their employability. Furthermore, the ethical implications of AI in education must be considered as these trends develop. The responsible deployment of AI technologies is crucial for ensuring that educational practices remain equitable and just (Radanliev, 2024).

This includes addressing concerns related to data privacy, algorithmic bias, and the transparency of AI decision-making processes. By establishing robust ethical frameworks and governance structures, educators and policymakers can ensure that AI-integrated micro-credentials are developed and implemented in ways that prioritise learner welfare and promote social equity. In conclusion, the future of AI-integrated micro-credentials is poised to be shaped by several emerging trends, including the adoption of blockchain technology, the growing importance of soft skills and digital competencies, and the expansion of initiatives in developing countries. By proactively addressing these trends and their associated ethical considerations, educators and policymakers can ensure that micro-credentials continue to evolve in ways that meet the needs of learners and employers, ultimately contributing to a more skilled and adaptable workforce.

To maximise the potential of AI-enhanced micro-credentials, it is essential for educators, institutions, policymakers, and industry stakeholders to adopt actionable recommendations that foster collaboration, develop clear standards, and invest in necessary infrastructure. These recommendations aim to ensure that micro-credentials effectively meet the evolving needs of learners and employers while maintaining quality and credibility. One of the most critical steps in enhancing the relevance of micro-credentials is fostering collaboration between educational institutions and industry stakeholders. This collaboration can help ensure that micro-credentials are aligned with current job market demands and skill requirements.

Educational institutions must engage with employers to understand the competencies that are most valued in the workforce (Akavova, 2023). By establishing partnerships, institutions can co-create micro-credential programmes that reflect real-world needs, thereby enhancing the employability of graduates. Additionally, industry stakeholders should be involved in the design and assessment of micro-credentials to ensure that they are recognised and valued in the job market. This collaboration can take the form of advisory boards or partnerships that facilitate the exchange of knowledge and resources between educators and employers. By working together, both parties can contribute to the development of micro-credentials that are not only relevant but also credible and recognised across sectors.

Establishing clear standards and frameworks for micro-credentialing is essential for maintaining quality and credibility. There is a need for standardised definitions and criteria that outline what constitutes a micro-credential (Pendy, 2023). These standards should encompass aspects such as the learning outcomes, assessment methods, and the competencies being validated. By creating a common framework, stakeholders can ensure that micro-credentials are consistent, reliable, and comparable across different institutions and industries. Moreover, the development of a national or international registry for micro-credentials can facilitate the tracking and reporting of earned credentials. Such a system can enhance the visibility and recognition of micro-credentials among employers and other educational institutions (Kumar et al., 2022). By maintaining a centralised database, learners can easily share their achievements, and employers can verify the authenticity of the credentials, thereby fostering trust in the micro-credentialing system.

Investing in infrastructure and resources to support AI integration in micro-credentialing is another key recommendation. Institutions must ensure that they have the necessary technological infrastructure to deliver AI-driven micro-credential programmes (Alasmari, 2024). This includes investing in robust learning management systems, data analytics tools, and cybersecurity measures to protect learner data. Additionally, institutions should provide training and support for educators to effectively utilise AI technologies in their teaching practices. By equipping educators with the skills and knowledge to integrate AI into micro-credentialing, institutions can enhance the quality and effectiveness of their programmes.

Finally, addressing ethical considerations is paramount for the successful implementation of AI-enhanced micro-credentials. Stakeholders must ensure that AI systems are designed and deployed responsibly, with a focus on fairness, transparency, and accountability (Kim et al., 2022). This includes implementing measures to prevent algorithmic bias, protecting learner data, and providing clear explanations of AI decision-making processes. By prioritising ethical considerations, institutions can foster trust in AI technologies and ensure that they are used to support learner success without compromising individual rights or privacy. In conclusion, the successful implementation of AI-enhanced micro-credentials requires a collaborative effort among educators, institutions, policymakers, and industry stakeholders. By fostering collaboration, developing clear standards, investing in infrastructure, and addressing ethical considerations, stakeholders can ensure that micro-credentials effectively meet the evolving needs of learners and employers, ultimately contributing to a more skilled and adaptable workforce.

In conclusion, the integration of AI with micro-credentials presents a transformative opportunity for vocational and professional training. By leveraging AI to personalise learning experiences, streamline assessment processes, and enhance the credibility of micro-credentials, educational institutions can better meet the needs of learners and employers in a rapidly evolving job market. However, the successful implementation of AI-enhanced micro-credentials requires careful consideration of ethical implications, quality assurance measures, and collaboration among stakeholders. As the landscape of education continues to evolve, addressing these challenges will be essential for maximising the impact of micro-credentials in supporting workforce development and lifelong learning.

REFERENCES

Abdullah, F. (2023). Micro-credentials at higher education institutions: towards smooth sailing ahead., 118-126. https://doi.org/DOI: 10.2991/978-2-38476-196-8_11

Abulibdeh, A., Zaidan, E., & Abulibdeh, R. (2024). Navigating the confluence of artificial intelligence and education for sustainable development in the era of industry 4.0: Challenges, opportunities, and ethical dimensions. *Journal of Cleaner Production*, 437, 437. DOI: 10.1016/j.jclepro.2023.140527

Ahmad, K., Iqbal, W., El-Hassan, A., Qadir, J., Benhaddo, D., Ayyash, M., & Al-Fuqaha, A. (2023). Data-Driven Artificial Intelligence in Education: A Comprehensive Review. *IEEE Transactions on Learning Technologies*, 17, 12–31. DOI: 10.1109/TLT.2023.3314610

Akavova, A. (2023). Adaptive learning and artificial intelligence in the educational space. E3s Web of Conferences, 451, 06011. https://doi.org/DOI: 10.1051/e3sconf/202345106011

Alasmari, T. (2024). Reshaping vocational training: A study on the recognition of micro-credentials in job markets. *Education + Training*, 66(2/3), 233–251. DOI: 10.1108/ET-07-2023-0282

Albdrani, R., & Al-Shargabi, A. A. (2023). Investigating the effectiveness of ChatGPT for providing personalized learning experience: A case study. *International Journal of Advanced Computer Science and Applications*, 14(11). Advance online publication. DOI: 10.14569/IJACSA.2023.01411122

Alrayes, A., Henari, T. F., & Ahmed, D. A. (2024). Chatgpt in education – understanding the Bahraini academics perspective. *Electronic Journal of e-Learning*, 22(2), 112–134. DOI: 10.34190/ejel.22.2.3250

Anuyahong, B., Rattanapong, C., & Patcha, I. (2023). Analyzing the impact of artificial intelligence in personalized learning and adaptive assessment in higher education. *International Journal of Innovation and Scientific Research*, X(IV), 88–93. DOI: 10.51244/IJRSI.2023.10412

Arvin, N. (2023). Teacher experiences with ai-based educational tools. aitechbesosci, 1(2), 26-32. https://doi.org/DOI: 10.61838/kman.aitech.1.2.5

Azzam, A., & Charles, T. (2024). A Review of Artificial Intelligence in K-12 Education. *Open Journal of Applied Science*, 14(8), 2088–2100. DOI: 10.4236/ojapps.2024.148137

Baskara, R. (2023). Personalised learning with ai: Implications for ignatian pedagogy. *International Journal of Educational Best Practices*, 7(1), 1. DOI: 10.31258/ijebp.v7n1.p1-16

Brown, M., McGreal, R., & Peters, M. (2023). A strategic institutional response to micro-credentials: key questions for educational leaders. Journal of Interactive Media in Education, 2023(1). https://doi.org/DOI: 10.5334/jime.801

Bruguera, C. (2023). *Exploring learners' motivations and preferences for micro-credentials: a mixed-method study*. Ubiquity Proceedings., DOI: 10.5334/uproc.67

Chaka, C. (2022). Fourth industrial revolution—a review of applications, prospects, and challenges for artificial intelligence, robotics and blockchain in higher education. Research and Practice in Technology Enhanced Learning, 18, 002. https://doi.org/DOI: 10.58459/rptel.2023.18002

Chakravorty, D. K., Lawrence, R., He, Z., Brashear, W., Liu, H., Palughi, A. J., & Palsole, S. V. (2023). Access to Computing Education Using Micro-Credentials for Cyberinfrastructure. *Journal of Computational Science*, 14(2).

Charles, R., & Charles, T. (2024). High School Students' Perceptions of Using AI for Learning. *Voice of the Publisher*, 10(3), 284–297. DOI: 10.4236/vp.2024.103024

Charles, T. (2021). The past, present and future of assessments in the higher education sector. In Hill, C., Lamie, J., & Gore, T. (Eds.), *The Evolution of Transnational Education* (pp. 126–136). Routledge. DOI: 10.4324/9781003225386-13

Charles, T., & Hill, C. (2023). Remaining steadfast in the face of overwhelming change: Ethics and practice in emergency remote teaching–A case study in Dubai. In Lamie, J., & Hill, C. (Eds.), *The evolving nature of universities* (pp. 89–98). Routledge. DOI: 10.4324/9781003389361-7

Chen, L., Chen, P., & Lin, Z. (2020). Artificial intelligence in education: A review. *IEEE Access : Practical Innovations, Open Solutions*, 8, 75264–75278. DOI: 10.1109/ACCESS.2020.2988510

Clausen, J. (2021). Learning to fly: Development and design of a micro-credentialing system for an educator preparation program in the absence of a required educational technology course. *TechTrends*, 66(2), 276–286. DOI: 10.1007/s11528-021-00673-x PMID: 34664042

Deng, Y., Kamani, M., & Mahdavi, M. (2020). Adaptive personalised federated learning. https://doi.org//arxiv.2003.13461DOI: 10.48550

Desmarchelier, R., & Cary, L. (2022). Toward just and equitable micro-credentials: An Australian perspective. *International Journal of Educational Technology in Higher Education*, 19(1), 25. Advance online publication. DOI: 10.1186/s41239-022-00332-y PMID: 35669714

Drewery, D., Woodside, J., & Eppel, K. (2022). Artificial intelligence and résumé critique experiences. *Canadian Journal of Career Development*, 21(2), 28–39. DOI: 10.53379/cjcd.2022.338

Eidesen, P., Bjune, A. E., & Lang, S. I. (2023). "show me how to use a microscope" – the development and evaluation of certification as direct assessment of practical lab skills. *Ecology and Evolution*, 13(10), e10592. Advance online publication. DOI: 10.1002/ece3.10592 PMID: 37841223

Familoni, B.Babajide Tolulope FamiloniNneamaka Chisom Onyebuchi. (2024). Advancements and challenges in ai integration for technical literacy: A systematic review. *Engineering Science & Technology Journal*, 5(4), 1415–1430. DOI: 10.51594/estj.v5i4.1042

Gauthier, T. (2020). The value of microcredentials: The employer's perspective. *The Journal of Competency-Based Education*, 5(2), e01209. Advance online publication. DOI: 10.1002/cbe2.1209

Gligorea, I., Cioca, M., Oancea, R., Gorski, A.-T., Gorski, H., & Tudorache, P. (2023). Adaptive learning using artificial intelligence in e-learning: A literature review. *Education Sciences*, 13(12), 1216. DOI: 10.3390/educsci13121216

Göçen, A., & Aydemir, F. (2020). Artificial intelligence in education and schools. *Research on Education and Media*, 12(1), 13–21. DOI: 10.2478/rem-2020-0003

Güçlü Aydoğan, M., Draganović, S., & Elen, M. A. (2024). Online learning self-efficacy beliefs predict subjective well-being of college students during COVID-19 pandemic. *Journal of Educational Technology and Online Learning*, 7(3), 334–345. DOI: 10.31681/jetol.1513598

Halim, F. (2023). Development and validation of a questionnaire for microlearning requirements in micro-credentials: a pilot study. https://doi.org/DOI: 10.21203/rs.3.rs-3162218/v1

Healy, M. (2021). Microcredential learners need quality careers and employability support. *The Journal of Teaching and Learning for Graduate Employability*, 12(1), 21–23. DOI: 10.21153/jtlge2021vol12no1art1071

Hill, C., Abu-Ayyash, E., & Charles, T. (2023). By nature, a social animal: An exploration of perceptions of online group work. *Cambridge Journal of Education*, 53(5), 665–681. DOI: 10.1080/0305764X.2023.2206795

Holmes, W., Porayska-Pomsta, K., Holstein, K., Sutherland, E., Baker, T., Shum, S., & Koedinger, K. (2021). Ethics of ai in education: Towards a community-wide framework. *International Journal of Artificial Intelligence in Education*, 32(3), 504–526. DOI: 10.1007/s40593-021-00239-1

Hunt, T., Carter, R., Zhang, L., & Yang, S. (2020). Micro-credentials: The potential of personalised professional development. *Development and Learning in Organizations*, 34(2), 33–35. DOI: 10.1108/DLO-09-2019-0215

Kamenskih, A. (2022). The analysis of security and privacy risks in smart education environments. *Journal of Smart Cities and Society*, 1(1), 17–29. DOI: 10.3233/SCS-210114

Katiyar, P. (2024). Ai-driven personalized learning systems: enhancing educational effectiveness. eatp. https://doi.org/DOI: 10.53555/kuey.v30i5.4961

Kiiskilä, P., Kukkonen, A., & Pirkkalainen, H. (2023). Are micro-credentials valuable for students? perspective on verifiable digital credentials. *SN Computer Science*, 4(4), 366. Advance online publication. DOI: 10.1007/s42979-023-01797-y

Kim, J., Lee, H., & Cho, Y. (2022). Learning design to support student-ai collaboration: Perspectives of leading teachers for ai in education. *Education and Information Technologies*, 27(5), 6069–6104. DOI: 10.1007/s10639-021-10831-6

Kiyasseh, D., Laca, J., Haque, T., Miles, B., Wagner, C., Donoho, D., & Hung, A. (2023). A multi-institutional study using artificial intelligence to provide reliable and fair feedback to surgeons. *Communications Medicine*, 3(1), 42. Advance online publication. DOI: 10.1038/s43856-023-00263-3 PMID: 36997578

Klímová, B., Pikhart, M., & Kacetl, J. (2023). Ethical issues of the use of ai-driven mobile apps for education. *Frontiers in Public Health*, 10, 1118116. Advance online publication. DOI: 10.3389/fpubh.2022.1118116 PMID: 36711343

Kohler, M., Gamrat, C., Raish, V., & Gross, E. (2021). Microlearning and micro-credentials in higher education. In *Microlearning in the digital age* (pp. 109–128). Routledge. DOI: 10.4324/9780367821623-10

Kumar, J., Richard, R., Osman, S., & Lowrence, K. (2022). Micro-credentials in leveraging emergency remote teaching: The relationship between novice users' insights and identity in malaysia. *International Journal of Educational Technology in Higher Education*, 19(1), 18. Advance online publication. DOI: 10.1186/s41239-022-00323-z PMID: 35382441

Kwak, Y., Ahn, J., & Seo, Y. (2022). Influence of ai ethics awareness, attitude, anxiety, and self-efficacy on nursing students' behavioral intentions. *BMC Nursing*, 21(1), 267. Advance online publication. DOI: 10.1186/s12912-022-01048-0 PMID: 36180902

Lang, J. (2023). Workforce upskilling: Can universities meet the challenges of lifelong learning? *International Journal of Information and Learning Technology*, 40(5), 388–400. DOI: 10.1108/IJILT-01-2023-0001

Lee-Chavarria, D., Loucks, T. L., Paranal, R., Sampson, R., & Feghali-Bostwick, C. (2024). Supporting clinical research professionals through educational innovations. *Frontiers in Pharmacology*, 14, 1304415. Advance online publication. DOI: 10.3389/fphar.2023.1304415 PMID: 38259267

Li, X. (2024). Personalized learning path recommendation algorithm for english listening learning. jes, 20(6s), 2188-2199. https://doi.org/DOI: 10.52783/jes.3133

Lim, S., Phan, T., Law, M., Goh, G., Lukies, M., Joseph, T., & Clements, W. (2022). Non-radiologist perception of the use of artificial intelligence (ai) in diagnostic medical imaging reports. *Journal of Medical Imaging and Radiation Oncology*, 66(8), 1029–1034. DOI: 10.1111/1754-9485.13388 PMID: 35191186

Lin, J., Sha, L., Gašević, D., & Chen, G. (2022). Establishing trustworthy artificial intelligence in automated feedback. https://doi.org/DOI: 10.35542/osf.io/5efxn

Maina, M., Ortiz, L., Mancini, F., & Melo, M. (2022). A micro-credentialing methodology for improved recognition of he employability skills. *International Journal of Educational Technology in Higher Education*, 19(1), 10. Advance online publication. DOI: 10.1186/s41239-021-00315-5 PMID: 35224180

Mardisentosa, B., Rahardja, U., Zelina, K., Oganda, F. P., & Hardini, M. (2021, November). Sustainable learning micro-credential using blockchain for student achievement records. In *2021 Sixth International Conference on Informatics and Computing (ICIC)* (pp. 1-6). IEEE. DOI: 10.1109/ICIC54025.2021.9632913

Masrek, M., Susantari, T., Mutia, F., Yuwinanto, H. P., & Atmi, R. T. (2024). Enabling education everywhere: How artificial intelligence empowers ubiquitous and lifelong learning. *Environment-Behaviour Proceedings Journal*, 9(SI18), 57–63. DOI: 10.21834/e-bpj.v9iSI18.5462

McGreal, R. (2024). Empowering micro-credentials using blockchain and artificial intelligence. In *Global Perspectives on Micro-Learning and Micro-Credentials in Higher Education* (p. 16). IGI Global. DOI: 10.4018/979-8-3693-0343-6.ch006

McGreal, R., Mackintosh, W., Cox, G., & Olcott, D.Jr. (2022). Bridging the gap: Micro-credentials for development. *International Review of Research in Open and Distance Learning*, 23(3), 288–302. DOI: 10.19173/irrodl.v23i3.6696

McGreal, R., & Olcott, D.Jr. (2022). A strategic reset: Micro-credentials for higher education leaders. *Smart Learning Environments*, 9(1), 9. DOI: 10.1186/s40561-022-00190-1

Miao, M., Ahmed, M., Ahsan, N., & Qamar, B. (2023). Intention to use technology for micro-credential programs: Evidence from technology acceptance and self-determination model. *International Journal of Educational Management*, 38(4), 948–977. DOI: 10.1108/IJEM-02-2023-0066

Mir, U., Kar, A., & Gupta, M. (2021). Ai-enabled digital identity – inputs for stakeholders and policymakers. *Journal of Science and Technology Policy Management*, 13(3), 514–541. DOI: 10.1108/JSTPM-09-2020-0134

Murtaza, M., Ahmed, Y., Shamsi, J., Sherwani, F., & Usman, M. (2022). Ai-based personalized e-learning systems: Issues, challenges, and solutions. *IEEE Access : Practical Innovations, Open Solutions*, 10, 81323–81342. DOI: 10.1109/ACCESS.2022.3193938

Ng, D., Leung, J., Su, J., Ng, R., & Chu, S. (2023). Teachers' ai digital competencies and twenty-first century skills in the post-pandemic world. *Educational Technology Research and Development*, 71(1), 137–161. DOI: 10.1007/s11423-023-10203-6 PMID: 36844361

Öncü, S., Çolakoğlu, M., & Colak, H. (2024). Engagement dynamics in information technology education: A comparative analysis of online vs. face-to-face instruction. *Journal of Educational Technology and Online Learning*, 7(3), 321–333. DOI: 10.31681/jetol.1508735

Orak, C., & Turan, Z. (2024). Using artificial intelligence in digital video production: A systematic review study. *Journal of Educational Technology and Online Learning*, 7(3), 286–307. DOI: 10.31681/jetol.1459434

Orman, R., Şimşek, E., & Çakır, M. (2023). Micro-credentials and reflections on higher education. *Higher Education Evaluation and Development*, 17(2), 96–112. DOI: 10.1108/HEED-08-2022-0028

Pendy, B. (2023). Artificial intelligence: The future of education. *Jurnal Indonesia Sosial Sains*, 2(11). Advance online publication. DOI: 10.59141/jiss.v2i11.801

Peters, M. (2023). *Skills alignment for lifelong learners in higher education: smart catalogues for reskilling and upskilling pathways*. Ubiquity Proceedings., DOI: 10.5334/uproc.71

Radanliev, P., Santos, O., Brandon-Jones, A., & Joinson, A. (2024). Ethics and responsible ai deployment. *Frontiers in Artificial Intelligence*, 7, 1377011. Advance online publication. DOI: 10.3389/frai.2024.1377011 PMID: 38601110

Reed, A. (2023). Micro-credentials and the role of evidence: Increasing the potential for learner-centeredness, inclusivity and an expansive model of assessment and credentialing. *International Journal of Information and Learning Technology*, 40(5), 401–412. DOI: 10.1108/IJILT-12-2022-0228

Renumol, V. (2021). A systematic literature review on adaptive content recommenders in personalized learning environments from 2015 to 2020. *Journal of Computers in Education*, 9(1), 113–148. DOI: 10.1007/s40692-021-00199-4

Ruddy, C., & Ponte, F. (2019). Preparing students for university studies and beyond: A micro-credential trial that delivers academic integrity awareness. *Journal of the Australian Library and Information Association*, 68(1), 56–67. DOI: 10.1080/24750158.2018.1562520

Sabharwal, D., Kabha, R., & Srivastava, K. (2023). Artificial intelligence (ai)-powered virtual assistants and their effect on human productivity and laziness: Study on students of delhi-ncr (india) & fujairah (uae). *Journal of Content Community and Communication*, 17(9), 162–174. DOI: 10.31620/JCCC.06.23/12

Sarı, T., Nayir, F., & Bozkurt, A. (2024). Reimagining education: Bridging artificial intelligence, transhumanism, and critical pedagogy. *Journal of Educational Technology and Online Learning*, 7(1), 102–115. DOI: 10.31681/jetol.1308022

Schumacher, C., & Ifenthaler, D. (2018). Features students really expect from learning analytics. *Computers in Human Behavior*, 78, 397–407. DOI: 10.1016/j.chb.2017.06.030

Selvaratnam, R. M., & Sankey, M. D. (2021). An integrative literature review of the implementation of micro-credentials in higher education: Implications for practice in Australasia. *Journal of Teaching and Learning for Graduate Employability*, 12(1), 1–17. DOI: 10.21153/jtlge2021vol12no1art942

Seo, K., Tang, J., Roll, I., Fels, S., & Yoon, D. (2021). The impact of artificial intelligence on learner–instructor interaction in online learning. *International Journal of Educational Technology in Higher Education*, 18(1), 54. Advance online publication. DOI: 10.1186/s41239-021-00292-9 PMID: 34778540

Seo, K., Tang, J., Roll, I., Fels, S., & Yoon, D. (2021). The impact of artificial intelligence on learner–instructor interaction in online learning. *International Journal of Educational Technology in Higher Education*, 18(1), 54. Advance online publication. DOI: 10.1186/s41239-021-00292-9 PMID: 34778540

Sharma, H., Jain, V., Mogaji, E., & Babbilid, A. S. (2024). Blended learning and augmented employability: A multi-stakeholder perspective of the micro-credentialing ecosystem in higher education. *International Journal of Educational Management*, 38(4), 1021–1044. DOI: 10.1108/IJEM-12-2022-0497

Shehzad, N., & Charles, T. (2023). Exploring the impact of instructor social presence on student engagement in online higher education. *Contemporary Educational Technology*, 15(4), ep484. DOI: 10.30935/cedtech/13823

Soon, J. J., & Ismail, R. (2021). Professional Jobs and Structural Unemployment in the Post-Pandemic World: Is Micro-Credentialing the Missing Bridge. *The New Normal: Reinventing Professional Life and Familial Bonding in the Post COVID, 19.*

Subasinghe, C., & Giridharan, B. (2023). Introducing multidisciplinary micro-credentialing: rethinking learning and development for higher education and industry. In *Introducing Multidisciplinary Micro-credentialing: Rethinking Learning and Development for Higher Education and Industry* (pp. 3–16). Emerald Publishing Limited. DOI: 10.1108/978-1-80382-459-820231002

Surono, S. (2023). Development of micro credential design for project management to improve the quality of engineering practices. *International Journal of Social Service and Research*, 3(11), 2910–2920. DOI: 10.46799/ijssr.v3i11.598

Tammeleht, A. (2023). Development and piloting of a micro-credential programme in research ethics and integrity leadership – an example from estonia., 733-740. https://doi.org/DOI: 10.4995/HEAd23.2023.16220

Tamoliūnė, G., Teresevičienė, M., Volungevičienė, A., Trepulė, E., & Daukšienė, E. (2023). Exploring the potential of micro-credentials: A systematic literature review. *Frontiers in Education*, 7, 1006811. Advance online publication. DOI: 10.3389/feduc.2022.1006811

Tee, P., Cham, T.-H., Aw, E. C.-X., Khudaykulov, A., & Zhang, X. (2023). Marketing micro-credentials: Understanding learners' engagement and willingness to pay more. *International Journal of Educational Management*, 38(4), 1001–1020. DOI: 10.1108/IJEM-03-2023-0096

Tuomi, I. (2022). Artificial intelligence, 21st century competences, and socio-emotional learning in education: More than high-risk? *European Journal of Education*, 57(4), 601–619. DOI: 10.1111/ejed.12531

Wheelahan, L., & Moodie, G. (2021). Analysing micro-credentials in higher education: A Bernsteinian analysis. *Journal of Curriculum Studies*, 53(2), 212–228. DOI: 10.1080/00220272.2021.1887358

Yang, B. (2022). An empirical study on the application of machine learning for higher education and social service. *Journal of Global Information Management*, 30(7), 1–16. DOI: 10.4018/JGIM.296723

Zhang, G. (2024). Optimization and application of english word memory algorithm based on reinforcement learning. jes, 20(6s), 1786-1799. https://doi.org/DOI: 10.52783/jes.3096

Zhang, X., Liu, C., Chai, K., & Poslad, S. (2020). A challenge-response assisted authorisation scheme for data access in permissioned blockchains. *Sensors (Basel)*, 20(17), 4681. DOI: 10.3390/s20174681 PMID: 32825194

Zou, H., Ullah, A., Qazi, Z., Naeem, A., & Rehan, S. (2023). Impact of micro-credential learning on students' perceived employability: The mediating role of human capital. *International Journal of Educational Management*, 38(4), 897–915. DOI: 10.1108/IJEM-01-2023-0002

Chapter 11
Integration of Micro-Credentials With Artificial Intelligence in Open Education:
Developments and Challenges for Middle East Countries

Sehar un Nisa Hassan
College of Public Health and Health Informatics, University of Ha'il, Ha'il, Saudi Arabia

ABSTRACT

The global trends in higher education are moving toward skill-based credentials. Micro-credentials and digital badges are the buzzwords to demonstrate the acquisition of industry-specific skills of the candidates. Integration of AI in open education could enhance the deployment of personalized higher education for everyone and can address several challenges related to retention, assessment, and credibility of micro-credentials in open pedagogy. Timely sharing of these credentials across a wide range of international systems through AI will widen the prospects of continuing education and employment for learners. The Middle East is making timely responses to the digitization of education systems. According to some market forecasts, the market for AI tools in the Middle East region will reach nearly eight billion dollars by the year 2027. There are several ethical dilemmas surrounding use of AI in education and micro-credential programs such as data privacy, biasness and fairness, equity in access, accountability, transparency, cultural sensitivity and the impacts on traditional education models and current review therefore stresses the need for comprehensive ethical guidelines and policies in the Middle East region rather blind

DOI: 10.4018/979-8-3693-5488-9.ch011

adoption. The book chapter offers an analysis of the existing scenario, emerging opportunities and challenges and makes specific recommendations to expand and integrate AI tools in open education in the Middle East region.

INTRODUCTION

Political, social, economic, scientific, and technological revolutions in the past intersected and influenced the role and purpose of tertiary education recognizing the need for continual learning for human development and agency. Access to good quality higher education is viewed as a human right and could play a significant role in addressing social and economic challenges. These revolutions have led to the emergence of open education initiatives, such as massive online courses and open educational resources, representing a paradigm shift in education (Blessinger & Bliss, 2016).

Middle East region is making a fast response to the adoption of the latest technological advancements in all fields including the education system. The traditional and open education systems in this region are employing new digital tools, and immersive techniques and creating learning environments that meet the unique and diverse educational needs of learners (Singh et al., 2019). The integration of advanced technologies like Artificial Intelligence (AI), is the emerging priority in the education system in the Middle East region. Despite recent and significant advancements in AI technologies within this region's education sector, several technological, attitudinal, and ethical issues are at the forefront and hinder the swift adoption and integration of digitized education. This chapter briefly introduces the significance of micro-credentials in job skills development and enhancement, the potential benefits of AI integration in open education and lists a few AI tools currently employed for the delivery of micro-credentials. Micro-credentials hold significant importance in the Middle East region as they provide effective quick solutions to diminish the wide gaps in the job skills market. Integration of AI in the delivery of micro-credentials can support workforce development and will also contribute towards the achievement of strategic goals in the adoption of educational technology in these countries. The key focus of this book chapter is to provide an overarching overview of current developments and challenges in the deployment of educational technology in the Middle East region. The chapter also provides a comparative analysis with global trends and conducts a critical analysis of literature from the Middle East region to understand the educational, technological, sociocultural and ethical context for the development and implementation of AI-powered micro-credential programs. The exploratory and critical analysis of the recent literature provides the basis to make recommendations for competency-based digitized educational tools and assessment methods. It also provides the framework for the development of educational policies that are essential for creating an environment that supports the effective and equitable integration of AI in micro-credentials, ultimately enhancing the efficacy of competency-based online studies. The authors propose specific research questions to address identified gaps in research and emphasize the need for interdisciplinary research to expand and integrate AI in open education in the Middle East region.

Micro-Credentials in Open Education

A micro-credential is a certification of assessed learning that is additional, alternate, complementary to or a part of a formal qualification. In open education, a micro-credential refers to a certificate earned through Massive Open Online Courses (MOOCs) or other shorter forms of learning experiences. It can serve as a signal of achievement that stands alone or interacts with formal qualifications, providing alternative entry mechanisms to degree programs, value-added programs during degrees, and 'last mile' services connecting learners to work experience and employment (Oliver, 2019).

In the vocational education and training (VET) system, micro-credentials work by providing learners with smaller blocks of learning that are more focused and specific than traditional degrees or certificates. This allows learners to acquire targeted skills and knowledge quickly and efficiently. For employers, micro-credentials help identify candidates with specific skills needed for their industry, making the hiring process more streamlined. Providers benefit from offering these specialized courses, catering to the demand for flexible and relevant training options. Overall, micro-credentials offer a more agile and responsive approach to education and training in the VET system (McGovern, 2019); (Palmer, 2021).

Table 1 presents some of the job skills related to the fields of information technology and marketing that can be developed or enhanced through micro-credentials.

Table 1. Examples of job skills, tasks and assessment methods used in micro-credentials

Micro-credentials	Tasks	Assessment Indicators
Digital Marketing	Create a social media marketing campaign for a new product, including targeted ads and audience engagement strategies.	Submit a report outlining the campaign strategy, results, and reflections on areas for improvement.
Data Analysis	Analyze a dataset provided by the course instructor to identify trends, patterns, and insights.	Present findings through a data visualization tool and give a brief presentation explaining the analysis process and key takeaways.
Project Management	Lead a team in planning and executing a small project, including setting goals, delegating tasks, and managing timelines and resources.	Submit a project proposal, Gantt chart, and final report detailing the project's outcomes and lessons learned.
Coding and Programming	Complete a coding challenge or project that demonstrates your understanding of programming concepts and ability to write clean, efficient code.	Have your code reviewed by an instructor or industry professional, who will provide feedback on its correctness, efficiency, and readability.

Global Trends in the Integration of AI in Micro-credentials

Educational institutions in various regions of the world are employing various AI tools to improve the delivery of micro-credentials. The literature supports that integrating micro-credentials with artificial intelligence is likely to improve the delivery and credibility of micro-credentials in open education (Brown et al., 2021). AI can help personalize the learning experience for individuals pursuing micro-credentials. By tracking and analyzing learner behavior and preferences, AI can recommend additional resources or courses that align with their interests and goals. This can help learners make more informed choices about their educational pathways and stay engaged in their learning journey (Palmer, 2021).

The integration of technologies like virtual reality and chatbots significantly impacts teaching and learning processes. These tools provide immersive and interactive learning experiences that can enhance understanding and retention. Virtual reality can offer simulation-based learning, providing practical exposure, while chatbots facilitate personalized support and instantaneous feedback. These technologies contribute to better engagement and improved learning outcomes, which, in the long term, foster a more adaptive and responsive educational environment.

The assessment process for micro-credentials by integrating AI ensures quality and academic integrity by including authentic problem-solving in real-world applications, personalized feedback, and maintaining accountability for academic integrity in arrangements with any other party involved in the provision of higher education. Additionally, comprehensive reviews are conducted regularly to assess the design, content, learning outcomes, assessment methods, and learners' achievement of those outcomes (Oliver, 2019). Learners also have opportunities to provide feedback on their educational experiences, which informs monitoring, review, and improvement activities. These measures help to ensure robust assessment, feedback, academic integrity, and governance in the micro-credentialing process.

Some of the commonly employed AI tools in the open education system are presented in Table 2:

Table 2. Examples of AI tools used in open education systems

AI tools	Examples	Key Features
Learning Management Systems (LMS)	Blackboard, Canvas and Moodle	Incorporate AI features to support personalized learning experiences, adapt assessments to student needs, and provide analytics to monitor learner progress.
AI Chatbots	Intercom and Drift	Offer immediate support to learners by answering course-related questions, and help in navigation within micro-credential pathways.
Adaptive Learning Platforms	DreamBox and Smart Sparrow	Employ AI features to customize educational content based on each learner's individual requirements, facilitating skill acquisition relevant to micro credentials.
Interactive Content Creation	Articulate 360 and Genially	AI-driven platforms assist educators in developing adaptive learning materials or engaging content tailored for micro-credential courses.
Automated Grading Solutions	Gradescope and ProctorU	Utilize AI technologies for automating the grading process and ensuring academic integrity during assessments, which streamlines the evaluation of micro-credential programs.
Learning Analytics Tools	Brightspace Insights and Civitas Learning	Apply AI features to assess student data, make predictions about performance, and identify learners at risk, thereby enhancing the overall experience for those obtaining micro-credentials.
Skill Assessment Tools	Codility and HackerRank	Employs AI to assess technical competencies through coding challenges that align with micro-credentials in various technical fields

These AI tools contribute to a more effective and tailored educational experience for individuals pursuing micro-credentials as well as improve the accuracy in the assessment of job skills ensuring that learners acquire the necessary knowledge and competencies to meet the professional requirements for the target job market and/or positions.

A Scoping Review on the Adoption of Educational Technology and Integration of AI in Open Education in the Middle East

Educational institutions and systems in the Arab countries in the past few years especially post-COVID-19 have shown significant interest and shift towards the adoption of educational technology, and this is validated by the market forecasts for the educational technology industry which is projected to reach nearly eight billion dollars by the year 2027, only in the Middle East region. This is because the traditional education system can enhance the educational experiences of learners and efficiency in assessment by use of AI tools whereas the open education system can enhance their delivery and credibility. However, at present there is a dearth of scientific studies from the Middle East region and limited empirical evidence does not provide enough guidance on theoretical frameworks nor adequate knowledge about the implementation of AI tools in education that align with the local educational, socioeconomic, and cultural context (Zhang & Aslan, 2021); (Fadlelmula & Qadhi, 2024). Accumulative knowledge is imperative to the development of an appropriate action framework for AI integration in the open education system of Middle East countries.

This book chapter therefore aims to provide an overarching review of the current developments, challenges and specific gaps in educational technology adoption in the open education system in Middle Eastern countries. Moreover, this review will help determine the future priorities for research and development to accomplish the integration of AI in the delivery of open education and micro-credentials in the Middle East region. Technological transformations in open education require readiness to learn from prior projects and collaborations.

The scoping review presented in this book chapter is compiled after consulting several sources including newspaper articles, original research articles, expert opinions, review articles, government and other organizational reports, online educational resources, and professional guidelines. The literature search and preliminary exploratory analysis were carried out by employing AI-powered search engines (Semantic Scholar, Elicit & Scite). This literature search through AI-powered search engines supported the retrieval and review of the most relevant articles on the integration of AI in open education in Middle Eastern countries. The keywords and/or terms used in the prompts created for the literature search are listed in Table 3.

Table 3. Keywords used in the prompts for retrieval of most relevant literature on Integration of AI in micro-credentials in the Middle East

Digital credentials	Micro-credentialing	Online education	Educational technology
Artificial intelligence in micro-credentials	Competency-based online studies	Skill-based e-learning	Adaptation of online learning materials in local languages
AI-powered assessment in education	Micro-credentials in the Middle East	Workforce skills development in the Middle East	Ethical challenges in AI integration in education
Technological Innovations in open Education the Arab world	Learning Analytics Tools in Middle Eastern universities	Credentialing initiatives in online education and its societal implications	Social aspects of AI integration and expansion in education

The research articles and other literature retrieved through the initial search were screened for their appropriateness. The key studies were evaluated, and a scoping review was completed to answer the following research questions.

1. What are the current developments and challenges faced by educational institutions in the middle east region AI integration in open education?
2. What are the challenges in implementing personalized learning using AI tools for students with diverse backgrounds and varying levels of digital competence?
3. What is needed to increase awareness among learners from this region about specific activities or tasks that can be used to earn micro-credentials and how do they contribute to their overall learning goals?
4. In what ways does the use of technology, such as virtual reality and chatbots, impact the effectiveness of teaching and learning processes and long-term student outcomes?
5. What are the perceptions of students and teachers about associated ethical issues in the use of AI tools in open education and the role of teachers? How the ethical concerns surrounding AI integration in open education be best addressed moving forward?
6. How can AI tools help to achieve transparency in open courses and improve the methods of evaluation of learner's skills to gain the trust of employers in the Middle East region?
7. How do national, regional, and/or international quality assurance agencies and professional organizations improve the credibility of courses through the integration of AI in micro-credentials?
8. What measures are needed to increase the credibility and recognition of micro-credentials among learners, educational institutions, and employers?

9. What types of policy recommendations are needed to minimize the digital divide, improve technical infrastructure, improvement of procedures for the recognition of micro-credentials and training gaps to enhance the technical skills of users to gain maximum benefit?
10. What practical measures are needed in the adoption of specific AI innovations that can enable open education from this region to spearhead digital revolutions in micro-credentials?
11. What are the current gaps in existing research to understand emerging and ever-evolving dilemmas related to the use of AI tools in open education at regional and international level?

This exploratory and critical analysis of literature not only focuses upon the accumulation of empirical evidence about technological and educational accomplishments in this domain, but it also highlights the social and ethical challenges that are being ignored due to the fast pace of development in this field. The goal is to acquaint researchers with state-of-the-art research on technological innovations and developments and make them aware of the social and ethical implications associated with integrating and expanding AI tools in open education in the Middle East region. A holistic perspective provided in this book chapter will aid in building a context for future research studies that should focus on investigating and proposing solutions to handle ongoing and emerging educational, technological, social and ethical issues associated with the integration and expansion of AI in competency-based education.

Current Developments and Challenges in Educational Technology Adoption in the Arab World

Lack of infrastructure and a shortage of financial and human resources compromise access to quality education in traditional higher education systems and or institutions in various regions of the world (Tlili et al., 2020). The development of educational technologies around the globe created an alternative path in the form of online distance education that increases access to quality education for large sections of populations globally. However, open education systems and online studies are partially able to assert their credibility in Middle Eastern countries. This limited trust is attributable to several factors such as cultural context, quality assurance issues, employer perceptions, disparities in technology infrastructure, and lack of clear government policies have caused inconsistencies in the implementation of curriculum and assessment methods in e-learning. Despite these challenges, there is a growing acceptance and adoption of online education in some Middle Eastern countries, particularly accelerated by the COVID-19 pandemic. Initiatives by governments to promote digital literacy and encourage diverse educational pathways also reflect a shift toward greater acceptance of open education and online studies. The integration of AI and micro-credential initiatives in the Middle East has gained a significant pace of development in the education sector. The following section explores the nature, influence, and outcomes of these programs, emphasizing the potential benefits and obstacles encountered in the region.

The government of the United Arab Emirates (UAE) has introduced several initiatives and strategies to integrate AI technologies into the educational landscape seamlessly. This strategic move aligns with the UAE's focus on sustainability and aims to enhance academic excellence, student achievements, operational efficiency, and sustainability practices within higher education institutions (Shwedeh et al., 2024). One of the examples of these efforts is the opening of Micro-credential initiatives, which provide targeted education and training in specific skills, and are emerging as a vital component in addressing the educational gaps associated with AI. These initiatives can offer flexible learning opportunities that cater to the needs of professionals seeking to enhance their skills in AI and related technologies. They serve as a valuable pathway for individuals aiming to enhance their skills without the necessity of enrolling in traditional degree programs, thereby fostering a culture of lifelong learning (Zou et al., 2024). The effectiveness of such programs, however, largely depends on their alignment with industry needs and the extent to which they are recognized by employers. For example, the development of AI literacy curricula in K-12 education is crucial for preparing future generations to engage with AI technologies effectively (Zhang et al., 2024). This foundational education can solve the problem of a shortage of workforce with basic IT skills. These skills are needed to carry out various tasks in the healthcare and tourism industries that are growing at a fast pace in this region. Despite the promising potential of AI in education and micro-credential initiatives, several challenges persist. A lack of standardized curricula and recognition of micro-credentials across different sectors can hinder the effectiveness of these educational programs (Hasan et al., 2024).

In one project from Egypt designed an Intelligent Tutoring System (ITS) to teach Arabic grammar to fourth-grade students. The system, named AG TUTOR, encompasses a Tutoring Module, Question Selector Module, and Expert Module, leveraging Natural Language Processing (NLP) to enhance educational interactions (Mahmoud & Abo El-Hamayed, 2016). The company Kahoot have been working on several research projects aimed at integrating AI to enhance cognitive training and interactive learning experiences for university students in this region (Alawadhi & Abu-Ayyash, 2021); (Minton & Bligh, 2021). The use of AI and tools such as personalization, automation, virtual teacher aids, and smart campus planning can help overcome these challenges. Faculty members also demonstrate positive perceptions about the uses of AI in teaching and learning in higher education and are willing to adopt AI in their institutions considering it will be beneficial for improving student learning experiences, motivation for learning, reducing dropout rates, and providing personalized and adaptable learning path (Sharawy & Sherif Sharawy, 2023). However, the lack of existing evidence related to the implementation of AI in open education in these countries makes it difficult to fully understand and address the challenges of incorporating AI into teaching and learning.

The American University of Beirut has been involved in research on AI applications in education and has a special emphasis on improving access to quality education through adaptive learning technologies. Particularly education experts are talking about the potential of AI in remote education and language learning to support displaced communities impacted by the ongoing conflict in some countries of the region including Syria and Palestine (Habib, 2023). Youth and people from these regions can be supported to attain their educational goals through MOOCs and blended learning approaches without compromising the quality of higher education. These regions are in higher need to have open educational resources, digital libraries, and virtual labs to support education. The educational institutes from Iraq are also exploring AI applications in education amidst the challenges of rebuilding the education system post-conflict.

The University of Jordan and The Jordan University of Science and Technology are doing notable work in using AI for curriculum development and creating digital learning environments, however, there are currently wide gaps in educational accessibility and quality that can be enfolded through national-level initiatives on digital transformation in education (Obeidat et al., 2023). Higher Education Institutions (HEIs) in Oman, such as Sohar University, have adopted blended learning in response to the pandemic, utilizing platforms like the Sohar University Learning Management System (SULMS) and Microsoft Teams for educational purposes and communication. The advantages of online and blended learning include the capacity to host foreign university programs, provide elective courses, and effectively deliver courses to a higher number of students. Nevertheless, HEIS must ensure that their online and blended learning initiatives are meticulously planned with suitable assessment methods to uphold academic integrity and achieve educational objectives (Al-Fazari, 2023).

The King Abdullah University of Science and Technology (KAUST) and King Saud University from Saudi Arabia have spearheaded studies on AI in education, particularly in developing intelligent tutoring systems and automated grading systems (Al-Darrab & Rushdi, 2021). The government in KSA has launched initiatives like the Saudi AI Strategy, which includes a focus on modernizing education through AI (Elhajji et al., 2020).

One study demonstrated that AI-powered recommendation systems can be utilized in Middle Eastern history education to guide students in exploring relevant historical topics and primary sources by providing personalized suggestions based on their interests and learning objectives. These systems can recommend specific resources, such as articles, books, and primary documents, that align with the student's research questions and areas of inquiry. By leveraging AI algorithms, educators can help students navigate the vast amount of historical information available and focus on the most relevant sources for their research, thereby facilitating independent inquiry and critical analysis in Middle East history education (Ni, 2018). AI can be used to assess and validate the proficiency of learners who have completed micro-credential courses through automated grading of assessments, simulations or other types of evaluation, allowing learners to receive immediate feedback on their performance (Pirkkalainen et al., 2023). Furthermore, AI can also be used to enhance the credibility and acceptance of micro-credentials in the job market. By creating a transparent and secure credentialing system powered by blockchain technology, AI can help verify the authenticity of micro-credentials and ensure that they are recognized and valued by employers and institutions. This could help to gain the trust of learners and employers in the Middle East region.

A study from the United Arab Emirates (UAE) focuses on exploring virtual learning experiences of undergraduate students. Students were engaged in learning English as a Foreign Language (EFL) by employing 'Kahoot' which is a popular game-based interactive learning platform. The findings demonstrated potential benefits in enhancing student engagement and motivation for learning (Alawadhi & Abu-Ayyash, 2021).

Virtual reality enhances immersive learning experiences, making abstract concepts easier to understand. Chatbots provide instant feedback and personalized assistance, increasing engagement and comprehension. These technologies contribute to improved long-term student outcomes by facilitating interactive and adaptive learning environments. Technologies like virtual reality and chatbots enhance engagement and provide interactive learning experiences. However, the effectiveness depends on the quality of content and the teacher's ability to integrate these tools effectively.

The use of technology, such as virtual reality (VR) and chatbots, can significantly enhance the effectiveness of teaching and learning processes. VR provides immersive learning experiences, making complex concepts easier to understand. Chatbots offer personalized support and immediate feedback, improving student engagement and satisfaction. Another study demonstrated that instantaneous feedback was the key feature for higher acceptance of chatbots by students in classrooms where there is an imbalance in the teacher-student ratio (Essel et al., 2022). Chatbots offer instant feedback and support, which can enhance student engagement and provide personalized assistance. The long-term outcomes of integrating these technologies include improved retention rates, higher student satisfaction, and better preparedness for real-world tasks. The interactive and adaptive nature of these tools also helps students develop critical thinking and problem-solving skills, which are essential for their future careers (Ait Baha et al., 2023). These technologies can lead to better student outcomes by fostering a deeper understanding of the material and developing critical thinking skills.

AI tools such as ChatGPT can facilitate communication and collaboration between instructors and students in Arab universities by helping to identify research topics of interest to both parties, matching researchers with similar research interests, and providing suggestions for research topics. Additionally, AI tools can enhance data analysis processes, allowing instructors and students to analyze large amounts of data and identify patterns that can inform their research (Mellor, 2024).

Overall, the integration of micro-credentials with artificial intelligence in open education has the potential to revolutionize the way we learn, assess, and validate skills and knowledge. By leveraging AI technologies, we can create a more personalized, efficient, and reliable learning experience for individuals pursuing micro-credentials, ultimately empowering them to succeed in their personal and professional endeavors.

Overcoming Challenges in the Integration of Micro-Credentials with AI in Open Education in the Middle East Region:

Open Educational Resources (OER) and MOOCs are focused on eliminating conventional barriers to knowledge acquisition, academic credits, and degrees, such as financial constraints. They empower both students and educators by providing greater autonomy over content and technology. By engaging learners and teachers, these initiatives aim to enhance their influence and enhance the overall learning experience. The core objective is to democratize education and transition towards a model of abundant knowledge (Blessinger & Bliss, 2016). The integration of AI tools in expanding open education is expected to broaden access to high-quality educational materials and courses across the Arab world. This advancement could help bridge educational disparities, encourage continuous learning, and boost digital competencies among learners in the region (Jemni & Khribi, 2016). Furthermore, OER and MOOCs have the potential to foster innovative teaching approaches and collaborative learning environments, ultimately promoting educational inclusivity within the Arab world.

The status of OER in the Arab region is currently at a nascent stage. A recent systematic review of research and development in machine learning and AI in education in Egypt, Saudi Arabia, UAE, Bahrain, and Jordan concluded that successful implementation of AI and ML in Arab World Education requires a comprehensive strategy that should consider the unique context of the region (Rabie, 2023). There is a need to identify and address several challenges such as the digital divide, socio-economic barriers, and educational inequalities that hinder the adoption of AI and micro-credentials. Progress in OER adoption varies across countries in the region, with many lacking explicit policies or vision for supporting OER implementation except for select countries like Bahrain and Saudi Arabia. Educational institutions in the Middle East confront challenges related to inadequate digital infrastructure, varying levels of digital literacy among students, and resistance towards departing from traditional teaching methodologies. Moreover, there is a notable scarcity of OER development and utilization in Arab nations, particularly concerning resources available in Arabic (Tlili et al., 2020). Addressing these issues necessitates significant investments in technology infrastructure and training programs. It is imperative to focus on rectifying these challenges promptly as open and inclusive higher education systems are built upon UNESCO's three pillars of education rights – access, quality, and respect within learning environments – along with the responsibilities held by governments, educational entities, and organizations regarding resource provision and fostering conducive learning atmospheres (Blessinger & Bliss, 2016).

Technology plays a pivotal role in disseminating OER by enabling individuals, groups, and institutions to share educational content under open licenses. Effective resource discovery mechanisms are crucial elements of technological strategies for OER distribution as they ensure that users can find, utilize, and repurpose resources efficiently for their benefit. Leveraging technology within open education facilitates the management of content development, curation processes, licensing procedures, as well as dissemination efforts related to OERs – ultimately enhancing the accessibility and reusability of educational materials (Barker & Campbell, 2024). Despite this potential progress facilitated by technology-driven initiatives for OER promotion globally; limited measures have been implemented specifically aimed at empowering OER within the Arab region at present. The e-learning sector in Saudi Arabia is experiencing rapid growth; however, the academic credentials obtained through open education systems for postgraduate studies are not widely recognized by employers for hiring or promotion due to concerns regarding their credibility. Forecasts indicate that the e-learning market is projected to reach four billion dollars by 2027. The country is emphasizing nurturing local talent to reduce its reliance on outsourced human resources, particularly in the healthcare sector. Enhancing the quality of micro-credentials offered by open universities in this region can lead to cost savings and positive outcomes for workforce development within the community. In Saudi Arabia, interest in integrating AI-based learning outcomes into higher education institutions is growing; however, the actual deployment of AI remains at an early stage (Alzahrani, 2022). The notable contributions towards developing AI-based learning outcomes are primarily by King Abdulaziz University and Al Qasim University (Alotaibi & Alshehri, 2023). We as instructors at the University of Ha'il, endorse that the university has started several workshops to train instructors in the use of AI tools in assessment and to orient faculty about ethical and practical issues in deployment of AI tools in education. The moral dilemmas associated with artificial intelligence and micro-credential programs in education are complex, addressing topics such as data protection, biases in algorithms, and the effects on fairness in education. These issues are particularly pertinent in the context of the Middle East, where rapid technological advancements intersect with diverse socio-economic landscapes.

Privacy and data security concerns accompany the use of AI tools within educational settings. Users of these tools express apprehensions regarding data privacy and security issues. The collection and analysis of vast amounts of student data raises significant questions about consent, security, and the potential for misuse. As AI systems increasingly rely on personal data to tailor educational experiences, the risk of breaches and unauthorized access becomes a pressing issue. Institutions must navigate the complexities of data protection laws, such as the General Data Protection Regulation (GDPR) in Europe, which sets stringent guidelines for data handling (Burton et al., 2017). The ethical implications of data privacy extend beyond compliance; they encompass the moral responsibility of educational institutions to safeguard student information and maintain trust. Failure to adequately protect data can lead to severe consequences, including reputational damage and loss of student confidence (Valerio, 2024).

Algorithmic bias represents a significant ethical challenge in implementing artificial intelligence in educational environments. AI technologies can unintentionally carry forward pre-existing biases within their training datasets, resulting in unequal outcomes for various student populations. For example, if an AI model is developed using data that reflects previous inequalities, it may exacerbate these issues by delivering skewed recommendations or evaluations. This concern is especially critical in the realm of micro-credentials, as the success of these initiatives could be compromised if they disproportionately benefit specific demographic groups (Yu & Yu, 2023). Addressing this issue necessitates a commitment to making AI algorithms transparent and accountable, with regular assessments to detect and address biases. Educators and decision-makers must focus on creating equitable AI systems that foster inclusivity and equal access to educational resources for all students.

Educational Equity in Micro-Credentials

Research from other Middle East countries has demonstrated that disparities in digital skills and technology access pose a significant barrier, impacting the implementation of personalized learning through AI tools and effective utilization of AI tools (Teniou & Dehane, 2019). For instance, a recent study from Jordan reported varying levels of digital literacy among students, with limited exposure to formal AI education in their curriculum. This points to a potential gap between AI advancements and its integration into medical education in Jordan. Infrastructural discrepancies, such as uneven internet access and outdated digital devices, further complicate the incorporation of technology into personalized learning (Al-Qerem et al., 2023). Moreover, the implementation of micro-credential programs must consider the varying levels of access to technology and resources among different populations. In regions with significant disparities in educational infrastructure, the digital divide can hinder equitable access to micro-credential opportunities (Bruguera, 2023). The rise of micro-credentials presents both opportunities and challenges for educational equity. On one hand, micro-credentials can democratize access to education by providing flexible, targeted learning opportunities that cater to diverse learner needs (Abdullah & Ghazali, 2024). However, the effectiveness of micro-credentials in promoting educational equity hinges on their recognition by employers and educational institutions. Without widespread acknowledgement, they risk deepening existing disparities by creating a hierarchy of qualifications where only specific credentials are valued (Sharma et al., 2024). Therefore, stakeholders must collaborate in developing frameworks that ensure micro-credentials are accessible to all learners, regardless of their socio-economic background.

Addressing the ethical concerns of data privacy, algorithmic bias, and educational equity is essential for the successful integration of AI and micro-credential initiatives in the Middle East. Educational institutions must adopt a proactive approach to these challenges, fostering an environment that prioritizes ethical considerations while leveraging the benefits of technological advancements. Engaging in ongoing dialogue and feedback loops with all stakeholders is crucial for proactively tackling ethical dilemmas (Murtaza et al., 2022). Concerns regarding data privacy, bias, and the potential displacement of human interaction by AI are shared by students and educators. Mitigating these apprehensions necessitates the establishment of well-defined ethical standards, ensuring transparency in AI algorithms, and striking a balance between AI utilization and human supervision within educational settings. Key elements such as maintaining data privacy, addressing bias in AI algorithms, and preventing the dehumanization of education can be addressed through the implementation of clear guidelines, transparent AI operations, and continuous ethical training for educators. Furthermore, the presence of cultural and linguistic diversity poses a significant hurdle in developing inclusive AI-driven educational experiences. Limited research exists on adapting AI tools to cater to the diverse cultural and linguistic requirements of students from varied backgrounds. The absence of customized regional AI solutions tailored to specific educational needs exacerbates this challenge. There is a consensus that involving stakeholders in the development and application of AI tools is essential to navigate the practical and ethical challenges effectively (Zhang & Aslan, 2021; Shwedeh et al., 2024).

There is a growing concern that AI might encroach upon traditional teaching roles, diminishing interpersonal interactions in learning environments. To address these ethical issues effectively, it is imperative to implement precise guidelines and protocols that safeguard data privacy while promoting transparency in AI applications. Teachers should be actively engaged in crafting and deploying AI-driven tools to ensure a harmonious blend of technological advancement and human touch. Continuous professional growth opportunities coupled with open discussions on ethics can equip educators to effectively navigate these complexities (Besser & Newby, 2020).

These combined factors underscore the need for customized approaches toward implementing AI technologies to deliver equitable educational experiences for all learners. Overcoming existing hurdles related to acceptance, integration, implementation, and expansion of AI-based educational technologies requires broader stakeholder involvement encompassing university administrators, educators, publishers, ICT providers, and internet service providers. This collaborative effort aims to enhance Open Educational Resources (OER) adoption rates while fostering social equity and enhancing learning outcomes (Tlili et al., 2020).

Role of AI tools to Achieve Transparency in Open Education in the Middle East Region

To gain the trust of employers in the Middle East, institutions can share detailed reports generated by AI that highlight the specific competencies and skills acquired by learners. Additionally, involving industry stakeholders in the development of AI-driven assessment tools can align educational outcomes with employer expectations, further AI tools can enhance transparency in open courses by providing clear, data-driven insights into student performance. These tools can offer objective assessments, reducing biases in evaluation methods and helping to gain the trust of employers. Implementing blockchain technology for credential verification can further improve transparency and trust. bolstering confidence in the capabilities of graduates. AI tools can standardize evaluation methods and provide consistent feedback, enhancing transparency. This can build trust among employers by ensuring that learners meet defined competencies. AI tools can enhance transparency in open courses by providing clear, traceable, and verifiable records of learner achievements, often through blockchain technology. These tools can also improve the evaluation methods by offering a more accurate, consistent, and unbiased assessment of skills and competencies. This reliability builds trust among employers regarding the validity of the demonstrated skills, making micro-credentials more acceptable and valued in the job market. AI tools can provide real-time data analytics to monitor learner progress and skill acquisition. By using standardized assessment algorithms, AI can ensure fair and consistent evaluation methods, thereby increasing transparency and gaining the trust of employers.

Recommendations to Improve Credibility and Delivery of Micro-credentials using AI tools:

National, regional, and international quality assurance agencies, along with professional organizations, can improve course credibility by setting standards, guidelines and benchmarks for AI applications and micro-credentials (Chakroun & Keevy, 2018). Open universities in the Middle East can ensure the credibility and recognition of micro-credentials using AI tools by partnering with renowned global institutions and industry leaders. Establishing clear criteria for awarding micro-credentials and maintaining rigorous standards can also enhance their validity. Providing platforms where learners can showcase their micro-credentials to employers and peers, such as digital portfolios or credentialing networks, can further support recognition. Continuous engagement with stakeholders and adapting credentials to meet evolving industry needs can maintain their relevance and acceptance. Open universities can ensure the credibility and recognition of micro-credentials by aligning them with industry standards, involving employers in the credential design process, and offering transparent and rigorous assessment methods. Establishing partnerships with other educational institutions and employers can also help in gaining wider recognition. Open universities should collaborate with industry partners and international bodies to ensure that micro-credentials are recognized. They should also maintain rigorous standards and provide clear pathways for learners to demonstrate their skills. Open universities can establish partnerships with reputed institutions and industry players, promote success stories of micro-credential holders, and ensure that their courses meet international standards. By collaborating with educational institutions and industry partners, they can ensure that the micro-credentials are relevant, reliable, and reflective of the actual skills required in the job market. These agencies can develop standardized frameworks for AI integration, conduct regular audits, and provide accreditation for AI-enabled courses. Collaboration with industry leaders can also ensure that the AI tools used are aligned with current job market demands. Setting standards for AI integration in micro-credentials will ensure global recognition of these credentials. Regular audits, certification processes, and collaboration with educational institutions to ensure adherence to these standards are necessary. Providing accreditation for courses that meet these criteria can enhance their credibility. These bodies should collaborate with educational institutions to ensure that AI tools are used ethically and effectively, providing frameworks for continuous improvement and evaluation. Regular audits and the endorsement of high-quality AI-driven programs can reassure learners and employers of the credibility and relevance of these courses. Regularly updating course content to reflect industry needs can also enhance credibility, acceptance and recognition among learners and employers. Additionally, organizing forums and conferences to discuss best practices and innovations in AI can foster a culture of quality and excellence in education.

Practical measures are needed in the adoption of specific AI innovations that can enable open education from this region to spearhead digital revolutions in micro-credentials. These include investing in AI research and development, creating pilot programs to test AI innovations, and fostering public-private partnerships to fund and support AI initiatives (Murtaza et al., 2022). A systematic review of research from the Arab region recommended that the use of AI tools should be encouraged for a wide range of subjects including applied languages, medicine, and science. There is a need to develop AI-based programs and systems to enhance teaching and learning processes and provide incentives for institutions to adopt AI tools (Alzahrani, 2022).

Policies should focus on improving technical infrastructure, providing access to digital tools, and offering training programs to enhance digital literacy. Support for marginalized groups is also crucial to bridge the digital divide. To minimize the digital divide and improve technical infrastructure, policies should focus on providing universal access to digital tools and internet connectivity, particularly in underserved areas (Brown et al., 2021). Investments in digital literacy programs are essential to equip learners and educators with the necessary technical skills. Moreover, standardized procedures for the recognition of micro-credentials and continuous professional development opportunities for educators will ensure that the benefits of AI in education are maximized and widely distributed. Policies should focus on providing affordable access to digital tools, investing in robust technical infrastructure, and developing clear guidelines for micro-credential recognition.

Several measures are needed to enable open education in the Middle East to spearhead digital revolutions in micro-credentials:

a. **Involving Local Expertise:** Designing micro-credentials in consultation with local educationists, field experts and industry personnel, who understand the community's conditions and needs is crucial for success. This ensures that the content is relevant and tailored to the specific challenges faced by the labor market in the Arab world (Alawadhi & Abu-Ayyash, 2021).
b. **Infrastructure Development:** Investments in robust digital infrastructure to ensure reliable internet connectivity and access to modern technological tools for both educators and students. This foundational support is crucial for leveraging AI capabilities effectively (Alotaibi & Alshehri, 2023).
c. **Customize Content**: Middle Eastern countries are especially struggling to meet the labor market needs in the healthcare sector. There is need to overcome the challenges of knowledge and skills gap in this area, the content of online med-

ical education programs should be customized by adapting them to the local language, environment, and Arab culture. This will help engage learners and make the material more impactful and relevant to their daily practice (Dashash, 2023).

d. **Professional Development**: Educators play a main role in designing and employing instructional methods and classroom activities for students. Factors such as instructors' knowledge, skills and attitudes do impact the integration of AI in educational practices within higher education institutions. Therefore, it is necessary to conduct comprehensive training programs for educators to enhance their technical proficiency and understanding of AI tools. This will equip them to utilize AI-driven resources and significantly improve the integration of AI-driven innovations into their teaching methodologies effectively (Almurayh, 2021).

e. **Curriculum Integration:** Incorporate AI-related content into the curriculum to improve AI literacy among students. Teaching both with AI tools and about AI technologies ensures that students are not just consumers of technology but also understand its underlying principles and potential applications (Murtaza et al., 2022). The effectiveness and usefulness of online education depend significantly on the quality of the educational material and scientific content. Ensuring that the content is accurate, up-to-date, and well-presented is essential for engaging learners and improving their skills and knowledge (Ofosu-Ampong, 2024).

f. **Stakeholder Collaboration**: Foster partnerships with global educational institutions tech companies, and industry stakeholders to keep pace with advancements in AI and to ensure the relevancy and high standards of micro-credentials. Providing recommendations for improving the quality of Arabic content and practices in online education can inform policies and strategies to enhance online medical education in the Arab world. By implementing these recommendations, stakeholders can work towards raising the standards of online education in the region (Almurayh, 2021).

g. **Ethical Guidelines**: Establish clear ethical guidelines and data protection policies to address privacy concerns and ensure the responsible use of AI in education. Transparent governance models will help build trust among students, educators, and other stakeholders. The institution addresses potential biases in AI algorithms used in educational technologies by ensuring transparency, equity, and accountability in decision-making processes. This helps nurture trust among stakeholders and mitigate any potential risks and biases. Additionally, establishing robust regulatory frameworks and comprehensive policy guidelines is imperative to govern the responsible use of AI within higher education, which also helps in addressing biases (Shwedeh et al., 2024).

h. **Ensuring Data Privacy:** The institution ensures the protection of sensitive information and data privacy for all stakeholders by implementing robust security protocols to shield sensitive data from unauthorized access or breaches. This approach creates a secure and comfortable educational setting where students feel comfortable sharing personal information and actively participating in their academic pursuits (Shwedeh et al., 2024).
i. **Research and Continuous Evaluation**: Implement a continuous feedback loop involving educators, students, and employers to regularly assess the effectiveness of AI tools. This approach helps in making necessary adjustments and ensures that the AI innovations remain aligned with educational goals and market demands to enhance digital literacy and technical skills is essential. Conducting qualitative and quantitative studies to explore health professionals' experiences participating in online medical courses can provide valuable insights for improving the design and delivery of online education in the Arab world. This research can help identify best practices and areas for improvement (Dashash, 2023).

Implications and Directions for Future Research for Integration of Micro-Credentials with AI

This exploratory and critical review on integration of AI in micro-credentials in the Middle East regions demonstrates that there is a recognition and acceptance to employ AI tools in open education in this region and that can significantly contribute to workforce skills development in the Middle East. These advanced technologies increase the interactivity and engagement in learning and enhance practical understanding of subjects. Use of AI tools will likely to improve the validity of courses by designing course contents that address specific skills gaps and knowledge requirements of learners in this region and will contribute to educational progress of people (Hooda et al., 2022). The AI tools potentially create a more interactive and empathic learning environment for users that enhance retention in open education. The transparency of assessment methods could be ensured through the integration of AI thus enhancing the trust of learners and the labor market in open courses. The AI era has brought significant changes in how people interact and work, with innovation outpacing policy development and educational reform. As AI use continues to grow, education systems need to adapt quickly to provide both job-specific skills and transversal skills for navigating new ways of working. Institutions must invest in infrastructure, staff development, and curriculum updates to prepare students for the changing workforce. Despite challenges, embracing AI offers new tools and solutions to old problems. COVID-19 highlighted the digital divide but also led to increased flexibility in learning methods. Integration of AI in open education will ensure the timely sharing of these credentials across a wide range of international systems that will widen the prospects of continuing education and employment for learners even in resource-constrained environments. With international cooperation and targeted investments, AI could lead to inclusive growth and development through continuous learning opportunities and industry collaborations (UNESCO, 2021).

Current research gaps include a need for longitudinal studies on the impact of AI in education, particularly on long-term learning outcomes and equity. There is also a need for more research on the development of AI tools that cater to diverse cultural and educational contexts and the ethical implications of such technologies. Currently, there is a shortage of evidence about the effectiveness of E-learning and AI in various countries of the Arabic world. There are several research gaps, such as a lack of knowledge to develop specialized AI strategies for the enhancement of concurrent thinking. There is a need to assess the barriers to the use of AI in academic research, explore the challenges that students are facing and the role of AI in addressing them, identifying differences in perceived challenges between genders, examining the applications of AI in teaching from university lecturers' perspectives, evaluating faculty members' awareness of AI skills and their relationship with experience and training, and investigating obstacles and proposals for improving the use of AI techniques in developing teacher preparation programs (Alzahrani, 2022). Addressing these gaps requires collaborative efforts among researchers, educators, and policymakers at both regional and international levels (Ahsan et al., 2023).

Empirical research can be conducted to assess the effectiveness of AI-powered educational tools in improving student engagement, comprehension, and critical thinking skills in the context of Middle East history education by developing and implementing AI-enhanced educational interventions within diverse classroom settings. This can be followed by a rigorous evaluation of their impact on student learning outcomes. By synthesizing existing knowledge with empirical findings, evidence-based strategies can be developed to harness the transformative potential of AI in Middle East history education (Ni, 2018).

Importance of Interdisciplinary Research

Interdisciplinary research plays a crucial role in addressing the complex challenges of integrating AI into education by bringing together experts from various fields such as computer science, education, psychology, and more. This collaboration allows for a holistic understanding of how AI can be effectively utilized in education to create adaptive and personalized learning environments that cater to individual student needs. Additionally, interdisciplinary research helps explore the ethical implications, social impact, and potential biases of AI in education, ensuring responsible and equitable implementation. This comprehensive approach is essential for optimizing the use of AI in education and maximizing its benefits while minimizing potential harm (Kusters et al., 2020). Currently, there are gaps in research such as the long-term impacts of AI on learning outcomes, ethical implications, and strategies to effectively integrate AI into diverse settings. Addressing these gaps requires interdisciplinary research, collaboration across regions, and continuous monitoring of emerging trends and challenges in AI integration in education (Saheb & Saheb, 2023). Potential collaborations between technology experts, educators, and policymakers include developing innovative curricula integrating technology into education, improving access to technology resources in schools, promoting STEM education, and creating comprehensive programs supporting technology education and career readiness. Collaborations can involve developing and implementing new educational tools and resources, establishing policies for technology use in schools, conducting research on the impact of technology on learning outcomes, tailoring AI tools to meet specific needs, and promoting innovation in education technology. Joint research projects, policy development, and professional development programs for educators are also potential collaborations that can drive innovation in education and bridge the gap between research findings and policy decisions. Coordinating efforts to develop digital literacy programs, implementing technology standards, and creating supportive policies for innovation in the classroom are additional potential collaborations. Partnerships can create opportunities for students to work on projects involving generative AI, leading to innovative learning experiences and real-world applications, as well as the development of educational policies that support technology integration in classrooms.

The latest development in this area is the launch of a comprehensive global research initiative to explore the role of artificial intelligence (AI) in higher education, spearheaded by an award-winning AI company (WISE), the Institute of International Education, and seven partnered universities (Nuthall, 2024). The project aims to understand AI's influence on education and workforce skills, particularly how institutions can adapt and collaborate with industry. Central to this effort is the objective of developing evidence-based strategies for inclusive and effective AI integration. The research will cover various aspects, such as personalized learning, ethical AI usage, and its potential to improve access to education, especially in Africa. Each participating university will investigate local employment requirements, governance structures for AI in curricula, and how generative AI affects academic practices and equity outcomes. Overall, the initiative seeks to prepare students for future challenges while ensuring education evolves responsibly alongside technological advancements.

Interdisciplinary collaboration certainly can provide a comprehensive understanding of how AI can be effectively integrated into education while mitigating potential risks and ensuring ethical use. The potential of some renowned universities in Saudi Arabia and other institutes in the Middle East region to carry out state-of-the-art research in collaboration with international and regional organizations will be effective in the further development and implementation of AI-based learning outcomes in higher education institutions in Saudi Arabia (Alotaibi & Alshehri, 2023).

The insights and inferences drawn from this scoping review are useful for educational institutions, edtech companies, and policymakers to achieve expansion, integration, and sustainability of AI in open education in this region of the world. Integration of AI in education should not be approached as blind technological transformation but social and ethical challenges posed by integration of AI in the educational landscape of the Middle East, should be addressed through comprehensive policies and action frameworks.

CONCLUSION

Educational institutions in the Middle East face challenges like inadequate digital infrastructure, varying levels of digital literacy among students, and resistance to change from traditional teaching methods. Additionally, a limited number of projects are underway for the development or adaptation of AI tools to meet the diverse cultural and linguistic needs of students from different backgrounds. There is a pressing need for comprehensive studies that unravel the true impact of current AI tools on education over time in diverse contexts. Besides the lack of localized AI solutions tailored to the specific educational needs of the region, as well as users, are generally concerned about data privacy and security. Educational institutions also need to address the concerns of privacy and data security that accompany the use of AI. Collectively, these factors necessitate tailored approaches to AI implementation to ensure equitable and effective educational experiences for all students. Addressing these requires substantial investment in technology and training. Moreover, there is a need to increase awareness among learners about specific activities or tasks that can be used to earn micro-credentials, institutions should develop clear, comprehensive communication strategies that explain the benefits and processes of earning these credentials. Targeted campaigns, workshops, and information sessions are needed to increase awareness about micro-credentials. This includes highlighting how micro-credentials align with career goals and learning objectives. Campaigns can be run to engage students, faculty, and other stakeholders, ensuring the relevance and acceptance of these credentials in both educational and professional contexts. Educational institutions should collaborate with employers to highlight the value of micro-credentials in career advancement and incorporate them into overall learning objectives. There is a need to integrate micro-credential information into existing courses and providing clear examples of how micro-credentials can enhance career prospects and contribute to overall learning goals is essential. Collaboration with local industry partners to validate and recognize these credentials can also help in increasing their value and acceptance in this region and will be effective in meeting the workforce needs of the region. Highlighting success stories and real-life applications of these credentials can motivate learners by showing how micro-credentials align with career advancement and personal development goals. Additionally, integrating discussions on micro-credentials into the curriculum can help students understand their role in achieving broader educational and professional objectives. Existing research gaps include a lack of longitudinal studies on the impact of AI tools in education, insufficient analysis of cultural and contextual factors in AI implementation, and limited exploration of the ethical implications of AI use. By addressing these gaps, researchers and educators can better navigate the complexities and harness the full potential of AI in open education that could achieve beneficial outcomes for teachers, learners, and the broader community.

ACKNOWLEDGMENT

I would like to acknowledge Moied Ihsan's contribution in accomplishing the extensive literature search and filtering out relevant authentic sources and information using various techniques and AI tools.

REFERENCES

Abdullah, F., & Ghazali, N. (2024). Micro-credentials at Higher Education Institutions: Towards Smooth Sailing Ahead. *4th International Conference on Communication, Language, Education and Social Sciences (CLESS 2023)*, 118–126.

Ahsan, K., Akbar, S., Kam, B., & Abdulrahman, M. D.-A. (2023). Implementation of micro-credentials in higher education: A systematic literature review. *Education and Information Technologies*, 28(10), 13505–13540. DOI: 10.1007/s10639-023-11739-z

Ait Baha, T., El Hajji, M., Es-Saady, Y., & Fadili, H. (2023). The impact of educational chatbot on student learning experience. *Education and Information Technologies*, •••, 1–24.

Al-Darrab, A., & Rushdi, A. M. (2021). On national research and educational networks. *Journal of King Abdulaziz University-Computing and Information Technology Sciences*, 10(1), 1–35.

Al-Fazari, H. (2023). Delivery of Online and Blended-Learning Higher Education Programs in the Arab world---A Case Study from Sohar University in Oman. In Badran, A., Baydoun, E., Hillman, S., & Mesmar, J. (Eds.), *Higher Education in the Arab World: E-Learning and Distance Education* (pp. 99–109). Springer Nature Switzerland., DOI: 10.1007/978-3-031-33568-6_6

Alawadhi, A., & Abu-Ayyash, E. A. S. (2021). Students' perceptions of Kahoot!: An exploratory mixed-method study in EFL undergraduate classrooms in the UAE. *Education and Information Technologies*, 26(4), 3629–3658. DOI: 10.1007/s10639-020-10425-8

Almurayh, A. (2021). The Challenges of Using Arabic Chatbot in Saudi Universities. *IAENG International Journal of Computer Science*, 48(1).

Alotaibi, N. S., & Alshehri, A. H. (2023). Prospers and Obstacles in Using Artificial Intelligence in Saudi Arabia Higher Education Institutions—The Potential of AI-Based Learning Outcomes. *Sustainability (Basel)*, 15(13), 10723. Advance online publication. DOI: 10.3390/su151310723

Alzahrani, A. (2022). A systematic review of artificial intelligence in education in the arab world. *Revista Amazonia Investiga*, 11(54), 293–305. DOI: 10.34069/AI/2022.54.06.28

Barker, P., & Campbell, L. M. (2024). *3 . Technology Strategies for Open Educational Resource Dissemination.*

Besser, E. D., & Newby, T. J. (2020). Feedback in a Digital Badge Learning Experience: Considering the Instructor's Perspective. *TechTrends*, 64(3), 484–497. DOI: 10.1007/s11528-020-00485-5

Blessinger, P., & Bliss, T. J. (2016). Introduction to open education: Towards a human rights theory. *Open Education: International Persepectives in Higher Education*, 11–30. DOI: 10.11647/OBP.0103.01

Brown, M., Nic Giolla Mhichíl, M., Beirne, E., & Mac Lochlainn, C. (2021). *The global micro-credential landscape: Charting a new credential ecology for lifelong learning.*

Burton, E., Goldsmith, J., Koenig, S., Kuipers, B., Mattei, N., & Walsh, T. (2017). Ethical considerations in artificial intelligence courses. *AI Magazine*, 38(2), 22–34. DOI: 10.1609/aimag.v38i2.2731

Chakroun, B., & Keevy, J. (2018). *Digital credentialing: implications for the recognition of learning across borders.*

Dashash, M. (2023). The Implementation of Online Medical Education in the Arab World. In Badran, A., Baydoun, E., Hillman, S., & Mesmar, J. (Eds.), *Higher Education in the Arab World: E-Learning and Distance Education* (pp. 271–294). Springer Nature Switzerland., DOI: 10.1007/978-3-031-33568-6_14

Elhajji, M., Alsayyari, A. S., & Alblawi, A. (2020). Towards an artificial intelligence strategy for higher education in Saudi Arabia. *2020 3rd International Conference on Computer Applications & Information Security (ICCAIS)*, 1–7.

Essel, H. B., Vlachopoulos, D., Tachie-Menson, A., Johnson, E. E., & Baah, P. K. (2022). The impact of a virtual teaching assistant (chatbot) on students' learning in Ghanaian higher education. *International Journal of Educational Technology in Higher Education*, 19(1), 57. DOI: 10.1186/s41239-022-00362-6

Fadlelmula, , K. FQadhi, , S. M. (2024). Beyond the Classroom: Integrating the ORID Model for In-Depth Reflection and Assessment in Service-Learning. *Education Sciences, 14*(9), 987.

Habib, M. (2023). Digital transformation strategy for developing higher education in conflict-affected societies. *Social Sciences & Humanities Open*, 8(1), 100627. https://doi.org/https://doi.org/10.1016/j.ssaho.2023.100627. DOI: 10.1016/j.ssaho.2023.100627

Hooda, M., Rana, C., Dahiya, O., Rizwan, A., & Hossain, M. S. (2022). Artificial Intelligence for Assessment and Feedback to Enhance Student Success in Higher Education. *Mathematical Problems in Engineering*, 2022, 1–19. Advance online publication. DOI: 10.1155/2022/5215722

Jemni, M., & Khribi, M. K. (2016). Toward empowering open and online education in the arab world through OER and MOOCs. *Lecture Notes in Educational Technology*, 9783662529232, 73–100. DOI: 10.1007/978-3-662-52925-6_4

Kusters, R., Misevic, D., Berry, H., Cully, A., Le Cunff, Y., Dandoy, L., Díaz-Rodríguez, N., Ficher, M., Grizou, J., Othmani, A., Palpanas, T., Komorowski, M., Loiseau, P., Moulin Frier, C., Nanini, S., Quercia, D., Sebag, M., Soulié Fogelman, F., Taleb, S., & Wehbi, F. (2020). Interdisciplinary research in artificial intelligence: Challenges and opportunities. *Frontiers in Big Data*, 3, 577974. DOI: 10.3389/fdata.2020.577974 PMID: 33693418

Mahmoud, M. H., & Abo El-Hamayed, S. H. (2016). An intelligent tutoring system for teaching the grammar of the Arabic language. *Journal of Electrical Systems and Information Technology*, 3(2), 282–294. https://doi.org/https://doi.org/10.1016/j.jesit.2016.04.001. DOI: 10.1016/j.jesit.2016.04.001

McGovern, T. M. (2019). *Academic digital badges: Industry, employment, and prospects*. University of South Florida.

Mellor, N. (2024). Using AI to Develop Capabilities in Arab Universities. In *Studies in Big Data* (Vol. 144, Issue March). Springer Nature Switzerland. DOI: 10.1007/978-3-031-52280-2_16

Minton, M., & Bligh, B. (2021). Examining the use of Kahoot to support digital game-based formative assessments in UAE higher education. *Studies in Technology Enhanced Learning*, 1(2). Advance online publication. DOI: 10.21428/8c225f6e.32b8666f

Murtaza, M., Ahmed, Y., Shamsi, J. A., Sherwani, F., & Usman, M. (2022). AI-Based Personalized E-Learning Systems: Issues, Challenges, and Solutions. *IEEE Access : Practical Innovations, Open Solutions*, 10, 81323–81342. DOI: 10.1109/ACCESS.2022.3193938

Ni, L. B. (2018). AI-Enhanced Digital Learning : Revolutionizing Middle East. *History of Education*, 1(1), 40–44.

Nuthall, K. (2024, September). No Title. *University World News*. https://www.universityworldnews.com/post.php?story=20240920144632455

Obeidat, N. M., Shibli, R. A., Khasawneh, M. A., & Thaher, N. H. (2023). Distance Education: Is It Any Longer a Paradigm of Choice? The University of Jordan; A Case Study. In Badran, A., Baydoun, E., Hillman, S., & Mesmar, J. (Eds.), *Higher Education in the Arab World: E-Learning and Distance Education* (pp. 79–98). Springer Nature Switzerland., DOI: 10.1007/978-3-031-33568-6_5

Ofosu-Ampong, K. (2024). Beyond the hype: Exploring faculty perceptions and acceptability of AI in teaching practices. *Discover Education*, 3(1), 38. DOI: 10.1007/s44217-024-00128-4

Oliver, B. (2019). *Making micro-credentials work for learners, employers and providers* (pp. 1435129097-1637135585). Available at https://www.researchgate.net/publication/335109512_Making_micro-credentials_work_for_learners_employers_and_providers

Palmer, B. (2021). *An analysis of'micro-credentials' in VET*. Available at https://www.ncver.edu.au/__data/assets/pdf_file/0041/9666257/An-analysis-of-micro-credentials-in-VET.pdf

Pirkkalainen, H., Sood, I., Padron Napoles, C., Kukkonen, A., & Camilleri, A. (2023). How might micro-credentials influence institutions and empower learners in higher education? *Educational Research*, 65(1), 40–63. DOI: 10.1080/00131881.2022.2157302

Saheb, T., & Saheb, T. (2023). Topical review of artificial intelligence national policies: A mixed method analysis. *Technology in Society*, 74, 102316. https://doi.org/https://doi.org/10.1016/j.techsoc.2023.102316. DOI: 10.1016/j.techsoc.2023.102316

Sharma, H., Jain, V., Mogaji, E., & Babbilid, A. S. (2024). Blended learning and augmented employability: A multi-stakeholder perspective of the micro-credentialing ecosystem in higher education. *International Journal of Educational Management*, 38(4), 1021–1044. DOI: 10.1108/IJEM-12-2022-0497

Shwedeh, F., Salloum, S. A., Aburayya, A., Fatin, B., Elbadawi, M. A., Al Ghurabli, Z., & Al Dabbagh, T. (2024). AI Adoption and Educational Sustainability in Higher Education in the UAE. *Studies in Big Data*, 144(March), 201–229. DOI: 10.1007/978-3-031-52280-2_14

Singh, A. D., Abuhamdeih, S., & Raghunathan, S. (2019). *Inspiring the Advancement of MOOCs in the Middle East. MOOCs and Open Education in the Global South: Challenges*. Successes, and Opportunities.

Tlili, A., Jemni, M., Khribi, M. K., Huang, R., Chang, T. W., & Liu, D. (2020). Current state of open educational resources in the Arab region: An investigation in 22 countries. *Smart Learning Environments*, 7(1), 11. Advance online publication. DOI: 10.1186/s40561-020-00120-z

UNESCO. (2021). Understanding the impact of artificial intelligence on skills development. In *United Nations Educational*. Scientific and Cultural Organization.

Valerio, A. (2024). Anticipating the Impact of Artificial Intelligence in Higher Education: Student Awareness and Ethical Concerns in Zamboanga City, Philippines. *Cognizance Journal of Multidisciplinary Studies*, 4(6), 10–47760. DOI: 10.47760/cognizance.2024.v04i06.024

Yu, L., & Yu, Z. (2023). Qualitative and quantitative analyses of artificial intelligence ethics in education using VOSviewer and CitNetExplorer. *Frontiers in Psychology*, 14, 1061778. DOI: 10.3389/fpsyg.2023.1061778 PMID: 36968737

Zhang, H., Lee, I., & Moore, K. (2024). An Effectiveness Study of Teacher-Led AI Literacy Curriculum in K-12 Classrooms. *Proceedings of the AAAI Conference on Artificial Intelligence*, 38(21), 23318–23325. DOI: 10.1609/aaai.v38i21.30380

Zhang, K., & Aslan, A. B. (2021). AI technologies for education: Recent research & future directions. *Computers and Education: Artificial Intelligence*, 2, 100025. DOI: 10.1016/j.caeai.2021.100025

Zou, H., Ullah, A., Qazi, Z., Naeem, A., & Rehan, S. (2024). Impact of micro-credential learning on students' perceived employability: The mediating role of human capital. *International Journal of Educational Management*, 38(4), 897–915. DOI: 10.1108/IJEM-01-2023-0002

Chapter 12
Redefining Learning Pathways:
The Impact of AI-Enhanced Micro-Credentials on Education Efficiency

Andi Asrifan
https://orcid.org/0000-0002-9934-6129
Universitas Negeri Makassar, Indonesia

Sadaruddin Sadaruddin
https://orcid.org/0000-0001-6890-1540
Universitas Islam Makassar, Indonesia

Ashar Ashar
Universitas Islam Makassar, Indonesia

Jusmaniar Nonci
Universitas Islam Makassar, Indonesia

Trisno Setiawan
Universitas Negeri Makassar, Indonesia

Erniati Erniati
Universitas Islam Makassar, Indonesia

ABSTRACT

AI-enhanced micro-credentials can optimize learning pathways, improve access to education, and boost workforce skills, according to this report. It addresses traditional education delivery model issues and an increasing requirement for lifelong learning. An AI expert system tool called EDMENTUM validates credentials and customizes learning routes in the quasi-experimental study on AI-enhanced micro-credentials and learning efficiency. Discussing micro-credentials history and integration with AI, case examples show their practical use. The document also emphasizes linking education with industrial demands and addressing fairness, access, data privacy,

DOI: 10.4018/979-8-3693-5488-9.ch012

and security issues for policy and practice. AI-enhanced micro-credentials have many benefits, but careful design and execution are needed to maintain data transparency, trust, and management.

INTRODUCTION

Micro-credentials can help to address both challenges by providing granular learning pathways, assessment, and digital records (Pirkkalainen et al., 2023) (Ward et al., 2023) (Laughlin, 2021). Recent progress in AI technology promises to further enrich the potential of micro-credentials as tools to manage the evolving talent needs of employers. In this paper, we review the promise, challenges, and implications of AI-enhanced micro-credentials for creating learning pathways that are more efficient for a rapidly changing job market.

The capacity of the education sector to support workforce skills development has significant implications for economic growth and social equity. However, traditional education delivery models face a number of constraints for this purpose. One challenge is how to effectively combine, sequence, and integrate a broader range of learning experiences throughout individuals' working lives (Ajjawi et al., 2020) (Cantor et al., 2021) (Pohl et al., 2021). A second challenge is that education credentials often poorly capture rapid and typically experiential learning in the workplace. As a result, talented individuals from socioeconomically disadvantaged backgrounds, recent immigrants/returnees whose education was otherwise interrupted, or who gained workforce experience as a primary path to personal development may be excluded from consideration for desirable job opportunities, with resulting higher unemployment, lower incomes, and weaker labor force participation.

1.1. Background and Rationale

We describe an AI-enhanced methodology for providing micro-credential feedback to learning professionals, known as mentors, who can use the feedback to enhance the quality of educational pathways. Because these pathways can be online, security is enhanced due to the use of secure micro-credentials. The feedback is based on quality, personalized insights that come from DCS according to individual learning using machine learning models (Song et al., 2023) (Guni et al., 2021) (Tulloch et al., 2020). The result is that both the learning professional rewards and the education pathways are optimized more quickly and efficiently than possible through traditional benchmarks, with possible impacts on both cost and time-to-outcome for the education process.

In its never-ending quest to make things work more efficiently, intent-based AI has been brought to bear on numerous aspects of daily life, from getting along in traffic to optimizing retail footprints (Leivadeas & Falkner, 2022). Education and learning have not been neglected in this headlong rush to ensure that every process runs at maximum capacity. The ascent of online education to what seems to be a permanent place at the forefront of many families' educational choices has hardly been a secret, fueled by their attraction as a low-overhead and, some would say, easy-to-operate educational experience for students and their families (Ferri et al., 2020) (Ionescu et al., 2020) (Pregowska et al., 2021). In recent years, widespread acknowledgment of the need for learning to happen over the lifetime of the professional has, if anything, drawn that attention into an even tighter focus, as professionals and professionals-to-be alike embrace learning to provide themselves with the knowledge bases necessary to prosper in an ever-competitive job market.

THEORETICAL FRAMEWORK

This is causing many educated workers to be insufficient for new jobs because the acquisition of skills does not match the needs of all kinds of jobs at the organizational level. Therefore, it is imperative to develop a new education method that can adapt to the rapid adjustment of social and market needs. The revolution in science and information technology has given new vitality to a diploma reform with "micro-credential" as its core concept (Jung, 2024) (Sykes, 2023). In response to questions of financing and marketing in a rapidly changing educational structure, the micro-credential method can tackle each challenge in formal and non-formal psychology.

Micro-credentials are not an unprecedented innovation in education (Tamoliune et al., 2023) (Subasinghe & Giridharan, 2023) (Rajabalee, 2023) (Keoy et al., 2024). Their operational concept is to categorize them as the smallest unit of a course to complete the learning objectives, which in turn constitute the individual's career plan pathway. In the COVID-19 era, micro-credentials, which emphasize self-study and mobile education, are noteworthy. It is self-evident that learning and work should not be completely separate; "work-study" is the mainstream of education. With the transformation of the Chinese economic structure, traditional educational forms isolate the feedback effect (Li & Wei, 2022) (Xin & Corpuz, 2024).

This study concentrates on the relationship between the effectiveness of micro-credential-based learning models and "artificial intelligence-mediated" technology from the theoretical perspective. We first discuss the potential values of micro-credential-based learning by comparing them with the traditional training model.

Then, we look at a series of "inefficient learning" phenomena in the micro-credential application process. Finally, we interpret how artificial intelligence technology can solve the inefficiency problem in the training process. This study sheds light on the deep integration of AI technology and learning-based micro-credentialing.

2.1. Micro-credentials in Education

A brief definition of micro-credentials. Micro-credentials are not new (Zou et al., 2023) (Wheelahan & Moodie, 2021) (De Rosa, 2024). It asks a digital collector to include coursework and practical experience competencies relevant to skills-based professions. It focuses on seamless learning, flavored by competency-based education: a universal high-quality micro-credential designed via modules that are constantly updated on global standards, like Chinese micro-credentials, to guard against credential inflation (Rajabalee, 2023) (Subasinghe & Giridharan, 2023). Theory, practice, and strategy generalization among users, platforms, courses, and micro-credentials create a dynamic business ecosystem along the edge to offer fairness to individuals, universities, and the workforce (Abulibdeh et al., 2024). 2023 (Farmer). The feasibility study of the Channel Cooperation Conditions revealed enormous collaboration.

Micro-credentials began with career skill badges (Piedra, 2021) (Yanek, 2020) (Abdelhafid, 2024). The 2.0 edition of Mustangs, the world's first Chinese MOOC platform run by leading state-owned universities, used micro-credentials. Its mini-degrees, which students and employers increasingly acknowledge, fuel its widespread adoption in China. The xuetangX platform's MOOC learners automatically receive such a combination from the 3.0 platform, a specialized MOOC-derived system. This platform partners with edX to offer a specialized course function that delivers micro-credentials from top universities worldwide. With major partners like MIT and Harvard University, EdX has over 13 million registered users from every country and 600 partners. Harvard and MIT founded it in 2012 (Davies et al., 2022; Bagdi, 2023).

2.2. Artificial Intelligence in Education

As intelligent tutors can diagnose learners' knowledge gaps, tailor content, adjust feedback, and provide precise instruction at the right time, they create a big quality jump compared to other mediocre quality e-learning materials (Azevedo et al., 2022) (Kharbat et al., 2021) (Gan et al., 2022) (Yilmaz et al., 2022). This will significantly increase learners' efficiency in acquiring knowledge, skills, and qualifications. Model-supported collaborative learning has been introduced to solve the limitations of the pure human-computer model by integrating other stakeholders associated with teaching and learning, facilitating social interaction and collaboration. For example, learning analytics can be used to collect and analyze students' interactions with online educational content; intelligent tutors and collaborative scripts can monitor the interactions between novice learners with expertise to guide problem-solving processes in CSCL settings. AI can also offer practical advantages in aiding access to knowledge for reference, self-regulating learning, and autonomy in problem-solving, thus promoting personalized learning and collaborative learning (Stahl, 2021) (Hassani et al., 2020) (Borges et al., 2021) (Okunlaya et al., 2022).

Artificial intelligence has been pervasively influencing and transforming various aspects of education (Okunlaya et al., 2022) (Lameras & Arnab, 2021) (Pham & Sampson, 2022) (Emmert-Streib, 2021). It is used as an umbrella term for a variety of subfields of technology, such as brain-inspired computing, robotics, virtual and augmented reality, visualization applications, and adaptive learning technologies. A more familiar reference might be 'intelligent tutoring,' which captures the idea of a technology that can mimic the pedagogical role of an exemplary teacher. AI in education was built upon earlier learning technologies and was initially focused on intelligent computer-assisted instruction and the machine-learning developments behind it (Guan et al., 2020) (Pham & Sampson, 2022) (Chen et al., 2020). It then focused on more advanced learning technologies or next-generation learning technology.

2.3. Integration of AI and Micro-credentials

In reskilling and lifelong learning, the appearance and influence of micro-credentials will offer more diverse and customized content to fit the knowledge demands of individuals and the changes of industries, compared with traditional diplomas and certificates such as an undergraduate or a master's degree (Desmarchelier & Cary, 2022) (Lang, 2023). Since these changes often occur before or around work, micro-credentials are sometimes scattered and unorganized compared with diplomas and degrees, leading to a negative effect on the diffusion to employers, especially for developed economies that emphasize highly knowledge and skill economy. The attributes of courses will be obtained or transformed regarding value and difficulty through related cloud services with a trained knowledge-based panel (Xin et al., 2022) (Schneider et al., 2020) (Liu et al., 2020) (Thakur et al., 2022). A novel AI panel design of the algorithm will help predict parameter changes. The algorithm can be deployed on top of many micro-credentials and large online labor platforms to guide learners, upskill current workers, and reduce time waste during college (Chukowry et al., 2021) (Hearn et al., 2023).

Many employed machine learning models are designed for matching, predicting, and clustering metadata, thus optimizing micro-credential compression and enhancement. The research will propose to reduce a 16-week learning content to around 40 hours with the optimized parameters. Hypothesis testing will help to confirm the method. With the increasing volume and variety of courses, this research constructed a more effective learning pathway system to fulfill the intelligence era by integrating micro-credentials. Integrating AI and micro-credentials will help optimize course compression, teacher management, and clustering. The contribution is revealing the potential of AI techniques in enhancing micro-credentials and compressing them to a reachable study amount, which leads to an optimized saving of learners and teaching resources.

METHODOLOGY

Micro-data is a major obstacle to adopting IO and AI findings (Jaakkola & Thalheim, 2020). According to this article, improved learning paths using AI-enhanced micro-credentials may overcome the absence of path-related individual educational data. EDMENTUM, the AI expert system tool, implements a novel AI-enhanced micro-credential-based learning approach. EDMENTUM and micro-credential data give students fresh data beyond offline learning. This paper proposes personalized credentialing, personalized learning pathways, and eligibility cancellation in exchange for scholarship as innovative learning efficiency investigation applications. Recent technological advances and micro-credential resources make them possible. Advanced capabilities may alleviate learning efficiency study concerns and increase acceptance. EDMENTUM validates each micro-credential using AI deep learning to deliver accurate learning performance snapshots. It also allows cost-benefit maximization-based student-specific learning pathways to maximize learning efficiency (Kholbutaevich & Anarbaevich, 2024) (House, 2020) (Chang & Liu, 2024). EDMENTUM is an AI expert system tool for online education for senior high school pupils (Roll et al., 2021) (Barrett, 2022). They can take online courses and tests, get micro-credentials, and create tailored learning pathways based on their learning outcomes. The solution also provides encrypted AI-enhanced blockchain certifications that only students and the AI can read. This prevents cheating and promotes learning. This case study uses EDMENTUM, an AI expert system tool, to examine the learning efficiency of AI-enhanced micro-credentials. Taiwan's AI Excellence Program funded EDMENTUM's trial use at a senior high school.

3.1. Research Design

The paper's final variable was e-Learning at T2, absent T1. Such models could test numerous hypotheses, account for group-level extra differences, or illuminate school-level variations impacting individual students, their growth, and learning routes. The HLM can characterize higher-level distributions and implications (Otani et al., 2020) (Dao et al., 2021) (Bash et al., 2021). This study utilized and compared Level-1 models, including multi-session growth trajectories, the time-indexed number of learning sessions, linear and quadratic model parameters, and other mediation and strategy variables inherent in school-student e-learning as part of the total variation. In several ways, these models referenced and extended earlier research on learning behavior, self-regulation, and development. Presenting and comparing strategies with value-added prediction accuracy and coupled evaluation of AI-enhanced educational tools in actual school administrative practices (Wang et al., 2023) (Meng et al., 2022).

The study used a quasi-experimental, TAG, CQ, QUAN, and MAL-TI-C design. The study included 200 junior secondary school students who took the research team's AI-enhanced micro-credentials (TAG). The comparison group consisted of 200 junior secondary school kids who did not receive the research team's treatment. The present research used the quantitative research approach to collect data on school absences and assignment completion from the college's Discipline Learning Analytics platform, including the school's e-learning plan and experimental student identification. Multi-level linear and logistic regression uses mathematical models for multilevel learning. The study analyzed data using hierarchical linear modeling (HLM) or multilevel modeling (MLM).

3.2. Data Collection Methods

Manually evaluating ERIC search results yielded the first dataset. Both authors did this concurrently. The reviewers and the rest of the team separately checked the search results' titles and abstracts for relevant literature. Next, full-text articles were relevance-assessed. The review covered publications on micro-credentials influence independent of study methodology, data sources, or research objectives. The initial dataset was "RP-ERIC." Manually collecting the second dataset used ScienceDirect, but the method was identical. The second dataset was "RP-SD." Our database included all manual-searched publications. In October 2020, we ran a thorough literature search to find micro-credential studies on education. The search used ERIC, ScienceDirect, and Google Scholar. Google Scholar was unsuitable owing to poor or slow data retrieval. We searched in English and German. Several relevant studies were found using various search criteria. The search term was "micro-credential*" (title and/or abstract) AND "impact" (title and/or abstract), updated for each publication search. This initial search query appeared interesting because a 2019 systematic study of educational micro-credentials used a similar query.

Table 1. Search process for literature datasets

Step	Description	Dataset Label
Initial Search	Conducted a manual review of search results from ERIC	RP-ERIC
Parallel Review	Both authors independently reviewed titles and abstracts to identify potentially relevant papers	RP-ERIC
Full-Text Assessment	Assessed full-text articles for relevance	RP-ERIC
Inclusion Criteria	Included publications focusing on the impact of micro-credentials, regardless of study methods, data sources, or research objectives	RP-ERIC
Search in ScienceDirect	Conducted a manual review of search results from ScienceDirect	RP-SD
Parallel Review	Both authors independently reviewed titles and abstracts to identify potentially relevant papers	RP-SD
Full-Text Assessment	Assessed full-text articles for relevance	RP-SD
Inclusion Criteria	Included publications focusing on the impact of micro-credentials, regardless of study methods, data sources, or research objectives	RP-SD
Data Import	Imported every publication found into the database as an independent entry	RP-ERIC & RP-SD

Table 2. Number of hits and exclusion process

Dataset Label	Initial Hits	Titles and Abstracts Reviewed	Full-Text Assessed	Included Publications
RP-ERIC	150	150	75	50
RP-SD	200	200	100	60

Table 3. Systematic literature search details

Aspect	Description
Date of Search	October 2020
Research Databases	ERIC, ScienceDirect, Google Scholar
Language	English, German
Search Queries	"micro-credential*" (title and/or abstract) AND "impact" (title and/or abstract)
Modifications	Search query was slightly modified for each database
Challenges	Google Scholar proved to be less suitable due to unreliable or time-consuming data retrieval processes
Search Basis	Search query was based on a literature review on educational micro-credentials published in 2019

3.3. Data Analysis Techniques

Expected outcomes of the implementation of micro-credentials unique contribution: The case study mainly focuses on analyzing the impact, thereby verifying the credibility of using micro-credentials in university education. The research conclusions required to address the above questions will help promote the establishment of a new learning pathway, AI educational practice, and alternative education system in the future.

First, three databases are used in the study: the assessment training practice data with five-course projects, the case application data, and the user information data. Micro-credential items' relevance, accuracy, and representativeness are confirmed through data label prediction. For the model learning information, having confirmed the relevance, accuracy, and representativeness of the micro-credentials, we finally conduct the impact analysis on the performance of auto-derived micro-credentials and traditional course certificates.

This section details the data analysis techniques used to address the research questions. We discuss the assessment practice, case, and student demographics data used for the relevance analysis, accuracy, representativeness, and learning goal model experimentation. We then propose a framework for conducting impact analysis between auto-generated micro-credentials and human-issued course-based credentials.

AI-ENHANCED MICRO-CREDENTIALS: A LITERATURE REVIEW

This chapter presents a survey of the most specific research about micro-credentials evolution. We first discuss their purpose, how to create them, and the technology that can be used to manage them effectively. In a later section, we discuss the essential challenge of certifying student achievement, particularly in cases where students create their micro-credentials. The chapter ends with a few specific lessons learned.

Growing interest in micro-credentials - akin to badges, nanodegrees, and other mini-programs - offers alternative qualifications for today's rapidly changing workforce demands. Micro-credentials remain closely associated with 21st-century teaching and learning in which "students collaborate, innovate, create, think critically, and communicate. (Wheelahan & Moodie, 2021) (Yanek, 2020) (Barty et al., 2024)" As digital badges, micro-credentials are effective signals to certify specific skills and competencies of individual students compared to traditional credentials.

4.1. Historical Development of Micro-credentials

It was difficult to distribute resources because anyone may offer certificates, calling their efficacy into question. Again, micro-certificates did not interface with metadata display systems like CDS, and their influence was unknown (McGovern2020). Today's base information issues and development mechanisms are similar. A vast number of educational service providers caused teachers who could not learn, which led to many educational intermediaries creating micro-credential alternatives for formal authorized schooling. With blockchain to unify certification, micro-credential development becomes comprehensive. Internet companies, including Mozilla, IBM Design, and UNESCO, contributed to suggestions, standards, competitions, conferences, and more (Uzwyshyn et al., 2022). Micro-credentials were less relevant than foreign ones at Macau X. It explored micro-credentials as part of an educational program, but operational complexity prevented development. Micro-credential learning ideas are mainly united and focus on macro-learning. High-tech companies have advocated micro-certification since the 1970s (Shi et al., 2022) (Inayatullah, 2020). It focused on customizing employee training for business purposes. Moore and Kreger's original informal labor market model included micro-credentials, later becoming Internet development certification. Its effect was limited and rarely useful. Workers who earned micro-credentials for subsequent achievement were called "doers," "volunteers," not workers. Companies used claimed experience instead of certified ability to cut hiring expenses during the post-.com labor shortage (Vogel & Ouagrham-Gormley, 2023) (Burrell & Mcandrew, 2023) (Antonisse, 2021). However, without formal schooling norms, defining ability became difficult. Society doubted if higher education could improve job prospects. It led to MOOCs, boot camps, other informal venues, simulation teaching experience, specialized training programs, and additional training to compensate for educational institutions.

4.2. Applications of AI in Education

However, much AI-based educational research has focused on improving individual learning processes or helping teachers analyze and grade student performance (Bond et al., 2020). (Zhai, 2021; Chiang, 2022). Developing technologies that improve a holistic approach to teaching and learning requires public and commercial research.

AI tools that support and enhance teachers' activities include intelligent tutoring or the ability to grade student assignments automatically, enrollment support or applicant performance assessment, and targeted feedback through peer assessment or computer-aided project collaboration. AI-enhanced micro-credentials enable tailored learning and skill acquisition, which could boost education efficiency. Active learning and chatbot involvement can improve learning outcomes. Three types of personalized learning resources use AI, machine learning, and educational data mining to create predictive models and recommend students: psycho-pedagogical models, learning analytics, and artificial intelligence to create responsive learning systems; and intelligent tutors that offer personalized online learning experiences; and AI can customize learning through adaptive learning resources and improve teaching with AI technologies that instructor guide teachers (Bhutoria, 2022) (Somasundaram et al., 2020).

4.3. Case Studies of AI-Enhanced Micro-credentials

In this section, we describe the first two fields for which it is an appropriate mechanism and also provide a case study from each field. We also summarize reflections on applying the proposed mechanism to these and other areas. The main objective is to illustrate the potential effects. In this work, we do not propose to examine the data, but we note where such data exists and could be used to check the proposed hypotheses.

The industry is where vast amounts of data on many different phenomena are collected and analyzed in real-time (Kabugo et al., 2020) (Ranjan & Foropon, 2021). In particular, companies regularly use statistical information on employee behavior for compensation and promotion decisions. On the other hand, despite the extensive use of data-based research in the field, education does not systematically collect information on behavior and use it to guide learners (Mandinach & Schildkamp, 2021) (Hase et al., 2022) (Henderson and Corry2021). We propose to create micro-credentials composed of AI-enhanced lifelong model parameters and show that using these micro-credentials in employment is a productive economic activity. This approach leads to a financial incentive to AI-enhance model parameters because the proceeds of that enhancement are greater earnings, a form of future personal capital.

THE IMPACT OF AI-ENHANCED MICRO-CREDENTIALS ON EDUCATION EFFICIENCY

Several elements boost course efficiency in the model. Wraparound services, which assist kids in focusing on learning without being distracted by a variety of developmental challenges, have been demonstrated to boost completion rates, comprehension, and retention. Computer coaches and AIED tools emphasize understanding, which improves retention (Khosravi et al., 2022) (Alam, 2021) (Srinivasa, 2022). Reduce dropout rates around pauses to increase understanding. Traditional online course completion rates vary because students might drop out without personal interaction from cheap, replaceable instructors. AI-enhanced classrooms with high completion rates, consistent weekly rates, and student learning rates instead of clock times (Yu & Lu, 2021). Srinivasa et al. (2022)D'Mello & Graesser (2023) Um (2023). Wraparound services may take longer or cost more. We double-understand improvements with maximum time and wraparound effectiveness, comparable to motivational emails. The promise of artificial intelligence (AI) to transform education has generated excitement in the previous decade. Identifying pathways that allow people to reap the benefits of this transformation is a major problem (Chiles et al., 2021) (Krafft, 2020) (Fazey, 2020) (Barrett & Rose, 2022). Work-oriented and industry-linked micro-credentials and wraparound services can improve job prospects, especially for middle-skill workers, who are best served by learning techniques, but this approach scales to few students. The micro-credentials with wraparound concepts may increase reach and cost-effectiveness by using AI-enhanced teachers and mixed-mode teaching. It equalizes work-oriented, low-cost, less-time-consuming, and traditional education.

5.1. Enhanced Personalization and Adaptive Learning

With the use of AI to enhance micro-credentials, the task of talent cultivation in dynamic specialization is achievable (Sharma et al., 2024) (Ng & Keng, 2023) (Fitzgerald and Huijser2023) (Ling & Ling, 2023). With the dynamic generation and retrieval of micro-credentials issued, a real-time, dynamic, hierarchical scope of potential users and the development status of learning paths can be known. Since the value of a micro-credential depends on the market supply and the demand, the time constraint is more attractive. The demand constraint is relatively relaxed as compared with time restriction if a particular user's learning path is drawn from the real-time issuer. A sufficient number of verifiable historical documents can be obtained (Wheelahan & Moodie, 2021) (Wheelahan & Moodie, 2022) (Zou et al., 2023) (De Rosa et al., 2024). Since the management policy of micro-credentials is constantly learning and improving the mismatch between supply and demand with time constraints, a "guaranteed" job for a micro-credential learner can be achieved. Moreover, it is more cost effective than traditional one-on-one education services. AI-enhanced micro-credential systems can provide users with personalized and adaptive learning pathways. For instance, the system can autocomplete learners' goals and interests from their profiles, construct learning paths for them by issuing micro-credential documents, and enable learners to pursue their learning paths through different routes, one after another. Personalization is a key factor in influencing e-learning success. Interaction extension is also essential to be provided to learners in different respects, simultaneously to ease the pressure on teachers to interact with learners and draw closer an e-learning system to the real world (Wu et al., 2022) (Sidhu & Gage, 2021) (Lopes et al., 2022).

5.2. Efficiency in Skill Acquisition and Recognition

In skill acquisition, learning efficiency often suffers because trainees are too heterogeneous in their prior knowledge of the field (Castillo-Segura et al., 2021) (Xie et al., 2021) (Santana-Dominguez et al., 2022). Standard prescriptive training takes the approach of the great blackboard in the sky from AI, which is too abstract, standard, and theoretical and, therefore, does not fit the specifics of the local world. This paper argues that a domain-specific tutoring system developed using knowledge-engineering prototyping methods is the perfect teaching tool for educating people to perform domain-specific tasks. We expect this hybrid mixture of AI with knowledge-engineering prototyping to usher in a golden training era. The golden era of training should also facilitate a parallel golden era of domain-specific expert systems; our prediction for the next decade is not just positive about expert systems, but it seems exceptionally so (Singla et al., 2020) (Xu et al., 2021) (Rouf et al., 2021).

5.3. Cost-Effectiveness and Scalability

Higher efficiency of mastery learning AI-ETs can influence future learning by supporting short-term learning "sprints." A "personal a-ha" moment advances a student in Kennedy's education theory. The individual pauses for reflection and consolidation after reaching the next learning milestone, then enthusiastically continues on the next learning trajectory. AI-enhanced mastery learning micro-credentials enable short-term learning sprints and provide reflection and consolidation tools at predetermined learning pathway milestones. The learning sprint can solve most 21st-century knowledge service sector difficulties in about three months. Lean startup model emphasises minimising product (P) to save time and money (Chengbin et al., 2022). (Lizarelli et al., 2022). To save time and money, mastery learning AI-ETs claim to help us build no more curriculum (C) and learning (L) trajectories. Deep learning has revolutionized natural language processing (NLP), computer vision, and reinforcement learning in the age of AI (Sorin et al., 2020) (Guo et al., 2020) (Zhang et al., 2020). NLP has enabled automatic essay grading, eliminated the 12-hour manual grading bottleneck, and made scaling short answer and multiple choice methods cost-effective. Deep learning-based AI-ETs can ensure cost-effectiveness and scalability by fully and deeply designing a small curriculum like cyber training, in this chapter, with links between exercises and micro-credentials and extensive training data.

CHALLENGES AND ETHICAL CONSIDERATIONS

Income constraints have always been a major source of inequality in higher education, and AI-enhanced micro-credentials may still bring about a greater digital divide (Higgs, 2020) (Williamson & Hogan, 2021) (Kuo et al., 2023). Courses with AI-enhanced grading, e-tutoring, or e-mentoring based on technologies such as learning analytics and natural language processing may be prohibitively expensive because platform design, content creation, and web infrastructure build-up costs are comparatively high. Even though some existing platforms, such as Coursera, are opening up access to free micro-credentialing, the availability and quality of the platform-supported features are not as attractive or accessible as those for fee-paying learners. Schools or universities are also now required to be involved, possibly pushing disadvantaged groups further into the margins of the learning community (Peele-Eady & Moje, 2020) (Networked, 2021) (Foreshew & Al-Jawad, 2022). The value of micro-credentials needs to be weighed against their potential societal impact, as multiple categories of marginalized groups may face additional challenges in using them (Pirkkalainen et al., 2023) (Varadarajan et al., 2023) (Ahsan et al., 2023) (Wheelahan & Moodie, 2022). Overall, AI-enhanced micro-credentials have the potential to exacerbate disparities, putting underprivileged minority populations, those who cannot afford the cost of micro-credential acquisition, or those who do not have the time to invest in continuous learning at an economic disadvantage. Selective access to micro-credentials may form an additional layer of social stratification.

6.1. Data Privacy and Security

Micro-credentialing, especially biometrics, poses hazards to children and students (Khan et al., 2021). Elliott, 2021; Leoste et al., 2021. Key issues include (a) collecting sensitive information (biometric) from children and students; (b) security, safety, and privacy concerns, such as biometric technology misuses; and (c) potential stigmatization and/or exclusion or other adverse consequences on children and students. A advice on protecting learners' data would be great. Educational technology should fit with educational ethics and promote democratic principles, as well as children's and students' rights and welfare (Shonfeld et al., 2021). Zakharova & Jarke (2021) Thus, educators, parents, learners, governmental authorities, and industry should collaborate on AI applications, including educational and micro-credentialing ones. Educational micro-credentials they support are social entities in a communication ecosystem where learners, teachers, and schools have agency and power.

Due to recent media reports on the dangers of biometric technologies used by educational institutions, such as surveillance or profiling, AI-enhanced next-generation micro-credentialing has raised concerns about student data safety and privacy (Ryoo & Winkelmann, 2021). In addition to privacy and security concerns, the platform could manipulate users with specialized, targeted manipulation due to rich data and profile clues. Therefore, technology composition and design should be carefully considered to defend student interests. This may inhibit the free use and productive deployment of digital education services.

FUTURE DIRECTIONS AND RECOMMENDATIONS

AI-enhanced micro-credentialing solutions should be designed carefully to enhance but not detract from the educational outcomes they are intended to serve (Abulibdeh et al., 2024). As such, it is the responsibility of researchers and/or education professionals to remain conscious of their roles in supporting learners and encouraging AI to position itself as a supportive tool in enhancing learning experiences. Data security and privacy are important considerations. Organizations should prioritize maintaining transparency, trust, and control through data privacy and compliance with surrounding regulatory requirements (Wylde et al., 2022) (Aldboush & Ferdous, 2023). Practical and ethical concerns about using AI in micro-credentials should not cause faculty to be reluctant to embrace their role in contributing to AI-enhanced micro-credentials. Online platforms are part of the educational mix and are in the hands of higher education institutions to adequately regulate and guide intelligent learning processes.

7.1. Policy Implications and Regulatory Frameworks

Diversity in education needs individuals who are in demand fit. An unorthodox definition of in-demand fit individuals is those with the knowledge and skills that industries truly need (Lauder & Mayhew, 2020) (Sale, 2023). This article is founded on the ideation of breaking through the boundaries of structures and formats of the education system to increase friendships and partnerships between education organizations and industries. Two research studies in co-devising 'Badging K-12 Japan (BK-JP)' contribute towards developing open badge credentials designed for the Japanese fundamental education system and its approach. This article reports that open badges, such as digital mini certificates, endorse individual exceptionality for knowledge and skills for the present and future world and secure equity by diversifying criteria for excellent learning norms among underserved populations. The results of the two studies uncovered diverse perspectives toward open badges that require careful attention to implement equitable open badge credentialing systems in the educational environment.

7.2. Professional Development and Training Programs

Utilizing AI-enhanced micro-credentials to enhance employees' actual performance in jobs is also addressed (North, 2021) (Abulibdeh et al., 2024) (Sandhu et al., 2024). A series of AI-enhanced learning modules (ACTR) tackle knowledge fragmentation in traditional training courses. These smart learning sequences contain important information regarding the classes and grasp algorithms that enhance prolonged learning capability by spatiotemporally considering the former and future learning conditions. Taking advantage of time and depth adjustment of the scheduled learning units, the offered probabilistically generated AI-enhanced micro-credentials adapt to the staff's available learning time (Williams, 2023). Finally, a congruence-measurement-infused learning effect monitoring and certificate designing method is proposed to test whether the contents received differ from the provided credential and actual job performance.

Improper training implementation decreases the effectiveness of on-the-job training and can lead to a high turnover of employees and a waste of resources (Chukwuemeka and Endurance, 2022) (Shuibin et al., 2020) (Taye & Getnet, 2020). Especially for newly-recruited employees, training in high frequency but low rule-based expertise is necessary. Video lectures and quizzes still dominate online courses and are characterized by a high time-investment tendency for watching lectures. The certification from MOOCs with a high dropout rate has not received enough attention yet (Wang et al., 2023) (Aydin & Yazici, 2020) (Goopio & Cheung, 2021) (Aldowah et al., 2020) (Jin, 2023). This said, the impact of online course achievement placed in open platforms on employees' job performance is less testified.

CONCLUSION

The integration of AI-enhanced micro-credentials in education represents a significant advancement in optimizing learning pathways, improving access to education, and enhancing workforce skills development. The research underscores the transformative potential of AI in personalizing learning experiences, validating credentials, and tailoring educational content to meet individual needs. The use of AI expert systems like EDMENTUM has demonstrated practical applications and positive impacts on learning efficiency through a quasi-experimental design. The historical development of micro-credentials and their integration with AI highlight the importance of aligning educational outcomes with industry needs and the growing demand for lifelong learning. Case studies presented in the research illustrate the potential effects of AI-enhanced micro-credentials, showcasing their ability to provide personalized credentialing, optimize learning pathways, and even influence eligibility for scholarships. However, the implementation of AI-enhanced micro-credentials is not without challenges. Issues related to equity, access, data privacy, and security must be carefully addressed to ensure that the benefits are equitably distributed and that learners' data is protected. The research emphasizes the need for thoughtful design and implementation of AI solutions in education to enhance learning outcomes while maintaining transparency, trust, and control over data. In conclusion, while AI-enhanced micro-credentials offer promising advancements in education, their success depends on careful consideration of the associated challenges. Ensuring transparency, trust, and control over data is crucial to maximizing the potential of these innovative technologies and achieving meaningful improvements in education efficiency and workforce development. The findings suggest that with careful design and implementation, AI-enhanced micro-credentials can significantly contribute to the future of education and workforce training.

List of Abbreviations:

DCS: Dynamic Content System
MOOC: Massive Open Online Course
CSCL: Computer-Supported Collaborative Learning
IO: Input-Output
AI: Artificial Intelligence
EDMENTUM: "education" (ED) with "momentum" (MENTUM)

T2: timepoint in a longitudinal study or experimental design
T1: the initial timepoint
HLM: Hierarchical Linear Modeling
TAG: Treatment and Group
CQ: Comparison and Question
QUAN: Quantitative
QUAL: Qualitative
MAL-TI-C: Multi-level Analysis
MLM: Multilevel modeling
CSCL: Computer-Supported Collaborative Learning
RP-SD: Research Papers - ScienceDirect
NLP: Natural Language Processing
AI-ETs: Artificial Intelligence-Enhanced Tutors
ACTR: AI-Enhanced Cognitive Tutoring Resources

REFERENCES

Abdelhafid, F. (2024). E-Badges System and Online Credits Recognition of Digital Skills: Digital Badges' Place in the Current Accreditation System. In Embracing Technological Advancements for Lifelong Learning (pp. 59-71). IGI Global. [HTML]

Abulibdeh, A., Zaidan, E., & Abulibdeh, R. (2024). Navigating the confluence of artificial intelligence and education for sustainable development in the era of industry 4.0: Challenges, opportunities, and ethical …. Journal of Cleaner Production. sciencedirect.com

Ahsan, K., Akbar, S., Kam, B., & Abdulrahman, M. D. A. (2023). Implementation of micro-credentials in higher education: A systematic literature review. [springer.com]. *Education and Information Technologies*, 28(10), 13505–13540. DOI: 10.1007/s10639-023-11739-z

Ajjawi, R., Tai, J., Huu Nghia, T. L., Boud, D., Johnson, L., & Patrick, C. J. (2020). Aligning assessment with the needs of work-integrated learning: The challenges of authentic assessment in a complex context. [tandfonline.com]. *Assessment & Evaluation in Higher Education*, 45(2), 304–316. DOI: 10.1080/02602938.2019.1639613

Alam, A. (2021, December). Should robots replace teachers? Mobilisation of AI and learning analytics in education. In 2021 International Conference on Advances in Computing, Communication, and Control (ICAC3) (pp. 1-12). IEEE. [HTML] DOI: 10.1109/ICAC353642.2021.9697300

Aldowah, H., Al-Samarraie, H., Alzahrani, A. I., & Alalwan, N. (2020). Factors affecting student dropout in MOOCs: A cause and effect decision-making model. *Journal of Computing in Higher Education*, 32(2), 429–454. coventry.ac.uk. DOI: 10.1007/s12528-019-09241-y

Antonisse, L. (2021). Strengthening the right to Medicaid home and community-based services in the post-COVID era. Columbia Law Review. columbialawreview.org

Aydin, I. E., & Yazici, M. (2020). Drop-Out in MOOCs. [ed.gov]. *Turkish Online Journal of Educational Technology-TOJET*, 19(3), 9–17.

Azevedo, R., Bouchet, F., Duffy, M., Harley, J., Taub, M., Trevors, G., Cloude, E., Dever, D., Wiedbusch, M., Wortha, F., & Cerezo, R. (2022). Lessons learned and future directions of metatutor: Leveraging multichannel data to scaffold self-regulated learning with an intelligent tutoring system. [frontiersin.org]. *Frontiers in Psychology*, 13, 813632. DOI: 10.3389/fpsyg.2022.813632 PMID: 35774935

Bagdi, H., Pothabathula, S. V., Sharma, L., & Bulsara, H. P. (2023). The global market upsurge in web traffic and revenues during the epidemic: An exploratory research of e-learning companies. [HTML]. *International Journal of Development Issues*, 22(3), 418–444. DOI: 10.1108/IJDI-06-2023-0147

Barrett, H. & Rose, D. C. (2022). Perceptions of the fourth agricultural revolution: What's in, what's out, and what consequences are anticipated?. Sociologia Ruralis. wiley.com

Barrett, M., Czerwinski, E., Goodell, J., Jacobs, D., Ritter, S., Sottilare, R., & Thai, K. P. (2022). Learning engineering uses data (Part 2): Analytics. In Learning Engineering Toolkit (pp. 175-198). Routledge. [HTML]

Barty, G., Boyer, N., Chrysikos, A., Griffith, M., House, K., Laughlin, T., . . . Zanville, H. (2024). Developing a more granular and equitable approach to the learner-earner journey: The role of badging, micro-credentials and 21st Century Skills within higher education to enable future workforce development. londonmet.ac.uk

Bash, K. L., Howell Smith, M. C., & Trantham, P. S. (2021). A systematic methodological review of hierarchical linear modeling in mixed methods research. [HTML]. *Journal of Mixed Methods Research*, 15(2), 190–211. DOI: 10.1177/1558689820937882

Bhutoria, A. (2022). Personalized education and artificial intelligence in the United States, China, and India: A systematic review using a human-in-the-loop model. Computers and Education: Artificial Intelligence. sciencedirect.com

Bond, M., Buntins, K., Bedenlier, S., Zawacki-Richter, O., & Kerres, M. (2020). Mapping research in student engagement and educational technology in higher education: A systematic evidence map. [springer.com]. *International Journal of Educational Technology in Higher Education*, 17(1), 1–30. DOI: 10.1186/s41239-019-0176-8

Borges, A. F., Laurindo, F. J., Spínola, M. M., Gonçalves, R. F., & Mattos, C. A. (2021). The strategic use of artificial intelligence in the digital era: Systematic literature review and future research directions. [HTML]. *International Journal of Information Management*, 57, 102225. DOI: 10.1016/j.ijinfomgt.2020.102225

Burrell, D. N. & Mcandrew, I. (2023). Addressing Bio-Cybersecurity Workforce Employee Shortages in Biotechnology and Health Science Sectors in the US. Scientific Bulletin. sciendo.com

Cantor, P., Osher, D., Berg, J., Steyer, L., & Rose, T. (2021). Malleability, plasticity, and individuality: How children learn and develop in context 1. In The science of learning and development (pp. 3-54). Routledge. tandfonline.com

Castillo-Segura, P., Fernández-Panadero, C., Alario-Hoyos, C., Muñoz-Merino, P. J., & Kloos, C. D. (2021). A cost-effective IoT learning environment for the training and assessment of surgical technical skills with visual learning analytics. [sciencedirect.com]. *Journal of Biomedical Informatics*, 124, 103952. DOI: 10.1016/j.jbi.2021.103952 PMID: 34798158

Celik, I. (2023). Towards Intelligent-TPACK: An empirical study on teachers' professional knowledge to ethically integrate artificial intelligence (AI)-based tools into education. Computers in Human Behavior. sciencedirect.com

Chang, J., & Liu, D. (2024). Optimising Learning Outcomes: A Comprehensive Approach to Virtual Simulation Experiment Teaching in Higher Education. [HTML]. *International Journal of Human-Computer Interaction*, •••, 1–21. DOI: 10.1080/10447318.2024.2314825

Chen, X., Xie, H., Zou, D., & Hwang, G. J. (2020). Application and theory gaps during the rise of artificial intelligence in education. [sciencedirect.com]. *Computers and Education: Artificial Intelligence*, 1, 100002. DOI: 10.1016/j.caeai.2020.100002

Chengbin, W., Hongbin, W., Min, D., & Yongyan, F. (2022). Lean startup approaches (LSas): Convergence, integration and improvement. [HTML]. *Technological Forecasting and Social Change*, 179, 121640. DOI: 10.1016/j.techfore.2022.121640

Chiang, F. K., Shang, X., & Qiao, L. (2022). Augmented reality in vocational training: A systematic review of research and applications. [HTML]. *Computers in Human Behavior*, 129, 107125. DOI: 10.1016/j.chb.2021.107125

Chiles, R. M., Broad, G., Gagnon, M., Negowetti, N., Glenna, L., Griffin, M. A., Tami-Barrera, L., Baker, S., & Beck, K. (2021). Democratizing ownership and participation in the 4th Industrial Revolution: Challenges and opportunities in cellular agriculture. [springer.com]. *Agriculture and Human Values*, 38(4), 943–961. DOI: 10.1007/s10460-021-10237-7 PMID: 34456466

Chukowry, V., Nanuck, G., & Sungkur, R. K. (2021). The future of continuous learning–Digital badge and microcredential system using blockchain. Global Transitions Proceedings. sciencedirect.com

Chukwuemeka, O., & Endurance, G. W. (2022). Impact of Training and Development on Employees' Performance in Epenal Group Ltd. [HTML]. *International Journal on Integrated Education*, 5(5), 281–293.

D'Mello, S. K., & Graesser, A. (2023). Intelligent tutoring systems: How computers achieve learning gains that rival human tutors. Handbook of educational psychology. [HTML]

Dao, T. T., Mai, X. T., Ngo, T., Le, T., & Ho, H. (2021). From efficiency analyses to policy implications: A multilevel hierarchical linear model approach. [HTML]. *International Journal of the Economics of Business*, 28(3), 457–470. DOI: 10.1080/13571516.2021.1981750

Davies, T. E., Li, H., Bessette, S., Gauvin, R., Patience, G. S., & Dummer, N. F. (2022). Experimental methods in chemical engineering: Scanning electron microscopy and X-ray ultra-microscopy—SEM and XuM. [wiley.com]. *Canadian Journal of Chemical Engineering*, 100(11), 3145–3159. DOI: 10.1002/cjce.24405

De Rosa, M., Glumac, O., Bianco, V., & Pallonetto, F. (2024). A micro-credential approach for life-long learning in the urban renewable energy sector. Renewable Energy. sciencedirect.com

Desmarchelier, R., & Cary, L. J. (2022). Toward just and equitable micro-credentials: An Australian perspective. [springer.com]. *International Journal of Educational Technology in Higher Education*, 19(1), 25. DOI: 10.1186/s41239-022-00332-y PMID: 35669714

Elliott, A. (2021). Making sense of AI: Our algorithmic world. [HTML]

Emmert-Streib, F. (2021). From the digital data revolution toward a digital society: Pervasiveness of artificial intelligence. Machine Learning and Knowledge Extraction. mdpi.com

Farmer, L. S. (2023). Technology use and its changing role in community education. In *Handbook of Research on Andragogical Leadership and Technology in a Modern World* (pp. 358–383). IGI Global. [HTML] DOI: 10.4018/978-1-6684-7832-5.ch019

Fazey, I., Schäpke, N., Caniglia, G., Hodgson, A., Kendrick, I., Lyon, C., & Saha, P. (2020). Transforming knowledge systems for life on Earth: Visions of future systems and how to get there. [sciencedirect.com]. *Energy Research & Social Science*, 70, 101724. DOI: 10.1016/j.erss.2020.101724

Ferri, F., Grifoni, P., & Guzzo, T. (2020). Online learning and emergency remote teaching: Opportunities and challenges in emergency situations. Societies. mdpi.com

Fitria, T. N. (2021, December). Artificial intelligence (AI) in education: Using AI tools for teaching and learning process. In Prosiding Seminar Nasional & Call for Paper STIE AAS (pp. 134-147). stie-aas.ac.id

Fitzgerald, R., & Huijser, H. (2023). The Opportunities and Challenges in the Portability and Authentication of Micro-credentials and Short Courses in a Post-COVID Landscape. Technology-Enhanced Learning and the Virtual University, 465-477. [HTML]

Foreshew, A., & Al-Jawad, M. (2022). An intersectional participatory action research approach to explore and address class elitism in medical education. [HTML]. *Medical Education*, 56(11), 1076–1085. DOI: 10.1111/medu.14857 PMID: 35718997

Gan, W., Sun, Y., & Sun, Y. (2022). Knowledge interaction enhanced sequential modeling for interpretable learner knowledge diagnosis in intelligent tutoring systems. [HTML]. *Neurocomputing*, 488, 36–53. DOI: 10.1016/j.neucom.2022.02.080

Goopio, J., & Cheung, C. (2021). The MOOC dropout phenomenon and retention strategies. [HTML]. *Journal of Teaching in Travel & Tourism*, 21(2), 177–197. DOI: 10.1080/15313220.2020.1809050

Guan, C., Mou, J., & Jiang, Z. (2020). Artificial intelligence innovation in education: A twenty-year data-driven historical analysis. International Journal of Innovation Studies. sciencedirect.com

Guni, A., Normahani, P., Davies, A., & Jaffer, U. (2021). Harnessing machine learning to personalize web-based health care content. [jmir.org]. *Journal of Medical Internet Research*, 23(10), e25497. DOI: 10.2196/25497 PMID: 34665146

Guo, J., He, H., He, T., Lausen, L., Li, M., Lin, H., & Zhu, Y. (2020). Gluoncv and gluonnlp: Deep learning in computer vision and natural language processing. [jmlr.org]. *Journal of Machine Learning Research*, 21(23), 1–7.

Hase, A., Kahnbach, L., Kuhl, P., & Lehr, D. (2022). To use or not to use learning data: A survey study to explain german primary school teachers' usage of data from digital learning platforms for purposes of …. Frontiers in Education. frontiersin.org

Hassani, H., Silva, E. S., Unger, S., TajMazinani, M., & Mac Feely, S. (2020). Artificial intelligence (AI) or intelligence augmentation (IA): What is the future? [mdpi.com]. *AI*, 1(2), 8. DOI: 10.3390/ai1020008

Hearn, G., Williams, P., Rodrigues, J. H. P., & Laundon, M. (2023). Education and training for industry 4.0: A case study of a manufacturing ecosystem. [HTML]. *Education + Training*, 65(8/9), 1070–1084. DOI: 10.1108/ET-10-2022-0407

Henderson, J., & Corry, M. (2021). Data literacy training and use for educational professionals. [emerald.com]. *Journal of Research in Innovative Teaching & Learning*, 14(2), 232–244. DOI: 10.1108/JRIT-11-2019-0074

Higgs, L. (2020). Labour Rights, Artificial Intelligence and Automation in the context of the UK, Brexit, and Covid-19 with a comparative study of Singapore. gchumanrights.org

House, K. M. (2020). Student perceptions of personalized learning in a rural school district.. louisville.edu

Inayatullah, S. (2020). Scenarios for Teaching and Training: From Being "Kodaked" to Futures Literacy and Futures-Proofing. CSPS Strategy and Policy Journal. metafuture.org

Ionescu, C. A., Paschia, L., Gudanescu Nicolau, N. L., Stanescu, S. G., Neacsu Stancescu, V. M., Coman, M. D., & Uzlau, M. C. (2020). Sustainability analysis of the e-learning education system during pandemic period—Covid-19 in Romania. [mdpi.com]. *Sustainability (Basel)*, 12(21), 9030. DOI: 10.3390/su12219030

Jaakkola, H., & Thalheim, B. (2020). Sixty years–and more–of data modelling. In Information Modelling and Knowledge Bases XXXII (pp. 56-75). IOS Press. iospress.nl DOI: 10.3233/FAIA200820

Jin, C. (2023). MOOC student dropout prediction model based on learning behavior features and parameter optimization. [HTML]. *Interactive Learning Environments*, 31(2), 714–732. DOI: 10.1080/10494820.2020.1802300

Jung, J. (2024). When massified higher education meets shrinking birth rates: the case of South Korea. Higher Education. springer.com

Kabugo, J. C., Jämsä-Jounela, S. L., Schiemann, R., & Binder, C. (2020). Industry 4.0 based process data analytics platform: A waste-to-energy plant case study. [sciencedirect.com]. *International Journal of Electrical Power & Energy Systems*, 115, 105508. DOI: 10.1016/j.ijepes.2019.105508

Keoy, K. H., Koh, Y. J., Iqbal, J., Anjum, S. S., Yeo, S. F., Cherukuri, A. K., Teoh, W. Y., & Piut, D. A. A. (2024). Streamlining micro-credentials implementation in higher education institutions: Considerations for effective implementation and policy development. [worldscientific.com]. *Journal of Information & Knowledge Management*, 23(01), 2350069. DOI: 10.1142/S0219649223500697

Khan, A. H., Ejaz, N., Matthews, S., Snow, S., & Matthews, B. (2021, June). Speculative design for education: Using participatory methods to map design challenges and opportunities in Pakistan. In *Proceedings of the 2021 ACM Designing Interactive Systems Conference* (pp. 1748-1764). [HTML] DOI: 10.1145/3461778.3462117

Kharbat, F. F., Alshawabkeh, A., & Woolsey, M. L. (2021). Identifying gaps in using artificial intelligence to support students with intellectual disabilities from education and health perspectives. [HTML]. *Aslib Journal of Information Management*, 73(1), 101–128. DOI: 10.1108/AJIM-02-2020-0054

Kholbutaevich, T. O., & Anarbaevich, A. R. (2024). ELECTRONIC EDUCATION: TASKS, PROSPECTS, AND RESULTS. Global Book Publishing Services, 1-76. scientificpublication.org

Khosravi, H., Shum, S. B., Chen, G., Conati, C., Tsai, Y. S., Kay, J., & Gašević, D. (2022). Explainable artificial intelligence in education. [sciencedirect.com]. *Computers and Education: Artificial Intelligence*, 3, 100074.

Krafft, M., Sajtos, L., & Haenlein, M. (2020). Challenges and opportunities for marketing scholars in times of the fourth industrial revolution. [sciencedirect.com]. *Journal of Interactive Marketing*, 51(1), 1–8. DOI: 10.1016/j.intmar.2020.06.001

Kuo, B. C., Chang, F. T. Y., & Lee, Y. L. (2023). Trends and Issues of Digital Learning in Taiwan. Trends and Issues of Promoting Digital Learning in High-Digital-Competitiveness Countries: Country Reports and International Comparison. ed.gov

Lameras, P. & Arnab, S. (2021). Power to the teachers: an exploratory review on artificial intelligence in education. Information. mdpi.com

Lang, J. (2023). Workforce upskilling: Can universities meet the challenges of lifelong learning? [HTML]. *The International Journal of Information and Learning Technology*, 40(5), 388–400. DOI: 10.1108/IJILT-01-2023-0001

Lauder, H. & Mayhew, K. (2020). Higher education and the labour market: an introduction. Oxford Review of Education. tandfonline.com

Laughlin, T. (2021). A vision for deeper agency and personalization in micro-credentials. Career ready education through experiential learning. [HTML]

Lee, S., & Geum, Y. (2021). How to determine a minimum viable product in app-based lean start-ups: Kano-based approach. [HTML]. *Total Quality Management & Business Excellence*, 32(15-16), 1751–1767. DOI: 10.1080/14783363.2020.1770588

Leivadeas, A., & Falkner, M. (2022). A survey on intent-based networking. [HTML]. *IEEE Communications Surveys and Tutorials*, 25(1), 625–655. DOI: 10.1109/COMST.2022.3215919

Leoste, J., Õun, T., Loogma, K., & San Martín López, J. (2021). Designing Training Programs to Introduce Emerging Technologies to Future Workers—A Pilot Study Based on the Example of Artificial Intelligence Enhanced .... Mathematics. mdpi.com

Li, J. & Wei, Z. (2022). Intelligent Optimization Method of the Higher Vocational Education System for Labor Market Demand in Guangdong-Hong Kong-Macao Greater Bay Area. Mathematical Problems in Engineering. wiley.com

Ling, P., & Ling, L. (2023). Micro-credentials and Higher Education: The Bottom Line. In Introducing Multidisciplinary Micro-credentialing: Rethinking Learning and Development for Higher Education and Industry (pp. 149-167). Emerald Publishing Limited. [HTML]

Liu, Z. Q., Deryagin, A., & Glushkov, S. (2020). IT-architecture for corporate knowledge management systems. [iJET]. *International Journal of Emerging Technologies in Learning*, 15(14), 65–82. DOI: 10.3991/ijet.v15i14.14673

Lizarelli, F. L., Torres, A. F., Antony, J., Ribeiro, R., Salentijn, W., Fernandes, M. M., & Campos, A. T. (2022). Critical success factors and challenges for Lean Startup: A systematic literature review. [HTML]. *The TQM Journal*, 34(3), 534–551.

Lopes, C., Bernardes, Ó., Gonçalves, M. J. A., Terra, A. L., da Silva, M. M., Tavares, C., & Valente, I. (2022). E-learning enhancement through multidisciplinary teams in higher education: Students, teachers, and librarians. [mdpi.com]. *Education Sciences*, 12(9), 601. DOI: 10.3390/educsci12090601

Mandinach, E. B. & Schildkamp, K. (2021). Misconceptions about data-based decision making in education: An exploration of the literature. Studies in Educational Evaluation. sciencedirect.com

McGovern, T. (2020, June). Exploratory Study: Digital Badging. In InSITE 2020: Informing Science+ IT Education Conferences: Online (pp. 185-204). informing-science.org

Meng, N., Dhimolea, T. K., & Ali, Z. (2022). AI-enhanced education: Teaching and learning reimagined. In *Bridging human intelligence and artificial intelligence* (pp. 107–124). Springer International Publishing. [HTML] DOI: 10.1007/978-3-030-84729-6_7

Networked, L. E. C. (2021). Networked learning in 2021: A community definition. [springer.com]. *Postdigital Science and Education*, 3(2), 326–369. DOI: 10.1007/s42438-021-00222-y

Ng, D. W. L., & Keng, L. K. N. (2023). Innovative and Emerging Intersections Between Industry and Academia: Rationale for Micro-credentialing. In Introducing Multidisciplinary Micro-credentialing: Rethinking Learning and Development for Higher Education and Industry (pp. 49-77). Emerald Publishing Limited. [HTML]

North, K. (2021). Learning in the Year 2030. Managing Work in the Digital Economy: Challenges, Strategies and Practices for the Next Decade, 223-238. [HTML]

Okunlaya, R. O., Syed Abdullah, N., & Alias, R. A. (2022). Artificial intelligence (AI) library services innovative conceptual framework for the digital transformation of university education. [HTML]. *Library Hi Tech*, 40(6), 1869–1892. DOI: 10.1108/LHT-07-2021-0242

Osman, S. A., & Ahmed, Z. E. (2024). *Navigating AI Integration: Case Studies and Best Practices in Educational Transformation.* AI-Enhanced Teaching Methods. [HTML] DOI: 10.4018/979-8-3693-2728-9.ch011

Otani, K., Deng, Y., Herrmann, P. A., & Kurz, R. S. (2020). Patient satisfaction, quality attributes, and organizational characteristics: A hierarchical linear model approach. [sagepub.com]. *Journal of Patient Experience*, 7(5), 801–806. DOI: 10.1177/2374373519892410 PMID: 33294618

Ozmen Garibay, O., Winslow, B., Andolina, S., Antona, M., Bodenschatz, A., Coursaris, C., Falco, G., Fiore, S. M., Garibay, I., Grieman, K., Havens, J. C., Jirotka, M., Kacorri, H., Karwowski, W., Kider, J., Konstan, J., Koon, S., Lopez-Gonzalez, M., Maifeld-Carucci, I., & Xu, W. (2023). Six human-centered artificial intelligence grand challenges. [tandfonline.com]. *International Journal of Human-Computer Interaction*, 39(3), 391–437. DOI: 10.1080/10447318.2022.2153320

Peele-Eady, T. B., & Moje, E. B. (2020). Communities as contexts for learning. In Handbook of the cultural foundations of learning (pp. 230-246). Routledge. taylorfrancis.com DOI: 10.4324/9780203774977-16

Pham, S. T., & Sampson, P. M. (2022). The development of artificial intelligence in education: A review in context. [HTML]. *Journal of Computer Assisted Learning*, 38(5), 1408–1421. DOI: 10.1111/jcal.12687

Piedra, D. (2021). Open digital badges: The future of skill validation and credentialing. In *Handbook of Research on Innovations in Non-Traditional Educational Practices* (pp. 1–14). IGI Global. [HTML] DOI: 10.4018/978-1-7998-4360-3.ch001

Pirkkalainen, H., Sood, I., Padron Napoles, C., Kukkonen, A., & Camilleri, A. (2023). How might micro-credentials influence institutions and empower learners in higher education? [tandfonline.com]. *Educational Research*, 65(1), 40–63. DOI: 10.1080/00131881.2022.2157302

Pohl, C., Klein, J. T., Hoffmann, S., Mitchell, C., & Fam, D. (2021). Conceptualising transdisciplinary integration as a multidimensional interactive process. [sciencedirect.com]. *Environmental Science & Policy*, 118, 18–26. DOI: 10.1016/j.envsci.2020.12.005

Pregowska, A., Masztalerz, K., Garlińska, M., & Osial, M. (2021). A worldwide journey through distance education—from the post office to virtual, augmented and mixed realities, and education during the COVID-19 pandemic. Education Sciences. mdpi.com

Rajabalee, Y. B. (2023). The Implementation of Micro-Credentials in Formal and Informal Learning: A Systematic. semanticscholar.org

Ranjan, J., & Foropon, C. (2021). Big data analytics in building the competitive intelligence of organizations. [HTML]. *International Journal of Information Management*, 56, 102231. DOI: 10.1016/j.ijinfomgt.2020.102231

Roll, I., McNamara, D., Sosnovsky, S., Luckin, R., & Dimitrova, V. (2021). *Artificial intelligence in education*. Springer International Publishing. [HTML]

Rouf, N., Malik, M. B., Arif, T., Sharma, S., Singh, S., Aich, S., & Kim, H. C. (2021). Stock market prediction using machine learning techniques: A decade survey on methodologies, recent developments, and future directions. [mdpi.com]. *Electronics (Basel)*, 10(21), 2717. DOI: 10.3390/electronics10212717

Ryoo, J. & Winkelmann, K. (2021). Innovative learning environments in STEM higher education: Opportunities, challenges, and looking forward. oapen.org

Sale, R. R. (2023). The Composition of Opportunity: Organizational Approaches to Developing Workforce Education Pathways Through Cross-Sector Partnerships. proquest.com

Sandhu, R., Channi, H. K., Ghai, D., Cheema, G. S., & Kaur, M. (2024). An Introduction to Generative AI Tools for Education 2030. Integrating Generative AI in Education to Achieve Sustainable Development Goals, 1-28. [HTML]

Santana-Dominguez, I., Ballesteros-Rodriguez, J. L., & Domínguez-Falcón, C. (2022). An application of training transfer literature to the analysis of training for entrepreneurship: A conceptual model. [sciencedirect.com]. *International Journal of Management Education*, 20(2), 100649. DOI: 10.1016/j.ijme.2022.100649

Schneider, G. F., Kontes, G. D., Qiu, H., Silva, F. J., Bucur, M., Malanik, J., Schindler, Z., Andriopolous, P., de Agustin-Camacho, P., Romero-Amorrortu, A., & Grün, G. (2020). Design of knowledge-based systems for automated deployment of building management services. [sciencedirect.com]. *Automation in Construction*, 119, 103402. DOI: 10.1016/j.autcon.2020.103402

Sharma, H., Jain, V., Mogaji, E., & Babbilid, A. S. (2024). Blended learning and augmented employability: A multi-stakeholder perspective of the micro-credentialing ecosystem in higher education. [HTML]. *International Journal of Educational Management*, 38(4), 1021–1044. DOI: 10.1108/IJEM-12-2022-0497

Shi, D., Zhou, J., Wang, D., & Wu, X. (2022). Research status, hotspots, and evolutionary trends of intelligent education from the perspective of knowledge graph. Sustainability. mdpi.com

Shonfeld, M., Cotnam-Kappel, M., Judge, M., Ng, C. Y., Ntebutse, J. G., Williamson-Leadley, S., & Yildiz, M. N. (2021). Learning in digital environments: A model for cross-cultural alignment. [springer.com]. *Educational Technology Research and Development*, 69(4), 1–20. DOI: 10.1007/s11423-021-09967-6 PMID: 33654347

Shuibin, G., Benjamin, T., & Naam, Y. D. (2020). AN ASSESSMENT ON THE IMPACT OF TRAINING AND DEVELOPMENT ON EMPLOYEE PRODUCTIVITY IN GHANA EDUCATION SERVICE, WA. [HTML]. *International Journal of Information, Business and Management*, 12(1), 42–70.

Sidhu, R. & Gage, W. H. (2021). Enhancing the odds of adopting e-learning or community-focused experiential learning as a teaching practice amongst university faculty. Heliyon. cell.com

Singla, J., Kaur, B., Prashar, D., Jha, S., Joshi, G. P., Park, K., Tariq, U., & Seo, C. (2020). A Novel Fuzzy Logic-Based Medical Expert System for Diagnosis of Chronic Kidney Disease. [wiley.com]. *Mobile Information Systems*, 2020(1), 8887627. DOI: 10.1155/2020/8887627

Smolenski, N. (2021). Blockchain for Education: A New Credentialing Ecosystem. OECD Digital Education Outlook 2021 Pushing the Frontiers with Artificial Intelligence, Blockchain and Robots: Pushing the Frontiers with Artificial Intelligence, Blockchain and Robots, 209. google.com

Somasundaram, M., Junaid, K. A. M., & Mangadu, S. (2020). Artificial intelligence (AI) enabled intelligent quality management system (IQMS) for personalized learning path. Procedia Computer Science. sciencedirect.com

Song, T., Choi, Y., Jeon, J. H., & Cho, Y. K. (2023). A machine learning approach to discover migration modes and transition dynamics of heterogeneous dendritic cells. Frontiers in Immunology. frontiersin.org

Sorin, V., Barash, Y., Konen, E., & Klang, E. (2020). Deep learning for natural language processing in radiology—Fundamentals and a systematic review. [HTML]. *Journal of the American College of Radiology*, 17(5), 639–648. DOI: 10.1016/j.jacr.2019.12.026 PMID: 32004480

Srinivasa, K. G., Kurni, M., & Saritha, K. (2022). Harnessing the Power of AI to Education. In *Learning, teaching, and assessment methods for contemporary learners: pedagogy for the digital generation* (pp. 311–342). Springer Nature Singapore. [HTML] DOI: 10.1007/978-981-19-6734-4_13

Stahl, B. C. (2021). Artificial intelligence for a better future: an ecosystem perspective on the ethics of AI and emerging digital technologies. oapen.org

Subasinghe, C., & Giridharan, B. (2023). Introducing Multidisciplinary Micro-credentialing: Rethinking Learning and Development for Higher Education and Industry. In Introducing Multidisciplinary Micro-credentialing: Rethinking Learning and Development for Higher Education and Industry (pp. 3-16). Emerald Publishing Limited. [HTML]

Sykes, J. (2023). A self-reflective design study of three visio and visio-haptic artifacts for use in mechanical engineering design education. umanitoba.ca

Tamoliune, G., Greenspon, R., Tereseviciene, M., Volungeviciene, A., Trepule, E., & Dauksiene, E. (2023, January). Exploring the potential of micro-credentials: A systematic literature review. [). Frontiers Media SA. frontiersin.org]. *Frontiers in Education*, 7, 1006811. DOI: 10.3389/feduc.2022.1006811

Taye, D. & Getnet, B. (2020). The impact of employee turnover on organizational performance: A case study of Mada Walabu University, Bale Robe, Ethiopia. American journal of pure and applied biosciences. academia.edu

Thakur, N., Singh, A., & Sangal, A. L. (2022). Cloud services selection: A systematic review and future research directions. [HTML]. *Computer Science Review*, 46, 100514. DOI: 10.1016/j.cosrev.2022.100514

Tulloch, J., Zamani, R., & Akrami, M. (2020). Machine learning in the prevention, diagnosis and management of diabetic foot ulcers: a systematic review. IEEE Access. ieee.org

Tzimas, D., & Demetriadis, S. (2021). Ethical issues in learning analytics: A review of the field. [HTML]. *Educational Technology Research and Development*, 69(2), 1101–1133. DOI: 10.1007/s11423-021-09977-4

Um, H., Kim, H., Choi, D., & Oh, H. (2023). An AI-based English education platform during the COVID-19 pandemic. Universal Access in the Information Society. springer.com

Uzwyshyn, R., Balnaves, E., Boffy, F. X., Chakarova, J., Kleinveldt, L., Sánchez Nogales, E., ... & IFLA Information Technology Standing Committee. (2022). Trends and Issues in Library Technology, June 2022. ifla.org

Varadarajan, S., Koh, J. H. L., & Daniel, B. K. (2023). A systematic review of the opportunities and challenges of micro-credentials for multiple stakeholders: Learners, employers, higher education institutions and government. [springer.com]. *International Journal of Educational Technology in Higher Education*, 20(1), 13. DOI: 10.1186/s41239-023-00381-x PMID: 36874535

Vogel, K. M. & Ouagrham-Gormley, S. B. (2023). Scientists as spies?: Assessing US claims about the security threat posed by China's Thousand Talents Program for the US life sciences. Politics and the Life Sciences. cambridge.org

Wang, W., Zhao, Y., Wu, Y. J., & Goh, M. (2023). Factors of dropout from MOOCs: A bibliometric review. [HTML]. *Library Hi Tech*, 41(2), 432–453. DOI: 10.1108/LHT-06-2022-0306

Wang, X., Li, L., Tan, S. C., Yang, L., & Lei, J. (2023). Preparing for AI-enhanced education: Conceptualizing and empirically examining teachers' AI readiness. Computers in Human Behavior. e-tarjome.com

Ward, R., Crick, T., Hanna, P., Hayes, A., Irons, A., Miller, K., & Walters, J. (2023). Using skills profiling to enable badges and micro-credentials to be incorporated into higher education courses. *Journal of Interactive Media in Education*, 2023(1), 1–22. ulster.ac.uk. DOI: 10.5334/jime.807

Wheelahan, L. & Moodie, G. (2021). Analysing micro-credentials in higher education: a Bernsteinian analysis. Journal of Curriculum Studies. tandfonline.com

Wheelahan, L. & Moodie, G. (2022). Gig qualifications for the gig economy: micro-credentials and the 'hungry mile'. Higher Education. springer.com

Williams, P. (2023). AI, Analytics and a New Assessment Model for Universities. Education Sciences. mdpi.com

Williamson, B., & Hogan, A. (2021). Pandemic privatisation in higher education: Edtech and university reform. qut.edu.au

Wu, L., Hsieh, P. J., & Wu, S. M. (2022). Developing effective e-learning environments through e-learning use mediating technology affordance and constructivist learning aspects for performance impacts.... [HTML]. *The Internet and Higher Education*, 55, 100871. DOI: 10.1016/j.iheduc.2022.100871

Xie, B., Liu, H., Alghofaili, R., Zhang, Y., Jiang, Y., Lobo, F. D., Li, C., Li, W., Huang, H., Akdere, M., Mousas, C., & Yu, L. F. (2021). A review on virtual reality skill training applications. [frontiersin.org]. *Frontiers in Virtual Reality*, 2, 645153. DOI: 10.3389/frvir.2021.645153

Xin, X., Shu-Jiang, Y., Nan, P., ChenXu, D., & Dan, L. (2022). Review on A big data-based innovative knowledge teaching evaluation system in universities. Journal of innovation & knowledge, 7(3), 100197. sciencedirect.com

Xin, Y. & Corpuz, G. V. (2024). The challenge of labor education in higher vocational colleges. Frontiers in Educational Research. francis-press.com

Xu, Y., Liu, X., Cao, X., Huang, C., Liu, E., Qian, S., ... & Zhang, J. (2021). Artificial intelligence: A powerful paradigm for scientific research. The Innovation, 2(4). cell.com

Yanek, J. J. (2020). Digital Badges: A Study of K-12 Educators' Degree of Exposure to 21st Century Skills Developed through Micro-Credentials. [HTML]

Yilmaz, R., Yurdugül, H., Yilmaz, F. G. K., Şahin, M., Sulak, S., Aydin, F., & Ömer, O. R. A. L. (2022). Smart MOOC integrated with intelligent tutoring: A system architecture and framework model proposal. [sciencedirect.com]. *Computers and Education: Artificial Intelligence*, 3, 100092. DOI: 10.1016/j.caeai.2022.100092

Yu, S. & Lu, Y. (2021). An introduction to artificial intelligence in education. [HTML]

Zakharova, I., & Jarke, J. (2022). Educational technologies as matters of care. *Learning, Media and Technology*, 47(1), 95–108.

Zhai, X., Chu, X., Chai, C. S., Jong, M. S. Y., Istenic, A., Spector, M., Liu, J.-B., Yuan, J., & Li, Y. (2021). A Review of Artificial Intelligence (AI) in Education from 2010 to 2020. [wiley.com]. *Complexity*, 2021(1), 8812542. DOI: 10.1155/2021/8812542

Zhang, W. E., Sheng, Q. Z., Alhazmi, A., & Li, C. (2020). Adversarial attacks on deep-learning models in natural language processing: A survey. [TIST]. *ACM Transactions on Intelligent Systems and Technology*, 11(3), 1–41. DOI: 10.1145/3374217

Zou, H., Ullah, A., Qazi, Z., Naeem, A., & Rehan, S. (2023). Impact of micro-credential learning on students' perceived employability: The mediating role of human capital. [HTML]. *International Journal of Educational Management*.

Chapter 13
Flipped Classroom Approach to Incorporate MOOCs as Micro-Credentials Into Higher Education

Amine Hatun Atas
https://orcid.org/0000-0001-6325-353X
Education Application and Research Center, Galatasaray University, Turkey

ABSTRACT

Micro-credentials, which signify the attainment of particular skills, have attracted considerable interest due to their adaptability, alignment with industry requirements, and congruence with lifelong learning endeavors. While encompassing various types, micro-credentials are often linked with Massive Open Online Courses (MOOCs). Despite the increasing number of MOOCs and the rising enrollment of students acquiring micro-credentials, there is a challenge regarding the recognition of these micro-credentials within formal educational contexts. At this stage, the Flipped Classroom (FC), which involves both online and in-class phases, could present a suitable approach for integrating micro-credentialing into formal educational contexts under the guidance of course instructors. Accordingly, the aim of this chapter is to advance a conceptual proposal for acknowledging and recognizing MOOCs as a source of micro-credentials within the context of higher education environments while accounting for the intricate interactions among micro-credentialing, MOOCs, and the FC approach.

DOI: 10.4018/979-8-3693-5488-9.ch013

1. INTRODUCTION

The importance of skills acquired at the end of the educational process has become evident, alongside awarding diplomas based on educational outcomes in higher education (HE). There is an emphasis on the future of the job market being measured by skills rather than diplomas; in other words, the preference lies in skills rather than degrees (Kasriel, 2018). Although the function of HE extends beyond skill acquisition, enabling students to adapt to the workforce and effectively utilize the knowledge and skills acquired during university education is one of its objectives.

In recent years, micro-credentials that indicate the acquisition of specific skills or competencies have garnered attention because of their flexibility, alignment with industry needs, and compatibility with lifelong learning initiatives. According to the European Union (2021), a micro-credential denotes the accomplishment in learning that a learner has gained after completing a concise period of learning. Such short learning opportunities, like abbreviated courses leading to micro-credentials, facilitate the focused attainment of abilities and proficiencies tailored to a rapidly evolving society and job market, serving as supplements to conventional qualifications without displacing them. The extensive and swift expansion of micro-credentials in various forms, durations, assessment methods, and delivery modes poses challenges for their recognition in educational, training, or employment contexts (European Training Foundation, 2022). Primarily, micro-credentials are situated outside the formal qualification frameworks. However, these frameworks offer formal direction, as learners typically seek transparency and relevance of micro-credentials to formal qualifications (McGreal & Olcott, 2022). Hence, the acknowledgment of micro-credentials within formal educational procedures holds significance.

There exist various categories of micro-credentials, each validating learning, skill acquisition, or competencies through an accepted assessment method. Certain certificates merely confirm attendance and are not classified as micro-credentials. However, specific badges grounded in competencies may meet the criteria for micro-credentials if they authenticate learning and are connected with a dependable assessment procedure (McGreal & Olcott, 2022). Micro-credentials are frequently associated with Massive Open Online Courses (MOOCs) (European MOOC Consortium (EMC), 2020). The expansion of MOOCs over the span of ten years culminated in a peak of 19.4 thousand MOOCs available in December 2021, offered by around 950 universities globally (Shah, 2021). Despite the increasing number of MOOCs and the rising enrollment of students acquiring education and micro-credentials through MOOCs, there exists a challenge regarding the appropriateness, assessment, and recognition of these micro-credentials within educational contexts. When the importance of various qualifications isn't obvious, students in universities might hesitate to get their extra learning recognized. Likewise, employers might find it hard to understand or judge the quality of different micro-credentials to meet their skill needs (Desmarchelier & Cary, 2022; MicroHE Consortium, 2019).

Incorporating micro-credentials into formal educational procedures at HE requires choosing and endorsing MOOCs that either correspond with and/or enhance learning objectives, integrating them in a way that complements the current curriculum, and verifying the suitability of assessment and evaluation systems. At this juncture, the Flipped Classroom (FC) approach, comprising both online and face-to-face/in-class components, may offer an appropriate framework for incorporating micro-credentialing into a formal education context. This instructional strategy utilizes technology to relocate lectures from the classroom setting and transfer practice sessions involving concepts into the classroom (Bergmann & Sams, 2012). This study examines how global MOOCs as micro-credentials can be integrated into HE using the FC model. In doing so, MOOCs, micro-credentials, and the FC approach are examined separately, allowing the reader to see the dynamics of these three components and presenting an conceptual integration strategy. Additionally, the existing conceptual models/methods proposed through current micro-credential studies are discussed.

The chapter begins by defining the terminology and various types of micro-credentials. It highlights the challenges and opportunities associated with their integration into HE and discusses how MOOCs can serve as a source for these credentials. Additionally, it underscores the importance of aligning micro-credentials with formal educational processes and explores how the FC approach can facilitate this alignment.

2. BACKGROUND

2.1. Nomenclature of Micro-Credentials

The term micro-credential lacks universal agreement worldwide (Brown, 2021; Oliver, 2019). A credential is a broad term that refers to the outcome of an educational effort, signifying a respected third party's verification that learning has been achieved and that the individual can effectively apply this knowledge (International Council of Distance Education-ICDE, 2019). Micro-credentials, the emphasis on "micro," are certifications that indicate the completion of learning objectives via shortened courses or training programs. They provide acknowledged recognition of abilities that are learned more quickly (McGreal & Olcott Jr., 2022). Similarly, Oliver (2019) describes a micro-credential as a certification for assessed learning that is less formal than a traditional qualification, stressing its brevity. Pickard et al.

(2018) define a micro-credential as a certification that consists of several courses, but is not equal to a full degree.

Concerning the lower and upper workload limits, a micro-credential is defined as a section of a credential that awards a minimum of 5 European Credit Transfer System (ECTS) credits, which can be combined into a larger credential or included in a portfolio (Brown et al., 2021; MicroHE Consortium, 2020; Varadarajan et al., 2023). For micro-credentials, the New Zealand Qualifications Authority (NZQA) (2024) sets a maximum of 40 credits. Some experts argue that an initial threshold of 5 ECTS is appropriate when it pertains to the workload cap, while others argue that there shouldn't be a minimum at all (European Commission, 2020).

2.2. Types of Micro-Credentials

Exploring the different categories of micro-credentials is beneficial for gaining a better understanding of their nature and characteristics. Numerous terms are often used interchangeably with or in addition to micro-credentials. According to UNESCO, the term micro-credential serves as an overarching category covering a range of credentials, such as "nano-degrees, micro-masters credentials, certificates, badges, licenses, and endorsements." (European Commission, 2020, p. 11).

A set of micro-credentials is associated with MOOCs (McGreal & Olcott Jr., 2022). Many MOOC providers have introduced their own designations, such as MicroMasters (EdX), Nanodegree (Udacity), and Specialization (Coursera) (Brown et al, 2021). As with the ones offered by MOOCs, Micro-credentials can be issued in digital form and are often known as Alternative Digital Credentials (ADCs). In this definition, *alternative* refers to credentials that are distinct from formal academic certifications; *digital* relates to the way these credentials are presented, managed, and stored using digital technology to handle and transmit information, including the credentials and their embedded data; and *credential* is describing the result of an educational endeavor, representing validation by a respected third party, often HE institutions (ICDE, 2019).

Besides the micro-credential denominations provided by MOOCs, badges are also utilized with a credential function. Cheng et al. (2018) state that badges have served a unique purpose for thousands of years, acting as a way to share and convey information. These digital icons can represent connections, skills mastered, or personal passions. Accessible online, this kind of ADC comes with embedded details (metadata) and links that explain the activity's background, importance, steps involved, and final results (Gibson et al., 2015). Cheng et al. (2018) define Open Digital Badges (ODBs) as comprehensive credentials that can be easily exchanged within a network of individuals and institutions thorugh an open and shared infrastructure. The functions of ODBs are flexible and depend on what they're meant to achieve.

They can serve a variety of purposes beyond simply conveying information. Ahn et al. (2014) offer a concise breakdown of how badge research can be understood. They categorize badge applications into three main areas: 1) rewarding desired behaviors, 2) enhancing learning experiences, and 3) acting as verifiable credentials that can influence social and economic opportunities. In other words, the use of badges as credentials has been identified as just one of their many functions. Cheng et al. (2018) identify four main types of ODBs. "Recognition ODBs" acknowledge achievements, "Candy ODBs" motivate progress, "Credential ODBs" serve as detailed certifications, and "Instructional ODBs" function as learning tools to organize and deliver educational materials (p. 194). It is noteworthy that the term "microcredential/micro-credential" emerged relatively later compared to other related terms. A Google trend analysis from June 2021 indicated that the term "microcredentials" first appeared in search results in 2013, followed by "micro-credentials" in 2015. However, other terms like "digital badge," "short online course," "micromasters," "alternative credential," and "digital credential" were already appearing in searches before 2004 (Brown et al., 2021, p. 231).

2.3. Affordances of Micro-Credentials

Micro-credentialing might offer a more adaptable model of lifelong learning, enabling learners to take greater control of their professional development and better address their individual needs (Ralston, 2021). Compared to traditional university degrees, micro-credentials provide several advantages for busy professionals, including a reduced course load, quicker completion time, affordability, career relevance, and flexible learning options (Moroder, 2014). Moreover, micro-credentials enable the documentation of diverse skills and experiences acquired throughout one's career, offering additional insights to employers beyond conventional transcripts (Maina et al., 2022). Micro-credentials offer learners significant opportunities by fostering student-centered learning and increasing motivation through personalized and flexible pathways. They encourage lifelong learning and skill enhancement, offering proof of competencies and improving employability. Moreover, they cultivate vital 21st-century skills and expand access to affordable formal education; however, a summary of the main challenges for learners with micro-credentials highlights gaps in broad knowledge, the narrow job-specific nature of the credentials, and restricted accessibility caused by the lack of federal or independent financial aid (Varadarajan et al., 2023). Overall, micro-credentials present a multitude of advantages for individuals, businesses, and organizations of various scales, offering flexibility, portability, and cost-effectiveness when appropriately designed, while also potentially enhancing employee engagement and facilitating precise monitoring of employee progress for employers. Micro-credentials afford personalized, flexible, and cost-effective training options, recognizing and structuring skills, while enabling scalability, lifelong learning, multidisciplinary training, employee engagement, on-demand delivery, and competitive advantage (DeakinCo, 2017).

2.4. Challenges of Integrating Micro-Credentials into Higher Education

A key factor leading to the skill gap is reported as the lack of sufficient focus in HE institutions on aiding students in obtaining the vital skills required for smooth integration into the labor market, underscoring the necessity for a curriculum to be centered on competency (Kabita & Ji, 2017). Despite the enthusiastic promotion of engaging in the micro-credential market, a contrary perspective is held, contending that institutions should conduct a comprehensive analysis and evaluation of the existing landscape. This includes conducting an inventory of their institutional capabilities to strategically realign their priorities before entering the credential market (McGreal & Olcott, 2022).

The situation of accrediting and incorporating existing micro-credentials offered by MOOC providers and private institutions into formal education stands as a solution due to the high cost and effort required for HE professionals to prepare their own micro-credentials. Micro-credentials will encounter financial hurdles if they are perceived as optional or supplementary (McGreal & Olcott Jr., 2022). Whether HE institutions develop their own MOOCs or students choose to participate in global MOOCs individually, both the creation and accreditation of these courses will demand significant labor and cost. The truth is that regardless of how we frame the discussion, micro-credentials will incur cost, and resources will play a crucial function for funders, suppliers, learners, and companies. Ultimately, someone will have to bear that expense (McGreal & Olcott Jr., 2022).

Research regarding the capacity of HE institutions, conducted among university staff in the Philippines, highlighted obstacles that should be taken into account when developing micro-credentials. These obstacles include inadequate comprehension or limited awareness of micro-credentials, the formulation of micro-credential designs, accreditation and acknowledgment processes, quality assurance mechanisms, potential redundancy with current non-formal educational initiatives, faculty qualifications and professional development, and the extension of micro-credentials into primary and secondary education contexts (Pawilen et al., 2022). The perspectives emphasize either the restructuring of HE institutions' curricula based on competency or the integration of existing micro-credentials into formal education through accreditation/validation. Although various methods exist for providing micro-credentials, the ongoing discussion revolves around the optimal approach to authenticating these credentials, particularly when considering their transferability across different institutions and industries (Selvaratnam & Sankey, 2021).

2.5. Recognition Issues of Micro-Credentials Within Higher Education Settings

Micro-credentials come in various forms. While some certificates confirm attendance and don't count as micro-credentials, others, like competency-based badges, can qualify as micro-credentials when they validate learning and are linked to trustworthy assessments (McGreal & Olcott Jr., 2022). Whether as a badge or certificate format, the importance of defining micro-credentials and their characteristics stems from acknowledging them as credit-bearing learning activities. Credit-bearing micro-credentials entail assessments that match a recognized qualification level. Successful attainment of the learning objectives results in an opportunity for admission to or credit toward a formal qualification, regardless of the learner's decision to accept it. These micro-credentials reflect and enhance the academic standards expected in the related qualification(s). With credit-bearing micro-credentials, the time and effort invested by the learner are proportional to the amount of credit awarded for the corresponding qualification(s) (Oliver, 2019).

According to Kazin and Clerkin (2018), for micro-credentials to achieve their full potential, the following elements will need to be established: Transparency, transferability, stackability, transition from non-credit to credit pathways, and alignment and currency. The current lack of *transparency* necessitates a shift towards embedding digital information in easily understandable terms, replacing grades and conventional transcripts. The current state of *portability* highlights the necessity for reliable competency-based learning records supported by an accessible credential registry, while *stackability* requires the capability for individuals to combine or add credentials along career paths. *The transition from non-credit to credit pathways* should be based on skills and competencies, enabling individuals to obtain credentials that integrate training and experience into career pathways. Lastly, *alignment and currency* necessitate an updated credential registry reflecting industry standards and employer input.

According to the International Standard Classification of Education (ISCED) definition, micro-credentials are best suited to non-formal education as they are planned by providers to supplement, alternate, or complement formal education in lifelong learning. However, when they count towards formal qualifications, they become part of formal education. Credit-bearing micro-credentials, which provide admission or credit towards formal qualifications, require further clarification, particularly regarding expected standards (Oliver, 2019). Based on Australia's Higher Education Standards Framework (Australian Government Department of

Education, 2015), Oliver (2019) offered a list of standards that may apply to credit-bearing micro-credentials. The highlighted standard categories include "admission, orientation and progression, learning outcomes and assessment, qualifications and certification, staffing, learning resources and educational support, academic integrity, monitoring, review and improvement, delivery with other parties, and representation, information, and information management" (pp. 39-40). According to the updated standards, seven categories of standards are identified: "student participation and attainment, learning environment, teaching, research and research training, institutional quality assurance, governance and accountability, representation, information and information management" (Australian Government Department of Education, 2021, p. 2). The Council of the European Union (2022) outlines the standard elements for describing micro-credentials across Europe, recommended as a resource to aid implementation. These standard elements to describe a micro-credential include the mandatory components, which are learner's identification, micro-credential title, issuer's country or region, awarding bodies, issuance date, learning outcomes, notional workload (in ECTS credits if possible), level and cycle of the learning experience, type of assessment, participation form, and quality assurance type. Optional features, when applicable, consist of prerequisites, oversight and identity verification during assessments, the grade obtained, integration or stackability options, and additional details. A few conceptual models for integrating micro-credentials have been proposed. Pawilen et al. (2022), present an instructional framework tailored for curriculum design in the Philippine context. Their framework for micro-credential curriculum development emphasizes a cyclical process that starts with a three-part needs analysis (external, internal, and organizational). It guides educators through five steps, which are selecting micro-credentials to offer, specifying learning objectives, outlining content and activities, designing learning materials and experiences, and crafting assessment tools. Following development, implementation and evaluation phases come, with the letter informing a crucial fifth step, named curriculum improvement based on national standards and learner outcomes. Throughout this cycle, educators are central to both developing and delivering the micro-credentials.

Kato et al. (2020) offer a framework with three types for integrating micro-credentials: embedding, recognition of prior learning, and a modular system. The embedded approach integrates micro-credentials into existing programs, replacing specific content and assessments. Alternatively, the recognition method acknowledges prior learning through alternative credentials for admission purposes. Lastly, the modular system presents micro-credentials as building blocks that can be combined into larger programs. For example, universities might offer Master's degrees of micro-credential modules delivered through online platforms like edX's MicroMasters or Coursera's MasterTrack Certificates.

Although not providing a model exemplifying the process of obtaining micro-credentials, Rossiter and Tynan (2019) offer a series of steps in gathering the micro-credential. The steps are stated as being aware and understanding, choosing, committing, pre-commencing, commencing and focusing, completing, celebrating, using, sharing, and reconnecting. That is, the learner embraks a period of exploration, collecting information, and understanding, then chooses the micro-credential(s) of interest and decides to enroll. Antonaci et al. (2021) introduce the Common Micro-credentials Framework (CMF), developed by the European MOOCs Consortium to facilitate the creation and recognition of such programs among traditional institutions and MOOC providers. The CMF employs 'Bologna tools' like the European Qualifications Framework (EQF), the European Credit Transfer and Accumulation System (ECTS), and the Diploma Supplement (DS) to promote mutual trust and transparency. It establishes a unified terminology across institutions. Courses that adhere to CMF standards must entail a workload of 100-150 hours (corresponding to 4-6 ECTS), fall within EQF levels 6 (bachelor) or 7 (master) (with level 5 as an option), offer assessment for academic credit or recognition of prior learning, authenticate IDs during assessment, and provide a transcript outlining learning objectives, study hours, EQF level, and credits earned.

The European Short Learning Programmes project (E-SLP), undertaken by a consortium comprising HE institutions from 13 European countries (Belgium, Cyprus, Finland, Germany, Greece, Italy, Lithuania, Poland, Portugal, Spain, The Netherlands, Türkiye, and the United Kingdom), stands as a pioneering European endeavor focused on elucidating the SLP concept and formulating institutional approaches and directives for crafting, advancing, imparting, and validating SLPs (Antonaci et al., 2021). SLPs encompass a set of courses (units, modules, or similar educational components) centered around a shared topic, addressing particular societal requirements. These SLPs serve as modular components that can be accumulated toward broader formal degrees, designed specifically to unconventional and adult learners (Melai et al., 2020). Key features of SLPs include: structured learning units leading to qualifications, ranging from 5 to 30 ECTS and EQF levels 5 to 8, offered solely by HE institutions, adaptable to online or blended learning, compatible with broader academic programs, documented with achievements like a diploma supplement, and undergo internal quality assurance with possible external review (Antonaci et al., 2021; Melai et al., 2020). While SLPs are confined to delivery by HE institutions, they can be deemed compliant with CMF criteria and serve as guiding principles for the integration of other micro programs into higher education.

2.6. MOOCs as a Source of Micro-Credentials

The term MOOC was first introduced in Canada in 2008 by Dave Cormier. Initially, MOOCs were online courses advocated by supporters of open educational resources to freely distribute educational materials, utilizing learning designs that fostered interaction between educators and learners in networked environments (Bonk et al., 2017; Porter & Beale, 2015). There is ongoing debate over the definition of a MOOC, with some contending that they lack true openness due to limited content reuse, while others find the term massive vague. Additionally, certain courses may be mislabeled as MOOCs if they aren't accessible to all (Bonk et al., 2017). According to OpenUpEd (2015), MOOCs are online courses that are intended for a considerable number of students. They are free to enroll in, accessible to anybody with an internet connection anywhere, and provide students with a full course experience at no cost. In another definition, Tschofen and Mackness (2012) state that MOOCs are similar to courses in that they offer an structured curriculum centered around a particular theme or topic, but learners are required to be self-reliant and manage their own learning by creating their own conceptual and social connections to meet their own requirements. Based on the existing definitions and current practices, it can be seen that the massiveness and openness criteria of MOOCs are controversial, whereas there is a consensus on being fully an online course.

MOOC pedagogy is generally divided into two types: xMOOC and cMOOC (Wong, 2021). While the xMOOC format is often characterized by its foundation in cognitive-behaviorist principles, cMOOCs are predicated on the explicit connectivist concepts of autonomy, variety, openness, and interaction, as well as the processes of gathering, remixing, repurposing, and sharing knowledge and resources (Rodriguez, 2012). Unlike cMOOCs, which emphasize connectivity and collaboration, xMOOCs prioritize content delivery and individual learning (Bonk et al., 2018). Starting in 2013, the constructivist pMOOC model started to develop (Reeves & Hedberg, 2014). In this model, participants collaborate online to complete a project or solve a problem (Bonk et al., 2017).

Since their establishment in 2008, MOOCs have rapidly gained popularity (Wong, 2021). It's been over ten years since MOOCs became popular, and they have attracted 220 million learners with 19.4k courses, 1670 micro-credentials, and 70 MOOC-based degrees. It is also reported that three leading MOOC providers are Coursera, with 97 million learners, over 6,000 courses, 910 micro-credentials, and 34 degrees; edX, with 42 million learners, 3,550 courses, 480 micro-credentials, and 13 degrees; and FutureLearn, with 17 million learners, 1,400 courses, 180 micro-credentials, and 22 degrees (Shah, 2021). Examining the types of online courses offered by Coursera (2024) reveals options including free courses, certificate programs, and degree programs. EdX (2024) presents a range of educational offerings, including courses, boot camps, certificates, micro-bachelor and micro-master programs. Similarly, FutureLearn (2024) categorizes its course offerings into short online courses, online certifications, and online degrees. Some nano-MBA programs offered by FutureLearn specify that earned credits can be transferred to partner universities. Upon completing the program, participants will receive university credits that can be applied to relevant MBA programs. Additionally, a course completion certificate will be granted, affirming the acquisition of specific skills and knowledge throughout the course.

2.7. The Flipped Classroom Approach

The FC concept is that tasks typically performed during in-person class time are undertaken outside of class, while activities traditionally assigned as homework are tackled during class sessions (Bergmann & Sams, 2012). Bergmann and Sams (2012) assert that the decision to record lessons for outside of the class stemmed from a sense of self-interest. They found themselves dedicating excessive time to reviewing lessons with absent students, prompting them to rely on recorded lectures as a primary solution. Throughout their combined 37 years of teaching experience, they encountered frustration with students' challenges in effectively applying lecture content to homework assignments. As indicated by its nomenclature, the activities done inside class and outside of class are flipped/converted. In the FC approach, time is reorganized significantly. Students pose questions regarding the video-delivered content, typically addressed in the initial minutes of class, enabling clarification of misconceptions before they are improperly applied. The rest of the class is dedicated to in-depth hands-on activities and/or directed problem-solving sessions. In their later research, Bergmann and Sams (2014) described FC as an instructional approach in which direct teaching transitions from the traditional classroom setting to individualized environments. This transformation results in the communal space evolving into a vibrant, engaging learning environment, where educators provide guidance to students in applying concepts and engaging creatively with the material. In other words, instructional content is delivered via video or other self-paced learning materials for students to engage with them independently before class. This adjustment in timing enables teachers to utilize class time for activities that are more effectively conducted in a group setting or demand personalized teacher guidance. Schmidt and Ralph (2016) describe the FC as one where students engage in preparatory activities at home, such as watching videos, viewing slides, and completing readings. Once students have completed this preparatory work, they come to class ready to solve problems, analyze texts, or explore solutions. Gilboy et al. (2015) elaborate on the FC model on a specific subject-matter; that is, rather than attending a lecture on public policy in class and subsequently finishing a paper at home, students engage in preparatory activities such as reviewing materials and watching policy-related videos before class. During class time, they actively participate in learning activities such as discussions on current policy issues and analysis of case studies. In fact, taking into account the learning objectives, they link FC approach with Bloom's Taxonomy (BT) (Bloom et al., 1956; Krathwohl, 2002) by highlighting how the FC facilitates the instructor's presence with students during activities that encompass higher levels of BT, including application, analysis, and synthesis.

Although some research highlights numerous positive educational outcomes of FCs, other studies point out the limitations associated with this approach. A comprehensive systematic literature review demonstrates that the most commonly reported benefits of the FC include enhanced student learning performance, increased satisfaction, and greater engagement. However, several challenges were also identified, mainly associated with out-of-class activities. These challenges include inadequate student preparation before class, the time-consuming nature of the approach, and concerns about the quality of the videos (Akçayır & Akçayır, 2018). Gilboy et al. (2015) discovered that students valued the flexibility afforded by the FC, allowing them to work at their own pace and schedule, thereby facilitating the application of their learning during face-to-face (F2F) classes and throughout the course. However, students expressed concerns about the lack of immediate access to the instructor for questions during out-of-class periods and the potential unpreparedness of peers for F2F active learning activities. Drawing from the findings reported by Zainuddin and Halili (2016), the FC generates positive effects on various aspects of students' learning experiences, including performance, motivation, engagement, and interaction. However, some issues associated with the implementation of the FC remain to be explored further by future researchers, such as concerns about the quality of video lectures and ensuring that faculty members were adequately trained to use this teaching and learning method. In response to the interpretation that Gilboy et al. (2015) reported, Zainuddin and Halili (2016) stated that in the FC, the lower levels of BT (understanding, remembering) are often covered stepwise prior to the F2F sessions—using videotaped lectures, films, assigned readings, and/or simulations. This foundational support aims to prepare students for engaging in higher-order learning activities during in-class time, ranging from application to evaluation level of BT. Ghafoor and Abiodullah (2024) investigated the impact of the FC on the academic performance of higher secondary students using a quasi-experimental research design. The findings strongly indicate that the FC substantially improves students' learning and enhances students' critical thinking skills. Furthermore, they suggested that institutes should adopt the FC approach, manage the online component effectively, and provide training workshops for students. Clear assessment systems should offer constructive feedback, and the model should account for students' prior knowledge. Necessary technological infrastructure must be supported to facilitate this approach. Galindo-Domínguez (2021) conducted a comprehensive systematic review comparing the effectiveness of the FC approach with other teaching approaches. Analyzing 61 studies with pre-post designs and control groups, the findings suggest that the FC is more effective for learning achievement in secondary and HE levels. It may also provide advantages in motivation, self-efficacy, cooperativeness, and engagement. However, they noted that FC may not be as advantageous in other educational levels where traditional methods are less commonly utilized, such as in primary education.

Although the FC approach proves effective in various aspects, creating high-quality video materials is a time-consuming process (Akçayır & Akçayır, 2018). Other studies have also indicated that instructional videos were overly lengthy, resulting in students' difficulty sustaining attention while viewing them (Lo & Hew, 2017; Snyder et al., 2014). Nevertheless, students appreciated the flexibility of watching videos at their convenience, without time constraints or the pressure of instructor supervision or peer observation. This highlights the convenience, accessibility, and enjoyment students experience when using videos for preparation in the FC (Olakanmi, 2017). Khan Academy, a non-profit entity associated with the FC (Olakanmi, 2017), offers learners with practice exercises, instructional videos, and a customized learning dashboard, enabling them to progress at their own speed both within and beyond traditional classroom settings (Khan, 2011). The platform has been noted for its effectiveness in enhancing student learning (e.g., Ferman et al., 2019; Weeraratne & Chin, 2018). In the context of the beneficial impact of the FC approach on numerous pedagogical outcomes, emphasis is placed on the quality of videos used at online phase of FC. At this juncture, it is contemplated that the utilization of existing MOOCs as learning materials in the online phase of the FC approach may be considered a potential solution. The rich content repository of global MOOCs, coupled with the workload incurred by preparing videos for the online component of FC (Akçayır & Akçayır, 2018), may render the concurrent utilization of these two educational components feasible.

2.8. Exemplary Research on MOOC-Based FC Practices in Higher Education

In the scope of HE, it has been noted that the implementation of MOOC-based FC practices has been conducted across various fields, particularly utilizing local MOOCs/ Small Private Online Courses (SPOCs). In one of these studies, Wang and Zhu (2019) conducted a quasi-experiment to assess the impact of a MOOC-based FC in an inorganic chemistry course. They compared student performance between the MOOC-based FC and a traditional classroom model. In the FC, students were required to create an account on the Chinese University MOOC platform to access micro-lectures and complete online exercises. The FC structure included before-class and in-class activities, with learners watching two to three micro-lectures on the platform prior to each session. The study found that, on average, students in the MOOC-based FC outperformed those in the traditional classroom. The majority of students indicated a favorable experience with the FC, particularly regarding peer interaction, learning resources, and active learning outcomes. However, no noticeable enhancements in self-efficacy or self-regulated learning were recorded by the conclusion of the course.

In another study, Pertuz et al. (2023) conducted a case study with 23 students enrolled in a Digital Signal Processing course as part of an Undergraduate Electronics Engineering Program. They explored the integration of MOOCs into traditional course. The course resources supported by MOOCs were implemented and made available through Moodle. The findings indicate that the MOOC-based FC approach is gaining traction in undergraduate engineering education, showing potential to enhance active learning during in-class sessions while promoting the adoption and use of MOOCs.

Another experimental study sought to redesign a conventional undergraduate course by integrating MOOC content and FC practices, assessing its effectiveness based on students' experiences and perceptions in an Internet and Distance Education course that was provided to 15 students. For the online portion of FC, the instructor and two teaching assistants explored multiple MOOC platforms to select an appropriate course. They chose Emerging Trends and Technologies in the Virtual K-12 Classroom due to its relevance, convenient scheduling, and compatibility with students' language skills. Students completed the Coursera course or accessed other online materials at their own pace using their laptops, while the instructor and teaching assistants remained present in the classroom to provide support and observe. Satisfaction surveys revealed that students were largely pleased with the redesigned course, valuing the instructor's responsiveness, positive attitude towards technology, adaptability of the course, and the quality of both the technology and internet access. However, students reported lower satisfaction regarding their perceived interaction with peers (Li et al, 2015).

In a study where the FC approach was implemented using Small Private Online Courses (SPOCs), an Installation Engineering Cost was developed, incorporating teaching activities across pre-class, in-class, and post-class phases over two academic years for both large and small classes. In the online segment of the FC, students engaged in autonomous learning to develop their understanding and initial grasp of new concepts before and after class. This process utilized a platform called Superstar Learning, where instructors could upload course materials (videos, lecture slides, documents, etc.), assign learning tasks, and facilitate online communication. The results indicated that students' exam scores, awareness, participation, and satisfaction in FCs were higher compared to traditional classrooms. Additionally, small class settings proved to be more effective than large class settings in fostering students' comprehensive abilities (Zhang et al., 2020).

Another study evaluates the effectiveness of a FC method utilizing MOOCs for standardized training of Oncology Radiotherapy residents. It involved 48 junior residents, with the control group undergoing traditional training and the experimental group participating in a MOOC-based blended FC approach. In the online segment of FC, students were expected to engage in independent study through a MOOC on the China University platform. This study concentrated on identifying and addressing challenges encountered during the learning process, as well as understanding key and complex concepts. The findings indicated that the research group significantly outperformed the control group in areas such as theoretical foundations, skill application, and case analysis. The research group demonstrated substantial enhancements in theoretical knowledge, problem-solving abilities, self-directed learning, teamwork, and communication skills. They also achieved higher scores in self-motivation, task analysis, self-monitoring, and self-evaluation, alongside increased satisfaction regarding their interest in learning, clinical reasoning, problem-solving capabilities, team collaboration, and skills in delineating radiotherapy targets. Overall, the MOOC-based FC blended teaching approach had a positive effect on the standardized training of oncology radiotherapy residents (Yu et al., 2024).

To conclude, these exemaplary studies collectively highlight the growing effectiveness and adaptability of MOOC-based FC implementations across diverse disciplines in HE, demonstrating significant improvements in student performance and engagement. In the exemplary studies, it is often observed that instead of integrating well-known/global MOOC platforms into the course, SPOCs were used. However, the creation of content by the teacher for the local MOOCs/SPOCs used in the online phase of FC creates a workload (Akçayır & Akçayır, 2018). At this point, creating MOOCs in a format that meets certain standards as micro-credentials and/or selecting global MOOCs that align with the micro-credential standards and course content can be considered an alternative.

3. THE FLIPPED CLASSROOM APPROACH FOR INTEGRATING MOOCS INTO HIGHER EDUCATION

This part details the proposal for integrating MOOC materials into the pre-class phase of the two-phased FC approach under teacher supervision and monitoring students' progress in achieving the learning outcomes. As Schmidt and Ralph (2016) and Gilboy et al. (2015) underscored the importance of BT cognitive process levels in the learning outcomes to be obtained across FC phases, it becomes crucial to initially *set and separate the learning objectives to be covered in both the online and in-person phases of FC*. It would be beneficial to consider aligning the learning objectives corresponding to the lower levels of BT with the pre-class online phase while setting higher-level learning outcomes for the in-class sessions. Additionally, it is necessary to establish the relationships between the learning outcomes targeted in the online pre-class and face-to-face in-class components.

Once the learning outcomes have been identified, it is necessary to *select the global MOOCs that align with the learning objectives*. These MOOCs should also be recognized as micro-credentials and included as part of the diploma; hence, they must adhere to CMF standards based on Bologna tools such as ECTS and DC, as outlined by Antonaci et al. (2021). The selection of MOOCs to be integrated into the formal process should be based on criteria such as their suitability for grade levels (undergraduate, graduate), the learning outcomes, the quality of learning materials, and assessment activities. The key point here is that the learning outcomes of the selected MOOC must align with the course, and the prepared learning materials must meet these learning outcomes.

In the online pre-class phases of the FC, it is essential to *establish communication channels* such as discussion groups and e-mails through which students can reach the instructor for support while completing the MOOCs. In this context, establishing a collaboration with MOOC providers and utilizing the learning analytics available within the MOOC system can be beneficial for instructors in monitoring student learning progress.

In the subsequent step, deciding how the selected MOOC to be followed in the online phase of FC *will be linked to the in-class learning activities is essential*. The key focus here is on planning learning activities within the classroom to elevate the skills acquired through MOOCs to higher cognitive levels of BT, emphasizing the transfer of skills from the online environment to the classroom setting. In this phase, classroom activities can include discussions, group work, and collaborative learning exercises where the learning outcomes from the MOOC can be applied.

The predominance of MOOCs as primarily informal learning activities is closely associated with the validity and reliability of the assessments conducted. Presently, many existing MOOCs primarily fall under the category of xMOOCs (Bonk et al., 2018; Wong, 2021), focusing on self-paced learning where learners follow a structured format autonomously. However, for these MOOCs to be integrated into formal processes, it is necessary to ensure robust assessment practices. The assessment of MOOCs integrated with FC within the scope of the course, under the supervision of subject matter experts, would provide a reliable method for recognizing the micro-credentials obtained from MOOCs as part of the diploma supplement. In FC, the completion of MOOC activities in the online phase can be interpreted either by teachers and/or through AI-driven learning analytics. Alongside these emerging technological options, in-class activities such as quizzes to evaluate the learning objectives to be covered through MOOC can be conducted to monitor students' performance. The steps toward integrating MOOCs into HE using the FC approach are summarized in the following Figure 1.

Figure 1. Integrating MOOCs into HE using the FC approach

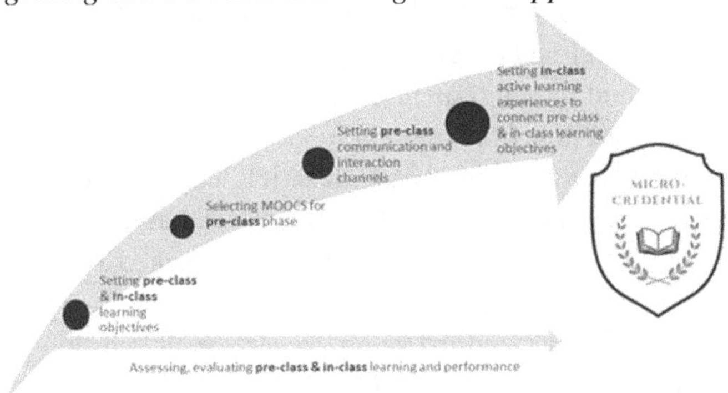

As a preparatory phase for the applicability of the offered model, rather than having MOOCs completely transform the entire course structure, a basic or moderate level of MOOC integration can be viewed as a preliminary testing step. Although the most of the current models do not address the use of global MOOCs as micro-credentials, presenting FC as an implementation method and providing a spectrum for MOOC integration could be useful for understanding and applying the model proposed in this study. In line with this, Pérez-Sanagustín et al. (2015) offered the MOOC-based hybrid pedagogies framework, which organizes pedagogical approaches along a spectrum defined by two key factors: the extent of integration between the MOOC and the traditional course, and the amount of support provided to students within these courses. A MOOC that is not tied to a specific course but is accessible to students at all times represents a low level of integration, even if it includes materials relevant to on-campus course topics. When professors use a MOOC as a supplementary resource, it indicates a medium level of integration. At a high level of integration, professors structure their classes around the MOOC, using it as the primary course reference, a method referred to as Flipped MOOC-based pedagogy (Pérez-Sanagustín et al., 2015). The MOOC structure can be piloted by first testing low or medium levels of integration before progressing to high-level integration. In terms of integrating MOOCs into face-to-face classes, Delgado Kloos et al. (2015) outline six types of experiences: "Local Digital Prelude, Flipping the Classroom, Canned Digital Teaching with Face-to-Face Tutoring, Face-to-Face and Canned Teaching, Face-to-Face Teaching with Remote Tutoring, and Canned

Digital Teaching with Remote Tutoring" (p. 967). Although these approaches do not focus using MOOCs as micro-credentials, they suggest various ways to incorporate MOOCs into in-person courses. These models include more flexible, low-level integration suggestions for using MOOCs or local MOOCs, known as SPOCs, as supplementary course materials.

In another study, Pérez-Sanagustín et al. (2017) introduced a Hybrid MOOC (H-MOOC) framework aimed at explaining how a current MOOC can be reused and integrated into the educational program, focusing on two main factors: the required institutional support and the alignment of the hybrid initiative with the curricular content. They suggested four fundamental models as guidelines: (1) "MOOC as a service," where students voluntarily enroll in a MOOC that is not directly related to any course in the curriculum; (2) "MOOC as a replacement," in which the MOOC replaces a conventional course, with its content closely aligned to existing curriculum courses; (3) "MOOC as a driver," where a traditional course is organized around a MOOC; and (4) "MOOC as an added value," where the institution provides all the necessary support for students' success in the course, even if the course does not directly correspond to any curricular content (p. 51). Although this framework does not explicitly mention the use of FC and integration of MOOCs as micro-credentials, the "MOOC as a driver" model suggests a requirement for high integration, similar to the Flipped MOOC-based pedagogy presented by Pérez-Sanagustín et al. (2015). Lastly, Defaweux et al. (2019) identified three distinct strategies employed by instructors at the University of Liège (Belgium) to integrate MOOCs with in-person courses. Shortly, the first strategy, "*Pendulum*", involves a deliberate alternation between MOOC sessions and face-to-face classes in a FC model. During these in-person sessions, local students engage in classroom lessons that assess, clarify, and expand their understanding of the MOOC modules. The second strategy, known as "*Sandwich*", positions the MOOC as the central element of a hybrid instructional design, with on-campus sessions designed to introduce and conclude the course centered around the MOOC content. Finally, the "*Tetris*" strategy, reflects professors' efforts to create a MOOC that serves as a foundational building block applicable to various courses. These strategies also include suggestions for making the MOOC or the face-to-face course the central element of the instructional design.

4. CONCLUSION

To conclude, the integration of micro-credentials, in particular those awarded through MOOCs, into formal education is a two-sided opportunity: on the one hand, an opportunity to provide better recognition of the knowledge attained through MOOCs, and on the other hand, a challenge to address the quality assurance issues posed by such integration. Recognizing micro-credentials as credible learning activities requires defining the characteristics of micro-credentials and meeting accepted qualification standards. The use of the FC model is one potential path for incorporating MOOCs into formal education. If the adopting institutions find the content quality of MOOCs acceptable and can bridge the gap in the learning activities implemented in the face-to-face models and MOOCs, then the institutions can make use of the vast amount of content available in MOOCs to save effort in producing materials. However, the maintenance of the quality of MOOCs and their alignment with the required learning objectives and assessment elements are crucial in this case. In general, the integration of MOOCs into formal education through the FC model requires careful planning with respect to MOOC selection, learning activity design, and developing robust assessment strategies. Overall, incorporating MOOCs and micro-credentials into formal education holds potential for enhancing student learning experiences and outcomes.

5. FUTURE RESEARCH DIRECTIONS

Before the implementation of MOOCs within formal educational settings/HE, or even to consider them as an extrinsic micro-credential, legal specifications that will govern the application processes should first be set up. Meanwhile, it is mandatory to carry out study practices on the potential effectiveness of implementation of MOOCs in the settings of HE. Particularly, existing literature on micro-credentials primarily comprises reports rather than empirical studies. Therefore, theoretical frameworks such as FC and similar approaches (e.g. Kato et al., 2020; Pawilen et al., 2022; Rossiter & Tynan, 2019) presenting how micro-learning content like MOOCs can be integrated into HE hold significance in laying the groundwork for research. Hence, it is recommended to investigate the method of integrating MOOCs, not SPOCs, into the curriculum using the proposed FC approach from administrative, student, and teacher perspectives, as well as from the standpoint of technological feasibility.

The integration of MOOCs with FC into the HE setting will help meet the micro-credential criteria (e.g. Antonaci et al., 2021; Kazin & Clerkin, 2018; Melai et al., 2020). The verification and validation of micro-credentials by HE professionals, followed by their addition to diplomas, will contribute to the achieving of the potential of micro-credentials. In addition, evolving AI technologies will make significant contributions to evaluating students' learning analytics and understanding their learning and interactions within MOOCs. Particularly, obtaining such data for ensuring the identity and monitoring/evaluating learning analytics of learners completing MOOC content is crucial for integrating them into HE Learning Management Systems and recognizing micro-credentials by HE institutions.

The integration of MOOCs into HE courses and their recognition as micro-credentials will inevitably impact the workload of instructors and the number of courses they offer. If micro-credentials are counted in terms of ECTS credits, students may opt for these short programs instead of elective courses. Consequently, this situation may necessitate a regulatory adjustment concerning instructors' workload. Moreover, the integration of MOOCs as micro-credentials into HE will require training for the teachers who will utilize them.

While MOOCs are often marketed as cost-free, many MOOC providers do charge fees for issuing micro-credentials. Therefore, embedding MOOCs into HE courses may necessitate an access arrangement requiring collaboration between MOOC providers and HE institutions. Indeed, the fact that MOOC providers offer campus solutions (e.g., Cousera for campus) indicates their readiness to engage in regulatory frameworks facilitating collaboration with HE institutions.

REFERENCES

Ahn, J., Pellicone, A., & Butler, B. S. (2014). Open badges for education: What are the implications at the intersection of open systems and badging? *Research in Learning Technology*, 22.DOI: 10.3402/rlt.v22.23563

Akçayır, G., & Akçayır, M. (2018). The flipped classroom: A review of its advantages and challenges. *Computers & Education*, 126, 334–345. DOI: 10.1016/j.compedu.2018.07.021

Antonaci, A., Henderikx, P., & Ubachs, G. (2021). The Common Microcredentials Framework for MOOCs and short learning programmes. *Journal of Innovation in Polytechnic Education*, 3(1), 5–9. DOI: 10.69520/jipe.v3i1.89

Australian Government Department of Education. (2015). *Higher Education Standards Framework (Threshold Standards) 2015*. Federal Register of Legislation. https://www.legislation.gov.au/F2015L01639/latest/versions

Australian Government Department of Education. (2021). *Higher Education Standards Framework (Threshold Standards) 2021*. Federal Register of Legislation. https://www.legislation.gov.au/F2021L00488/latest/text

Bergmann, J., & Sams, A. (2012). *Flip Your Classroom: Reach Every Student in Every Class Every Day*. International Society for Technology in Education.

Bergmann, J., & Sams, A. (2014). The flipped model. In *Flipped learning: Gateway to student engagement*. International Society for Technology in Education.

Bloom, B. S., Engelhart, M. D., Furst, E. J., Hill, W. H., & Krathwohl, D. R. A. (1956). *Taxonomy of Educational Objectives: The Classification of Educational Goals. Handbook 1: Cognitive Domain*. David McKay.

Bonk, C. J., Lee, M. M., Reeves, T. C., & Reynolds, T. H. (2017). The emergence and design of massive open online courses (MOOCs). In Reiser, R. A., & Demsey, J. V. (Eds.), *Trends and issues in instructional design and technology* (4th ed., pp. 250–268). Pearson.

Bonk, C. J., Zhu, M., Kim, M., Xu, S., Sabir, N., & Sari, A. R. (2018). Pushing toward a more personalized MOOC: Exploring instructor selected activities, resources, and technologies for MOOC design and implementation. *International Review of Research in Open and Distance Learning*, 19(4). DOI: 10.19173/irrodl.v19i4.3439

Brown, M., Giolla Mhichil, M. N., Beirne, E., & Mac Lochlainn, C. (2021). The global micro-credential landscape: Charting a new credential ecology for lifelong learning. *Journal of Learning Development*, 8(2), 228–254. DOI: 10.56059/jl4d.v8i2.525

Cheng, Z., Watson, S. L., & Newby, T. J. (2018). Goal setting and open digital badges in higher education. *TechTrends*, 62(2), 190–196. DOI: 10.1007/s11528-018-0249-x

Coursera. (2024). *Explore-Goals.*https://www.coursera.org/

DeakinCo. (2017). *What are micro-credentials and how can they benefit both businesses and employees?* Deakin Co., https://deakinco.com/resource/what-are-micro-credentials-and-how-can-they-benefit-both-businesses-and-employees/#:~:text=Micro%2Dcredentialing%20offers%20you%20and,and%20learning%20on%20the%20job.&text=The%20flexibility%20and%20incremental%20nature,they%20accumulate%20in%20their%20role

Delgado Kloos, C., Muñoz-Merino, P. J., Alario-Hoyos, C., Estévez Ayres, I., & Fernández-Panadero, C. (2015). Mixing and blending MOOC technologies with face-to-face pedagogies. *2015 IEEE Global Engineering Education Conference (EDUCON)*, Tallinn, Estonia, 967–971. DOI: 10.1109/EDUCON.2015.7096090

Desmarchelier, R., & Cary, L. J. (2022). Toward just and equitable micro-credentials: An Australian perspective. *International Journal of Educational Technology in Higher Education*, 19(1), 25. DOI: 10.1186/s41239-022-00332-y PMID: 35669714

edX (2024). *Enterprise-For Campus.*https://business.edx.org/campus

European Commission. (2020). *A European approach to micro-credentials: Background paper for the first meeting of the consultation group on micro-credentials.* https://education.ec.europa.eu/sites/default/files/document-library-docs/european-approach-micro-credentials-higher-education-consultation-group-output-annex-1.pdf

European MOOC Consortium (EMC). (2020). EMC common microcredential framework. *European MOOC Consortium*, 1–13. https://emc.eadtu.eu/images/EMC_Common_Microcredential_Framework_.pdf

European Training Foundation. (2022). *Guide to design, issue and recognise micro-credentials.*https://etf.europa.eu/sites/default/files/2023-05/Micro-Credential%20Guidelines%20Final%20Delivery.pdf. Accessed: April 2024.

European Union. (2021). *A European approach to micro-credentials.* https://education.ec.europa.eu/sites/default/files/2022-01/micro-credentials%20brochure%20updated.pdf

Ferman, B., Finamor, L., & Lima, L. (2019). A*re Public Schools Ready to Integrate Math Classes with Khan Academy?* Munich Personal RePEc Archive. https://mpra.ub.uni-muenchen.de/94736/

FutureLearn. (2024). C*ourses*.https://www.futurelearn.com/?main-nav-submenu=main-nav-courses

Galindo-Domínguez, H. (2021). Flipped classroom in the educational system: Trend or effective pedagogical model compared to other methodologies? *Journal of Educational Technology & Society*, 24(3), 44–60. .https://www.jstor.org/stable/27032855

Ghafoor, S., & Abiodullah, M. (2024). Effect of flipped classroom approach on higher secondary students' academic performance. *Educational Research and Innovation, 4*(1). https://eri.com.pk/index.php/Journal/article/view/116/74

Gibson, D., Ostashewski, N., Flintoff, K., Grant, S., & Knight, E. (2015). Digital badges in education. *Education and Information Technologies*, 20(2), 403–410. DOI: 10.1007/s10639-013-9291-7

Gilboy, M. B., Heinerichs, S., & Pazzaglia, G. (2015). Enhancing student engagement using the flipped classroom. *Journal of Nutrition Education and Behavior*, 47(1), 109–114. DOI: 10.1016/j.jneb.2014.08.008 PMID: 25262529

International Council of Distance Education (ICDE). (2019). *Report of the ICDE Working Group on the Present and Future of Alternative Digital Credentials* (ADCs). https://static1.squarespace.com/static/5b99664675f9eea7a3ecee82/t/5cc69fb771c10b798657bf2f/1556520905468/ICDE-ADC+report-January+2019+%28002%29.pdf

Kabita, N. D., & Ji, L. (2017). *The why, what and how of competency-based curriculum reforms: The Kenyan experience*.https://unesdoc.unesco.org/ark:/48223/pf0000250431

Kasriel, S. (2018). *The future of work won't be about college degrees; it will be about job skills. Consumer News and Business Channel*.https://www.cnbc.com/2018/10/31/the-future-of-work-wont-be-about-degrees-it-will-beabout-skills.html

Kato, S., Galán-Muros, V., & Weko, T. (2020). *The emergence of alternative credentials (OECD Education Working Papers No. 216)*. OECD Publishing. DOI: 10.1787/19939019

Kazin, C. J., & Clerkin, K. M. (2018). *The potentials and limitations of microcredentials. Service Members opportunity Colleges*.https://supportsystem.livehelpnow.net/resources/23351/Potential%20and%20Limitations%20of%20Microcredentials%20FINAL_SEPT%202018.pdf

Khan, S. (2011). *About Khan Academy*. http://www.khanacademy.org/about

Krathwohl, D. R. (2002). A revision of Bloom's taxonomy: An overview. *Theory into Practice*, 41(4), 212–218. DOI: 10.1207/s15430421tip4104_2

Li, Y., Zhang, M., Bonk, C. J., & Guo, N. (2015). Integrating MOOC and flipped classroom practice in a traditional undergraduate course: Students' experience and perceptions. [iJET]. *International Journal of Emerging Technologies in Learning*, 10(6), 4–10. DOI: 10.3991/ijet.v10i6.4708

Lo, C. K., & Hew, K. F. (2017). A critical review of flipped classroom challenges in K-12 education: Possible solutions and recommendations for future research. *Research and Practice in Technology Enhanced Learning*, 12(4), 4. DOI: 10.1186/s41039-016-0044-2 PMID: 30613253

Maina, M. F., Guàrdia Ortiz, L., Mancini, F., & Martinez Melo, M. (2022). A micro-credentialing methodology for improved recognition of HE employability skills. *International Journal of Educational Technology in Higher Education*, 19(10), 10. DOI: 10.1186/s41239-021-00315-5 PMID: 35224180

McGreal, R., & Olcott, D.Jr. (2022). A Strategic Reset: Micro-Credentials for Higher Education Leaders. *Smart Learning Environments*, 9(1), 9. DOI: 10.1186/s40561-022-00190-1

Melai, T., van der Westen, S., Winkels, J., Antonaci, A., Henderikx, P., & Ubachs, G. (2020). *Concept and role of Short Learning Programmes in European higher education*. (Research Report No. 02.1). https://eslp.eadtu.eu/images/Concept_and_role_of_SLPs.pdf

Micro, H. E. Consortium. (2019). *A briefing paper on the award, recognition, portability and accreditation of microcredentials: An investigation through interviews with key stakeholders & decision makers*. https://microcredentials.eu/wp-content/uploads/sites/20/2019/12/WP3-Interviews-with-Key-Stakeholders-Decision-Makers-Overall-Summary-Report.pdf. Accessed: April 2024.

Moroder, K. (2014). *Micro-credentials: empowering lifelong learners*. Edutopia, https://www.edutopia.org/blog/micro-credentials-empowering-lifelong-learners-krista-moroder

New Zealand Qualifications Authority (NZQA). (2024). *Guidelines for Applying for Approval of a Training Scheme or a Micro-credential*. https://www2.nzqa.govt.nz/assets/Tertiary/Approval-accreditation-and-registration/Micro-credentials/Guidelines-for-micro-credentials-January-2024.pdf

Olakanmi, E. E. (2017). The Effects of a Flipped Classroom Model of Instruction on Students' Performance and Attitudes Towards Chemistry. *Journal of Science Education and Technology*, 26(1), 127–137. DOI: 10.1007/s10956-016-9657-x

Oliver, B. (2019). *Making micro-credentials work for learners, employers and providers. Deakin University*.https://dteach.deakin.edu.au/wp-content/uploads/sites/103/2019/08/Making-micro-credentials-work-Oliver-Deakin-2019-full-report.pdf

OpenUpEd. (2015). *Definition Massive Open Online Courses (MOOCs)*. https://www.openuped.eu/images/docs/Definition_Massive_Open_Online_Courses.pdf

Pawilen, G. T., Lubong, K. S., & Fausto, C. J. R. S. (2022). A proposed model in designing curriculum for microcredentials in the Philippines. *International Journal of Curriculum and Instruction*, 15(1), 508–520. https://files.eric.ed.gov/fulltext/EJ1382892.pdf

Pérez-Sanagustín, M., Hilliger, I., Alario-Hoyos, C., Delgado Kloos, C., & Rayyan, S. (2017). H-MOOC framework: Reusing MOOCs for hybrid education. *Journal of Computing in Higher Education*, 29(1), 47–64. DOI: 10.1007/s12528-017-9133-5

Pérez-Sanagustín, M., Hilliger, I., Schwarzenberg, P., & Parra, D. (2015). A framework of hybrid MOOC-based pedagogies. In Changee, W., & Wapla, M. (Eds.), *EC-TEL 2015 workshops* (pp. 6–10). https://educate.gast.it.uc3m.es/wp-content/uploads/2015/09/A-Framework-of-Hybrid-MOOC-based-pedagogies-HybridED-ECTEL2015.pdf

Pertuz, S., Reyes, O., Cristobal, E. S., Meier, R., & Castro, M. (2023). MOOC-based flipped classroom for on-campus teaching in undergraduate engineering courses. *IEEE Transactions on Education*, 66(5), 468–478. DOI: 10.1109/TE.2023.3282896

Pickard, L., Shah, D., & De Simone, J. J. (2018). Mapping microcredentials across MOOC platforms. *In 2018 Learning with MOOCs (LWMOOCS), Madrid, Spain.* (pp. 17-21). IEEE. DOI: 10.1109/LWMOOCS.2018.8534617

Porter, D., & Beale, R. (2015). *A policy brief on MOOCs*. The Commonwealth of Learning. https://oasis.col.org/server/api/core/bitstreams/7365921f-bb0b-4a25-be44-fa7e25981fe2/content

Ralston, S. J. (2021). Higher education's microcredentialing craze: A postdigital-Deweyan critique. *Postdigital Science and Education*, 3(1), 83–101. DOI: 10.1007/s42438-020-00121-8

Reeves, T. C., & Hedberg, J. G. (2014). MOOCs: Let's get REAL. *Educational Technology*, 54(1), 3–8. https://www.jstor.org/stable/44430228

Rodriguez, C. O. (2012). MOOCs and the AI-Stanford like courses: Two successful and distinct course formats for massive open online courses. *European Journal of Open, Distance and E-Learning*. https://files.eric.ed.gov/fulltext/EJ982976.pdf

Rossiter, D., & Tynan, B. (2019). *Designing and Implementing Micro-Credentials: A Guide for Practitioners. Commonwealth of Learning*. https://oasis.col.org/server/api/core/bitstreams/770ff842-9a5e-424b-a253-0757fa539086/content

Schmidt, S. M. P., & Ralph, D. L. (2016). The Flipped Classroom: A twist on teaching. C*ontemporary Issues in Education Research (CIER), 9*(1), 1–6. https://files.eric.ed.gov/fulltext/EJ1087603.pdf

Selvaratnam, R. M., & Sankey, M. D. (2021). An integrative literature review of the implementation of micro-credentials in higher education: Implications for practice in Australasia. *Journal of Teaching and Learning for Graduate Employability*, 12(1), 1–17. https://files.eric.ed.gov/fulltext/EJ1293818.pdf. DOI: 10.21153/jtlge2021vol12no1art942

Shah, D. (2021). By the numbers: MOOCs in 2021. *Class Central*. https://www.classcentral.com/report/mooc-stats-2021

Snyder, C., Paska, L. M., & Besozzi, D. (2014). Cast from the Past: Using Screencasting in the Social Studies Classroom. *Social Studies*, 105(6), 310–314. DOI: 10.1080/00377996.2014.951472

The Council of the European Union. (2022). Council recommendation of 16 June 2022 on a European approach to micro-credentials for lifelong learning and employability. *Official Journal of the European Union*.https://eur-lex.europa.eu/legal-content/EN/TXT/PDF/?uri=CELEX:32022H0627(02)

Tschofen, C., & Mackness, J. (2012). Connectivism and dimensions of individual experience. *International Review of Research in Open and Distance Learning*, 13(1), 124–143. DOI: 10.19173/irrodl.v13i1.1143

Varadarajan, S., Koh, J. H. L., & Daniel, B. K. (2023). A systematic review of the opportunities and challenges of micro-credentials for multiple stakeholders: Learners, employers, higher education institutions and government. *International Journal of Educational Technology in Higher Education*, 20(13), 13. DOI: 10.1186/s41239-023-00381-x PMID: 36874535

Wang, K., & Zhu, C. (2019). MOOC-based flipped learning in higher education: Students' participation, experience and learning performance. *International Journal of Educational Technology in Higher Education*, 16(1), 33. DOI: 10.1186/s41239-019-0163-0

Weeraratne, B., & Chin, B. (2018). Can Khan Academy e-learning video tutorials improve mathematics achievement in Sri Lanka? *International Journal of Education and Development using Information and Communication Technology (IJEDICT), 14(*3), 93-112. https://files.eric.ed.gov/fulltext/EJ1201489.pdf

Wong, B. T. (2021). A survey on the pedagogical features of language massive open online courses. *Asian Association of Open Universities Journal*, 16(1), 116–128. DOI: 10.1108/AAOUJ-03-2021-0028

Yu, D.-Y., Zhang, L., Li, Y.-L., Lan, T., Gu, L.-N., & Yang, S.-S. (2024). The implementation of a MOOC-based flipped classroom teaching method in the context of oncology radiotherapy residency training. *Journal of Cancer Education*. DOI: 10.1007/s13187-024-02513-x PMID: 39369377

Zainuddin, Z., & Halili, S. (2016). Flipped Classroom Research and Trends from Different Fields of Study. *International Review of Research in Open and Distance Learning*, 17(3), 313–340. DOI: 10.19173/irrodl.v17i3.2274

Zhang, L., Xuan, Y., & Zhang, H. (2020). Construction and application of SPOC-based flipped classroom teaching mode in Installation Engineering Cost curriculum based on OBE concept. *Computer Applications in Engineering Education*, 28(6), 1503–1519. DOI: 10.1002/cae.22320

ADDITIONAL READING

Bergmann, J., & Sams, A. (2014). The flipped model. In *Flipped learning: Gateway to student engagement*. International Society for Technology in Education.

Bonk, C. J., Zhu, M., Kim, M., Xu, S., Sabir, N., & Sari, A. R. (2018). Pushing toward a more personalized MOOC: Exploring instructor selected activities, resources, and technologies for MOOC design and implementation. *International Review of Research in Open and Distance Learning*, 19(4). DOI: 10.19173/irrodl.v19i4.3439

Varadarajan, S., Koh, J. H. L., & Daniel, B. K. (2023). A systematic review of the opportunities and challenges of micro-credentials for multiple stakeholders: Learners, employers, higher education institutions and government. *International Journal of Educational Technology in Higher Education*, 20(13), 13. DOI: 10.1186/s41239-023-00381-x PMID: 36874535

KEY TERMS AND DEFINITIONS

Credential: A credential is a broad term that refers to the outcome of an educational effort, signifying a respected third party's verification that learning has been achieved and that the individual can effectively apply this knowledge (International Council of Distance Education-ICDE, 2019).

Flipped Classroom: The FC concept is that tasks typically performed during in-person class time are undertaken outside of class, while activities traditionally assigned as homework are tackled during class sessions (Bergmann & Sams, 2012).

Micro-Credential: Micro-credentials, the emphasis on "micro," are certifications that indicate the completion of learning objectives via shortened courses or training programs. They provide acknowledged recognition of abilities that are learned more quickly (McGreal & Olcott Jr., 2022).

MOOC: MOOCs are online courses that are intended for a large number of students. They are free to enroll in, accessible to anybody with an internet connection anywhere, and provide students with a full course experience at no cost (OpenUpEd, 2015). MOOCs offer an organized curriculum centered around a particular theme or topic, in which learners are expected to be self-reliant and manage their own education by creating their own conceptual and social connections to meet their own requirements (Tschofen and Mackness, 2012)

Chapter 14
Artificial Intelligence in Micro-Credentials for Open and Distance Learning: A Technologically-Enhanced Systematic Review

Siti Haslina Md Harizan
Universiti Sains Malaysia, Malaysia

Mohamed Ally
Athabasca University, Canada

ABSTRACT

Micro-credentials are growing rapidly, meeting the demand for a flexible workforce and aligning well with the ODL environment. The use of artificial intelligence is pushing education to new heights. However, AI's integration in micro-credentials for ODL is fragmented, limiting the field's expansion. This research aims to address this gap by conducting a systematic review using software to analyse the relevant literature comprehensively. Employing a hybrid approach of bibliometric and thematic analysis, the review examines forty-six articles on AI integration into micro-credentials in ODL, identifying research gaps and suggesting future directions. The review provides updated insights, benefiting both theoretical and practical applications. It offers a comprehensive reference for industry practitioners to bridge the gap between theory and practice, contributing new knowledge and identifying future research opportunities.

DOI: 10.4018/979-8-3693-5488-9.ch014

INTRODUCTION

The integration of Artificial Intelligence (AI) into micro-credentials courses within open and distance learning (ODL) in higher educational institutions marks a pivotal shift in the educational paradigm, aimed at enhancing accessibility, personalisation, and efficiency. This evolution aligns with the rapid technological advancements and the increasing demand for flexible, lifelong learning opportunities that cater to a diverse global learner population. It is known that AI plays an important role in transforming ODL through micro-credentials by involving adaptive learning systems, personalised content delivery, and the automation of administrative tasks, which collectively aim to improve learning outcomes and student engagement. By leveraging AI technologies, institutions can offer more personalised and adaptive learning experiences, meeting the individual needs of learners and addressing the diverse competencies required in today's dynamic job market. This integration also promises to enhance the scalability and effectiveness of ODL programs, making higher education more accessible to a broader audience. However, the integration of AI into micro-credential courses within ODL contexts is not without its challenges. Many areas are yet to be explored given the current state of knowledge.

Nevertheless, emerging trends and innovative practices in the use of AI in micro-credentials within ODL highlight the potential for significant improvements in personalised learning, accessibility, and learner support. Thus, the integration of AI into micro-credential courses within ODL in higher education institutions may offer promising opportunities to redefine the learning experience, making it more personalised, accessible, and aligned with the needs of the 21st-century learner. By addressing the challenges and leveraging the emerging trends, higher education institutions can harness the power of AI to enhance the value and impact of their ODL programs and micro-credentials.

Background of Study

Open and Distance Learning (ODL) is an educational system that removes barriers related to time, location, and access, emphasizing the role of technology in facilitating education for learners who are physically separated from their instructors (Ghosh et al., 2012). ODL leverages technology and flexible methodologies to provide accessible, inclusive, and learner-centered education. In particular, micro-credentials provide a flexible learning pathway that caters to the needs of learners looking to upskill or reskill, making them particularly relevant in ODL settings. Micro-credentials, aligned with the gig economy, are short, industry-based learning units facilitated by digital platforms that contribute to education privatisation, transferring employment preparation costs to individuals and tightening higher education's ties to immediate workplace demands, rather than broader occupational skills (Wheelahan & Moodie, 2022). Micro-credentials are also known as short, focused, and competency-based certifications designed to support reskilling and upskilling, making them highly relevant in today's fast-paced and dynamic job market. Micro-credentials offer a means for learners to gain new skills or enhance existing ones without committing to long-term educational programs (Orman et al., 2023). These credentials are often delivered online and can be obtained through platforms like Coursera, Udemy, and EdX. Micro-credentials typically include metadata that transparently shows the learner's identity, awarding body, date of issue, study hours needed, type of assessment, and form of participation (Caetano et al., 2023).

The rise of micro-credentials reflects a shift towards more flexible, affordable, and accessible education options, stackable, and tailored to the evolving needs of learners and the job market. Its flexibility allows learners to study at their own pace and from any location. It is designed to provide specific skills or knowledge that can be immediately applicable in the workplace This has become increasingly important in the context of the COVID-19 pandemic, which has accelerated the adoption of online learning and highlighted the need for adaptable educational models (Ahmat et al., 2021). In particular, micro-credentials are valuable for professional development as it enables educators and other professionals to update their skills, stay current with industry trends, and demonstrate their competencies to employers. This form of credentialing is increasingly being recognised and valued by employers, enhancing employability and career progression (Hunt et al., 2020). Micro-credentials can be standalone certifications or combined (stacked) to contribute towards broader qualifications such as degrees or professional certifications. Stackability makes them a versatile tool in the educational landscape, allowing learners to build a portfolio of skills progressively (Sargent et al., 2023). Micro-credentials offer a new approach to professional development by providing opportunities to document learning using work samples, videos, and other artifacts. This method enables teachers and other professionals to share their learning and achievements more broadly and can lead to recognition and rewards in their careers (Berry et al., 2016).

Artificial intelligence has emerged as the leading-edge technological trend. AI holds significant potential to transform ODL by addressing various challenges and enhancing the learning experience for students and educators. AI has the potential to significantly enhance ODL by providing personalised learning experiences, automating administrative tasks, and improving student engagement and performance. AI enables personalised learning by tailoring educational content to meet the individual needs of learners. This customisation can improve engagement and comprehension by adjusting the pace and complexity of material based on each student's progress and learning style (Yu et al., 2017). On top of that, AI-powered support systems, such as chatbots and virtual tutors, provide instant feedback and assistance to students. These systems can answer common questions, guide learners through difficult concepts, and offer personalised tutoring, and thereby, enhancing the overall learning experience (Wen & Lin, 2008). AI can also analyse vast amounts of data to identify patterns and predict student outcomes which helps educators to intervene early when a student is struggling while personalising instruction to improve academic performance (Doğan et al., 2023). AI-driven interactive platforms, including virtual and augmented reality, can create immersive learning environments. These technologies engage students more deeply by providing hands-on experiences and simulations that enhance understanding and retention (Rad et al., 2018). Besides, AI can also automate administrative tasks such as grading, scheduling, and plagiarism detection, allowing educators to focus more on teaching and student interaction. This increases efficiency and reduces the workload on educators (Fadzil & Munira, 2008). The adaptability of AI systems to the diverse needs and backgrounds of learners, offering a more inclusive educational environment. This ensures that all students, have the opportunity to succeed regardless of their starting point (Holmes & Anastopoulou, 2019). By leveraging AI technologies, educational institutions can offer more flexible, efficient, and effective learning solutions.

The integration of AI into micro-credentials within Open and Distance Learning can significantly enhance the effectiveness, accessibility, and personalisation of learning experiences. AI technologies facilitate various aspects of the educational process, from personalised learning paths to automated support systems, making education more adaptable to individual learner needs. AI enables personalised learning by tailoring educational content to meet the unique needs of each learner. This is achieved through adaptive learning systems that adjust the complexity and pace of material based on the learner's progress and preferences. Such systems are particularly beneficial in ODL settings, where direct interaction with instructors is limited (Fadzil & Munira, 2008). The development of AI-powered virtual teaching assistants, such as T-BOT and Q-BOT, helps both students and tutors by providing real-time tutoring and evaluation. These AI agents can engage with students through natural language, offering support and feedback, which enhances the learning experience on platforms like Moodle (Rodriguez et al., 2008). Integrating AI into the Learning Management System (LMS) may streamline and enhance various educational processes, such as content delivery, student assessment, and feedback. AI technologies can automate administrative tasks, provide personalised learning paths, and offer analytics to monitor and improve student performance (Firat, 2023). AI-driven insights can also help educators design more effective courses by analysing student data to identify learning patterns and areas for improvement. This can lead to the creation of more engaging and effective educational content (Goksel & Bozkurt, 2019).

Despite the emerging interest in AI which is significantly impactful to the landscape of the higher educational research landscape, systematic literature reviews concerning the integration of AI in MCs particularly in the context of ODL are relatively new and rarely focused. To date, the existing systematic literature reviews have yet to provide a holistic, comprehensive, non-fragmented, and updated state of research and development of the integration of AI in micro-credentials particularly in the context of ODL. The extent of the research is fragmented, potentially impeding the field's advancement when challenged with conflicting viewpoints and limited replications.

A review done by Thi Ngoc Ha et al. (2023) assesses micro-credential research and practices in higher education, based on academic literature from 2012 to 2022. Through analysing 29 articles, it explores awareness, benefits, challenges, and factors impacting the effectiveness of micro-credentials. The findings indicate that micro-credentials hold potential advantages for higher education, but their implementation is not straightforward for students or institutions. Currently, micro-credentials are in the early stages of integration into higher education, and more research is needed to fully understand their long-term viability and impact. However, the review underscored challenges associated with the implementation of micro-credentials whereby micro-credentials are not micro tasks for students to complete or for higher education providers to offer meaningful learning experiences for students. Therefore, the viability and effectiveness of micro-credentials in higher education, especially in the long term have yet to be assessed.

Alsobhi et al. (2023) conducted a systematic literature review of studies published between 2016-2022, assessing them against established requirements for blockchain-based systems and identifying research gaps, thus providing insights into recent developments in micro-credentialing systems for higher educational institutions. Nevertheless, the review suggested that an intelligent blockchain-based micro-credential framework for higher education students to manage micro-credentials and provide learning recommendations for students is yet to be explored and further developed.

Ahsan et al. (2023) reviewed the emerging role of micro-credentials and digital badges in higher educational institutions, suggesting they represent a significant shift in learning models through technology. By reviewing 56 peer-reviewed articles from 2015 to 2021, the research highlights the increasing interest in MCs within higher education (HE). The findings suggest a need for further investigation into the technological impacts and various stakeholder perspectives on MCs. The study synthesizes key themes into a conceptual framework for MC implementation in HE and points out research gaps, contributing to the evolving discussion on the way micro-credentials can revolutionise higher education degree delivery and student learning achievements. However, the use of machine learning or other artificial intelligence-based research tools were not identified in the review.

A review by Mena-Guacas et al. (2023) examines the progression of teaching methods in short-term courses through a systematic PRISMA methodology-based review. It focused on selecting studies that detail the teaching methods designed for courses not exceeding 90 days, excluding longer courses and incomplete studies. Conducted on April 9, 2022, the research utilised the SCOPUS database, rigorously reviewing and analysing articles multiple times by different researchers. Out of the selected 42 articles, the findings are categorised into the learning experience, teaching methodology, technological resources, and assessment methods, highlighting a shift towards experiential learning in short-term courses over traditional memory-based activities.

Besides, it is also important to get acquainted with gaps which render the integration of AI into micro-credentials in ODL. Since ODL often lacks personalised learning pathways tailored to individual student needs, making it challenging to address diverse learning preferences and requirements effectively, AI can help by providing adaptive learning experiences (Garrido et al., 2016). As ODL programs grow, scaling personalised support becomes increasingly difficult and thus, AI solutions can scale efficiently, providing consistent support to a large number of learners simultaneously (Dai et al., 2022). It is also learned that ODL learners often face delays in receiving feedback, which can hinder their progress (Forkan et al., 2023). AI is believed to provide instant feedback and guidance, thus, enhancing the learning experience and keeping students engaged. Moreover, the administrative workload in managing micro-credentials, such as grading and verification, is high and therefore, AI can help in automating these processes, improving efficiency and allowing educators to focus more on teaching (Hatzi et al., 2012).

Based on the coverage of past reviews as well as gaps identified, there is an urgent need to undertake a systematic literature review which is motivated by lacking insights that focus on the integration of AI into micro-credentials that render sufficient basis for reviews on current research that has been done to date. The availability of research on artificial intelligence across various disciplines also limits a comprehensive understanding of the areas. The dearth of reviews that incorporate the essence of AI in micro-credentials within ODL has triggered an urgency to provide a comprehensive and holistic state-of-the-art review that captures the current and potential state-of-the-art research and development of AI in micro-credentials for ODL settings. This has raised several questions as follows:

RQ1: What is the trend of publication and citation in research that incorporates AI in micro-credential courses within the ODL context?

RQ2: What are the major themes in AI in micro-credentials for ODL research?

RQ3: What are research avenues available for future research that intends to incorporate AI in micro-credential courses within the ODL context?

This study will review the integration of artificial intelligence in micro-credentials within the context of open and distance learning. The review aims to address the knowledge gaps by highlighting comprehensive, holistic, and updated insights on the development and integration of AI in micro-credentials within the open and distance learning context, which could stimulate future research agendas in its relevant domains. The objectives of the study are (1) to address and map the existing research that incorporates AI in micro-credentials courses within the ODL context by employing review protocol together with the analytical techniques supported by bibliometric software technology, (2) to identify major themes in the current body of knowledge that constitutes AI in micro-credentials for ODL, and (3) to propose and suggest potential future trends for further understanding and benefits both theoretically and practically. The subsequent parts of the study highlight the methodology and research protocol to be followed, findings about the current trends and developments, major themes, as well as discussions on the gaps in the research for future research avenues of the abovementioned topics.

Methodology

A domain-based review will be employed using a hybrid approach that combines both bibliometric and thematic analysis with the aid of appropriate and latest software. The review will observe the Scientific Procedures and Rationales for the Systematic Literature Reviews (SPAR-4-SLR) protocol (Paul et al., 2021). SPAR-4-SLR provides a comprehensive methodological framework for conducting systematic literature reviews. This protocol emphasizes a rigorous and transparent approach to the literature review, incorporating clearly defined steps such as formulating research questions, systematic searching, screening for relevance, quality appraisal, data extraction, and synthesis of findings. SPAR-4-SLR aims to enhance the reliability and reproducibility of systematic literature reviews by ensuring methodological rigor and reducing biases. SPAR-4-SLR has been applied in various research contexts to improve the systematic review process. For instance, Ahiadu and Abidoye (2023) used this protocol to review the impact of economic uncertainty on property performance, highlighting the utility of SPAR-4-SLR in organizing and analyzing large datasets systematically. Similarly, Alkadi and Abed (2023) applied the SPAR-4-SLR protocol in their review of consumer acceptance of fintech payment services, demonstrating its effectiveness in structuring and analysing comprehensive literature datasets.

SPAR-4-SLR consists of three stages (assembling, arranging, and assessing) and six substages that follow sequentially (identification, acquisition, organisation, purification, evaluation, and reporting). The assembly stage involves gathering all relevant studies from various databases using predefined search criteria. This stage focuses on ensuring a comprehensive collection of articles that align with the research questions. It includes defining search terms, selecting appropriate databases, and applying inclusion and exclusion criteria to filter the initial search results. The arranging stage entails the organising and categorising of the collected studies from the assemble stage. This includes systematically sorting the studies based on relevance, thematic areas, and research questions. It also involves the removal of duplicates and the initial screening of titles and abstracts to ensure the studies meet the predefined criteria for further detailed analysis. The assessing stage in the SPAR-4-SLR protocol implies the evaluation of the quality and relevance of the selected studies. This includes critical appraisal using predefined criteria to assess the methodological rigour, validity, and reliability of the studies, ensuring only high-quality research contributes to the final synthesis.

During the final synthesis, the articles will be arranged and assessed with the aid of appropriate software before being coupled into several major research streams. The articles will be further reviewed through a subsequent thematic analysis whereby different authors will independently read the articles to identify major thematic themes discussed in each research stream. An inductive coding approach will be employed to explore the essence of each generated cluster and distinguish between major thematic themes across the earlier identified research streams. The gaps across the research streams will be highlighted for the identification of future research considerations and suggestions.

Assemble

This stage involves the identification and acquisition of publications for review. Only articles published in the World of Science (WoS) and Scopus databases between 2010 to 2024 are considered since these are the largest multidisciplinary databases that host the mostly used publications in bibliometric studies (Galetsi et al., 2019; Visser et al, 2021). The assembly stage ended on 13th March 2024. The search query used comprises Boolean operator “AND”, and truncation of major keywords of the topic i.e. “micro-credentials” AND “open and distance learning” AND “artificial intelligence”. Based on the search query, a total of 108 publications was assembled which signifies the maturity of the domain for review.

Arrange

The ‘arrange’ stage involves the organisation and purification of published articles through inclusion and exclusion criteria. Only full research articles, early access, and review articles were included. Proceedings papers, book chapters, and data papers were excluded. A total of 95 articles comprising 75 articles from WoS and 20 articles from Scopus gathered in the assemble stage were finally retained for the subsequent stage.

Assess

The final stage of the review protocol involves the evaluation and reporting of the articles. The evaluations of articles were performed by performing bibliometrics analysis that runs algorithms and quantitative techniques that extract a specific compilation of the research stream of the scholarly literature (Kraus et. al., 2022). There were two components of bibliometric analysis involved in this study namely science mapping and performance analysis (Lim & Kumar, 2023). By employing performance analysis, the study assesses the publication and citation in the shared field of AI, micro-credentials, and ODL. In addition, this study also presents science mapping using keyword co-occurrence analysis (Igami et. al. 2014) and bibliographic coupling (Waltman et. al., 2010) in forming clusters of publication based on the co-occurrence of keywords and similarities in shared reference respectively. The analyses were performed using Bibliometrix-R and visualised using VOSViewer.

The outcome of the analyses exhibited a two-dimensional map, which locates items based on the similarity of the keywords and references. A higher degree of relatedness between the articles is indicated by closer proximity between the items. A minimum threshold for keyword co-occurrence and bibliographic coupling was established to ensure the inclusion of all selected articles in the analysis. To better ensure a sharper focus on the core articles for each cluster, a minimum number of occurrences of keywords and total citation link strength was set at three. This led to the 46 articles coupled into six major thematic clusters. The articles in the clusters were conscientiously reviewed using interpretive analysis. Each of the researchers read the articles independently and picked out important and major thematic themes for each research stream.

Figure 1. SPAR-4-SLR protocol (Paul et al., 2021)

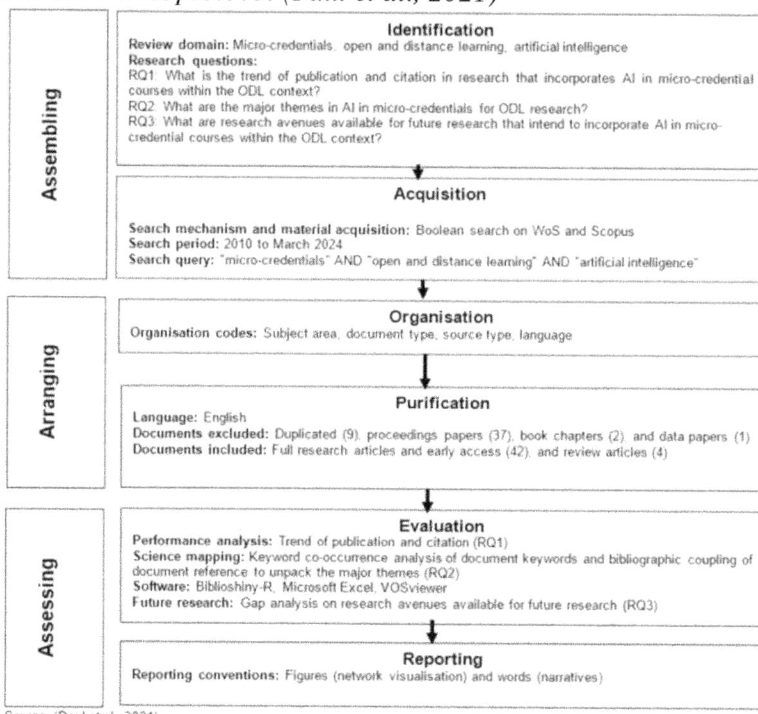

Source: (Paul et al., 2021)

Results and Findings

Trends of publication and citation (RQ1)

The publication years of the body of knowledge focusing on artificial intelligence in micro-credentials for open and distance learning range between 2010 and March 2024 (*see*Figure 2). The majority of the articles were published as full research articles (91.3%), while the remainder 8.75% comprising review articles. The annual growth rate of publication is 8.16% with average citations per document of 4.63. The total number of authors recorded was 333, whereby 30 authors published in single-authored documents while international co-authorship comprised 20.31%. The average co-authorship per document is 2.82. A total of 4014 references were used in composing the articles with average citations per document at 4.63.

Figure 2. Number of articles published between 2010 and 2023

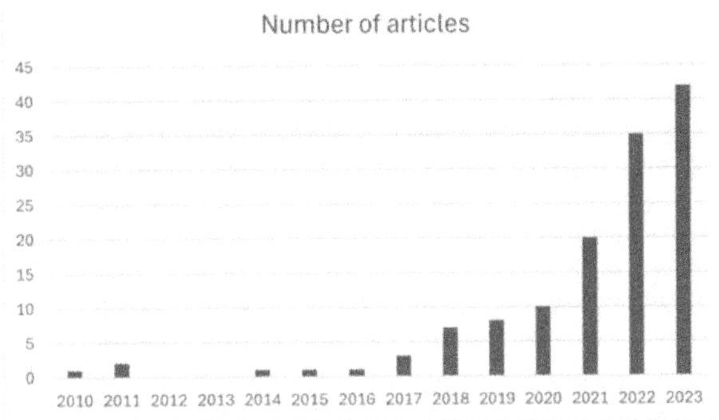

Figure 3. Countries of citations (total article citations)

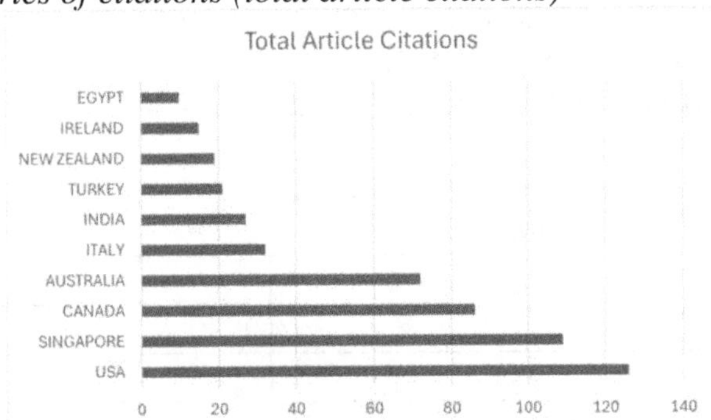

Figure 3 shows the countries of citations. The most cited country is the United States of America, with a total citation article of 126, followed by Singapore, with 109 citations, Canada with 86 citations, Australia (72 citations), Italy (32 citations), India (27 citations), Türkiye (21 citations), New Zealand (19 citations), Ireland (15 citations), and Egypt (10 citations).

Figure 4. Average article citations by country

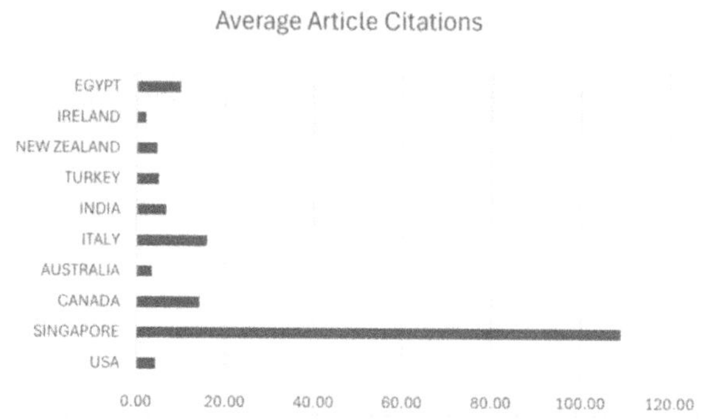

In terms of average article citations by country (*see*Figure 4), Singapore has the highest number of average article citations (109), followed by Italy (16 citations), Canada (14.3 citations), Egypt (10 citations), India (6.8 citations), Türkiye (5.2 citations), New Zealand (4.8 citations), United States of America (4.5 citations), Australia (3.6 citations), and Ireland (2.1 citations).

Table 1 . Most frequent keywords

Terms	Frequency
higher-education	8
students	8
perceptions	6
digital badges	5
education	5
badges	4
motivation	4
achievement	3
curriculum	3
engagement	3

In Table 1, the most frequent keywords used in the publication are higher education (n=8) and students (n=8), followed by perceptions (n=6), digital badges (n=5), education (n=5), badges (n=4), motivation (n=4), achievement (n=3), curriculum (n=3), and engagement (n=3).

Figure 5. Annual total citation per year

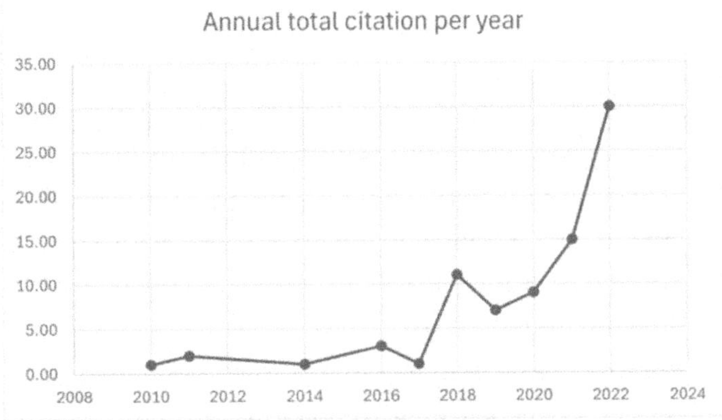

There is an increasing trend in the annual total citations per year from 2010 to 2022 (*see*Figure 5). The humble trend started with one citation per year in 2010, followed by two citations in 2011, one citation in 2014, and three citations in 2016, which dropped to one citation in 2017 before spiking to eleven citations in 2018 and down to seven and nine citations in 2019 and 2020 respectively. The latter trend saw a dramatic increase in the annual total citations per year with fifteen citations in 2021 to thirty citations in 2022. Both 2023's and 2024's figures are yet to be available.

Major thematic cluster (RQ2)

Keyword co-occurrence analysis

A keyword co-occurrence analysis has been conducted to identify major themes that emerge in the literature that integrate artificial intelligence into micro-credentials within the ODL context. The resulted outcome of the keyword co-occurrence network uncovers major areas of interest via the mapping of keywords that have been enlisted by authors in their articles (Donthu et al., 2019). Figure 6. shows the keyword co-occurrence network of between artificial intelligence, micro-credentials, and ODL. This network is generated and visualised using VOSviewer apps. The distance between two keywords in the visualization approximately indicates the relatedness of the keywords in terms of co-citation links. In general, the closer two keywords are located to each other, the stronger their relatedness. The strongest co-citation links between keywords are also represented by lines.

There are six thematic clusters generated as the result of the keywords co-occurrence analysis. Each cluster is represented by different colours of the network (*see*Figure 6). Red networks denote motivational drives underlying micro-credentials, green networks represent alternative aspects of micro-credentials, blue networks manifest motives underlying lifelong learning, and yellow networks signify AI-based learning. Purple networks indicate micro-credentials for teacher education while cyan networks exhibit equity and inclusivity of open education.

Supplementing the keyword co-occurrence network is the bibliometric information that demonstrates co-occurrences among all keywords in Table 2). The explanation of the keyword co-occurrence and relationships between topics in each cluster is formed based on the logical sensemaking manner (Lim & Kumar, 2023), whereby keywords are organised in a logical way to present a coherent narrative of each cluster (Donthu et. al., 2022).

Figure 6. Keyword co-occurrence network between artificial intelligence, micro-credentials, and ODL research

Table 2. Major keyword co-occurrence clusters in the research

Themes and keywords	
Co-word cluster 1: Motivational drives underlying micro-credentials (red network)	**Co-word cluster 4: AI-based learning (yellow network)**
Achievement	Artificial intelligence
Badges	Classification
Competency-based education	Cloud computing
Covid-19	Deep learning
Curriculum	Machine learning
Digital badge	Metaheuristics

continued on following page

Table 2. Continued

Themes and keywords	
Micro-credential	
Motivation	**Co-word cluster 5: Micro-credentials for teacher education (purple network)**
Performance	Design
Self-efficacy	Digital badges
	Distance learning
Co-word cluster 2: Alternative aspects of micro-credentials (green network)	Micro-credentials
Alternative credentials	Pre-service teachers
Competencies	Teacher education
e-learning	
Engagement	**Co-word cluster 6: Equity and inclusivity of open education (cyan network)**
MOOC	Equity
Online learning	Higher education
Open badges	OER
Skills	Open source
	policy
Co-word cluster 3: Motives underlying lifelong learning (blue network)	
Education	
Employability	
Higher education	
Knowledge	
Lifelong learning	
MOOCS	
Perceptions	
Students	

Keyword Co-Occurrence Cluster 1: Motivational Drives Underlying Micro-Credentials (Red Network)

The first keyword co-occurrence cluster focuses on motivational factors that drive a learner to undertake micro-credentials courses. From the perspective of policymakers and higher educational institutions, this cluster can be viewed as the objectives of offering chunk-based micro-credentials courses and programmes that utilise it. This cluster is formed by ten keywords, namely "achievement", "badges", "competency-based education", "Covid-19", "curriculum", "digital badge", "micro-credentials", "motivation", "performance", and "self-efficacy". The motivational drives underlying micro-credentials are driven by the desire for achievement, enhanced self-efficacy, and the practical benefits of competency-based education. Digital badges serve as powerful motivators, providing visible recognition of skills and fostering a culture of continuous learning and improvement, especially in the context of the evolving educational landscape post-COVID-19. The motivational drives underlying micro-credentials are multi-faceted, and deeply rooted in the pursuit of achievement, self-efficacy, and the need for competency-based education, especially in the wake of the Covid-19 pandemic.

Keyword Co-Occurrence Cluster 2: Alternative Aspects of Micro-Credentials (Green Network)

The second keyword co-occurrence cluster deals with alternative aspects of micro-credentials. This cluster is formed by eight keywords namely "alternative credentials", "competencies", "e-learning", "engagement", "MOOC", "online learning", "open badges", and "skills". The alternative aspects are transforming education by fostering engagement, enhancing employability, and promoting lifelong learning. These credentials offer a practical and flexible approach to skill acquisition, preparing learners for the dynamic demands of the modern workforce. Micro-credentials provide a targeted approach to learning, focusing on the acquisition of discrete, job-relevant skills rather than traditional, time-bound degrees. This shift is particularly significant in the context of online learning, where engagement and flexibility are paramount. By integrating micro-credentials into MOOCs (Massive Open Online Courses) and other e-learning environments, educators can create more personalized and interactive learning experiences that cater to the diverse needs of students.

Keyword Co-Occurrence Cluster 3: Motives Underlying Lifelong Learning (Blue Network)

The third keyword co-occurrence cluster encapsulates of motives underlying lifelong learning which comprises eight keywords such as "education", "employability", "higher education", "knowledge", "lifelong learning", "MOOCs", "perceptions", and "students". The motives underlying lifelong learning are deeply intertwined with the evolving demands of education, employability, and the pursuit of knowledge. The motives underlying lifelong learning encompass a blend of practical and aspirational goals, which are centred on the continuous pursuit of education, employability, and knowledge in an ever-changing world. In today's world, the concept of lifelong learning has gained significant importance, driven by the need to stay relevant in the workforce and adapt to new technologies and methodologies. Education is no longer confined to the traditional boundaries of primary, secondary, and higher education. It has expanded to encompass a continuous, self-directed process that extends throughout an individual's life. This shift is motivated by the recognition that knowledge and skills must be constantly updated to meet the demands of an ever-evolving job market.

Keyword Co-Occurrence Cluster 4: AI-Based Learning (Yellow Network)

The fourth keyword co-occurrence cluster focuses on AI-based learning. This cluster is made up of six keywords namely "artificial intelligence", "classification", "cloud computing", "deep learning", "machine learning", and "metaheuristics". AI-based learning represents a significant leap forward in education, driven by artificial intelligence, machine learning, deep learning, and cloud computing. Through classification algorithms, AI can assess a student's strengths and weaknesses, enabling more targeted interventions that optimise learning outcomes. Meanwhile, metaheuristics, which is the advanced optimisation algorithms used in AI, also contribute to educational advancements by solving complex problems related to resource allocation and curriculum planning. These algorithms help institutions optimise their operations, ensuring that resources are used efficiently and effectively to support student learning.

Keyword Co-Occurrence Cluster 5: Micro-Credentials for Teacher Education (Purple Network)

The fifth keyword co-occurrence cluster taps on micro-credentials for teacher education. This cluster is formed by six keywords namely "design", "digital badges", "distance learning", "micro-credentials", "pre-service teachers", and "teacher education". The integration of micro-credentials and digital badges into teacher education is a transformative development that supports the professional growth of pre-service teachers. By leveraging these innovative tools, teacher education programs can better prepare educators for the dynamic and technologically advanced educational landscape, ultimately leading to improved teaching outcomes and student success.

Keyword Co-Occurrence Cluster 6: SDG's Equity and Inclusivity of Open Education (Cyan Network)

The sixth and the last keyword co-occurrence cluster concentrates on the equity and inclusivity of open education. This cluster is made up of five keywords, which consist of "equity", "higher education", "Open Educational Resources (OER)", "open source", and "policy". This cluster contains the least number of keywords, indicating possible future research avenues for educational policies and sustainable development goals 4 (SDG4) studies. (SDG4 is a commitment to "ensure inclusive and equitable quality education and promote lifelong learning opportunities for all (United Nations, n.d.).

In an increasingly interconnected world, the principles of equity and inclusivity are becoming paramount in the realm of liberalisation of education. Open Education Resources (OER) and open-source policies play a pivotal role in democratising access to higher education. By providing free and openly licensed educational materials, OERs eliminate financial barriers that often prevent marginalised communities from accessing quality learning resources. This inclusivity ensures that students, regardless of their socioeconomic background, have the opportunity to engage with high-quality educational content, fostering a more equitable learning environment. In short, the equity and inclusivity of open education, bolstered by OER and open-source policies, represent a transformative approach to higher education. By championing these principles, educational institutions can create a more equitable and inclusive future, where knowledge is accessible to all, regardless of their background or circumstances.

Bibliographic Coupling of the Research

Bibliographic coupling was done using data clustering techniques. Similar articles based on common referencing pattern coverage are categorised under the same cluster (Weinberg, 1974). Figure 7 shows the articles network that was generated and visualised using VOSviewer. Six main thematic clusters that emerged from the bibliographic coupling analysis are indicated by the colours of the network that made up the body of knowledge. Each colour of network represents each theme identical to those generated earlier in the keywords co-occurrence analysis. Motivational drives underlying micro-credentials is denoted by red networks while alternative aspects of micro-credentials are represented by green networks. Motives underlying lifelong learning is manifested by blue networks while and AI-based learning is signified by yellow networks. Micro-credentials for teacher education is indicated by purple networks while equity and inclusivity of open education are expressed by cyan networks. The bibliographic coupling network detailing the authors and publication in

Figure 7 distinguishes the semantic association among the articles to identify and uncover latent research themes that may guide future research directions.

Figure 7. Bibliographic coupling network between artificial intelligence, micro-credentials, and open and distance learning research

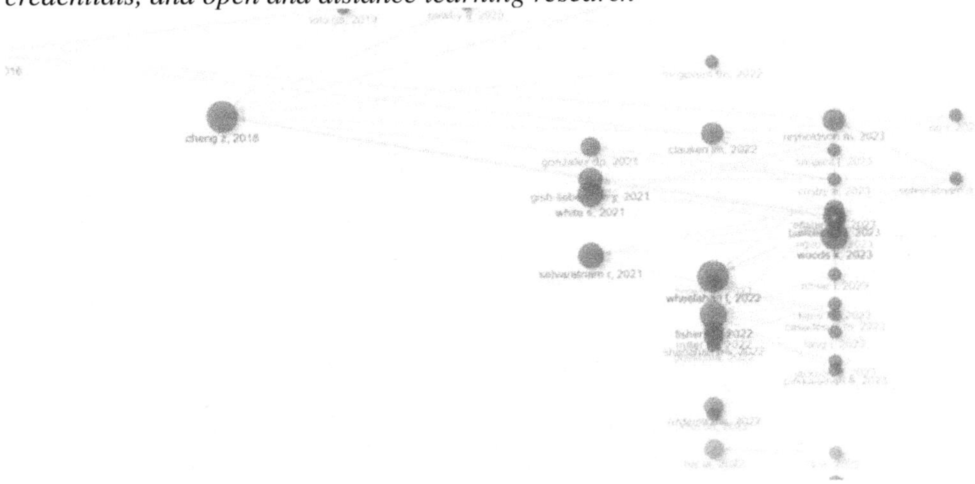

Table 3 . Most prolific articles in the major bibliographic clusters

Cluster and article title	Author(s), year
Bibliographic cluster 1: Motivational drives underlying micro-credentials	
Goal Setting and Open Digital Badges in Higher Education.	Cheng et al., (2018)
Instructional digital badges: effective learning tools.	Newby & Cheng (2020)
Student, Interrupted: Can Digital Badging Improve Programmatic Agility and Help IS Students During Crises?	McGovern & Gogan (2022)
Advancing Professional Development in Health Literacy: The Health Literacy Specialist Certificate Program and the Health Literacy Solutions Center.	Gonzalez & Villaire (2021)
Learning to Fly: Development and Design of a Micro-Credentialing System for an Educator Preparation Program in the Absence of a Required Educational Technology Course.	Clausen (2022)
Marketing micro-credentials: An analysis of actors, voices and messages in educational innovation discourse.	Reynoldson (2023)
Achieving professional qualifications using micro-credentials: a case of small packages and big challenges in higher education.	Raj et al. (2024)
Micro-Credentials and Badges in Education: a Historical Overview.	Gish-Lieberman et al. (2021)

continued on following page

Table 3 . Continued

Cluster and article title	Author(s), year
Developing credit based micro-credentials for the teaching profession: An Australian descriptive case study.	White (2021)
The State of Micro-Credentials Implementation and Practice in Australasian Higher Education.	Selvaratnam & Sankey (2021)
Analysing micro-credentials in higher education: a Bernsteinian analysis.	Wheelahan & Moodie (2021)
Gig qualifications for the gig economy: micro-credentials and the "hungry mile."	Wheelahan & Moodie (2022)
An assessment of micro-credentials in New Zealand vocational education.	Fisher & Leder (2022)
Less Is More: Exploring the Value of Micro-Credentials Within a Graduate Program.	Woods & Woods (2023)
Bibliographic cluster 2: Alternative aspects of micro-credentials	
Designing MOOCs with LITTLE.	Tang & Qian (2022)
Gamification to Enhance Motivation and Engagement in Blended eLearning for Technical and Vocational Education and Training.	Jayalath & Esichaikul (2022)
Massive Open Online Courses in Digital Workplace Learning.	Egloffstein (2018)
Employee Perspectives on MOOCs for Workplace Learning.	Egloffstein & Ifenthaler (2017)
Participation and Achievement in Enterprise MOOCs for Professional Development: Initial Findings from the openSAP University.	Egloffstein & Schwerer (2019)
Acknowledging All Learning: Alternative, Micro, and Open Credentials.	West et al. (2020)
Signals and noise: communicating achievement through alternative credentials.	Bean et al. (2023)
A Vision for Deeper Agency and Personalization in Micro-Credentials.	Laughlin (2021)
Getting started with open badges and open micro-credentials.	Clements et al. (2020)
Bibliographic cluster 3: Motives underlying lifelong learning	
Workforce upskilling: can universities meet the challenges of lifelong learning?	Lang (2023)
Streamlining Micro-Credentials Implementation in Higher Education Institutions: Considerations for Effective Implementation and Policy Development.	Keoy et al. (2023)
Employability-related activities beyond the curriculum: how participation and impact vary across diverse student cohorts.	Jackson & Dean (2023)
Bibliographic cluster 4: AI-based learning	
Evolutionary Algorithm Based Feature Subset Selection for Students Academic Performance Analysis.	Babu et al. (2023)
Emphasizing privacy and security of edge intelligence with machine learning for healthcare.	Rajendran et al. (2022)
How Should Chemistry Educators Respond to the Next Generation of Technology Change?	Pence (2020)
Bibliographic cluster 5: Micro-credentials for teacher education	

continued on following page

Table 3 . Continued

Cluster and article title	Author(s), year
Pre-service Teachers Computational Thinking (CT) and Pedagogical Growth in a Micro-credential: A Mixed Methods Study.	Bal et al. (2022)
Instructional digital badges: effective learning tools.	Newby & Cheng (2020)
Engineering Pedagogy and Engineering Educators' Competency Model for Effective Teaching and Learning Steam. Problems of Education in the 21st Century.	Rüütmann (2023)
Bibliographic cluster 6: Equity and inclusivity of open education	
Open educational resources (OER) and some of the United Nations sustainable development goals.	Ossiannilsson (2023)
Bridging the Gap: Micro-credentials for Development UNESCO Chairs Policy Brief Form - Under the III World Higher Education Conference (WHEC 2021) Type: Collective X.	McGreal et al. (2022)
Open For All: The OERu's Next Generation Digital Learning Ecosystem.	Lane & Goode (2021)

Bibliographic Cluster 1: Motivational Drives Underlying Micro-Credentials

The first bibliographic cluster focuses on the motivational drives underlying micro-credentials. Fourteen prolific studies formed this cluster. Wheelahan and Moodie (2021) asserted the importance of having micro-credentials in higher education, by arguing that it aligns curricula with labour market demands, emphasizing employability and 21st-century skills. Using Basil Bernstein's sociology, it examines how micro-credentials shape education through the lens of human capital theory, focusing on re-contextualisation and the market-oriented "homo economicus. In another study, Wheelahan and Moodie (2022) stressed that micro-credentials which are indeed aligned with the gig economy contribute to education privatisation, transferring employment preparation costs to individuals, and tightening higher education's ties to immediate workplace demands, rather than broader occupational skills.

The study by Cheng et al. (2018) argued for integrating open digital badges with a goal setting of optimising learning and providing design recommendations for incorporating open digital badges as technological tools. Another study by Newby and Cheng (2020) found that pre-service teachers using digital badges with instructional scaffolding reported higher confidence and achieved better grades compared to those with traditional projects, highlighting their potential to enhance learning performance. McGovern and Gogan (2022) asserted that a stackable badged micro-credential system can enhance academic flexibility, helping students manage personal and societal crises by certifying mastery in modules of a graduate-level course. It also offers structure, temporal flexibility, and portability, easing course interruption and resumption.

In 2018, the New Zealand Qualifications Authority (NZQA) recognised micro-credentials, defining their credit limits and allowing publication on the NZQA website. The framework applies to Tertiary Education Organisations, while universities create their recognition schemes (Fisher & Leder, 2022). The rules address international and non-TEO providers and identify potential issues like qualification disaggregation and future recognition.

White (2021) critiques the development of credit-bearing micro-credentials for Australian teachers' professional development which are designed to support learning and create pathways to advanced education by examining design stages, challenges, and benefits.

Through Selvaratnam and Sankey (2021), surveys done by the Australasian Council on Open, Distance, and eLearning showed increased interest and policy work, but with note that significant implementation efforts are needed. In a later study, Selvaratnam et al. (2024) suggested that as demand for micro-credentials rises, education providers need guidance to enhance their capacity and capability for high-quality, profitable learning outcomes. This study developed a maturity model to help providers assess and improve their micro-credential delivery. A survey of Australasian higher education providers validated the model, finding technical infrastructure most mature, while quality, resourcing, standards, and strategy were least mature. In another study, Reynoldson (2023) emphasizes neoliberal ideals, which view students as independent consumers managing their employability, but lacks student perspectives. In this study, micro-credentials in Australian higher education are seen as innovative, industry-linked educational credits. Proponents include public institutions, private companies, and governments.

In the United States of America, Gonzalez and Villaire (2021) elaborated on Healthy People 2030 which emphasises increasing organisational health literacy. To support this, the Institute for Healthcare Advancement offers the Health Literacy Specialist Certificate Program and the Health Literacy Solutions Center for professional development and networking. The Certificate includes seven micro-credentials developed by experts, and the Solutions Centre serves over 10,000 members with resources and education. Clausen (2022) highlighting both opportunities and challenges of a comprehensive micro-credentialing system aligned with the ISTE (standards that serve as a framework for innovation and excellence in learning, teaching, and leading adopted by the United States of America and many countries worldwide) to prepare teachers for technology integration. This system addresses the lack of a required educational technology course and receives feedback for further improvement. Given the current U.S. higher education climate, whereby university faculty and staff are tasked with doing more with less, Woods & Woods (2023) explored the benefits of micro-credentials for students and universities, detailing the creation of graduate certificates within a Master's program, and offering insights on design challenges and opportunities.

Gish-Lieberman et al. (2021) asserted that micro-credentials support self-directed learning by providing visible learning pathways with digital badges. Rooted in historical badge systems, self-regulated learning phases which comprise forethought, performance, and self-reflection are suggested for micro-credentials because the effective implementation requires standards, best practices, and integration with feedback and collaborative learning. Study by Raj et al. (2024) identifies key barriers to micro-credential implementation which hinder the motivation to enroll namely unclear definitions, ambiguous courses, lack of accreditation, quality assurance, remuneration policies, coordination issues, inadequate learning volume, and low acceptance by individuals and organisations. The findings are derived from literature, expert input, and ranking methods, which guide educational institutions and policymakers.

Meeting the contemporary rapid labour market demand, facilitating the flexibility of 21st-century learning, the need to integrate with the national education frameworks and systems, suitability with self-directed learning orientations, and overcoming barriers that hinder motivation underlying micro-credentials undertakings are among the issues covered by the prominent articles in this cluster.

Bibliographic Cluster 2: Alternative Aspects of Micro-Credentials

The second bibliographic cluster concentrates on the alternative aspects of micro-credentials. The cluster also includes MOOCs which can be inferred from the near-similar characteristics of micro-credentials, innovations in current pedagogy, and ideal applicability for corporate training. Nine prominent studies are comprised in this cluster. Traditional education systems inadequately prepare learners for the future of work, using standardised, and inequitable approaches. Based on this assumption, Laughlin (2021) envisioned the integration of emerging learner-centred paradigms and micro-credentialing which can create relevant, learner-focused educational experiences, and benefit future workforce preparation while addressing individual needs. West et al. (2020) reviews societal, educational, employer, and learner needs for new alternative credentials and provides a theoretical rationale for open micro-credentials and examines their credentialing, motivational, and technological functions, including open badges. At global scale, Bean et al. (2023) highlights the evolution, key development challenges, and opportunities of alternative credentials as the implications for higher education based on lessons learned from the researchers' extensive experience in credential initiatives across continents and sectors of North America, Europe, and Australasia.

Innovation in current pedagogy is also emphasized. Tang and Qian (2022) proposes the LITTLE framework, emphasizing learner-centered, inquiry-based, technology-enriched, trophy-driven, literature-guided, and evidence-based design strategies to enhance the effectiveness of existing micro-credentials and MOOCs which are seen as a disruptive, low-cost higher education option but face issues like low retention and forum participation. Examples and theoretical justifications are provided to illustrate these guidelines. When delivering blended-mode eLearning in TVET is challenging due to motivational and engagement issues, Jayalath and Esichaikul (2022) proposed a gamified operational model to enhance learner success in TVET by embedding motivational (attention, relevance, confidence, satisfaction) and engagement (behavioural, emotional, cognitive) frameworks. Fifteen game dynamics, mechanics, and components are suggested, and tested in a sample online course. In Rüütmann (2023)'s research, the psycho-didactical model of Engineering Pedagogy for effective STEAM education is outlined, whereby it presents the attributes and skills of 21st-century engineering graduates, the IGIP competency model for educators, and describes a micro-credentials program for STEAM teachers in which the model emphasizes interconnected learning activities to achieve specific educational goals.

In corporate training, Egloffstein and Ifenthaler (2017) investigated employee perspectives on MOOCs for workplace learning, focusing on motivation, credentials, and incentives. Surveying 119 employees, findings show high interest in career development through MOOCs but low acceptance of MOOC credentials among stakeholders. Implications for MOOC design and implementation in professional contexts are discussed. In the later study, Egloffstein (2018) explores MOOCs for digital workplace learning, discussing basic designs, platform features, and current providers which later highlighted the strengths, weaknesses, opportunities, and threats. The study offers insights on implementing MOOCs in corporate settings and future developments. In another study, Clements et al. (2020) provides a practical guide for organisations in designing and implementing open badging systems which cover key terms, past uses, and technologies for creating badges, including a framework with step-by-step instructions for implementation to recognise diverse skills and experiences across various settings. Given MOOCs are a growing trend in professional learning, explored SAP's openSAP as an example of Enterprise MOOCs and found that they are valuable for global professional learning. However, it often does not focus on digital workplace learning whereby alternative achievement metrics are required.

The increasing preferences for micro-credentials and MOOCs in organisational and corporate training through alternative credentials and open badges are among the issues highlighted in this cluster. Indeed, the expected outcomes are commonly shared, which consistently focus on enhancing the competencies, and skills, and better student engagement through innovative technology including e-learning and online learning.

Bibliographic Cluster 3: Motives Underlying Lifelong Learning

The third bibliographic cluster encapsulates motives underlying lifelong learning. It is known that the rise of digital micro-credentials in education has led to confusion among stakeholders, which prompts global efforts to define the quality of learning and its beneficial impacts. Therefore, in response to the Fourth Industrial Revolution, Lang (2023) came out with commentary reviews of literature on micro-credentials, that emphasized their role in lifelong learning and workforce upskilling. In another study, Keoy et al. (2023) examines the adoption of micro-credentials in Malaysia from the perspectives of higher education providers, whereby It identifies technological, organisational, and people-related challenges while proposing a framework for successful implementation. By addressing these recommendations, the study is hoped to enhance student learning and transform higher education, thus, meeting digital age demands. Jackson and Dean (2023) surveyed 84,000 Australian graduates on their participation in employability-related activities and the impact on work readiness and employment outcomes whereby over half have participated with notable differences by age, gender, disability, citizenship, and socio-economic background. It was also found that graduates from disadvantaged backgrounds saw significant benefits, especially from leadership roles, awards, and mentoring programs. In short, the cluster wraps up the underlying factors that motivate lifelong learning. The important issue is the focus on the pursuance of lifelong learning through micro-credentials and MOOCs are largely driven by the need to acquire higher education and knowledge about employability based on perceptions of students.

Bibliographic Cluster 4: AI-Based Learning

In this cluster, AI-based learning has come into the picture. This cluster illustrates the significance of AI in supporting students learning. With AI, online learning can be made conveniently accessible and flexible. Important studies underlying this cluster comprising Babu et al. (2023), Pence (2020), and Rajendran et al. (2022).

Babu et al. (2023) utilised AI techniques to predict student performance by analysing large educational datasets. The study proposed the MOFSS-ODL model, which combines feature selection and deep learning to enhance predictive accuracy.

Tested on a UCI dataset, the model achieved a 96.49% accuracy, which outperformed the recent methods of Educational Data Mining. Rajendran et al. (2022) highlights the significance of edge computing for decentralised healthcare by leveraging wearable devices and mobile apps for immediate diagnosis and treatment which are supported by scalable data privacy mechanisms. The study found that AI and edge computing could enhance medical care by integrating deep learning with medical technology, reducing latency, and improving real-time patient monitoring. In the study by Pence (2020), it is acknowledged that new instructional technologies like smartphones, cloud computing, AI, 3D printing, virtual reality, and augmented reality are transforming chemistry education by extending learning beyond the classroom. However, it is also important to note that these technologies can lead to student isolation and pose challenges for faculty in fostering essential social skills and managing individualised learning.

AI-based learning forms an important catalyst for future design and implementation of micro-credentials. It is therefore important to utilise and design the available AI tools and techniques to enhance the practicality and significance of micro-credentials in the ODL context.

Bibliographic Cluster 5: Micro-Credentials for Teacher Education

This cluster addresses the importance of designing and developing micro-credentials for teachers' training and curriculum. A Maryland university developed a micro-credential in Computational Thinking (CT) for K-8 pre-service and in-service teachers (Bal et al., 2022). Based on the analysis of surveys, journal entries, and lesson plans showed growth in CT awareness and integration, the micro-credential effectively adds CT content to an already packed curriculum which enhances teachers' knowledge and implementation skills.

Given the effectiveness of digital badges, as micro-credentials in improving learning are unclear, Newby and Cheng (2020)'s attempts have found that pre-service teachers who used digital badges with instructional scaffolding reported higher confidence and achieved better grades compared to those with traditional projects. This outcome has led micro-credentials to be further recognised in effectively enhancing learning performance. Through a niche study, Rüütmann (2023) outlined the psycho-didactical model of Engineering Pedagogy for effective STEAM education (STEAM Education is an approach to learning that uses Science, Technology, Engineering, the Arts, and Mathematics) by presenting the attributes and skills of 21st-century engineering graduates, introducing the IGIP competency model for educators, and describing a micro-credentials program for STEAM teachers. The model emphasizes interconnected learning activities to achieve specific educational goals.

Given evidence of micro-credential development across various fields of teacher education, it is therefore important to implement more micro-credentials for the educational sector to reap its benefits in facilitating teachers' training and enhancing their skills and competencies.

Bibliographic Cluster 6: SDG's Equity and Inclusivity of Open Education

This cluster projected on the equity and inclusivity of open education, despite niche focuses on AI, micro-credentials, and ODL aspects. Three important studies are elaborated. The Covid-19 pandemic, rising education costs, and employer concerns about skills have driven universities, colleges, and credentialing agencies to rethink credentials that focus on open education and micro-credentials. By providing affordable, flexible options for students and meeting employer needs for skilled employees, micro-credentials ensure acceptance, stackability, and secure digital records of skills while supporting Education for All (SDG4). Based on these findings, McGreal et al. (2022) recommended institutions, governments, UNESCO, and NGOs to undertake and implement micro-credentials in their respective entities.

By highlighting the technological benefits of the *Open Education Resource universitas (OERu)*, an international consortium offering stackable micro-credentials through an open-source Next Generation Digital Learning Ecosystem (NGDLE), Lane and Goode (2021) details the cost-effective implementation of open-source technologies, supporting hundreds of thousands of learners with an annual budget under US$10,000. The NGDLE was found to enhance technological autonomy, resilience, and educational opportunities for learners and educators globally.

In another study, Ossiannilsson (2023) highlights the UNESCO OER Recommendation, which was adopted in 2019, and aligned with multiple UN Sustainable Development Goals (SDGs), particularly SDG 4 (education), SDG 5 (gender equality), SDG 9 (industry, innovation, and infrastructure), SDG 10 (reducing inequalities), SDG 16 (peace, justice, and strong institutions), and SDG 17 (partnerships). The author also explored ways in which OER supports these goals, advocates for stakeholder involvement, and addresses accessibility and quality issues by highlighting the interconnectedness of OER with universal values like equality and social justice and proposing a model that links OER implementation with achieving these SDGs.

Open education significantly contributes to the SDGs related to equity and inclusivity by providing accessible, affordable, and flexible learning opportunities for all individuals, regardless of their socio-economic status, geographic location, or background. By leveraging digital platforms and resources, open education reduces barriers to education, enabling marginalised and underserved populations to acquire essential skills and knowledge. By aligning with SDGs, open education not only addresses immediate educational disparities but also contributes to long-term societal transformation by creating a more informed, skilled, and equitable global community.

Discussion, Gaps, and Future Research Avenue (RQ3)

The reflection part of the review identified and discussed notable knowledge gaps encountered which address and suggest future research that can be pursued.

Gap 1: Lack of research in the actual implementation of micro-credentials.

Although open digital badges are recognised as micro-credentials, their potential to enhance learning through goal setting is under-researched (Cheng et al., 2018) while their effectiveness in improving learning is unclear (Newby & Cheng, 2020). More research is needed to refine and assess the designs and effective implementation through standards, best practices, and integration with feedback and collaborative learning in micro-credentials (Gish-Lieberman et al., 2021). In Selvaratnam et al., (2024)'s study, future research is demanded for the refinement and extension of a maturity model that helps providers assess and improve their micro-credential delivery.

Gap 2: Lack of research in measuring the achievement of micro-credentials in workplace settings

Gaps remained in adhering to the motivational and engagement issues for example, Jayalath and Esichaikul (2022)'s suggested game dynamics, mechanics, and components are to be further tested in a sample online course. Enterprise MOOCs are found to be valuable for global professional learning. However, they do not focus on digital workplace learning (Egloffstein & Schwerer, 2019). Therefore, alternative achievement metrics are needed.

Gap 3: Lack of research on micro-credentials for teacher education

Despite the importance of teacher empowerment as far as their roles are concerned, there has been limited studies done on micro-credentials that are specifically designed for teachers' training and educational programmes. More studies should be undertaken to calibrate the skills and competencies of teachers in alignment with the learning outcomes achievable through micro-credentialing. This will hope to provide more flexibility to the teachers in engaging with the evolving learner generation that is closely shaped by the latest technological trends.

Gap 4: Lack of studies that research equity and inclusivity of open education

Not many research articles specifically tapped into the issues of equity and inclusivity of open education. To date, much attention has been paid to the role of OER in achieving SDGs (Ossiannilsson, 2023), recommendations for universities, colleges, and credentialing agencies to rethink credentials by focusing on open education and micro-credentials (McGreal et al., 2022), and cost-effective strategies in the implementation of open-source technologies (Lane & Goode, 2021). Insights from the operationality of micro-credentials in actual implementation have yet to be understood, particularly in developing countries where the accessibility to education is not always at its ideal state.

Gap 5: Lack of research in the actual integration of AI into micro-credentials within ODL settings

Despite its benefits, implementing micro-credentials faces challenges such as ensuring quality assurance, integrating them into existing educational frameworks, and gaining recognition from employers. Addressing these challenges is crucial for the widespread adoption and success of micro-credentials in higher education. Although it is acknowledged that new instructional technologies like smartphones, cloud computing, AI, 3D printing, virtual reality, and augmented reality are transforming chemistry education by extending learning beyond the classroom (Pence, 2020), these technologies can lead to student isolation and pose challenges for faculty in fostering essential social skills and managing individualised learning. Future research may delve into this issue in smoothening the impact of AI usage for micro-credentials within the ODL context.

Gap 6: Lack of research in the ethical and effective use of AI in the implementation of micro-credentials in ODL settings

Data privacy, ethical considerations, and the digital divide pose significant barriers to the widespread adoption of AI in education. Although there are concerns regarding the quality assurance and recognition of AI-enhanced micro-credentials, which are crucial for their acceptance and value in the job market, study to date has yet to delve into these aspects, highlighting the importance of developing robust frameworks and standards to ensure the ethical and effective use of AI in the implementation of micro-credentials in ODL settings.

CONCLUSION, IMPLICATIONS, AND LIMITATIONS

Micro-credentials represent a significant innovation in education, offering flexible, accessible, and targeted learning opportunities that cater to the needs of modern learners and employers. While challenges remain, their potential to complement and enhance traditional education systems is substantial. The integration of AI in micro-credentials within ODL is deemed to significantly enhance the learning experience by providing personalised education, automating support systems, and improving accessibility. AI technologies make it possible to offer more flexible, efficient, and tailored learning experiences, thus meeting the diverse needs of learners in an open and distance learning environment.

This review presents the trends of publications in the domains of AI integration into micro-credentials in the ODL context namely years and countries of publications, authors' affiliations, sub-topics of the domains, and the number of citations over time. Major thematic clusters based on keyword co-occurrences and bibliographic coupling of research topics are also generated. The keyword co-occurrences analysis has produced six thematic clusters about the integration of AI into micro-credentials in ODL. These clusters have been well triangulated using two bibliometric information sources i.e. keywords and publication citations which comprise motivational drives underlying micro-credentials (Cluster 1), alternative aspects of micro-credentials (Cluster 2), motives underlying lifelong learning (Cluster 3), AI-based learning (Cluster 4), micro-credentials for teacher education (Cluster 5), and SDGs' equity and inclusivity of open education (Cluster 6). A reflection of bibliometric review reveals notable gaps encountered in the current literature which can be addressed and suggested for future research to be pursued. The review provides a theoretical understanding of advancing the subject areas while addressing its practical applications among future researchers, scholars, and practitioners. It also serves as a main and quick reference in providing state-of-the-art literature while enabling industry practitioners to unleash the full benefits of bridging the theoretical and practical gap.

The integration of AI in micro-credentials plays a crucial role in advancing lifelong learning, particularly within the framework of SDGs aimed at equity and inclusivity in education. Micro-credentials provide an alternative to traditional degrees by offering flexible, competency-based certifications that address the diverse needs and motivations of learners. For educators, micro-credentials facilitate continuous professional development, ensuring that teaching practices evolve to meet the demands of modern education systems. Through micro-credentials and the booming of AI, a progressive education system should offer meaningful qualifications valued in both labour markets and society made possible via ODL settings.

Motivational drives for micro-credentials stem from the need for accessible, personalized learning paths that accommodate the varying schedules and learning preferences of students. AI-enhanced learning systems offer tailored educational experiences, providing real-time feedback and adaptive learning pathways that support individual progress. This approach not only enhances the learning experience but also ensures that education is inclusive, catering to all learners regardless of their socio-economic background or geographic location.

The role of micro-credentials in teacher education is particularly significant. By leveraging AI, educators can engage in ongoing professional development, acquiring new skills and knowledge that are immediately applicable in the classroom. This continuous learning process is essential for maintaining high educational standards and adapting to new teaching methodologies. Furthermore, the focus on equity and inclusivity aligns with the SDGs by removing traditional barriers to education, such as cost and accessibility. Open education initiatives supported by AI-driven micro-credentials provide flexible learning opportunities that are crucial for fostering a more equitable global education landscape.

In summary, the integration of AI in micro-credentials enhances lifelong learning, supports teacher education, and promotes the SDGs' goals of equity and inclusivity in open education. This comprehensive approach ensures that all learners have the opportunity to succeed in an increasingly digital and interconnected world. Despite its contributions and insights, the review had several methodological limitations. First, only articles published in WoS and Scopus databases were considered. Other possible and relevant studies which are searchable using the same search query may be overlooked. This may limit the scope of insights provided by the review. The review also included only articles strictly related to the integrated domains of AI, micro-credentials, and ODL. Other articles that might have been related to the domains were not included due to misalignment with the keyword entry or other technical aspects related to the metadata of its listings. New reviews that capture these alternative domains are highly welcomed.

ACKNOWLEDGMENT

We would like to express our heartfelt gratitude to the Commonwealth of Learning for providing the exposure, resources, training, and support essential for this study. This work is a subsequent result of the ODL Practitioner Research Training and Mentorship programme for the year 2023.

REFERENCES

Ahiadu, A., & Abidoye, R. (2023). Economic uncertainty and direct property performance: A systematic review using the SPAR-4-SLR protocol. *Journal of Property Investment & Finance*, 42(1), 89–111. DOI: 10.1108/JPIF-08-2023-0073

Ahmat, N. H. C., Bashir, M. A. A., Razali, A. R., & Kasolang, S. (2021). Micro-Credentials in Higher Education Institutions: Challenges and Opportunities. *Asian Journal of University Education*, 17(3), 281–290. DOI: 10.24191/ajue.v17i3.14505

Ahsan, K., Akbar, S., Kam, B., & Abdulrahman, M. D. A. (2023). Implementation of micro-credentials in higher education: A systematic literature review. *Education and Information Technologies*, 28(10), 13505–13540. DOI: 10.1007/s10639-023-11739-z

Alkadi, R., & Abed, S. (2023). Consumer Acceptance of Fintech App Payment Services: A Systematic Literature Review and Future Research Agenda. *Journal of Theoretical and Applied Electronic Commerce Research*, 18(4), 1838–1860. DOI: 10.3390/jtaer18040093

Alsobhi, H. A., Alakhtar, R. A., Ubaid, A., Hussain, O. K., & Hussain, F. K. (2023). Blockchain-based micro-credentialing system in higher education institutions: Systematic literature review. *Knowledge-Based Systems*, 265, 110238. DOI: 10.1016/j.knosys.2022.110238

Babu, I., MathuSoothana, R., & Kumar, S. (2023). Evolutionary Algorithm Based Feature Subset Selection for Students Academic Performance Analysis. *Intelligent Automation & Soft Computing*, 36(3), 3621–3636. DOI: 10.32604/iasc.2023.033791

Bal, I. A., Alvarado-Albertorio, F., Marcelle, P., & Oaks-Garcia, C. T. (2022). Pre-service Teachers Computational Thinking (CT) and Pedagogical Growth in a Micro-credential: A Mixed Methods Study. *TechTrends*, 66(3), 468–482. DOI: 10.1007/s11528-022-00732-x PMID: 35499060

Bean, M., Grant, S., Hardaker, G., & Ward, R. (2023). Signals and noise: communicating achievement through alternative credentials. *International Journal of Information and Learning Technology*. DOI: 10.1108/IJILT-02-2023-0020

Berry, B., Airhart, K. M., & Byrd, P. A. (2016). Microcredentials: Teacher learning transformed. *Phi Delta Kappan*, 98(3), 34–40. DOI: 10.1177/0031721716677260

Caetano, F. J. P., Casanova, D. G., & Moreira, D. M. P. (2023). Microcredentials: an opportunity towards the digital transformation. *International Conference on Higher Education Advances*, 665–673. DOI: 10.4995/HEAd23.2023.16125

Cheng, Z., Watson, S. L., & Newby, T. J. (2018b). Goal Setting and Open Digital Badges in Higher Education. *TechTrends*, 62(2), 190–196. DOI: 10.1007/s11528-018-0249-x

Clausen, J. M. (2022). Learning to Fly: Development and Design of a Micro-Credentialing System for an Educator Preparation Program in the Absence of a Required Educational Technology Course. *TechTrends*, 66(2), 276–286. DOI: 10.1007/s11528-021-00673-x PMID: 34664042

Clements, K., West, R. E., & Hunsaker, E. (2020). Getting started with open badges and open microcredentials. *International Review of Research in Open and Distance Learning*, 21(1), 134–152. DOI: 10.19173/irrodl.v21i1.4529

Dai, J. J., Ding, D., Shi, D., Huang, S., Wang, J., Qiu, X., Huang, K., Song, G., Wang, Y., Gong, Q., Song, J., Yu, S., Zheng, L., Chen, Y., Deng, J., & Song, G. (2022). BigDL 2.0: Seamless Scaling of AI Pipelines from Laptops to Distributed Cluster. *2022 IEEE/CVF Conference on Computer Vision and Pattern Recognition (CVPR)*, 21407–21414. DOI: 10.1109/CVPR52688.2022.02076

Dogan, M. E., Goru Dogan, T., & Bozkurt, A. (2023). The Use of Artificial Intelligence (AI) in Online Learning and Distance Education Processes: A Systematic Review of Empirical Studies. *Applied Sciences (Basel, Switzerland)*, 13(5), 3056. Advance online publication. DOI: 10.3390/app13053056

Donthu, N., Kumar, S., Mukherjee, D., Pandey, N., & Lim, W. M. (2021). How to conduct a bibliometric analysis: An overview and guidelines. *Journal of Business Research*, 133, 285–296. DOI: 10.1016/j.jbusres.2021.04.070

Egloffstein, M. (2018). Massive Open Online Courses in Digital Workplace Learning. In *Digital Workplace Learning* (pp. 149–166). Springer International Publishing., DOI: 10.1007/978-3-319-46215-8_9

Egloffstein, M., & Ifenthaler, D. (2017). Employee Perspectives on MOOCs for Workplace Learning. *TechTrends*, 61(1), 65–70. DOI: 10.1007/s11528-016-0127-3

Egloffstein, M., & Schwerer, F. (2019). Participation and Achievement in Enterprise MOOCs for Professional Development: Initial Findings from the openSAP University. In *Learning Technologies for Transforming Large-Scale Teaching, Learning, and Assessment*. Springer International Publishing., DOI: 10.1007/978-3-030-15130-0_6

Fadzil, M., & Munira, T. A. (2008). Applications of Artificial Intelligence in an Open and Distance Learning institution. *2008 International Symposium on Information Technology, 1*, 1–7. DOI: 10.1109/ITSIM.2008.4631532

Firat, M. (2023). Integrating AI Applications into Learning Management Systems to Enhance e-Learning. *Öğretim Teknolojisi ve Hayat Boyu Öğrenme Dergisi - Instructional Technology and Lifelong Learning*, 1–14. DOI: 10.52911/itall.1244453

Fisher, R. M., & Leder, H. (2022). An assessment of micro-credentials in New Zealand vocational education. *International Journal of Training Research*, 20(3), 232–247. DOI: 10.1080/14480220.2021.2018018

Forkan, A. R. M., Kang, Y.-B., Jayaraman, P. P., Du, H., Thomson, S., Kollias, E., & Wieland, N. (2023). VideoDL: Video-Based Digital Learning Framework Using AI Question Generation and Answer Assessment. [IJAC]. *International Journal of Advanced Corporate Learning*, 16(1), 19–27. DOI: 10.3991/ijac.v16i1.35207

Galetsi, P., Katsaliaki, K., & Kumar, S. (2019). Values, challenges and future directions of big data analytics in healthcare: A systematic review. In *Social Science and Medicine* (Vol. 241). Elsevier Ltd., DOI: 10.1016/j.socscimed.2019.112533

Garrido, A., Morales, L., & Serina, I. (2016). On the use of case-based planning for e-learning personalization. *Expert Systems with Applications*, 60, 1–15. https://doi.org/https://doi.org/10.1016/j.eswa.2016.04.030. DOI: 10.1016/j.eswa.2016.04.030

Gish-Lieberman, J. J., Tawfik, A., & Gatewood, J. (2021). Micro-Credentials and Badges in Education: A Historical Overview. *TechTrends*, 65(1), 5–7. DOI: 10.1007/s11528-020-00567-4

Goksel, N., & Bozkurt, A. (2019). *Artificial Intelligence in Education.*, DOI: 10.4018/978-1-5225-8431-5.ch014

Gonzalez, D. P., & Villaire, M. (2021). Advancing Professional Development in Health Literacy: The Health Literacy Specialist Certificate Program and the Health Literacy Solutions Center. *American Journal of Health Education*, 52(6), 333–337. DOI: 10.1080/19325037.2021.1985020

Hatzi, O., Vrakas, D., Nikolaidou, M., Bassiliades, N., Anagnostopoulos, D., & Vlahavas, I. (2012). An Integrated Approach to Automated Semantic Web Service Composition through Planning. *IEEE Transactions on Services Computing*, 5(3), 319–332. DOI: 10.1109/TSC.2011.20

Holmes, W., & Anastopoulou, S. (2019). What do students at distance universities think about AI? *Proceedings of the Sixth (2019) ACM Conference on Learning @ Scale*. DOI: 10.1145/3330430.3333659

Hunt, T., Carter, R., Zhang, L., & Yang, S. (2020). Micro-credentials: The potential of personalized professional development. *Development and Learning in Organizations*, 34(2), 33–35. DOI: 10.1108/DLO-09-2019-0215

Igami, M. Z., Bressiani, J., & Mugnaini, R. (2014). A new model to identify the productivity of theses in terms of articles using co-word analysis. *Journal of Scientometric Research*, 3(1), 3. DOI: 10.4103/2320-0057.143660

Jackson, D., & Dean, B. A. (2023). Employability-related activities beyond the curriculum: How participation and impact vary across diverse student cohorts. *Higher Education*, 86(5), 1151–1172. DOI: 10.1007/s10734-022-00966-x

Jayalath, J., & Esichaikul, V. (2022). Gamification to Enhance Motivation and Engagement in Blended eLearning for Technical and Vocational Education and Training. *Technology. Knowledge and Learning*, 27(1), 91–118. DOI: 10.1007/s10758-020-09466-2

Keoy, K. H., Koh, Y. J., Iqbal, J., Anjum, S. S., Yeo, S. F., Cherukuri, A. K., Teoh, W. Y., & Piut, D. A. A. (2023). Streamlining Micro-Credentials Implementation in Higher Education Institutions: Considerations for Effective Implementation and Policy Development. *Journal of Information & Knowledge Management*. DOI: 10.1142/S0219649223500697

Kraus, S., Breier, M., Lim, W. M., Dabić, M., Kumar, S., Kanbach, D., Mukherjee, D., Corvello, V., Piñeiro-Chousa, J., Liguori, E., Palacios-Marqués, D., Schiavone, F., Ferraris, A., Fernandes, C., & Ferreira, J. J. (2022). Literature reviews as independent studies: Guidelines for academic practice. *Review of Managerial Science*, 16(8), 2577–2595. DOI: 10.1007/s11846-022-00588-8

Lane, D. C., & Goode, C. (2021). Open For All: The OERu's Next Generation Digital Learning Ecosystem. *International Review of Research in Open and Distance Learning*, 22(4), 146–163. DOI: 10.19173/irrodl.v23i1.5763

Lang, J. (2023). Workforce upskilling: Can universities meet the challenges of lifelong learning? *International Journal of Information and Learning Technology*, 40(5), 388–400. DOI: 10.1108/IJILT-01-2023-0001

Laughlin, T. (2021). A Vision for Deeper Agency and Personalization in Micro-Credentials. In Northrup, P., Rasmussen, K., & Colson, R. (Eds.), *Career Ready Education Through Experiential Learning* (pp. 19–45). IGI Global., DOI: 10.4018/978-1-7998-1928-8.ch002

Lim, W. M., & Kumar, S. (2023). Guidelines for interpreting the results of bibliometrics analysis: A sensemaking approach. *Global Business and Organizational Excellence*. https://api.semanticscholar.org/CorpusID:260600560

McGovern, T. M., & Gogan, J. L. (2022). Student, Interrupted: Can Digital Badging Improve Programmatic Agility and Help IS Students During Crises? *Communications of the Association for Information Systems*, 51(1), 51. DOI: 10.17705/1CAIS.05119

McGreal, R., Mackintosh, W., Cox, G., & Olcott, D.Jr. (2022). Bridging the Gap: Micro-credentials for Development UNESCO Chairs Policy Brief Form - Under the III World Higher Education Conference (WHEC 2021) Type: Collective X. *International Review of Research in Open and Distance Learning*, 23(3), 288–302. DOI: 10.19173/irrodl.v23i3.6696

Mena-Guacas, A. F., Chacón, M. F., Munar, A. P., Ospina, M., & Agudelo, M. (2023). Evolution of teaching in short-term courses: A systematic review. *Heliyon*, 9(6), e16933. Advance online publication. DOI: 10.1016/j.heliyon.2023.e16933 PMID: 37332952

Newby, T. J., & Cheng, Z. (2020). Instructional digital badges: Effective learning tools. *Educational Technology Research and Development*, 68(3), 1053–1067. DOI: 10.1007/s11423-019-09719-7

Orman, R., Şimşek, E., & Kozak Çakır, M. A. (2023). Micro-credentials and reflections on higher education. *Higher Education Evaluation and Development*, 17(2), 96–112. DOI: 10.1108/HEED-08-2022-0028

Ossiannilsson, E. (2023). Open educational resources (OER) and some of the United Nations sustainable development goals. *International Journal of Information And Learning Technology*, 40(5), 548–561. DOI: 10.1108/IJILT-01-2023-0002

Paul, J., Lim, W. M., O'Cass, A., Hao, A. W., & Bresciani, S. (2021). Scientific procedures and rationales for systematic literature reviews (SPAR-4-SLR). *International Journal of Consumer Studies*, 45(4). Advance online publication. DOI: 10.1111/ijcs.12695

Pence, H. E. (2020). How Should Chemistry Educators Respond to the Next Generation of Technology Change? *Education Sciences*, 10(2), 34. Advance online publication. DOI: 10.3390/educsci10020034

Rad, P., Roopaei, M., Beebe, N., Shadaram, M., & Au, Y. A. (n.d.). *AI Thinking for Cloud Education Platform with Personalized Learning*. http://hdl.handle.net/10125/49890

Raj, R., Singh, A., Kumar, V., & Verma, P. (2024). Achieving professional qualifications using micro-credentials: A case of small packages and big challenges in higher education. *International Journal of Educational Management*, 38(4), 916–947. Advance online publication. DOI: 10.1108/IJEM-01-2023-0028

Rajendran, S., Mathivanan, S. K., Jayagopal, P., Janaki, K. P., Bernard, B., Pandy, S., & Somanathan, M. S. (2022). Emphasizing privacy and security of edge intelligence with machine learning for healthcare. *International Journal of Intelligent Computing And Cybernetics*, 15(1), 92–109. DOI: 10.1108/IJICC-05-2021-0099

Reynoldson, M. (2023). Marketing micro-credentials: An analysis of actors, voices and messages in educational innovation discourse. *Innovations in Education and Teaching International*, 60(6), 953–963. DOI: 10.1080/14703297.2022.2083657

Rodriguez, E., Burguillo, J. C., Rodriguez, D. A., Mikic, F. A., Gonzalez-Moreno, J. C., & Novegil, V. (2008). Developing virtual teaching assistants for open e-learning platforms. *2008 19th EAEEIE Annual Conference*, 193–198. DOI: 10.1109/EAEEIE.2008.4610185

Rüütmann, T. (2023). Engineering Pedagogy and Engineering Educators' Competency Model For Effective Teaching And Learning Steam. *Problems Of Education In The 21st Century, 81*(4), 531–546. DOI: 10.33225/pec/23.81.531

Sargent, J., Rienties, B., Perryman, L. A., & Fitzgerald, E. (2023). Investigating the Views and Use of Stackable Microcredentials within a Postgraduate Certificate in Academic Practice. *Journal of Interactive Media in Education, 2023*(1). DOI: 10.5334/jime.805

Selvaratnam, R., & Sankey, M. (2021). The State of Micro-Credentials Implementation and Practice in Australasian Higher Education. *Open Praxis*, 13(2), 228–238. DOI: 10.5944/openpraxis.13.2.130

Selvaratnam, R. M., Warburton, S., Parrish, D., & Crew, S. (2024). A maturity model for micro-credentialing and shorter forms of learning practice in Australasian universities. *Journal of Higher Education Policy and Management*, 46(4), 409–424. Advance online publication. DOI: 10.1080/1360080X.2023.2299150

Tang, H., & Qian, Y. (2022). Designing MOOCs with LITTLE. *Cogent Education*, 9(1), 2064411. Advance online publication. DOI: 10.1080/2331186X.2022.2064411

Thi Ngoc Ha, N., Spittle, M., Watt, A., & Van Dyke, N. (2023). A systematic literature review of micro-credentials in higher education: A non-zero-sum game. *Higher Education Research & Development*, 42(6), 1527–1548. DOI: 10.1080/07294360.2022.2146061

United Nations, Department of Economic and Social Affairs. (n.d.). Goals 4: Ensure inclusive and equitable quality education and promote lifelong learning opportunities for all. Retrieved June 5, 2024, from https://sdgs.un.org/goals/goal4

Visser, M., van Eck, N. J., & Waltman, L. (2021). Large-scale comparison of bibliographic data sources: Scopus, web of science, dimensions, crossref, and microsoft academic. *Quantitative Science Studies*, 2(1), 20–41. DOI: 10.1162/qss_a_00112

Weinberg, B. H. (1974). Bibliographic coupling: A review. *Information Storage and Retrieval, 10*(5), 189–196. https://doi.org/https://doi.org/10.1016/0020-0271(74)90058-8

Wen, D., & Lin, F. (2008). Ways and Means of Employing AI Technology in E-Learning Systems. *2008 Eighth IEEE International Conference on Advanced Learning Technologies*, 1005–1006. DOI: 10.1109/ICALT.2008.304

West, R. E., Newby, T., Cheng, Z., Erickson, A., & Clements, K. (2020). Acknowledging All Learning: Alternative, Micro, and Open Credentials. In *Handbook of Research in Educational Communications and Technology: Learning Design: Fifth Edition*. Springer International Publishing. DOI: 10.1007/978-3-030-36119-8_27

Wheelahan, L., & Moodie, G. (2021). Analysing micro-credentials in higher education: A Bernsteinian analysis. *Journal of Curriculum Studies*, 53(2), 212–228. DOI: 10.1080/00220272.2021.1887358

Wheelahan, L., & Moodie, G. (2022). Gig qualifications for the gig economy: Micro-credentials and the "hungry mile.". *Higher Education*, 83(6), 1279–1295. DOI: 10.1007/s10734-021-00742-3 PMID: 34366441

White, S. (2021). Developing credit based micro-credentials for the teaching profession: An Australian descriptive case study. *Teachers and Teaching*, 27(7), 696–711. DOI: 10.1080/13540602.2021.2003324

Woods, K., & Woods, J. A. (2023). Less Is More: Exploring the Value of Micro-Credentials Within a Graduate Program. *The Journal of Continuing Higher Education*, 71(2), 215–223. DOI: 10.1080/07377363.2021.1966923

Yu, H., Miao, C., Leung, C., & White, T. J. (2017). Towards AI-powered personalization in MOOC learning. In *npj Science of Learning* (Vol. 2, Issue 1). Springer Nature. DOI: 10.1038/s41539-017-0016-3

KEY TERMS AND DEFINITIONS

Artificial Intelligence: Is the simulation of human intelligence in machines programmed to think, learn, and perform tasks autonomously.

Bibliometric Analysis: Is a quantitative method for evaluating academic literature, measuring research impact, trends, and patterns through citation data and publication metrics.

Micro-Credentials: Are short, focused certifications that validate specific skills or knowledge, offering flexible, competency-based learning tailored to immediate professional needs

Open and Distance Learning (ODL): Is an educational approach that provides flexible, accessible education using technology, allowing learners to study independently from remote locations.

SPAR-4-SLR: Is a systematic protocol for conducting literature reviews, ensuring rigorous, transparent, and replicable research synthesis through structured stages of assembling, arranging, assessing, and analysing studies.

Systematic Review: Is a methodical, comprehensive literature review that synthesises all relevant studies on a specific topic, ensuring rigour and minimising bias.

Thematic Analysis: Is a qualitative method for identifying, analysing, and reporting patterns (themes) within data, providing insights into meanings and experiences.

Chapter 15
Micro-Credentials in Higher Education and the Learning Compass 2030:
Intersections and Reflections

Ana Galvão
https://orcid.org/0000-0001-9978-9563
Instituto Politécnico de Bragança, Portugal

Isabel Chumbo
https://orcid.org/0000-0002-9630-2905
Instituto Politécnico de Bragança, Portugal

Eugénia Anes
https://orcid.org/0000-0001-8474-3474
Instituto Politécnico de Bragança, Portugal

ABSTRACT

Globalization in higher education is embodied in the articulation between micro-credentials and the Learning Compass, especially in the context of the Organization for Economic Cooperation and Development's (OECD) Learning Compass 2030, revealing a promising intersection for the future of education and skills development. Both concepts support the idea that education should be a continuous process, adaptable and aligned with the emerging needs of society and the labor market. The mission of this chapter is to understand how micro-credentials can help teachers sculpt their profile and train skills to help students on their learning path while promoting their well-being, as well as providing students with micro-credentials that enable them to develop knowledge and skills in specific areas and attitudes and values.

DOI: 10.4018/979-8-3693-5488-9.ch015

INTRODUCTION

In the fluid modernity of information and the learning process, we have the *Education 2030: Future of Education and Skills* project, proposed by the OECD in 2015, which highlights a conceptual learning matrix and the creation and development of an international curriculum based on the "*Learning Compass 2030*".(Directorate for Education and Skills - Education Policy Directorate, 2019; OECD, 2018c; Rodrigo Castañeda Valle et al., 2015). The *Future of Education and Skills 2030* sets out a new vision for education in the coming years, with the most important values driving this vision being inclusion and equality, thus meeting Education for Sustainable Development, Goal 4 of the Sustainable Development Goals (SDGs), namely "Ensure access to inclusive, quality and equitable education and promote lifelong learning opportunities for all". (United Nations, 2015, 2018). The aim is to, by 2030, ensure equal access for all women and men to quality and affordable technical, vocational and tertiary education, including university, and substantially increase the number of young people and adults with relevant skills, including technical and vocational skills, for employment, decent work and entrepreneurship (United Nations, 2015, 2018). This conceptualization is in line with the philosophy behind micro-credentials, as set out by the European Council: "People need access to quality education and learning, provided in different ways and environments, to develop their personal, social, cultural and professional knowledge, skills and competences". (The Council of the European Union, 2022). Member States are recommended to adopt a European approach to micro-credentials with the aim of promoting inclusion, access and equal opportunities and contributing to the achievement of resilience, social justice and prosperity for all, in a context of demographic and social change and throughout all phases of economic cycles. They also recommend, where appropriate, integrating micro-credentials into both education and training systems and skills policies, including through micro-credentials to improve access to education and training for all learners, including disadvantaged and vulnerable groups (such as people with disabilities, older people, people with low qualifications/skills, minorities, people with a migration background, refugees and people with fewer opportunities due to their geographical location and/or disadvantaged socio-economic situation), where appropriate.

In 2019, at the *Forum on Transforming Education, Global Peace Convention,* Andreas Schleicher, head of the OECD's Directorate for Education and Skills, stated that "Education is no longer just about teaching students something specific; it is more important to teach them to develop a reliable compass and navigational tools so that they can find their own way in an increasingly complex, volatile and uncertain world. Our imagination, conscience, knowledge, skills and, most importantly, our common values, intellectual and moral maturity and sense of responsibility are what will guide us to make the world a better place." Within this framework, the design of the Education 2030 project highlights competences (knowledge, skills, attitudes and values) as fundamental, which should be included in countries' school curricula (Directorate for Education and Skills - Education Policy Directorate, 2019). The Learning Compass proposed by the OECD thus lays the foundations for a common international curriculum - applicable to all types and levels of education and dynamic, in which the different subjects and disciplines are interrelated, and each student takes an idiosyncratic learning path according to their previous skills, talents and motivations. It also envisages "different types of assessment for different purposes", rather than standardized tests (OECD, 2018a, p. 13). Education and training systems must respond to the diverse individual needs, skills and abilities of all learners (The Council of the European Union, 2022). The 2030 education framework focuses on "how to implement curricula and learning environments that make the identified competences effective by 2030" (OECD, 2018c). While technology can be a valuable tool, teachers, tutors, mentors and the relational aspects of teaching will be key to learning, personal fulfilment and well-being.

To begin with, we kept in mind the following challenging question: What are the teacher profiles/competencies (knowledge, skills, attitudes and values) needed to help students learn and improve their well-being?

Background

In 2015, the OECD's Education Policy Committee launched the 'OECD Future of Education and Skills 2030' project as an opportunity to reflect, explore the long-term challenges facing education and help make the process of curriculum design and development more evidence-based and systematic (Directorate for Education and Skills - Education Policy Directorate, 2019; OECD, 2018c). The aim of the project was to help countries find answers to two far-reaching questions:

- What knowledge, skills, attitudes and values will today's students need to thrive and shape their world?
- How can education systems develop this knowledge, skills, attitudes and values effectively?

For today's students to thrive and positively influence the world, it is essential that they develop an integrated set of knowledge, skills, attitudes and values. **Knowledge:** Emerging Technologies, understanding of AI, robotics, biotechnology, and others; Sustainability and Environmental Sciences, knowledge about sustainable practices, climate change and environmental impacts; Global Economy, understanding of global economic dynamics and their local and international impacts; Health and

Wellness, fundamental knowledge about physical and mental health, nutrition and well-being; History and Culture, knowledge about diverse cultures and histories to foster a global understanding. **Skills:** Critical and Analytical Thinking, evaluating information and arguments, identifying biases, and making informed decisions; Multimodal Communication, ability to express ideas clearly both verbally and in writing, including through digital media; Interdisciplinary Collaboration, ability to work on projects that require knowledge of multiple disciplines; Information Management, ability to locate, evaluate and use information effectively; Emotional Resilience and Flexibility, ability to adapt to change and overcome challenges. **Attitudes:** Curiosity and Innovation, a proactive approach to learning and exploring new ideas; Empathy and Intercultural Respect, appreciating and respecting cultural and individual differences; Responsibility and Self-Discipline, commitment to fulfilling one's responsibilities and maintaining personal integrity; Openness to New Experiences, willingness to experiment and accept new ideas and practices; Proactivity and Leadership, willingness to lead initiatives and projects, inspiring others. **Values:** Ethics and Integrity, strong moral principles that guide behavior and decisions; Justice and Fairness, commitment to promoting justice, equality and inclusion; Sustainability, valuing practices that promote environmental, economic and social sustainability; Collaboration and Community, valuing teamwork and strengthening communities; Respect for Diversity, recognizing and valuing diverse ways of life and perspectives.(Directorate for Education and Skills - Education Policy Directorate, 2019; OECD, 2018c).

By developing this knowledge, skills, attitudes and values, students will be better equipped to face future challenges, lead significant innovations and contribute positively to global society.Top of the form

To answer the questions posed above, the OECD Future of Education and Skills 2030 project conceptualized the OECD Learning Compass 2030, an evolving learning framework that sets out an aspirational vision for education in 2030, providing guideposts towards the future we want to achieve: individual and collective well-being. The Learning Compass 2030 (Figure 1) focuses on curriculum design and the development of a conceptual framework for learning. It is also geared towards identifying the teacher profiles/competencies **(knowledge, skills, attitudes and values**) needed to help students learn and improve their well-being.

Figure 1. OECD learning compass 2030 (OECD, 2018c)

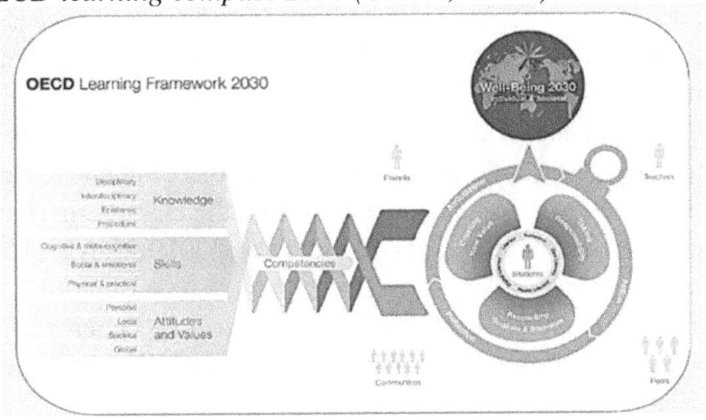

For teachers to be able to effectively help students learn and improve their well-being, it is essential that they possess a robust set of competencies, including knowledge, skills, attitudes and values. These aspects are fundamental to creating an educational environment that promotes learning and the holistic development of students. **Knowledge:** Pedagogy and Teaching Methods, in-depth knowledge of modern educational theories and practices, including differentiated methods to meet the diversity of learners; Educational Technology, familiarity with digital tools and emerging technologies that can be integrated into teaching; Developmental Psychology, understanding of the different stages of students' cognitive and emotional development; Curriculum and Disciplinary Content, mastery over the content they teach and the ability to relate it to interdisciplinary concepts; Educational Legislation and Education Policies, knowledge of the laws, regulations and policies that influence education. **Skills:** Effective Communication, ability to communicate clearly with students, family and other educational agents; Adaptation and Flexibility, ability to adapt teaching methods to individual student needs and technological and cultural changes; Assessment and Constructive Feedback, ability to assess student performance fairly and provide feedback that promotes learning and growth; Classroom Management, ability to create an organized learning environment conducive to student engagement; Leadership and Mentoring, abilities to inspire and guide students, promoting leadership among them. **Attitudes:** Empathy and Sensitivity, the ability to understand the emotional experiences and needs of students; Commitment to Continuous Learning, willingness to continually update oneself in relation to best practices and new educational technologies; Patience and Persistence, patience to deal with daily challenges and persistence to help all students reach their potential; Innovation and Creativity, openness to experimenting with new approaches and teaching methods; Professional Responsibility, commitment to the ethical standards of the profession and responsibility for the development of students. **Values,** Justice and Fairness, dedication to ensuring that all students have equal access to learning opportunities; Respect for Diversity: Valuing and promoting an inclusive environment that respects cultural, social and individual differences; Integrity, adherence to ethical principles in all interactions and decisions; Collaboration, valuing teamwork and cooperation between colleagues and the school community; Sustainability, promoting sustainable practices inside and outside the classroom. (Directorate for Education and Skills - Education Policy Directorate, 2019; Galvão, 2020a, 2020b; OECD, 2018c).

By developing this profile and skills, teachers will be better equipped to face the challenges of modern education and to help their students become effective and well-adapted learners.

A Brief Description of the Inseparable and Complementary Elements That Make Up Compass 2030

At the center of the learning compass is the student, confronted with three actions: creating new values, taking responsibility and reconciling tensions and dilemmas (OECD, 2018c). These actions bring together three capacities considered fundamental: anticipation, reflection and action. On the left are the competences (knowledge, skills, attitudes and values) with their respective contents acting in an interconnected way. In addition, the compass conveys the idea of learning as a collective attribute, occurring through teachers' recognition of how people learn in different ways, requiring support according to individual needs, building strong relationships between teachers or peers, with parents and with communities. This involves interactive, mutually supportive relationships that guide students in developing their ability to act. It also means teachers who recognize the individuality of students and know how to establish relationships with other teachers or peers, families and communities. (Directorate for Education and Skills - Education Policy Directorate, 2019; OECD, 2018c).

Student agency - This is defined as the ability to set goals, reflect and act responsibly to effect change. It involves acting rather than being directed; shaping rather than being shaped; and making responsible decisions.

Core fundamentals. Defined as the basic skills, knowledge, attitudes and values that are prerequisites for continued learning across the curriculum. Cognitive foundations; Health foundations, including physical and mental health, and well-being; Social and emotional foundations, including morals and ethics.

Transformative competencies to transform society and shape the future. It defines transformative competences as the kinds of knowledge, skills, attitudes and values that students need to transform society and shape the future for better lives

(OECD, 2018c). It identifies the following as transformative competences: Creating new value; Reconciling tensions and dilemmas; Taking responsibility.

Knowledge. Knowledge includes theoretical concepts and ideas, as well as practical understanding based on experiential learning. It identifies four types of knowledge: disciplinary, interdisciplinary, epistemic and procedural. The opportunity to acquire disciplinary knowledge is also fundamental to equality.

Skills. Defined as the ability to carry out processes and use knowledge responsibly to achieve a goal. Skills are part of a holistic concept of competence, involving the use of knowledge, skills, attitudes and values to meet complex demands. It distinguishes three different types of skills: Cognitive and metacognitive; Social and emotional; Physical and practical. (OECD, 2019).

Attitudes and Values. Defined as: the principles and beliefs that influence one's choices, judgments, behaviors and actions on the path to individual, social and environmental well-being. (Directorate for Education and Skills - Education Policy Directorate, 2019).

The Anticipation-Action-Reflection (AAR) cycle is an interactive learning process through which students continuously improve their thinking and act intentionally and responsibly, moving forward over time towards long-term goals that contribute to collective well-being.

The main objective of the Compass is the transition from a static and fragmented curriculum to an adaptable and dynamic curriculum that is as scientific as possible and reflects the demands of post-modern societies.

The inclusion of well-being among the 21st century competences for the year 2030, as part of the OECD's Education 2030 project, is significant for several reasons: Holistic Development, modern paradigms of education emphasize the holistic development of students, not only academically, but also emotionally, physically and socially. Well-being is fundamental to developing well-adapted individuals who can deal effectively with life's challenges; Improved Academic Performance, there is a strong correlation between well-being and academic success. Students who are mentally and physically healthy are more likely to perform better academically because they can concentrate better, are more engaged and have higher levels of motivation. Evidence has shown that well-being is linked to increased productivity and engagement, both in educational environments and in the workplace (Galvão, Anes, et al., 2019; Galvão et al., 2016; Galvão, Pinheiro, et al., 2019). Students and teachers who are well, tend to perform better and contribute positively to their environments; Mental Health Concerns, with the increased awareness and incidence of mental health problems among young people and adults, incorporating wellbeing into educational curricula can provide the tools and support needed to manage these challenges effectively. This not only helps in the early detection and management of mental health problems, but also destigmatizes mental health challenges; wellbeing skills, such as resilience, stress management and emotional regulation, are essential for lifelong learning and adaptability (Galvão, Anes, et al., 2019). These skills help individuals navigate the complexity of modern life and the rapidly changing job market; preparing for the job market, employers increasingly value social skills such as emotional intelligence, adaptability and collaborative skills, all enhanced by a solid foundation in well-being. Preparing students with these skills makes them more effective and valuable in the workplace; Social Benefits, promoting wellbeing within education can lead to wider social benefits, including reduced health costs, decreased levels of crime, increased economic productivity and more cohesive communities. These outcomes together contribute to a healthier and more stable society. A focus on well-being is not just an educational asset, but a necessary foundation for thriving in the 21st century. This inclusion reflects the understanding that the challenges of the modern world require more than traditional cognitive skills; they require strong, resilient individuals who can contribute positively to society. Thus, the focus on well-being within the OECD's Education 2030 framework reflects the understanding that education systems must adapt to prepare individuals not only for the job market, but also for the challenges of life in the 21st century (Directorate for Education and Skills - Education Policy Directorate, 2019; OECD, 2019).

Development and learning are more effective in a state of well-being. Educational institutions have a responsibility to promote well-being in the school context. Schools can make a substantial contribution to students' health and well-being. This has been widely recognized by various initiatives, including those promoted by the World Health Organization (WHO), UNICEF, UNESCO, the United States Centers for Disease Control and Prevention (CDC), the International Union for Health Promotion and Education (UIPES) and others. Portugal is one of the 46 members of the European Platform for Health Promotion at School, Schools for Health in Europe (SHE) - Health Promoting Schools, advocating that health promotion be an integral part of education and health development policies in Europe. (Vilaça et al., 2019). A health promoting school: Promotes students' health and well-being; Improves school results; Upholds the principles of social justice and equity; Provides a safe and supportive environment; Encourages students' participation and develops their skills (empowerment); Links health and education issues and systems; Addresses the health and well-being issues of the entire educational community; Collaborates with students' parents and the community; Integrates health into current school activities, the curriculum and assessment criteria; Sets realistic goals based on accurate data and solid scientific evidence; Strives for constant improvement through supervision and continuous evaluation.

Promoting Sustainable Well-Being at School

The Health Promoting School (HPS) is based on the principles of the World Health Organization's Ottawa Charter for Health Promotion. In this sense, it identifies six essential elements in promoting health in the school environment: Healthy school policies are clearly defined in documents or generally accepted practices that promote health and well-being. Various policies promote health and well-being, such as those that provide healthy eating practices at school or those that minimize *bullying*; The physical environment of the school, the physical environment refers to the buildings, grounds, playgrounds and equipment on and around the school grounds: the design and location of the building; access to natural light and adequate shade; the creation of spaces for physical activity; and adequate facilities for learning and healthy eating, it also refers to basic facilities: the maintenance of the building and sanitary hygiene practices to prevent the transmission of diseases; the availability of drinking water and fresh air; the absence of environmental contaminants, biological or chemical, harmful to health; the social environment of the school, the social environment of the school is a combination of the quality of relationships within the staff, within the students and between each other. It is influenced by relationships with parents and the wider community; Individual health competencies and action competencies, refers to the formal and informal curriculum and associated activities through which students, depending on their age, acquire knowledge, skills and undertake experiences that enable them to develop action competencies to improve their own health and well-being and that of others in the community, which improves their educational outcomes; Community liaison, community liaison consists of relations between the school and the students' families, plus relations between the school and key groups and people in the local community. Real partnerships (consultation, appropriate participation) with these partners reinforce the EPS and provide students and staff with a context and support for their actions; Health services, these are the local and regional health services, in the school itself or linked to it, which are responsible for the health care and health promotion of children and adolescents, through the direct provision of services to students (including those with specific needs), including: medical screenings and assessments by accredited and qualified professionals; mental health services (including counseling) to promote students' social and emotional development; to prevent or reduce obstacles to intellectual development and learning; to reduce or prevent stress and mental, emotional and psychological disorders, and to improve social interactions among all students

(International Union for Health Promotion and Education, 2009). Building health promoting schools: "Guidelines for promoting health in the school environment."

The SHE Manual for schools 2.0 (Vilaça et al., 2019) simultaneously addresses health and well-being through the six components, which meet the essential elements set out in the Ottawa Charter, which reinforce each other and make efforts to promote health and, consequently, general well-being more effective. See Figure 2.

Figure 2. SHE Manual for Schools 2.0 (Vilaça et al., 2019)

Component 1	The policies of school health are clearly defined documents or accepted practices, which aim at promoting health and well-being. These policies may regulate which foods may be offered by the school or describe the way to prevent or fight bullying. Policies are part of the school plan.
Component 2	The school environment includes buildings, lands and the atmosphere around the school. For instance, the creation of a healthy physical environment may be done through more attractive surroundings for physical and leisure activities.
Component 3	The social school environment is related to the quality of relationships among community members, for example among students, students and faculty, students and staff. The social environment is influenced by the social competences of the members of the school community, as well as by the relations with parents and society in general.
Component 4	Individual action competences regarding health may be promoted through the curriculum and other activities requiring knowledge and skills which allow students to make informed decisions about their health, well-being and school performance. These activities must be included in the school's daily routine and must consider healthy eating, daily physical activity, the development of social competences and health literacy.
Component 5	Community bonds are connections between the school and student's families, as well as between the school and the relevant community stakeholders which support the efforts regarding health promotion.
Component 6	Health services concern local and regional services connected to schools, responsible for healthcare and health promotion for students through the direct implementation of services to students, including special needs' students. The healthcare professionals may work with teachers on specific topics, for instance hygiene and sexual education.

The process of co-creation in the context of Health Promoting Schools is highlighted and recommended, a process shared by Galvão et al. (2023). This co-creation process will involve agents from the educational community together with experts and/or other stakeholders (such as a psychologist, nutritionist, nurse, a representative from the city council, a representative from the local sports club, etc. (Galvão, 2020a, 2020b). In this process of co-creating health promotion using the *whole-school approach*, all ideas and knowledge (scientific or contextual) are equally valid and valued throughout a cyclical, participatory process of sustainable dialog. Therefore, co-creation is a form of collaborative innovation, because ideas are shared and improved together for the collaborative development of new values (concepts, solutions, products and services) (Vilaça et al., 2019).

Schools are contexts where students spend most of their time, so they have a responsibility to promote well-being among their students while they are students and to prepare them for the challenges of the job market. Schools are most successful and effective when they create environments that consider the broader developmental needs of adolescents, young people and adults, including their physical, social, emotional and psychological needs. Top of the form

Learning theory suggests the need to incorporate a wide range of skills and competencies into the learning process, not just cognitive skills, and development depends on these interactions (Schoon et al., 2015). Therefore, education requires the holistic development of the adolescent, young adult and adult to be fully successful. Well-being can be promoted by schools for all aspects of an individual student; however, certain aspects of well-being can be effectively promoted through educational curricula, while other aspects are more effectively promoted by other aspects of schooling, such as mentoring, classroom and group activities, information campaigns, sports, and the arts (Directorate for Education and Skills - Education Policy Directorate, 2019).

How does well-being relate to other competencies for 2030? Well-being, encompassing both physical and psychological health, is deeply integrated with other competencies deemed crucial for 2030. The relationship can be understood through a few key points: Foundation for Learning, physical well-being ensures that individuals are healthy enough to engage in learning, while psychological well-being impacts motivation, stress management, and overall mental health, all of which are critical for cognitive processing and learning retention; Enhancement of Cognitive Competencies, there's growing evidence suggesting that good physical and psychological health can enhance cognitive abilities. For example, physical fitness is linked to improved executive functions like memory and attention, while psychological well-being can foster better decision-making and problem-solving skills; Interrelation with Social and Emotional Competencies, well-being supports and is supported by social and emotional competencies. For instance, emotional regulation, a key component of psychological well-being, helps in managing interpersonal relationships and navigating social contexts. Conversely, supportive social interactions can bolster individual well-being; Meta-competencies, well-being influences meta-competencies like adaptability, resilience, and self-efficacy. These competencies are essential for managing the complexities and challenges of the modern world and are closely tied to one's physical and psychological states.

Social and emotional skills, including perseverance, self-esteem and sociability, communication, curiosity and interest in others are also associated with well-being and, increasingly, employers see these skills as complementary rather than secondary to cognitive skills (Deming, 2017; OECD, 2018a).

In the framework of Education 2030, acknowledging the integral role of well-being is crucial not just for fostering other competencies but also for ensuring that educational strategies are holistic, supporting not just academic success but also the overall health and happiness of students.

The Council of Europe (2022) considers that "people need access to quality education and learning, delivered in different ways and in different contexts, in order to develop their personal, social, cultural and professional knowledge, skills and competences. There have been calls for education and training systems to become more flexible and find solutions to provide more learner-centered, accessible and inclusive learning to a wider range of profiles. Non-formal education and training providers are also addressing this need by providing new and innovative upskilling and reskilling opportunities."

We return to the original question: How can micro-credentials help teachers to sculpt their profile and train skills to help students along their learning path while promoting their well-being.

Teachers in higher education face unique challenges and must develop a diverse set of skills to be effective in their roles. We summarize these with the core competencies identified above: Pedagogical Competence, mastering teaching-learning strategies that promote engagement and active learning. This includes the ability to develop and implement innovative teaching methodologies, such as project-based learning, flipped learning and active learning (Galvão, 2020a, 2020b). In-depth knowledge of the scientific field, it is essential that teachers have an in-depth knowledge of their area of specialization, keeping up to date with the latest research and developments; Digital skills, the ability to integrate educational technologies is crucial, especially in this digital age. This can include the use of online learning platforms, virtual collaboration tools and digital resources to enrich the teaching process and facilitate learning; Communication and Presentation Skills; communicating clearly and presenting information in a way that is accessible and engaging for students, regardless of their background or initial level of preparation; Effective Assessment and Feedback, developing assessment methods that adequately measure student learning and providing constructive feedback that encourages them to continually improve; Curriculum Development and Design, the ability to plan, develop and evaluate curricula and educational programs that meet student needs and institutional objectives; Mentoring and Guidance, providing academic and professional guidance to students, helping them navigate the challenges of higher education and plan their future careers; Research and Innovation, in addition to teaching, higher education professors often carry out research. Developing research skills and contributing to the body of knowledge in their scientific field is essential; Adaptation and Flexibility, the ability to adapt to changes in the educational environment, such as changes in educational policies, student demographics or technology, is crucial; Interdisciplinary Collaboration, working effectively in multidisciplinary teams to enrich students' educational experience and collaborate on research.

The skills identified can be acquired through micro-credentials for teachers. Developing these skills will enable higher education teachers not only to improve their own teaching practice, but also to contribute significantly to the academic and personal development of students.

Interconnection Between micro-credentials and the Elements that Make up the OECD 2030 Learning Compass

In 2015, Portugal formulated the National Skills Strategy (OECD, 2018b)which involved a strategic assessment of the country's national skills system, see Figure 3. The National Skills Strategy used a framework to analyze the country's strengths and weaknesses. It then used these results as a basis for taking concrete action according to three pillars: 1) developing relevant skills from childhood to adulthood; 2) activating the supply of skills in the labor market; and 3) using skills effectively in the economy and society. An effective skills strategy ensures policy coherence between these three pillars, while strengthening the conditions for effective governance and funding - which underpin the skills system as a whole (OECD, 2018b). To make these three pillars a reality, it will be useful to offer micro-credentials for students to develop the necessary skills.

Figure 3. Skills strategy for Portugal: results of the diagnostic phase (2014-15)

12 SKILLS CHALLENGES FOR PORTUGAL

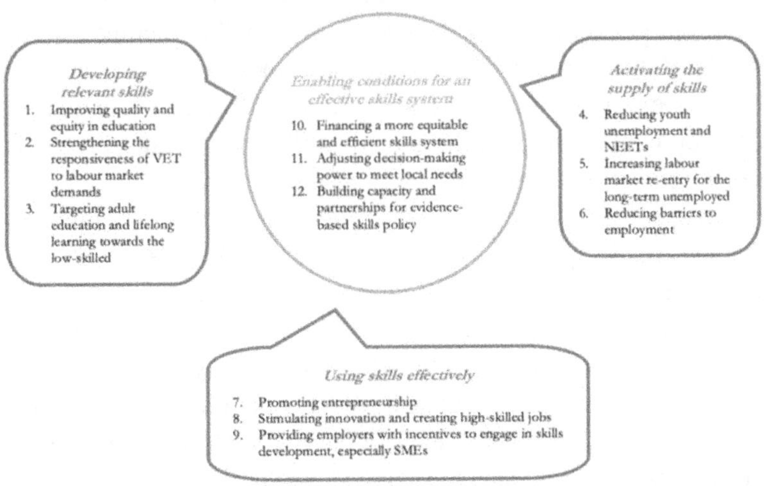

Micro-credentials have become an important component of the European higher education skills agenda and are considered a core offering of several pan-European institutions and alliances of higher education institutions that are currently adopting micro-credentials. It has been proposed that micro-credentials could complement bachelor's, master's and doctoral curricula, while providing value to professionals who already hold certain degrees. We therefore consider it an asset to make a set of micro-credentials available to both teachers and students. To realize the potential of micro-credentials, Member States are recommended, where appropriate, to integrate micro-credentials into both education and training systems and skills policies, including by: h) promoting the understanding and use of micro-credentials through the continuous professional development of teachers and trainers, educational advisors (e.g. in the context of Erasmus+ Teacher Academies), as well as academics, researchers and other related staff members. In this way, micro-credentials can help teachers sculpt their profile and train skills to help students on their learning path while promoting their well-being.

The European Council recommends: Supporting the exploration by higher education institutions of the role of micro-credentials in providing learning opportunities for diverse learners, including by extending an attractive, accessible, inclusive and learner-centered offer of lifelong learning activities, including through the activities of the "European Universities" alliances. Promote the use of micro-credentials in Erasmus+ Teacher Academies and with other teacher education and training providers to meet teachers' needs for continuous professional development, where relevant. (The Council of the European Union, 2022). In this context, it seems appropriate to make micro-credentials available to teachers to help them sculpt their profile and train skills to help students on their learning path while promoting their well-being.

Teachers can benefit from a portfolio of micro-credentials in the following areas: Personal development; Promotion of general well-being (health literacy); Healthy work contexts (relaxation techniques, etc.). (Tang et al., 2015).

It also provides students with micro-credentials that enable them to develop knowledge and skills in specific areas and attitudes and values:

"... In addition to full curricula, and while preserving their right to design study programs and regulate credit transfer issues independently, a number of higher education institutions offer or plan to offer shorter learning units that can help learners develop or update their cultural, professional and transversal skills and competences at various stages of life. An effective culture of lifelong learning is key to ensuring that everyone has the knowledge, skills and competences needed to thrive in society, on the job market and in their personal lives..." (The Council of the European Union, 2022). We therefore propose to offer four micro-credentials to students in the areas of Personal Development; Vocational Guidance; Decision Making; Professional Development; Financial Literacy.

Micro-credentials that can be validated and transferable in a global European context.

The articulation between micro credentials and the Learning Compass, especially in the context of the OECD Learning Compass 2030, reveals a promising intersection for the future of education and skills development. Both concepts support the idea that education should be a continuous process, adaptable and aligned with the emerging needs of society and the labor market. Let's see how these two ideas connect and complement each other:

Intersections of Micro-credentials and Learning Compass 2030

Personalized Learning: Micro-credentials allow for a more personalized learning experience that is aligned with Learning Compass' focus on learner agency. Learners can choose pathways that best suit their career goals and learning styles, allowing for a more tailored educational experience that fosters intrinsic motivation and engagement.

Relevance to the Job Market: Micro-credentials are directly linked to emerging market demands, facilitating the acquisition of up-to-date and highly relevant skills and competencies.

Lifelong Learning: The flexibility of micro-credentials supports Learning Compass' emphasis on lifelong learning. They enable individuals to continually update their skills or make career transitions as needed, which is crucial in a rapidly changing job market.

Skills Development: Both Learning Compass and micro-credentials emphasize the importance of developing a broad set of skills. Micro-credentials often focus on specific competencies that are highly relevant to the emerging needs of the workforce, such as digital literacy, critical thinking and collaboration, which are also central to Learning Compass 2030.

Educational Equity: Micro-credentials can potentially increase equity in education by providing alternative pathways to learning and qualifications, particularly for learners who may face barriers to traditional educational settings. This approach is aligned with the Learning Compass goal of making education more inclusive and accessible (OECD, 2019).

OECD Learning Compass 2030: Vision and Direction

Individual and Collective Well-Being: The Learning Compass emphasizes the development of competencies that not only benefit the individual, but also contribute to collective and global well-being.

Skills, Attitudes and Values: In addition to technical skills, the compass highlights the importance of attitudes, values and transversal skills, such as critical thinking, creativity and collaboration.

Adaptability and Resilience: Encourages education systems to prepare students to face future uncertainties and challenges by promoting adaptability and resilience.

Articulation between Micro-credentials and Learning Compass

Complementarity: Micro-credentials can be seen as practical instruments for achieving the objectives outlined by the Learning Compass, offering tangible means of acquiring the necessary competencies, skills, attitudes and values.

Educational Innovation: Both encourage innovation in education and training systems, promoting learning methods that are more flexible, inclusive and adapted to individual and social needs.

Preparing for the Future: Together they provide a framework to prepare students not only for current challenges, but also for future ones, aligning education, training and professional development with the demands of a constantly evolving society.

In short, the combination of micro-credentials with the vision provided by the OECD Learning Compass 2030 creates an educational ecosystem that is dynamic, inclusive and prepared to meet the demands of the 21st century. This ecosystem empowers individuals to successfully navigate their learning and career journeys, emphasizing the importance of education that is continuous, adaptable and deeply rooted in values that promote the well-being of all (Directorate for Education and Skills - Education Policy Directorate, 2019; OECD, 2018c, 2019).

Sustainable Development Goals (SDGs)

The SDGs are a collection of 17 global goals established by the United Nations (UN) in 2015 as part of the 2030 Agenda for Sustainable Development (United Nations, 2015, 2018).

Thus, the Learning Compass 2030 and micro-credentials have complementary roles in addressing the SDGs, specifically SDGs 3, 4 and 10. Here are some thoughts on how these tools and concepts can be integrated to achieve these goals.

SDG 3: Health and well-being

With regards to the Learning Compass 2030 this approach emphasizes the importance of developing skills that promote individuals' physical and mental well-being. Through its focus on developing self-management and emotional resilience, Learning Compass 2030 can make a significant contribution to health and well-being education, empowering individuals to make healthy choices and manage stress effectively.

Micro-credentials can be used to provide specific training in areas such as mental health, nutrition, physical exercise and first aid. Micro-credentials in health topics can enable professionals from a variety of fields, not just those linked to health, to integrate wellness practices into their daily routines and work environments, broadening the impact on community and individual health.

SDG 4: Quality Education

The Learning Compass 2030 is strongly focused on providing students with the skills and competencies they need to thrive in an ever-changing world, including the ability to learn continuously throughout their lives. So, the Learning Compass 2030 promotes teaching methods that are adaptive and inclusive, aligning directly with the goal of providing quality education for all.

Micro-credentials are essential tools for promoting lifelong learning, allowing individuals of all ages and backgrounds to acquire relevant and up-to-date skills quickly and affordably. This is especially valuable in contexts of rapid technological evolution and changing labor market needs.

SDG 10: Reducing Inequalities

The Learning Compass approach can help reduce educational inequalities by promoting an education that values diversity and inclusion. Developing global and social skills is crucial to understanding and valuing diverse perspectives, which is key to reducing social and economic inequalities.

By providing more flexible and democratic access to training and certification, micro-credentials can play a significant role in reducing barriers to educational and professional advancement. They are particularly beneficial in marginalized regions and groups, where access to traditional education may be limited.

In short, the combination of Learning Compass 2030 and micro-credentials offers a powerful tool to meet the global challenges outlined in the SDGs, promoting education adapted to the needs of the 21st century. By focusing on relevant skills and innovative teaching practices, this combination can drive significant progress in health and well-being, educational quality and the reduction of inequalities. Micro-credentials have significant potential to contribute to the SDGs through the promotion of accessible and relevant education, which supports both economic and social development. However, for this potential to be fully realized, a concerted effort is needed to ensure their quality, relevance and recognition in various sectors of society.

Ethical and legal aspects. European standard elements will be used to describe each micro-credential. The ten principles will be guaranteed (Quality; Transparency; Relevance; Valid assessment; Learning paths; Recognition; Portability; Learner-centered; Authenticity; Information and guidance) which highlight the fundamental characteristics of the European approach to micro-credentials that can promote their trust and quality.

Reflections on the Future of Microcredentials

As higher education institutions increasingly adopt microcredentials, they face both challenges and opportunities. Recognition of microcredentials among different institutions and employers remains a significant challenge. There is also a need for quality assurance mechanisms to ensure that these credentials maintain high educational standards and relevance to the changing demands of industry.

The future of micro-credentials in higher education looks promising, but requires careful integration into existing educational frameworks to maximize their potential benefits. This integration involves rethinking pedagogical approaches, adapting policies and fostering partnerships between educational institutions and industry. In doing so, micro-credentials can contribute significantly to the achievement of the Learning Compass 2030 goals, preparing students not only for the jobs of the future, but for lifelong resilience and personal development.

CONCLUSION

The Education 2030: The Future of Education and Skills project, set up by the OECD in 2015, proposes a conceptual learning matrix and the creation and management of an international curriculum based on a learning compass. This concept interweaves new competences (knowledge, skills, attitudes and values) to be included in countries' school curricula. It is a blueprint for an international definition of the knowledge, competencies, skills, attitudes and values that students will need to master in order to thrive and shape their lives and the world in 2030. The consensus of experts points in particular to the likelihood of micro-credentials gaining importance among educational institutions seeking to innovate, as well as networks of institutions looking for alternative approaches to traditional offers and study programs. While technology can be a valuable tool, teachers, tutors, mentors... and the relational aspects of teaching will be key to learning, personal fulfilment and well-being.

Limitations

"Despite their growing use, there is no common definition or standards for micro-credentials in Europe, which limits the understanding and adoption of micro-credentials and consequently undermines the potential of micro-credentials to facilitate flexible learning and career pathways" (The Council of the European Union, 2022).

REFERENCES

Deming, D. J. (2017). The growing importance of social skills in the labor market. *The Quarterly Journal of Economics*, 132(4), 1593–1640. DOI: 10.1093/qje/qjx022

Directorate for Education and Skills - Education Policy Directorate (2019). *Future of education and skills 2030: reflections on transformative competencies 2030.*

Galvão, A. (2020a). *"Cover" of pedagogical innovation processes and resources applied to learning*. Self-published.

Galvão, A. (2020b). The Design Thinking process as an enabler of motivation for learning. In de Jesus, S. N. (Ed.), *Inovação e partilha pedagógica na UAlg* (pp. 23–26). University of Algarve Editora.

Galvão, A., Anes, E., & Chumbo, I. (2023). Design Thinking to Promote Mental Health Literacy for Higher Education Students. In Rodrigues, S., & Mourato, J. (Eds.), *The Impact of HEIs on Regional Development: Facts and Practices of Collaborative Work With SMEs* (pp. 130–143). IGI Global., DOI: 10.4018/978-1-6684-6701-5.ch008

Galvão, A., Anes, E., Pinheiro, M., & Gomes, M. J. (2019). Happiness: one of the determinants of occupational health. *V Congresso Ibero-Americano e Luso-Brasileiro de Psicologia Da Saúde - I Congresso Promoção Da Saúde e Do Bem-Estar No Ensino Superior*, 45-50.

Galvão, A., Cabeceiro, S. F., & Pinheiro, M. (2016). Impact of the Coaching Process on Business Productivity. *3º Congresso Da Ordem Dos Psicólogos Portugueses*, 969-985. https://www.ordemdospsicologos.pt/ficheiros/documentos/livro_de_actas_3ao_congresso_opp_final.pdf

Galvão, A., Pinheiro, M., Antão, C., & Gomes, M. J. (2019). Happiness and mental health in higher education students: a comparative study. *V Congresso Ibero-Americano e Luso-Brasileiro de Psicologia Da Saúde - I Congresso Promoção Da Saúde e Do Bem-Estar No Ensino Superior*, 39-45.

International Union for Health Promotion and Education. (2009). *Building health-promoting schools: "Guidelines for promoting health in the school environment."* https://www.dge.mec.pt/sites/default/files/ficheiros/iuhpe_hps_guidelinesii_2009_portuguese.pdf

OECD (2018a). *Health at a Glance 2017: OECD Indicators*. OECD Publishing. DOI: 10.1787/health_glance-2015-en

OECD (2018b). *Skills strategy implementation guidance for Portugal* (OECD Skills Studies). OECD. DOI: 10.1787/9789264298705-en

OECD. (2018c). The Future of Education and Skills: Education 2030. In *OECD Education Working Papers*.http://www.oecd.org/education/2030/E2030 Position Paper (05.04.2018).pdf

OECD. (2019). *Learning compass 2030: Conceptual learning framework*.www.oecd.org/education/2030-project

Rodrigo Castañeda Valle. Simon Normandeau, & Gara Rojas González (2015). *Education at a glance interim report: update of employment and educational attainment indicators*. https://www.oecd.org/edu/eag.htm

Schoon, I., Nasim, B., Sehmi, R., & Cook, R. (2015). *The Impact of Early Life Skills on Later Outcomes*.

Tang, Y. Y., Hölzel, B. K., & Posner, M. I. (2015). The neuroscience of mindfulness meditation. *Nature Reviews. Neuroscience*, 16(4), 213–225. DOI: 10.1038/nrn3916 PMID: 25783612

The Council of the European Union. (2022). *Council recommendation of 16 June 2022 on a European approach to micro-credentials for lifelong learning and employability*. The Council of the European Union.

United Nations (2015). *Transforming our world: The 2030 agenda for sustainable development.* DOI: 10.1201/b20466-7

United Nations. (2018). Transforming Our World: The 2030 Agenda for Sustainable Development. In *A New Era in Global Health.* United Nations., DOI: 10.1891/9780826190123.ap02

Vilaça, T., Darlington, E., Velasco, M., Martinis, O., & Masson, J. (2019). *SHE Manual for schools 2.0.*www.schoolsforhealth.org/resources/materials-and-tools/

Chapter 16
Micro-Credentials in Higher Education:
A New Path for Gerontology

Ana Galvão
https://orcid.org/0000-0001-9978-9563
Instituto Politécnico de Bragança, Portugal

Isabel Chumbo
https://orcid.org/0000-0002-9630-2905
Instituto Politécnico de Bragança, Portugal

Eugénia Anes
https://orcid.org/0000-0001-8474-3474
Instituto Politécnico de Bragança, Portugal

ABSTRACT

The mission of this chapter is to provide a comprehensive overview of the importance and potential of microcredentials in advancing education and professional practice in Gerontology, emphasising the need for an adaptable, competency-oriented educational approach in this vital field. The following objectives are proposed: to reiterate the value of microcredentials as a strategic educational resource to meet the specific demands of Gerontology in higher education and to emphasise the need for a continued commitment to educational innovation and interdisciplinary collaboration to prepare trained gerontologists to meet the challenges of the Decade of Healthy Ageing 2021-2030.

DOI: 10.4018/979-8-3693-5488-9.ch016

BACKGROUND

Population ageing is a global trend that presents both challenges and opportunities for public policies, health systems and societies in general. By 2050, the global population of older individuals will have more than doubled, reaching a total of 2.1 billion people (Decade of Healthy Ageing 2021-2030).

Portugal is one of the countries in the European Union with the oldest population and where the ageing rate has grown exponentially in recent years. This brings challenges for all sectors, which means that networked responses are particularly important for healthy ageing. Overall, there is little evidence that older people today are in better health than previous generations. Good health prolongs life, this is a motto confirmed by medicine. The opportunities that come with increased longevity depend heavily on healthy ageing. People who experience these additional years of life in good health and continue to participate and be an integral part of families and communities strengthen societies; however, if the added years are dominated by poor health, social isolation or dependence on care, the implications for older people and society are much more negative.

The Decade of Healthy Ageing 2021-2030, proclaimed by the World Health Organisation (WHO) is a global initiative that seeks to catalyse significant changes in health and well-being policies for older people. The ageing of the global population is one of the most significant demographic transformations of the 21st century, with substantial implications for all aspects of society, including the economy, health systems, social structures and public policies.

The world's population is ageing at an unprecedented rate due to increased life expectancy and a falling birth rate, giving rise to different dynamics and challenges. The Decade of Healthy Ageing is not only a response to these challenges, but also an opportunity to restructure health and social systems in a way that promotes a long and healthy life for all.

Healthy Ageing encompasses the entire life course and is relevant to everyone, not just those who are currently disease-free. Intrinsic capacity at any time is determined by several factors, including underlying physiological and psychological changes, health behaviour and the presence or absence of disease. This is strongly influenced by the environments in which people have lived over the years. The social and economic resources and opportunities that people have over the life course influence their power to make healthy decisions and to give and receive support when they need it. Healthy ageing is therefore closely linked to social and economic inequality. Disadvantages in the areas of health, education, employment and income start early, reinforce each other and accumulate throughout life.

Naturally, older people in poor health work less, earn less and retire earlier. In this sense, healthy ageing means developing and maintaining the functional competences that enable well-being in old age. Functional competence is determined by an individual's intrinsic capacity (i.e. the combination of all the individual's physical and mental capacities), the environment in which they live (understood in the broadest possible sense and including the physical, social and political environments) and the interactions between them (Decade of Healthy Ageing 2021-2030).

It is possible to identify the following as strategies for Healthy Ageing: Lifelong Health Promotion, with a focus on preventive measures that can be incorporated at all stages of life to ensure healthy ageing; Favourable Environments, through the creation of physical and social environments that promote the health and well-being of older people; the Integration of Care, through the strengthening of health systems to offer integrated, person-centred care. Public Policies: Support for the Independence of Older People, through the development of policies that enable older people to live independently and safely in their communities; Capacity Building and Education, through continuing education programmes for health professionals and the community in general on the specific needs and rights of older people.

Urbanization and population ageing are transformative trends changing how we live, work, and experience our urban environments throughout our lives and into older age. By 2050, the world's urban population is expected to nearly double. Fifty-seven per cent of people 60 years and older live in towns and cities. Globally, the total number of people over 60 is set to double by 2050, rising from 1 billion to 2 billion, with 80% living in low- and middle-income countries. (WHO, 2018).

As such, the Decade of Healthy Ageing presents itself as a crucial opportunity to transform ageing-related policies and practices. International cooperation and innovation will also be essential to overcome the challenges of global ageing and to implement effective strategies that support the health and well-being of older people around the world. Increased life expectancy has undeniably brought with it significant challenges and unique opportunities for contemporary society. That's why the gerontologist's intervention is crucial in this context, aimed at improving the quality of life of the elderly and facilitating active and healthy ageing.

Gerontology is the science that studies the process of human ageing in its psychological, biological, social and cultural dimensions. It began to develop as an independent discipline in the middle of the 20th century. The term 'gerontology' was coined by Ilya Ilyich Mechnikov, a Russian biologist, in 1903. Mechnikov, who was working at the Pasteur Institute in Paris at the time, proposed the study of ageing with the hope that understanding this process could help improve people's health and longevity. Since then, gerontology has evolved to include various subfields, such as the biology of ageing, clinical gerontology, the psychology of ageing and the sociology of ageing, thus approaching ageing from a multidisciplinary perspective.

This discipline expanded significantly after the Second World War, especially with the increase in life expectancy and the growth of the global elderly population. As mentioned above, gerontology studies the social, psychological and biological aspects associated with the ageing process and assumes an unprecedented importance on the global stage. This emphasis on its recognition is largely due to the growing increase in life expectancy and the ageing of the world's population. With advances in medicine and public health, more people are living to advanced ages, which brings new challenges and opportunities for society. Thus, gerontology stands out as an essential field for understanding and meeting the specific needs of this expanding demography.

The World Health Organisation stresses the importance of understanding that there are considerable changes in health status, levels of independence, autonomy and social participation among older adults. Gerontology is, therefore, a key element in understanding the heterogeneity of older people, contributing to the definition of policies and programmes that guarantee opportunities for health, participation and security for people as they age.

Gerontology has also come to occupy a place in the educational offerings of various institutions, with generations of students taking courses and degrees with this designation. On this basis, we move on to link it to micro-credentials, which are emerging as an innovative and relevant educational solution. Characterised by their flexibility and adaptability, they allow for the quick and effective acquisition of specialisations in specific areas of study, including gerontology. Unlike traditional degree programmes, which require years of study, micro-credentials offer shorter courses focused on specific skills that are immediately applicable in the professional context. This approach allows professionals and students to adapt quickly to changes in the field of gerontology, updating their competencies in line with the emerging needs of care and support for the elderly population.

Scope

The higher education sector is responding to this learning landscape. This is particularly relevant to the massive open online courses (MOOCs) environment where there is the potential for thousands of participants to learn through multiple open-source tools with minimum intervention from educators. This social learning perspective can present a challenge for some educators (Adachi, C., Savage, J. & O'Donnell, M., 2017).

Oliver (2019) defines that "a micro-credential is a certification of assessed learning that is additional, alternate, complementary to or a formal component of a formal qualification." A micro-credential is a proof of the learning outcomes that a learner has acquired following a short learning experience. These learning outcomes have been assessed against transparent standards. The proof is contained in a certified document that lists the name of the holder, the achieved learning outcomes, the assessment method, the awarding body and, where applicable, the qualifications framework level and the credits gained. Micro-credentials are owned by the learner, can be shared, are portable and may be combined into larger credentials or qualifications. They are underpinned by quality assurance following agreed standards (Futures, H., Andersen, T., & Larsen, K., 2020).

Sadeq and Stanback (2021) have identified a total of 51 micro-credentials with an explicit aging-focus and searched for associated competencies for these micro-credentials. Moving forward, it is critical to ensure alignment between gerontological micro-credentials and established gerontological competencies and standards and to differentiate micro-credentials from formal academic programs.

This chapter aims at providing and innovative view of the value of micro-credentials as a valuable tool in the field of gerontology and therefore higher education.

These are short-term courses that offer specific and practical skills, providing a flexible way of learning. Here are some ways they can contribute to gerontology:

Specialization and Professional Updating

Focused Courses: Micro-credentials allow professionals from various fields (such as nursing, physiotherapy, psychology, and social work) to specialize in topics related to gerontology, such as geriatric care, mental health for the elderly, or public policies aimed at the elderly.

Constant Updating: Since gerontology is an ever-evolving field due to demographic changes and new scientific discoveries, micro credentials offer a quick and accessible way to stay updated on best practices and innovations.

Multidisciplinary Approach: Gerontology is an interdisciplinary field encompassing biological, psychological, social, and cultural aspects of ageing. Micro-credentials can provide knowledge in specific areas, such as nutrition for the elderly, assistive technology, or social interventions, promoting a more holistic and integrated view of elderly care.

Practical Skills for Professionals

Technical Training: Micro-credentials can focus on practical skills, such as using assistive technology, physiotherapy techniques for fall prevention, or effective communication strategies with elderly people with cognitive impairment.

Care Management: They can also offer training in areas such as managing elderly care services, administering long-term care institutions, and coordinating health programs for the elderly.

Flexibility for Various Professionals

Broadened Access: Professionals from different fields can gain specific knowledge in gerontology without enrolling in a long-term academic program. This includes caregivers, doctors, occupational therapists, physiotherapists, social workers, and even technology professionals who wish to develop innovative solutions for the elderly.

Customized Learning: Micro-credentials allow the choice of content that aligns with personal interests and professional needs, promoting more targeted and efficient training.

Promotion of Continuing Education: Micro-credentials promote continuing education, encouraging professionals to learn throughout their careers. This is especially important in gerontology, where new challenges and opportunities arise as the population ages.

Building a Specialized Workforce

With the growing number of elderly people, there is a demand for professionals trained in gerontology. Micro-credentials can help fill this gap by creating a workforce prepared to handle the unique needs of the elderly in different contexts, such as health, leisure, education, and social inclusion.

Contribution to Public Policies and Social Practices: Training in topics like public policies for ageing, elderly rights, and inclusive practices can be addressed through micro-credentials, empowering professionals to engage in the formulation and implementation of effective policies.

Stimulating Innovation: Through micro-credentials in areas like assistive technology and design for the elderly, professionals can be encouraged to develop innovative solutions that improve the quality of life for the elderly, from creating adapted products to implementing community support programs.

In summary, micro-credentials offer a quick, flexible, and practical way to develop essential skills in the field of gerontology, addressing the growing need for specialized training to deal with an ageing population.

Gerontology in Higher Education

The gerontology degree course in Portugal has been established in different higher education institutions over time, starting in 2001, and the offer has expanded as interest in the study of ageing and care for the elderly population has grown. These courses aim to train professionals who are able to intervene effectively and ethically in the ageing process, with an interdisciplinary approach that covers social, psychological, physical and healthcare management aspects for the elderly population.

Ministerial Order no. 841/2004 of 16 July creates the Degree in Gerontology taught at the Bragança Polytechnic University.

The bachelor degree in Gerontology is awarded to students who demonstrate, in this area, the ability to: a) Know the normal processes of ageing, detecting pathological deviations in good time; b) Evaluate problems of ageing, quality of life and well-being in elderly populations; c) Know the policies to support the elderly population in Portugal and in the European Union, namely the social solidarity and health systems; d) Know the different types of equipment and services to support the elderly; e) Know how to intervene in the community and in the family, with the elderly and carers (formal and informal); f) Know how to design, implement and manage active ageing programmes; g) Know how to accompany and/or refer the elderly in acute, rehabilitation and death situations; h) Integrate and work from an interdisciplinary and complementary perspective with the actors involved in the ageing phenomenon; i) Solve problems and introduce into their daily practice both the results of their reflection on practice and the results of additional scientific studies and research, with a view to innovation; j) Evaluate professional practice and promote its development, taking into account values and attitudes consistent with the standards of professional and ethical conduct subscribed to by Universal Rights.

This is a 180 ECTS course, whose syllabus includes the following scientific areas: Biology and Biochemistry; Political Science and Citizenship; Educational Sciences; Law; Philosophy and Ethics; Management and Administration; Medicine; Psychology; Health; Sociology; Therapy and Rehabilitation.

In 2012, the Association for Gerontology in Higher Education (AGHE) appointed two working groups, and in 2014 the Competences in Gerontology emerged, based on the literature on the foundations of gerontology and competence-based education. The document 'The Competences in Gerontology for Undergraduate and Postgraduate Education' (AGHE, 2020) resulted from the joint work of professors and students from more than 30 universities and colleges involved in gerontology education providing feedback for the consensus-building process besides giving rise to competence-based gerontology. This construct has contributed to the potential impacts of gerontology education. Competences can be applied to gerontology programmes at undergraduate, postgraduate, master's, doctoral and micro-credential levels.

There are three categories of competences (I, II and III). Category I competences represent the essential orientation towards the field of gerontology. Category II competences are 'interactional' competences that capture the processes of knowing and doing across the fields of gerontology. Category III competences aim to capture the competences most relevant to employment contexts in a variety of sectors and areas in which gerontologists can work, including education. Three categories of competences are recommended, 10 core and 8 specific. Each category identifies the domain for the competence, these are broad areas with specific competence statements related to the particular area and the content of each competence is also identified, as listed below:

> CATEGORY I - Foundational competencies to all fields of gerontology
> I.1 FRAMEWORKS FOR UNDERSTANDING HUMAN AGING. To utilize gerontological frameworks to examine human development and aging.
> I.2 BIOLOGICAL ASPECTS OF AGING. To relate biological theory and science to understanding senescence, longevity and variation in aging.
> I.3 PSYCHOLOGICAL ASPECTS OF AGING. To relate psychological theories and science to understanding adaptation, stability and change in aging.
> I.4 SOCIAL ASPECTS OF AGING. To relate social theories and science of aging to understanding heterogeneity, inequality and context of aging.
> I.5 THE HUMANITIES AND AGING. To develop comprehensive and meaningful concepts, definitions and measures for well-being of older adults and their families, grounded both in humanities and arts.
> I.6 RESEARCH AND CRITICAL THINKING. To distinguish factors related to aging outcomes, both intrinsic and contextual, through critical thinking and empirical research.
> CATEGORY II - Interactional competencies across fields of gerontology
> II.1 ATTITUDES AND PERSPECTIVES. To develop a gerontological perspective through knowledge and self-reflection.
> II.2 ETHICS AND PROFESSIONAL STANDARDS. To adhere to ethical principles to guide work with and on behalf of older people.
> II.3 COMMUNICATION WITH AND ON BEHALF OF OLDER PERSONS. To engage older persons, their families and the community in personal and public issues in aging through effective communication.
> II.4 INTERDISCPLINARY AND COMMUNITY COLLABORATION. To engage collaboratively with others to promote integrated approaches to ageing" (AGHE, 2020).

Then, eight specific competences:

> "CATEGORY III - Contextual competencies across fields of gerontology
> III.1 WELL-BEING, HEALTH AND MENTAL HEALTH. To promote older persons' strengths and adaptations to maximize well-being, health and mental health.

III.2 SOCIAL HEALTH. To promote quality of life and a positive social environment for older persons.
III.3 PROGRAM/SERVICE DEVELOPMENT. To employ and design programmatic and community development with and on behalf of the ageing population.
III.4 EDUCATION. To encourage older persons to engage in life-long learning opportunities.
III.5 ARTS AND HUMANITIES. To promote engagement of older people in the arts and humanities.
III.6 BUSINESS & FINANCE. To address the roles of older persons as workers and consumers in business and finance.
III.7 POLICY. To employ and generate policy to equitably address the needs of older persons.
III.8 RESEARCH, APPLICATION AND EVALUATION. To engage in research to advance knowledge and improve interventions for older persons" (AGHE, 2020).

At the end of the chapter, we will present a proposal for micro-credentials in Gerontology based on the AGHE document (2020) and the 'UN Decade of Healthy Ageing: Plan of Action 2021-2030'.

The Gerontologist's intervention in the world of longevity

Longer lives are an admirable achievement of humanity and are indicative of the social, economic and medical development that has succeeded in eliminating and minimising fatal childhood diseases, maternal mortality and delaying the mortality of the elderly. A longer life is an incredibly valuable resource that provides the opportunity to rethink not only what it is to be an older person, but also how all of life can unfold (UN Decade of Healthy Ageing: Plan of Action (2021-2030).

The core of longevity is undoubtedly health and well-being. Advances in preventive and personalised medicine allow healthcare professionals to identify and treat illnesses before they become serious. Balanced diets, regular exercise and stress management are key to keeping the body and mind in good condition as we age. The world of longevity is not just about increasing the number of years we live, but also about enriching the quality of those years. With collaboration between scientists, doctors, technologists, policymakers and educators, the future of longevity promises significant advances in how we age and live our extended lives. In addition, gerontology and geriatrics, which are studies and care specifically for the elderly, play vital roles.

The AGHE (2020) defines a gerontologist as a professional who contributes to improving the quality of life and promoting the well-being of people as they age, within their families, in the community and in society, through research, education and the application of interdisciplinary knowledge of the ageing process and ageing populations.

The integration of gerontologists into the labour market has proved to be an asset in supporting the whole person, with a holistic view of the ageing process, in humanising care for older adults and has contributed to a paradigm shift in the ageing process.

With reference to the definition of gerontologist, highlighting the multidisciplinary nature of their knowledge and, consequently, their interdisciplinary practice, presupposing work carried out in complementarity with other professionals, not replacing any professional class or practice. According to competence-based gerontology, three gerontologist profiles emerge: case manager, service provider/entrepreneur and consultant.

As a case manager, the Gerontologist has the ability to coordinate the different services that support older people, as well as their families, to identify and ensure effective administration of services according to their needs.

As a service provider/entrepreneur, they provide services for individual older people as well as for groups, based on their multidisciplinary knowledge of the ageing process. By (re)understanding the reality underlying his professional activity, he is able to anticipate future needs and implement innovative solutions in the field of services for the older population.

As a consultant, they assess the needs in a given area in order to help plan interventions that address those needs.

Gerontologists can develop interventions, programmes and projects in a variety of contexts, including social or private organisations, local authorities and public social security services; health structures within the scope of prevention programmes, health education and primary care; palliative care and hospital units.

Primary health care, the pillar of universal health coverage, is the main entry point for older people into the health system. It is also the most effective and efficient approach to improving physical and mental capacity and well-being. Strengthening primary health care to provide accessible, affordable, equitable, safe and community-based care for older people will require a competent workforce, appropriate legislation and regulation as well as sufficient sustainable funding. Essential to these activities will be the recognition of equity, social justice and social protection, as well as the elimination of the widespread ageism that limits older people's access to good quality health services.

The provision of person-centred, integrated care and primary health services that are comprehensive and responsive to the needs of older people will move countries one step closer to ensuring that more people benefit from universal health coverage by 2030.

Through their practice, gerontologists help ensure that the ageing process is planned, guided and well assisted.

Through their skills and training, they will be able to determine which professionals to mobilise, when and under what conditions, boosting the network of relationships with professionals, services and community resources in order to optimise and quickly and effectively solve the problems, difficulties and needs that may arise at any given time. This professional has specific skills that allow them to work in a variety of areas, including community intervention through the implementation of projects for ageing at home and in the community; management of organisations, services and gerontological social resources; and training and consultancy for institutions, companies and professionals working in the field of ageing.

Given the work contexts identified above, it is imperative that gerontologists update their knowledge and this can be done through micro-credentials.

Proposal for micro-credentials in the scientific field of Gerontology

Based on the AGHE document (2020) and the UN Decade of Healthy Ageing: Plan of Action 2021-2030, this proposal for nine micro-credentials is timely, as it meets the need for continuous professional development and training in the face of the challenges of the ageing process.

Need for Continuing Professional Development

Micro-credentials offer a path to continuous professional development in gerontology by enabling the acquisition of specific, emerging and highly relevant competences. With short, objective courses, students and professionals can learn about new technologies applied to the care of the elderly, such as telemedicine tools and remote monitoring devices, as well as innovative approaches that promote the independence and well-being of older people. As micro-credentials proliferate, the challenge for students/professionals looking to improve their skills is to figure out which micro-credential option will help them achieve their goals (Pickard, 2018, 18 July). Micro-credentials enable professionals to incorporate new knowledge and techniques into their repertoires, improving the quality of care and the effectiveness of gerontological interventions.

Training for the Challenges of the Ageing Process

The importance of training professionals to deal with the specific challenges of the ageing process cannot be underestimated. Issues such as mental health, physiotherapy, nutrition and public policies aimed at the elderly require in-depth understanding and specialised approaches. Micro-credentials in gerontology can focus on these critical areas by offering specialised training and equipping professionals with the skills needed to tackle these challenges effectively.

For example, micro-credential courses in geriatric mental health can address strategies for intervening in depression, anxiety and dementia in the elderly, while those focused on physiotherapy can teach advanced techniques for improving mobility and reducing pain. Similarly, micro-credentials in gerontological nutrition can update professionals on the specific nutritional needs of the elderly, and programmes focused on public policy can prepare professionals to advocate for more effective support systems for this population.

Implementation in Higher Education Institutions

According to the Council Recommendation on a European approach to micro-credentials for lifelong learning and employability (2022), micro-credentials will enable individuals to acquire, update and improve the knowledge, skills and competences they need to thrive in an evolving labour market and society and to be better prepared to deal with current and future challenges. Micro-credentials can be used to complement and improve education, training, lifelong learning and employability ecosystems.

The integration of micro-credentials in gerontology into the curricula of higher education institutions reflects an innovative approach to the teaching-learning process. Short courses, often completed in a few weeks, intensive workshops and online seminars provide an opportunity for students and professionals to update their competences or acquire specific new skills quickly. This type of education is particularly valuable in a field like gerontology, which covers a wide range of knowledge, from biological aspects of ageing to psychosocial issues and public policies aimed at the general well-being of older people.

We must also highlight the collaboration for the programme design, the effectiveness of which is significantly enhanced through collaboration between higher education institutions and a variety of strategic partners. Healthcare organisations, long-term care institutions and government bodies are teaming up with universities to develop micro-credential programmes that not only meet the educational needs of healthcare professionals, but also reflect the real needs of the aged care sector. This multidisciplinary partnership ensures that the content of the courses is not only theoretically sound, but also immediately applicable in the real context, thus maximising the impact of these programmes on improving the quality of care for the elderly.

This collaboration transcends content creation, extending to offering internships, field projects and research opportunities that enrich the educational experience. Long-term care facilities, for example, can serve as sites for the practical application of acquired knowledge, while healthcare organisations can share insights into emerging trends in the treatment and care of the elderly. Government bodies, meanwhile, play a crucial role in providing guidelines on public policy and identifying priority areas for professional development in gerontology.

Consequentially the introduction of micro-credentials in the gerontology curricula represents a significant evolution in higher education, bringing it more into line with contemporary needs for continuous learning and professional development. This link between higher education institutions and the various stakeholders in the health and elderly care sector not only enriches the content and relevance of micro-credential programmes, but also strengthens the aged care ecosystem, ensuring that professionals are adequately prepared to face the challenges of an ageing society.

Within this framework, we propose the following micro-credentials, each focused on the Sustainable Development Goals (SDGs) and their implications for healthy ageing and on the AGHE (2020) competences recommended for gerontological practice with their respective programme contents.

Delving into the micro-credentials in Context

These micro-credentials are intended to fulfil the document drawn up by the Council of Europe (2022), which in its paragraph d) admits the use of micro-credentials that can be integrated into curricula, or complement them when relevant.

(1) **Frameworks for understanding human aging:**

Healthy ageing means that older people contribute to society for longer, with opportunities for good health at all stages of life (SDG3).

Contents: Lifespan/Lifecourse perspectives to appreciate age over time in relation: To the human life cycle and stages of growth and development within the social context; To life transitions and adaptive resources; To the historical context of cohorts; To age, gender, race within social environments. Concepts and theories of aging from a bio-psycho-social framework. Bio-psycho-social understanding of aging to build a gerontological knowledge foundation. Gerontological frameworks in relation to aspects and problems of aging persons, their families, their environment and communities.

(2) **Biological aspects of aging. Contents:**

Normal biological aging changes from pathology including genetic factors. Cell- and organ-level systems change with age. Opportunities of reversibility and mutability in later life (e.g. frailty syndromes) and the plasticity of the human brain and body.

Common late-life syndromes and diseases and their related bio-psycho-social risk and protective factors. Implications of biomedical discoveries on individuals and society. Synthesize Biological with other gerontological ways of understanding human aging: Psychological; Sociological; Humanities.

(3) **Psychological aspects of aging. Contents:**

Human growth and development across the lifespan including late life outcomes such as life satisfaction, coping and adaptation. Normal age changes in intelligence and cognitive abilities including those that may impact late-life functioning. Signs, symptoms and impact of common cognitive and mental health problems in late life (e.g., dementia, depression, grief, anxiety). Older persons' potential for wisdom, creativity, life satisfaction, resilience, generativity, vital involvement and meaningful engagement. Synthesize psychological with other gerontological ways of understanding human aging: Biological; Sociological; Humanities.

(4) **Social aspects of aging:**

Healthy ageing requires lifelong learning, enabling older people to do what they value, retain decision-making capacity and preserve their purpose, identity and independence. This requires education, skills training and barrier-free participation, including digital skills (SDG4)

Contents: The diversity of the older population based on: Age; Functioning, Gender; Culture; Language; Religion; Immigration status; Sexual orientation; Other variables. The impact of inequality on individual and group life opportunities throughout the lifespan/ course impacting late-life outcomes. The changing dynamics of contemporary multigenerational families and their impact on social solidarity and interdependence. The changing population profile of the state/ province, nation. Contrast aging demographics globally among developed and developing countries. Impact of the demographic elements of: fertility, mortality, and immigration. How an older population mutually influences and is impacted by policies locally and globally. Synthesize sociological and other gerontological ways of understanding human aging: Biological; Psychological; Humanities.

(5) **Research and critical thinking. Contents:**

Research methodologies, interpretations and applications used by different disciplines to study aging. Gaps in research regarding both aging-related problems and successes in order to promote continued knowledge building. Research questions to solve problems and advance positive strategies related to older adults, their social networks, intergenerational relations and aging societies. Research studies using methods and procedures that produce reliable and valid gerontological knowledge. Critical thinking to evaluate information and its source (popular media and research publications). The strengths and limitations of reliance on either qualitative or quantitative questions, tools, methods and conclusions. The use of appropriate forms of evidence-based interventions and technologies for older adults, their families and caregivers.

(6) **Ethics and professional standards:**

Changing the way we think, feel and act about age and ageing. Despite older people's many contributions to society and their wide diversity, negative attitudes towards older people are common across societies and are rarely confronted. Stereotyping (the way we think), prejudice (the way we feel) and discrimination (the way we act) based on age have particularly deleterious effects on the health and well-being of older people (SDG10).

Contents: Respect the person's autonomy and right to real and meaningful self-determination. Respect interdependence of individuals of all ages and abilities. Respect cultural values and diversity.

Protect older persons from elder abuse of all types: Utilize programs and policies that address elder mistreatment and abuse. Mandatory legal reporting. Ethical standards and professional practices in all phases of work and research with and on behalf of older persons including but not limited to the following: Informed consent; Confidentiality; Beneficence; Non-malfeasance; Honesty and Integrity

(7) **Communication with and on behalf of older persons**

Ensuring that communities promote older people's capabilities. Physical, social and economic environments, both rural and urban, are important determinants of healthy ageing, having a powerful influence on the ageing process and the opportunities that ageing offers. Environments favourable to different age groups are better places to grow up, live, work, play and age. They are created by removing physical and social barriers and by implementing policies, systems, services, products and technologies aimed at: promoting health and building and maintaining physical and mental capacity throughout the life course; and enabling people, even if they lose their capacity, to continue doing things they value (SDG11).

Contents: Establish rapport and sustain working relationships with older persons, their families and caregivers. Listen and actively engage in problem solving to develop research, programs and policies with key stakeholders including: Older persons; Their families; Caregivers; Communities; Researchers; Policymakers. Advocate for and develop effective programs to promote the well-being of older persons. Demonstrate effective means to overcome challenges to communicating effectively with persons as they age including: Sensory deficits; Disabilities; Medical conditions. Apply and teach caregivers communication techniques to research and practice for elders with dementia. Use tools and technology to improve and enhance communication with and on behalf of older persons, their families, caregivers and communities. Consider heterogeneity in addressing communication styles and promoting the preferences of older persons including: Cultural; Racial/ethnic; Cohort; SES; Health literacy; Sexual preference; Immigration status; Geographical location. Analyze how older individuals are portrayed in public media and advocate for more accurate depictions of the diverse older population using research-based publications and multi-media dissemination methods. Develop and disseminate educational materials to increase accurate information regarding older persons and older person services. Inform the public of the spectrum of aging services that provide older persons with: Preventive; Treatment; Supportive programs.

(8) **Well-being, health and mental health. Contents:**

Build relationships that are respectful, confidential and engage positive change. Screen and provide referrals to evidence-based programs and interventions: Health promotion, disease prevention, assessment and treatment programs. Counsel older persons about healthcare and social program benefits; Provide care coordination services for persons with: Complex health and mental health problems; Geriatric syndromes. Facilitate optimal person-environment interactions: Assist in change in lived environment. Assist caregivers to identify, access and utilize resources that support responsibilities and reduce caregiver burden: Assistive devices; Technology; Professional services; Support groups and programs. Facilitate end of life planning, including: Advanced care planning; Palliative Care; Hospice.

(9) **Program/service development:**

The working-age population, which includes many older people, must have job opportunities and decent working conditions. Individual income and access to financial services will contribute to access to health services and products, reducing the risk of catastrophic expenditure. A healthy labour force increases productivity and reduces unemployment. Healthy ageing should leave no-one behind, thus creating a future for people of all ages. This will require active partnerships between various sectors and stakeholders, ignoring possible traditional barriers, with investments in favourable environments for all age groups and in integrated health and social care systems (SDG8).

Contents: Work collaboratively with older persons, local government and community organizations to advocate building age-friendly communities, including: Housing; Design techniques in public space and home environments; Neighbourhood safety; Transportation; Physical and social environments that benefit older persons. Construct and evaluate programs for older persons that promote inter-generational relationships. Design and evaluate leisure and recreational activities which enhance meaning and quality of late life. Encourage older persons to actively participate in the responsibilities of citizenship including: Volunteering; Intergenerational contributions; Identification of public issues and contributions to their solutions. Counsel individuals to utilize available services that promote well-being and quality of life. Consider the role of spirituality and religious needs and preferences when: Designing, delivering or; Supporting gerontology programs and services in both secular and faith-based organizations. Develop and implement programs and services for older persons in collaboration with communities that are founded in: Research; Policies; Procedures; Management principles; Documentation and Sound fiscal practice.

These micro-credentials can be used to complement and improve education, training, lifelong learning and employability ecosystems. The gerontologist's intervention is fundamental to facing the challenges of the world of longevity effectively. Through a holistic and interdisciplinary approach, gerontologists make a significant contribution to promoting healthy and active ageing, ensuring that the increase in life expectancy is accompanied by improvements in the quality of life of older people. The implementation of integrated strategies and the use of technology are essential for adapting care to the reality of global ageing. Learning experiences leading to micro-credentials are designed to provide the learner with specific knowledge, skills and competences that respond to societal, personal, cultural or labour market needs (Council of the European Union, 2022). And also to support the exploration by higher education institutions of the role of micro-credentials in offering learning opportunities to diverse learners, namely by extending an attractive, accessible, inclusive and learner-centred offer of lifelong learning activities, including activities of the ‘European Universities’ alliances, such as Bragança Polytechnic University, which is part of the Stars EU Alliance, a consortium that brings together the Hanze University of Applied Sciences (Netherlands), the Bragança Polytechnic University (Portugal), the Bremen University of Applied Sciences (Germany), the University of La Laguna (Spain), the University of Silesia in Opava (Czech Republic), the University of the West (Sweden), the Krakow University of Technology (Poland) and the Atlantic University of Technology (Ireland).

Challenges and Strategies

The implementation of micro-credentials in gerontology, while offering numerous opportunities for the advancement of knowledge and professional practice in this field, faces a number of significant challenges. These obstacles include issues related to standardisation, recognition of credentials on the market and ensuring quality education. Each of these elements plays a crucial role in the success and effectiveness of micro-credentials as professional development tools in gerontology.

Standardisation

One of the main challenges is the lack of standardisation in micro-credentials. Due to the emerging nature of this type of training, there is not yet a universal set of criteria or standards that defines what constitutes a micro-credential in gerontology. This can lead to great variability in the quality, content and learning outcomes of these courses. Without adequate standardisation, it becomes difficult for employers, professionals and educational institutions to assess the value and relevance of the micro-credentials acquired.

Recognition

Recognition of micro-credentials by employers and the health sector is another significant challenge. Even if a professional acquires valuable knowledge and skills through a micro-credential, if employers or regulatory bodies do not recognise these credentials as valid or useful, the potential impact on the individual's career development and on improving the quality of care provided to older people may be minimised. This recognition is crucial to ensure that micro-credentials in gerontology can translate into tangible improvements for both professionals and care recipients.

Quality Assurance

Ensuring quality education in micro-credential programmes represents another challenge. With the expansion of these programmes, ensuring that high educational standards are maintained is essential if micro-credentials are to be more than just meaningless certificates. This involves not only creating up-to-date and relevant content, but also implementing effective pedagogical methods and rigorously evaluating learning outcomes. Without this quality assurance, micro-credentials risk being viewed as inferior or less valuable than traditional qualifications.

Collaborative Networks of Higher Education Institutions in Consortium with Employers

To overcome these challenges, close collaboration between educational institutions, professional organisations, employers and regulators is essential. Developing sectoral or national standards for micro-credentials in gerontology can help establish a common basis for creating, evaluating and recognising these credentials. In addition, various awareness campaigns and education initiatives can promote the value of micro-credentials among employers and professionals, ensuring that these new forms of credentials are properly valued and recognised as a legitimate part of education and professional development in gerontology.

By addressing these challenges, the field of gerontology can maximise the potential of micro-credentials to foster a highly skilled workforce prepared to meet the complex needs of an ageing population.

To overcome the challenges associated with implementing micro-credentials in gerontology, it is crucial to establish effective strategies that guarantee the standardisation, recognition and quality of these educational programmes. The adoption of national and international accreditation standards, along with the active involvement of gerontology professionals in the design and evaluation of courses, are fundamental steps towards achieving these goals. We have outlined some strategies, which are in line with the European principles for designing and issuing micro-credentials set out in the Council recommendation on a European approach to micro-credentials for lifelong learning and employability (2022). These principles (Quality; Transparency; Relevance; Valid assessment; Learning process; Recognition; Validation and Authenticity; Updating and Follow-up; Portability and Accessibility) highlight the key features of the European approach to micro-credentials that can enable the trust and quality of micro-credentials. The principles are universal and can be applied to any area or sector, if appropriate.

Adoption of National and International Accreditation Standards

An effective approach to meeting the challenge of standardisation is the adoption of national and international accreditation standards for micro-credentials. This involves developing a clear and consistent set of criteria that all micro-credentials in Gerontology must meet in order to be officially recognised. These standards can cover aspects such as content relevance, teaching methods and student assessment. By aligning micro-credential programmes with these standards, educational institutions can ensure a consistent quality basis, facilitating the recognition of credentials by employers and society in general.

Involvement of Gerontology Professionals

Another crucial aspect of overcoming the challenges in implementing micro-credentials is the direct involvement of experienced gerontology professionals in the design and evaluation of courses. They can help identify key competences that are most valuable for today's labour market, as well as contributing insights to the creation of educational content that reflects the latest and most effective practices in elderly care.

Partnerships with Regulatory Bodies and Professional Associations

Establishing partnerships among educational institutions, regulatory bodies and professional associations in gerontology can facilitate the adoption of accreditation standards and the recognition of micro-credentials. These organisations can offer valuable insight into the needs of the sector and help define the quality and competence criteria that courses must meet. In addition, they can act as intermediaries to promote the recognition of micro-credentials in the labour market, ensuring that the professionals who obtain them are properly valued.

Development of Verification Platforms and Digital Portfolios

To make it easier for employers to recognise micro-credentials, investment can be made in the development of verification platforms and digital portfolios where professionals can present their credentials in a transparent and verifiable way. These digital tools allow employers to easily verify the authenticity and relevance of the micro-credentials acquired by candidates, increasing confidence in the value of these trainings.

Drawing to an end we must state that overcoming the challenges associated with implementing micro-credentials in Gerontology requires a multi-faceted approach involving the standardisation of quality criteria, the active involvement of professionals in the field and collaboration between educational institutions, regulatory bodies and professional associations. By adopting these strategies, it will be possible to ensure that micro-credentials in Gerontology offer relevant, recognised and high-quality training, making a significant contribution to continuing professional development and improving care for the older population.

DISCUSSION

Micro-credentials allow for a targeted acquisition of skills and competences while not replacing traditional qualifications. In 2019, the EU surpassed the 40% tertiary education attainment target in most EU countries (at least for women, but not for men). However, the knowledge and competences acquired through formal education and training must be adapted to a fast-changing society. High quality, innovative and learner-centred education and training would be further enhanced with the flexibility that micro-credentials can offer. Continuous learning recognised through micro-credentials can fill existing and emerging skills gaps. Hanne Shapiro Futures, Andersen, T., & Nedergaard Larsen, K. (2020). The growth of online education has spawned a variety of new "micro-credentials" – short-form, sub-degree awards that represent the completion of a learning module, course, or series of courses. Micro-credentials include both generic offerings such as digital badges as well as proprietary credential constructs such as "nanodegrees" or "MicroMasters." Given the trend in postsecondary education toward more targeted, affordable, and work-aligned offerings, great excitement has developed as millions of students and professionals have earned these non-degree credentials in just the last few years. Yet until now, little has been documented about HR leaders' experiences with and perceptions of micro-credentials in hiring. Gallagher, S. R. (2018). The World Health Organization (2018) states that: "The Decade of Action on *Healthy Ageing* should contribute to increasing healthy life expectancy. While men and women are living longer (increased life expectancy), the extra years are not necessarily healthy (i.e. healthy life expectancy). The next Decade should also contribute to reducing the inequities in both life expectancy and healthy life expectancy within and between cities and communities. The next decade should see cities and communities making measure- able changes in building and maintaining older people's functional ability. This has important implications for whether they can keep working, whether they are able to look after themselves or will need (and get) social care, or whether they can spend time with friends and family and maintain social relationships.

The next decade will see all countries developing age-friendly programmes. Cities and communities – because these are where people live, work, play and grow older – can control those factors that influence a person's functional ability. Creating age-friendly cities and communities can go a long way in creating environments that both promote health and build and maintain physical and mental capacity across the life-course; and enable people, even when experiencing capacity loss, to continue to do the things they value."

On the other hand, Sadeq and Stanback (2021) argue that micro-credentialing can offer value for employees unable or unwilling to pursue formal academic training but should be differentiated from such training. Moving forward, it is critical to ensure alignment between gerontological micro-credentials and established gerontological competencies and standards and to differentiate micro-credentials from formal academic programs. Futures, Andersen & Nedergaard Larsen (2020) add that in 2030, European citizens will be able to start their learning pathways into and through higher education at any stage in their lifetime. On top of the qualifications already achieved, micro-credentials will provide learners with rich opportunities to diversify their learning and improve their education by taking shorter courses. These micro-credentials can be linked thematically and be based on the expertise gained. Through this, micro-credentials will play a major role in encouraging and realising lifelong learning and a society of learning, which – through critical reflection of societal and business processes – will create better lives and better opportunities for all.

CONCLUSION

Population ageing will continue to affect all aspects of society, including the labour and financial markets, the demand for goods and services such as education, housing, health, long-term care, social protection, transport, information and communication, and family structures and intergenerational ties.

However, healthy ageing can be a reality for everyone. It will require a shift in focus from the paradigm of healthy ageing as the absence of disease to the paradigm of promoting functional ability that allows older people to be and do what they value. Actions will be needed to improve healthy ageing at multiple levels and in multiple sectors, in order to prevent illness, promote health, maintain intrinsic capacity and enable functional ability.

The Decade of Healthy Ageing 2021-2030 document, launched by the WHO in collaboration with international partners, sets out a global action plan to improve the lives of older people, their families and the communities in which they live. This plan recognises the need for policies, services and research focused on maximising the functionality and well-being of older people.

One of the focuses of the Decade of Healthy Ageing is to promote health and well-being among older people, with an emphasis on disease prevention. Micro-credentials in areas such as geriatric nutrition, physical exercise for the elderly, and chronic disease management are directly relevant, enabling professionals to implement effective prevention and health maintenance programmes. The plan emphasises the importance of continuing education for professionals who care for the elderly. Microcredentials are an ideal tool for this, as they offer flexible and focused learning opportunities that can be continually updated to reflect the latest evidence-based practices. Microcredentials in gerontology are aligned with the objectives of the Decade of Healthy Ageing 2021-2030, providing an educational methodology that supports the professional development needed to meet the challenges of a rapidly ageing global population.

Micro-credentials are beneficial as standalone certifications, to complement or supplement degree programs for greater employability, and to improve the level of lifelong learning. Beyond this emerging consensus, challenges still exist in terms of scaling up the use of micro-credentials.

REFERENCES

Adachi, C., Savage, J., & O'Donnell, M. (2017). Facilitating social learning through learning design – a perspective of collaborative academic development. In Partridge, H., Davis, K., & Thomas, J.. (Eds.), Me, *Us, IT! ProceedingsASCILITE2017: 34th International Conference on Innovation, Practice and Research in the Use of Educational Technologies in Tertiary Education* (pp. 7-11). DOI: 10.14742/apubs.2017.731

Council of the European Union. (2022). Council Recommendation on a European approach to micro-credentials for lifelong learning and employability. Official Journal of the European Union. C243:02. https://eur-lex.europa.eu/legal-content/EN/TXT/PDF/?uri=CELEX:32022H0627(02)

Damron-Rodriguez, J., Frank, J. C., Abushakrah, J., Jukema, J., Maiden, R. J., Mcdonnell, A. E., Pianosi, B., Sterns, H., & Van Dussen, D. (2020). *Gerontology competencies in higher education.* The Gerontological Society of America. www .geron.org

European Commission. (2020). A European approach to micro-credentials - output of the micro- credentials higher education consultation group - final report. *European Union*. Retrieved July 23, 2021, from

Gallagher, S. R. (2018). *Educational Credentials Come of Age: A Survey on the Use and Value of Educational Credentials in Hiring*. Center for the Future of Higher Education & Talent Strategy.

Hanne Shapiro Futures. Andersen, T., & Nedergaard Larsen, K. (2020). *[Title of the report, if available]* (Contract No. 1000245). Danish Technological Institute. Publications Office of the European Union. https://doi.org/DOI: 10.2766/30863

Oliver, B. (2019). *Making micro-credentials work for learners, employers, and providers.* Retrieved from https://www.researchgate.net/publication/335109512

Pickard, L. (2018, 18th July). Analysis of 450 MOOC-Based Microcredentials Reveals any Options But Little Consistency. Class Central.

Portugal. (2021). Decree Law 27/2021, of 16th April. *Diário da República,* n.º 74/2021, Série I. https://dre.pt/web/guest/pesquisa/-/search/161894401/details/normal?l=1 Parte superior do formulário

Sadeq, N., & Stanback, B. (2021, December 17). Adapting the Environmental Scan for Gerontology Graduate Students' Career Exploration. *Innovation in Aging*, 5(Suppl 1), 757. DOI: 10.1093/geroni/igab046.2806

The Global Network for Age-friendly Cities and Communities. looking back over the last decade, looking forward to the next. Geneva, Switzerland: World Health Organization; 2018 (WHO/FWC/ALC/18.4). Licence: CC BY-NC-SA 3.0 IGO.

WHO. (2021). *UN Decade of Healthy Ageing: plan of action 2021-2030.* Retrieved from https://cdn.who.int/media/docs/default-source/decade-of-healthy-ageing/decade-proposal-final-apr2020-en.pdf

Chapter 17
Applications of Artificial Intelligence Techniques in Education

M. Soundarya
https://orcid.org/0000-0001-7018-7972
Sathyabama Institute of Science and Technology, India

Joel Jebadurai Devapitchai
https://orcid.org/0000-0002-6947-8497
St. Joseph's College of Engineering, India

S. Krishnakumari
Sathyabama Institute of Science and Technology, India

Thirupathi Manickam
https://orcid.org/0000-0001-7976-6073
Christ University, India

ABSTRACT

In the rapidly evolving landscape of education, the integration of Artificial Intelligence (AI) has emerged as a transformative force, promising to revolutionize the way to teaching and learning. This book chapter presented the applications of AI tools in online education in these online learning environments, the interaction between learners and instructors significantly influences satisfaction and learning outcomes. Therefore, understanding how AI impacts this interaction is crucial for identifying potential challenges and ensuring safe and effective learning environments. Also, this book chapter presented the case studies, success stories, and benefits of AI applications in online education. This chapter will be useful for educational institutions to improve their efficiency with their stakeholders and learners.

DOI: 10.4018/979-8-3693-5488-9.ch017

INTRODUCTION

Artificial intelligence (AI) has become essential in modern society, providing enhanced efficiency and convenience across multiple industries. Its influence in educational institutions is also widespread, revolutionizing various aspects of education. AI-based education replaces traditional methods, bringing about significant transformations in the educational sectors. Additionally, stakeholders in educational systems are highly involved with AI-enabled educational platforms. The integration of AI in education offers promising opportunities alongside genuine concerns regarding its successful deployment. The potential uses of AI in online learning and teaching are vast, encompassing personalized student learning, automated instructor responsibilities, and AI-driven assessments. (Abulibdeh et.al. 2024). For instance, AI tutoring systems can offer tailored guidance and feedback based on individual learning patterns, while AI teaching assistants streamline instructors' workload by handling routine queries in online forums. Additionally, AI analytics empower instructors to gain insights into students' performance and progress through data analysis (Corba & Bennasar 2024). The internet has become integral to the educational landscape, enabling learning anytime and anywhere.

Enhancing student learning outcomes and satisfaction remains a primary goal of educational systems. To tailor teaching methods to individual student needs and preferences, accurate evaluations of their competencies are essential. However, in traditional classroom settings, limitations such as class size and the teacher's ability to accurately evaluate each student's characteristics hinder optimal education for all simultaneously (Domínguez et.al. 2024). Adaptive educational systems, which monitor learner characteristics and adjust instruction accordingly, are gaining prominence for their ability to provide tailored content and analysis. These systems actively adapt to individual student requirements, offering personalized support and enhancing the learning process.

There are five sections to this chapter. The goals and methodology are covered in the first section. The second section explores AI strategies used in corporate investment planning. The application of AI approaches to various functional areas of online education and courses.

This chapter comes out with the following objectives. They are,

1. The first objective of this study is to understand AI tools in online education. These tools can include Natural language processing (NLP); AI-powered grading systems, virtual reality, augmented reality, and chatbots.

2. The second objective covers the AI application in various functional areas of online education such as personalized learning, task automation, smart content creation, adaptable access; identifying classroom weaknesses, and AI examinations.
3. Benefits, challenges, case studies, and success stories of AI in online education are presented in the third objective.

METHODOLOGY

This book is purely based on secondary data from published articles, case studies, government reports, etc. Secondary data was covered with a focus on AI techniques such as adaptive learning platforms, intelligent tutoring systems, virtual classroom platforms, Chabot, and automated grading systems. Also, AI applied functional areas such as professional learning, task automation, smart content creation, adaptive access, and AI examinations. Finally, the benefits and challenges of AI in online education are presented in addition to the success story.

ARTIFICIAL INTELLIGENCE DECISION-MAKING TOOLS IN EDUCATION

Natural Language Processing (Nlp)

Natural Language Processing (NLP) is a Machine Learning technology that enables computers to understand, interpret, and manipulate human language. With vast amounts of voice and text data generated through communication channels like emails, text messages, social media, video, and audio, organizations utilize NLP software to process and analyze this information automatically. NLP helps identify the intent or sentiment behind messages, allowing for real-time responses to human communication (Devapitchai et.al. 2024). By effectively managing variations in dialects, slang, and grammatical inconsistencies found in everyday conversations, NLP plays a crucial role in the comprehensive and efficient analysis of both text and speech data.

Businesses employ NLP for various automated functions, including: (Wardat et.al. 2024)

- Processing, analyzing, and storing extensive documents
- Evaluating customer feedback or recordings from call centers
- Operating Chabot's for automated customer service

- Addressing inquiries involving who, what, when, and where
- Sorting and extracting textual content

AI-POWERED GRADING SOFTWARE

AI-powered grading software has revolutionized the way assessments are evaluated, blending machine learning algorithms with inputs from educators to streamline the grading process. These advanced tools are designed to understand and replicate human grading methods, which significantly reduces the time and effort required from teachers while maintaining consistent and reliable results. The emergence of AI in grading introduces a new approach to evaluating exams, one that addresses many of the inefficiencies associated with traditional grading methods. By automating this process, AI eliminates human biases, ensures accuracy, and speeds up the overall evaluation, allowing educators to focus more on personalized instruction and student engagement. As highlighted by Ocumpaugh et al. (2024), AI technology forms the foundation of these automated systems, driving a shift in educational assessment that promises to reshape the learning environment by offering a more efficient, fair, and scalable solution for grading.

Pattern Recognition

AI-driven systems are particularly adept at identifying patterns in students' responses, making them valuable tools for educators looking to enhance learning outcomes. By analyzing large volumes of student data, these systems can pinpoint specific areas where students struggle, such as recurring mistakes, misunderstandings of core concepts, or gaps in knowledge. This detailed insight enables educators to tailor their teaching methods to address these challenges more effectively. For example, if a significant number of students consistently make similar errors on a particular topic, teachers can adjust their instructional strategies, provide targeted feedback, or introduce additional resources to reinforce understanding (Devapitchai et.al 2024). In this way, AI systems not only streamline assessment but also empower educators with actionable insights, allowing them to proactively intervene and support student progress in a more personalized and efficient manner.

Adaptive Learning

AI-powered grading systems continuously evolve and enhance their effectiveness through adaptive learning mechanisms. These advanced technologies analyze extensive amounts of student data, including responses, performance metrics, and learning behaviors, to identify specific areas where students may struggle. By recognizing patterns and trends in this data, AI systems can offer targeted, personalized feedback and recommendations that address each learner's unique needs. This adaptability allows the grading system to tailor its assessments and feedback to help students improve in areas where they face challenges, fostering a more individualized learning experience (Raja et.al. 2024). As these AI systems learn from ongoing interactions and outcomes, they become increasingly proficient at delivering accurate, relevant, and actionable insights, ultimately supporting more effective teaching strategies and better learning outcomes.

Feedback Generation

AI algorithms play a crucial role in streamlining the feedback process for students by generating detailed and customized responses based on individual performance. These algorithms analyze students' answers, identify patterns, and assess areas of strength and weakness, producing nuanced feedback that addresses specific needs and suggests targeted improvements. This level of detailed analysis not only provides students with actionable insights to enhance their learning but also significantly reduces the time educators spend on grading and feedback. By automating the feedback generation process, AI frees up educators to focus more on personalized instruction and engagement, while ensuring that each student receives timely and relevant guidance. This efficiency not only improves the overall educational experience but also supports a more effective and responsive teaching environment.

VIRTUAL REALITY (VR)

Virtual reality (VR) has emerged as a transformative force in education, reshaping traditional teaching and learning methods by immersing students in dynamic, simulated environments. This cutting-edge technology offers an interactive learning experience, engaging students in ways that conventional methods cannot. Unlike typical computer interfaces that rely on screens, keyboards, or mice, VR places users directly inside a three-dimensional virtual world, allowing them to explore and interact with digital objects as if they were real (Arora 2024). Central to VR technology are specialized headsets equipped with high-resolution displays and motion-tracking sensors that monitor the user's head movements, adjusting the virtual scene to create a powerful sense of immersion. This real-time responsiveness gives students the feeling of "presence" within the virtual environment, enhancing their engagement and making the learning process more active. Beyond visual immersion, VR systems often integrate audio and haptic feedback, enabling users to hear sounds and physically interact with virtual objects, further amplifying the sense of realism. This immersive, hands-on learning experience has the potential to revolutionize education by allowing students to engage with complex concepts more tangibly and experientially.

An essential advantage of VR in education lies in its capacity to enrich experiential learning. Through VR simulations, students can delve into virtual realms, conduct experiments, and engage with intricate concepts firsthand (Lampropoulos & Kinshuk. 2024). This immersive approach nurtures a deeper grasp and lasting memory of subject matter spanning diverse disciplines, including science, mathematics, history, and literature. VR can cater to diverse learning styles and preferences, offering personalized learning experiences tailored to individual needs. Whether through interactive simulations, virtual field trips, or immersive storytelling, VR allows educators to cater to different learning modalities and adapt instruction to suit each student's unique learning pace and preferences. Kapoor & Kalia 2024 have explained that VR simulates real-world scenarios and provides interactive, three-dimensional environments, VR technology offers students the opportunity to engage with educational content in innovative and impactful ways, it provides,

a. **Immersive learning environment**

Virtual reality (VR) in education creates immersive learning environments that offer students a hands-on, experiential approach to understanding complex topics. By simulating real-world scenarios or abstract concepts, VR allows learners to engage deeply with the material in a way that traditional methods cannot. Students can explore historical events, conduct scientific experiments, or practice real-world skills, all within a controlled virtual space. The immersive nature of VR enhances engagement and retention, as students are not just passive observers but active participants in their learning journey. This technology promotes interactive, personalized education, making difficult concepts easier to grasp by allowing students to visualize and manipulate them in three-dimensional, lifelike environments. As a result, VR is transforming the educational landscape, fostering deeper understanding and sparking curiosity in learners.

b. **Enhanced engagement and motivation**

Virtual reality (VR) significantly enhances engagement and motivation in education by offering an immersive and interactive learning experience. Unlike traditional teaching methods, VR creates a captivating environment where students can actively participate in their learning journey. This immersive experience captures students' attention more effectively, making lessons more engaging and memorable.

The novelty and excitement of VR can also boost motivation, as students are more inclined to participate and explore when they are fully immersed in a dynamic, virtual world. By allowing learners to interact with and manipulate 3D objects, simulate real-world scenarios, and experience complex concepts firsthand, VR not only makes learning more enjoyable but also increases students' enthusiasm and commitment to their educational pursuits.

c. **Multi-sensory learning**

Virtual reality (VR) in education facilitates multi-sensory learning by engaging multiple senses simultaneously—sight, sound, and touch—thereby enhancing the overall learning experience. VR environments are designed to provide rich, interactive simulations where students can see, hear, and sometimes even feel virtual objects. For example, students can explore historical sites, conduct scientific experiments, or solve complex problems in a visually engaging 3D space. Audio cues and haptic feedback further immerse learners, making the educational content more accessible and impactful. This multi-sensory approach helps cater to different learning styles and reinforces understanding by providing diverse, sensory-rich experiences. By engaging multiple senses, VR not only makes learning more interactive and enjoyable but also improves retention and comprehension of the material.

d. **Experiential and authentic learning**

Virtual reality (VR) in education fosters experiential and authentic learning by immersing students in realistic simulations that mirror real-world scenarios. This hands-on approach allows learners to engage with content in a practical, interactive manner, providing experiences that closely resemble actual situations they might encounter outside the classroom. For instance, VR can transport students to historical events, enable them to practice complex surgical procedures or allow them to navigate intricate machinery—all within a controlled, virtual environment. These immersive experiences offer students a deeper understanding of concepts by allowing them to apply their knowledge in context, explore consequences, and solve problems as they would in real life. By bridging the gap between theoretical knowledge and practical application, VR not only enhances learning but also prepares students for real-world challenges, making education more relevant and impactful.

AUGMENTED REALITY (AR)

Augmented reality (AR) in online education refers to the integration of digital content and virtual objects into the real-world environment, thereby enhancing the learning experience through interactive and immersive elements. Unlike virtual reality, which creates entirely virtual environments, AR overlays digital information onto the physical world, allowing users to interact with both real and virtual elements simultaneously (Li et.al. 2024). AR enables educators to augment traditional learning materials, such as textbooks, worksheets, or presentations, with interactive digital content, such as 3D models, animations, videos, or simulations. This enhanced learning experience engages students' senses and promotes active participation, making abstract concepts more tangible and understandable. It allows students to visualize complex concepts and phenomena dynamically and interactively. For example, students studying anatomy can use AR apps to explore 3D models of the human body and its internal organs, rotate them, zoom in for detailed views, and interact with interactive labels or annotations to deepen their understanding of anatomical structures and functions.

Augmented Reality (AR) is revolutionizing the way we interact with mobile applications and visual graphic interfaces by overlaying computer-generated imagery onto real-world environments. This technology enables users to point their mobile cameras at physical spaces and see digital objects seamlessly integrated into their view of the real world (Yokutkhon 2024). Unlike virtual reality, which immerses users in a fully simulated environment, AR enriches the existing physical world with digital enhancements, blending virtual elements with real-world contexts. This creates a unique and highly interactive learning environment, where students can engage with educational content in a more dynamic and immersive way. For example, AR can project interactive 3D models of historical artifacts, biological structures, or geometric shapes into a classroom setting, allowing students to explore and manipulate these elements as if they were physically present. By combining approximately 25% of digital content with 75% of the real environment, AR maintains the integrity of the physical world while adding layers of virtual information, offering a balanced and enhanced learning experience that bridges the gap between physical and digital realms.

CHATBOT

Chatbots are computer programs that are designed to simulate human conversation, either through text or speech. They use artificial intelligence (AI) and natural language processing (NLP) technologies to understand user inputs and provide relevant responses They rely on NLP algorithms to understand and interpret human language. These algorithms analyze user inputs, identify keywords and phrases, and extract meaning to determine the user's intent or query (Ait Baha et.al 2024). Once the user's intent is identified, the Chabot generates a response based on predefined rules or machine learning algorithms. Responses can range from simple text messages to more complex actions, such as retrieving information from databases or external sources. Chatbots engage users in conversational interactions, mimicking the experience of chatting with a human (Jebadurai et.al. 2024) They can ask questions to gather more information, provide recommendations, offer assistance, or execute tasks on behalf of the user, Advanced Chabot can personalize interactions based on user preferences, history, and context. They may remember past interactions, adapt responses to individual users, and provide tailored recommendations or suggestions. It can integrate with external systems, databases, and APIs to access and retrieve information or perform specific tasks (Korda et.al. 2021). The development of chatbots has been driven by advances in artificial intelligence (AI) and natural language processing technologies. Modern chatbots are capable of understanding a wide range of user queries. It solves from simple requests for information to more complex interactions involving context and personalization. Lin & Yu, 2024 has mentioned that there are two main types of chatbots in education;

Rule-based Chatbots

These chatbots operate based on predefined rules and patterns. They follow a set of programmed instructions to interpret user inputs and generate responses. Rule-based chatbots are typically limited in their capabilities and may struggle to handle complex or ambiguous queries.

AI-powered Chatbots

These chatbots leverage machine learning algorithms continuously improving the learner's performance over time. They learn from user interactions and data to enhance the understanding of natural language and provide more accurate and personalized responses. AI-powered chatbots are capable of handling a wide range of queries and adapting to new contexts and scenarios.

Table 1. Types of chatbots

Sl.No	Types of chatbots	Applications	Uses
1	Voice bots	Voice bots, also known as voice assistants or conversational agents, have a wide range of applications across various industries. voice bots have the potential to streamline processes, improve efficiency, enhance user experiences, and provide new opportunities for automation across a wide range of industries.	a. Voice bots save time by responding quickly b. It will be available 24/7, ensuring users have access to information at any time.
2	Hybrid bots	Hybrid Chabot combines rule-based and AI-driven approaches and offers a more sophisticated and versatile user experience. it offers a powerful combination of automation and intelligence, enabling organizations to provide efficient and personalized experiences across various applications and industries.	a. Accessibility in the workplace. b. Increase sales. c. Suggest personalized opinions based on their purchase history.
3	Social Messaging Chatbots	Social messaging Chabot, which operates within messaging platforms such as Facebook Messenger, WhatsApp, and Slack, offers a convenient and accessible way for businesses to interact with customers. they engage with customers, streamline processes, and deliver personalized experiences.	a. Customer service can be done efficiently. b. Users can make bookings, place orders, and receive confirmations without leaving the chat interface, improving convenience and reducing friction in the transaction process.
4	Support Chatbots	Users can make bookings, place orders, and receive confirmations without leaving the chat interface, improving convenience and reducing friction in the transaction process. Users can make bookings, place orders, and receive confirmations without leaving the chat interface, improving convenience and reducing friction in the transaction process	a. Training and onboarding assistance. b. Product recommendation and guidance. c. Order tracking and status updates.

AI APPLICATION AREAS IN ONLINE EDUCATION

Personalised Learning

AI in education has revolutionized the way students engage with their curriculum by personalizing learning experiences to fit individual needs and preferences. Through advanced educational software, AI provides tailored learning paths that support each student's unique learning style, making the study process more efficient and effective (Ayeni 2024). Machine learning algorithms integrated into educational systems adapt to how students perceive and interact with lessons, significantly reducing the cognitive load and making learning more intuitive. The integration of AI and education is evident in features such as AI-powered games, customized learning programs, and other interactive tools that address specific student needs. These technologies facilitate instant query resolution, enabling students to receive immediate responses to their questions. Moreover, AI streamlines administrative tasks by automating actions such as assignment submissions, email responses, and feedback provision, allowing students and educators to focus more on meaningful learning and less on routine tasks. This fusion of AI with educational practices enhances both the learning experience and the overall efficiency of educational administration.

For instance, Platforms like Dreambox and Carnegie Learning utilize AI to offer customized math classes based on a student's proficiency, ensuring they grasp concepts thoroughly before advancing.

TASK AUTOMATION

In both virtual and in-person classrooms, AI technology has transformed educational environments by automating a wide range of value-added tasks beyond just personalizing instruction. AI software systems are capable of managing and executing various administrative functions with remarkable efficiency, including grading exams, verifying assignments, setting up research papers, and tracking student progress through reports. Additionally, AI can assist in creating presentations and notes, streamlining the preparation process for both students and educators. By automating these routine and time-consuming tasks, AI not only alleviates the administrative burden on teachers but also enhances the overall productivity of the learning environment. This automation allows educators to focus more on delivering high-quality instruction and engaging with students, while ensuring that administrative tasks are handled swiftly and accurately. Consequently, the integration of AI in education significantly improves operational efficiency, contributing to a more effective and streamlined educational experience. (Lima 2024). A practical example of this technology is Google's Smart Reply, which leverages machine learning algorithms to streamline email communication. This feature intelligently analyzes the content of incoming emails and generates suitable response suggestions, allowing users to quickly reply without having to type out full responses on their mobile devices. This convenience not only saves time but also enhances the efficiency of email correspondence.

An AI-driven system designed for English language learning excels at identifying students who are struggling with various aspects of the language, such as listening, speaking, reading, or writing. By analyzing performance data and recognizing patterns in student responses, the system tailors personalized exercises to address each learner's specific challenges. For instance, if a student struggles with pronunciation, the AI might generate targeted speaking drills; if difficulties are observed in reading comprehension, the system could provide customized reading passages and questions. Upon completion of these exercises, the AI promptly delivers detailed feedback, highlighting areas for improvement and offering suggestions for further practice. This immediate, personalized feedback helps students understand their mistakes and refine their skills more effectively, making the learning process more responsive and tailored to individual needs.

SMART CONTENT CREATION

Artificial intelligence (AI) and machine learning techniques are increasingly aiding teachers and researchers in the creation of smart content, which facilitates more effective teaching and learning. These advanced technologies enable the development of adaptive educational materials that are tailored to the needs of different learners. For instance, AI can analyze student performance data to generate personalized content that targets specific areas of difficulty or interest. Machine learning algorithms can also assist in curating and organizing educational resources, ensuring that the content is both relevant and engaging. Additionally, AI-powered tools can help educators by automating routine tasks such as grading and feedback, freeing up time for more interactive and personalized instruction. By leveraging AI and machine learning, teachers and researchers can generate innovative and high-quality educational materials, making the process of acquiring new knowledge more accessible and efficient for students. (Goel et.al 2024). Here are some examples of AI-powered content creation:

Visualisation of data

Traditional instructional methods, with the notable exception of lab experiments, frequently fall short in incorporating visual elements, which can limit students' understanding of complex concepts. AI-generated materials address this gap by enhancing the practical relevance of visualized online communication within educational settings (Vijayalakshmi et al. 2024). This technology enables the creation of dynamic 2D and 3D visualizations that bring abstract data and concepts to life, allowing students to interact with and explore information from multiple perspectives. By transforming static text and diagrams into immersive visual experiences, AI facilitates a deeper comprehension of subject matter, making it easier for students to grasp intricate details and relationships. This approach not only enriches the learning process but also supports diverse learning styles, ensuring that students can engage with content in a more meaningful and effective way.

Creating Digital Lessons

AI education can facilitate bit-size education by utilizing low-storage study materials and other digital lessons. In this way, students and professionals can use the entire content for research while taking up much computer space (Adel 2024). Furthermore, these materials will be accessible from any mobile device, removing the need for distance learning.

AI IN EXAMINATION

Artificial intelligence software has become a powerful tool for maintaining the integrity of online exams and interviews by actively detecting and reporting suspicious behavior. These AI systems utilize web cameras, microphones, and internet browsers to continuously monitor individuals during assessments. Through advanced keystroke analysis and real-time surveillance of webcam and microphone feeds, the software can identify irregular activities, such as the presence of unauthorized materials or additional individuals in the examination room (Mao et al. 2024). When such anomalies are detected, the AI promptly alerts the exam administrator, enabling immediate intervention to address any issues. This proactive approach helps ensure that the examination process remains secure and fair, making AI-driven monitoring one of the most effective solutions for online evaluations.

BENEFITS OF AI IN ONLINE EDUCATION

Automation of Routine Tasks

AI can automate administrative tasks such as grading assignments, managing course materials, and scheduling assessments. This frees up educators' time, allowing them to focus more on teaching and providing personalized support to students (Naseer et.al. 2024). The automation of routine tasks through AI in online education offers several significant benefits for educators, students, and educational institutions alike time efficiency, scalability, consistency and feedback, resource optimization, adaptability and personalization and data-driven insight are some of the positive factors.

Data-Driven Insights

AI algorithms can analyze vast amounts of educational data to provide actionable insights for educators and administrators. These insights can include trends in student performance, areas of difficulty, and effectiveness of teaching strategies, helping to inform instructional decisions and improve educational outcomes (Yuan, 2024). Data insights are found through the deep analysis of patterns and statistics within data. Through the interpretation of these patterns, organizations transform insights into forecasting customer needs, therefore promoting more effective decision-making.

Enhanced Accessibility

AI technologies, such as speech recognition and natural language processing, can improve accessibility for students with disabilities. For example, AI-powered transcription services can provide real-time captions for video lectures, making content more accessible to students with hearing impairments (Sappaile et.al. 2024). For instance, Accessibility is applied for a student who is blind or has low vision, AI can help them access information with screen readers.

24/7 Support

AI in education provides 24/7 support through virtual assistants, offering continuous assistance to students (Paul & Anuradha 2024). These AI-driven systems are capable of addressing queries, providing feedback, and offering guidance at any time, enhancing accessibility and support for learners around the clock.

CHALLENGES

Jafari & Keykha 2024 presented the following challenges of Artificial Intelligence in education. They are.

Data Privacy and Security

The collection and analysis of large amounts of student data raise concerns about privacy and security. Educational institutions must ensure that sensitive student information is protected from unauthorized access or misuse. Data privacy and security pose significant challenges in the realm of online education, where the collection and analysis of extensive student data are commonplace. Educational institutions face a complex landscape of technological, regulatory, and ethical considerations as they strive to safeguard sensitive student information.

Quality of Content and Feedback

While AI can automate certain aspects of content creation and feedback, there is a risk that the quality of generated content may not meet the standards expected in education. Educators need to ensure that AI-generated content is accurate, relevant, and engaging. Educators must navigate these challenges to ensure that AI-driven tools enhance rather than detract from the learning experience on accuracy and relevance, customization and personalization, engagement and interactivity, bias and ethical consideration, feedback quality, and timeliness are some of the major challenges.

Technical Issues and Reliability

AI-powered systems, while highly beneficial, are not without their challenges. Technical issues or malfunctions can occur, leading to potential disruptions in the learning process. For instance, system outages, software bugs, or connectivity problems may interrupt access to educational tools or interfere with real-time interactions, impacting both students and educators. Furthermore, the reliability of AI algorithms in delivering accurate assessments and feedback is an ongoing concern. These algorithms, which rely on vast amounts of data and complex computations, must be continuously monitored and refined to ensure they provide fair, precise, and contextually relevant evaluations. Regular updates and rigorous testing are essential to address any biases, inaccuracies, or limitations in the AI systems. As AI technology evolves, maintaining high standards of performance and reliability is crucial to maximizing its benefits and ensuring a smooth and effective learning experience.

Digital Divide

The digital divide highlights the significant disparities in access to technology and internet connectivity across various populations, which can impact educational opportunities. AI-powered online education initiatives, while offering innovative and personalized learning experiences, have the potential to exacerbate these existing inequalities if they are not designed with inclusivity in mind. Students from disadvantaged backgrounds may face challenges such as limited access to necessary devices, unreliable internet connections, or inadequate digital literacy skills, which can prevent them from fully participating in AI-enhanced educational programs. This gap in access can result in unequal learning opportunities, further widening the achievement gap between different socio-economic groups. To ensure that AI-driven educational tools benefit all students equitably, it is crucial to address these barriers by promoting greater access to technology, providing necessary support and training, and developing inclusive solutions that accommodate diverse needs and circumstances.

Ethical Consideration

The integration of AI in online education brings to the forefront a range of ethical concerns related to the responsible use of technology and its implications for students' autonomy, agency, and privacy (Marshall 2021). As AI systems become more prevalent in educational settings, it is crucial to address how these technologies impact students' control over their learning experiences and personal data. Ethical considerations include the potential for AI to influence or restrict students' decision-making, the need to protect sensitive information from misuse, and ensuring that AI tools do not perpetuate biases or inequalities. Establishing clear guidelines and ethical standards for AI deployment is essential to safeguard students' rights and foster a fair and transparent educational environment. These guidelines should focus on maintaining transparency about how AI systems collect and use data, ensuring data security, and providing students with the ability to make informed choices about their interactions with AI technologies. By proactively addressing these ethical issues, educational institutions can better harness the benefits of AI while mitigating potential risks and preserving the integrity of the learning experience.

Cost and Resource Constraints

Implementing AI technologies in online education requires significant investment in infrastructure, software development, and training. Educational institutions with limited resources may struggle to adopt and maintain AI systems effectively.

CASE STUDY AND SUCCESS STORIES OF AI IN EDUCATION

For instance, the iTalk2Learn system16, developed and tested by Carnegie Mellon University to evaluate its impact on young students learning fractions, utilized a learner model that incorporated details about each student's math knowledge, cognitive needs, emotional state, feedback received, and responses.

Thinkster Math is a math tutoring program that combines the expertise of human tutors with advanced artificial intelligence to provide personalized learning experiences for students. By leveraging AI technology, Thinkster Math tailors lessons to each student's unique learning style, strengths, and weaknesses, ensuring that the content is adaptive and responsive to individual progress. The human interaction component allows for personalized feedback and mentorship, making the program more engaging and supportive. This combination of AI and human guidance creates a dynamic learning environment that helps students build confidence, improve math skills, and achieve better outcomes.

Jill Watson is an AI-powered virtual teaching assistant introduced by the Georgia Institute of Technology in 2016, designed to assist students in an online course environment. Developed using IBM's Watson platform, Jill was created to handle the high volume of routine questions typically asked by students, such as inquiries about assignment deadlines, course policies, and other administrative details. Over time, Jill's AI capabilities were refined through machine learning, enabling her to provide accurate, timely, and human-like responses. Initially, students were unaware that they were interacting with an AI rather than a human TA, a testament to Jill's sophisticated design. Jill Watson's introduction marked a significant advancement in educational technology, showcasing the potential for AI to enhance teaching efficiency, student engagement, and scalability in online learning environments.

Cognii is a provider of AI-powered educational tools, offering innovative products designed to enhance learning in K-12 schools, higher education institutions, and corporate training programs. At the core of Cognii's offerings is its AI-based virtual learning assistant, which uses natural language processing (NLP) to engage students in interactive, open-ended conversations. This assistant provides personalized tutoring, instant feedback, and adaptive learning paths based on individual student needs. By allowing students to explain concepts in their own words and receiving constructive responses, Cognii fosters critical thinking and deep comprehension. In addition to K-12 and higher education, Cognii's technology is widely used in corporate training to streamline employee education and development, providing scalable solutions that optimize learning outcomes across various industries.

KidSense provides AI-driven educational solutions specifically designed for children, with a focus on enhancing learning experiences through speech recognition technology. One of its key innovations is a voice-to-text tool equipped with specialized algorithms that can accurately interpret the often complex and less predictable speech patterns of young learners. Recognizing that children's speech can be harder to translate due to varying pronunciation, developing language skills, and unique accents, KidSense's AI models are tailored to adapt to these challenges. This tool allows children to interact more naturally with educational platforms, promoting engagement and enabling personalized feedback based on their verbal responses. By bridging the gap between traditional learning methods and modern AI capabilities, KidSense helps to create more accessible and effective learning environments for young students.

CONCLUSION AND FUTURE DIRECTION OF RESEARCH

AI tools hold great promise for transforming education by personalizing learning, enhancing assessment, providing valuable insights, and automating administrative tasks. However, addressing ethical considerations, providing adequate training and support, ensuring equitable access, and maintaining the balance between technology and human interaction are critical challenges that need to be navigated for the successful implementation of AI tools in education. By examining the advancements, implementation, and impact of AI tools in education, this article provides a comprehensive overview of the potential and challenges associated with their use. The outlined structure ensures a thorough exploration of AI tools, their ethical considerations, and their transformative impact on teaching and learning

AI tools in education involve ongoing research, development, and careful implementation to maximize their potential while addressing associated challenges. Here are some key future directions and considerations for AI tools in education:

Ethical AI

As AI becomes increasingly integrated into educational systems, prioritizing ethical considerations is crucial to ensuring that these technologies are used responsibly and equitably. Establishing robust ethical frameworks and guidelines for the development and deployment of AI in education is essential to address potential risks and uphold the integrity of the educational process. These frameworks should encompass several key areas, including transparency, fairness, privacy, and accountability. Transparency involves communicating how AI systems operate, how data is collected and used, and how decisions are made. Fairness ensures that AI technologies do not reinforce existing biases or create new forms of inequality, and that all students have equitable access to the benefits of AI. Privacy concerns revolve around safeguarding students' personal and academic information from unauthorized access and misuse. Accountability requires that developers and educators are responsible for the impact of AI systems and can address any issues that arise. By creating and adhering to ethical guidelines, educational institutions can effectively harness the power of AI while mitigating potential negative effects, ultimately fostering a more inclusive, secure, and effective learning environment.

Explainable AI

Enhancing the transparency of AI algorithms is essential for building trust and understanding among educators, students, and stakeholders. To achieve this, initiatives must prioritize the development of explainable AI systems that can provide clear and understandable explanations for their decisions and recommendations. By making the inner workings of AI more transparent, users can better grasp how and why specific outcomes or suggestions are generated, which fosters greater confidence in the technology. Explainable AI not only demystifies complex algorithms but also helps users identify and address any potential biases or inaccuracies in the system. This transparency is crucial for ensuring that AI tools are used effectively and ethically in educational settings, as it empowers users to make informed decisions and promotes a more accountable and trustworthy use of technology.

Augmented Intelligence

Augmented intelligence emphasizes the role of AI as a supportive tool designed to enhance, rather than replace, the skills of educators. Rather than supplanting teachers, AI should be viewed as a valuable asset that assists in various aspects of teaching, such as generating content, conducting assessments, and analyzing data. By automating routine and administrative tasks, AI can free up teachers' time, allowing them to focus on more personalized instruction, mentorship, and building meaningful relationships with students. This collaborative approach ensures that AI complements the expertise and human touch of educators, ultimately enriching the learning experience and enabling teachers to provide more tailored and impactful support to their students.

Continuous Evaluation and Improvement

Continuous evaluation and research are imperative for gauging the efficacy and influence of AI tools in education. This involves assessing student outcomes, soliciting feedback from both educators and students and leveraging this data to iteratively enhance the design and utilization of AI tools.

ABBREVIATIONS

AI Artificial Intelligence
AIED Artificial Intelligence in Education
IoT Internet of Things
NLP Natural Language Processing
VR Virtual Reality
AG Augmented reality
ML Machine learning
EDTECH Education Technology

REFERENCES

Abulibdeh, A., Zaidan, E., & Abulibdeh, R. (2024). Navigating the confluence of artificial intelligence and education for sustainable development in the era of industry 4.0: Challenges, opportunities, and ethical dimensions. *Journal of Cleaner Production*, 437, 140527. DOI: 10.1016/j.jclepro.2023.140527

Adel, A. (2024). The convergence of intelligent tutoring, robotics, and IoT in smart education for the transition from industry 4.0 to 5.0. *Smart Cities*, 7(1), 325–369. DOI: 10.3390/smartcities7010014

Ait Baha, T., El Hajji, M., Es-Saady, Y., & Fadili, H. (2024). The impact of educational chatbot on student learning experience. *Education and Information Technologies*, 29(8), 10153–10176. DOI: 10.1007/s10639-023-12166-w

Arora, M. (2024). Virtual Reality in Education: Analyzing the Literature and Bibliometric State of Knowledge. *Transforming Education with Virtual Reality*, 379-402.

Ayeni, O. O., Al Hamad, N. M., Chisom, O. N., Osawaru, B., & Adewusi, O. E. (2024). AI in education: A review of personalized learning and educational technology. *GSC Advanced Research and Reviews*, 18(2), 261–271. DOI: 10.30574/gscarr.2024.18.2.0062

Devapitchai, J. J., Dheenadhayalan, K., Rajeshkumar, L., Meena, M. R., Soundarya, M., Sowmiya, M. S., & Manickam, T. (2024). Applications of Artificial Intelligence Techniques in Modern Banking Sectors. In *Blockchain Applications for Smart Contract Technologies* (pp. 279–298). IGI Global. DOI: 10.4018/979-8-3693-1511-8.ch014

Devapitchai, J. J., Krishnapriya, S. V., Karuppiah, S. P., & Saranya, S. (2024). Using AI-Driven Decision-Making Tools in Corporate Investment Planning. In *Generative AI for Transformational Management* (pp. 137–160). IGI Global. DOI: 10.4018/979-8-3693-5578-7.ch006

Forero-Corba, W., & Bennasar, F. N. (2024). Techniques and applications of Machine Learning and Artificial Intelligence in education: A systematic review. *RIED-Revista Iberoamericana de Educación a Distancia*, 27(1), 111–127.

Galindo-Domínguez, H., Delgado, N., Losada, D., & Etxabe, J. M. (2024). An analysis of the use of artificial intelligence in education in Spain: The in-service teacher's perspective. *Journal of Digital Learning in Teacher Education*, 40(1), 41–56. DOI: 10.1080/21532974.2023.2284726

Goel, P. K., Singhal, A., Bhadoria, S. S., Saraswat, B. K., & Patel, A. (2024). AI and Machine Learning in Smart Education: Enhancing Learning Experiences Through Intelligent Technologies. In *Infrastructure Possibilities and Human-Centered Approaches With Industry 5.0* (pp. 36-55). IGI Global.

Jafari, F., & Keykha, A. (2024). Identifying the opportunities and challenges of artificial intelligence in higher education: A qualitative study. *Journal of Applied Research in Higher Education*, 16(4), 1228–1245. DOI: 10.1108/JARHE-09-2023-0426

Jebadurai, D. J., Sheela, M. V., Rajeshkumar, L., Soundarya, M., Meena, R., Manickam, T., & Manikandan, M. (2024). AI-Driven Decision-Making and Optimization in Modern Agriculture Sectors. In *Using Traditional Design Methods to Enhance AI-Driven Decision Making* (pp. 269–288). IGI Global. DOI: 10.4018/979-8-3693-0639-0.ch012

Kapoor, S., & Kalia, G. (2024). Role of Virtual Reality in Education: Its Scope, Reach and Effect on Student Behavior. *Transforming Education with Virtual Reality*, 145-164.

14. Korda, D. R., Dapaah, E. O., & Akolgo, E. A. (2024). The role of AI chatbots in education: A review. *Academy Journal of Science and Engineering*, 18(1), 79–87.

Lampropoulos, G., & Kinshuk, . (2024). Virtual reality and gamification in education: A systematic review. *Educational Technology Research and Development*, 72(3), 1–95. DOI: 10.1007/s11423-024-10351-3

Li, K., Xirui, P., Song, J., Hong, B., & Wang, J. (2024). The application of augmented reality (ar) in remote work and education. *arXiv preprint arXiv:2404.10579*.

Lima, G. D. M., Ferreira, G. M. D. S., & Carvalho, J. D. S. (2024). Automation in education: Trending issues concerning Artificial Intelligence. *Educação e Pesquisa*, 50, e273857. DOI: 10.1590/s1678-4634202450273857por

Lin, Y., & Yu, Z. (2024). A bibliometric analysis of artificial intelligence chatbots in educational contexts. *Interactive Technology and Smart Education*, 21(2), 189–213. DOI: 10.1108/ITSE-12-2022-0165

Mao, J., Chen, B., & Liu, J. C. (2024). Generative artificial intelligence in education and its implications for assessment. *TechTrends*, 68(1), 58–66. DOI: 10.1007/s11528-023-00911-4

Naseer, F., Khalid, M. U., Ayub, N., Rasool, A., Abbas, T., & Afzal, M. W. (2024). Automated Assessment and Feedback in Higher Education Using Generative AI. In *Transforming Education With Generative AI: Prompt Engineering and Synthetic Content Creation* (pp. 433-461). IGI Global. DOI: 10.4018/979-8-3693-1351-0.ch021

Ocumpaugh, J., Roscoe, R. D., Baker, R. S., Hutt, S., & Aguilar, S. J. (2024). Toward asset-based instruction and assessment in artificial intelligence in education. *International Journal of Artificial Intelligence in Education*, •••, 1–40. DOI: 10.1007/s40593-023-00382-x

Paul, B. S., & Anuradha, A. (2024). Artificial Intelligence in Different Business Domains: Ethical Concerns. In *Exploring the Ethical Implications of Generative AI* (pp. 13-33). IGI Global.

Raja, S., Jebadurai, D. J., Ivan, L., Mykola, R. V., Ruslan, K., & Nadiia, P. R. (2024). Impact of Artificial Intelligence in Students' Learning Life. In *AI in Business: Opportunities and Limitations* (Vol. 2, pp. 3–17). Springer Nature Switzerland. DOI: 10.1007/978-3-031-49544-1_1

Sappaile, B. I., Vandika, A. Y., Deiniatur, M., Nuridayanti, N., & Arifudin, O. (2024). The Role of Artificial Intelligence in the Development of Digital Era Educational Progress. *Journal of Artificial Intelligence and Development*, 3(1), 1–8.

Vijayalakshmi, S., Madhavi, B., Jayanthi, N., Bansode, G. S., Sharma, N., & Shanthi, K. G. (2024, March). Smart Education With Iot And Ai: Revolutionizing Learning In The Digital Age. In *2024 2nd International Conference on Disruptive Technologies (ICDT)* (pp. 1282-1286). IEEE.

Wardat, Y., Tashtoush, M., AlAli, R., & Saleh, S. (2024). Artificial intelligence in education: Mathematics teachers' perspectives, practices and challenges. *Iraqi Journal for Computer Science and Mathematics*, 5(1), 60–77. DOI: 10.52866/ijcsm.2024.05.01.004

Yokutkhon, R. (2024). The use of virtual reality and augmented reality in education. *Journal of new century innovations, 48*(1), 157-161.

Yuan, L. (2024). Where does AI-driven Education, in the Chinese Context and Beyond, go next? *International Journal of Artificial Intelligence in Education*, 34(1), 31–41. DOI: 10.1007/s40593-023-00341-6

Chapter 18
Micro-Credentials: Not Working as Advertised

Stephen Murgatroyd
University of Alberta, Canada

ABSTRACT

The explicit intention of governments in making investments in micro-credentials in Canada was to respond to a growing skills gap in the human capital market. Employers complained that they were unable to find potential employees with the skills needed. Given the challenges faced by colleges and universities and the challenges within the Canadian economy, micro-credentials looked like a potentially effective response to the need to upskill and reskill the workforce. The results have demonstrated that this linking of higher education to human capital market needs is not working and is, in fact, a fiction. This chapter explores the state of play of micro-credentials in Canada against a background of institutional precarity, shifting government policies and a larger economic picture. It suggests that not only are micro-credentials a weak response to the labour market needs, they represent system "noise" rather than a reasoned response to a social and economic challenge.

INTRODUCTION

This chapter examines the launch and development of micro-credentials in Canada from 2020 to 2024 and how their emergence reflects underlying issues in which higher education is developing in Canada. Given the financial and operational precarity of colleges and universities and labour market challenges which confront governments in Canada, micro-credentials need to be understood both as political and economic instruments and as commercial opportunities for colleges and universities (Wheelahan & Moodie, 2022). Though some saw the potential of a

DOI: 10.4018/979-8-3693-5488-9.ch018

focus on micro-credentials as a harbinger of a significant change of programming at colleges and universities, it is already clear that they are "noise" rather than an agent of transformative change (Murgatroyd, 2022). The chapter will use available reports and evidence, exploring the extent to which policy and government expectations that led to investment in micro-credentials were matched by what happened in fact.

To understand the issues and concerns, some context is needed. It is important to understand the precarity of Canadian postsecondary institutions, the Canadian economy, and its human capital market.

The Precarious State of Post Secondary Education in Canada

Canada's higher education systems are complex and compartmentalized. Each of Canada's ten Provinces and three territories has sole and direct responsibility for all aspects of education, except for the provision of education on Indigenous reserves. The Government of Canada intrudes into this domain by offering financial support to students and funding for innovation related to labour market needs or research, which can impact postsecondary education. It can also impact the complex system by severely restricting access to higher education for international students, as it has just done (Usher, 2024a, 2024b).

Growth of the Student Population

Over the past thirty years, provincial and territorial governments have reduced per capita funding for postsecondary education, such that in some provinces, student fee revenues now exceed government investment, especially in the college sector. Using OECD 2024 data, investment in higher education as a percentage of total government funding has been falling at 7.5% each year in Canada since 2016 (OECD, 2024).

Despite declining government revenues, access to higher education has expanded significantly since 2016. In 2022-3, there were 2.22 million students (Usher & Balfour, 2024). This level of registration is a significant increase from the 2.05 million enrolled in 2016 (Statistics Canada, 2022). One-third of these students are enrolled in colleges, and two-thirds in universities. This significant enrollment growth was fuelled largely by international students, which accounted for 25% of students in colleges and 18% of students in universities in 2022-23.

At the same time, Canada's youth population (aged 18-21) declined by about 1.2% between 2012 and 2022, contributing to a degree of enrolment weakness in higher education. However, it is now clear that, largely due to immigration, the youth population numbers are set to increase substantially over the period 2022-2032, but the distribution of this growth will be uneven across the country. This demographic shift could lead to large increases in enrolments in some regions, ranging from 15%

in Ontario to around 35% in Alberta. Other regions and their institutions may see declines. Institutions were anticipating these demographic challenges when micro-credential funding and support were announced at the end of the pandemic.

Financial Precarity

Given that provincial government support for universities has fallen by about 15% since its peak in 2007, and tuition fees have been falling in real terms in recent years, institutions feel and are financially precarious. This situation is made worse by tuition freezes in some provinces (Ontario), below inflation caps on tuition increases in others (Alberta and Quebec), and by a dramatic curtailment of visa allocations for international students wishing to study in Canada – effectively a 50% cut. Given the dependency of many colleges and universities on such students – one Ontario college had 80% of its students as international students and one university in the Canadian Maritimes had 75% of its full-time student enrollment from this source[1] – the impact of these two factors has made institutions, specific programs, and certain key personnel precarious.

Without additional support or the ability to raise tuition, institutions will struggle to accommodate the anticipated growth in student numbers, potentially leading to issues with access to education. Colleges and universities are always looking for new sources of revenue and new ways to generate revenue from existing programs, courses, products, and services. They are now essentially commercial entities that, though regulated as publicly funded institutions, are seeking to become more entrepreneurial. This is no more explicit than in Ontario, where colleges now have significantly more revenue from student fees and other sources than from the Government of Ontario and the Government of Canada combined (Usher, 2024c). It is not surprising, therefore, to see Ontario lead Canada in its investment and support for micro-credentials and their development.

Canada's Economy and Human Capital Market

Canada is struggling economically. An indicator of this is a comparison of GDP per capita with that of other OECD nations. This measure indicates how the economic values we create connect to our demography and is a more helpful measure than GDP growth to show the health of the economy. The signs are not good:

"Canada is expected to record the lowest level of growth in living standards over the periods between 2020-2030 and 2030-2060 as measured by changes in per capita GDP. This means countries like the Czech Republic, Estonia, Israel, Italy, South Korea, New Zealand, Slovenia, and Turkey will surpass Canada in material standards of living. Indeed, by 2060, the OECD expects that Canada's average per person standard of living will be more than one-fifth less than the OECD average." Clemens, et al., (2023).

and also

"Canada has been the worst-performing advanced economy in the Organization for Economic Co-operation and Development since 1976. Governments of all partisan stripes have tried and failed to reverse the trend. If nothing changes, the OECD projects, our economic growth per capita will continue to stagnate for decades to come." Silcoff and O'Kane (2023).

The comparison with New Zealand, mentioned by Clemens et al. (2023), is telling. In 2020, the standard of living measured by GDP per capita was higher in Canada than in New Zealand by 4%. Projections show that, if nothing changes, Canada's standard of living will be 15.5% lower as New Zealand continues to enjoy significant economic growth. As Clemens et al. (2023) observe, to "catch up," working Canadians would need to work closer to six days a week to generate the same level of economic activity as their New Zealand counterparts.

Underlying this large issue are three sets of interrelated challenges: (a) stagnant productivity growth, (b) declining competitiveness, and (c) weak innovation. All made worse by deteriorating capital infrastructure. Given the challenges, investors prefer to invest in other jurisdictions, especially those with higher levels of productivity and economic growth (Williams & Finlayson, 2023). Many highly qualified Canadians can secure significantly higher earnings in other jurisdictions, which is why finding, developing, and retaining talent is a critical issue for all organizations.

Skill Shortages

The issue of skill shortages in Canada has been escalating for some time, best captured by a declining unemployment-to-job vacancy ratio, which is now 1:4, down from 4:4 in 2006. In 2022, Canada was unable to fill one million job vacancies, and 59% of employers struggled to find skilled labour (Deloitte, 2023). The economic cost of this shortfall has been estimated at $13 billion (Deloitte, 2023).

With an aging workforce, the situation is expected to worsen, with 700,000 skilled trades workers due to retire by 2030 and highly skilled workers needed in health care, information technology, education, and construction simply not being available at a level commensurate with demand. The Conference Board of Canada (2024) has suggested that, by 2030, Canada may face a shortage of close to 2 million jobs, even accounting for the disruptive potential of AI and related technology in terms of the future of work. The challenges are leading employers to be increasingly cautious about hiring recent graduates. Youth unemployment (15-24) was at 14% in May 2024 – more than twice the adult unemployment rate (6.3%).

To complicate matters, apprenticeships in Canada have experienced a 19% decline in enrollment from a peak of 470,000 enrollments in 2013 to a new low of 381,000 in 2020. Completion rates for apprenticeships are also low, with some skilled trades taking twice the time to secure their certification. Overall, on-time completion rates are 16%, and eventual completion after a significant time (up to five years after the scheduled completion date) is 36%.

Changing Policyscapes in Higher Education

Anticipatory governance, as expressed in policy decisions by governments and institutions, relies on assumed knowledge about the future and an understanding of the likely impacts of shifts in public policy (Anderson, 2010; Flyverbom & Garsten, 2021; Murgatroyd, 2024). Policies provide the appearance of credibility and competence in a world of contingencies" (Nelson et al., 2008). In the case of the launch of micro-credentials in Ontario and other Canadian jurisdictions, the projected transformation of the labour market linked to the phantasmagoric fiction that short-form learning would transform the skills, competencies and capabilities of would-be employees informed policymakers' thinking

COVID challenged an already fragile postsecondary system in three specific ways. First, all institutions had to grapple with the switch to remote instruction, despite some resistance from students and staff (Murgatroyd, 2022), which in turn also required rapid investment in new technology infrastructure (Lanthier et al., 2023); second, issues around mental health and student and staff wellbeing became a front-and-center issue, though many recognized that these challenges were not at all new (Chatoor et al. 2024). Third, issues of equity and inclusion, coupled with the real challenges many older students faced in terms of balancing work, family, and study, became acutely apparent – an indication of the changing composition of the student body.

A key underlying issue is access to affordable broadband, which remains problematic in Canada. According to the Telecommunications Regulatory Agency, just 62% of rural Canadians have access to broadband at 50/10 Mbps – the speed needed for interactivity online[2]. Canada also has some of the most expensive broadband in the world, making affordable, reliable access a challenge for many, even when broadband is widely available. Institutions and governments needed to access technology equity and inclusion as a component of any larger strategy to support a more focused shift to digital and hybrid learning.

Ontario led the way. The Ontario Virtual Learning Strategy (VLS) was announced in 2020, backed by an investment of over $70 million. Ontario is now home to a range of virtual learning offerings, including K-12 online courses, which saw 230,000 course registrations in 2023-24, certificates, diplomas, and degrees from universities, colleges, and Indigenous institutes, as well as courses and micro-credentials from various organizations. In all, there are over 42,000 fully online college and university courses, 2,130 micro-credentials, and 2,000 other qualifications available entirely online. Significant funds were allocated in 2020 for the development and deployment of micro-credentials - $59.9 million - with the then Minister making explicit their policy and strategic purpose: "*to help people retrain and upgrade their skills to find new employment.*"[3]. Additional funds were made available in subsequent years. The policy intention was crystal clear: micro-credentials were to be focused on labour market needs and the needs of the professions and trades. (Davidson & Ruparell, 2020).

A second policy feature, common to Alberta, Ontario, and some other jurisdictions in their launch of micro-credentials was a shift in institutional funding away from block operational base grants towards "outcome-based funding" (also known as performance-based funding – PBF), where a portion of available funds is related to a college or universities performance on key metrics, many of which relate to skills, employability and earnings – it will eventually represent 60% of government funding in Ontario[4]. The intention has been to incentivize institutions to better align their courses and programs with the needs of the labour market. Various forms of outcome or performance-based funding operate across 30 US states. An analysis by Ortagus, et al. (2020) reviewed twenty years of reports and concluded that such policies led to either no impact or a modest increase in retention and graduate rates in the US, but led to access and equity issues for disadvantaged students, worsened the situation of under-resourced schools and triggered schools to game the system. This is a clear example of phantasmagoric fiction.

The third policy shift is away from generalized and unspecific program funding and the growing use across Canada of what is known as "envelope" funding, where programs in high demand in the labour market receive targeted investment to grow capacity. For example, several governments have targeted growth in health practitioners, IT specializations (e.g. cybersecurity, artificial intelligence, preventative maintenance), and construction workers. Often, such funding is awarded whether institutional capacities can match the outcome expectations the government intends – a projected transformation that may, in fact, become a phantasmagoric fiction. Some micro-credentials were funded in this way, especially those aimed at upskilling health professionals, elder care assistants, and daycare workers.

Micro-Credentials and the Needs of the Human Capital Market

Given the explicit requirement to link micro-credentials to human capital market needs, several "frameworks" were developed to enable this connection. For example, Colleges and Institutes Canada (a network organization) suggested that all micro-credentials across Canada meet these proposed framework criteria[5]:

1. Micro-credentials can complement traditional credentials (certificate, diploma, degree, or post-graduate certificate) or stand-alone.
2. Micro-credentials are subject to a robust and rigorous quality assurance process.
3. Micro-credentials should represent competencies identified by employers/ industry sectors to meet employer needs.
4. Micro-credentials may provide clear and seamless pathways across different credentials (both non-credit and credit) and may be stackable.
5. Micro-credentials are based on assessed proficiency of a competency, not on time spent learning.
6. Micro-credentials are secure, trackable, and portable, and competency is documented in students' academic records.
7. Micro-credentials are to follow institutional approval processes.

E-Campus Ontario – a government-funded agency responsible for administering funding and support for micro-credentials in Ontario - also issued guidelines for their development which, though similar to that offered above, has some subtle differences:

1. The issuing body could be a college, university, an established agency, or employer.
2. Rather than certification and recognition through seat time, micro-credentials were to be harmonized by an agreed competency framework such as the European Skills, Competencies and Occupations Dictionary (ESCO)[6].
3. Assessment was to be based on competencies – knowledge, attitude, and skills. There must be a summative, outcome-based assessment that potential employers could review and assess when hiring.
4. Micro-credentials "will be validated by industry partners / external bodies where possible. This validation will confirm: (1) the competency is in demand by industry; (2) the established assessment is reflective of job performance in that industry."
5. Micro-credentials will be compatible with traditional transcripts, where possible.

These focused framework items reflected the commitment to employability skills assessed through competencies agreed with potential employers. This framework is now shown to be another phantasmagoric fiction. A few micro-credentials supported by funds from e-Campus Ontario were aligned with all aspects of their own framework. Almost none were validated by industry partners, though employer participation in credential development did increase, and few made use of competency-based assessment.

One issue none of these frameworks addressed directly was duration – how many hours of study should a micro-credential require of the student? Some made available by universities in Canada required 400 or more hours of graduate-level study – hardly a "short course." Others from colleges were 15-20 hours. This demonstrates another example of the rush to market so that funds could be accessed and deployed, often to leverage existing courses packaged in a new way.

Other jurisdictions, notably New Zealand and the European Union, explicitly linked micro-credentials to skills and competencies and created boundaries for their use and deployment so as not to overly disrupt already fragile systems (Karachalios & Papadakis, 2023; Omona & O'Dama, 2024). Canadian jurisdictions essentially encourage an open, competitive market and turn a blind eye to institutions that ignored the agreed frameworks for their deployment. Unlike Finland (Brauer, 2023) where the deployment of micro-credentials was highly regulated and supervised, Canadian micro-credential development was haphazard and serendipitous – a little like the "Wild West."

The Deployment of Micro-Credentials in Canada, 2019-2024

The take-up of available micro-credentials across Canada has been modest. In Ontario, which offers the largest number of micro-credentials, an evaluation study (Cathexis Consulting, 2024) shows that by the end of 2023, institutions had enrolled 2,609 individuals in one or more micro-credentials, 1,700 of whom had their fees paid for by the Ontario Student Assistance Program (OSAP). Completion rates for this group were 52%. Given that there were over 2,130 micro-credentials available, this must be seen as a low response.

Across Canada Murgatroyd (2024) estimated that, across Canada, some 10,000 micro-credentials were available, though some were so far removed from the stated labour market agenda as to border on the amusing – e.g. Chaucer's Friends. Some of these micro-credentials were deliberately intended as "teaser" courses for longer programs of study, especially diplomas and degrees. Some were offered to appease faculty and were essential "pet" project courses – e.g. "Fairytales – Meanings, Messages, and Morals." Others were more like micro-learning experiences requiring just one or two hours of study or less (.eil et al., 2021).

A part of the challenge was that both potential students and employers were unclear about what a micro-credential was, what it was supposed to deliver in terms of knowledge, skills, and capabilities, and how skills were to be assessed. The market reacted with caution and preferred established short courses offered by their employer, professional body, trade association, or private provider.

There are also significant concerns about quality, with some students and institutions expressing serious concerns about relevance, currency of the knowledge and skills being taught, and the value of assessment. The government asked the Post Secondary Quality Assessment Board (PEQAB) in Ontario to explore what could be done to strengthen the quality of micro-credentials. Their final report (PEQAB 2024) recommends a recalibration of micro-credentials through the award of a quality imprimatur – a legally protected term such as the "Ontario Micro-Credential (OMC)" – which would ensure it was compliant with a number of standards and frameworks. For example, its duration would "normally" be 12-16 hours of instructional time unless the credential was transferable to a diploma or degree program, in which case it should be equivalent to 40 hours of instructional time. It would also need to make use of a competency or skills framework for both course design and assessment.

Lane and Murgatroyd (2021), exploring the "wild west" of micro-credentials then emerging in Canada, documented eleven key actions needed to harness the potential of micro-credentials to deliver the strategic policy intention: help individuals develop and refine the skills they need to secure employment without having to undertake an extensive period of study. These actions include strengthening the role of employers or employer organizations in validating both the credential and the assessment of skills and the need to closely align a micro-credential with a competency framework sanctioned by employers and their organizations. None of the eleven recommendations appear to have been acted on.

Understanding the Response of Institutions

When the government offers significant funding at a time of precarity and vulnerability, college and university leaders want to secure their "slice of the pie." At one university in western Canada, the President instructed each of the Deans to submit five proposals when the provincial government made a call – they each had just one week to do so. Needless to say, some of these were poorly designed, and others were taken off the shelf from some other activity and re-purposed and packaged for the micro-credential fund. Not one of the proposals submitted involved industry or employer consultation.

To make matters worse, government rhetoric about focusing on closing the skills gap in terms of employability, upskilling, and reskilling came at the same time as high levels of inflation. Employers were laying off staff and downsizing to manage their growing costs. Colleges and universities found themselves being priced out of the market by MOOC providers and industry short course providers. Indeed, PEQAB (2024) points to the fact that the majority of those seeking upskilling and reskilling do so through their employer, an industry association or professional body, or a private skills training provider – accounting for 70% of enrolments in short-form training (page 22).

Micro-credentials cannot be seen to have any discernible impact on the skills gap challenge Canada faces. In some sectors, especially IT, health, and construction, employer demand for skilled labour is increasing and the supply is worsening. In the IT sector, 92% of employers in 2024 continue to say that the skills shortages are severe and 48% indicate that they are worsening when compared to the year before[7]. Overall, 89% of employers are challenged to find, develop and retain talent[8].

CONCLUSION

The challenge of skills for employment is not a simple one of improving a match between what students' study and what employers want – the underlying construct behind the push for micro-credentials. Indeed, we also know that degrees and diplomas often have very weak links to key skills in demand, which is why so many employers now use skills-based hiring rather than qualifications-based hiring (Fuller et al., 2022). We also know that a great many jobs do not require a degree or diploma, even though many who hold these jobs have these qualifications – in the US, around 41% of recent graduates hold jobs for which their degree is mainly irrelevant (Redden, 2020).

The neo-liberal phantasmagoric fiction that teaching and assessment can be closely aligned with the human capital markets needs is distorting the work of colleges and universities (Fleming, 2021), who are eager to find new sources of revenue and to demonstrate value and impact. Micro-credentials are the symbolic statement of this distortion. Given the poor response they have received, it may be best just to let them die on the vine.

REFERENCES

Anderson, B. (2010). Perception, precaution, preparedness: Anticipating action and future geographies. *Progress in Human Geography*, 34(6), 777–798. DOI: 10.1177/0309132510362600

Brauer, S. (2023). *Case study Finland: Micro-credentials for labour market education and training. First look at mapping micro-credentials in European labour-market-related education, training, and learning: take-up, characteristics, and functions.* CEDEFOP.

Cathexis Consulting. (2024). *Evaluation of Ontario's micro-credential strategy, 2020-23.* Minister of Colleges and Universities, Government of Ontario.

Chatoor, K., Pilla, N., Balata, L., & Kaufman, A. (2024). *Supporting student mental health in Ontario: Exploring best practices and identifying gaps.* Higher Education Quality Council of Ontario (mimeo). https://heqco.ca/pub/supporting-student-mental-health-in-ontario-exploring-best-practices-and-identifying-gaps/

Clemens, J., Globerman, S., & Palacios, M. (2023). Four-day week? With Canada's low productivity, we may need six-day work weeks. *Globe and Mail, 17th May.* https://www.theglobeandmail.com/business/commentary/article-four-day-workweek-productivity-canada/

Conference Board of Canada. (2024). *State of skills – Quality of work.* https://fsc-ccf.ca/projects/state-of-skills-quality-of-work/

Corbeil, R., Khan, B. H., & Corbeil, M. E. (2021). *Micro-learning in the digital age: The design and delivery of learning in snippets.* Routledge. DOI: 10.4324/9780367821623

Davidson, M., & Ruparell, S. (2020). *The future of Ontario workers.* June 24th (mimeo). https://cdn.agilitycms.com/colleges-ontario/documents-library/document-files/2020%20June%20-%20The%20Future%20of%20Ontarios%20Workers.pdf

Deloitte. (2023). *Strengthening Canada's labour market.* https://www2.deloitte.com/ca/en/pages/public-sector/blog/strengthening-canada-labour-market.html

Fleming, P. (2021). *Dark academia – How universities die.* Pluto Press.

Flyverbom, M., & Garsten, C. (2021). Anticipation and organization: Seeing, knowing, and governing futures. *Organizational Theory*, 2(3), 1–25. DOI: 10.1177/26317877211020325

Fuller, J. B., Langer, C., & Sigelman, M. (2022). Skills-based hiring is on the rise. Harvard Business Review Digital, February 11th. https://www.hbs.edu/faculty/Pages/item.aspx?num=62029

Karachalios, G. & Papadakis, N. (2023). Micro-credentials and skills – Towards a paradigm shift in reskilling. Advanced in Social Sciences Journal, 10 (5), 95:102. DOI: 10.14738/assrj.105.14691

Lane, J., & Murgatroyd, S. (2021). *Micro-credentials – Small qualifications, big deal.* Canada West Foundation, September. Available at https://cwf.ca/research/publications/what-now-micro-credentials-small-qualifications-big-deal/

Lanthier, S., Colyar, J., & Deakin, J. (2023). *Ontario college and university investments in digital learning during the pandemic.* Higher Education Quality Council of Ontario (mimeo). https://heqco.ca/pub/ontario-college-and-university-investments-in-digital-learning-during-the-pandemic/

Murgatroyd, S. (2022). The future is small – Micro-credentials and the skills agenda. *Revista Paraguaya de Education a Distancia, FACEN-UNA*, 3(1), 5–14.

Murgatroyd, S. (2024). *The future of higher education in an age of artificial intelligence.* Ethics Press.

Nelson, N., Geltzer, A., & Hilgartner, S. (2008). Introduction: The anticipatory state: making policy-relevant knowledge about the future. *Science & Public Policy*, 35(8), 546–550. DOI: 10.3152/030234208X370648

OECD. (2024). *Education at a glance.* OECD. https://www.oecd.org/en/publications/education-at-a-glance-2024_c00cad36-en.html

Omona, K., & O'Dama, M. L. (2024). *Global perspectives on micro-learning and micro-credentials in higher education.* IGI Global. DOI: 10.4018/979-8-3693-0343-6

Ortagus, J. C., Kelchen, R., Rosinger, K., & Voorhees, N. (2020). Performance-Based Funding in American Higher Education: A Systematic Synthesis of the Intended and Unintended Consequences. *Educational Evaluation and Policy Analysis*, 42(4), 520–550. DOI: 10.3102/0162373720953128

(PDF) Anticipation and Organization: Seeing, knowing, and governing futures. Available from: https://www.researchgate.net/publication/352470038_Anticipation_and_Organization_Seeing_knowing_and_governing_futures#fullTextFileContent [accessed Sep 30, 2024].

PEQAB. (2024). *Ontario micro-credentials: Harnessing the potential (mimeo).* Post Secondary Quality Assessment Board of Ontario. Available at https://www.peqab.ca/OMCReport.html

Redden, E. (2020). 41% of recent grads work in jobs that do not require a degree. *Inside Higher Education, February 17th*. https://www.insidehighered.com/quicktakes/2020/02/18/41-recent-grads-work-jobs-not-requiring-degree

Silcoff, J., & O'Kane, J. (2023). How the Liberals' multibillion tech plan created chaos instead of growth. *Globe and Mail, January 20th*. https://www.theglobeandmail.com/business/article-liberals-tech-plan-economic-growth/

Statistics Canada. (2022). Postsecondary enrolments and graduates, 2017-2018. 19 February. https://www150.statcan.gc.ca/n1/daily-quotidien/200219/dq200219b-eng.htm

Usher, A. (2024a). Three developments on the international student file. Feb 20th. https://higheredstrategy.com/three-developments-on-the-international-students-file/

Usher, A. (2024b). Marc Miller strikes again. Sept 23rdhttps://higheredstrategy.com/marc-miller-strikes-again/

Usher, A. (2024c). The eighth wonder of the world: Ontario college finances to 2023-4. https://higheredstrategy.com/the-eighth-wonder-of-the-world-ontario-college-finances-to-2023-24

Usher, A., & Balfour, J. (2024). *The State of Postsecondary Education in Canada, 2024*. Higher Education Strategy Associates.

Wheelahan, L., & Moodie, G. (2022). Gig qualifications for the gig economy: Micro-credentials and the 'hungry mile.'. *Higher Education*, 83(6), 1279–1295. DOI: 10.1007/s10734-021-00742-3 PMID: 34366441

Williams, D., & Finlayson, J. (2023). Canada faces 40 years of stagnant incomes – government economic strategy is failing. *Globe and Mail, September 12th*. https://www.theglobeandmail.com/business/commentary/article-canada-economic-growth-strategy/

ENDNOTES

1 See https://higheredstrategy.com/cape-breton-yet-again-%EF%BF%BC/

2 See https://crtc.gc.ca/eng/internet/internet.htm

3 See the budget announcement at https://budget.ontario.ca/2020/chapter-1c .html#s-9

4 See the Government of Ontario announcement at https://news.ontario.ca/en/release/59368/promoting-excellence-ontario-implements-performance-based -funding-for-postsecondary-institutions

5 See https://www.collegesinstitutes.ca/colleges-and-institutes-in-your -community/benefit-college-institute-credential/national-framework-for-microcredentials/

6 For details, see https://esco.ec.europa.eu/en/about-esco

7 As reported here https://www.hcamag.com/ca/specialization/hr-technology/how-is-the-tech-skills-gap-affecting-employers-in-2024/488616

8 For the most recent information, see https://www.benefitscanada.com/news/bencan/majority-of-canadian-employers-expecting-hiring-challenges-in-2024 -survey/

Compilation of References

(PDF) Anticipation and Organization: Seeing, knowing, and governing futures. Available from: https://www.researchgate.net/publication/352470038_Anticipation_and_Organization_Seeing_knowing_and_governing_futures#fullTextFileContent [accessed Sep 30, 2024].

Abbas, A. (2024). *Enhancing Student Engagement through AI-driven Analytics in Higher Education Institutions*. DOI: 10.13140/RG.2.2.28982.47682

Abdelhafid, F. (2024). E-Badges System and Online Credits Recognition of Digital Skills: Digital Badges' Place in the Current Accreditation System. In Embracing Technological Advancements for Lifelong Learning (pp. 59-71). IGI Global. [HTML]

Abdullah, F. (2023). Micro-credentials at higher education institutions: towards smooth sailing ahead., 118-126. https://doi.org/DOI: 10.2991/978-2-38476-196-8_11

Abdullah, F., & Ghazali, N. (2024). Micro-credentials at Higher Education Institutions: Towards Smooth Sailing Ahead. *4th International Conference on Communication, Language, Education and Social Sciences (CLESS 2023)*, 118–126.

Abulibdeh, A., Zaidan, E., & Abulibdeh, R. (2024). Navigating the confluence of artificial intelligence and education for sustainable development in the era of industry 4.0: Challenges, opportunities, and ethical …. Journal of Cleaner Production. sciencedirect.com

Abulibdeh, A., Zaidan, E., & Abulibdeh, R. (2024). Navigating the confluence of artificial intelligence and education for sustainable development in the era of industry 4.0: Challenges, opportunities, and ethical dimensions. *Journal of Cleaner Production*, 437, 437. DOI: 10.1016/j.jclepro.2023.140527

Adachi, C., Savage, J., & O'Donnell, M. (2017). Facilitating social learning through learning design – a perspective of collaborative academic development. In Partridge, H., Davis, K., & Thomas, J.. (Eds.), Me, *Us, IT! ProceedingsASCILITE2017: 34th International Conference on Innovation, Practice and Research in the Use of Educational Technologies in Tertiary Education* (pp. 7-11). DOI: 10.14742/apubs.2017.731

Adel, A. (2024). The convergence of intelligent tutoring, robotics, and IoT in smart education for the transition from industry 4.0 to 5.0. *Smart Cities*, 7(1), 325–369. DOI: 10.3390/smartcities7010014

Agasisti, T., Azzone, G., & Soncin, M. (2021). Assessing the effect of massive open online courses as remedial courses in higher education. *Innovations in Education and Teaching International*, 59(4), 462–471. DOI: 10.1080/14703297.2021.1886969

Ahiadu, A., & Abidoye, R. (2023). Economic uncertainty and direct property performance: A systematic review using the SPAR-4-SLR protocol. *Journal of Property Investment & Finance*, 42(1), 89–111. DOI: 10.1108/JPIF-08-2023-0073

Ahmad, K., Iqbal, W., El-Hassan, A., Qadir, J., Benhaddo, D., Ayyash, M., & Al-Fuqaha, A. (2023). Data-Driven Artificial Intelligence in Education: A Comprehensive Review. *IEEE Transactions on Learning Technologies*, 17, 12–31. DOI: 10.1109/TLT.2023.3314610

Ahmad, M. F., & Wan Abdul Ghapar, W. R. G. (2019). The Era of Artificial Intelligence in Malaysian Higher Education: Impact and Challenges in Tangible Mixed-Reality Learning System toward Self Exploration Education (SEE). *Procedia Computer Science*, 163, 2–10. DOI: 10.1016/j.procs.2019.12.079

Ahmad, N., Hoda, N., & Alahmari, F. (2020). Developing a Cloud-Based Mobile Learning Adoption Model to Promote Sustainable Education. *Sustainability (Basel)*, 12(8), 3126. DOI: 10.3390/su12083126

Ahmat, N. H. C., Bashir, M. A. A., Razali, A. R., & Kasolang, S. (2021). Micro-credentials in higher education institutions: Challenges and opportunities. *Asian Journal of University Education*, 17(3), 281–290. DOI: 10.24191/ajue.v17i3.14505

Ahn, J., Pellicone, A., & Butler, B. (2014). Open badges for education: What are the implications at the intersection of open systems and badging? *Research in Learning Technology*, 22. Advance online publication. DOI: 10.3402/rlt.v22.23563

Ahsan, K., Akbar, S., Kam, B., & Dan-Asabe Abdulrahman, M. (2023). Implementation of micro-credentials in higher education: A systematic literature review. *Education and Information Technologies*, 28(10), 13505–13540. DOI: 10.1007/s10639-023-11739-z

Ait Baha, T., El Hajji, M., Es-Saady, Y., & Fadili, H. (2023). The impact of educational chatbot on student learning experience. *Education and Information Technologies*, •••, 1–24.

Aithal, P. S., & Maiya, A. K. (2023). Innovations in higher education industry – Shaping the future. [IJCSBE]. *International Journal of Case Studies in Business, IT, and Education*, 7(4), 2581–6942. DOI: 10.47992/IJCSBE.2581.6942.0321

Ajjawi, R., Tai, J., Huu Nghia, T. L., Boud, D., Johnson, L., & Patrick, C. J. (2020). Aligning assessment with the needs of work-integrated learning: The challenges of authentic assessment in a complex context. [tandfonline.com]. *Assessment & Evaluation in Higher Education*, 45(2), 304–316. DOI: 10.1080/02602938.2019.1639613

Akavova, A. (2023). Adaptive learning and artificial intelligence in the educational space. E3s Web of Conferences, 451, 06011. https://doi.org/DOI: 10.1051/e3sconf/202345106011

Akçayır, G., & Akçayır, M. (2018). The flipped classroom: A review of its advantages and challenges. *Computers & Education*, 126, 334–345. DOI: 10.1016/j.compedu.2018.07.021

Akinwalere, S. N., & Ivanov, V. (2022). Artificial Intelligence in Higher Education: Challenges and Opportunities. *Border Crossing*, 12(1), 1–15. DOI: 10.33182/bc.v12i1.2015

Alam, A. (2021, December). Should robots replace teachers? Mobilisation of AI and learning analytics in education. In 2021 International Conference on Advances in Computing, Communication, and Control (ICAC3) (pp. 1-12). IEEE. [HTML] DOI: 10.1109/ICAC353642.2021.9697300

Alamri, H. A., Watson, S., & Watson, W. (2021). Learning Technology Models that Support Personalization within Blended Learning Environments in Higher Education. *TechTrends*, 65(1), 62–78. DOI: 10.1007/s11528-020-00530-3

Alasmari, T. (2024). Reshaping vocational training: A study on the recognition of micro-credentials in job markets. *Education + Training*, 66(2/3), 233–251. DOI: 10.1108/ET-07-2023-0282

Alasmari, T., & Alzahrani, A. (2024). Leveraging employment with micro-credentials: Policy and practice of the Middle East and North African Universities. *Educational Technology Research and Development*, 72(3), 1869–1891. DOI: 10.1007/s11423-024-10367-9

Alawadhi, A., & Abu-Ayyash, E. A. S. (2021). Students' perceptions of Kahoot!: An exploratory mixed-method study in EFL undergraduate classrooms in the UAE. *Education and Information Technologies*, 26(4), 3629–3658. DOI: 10.1007/s10639-020-10425-8

Albdrani, R., & Al-Shargabi, A. A. (2023). Investigating the effectiveness of ChatGPT for providing personalized learning experience: A case study. *International Journal of Advanced Computer Science and Applications*, 14(11). Advance online publication. DOI: 10.14569/IJACSA.2023.01411122

Albus, P. (2023). *Virtual reality in education: Impact of instructional design on learning outcomes and cognitive load.* https://oparu.uni-ulm.de/items/bc0bc5f9-464e-45c4-b6c1-811a90e5b852

Al-Darrab, A., & Rushdi, A. M. (2021). On national research and educational networks. *Journal of King Abdulaziz University-Computing and Information Technology Sciences*, 10(1), 1–35.

Aldowah, H., Al-Samarraie, H., Alzahrani, A. I., & Alalwan, N. (2020). Factors affecting student dropout in MOOCs: A cause and effect decision-making model. *Journal of Computing in Higher Education*, 32(2), 429–454. coventry.ac.uk. DOI: 10.1007/s12528-019-09241-y

Al-Fazari, H. (2023). Delivery of Online and Blended-Learning Higher Education Programs in the Arab world---A Case Study from Sohar University in Oman. In Badran, A., Baydoun, E., Hillman, S., & Mesmar, J. (Eds.), *Higher Education in the Arab World: E-Learning and Distance Education* (pp. 99–109). Springer Nature Switzerland., DOI: 10.1007/978-3-031-33568-6_6

Alkadi, R., & Abed, S. (2023). Consumer Acceptance of Fintech App Payment Services: A Systematic Literature Review and Future Research Agenda. *Journal of Theoretical and Applied Electronic Commerce Research*, 18(4), 1838–1860. DOI: 10.3390/jtaer18040093

Almurayh, A. (2021). The Challenges of Using Arabic Chatbot in Saudi Universities. *IAENG International Journal of Computer Science*, 48(1).

Alotaibi, N. S., & Alshehri, A. H. (2023). Prospers and Obstacles in Using Artificial Intelligence in Saudi Arabia Higher Education Institutions—The Potential of AI-Based Learning Outcomes. *Sustainability (Basel)*, 15(13), 10723. Advance online publication. DOI: 10.3390/su151310723

Alraimi, K. M., Zo, H., & Ciganek, A. P. (2015). Understanding the moocs continuance: The role of openness and reputation. Computers &Amp. *Computers & Education*, 80, 28–38. DOI: 10.1016/j.compedu.2014.08.006

Alrayes, A., Henari, T. F., & Ahmed, D. A. (2024). Chatgpt in education – understanding the Bahraini academics perspective. *Electronic Journal of e-Learning*, 22(2), 112–134. DOI: 10.34190/ejel.22.2.3250

Alsobhi, H. A., Alakhtar, R. A., Ubaid, A., Hussain, O. K., & Hussain, F. K. (2023). Blockchain-based micro-credentialing system in higher education institutions: Systematic literature review. *Knowledge-Based Systems*, 265, 110238. DOI: 10.1016/j.knosys.2022.110238

Alves, P., Lopes, A., Cruz-Correia, R., & Menezes, I. (2024). The interrupted journey: Factors and processes related to withdrawal, re-enrolment and dropout from doctoral education. *Higher Education*, 88(1), 225–242. DOI: 10.1007/s10734-023-01113-w

Alzahrani, A. (2022). A systematic review of artificial intelligence in education in the arab world. *Revista Amazonia Investiga*, 11(54), 293–305. DOI: 10.34069/AI/2022.54.06.28

Amer, M., Daim, T. U., & Jetter, A. (2013). A review of scenario planning. *Futures*, 46, 23–40. DOI: 10.1016/j.futures.2012.10.003

Anderson, B. (2010). Perception, precaution, preparedness: Anticipating action and future geographies. *Progress in Human Geography*, 34(6), 777–798. DOI: 10.1177/0309132510362600

Antonaci, A., Henderikx, P., & Ubachs, G. (2021). The Common Microcredentials Framework for MOOCs and short learning programmes. *Journal of Innovation in Polytechnic Education*, 3(1), 5–9. DOI: 10.69520/jipe.v3i1.89

Antoninis, M., Alcott, B., Al Hadheri, S., April, D., Fouad Barakat, B., Barrios Rivera, M., ... & Weill, E. (2023). Global Education Monitoring Report 2023: Technology in education: A tool on whose terms?. https://doi.org/10.54676/UZQV8501

Antonisse, L. (2021). Strengthening the right to Medicaid home and community-based services in the post-COVID era. Columbia Law Review. columbialawreview.org

Anuyahong, B., Rattanapong, C., & Patcha, I. (2023). Analyzing the impact of artificial intelligence in personalized learning and adaptive assessment in higher education. *International Journal of Innovation and Scientific Research*, X(IV), 88–93. DOI: 10.51244/IJRSI.2023.10412

Arora, M. (2024). Virtual Reality in Education: Analyzing the Literature and Bibliometric State of Knowledge. *Transforming Education with Virtual Reality*, 379-402.

Arvin, N. (2023). Teacher experiences with ai-based educational tools. aitechbesosci, 1(2), 26-32. https://doi.org/DOI: 10.61838/kman.aitech.1.2.5

Ashwin, P. (2022). The educational purposes of higher education: Changing discussions of the societal outcomes of educating students. *Higher Education*, 84(6), 1227–1244. DOI: 10.1007/s10734-022-00930-9

Ataizi, M., Öztürk, Ö., Demir, M., Kaya, S., İşcan, A., İşkol, S., & Kömür, İ. A. (2019). Examining Mooc Videos in Terms of Learning Theories. *Journal of Educational Technology and Online Learning*, 2(1), 34–55. DOI: 10.31681/jetol.516029

Australian Government Department of Education. (2015). *Higher Education Standards Framework (Threshold Standards) 2015*. Federal Register of Legislation. https://www.legislation.gov.au/F2015L01639/latest/versions

Australian Government Department of Education. (2021). *Higher Education Standards Framework (Threshold Standards) 2021*. Federal Register of Legislation. https://www.legislation.gov.au/F2021L00488/latest/text

Avella, J. T., Kebritchi, M., Nunn, S. G., & Kanai, T. (2016). Learning Analytics Methods, Benefits, and Challenges in Higher Education: A Systematic Literature Review. *Journal of Asynchronous Learning Networks*, 20(2), 13–29.

Aydemir, M. (2024). Micro-Credentials and Recognition of prior learning: Offering flexible and relevant learning opportunities for ODL learners. https://www.icetol.com/wp-content/uploads/2024/09/icetol2024_full_paper_proceedings.pdf

Aydin, I. E., & Yazici, M. (2020). Drop-Out in MOOCs. [ed.gov]. *Turkish Online Journal of Educational Technology-TOJET*, 19(3), 9–17.

Ayeni, O. O., Al Hamad, N. M., Chisom, O. N., Osawaru, B., & Adewusi, O. E. (2024). AI in education: A review of personalized learning and educational technology. *GSC Advanced Research and Reviews*, 18(2), 261–271. DOI: 10.30574/gscarr.2024.18.2.0062

A-young Park. J., & Vance, A. (2021, February 11). *Data privacy in higher education: Yes, students care*. Https://Er.Educause.Edu/Articles/2021/2/Data-Privacy-in-Higher-Education-Yes-Students-Care

Azevedo, R., Bouchet, F., Duffy, M., Harley, J., Taub, M., Trevors, G., Cloude, E., Dever, D., Wiedbusch, M., Wortha, F., & Cerezo, R. (2022). Lessons learned and future directions of metatutor: Leveraging multichannel data to scaffold self-regulated learning with an intelligent tutoring system. [frontiersin.org]. *Frontiers in Psychology*, 13, 813632. DOI: 10.3389/fpsyg.2022.813632 PMID: 35774935

Azzam, A., & Charles, T. (2024). A Review of Artificial Intelligence in K-12 Education. *Open Journal of Applied Science*, 14(8), 2088–2100. DOI: 10.4236/ojapps.2024.148137

Babiak, Z., Bodnar, O., & Plavutska, I. (2024). Artificial intelligence as a tool for modelling the educational environment. *Humanities Science Current Issues*, 1(73), 269–275. DOI: 10.24919/2308-4863/73-1-41

Babu, I., MathuSoothana, R., & Kumar, S. (2023). Evolutionary Algorithm Based Feature Subset Selection for Students Academic Performance Analysis. *Intelligent Automation & Soft Computing*, 36(3), 3621–3636. DOI: 10.32604/iasc.2023.033791

Bagdi, H., Pothabathula, S. V., Sharma, L., & Bulsara, H. P. (2023). The global market upsurge in web traffic and revenues during the epidemic: An exploratory research of e-learning companies. [HTML]. *International Journal of Development Issues*, 22(3), 418–444. DOI: 10.1108/IJDI-06-2023-0147

Bagherian, A., Gershon, M., Kumar, S., & Mishra, M. K. (2024). Analyzing the relationship between digitalization and energy sustainability: A comprehensive ISM-MICMAC and DEMATEL approach. *Expert Systems with Applications*, 236, 121193. DOI: 10.1016/j.eswa.2023.121193

Bakar, M. H. A., & Ghafar, N. H. Md., & Farid, A. (2024). Exploring the Integration of Artificial Intelligence in Technical and Vocational Education and Training (TVET): Applications, Benefits, Challenges, and Future Prospects Full Paper. In *Borneo Engineering & Advanced Multidisciplinary International Journal (BEAM)* (Vol. 3). https://beam.pmu.edu.my

Bal, I. A., Alvarado-Albertorio, F., Marcelle, P., & Oaks-Garcia, C. T. (2022). Pre-service Teachers Computational Thinking (CT) and Pedagogical Growth in a Micro-credential: A Mixed Methods Study. *TechTrends*, 66(3), 468–482. DOI: 10.1007/s11528-022-00732-x PMID: 35499060

Banerjee, P. (Dr) M., Sinha, P. (Dr) S., & Pandey, D. P. (2024). *ARTIFICIAL INTELLIGENCE IN EDUCATION: REVOLUTIONIZING LEARNING AND TEACHING*. Red Unicorn Publishing.

Barker, P., & Campbell, L. M. (2024). *3 . Technology Strategies for Open Educational Resource Dissemination*.

Barrett, H. & Rose, D. C. (2022). Perceptions of the fourth agricultural revolution: What's in, what's out, and what consequences are anticipated?. Sociologia Ruralis. wiley.com

Barrett, M., Czerwinski, E., Goodell, J., Jacobs, D., Ritter, S., Sottilare, R., & Thai, K. P. (2022). Learning engineering uses data (Part 2): Analytics. In Learning Engineering Toolkit (pp. 175-198). Routledge. [HTML]

Barty, G., Boyer, N., Chrysikos, A., Griffith, M., House, K., Laughlin, T., . . . Zanville, H. (2024). Developing a more granular and equitable approach to the learner-earner journey: The role of badging, micro-credentials and 21st Century Skills within higher education to enable future workforce development. londonmet.ac.uk

Bash, K. L., Howell Smith, M. C., & Trantham, P. S. (2021). A systematic methodological review of hierarchical linear modeling in mixed methods research. [HTML]. *Journal of Mixed Methods Research*, 15(2), 190–211. DOI: 10.1177/1558689820937882

Baskara, R. (2023). Personalised learning with ai: Implications for ignatian pedagogy. *International Journal of Educational Best Practices*, 7(1), 1. DOI: 10.31258/ijebp.v7n1.p1-16

Bates, T., Cobo, C., Mariño, O., & Wheeler, S. (2020). Can artificial intelligence transform higher education? *International Journal of Educational Technology in Higher Education*, 17(1), 42. DOI: 10.1186/s41239-020-00218-x

Bean, M., Grant, S., Hardaker, G., & Ward, R. (2023). Signals and noise: Communicating achievement through alternative credentials. *International Journal of Information and Learning Technology*, 40(4), 305–316. DOI: 10.1108/IJILT-02-2023-0020

Beattie, S. (2014). *Types of digital learning badges: Drawing on the xbox achievement experience*. HASTAC. https://www. hastac. org/blogs/scott-beattie/2014/06/30/types-digital-learning-badges-drawing-xbox-achievement-experience

Ben Messaoud, S., Ilahi, M., & Cheniti-Belcadhi, L. (2022). Towards a personalized micro-credentials approach based on learning analytics for reducing the gap university-industry. *2022 IEEE Global Engineering Education Conference (EDUCON)*, 1448–1454. DOI: 10.1109/EDUCON52537.2022.9766585

Bergmann, J., & Sams, A. (2012). *Flip Your Classroom: Reach Every Student in Every Class Every Day*. International Society for Technology in Education.

Bergmann, J., & Sams, A. (2014). The flipped model. In *Flipped learning: Gateway to student engagement*. International Society for Technology in Education.

Berry, B., Airhart, K. M., & Byrd, P. A. (2016). Microcredentials: Teacher learning transformed. *Phi Delta Kappan*, 98(3), 34–40. DOI: 10.1177/0031721716677260

Besser, E. D., & Newby, T. J. (2019). Exploring the Role of Feedback and its Impact within a Digital Badge System from Student Perspectives. *TechTrends*, 63(4), 485–495. DOI: 10.1007/s11528-019-00386-2

Besser, E. D., & Newby, T. J. (2020). Feedback in a Digital Badge Learning Experience: Considering the Instructor's Perspective. *TechTrends*, 64(3), 484–497. DOI: 10.1007/s11528-020-00485-5

Bezold, C. (2010). Lessons from using scenarios for strategic foresight. *Technological Forecasting and Social Change*, 77(9), 1513–1518. DOI: 10.1016/j.techfore.2010.06.012

Bhutoria, A. (2022). Personalized education and artificial intelligence in the United States, China, and India: A systematic review using a human-in-the-loop model. Computers and Education: Artificial Intelligence. sciencedirect.com

Bigelow, A., Booth, C., Brockerhoff-Macdonald, B., Cormier, D., Dinsmore, C., Grey, S., Harrison, L., Hobbs, A., Lee, S., Maher, P., McArthur, F., Mitchell-Ashley, T., Mosley, J., Papple, J., Porter, J., Presant, D., Sommer, J., & Zahedi, E. (2022). Ecampusontario's micro-credential toolkit. *Ontario Online Learning Consortium*. https://ecampusontario.pressbooks.pub/microcredentialtoolkit/front-matter/welcome-to-the-toolkit/

Binhammad, M. H. Y., Othman, A., Abuljadayel, L., Mheiri, H. A., Alkaabi, M., & Almarri, M. (2024). Investigating How Generative AI Can Create Personalized Learning Materials Tailored to Individual Student Needs. *Creative Education*, 15(7), 7. Advance online publication. DOI: 10.4236/ce.2024.157091

Blankenberger, B., & Phillips, A. D. (2016). Performance funding in Illinois higher education. *Educational Policy*, 30(6), 884–915. DOI: 10.1177/0895904814556748

Blessinger, P., & Bliss, T. J. (2016). Introduction to open education: Towards a human rights theory. *Open Education: International Persepectives in Higher Education*, 11–30. DOI: 10.11647/OBP.0103.01

Bloom, B. S., Engelhart, M. D., Furst, E. J., Hill, W. H., & Krathwohl, D. R. A. (1956). *Taxonomy of Educational Objectives: The Classification of Educational Goals. Handbook 1: Cognitive Domain*. David McKay.

Bond, M., Buntins, K., Bedenlier, S., Zawacki-Richter, O., & Kerres, M. (2020). Mapping research in student engagement and educational technology in higher education: A systematic evidence map. [springer.com]. *International Journal of Educational Technology in Higher Education*, 17(1), 1–30. DOI: 10.1186/s41239-019-0176-8

Bonk, C. J., Lee, M. M., Reeves, T. C., & Reynolds, T. H. (2017). The emergence and design of massive open online courses (MOOCs). In Reiser, R. A., & Demsey, J. V. (Eds.), *Trends and issues in instructional design and technology* (4th ed., pp. 250–268). Pearson.

Bonk, C. J., Zhu, M., Kim, M., Xu, S., Sabir, N., & Sari, A. R. (2018). Pushing toward a more personalized MOOC: Exploring instructor selected activities, resources, and technologies for MOOC design and implementation. *International Review of Research in Open and Distance Learning*, 19(4). DOI: 10.19173/irrodl.v19i4.3439

Borges, A. F., Laurindo, F. J., Spínola, M. M., Gonçalves, R. F., & Mattos, C. A. (2021). The strategic use of artificial intelligence in the digital era: Systematic literature review and future research directions. [HTML]. *International Journal of Information Management*, 57, 102225. DOI: 10.1016/j.ijinfomgt.2020.102225

Borodiyenko, O., Melnyk, O., & Nychkalo, N. (2023). The role of international co-operation in the development of vocational education in ukraine. *European Journal of Education*, 58(4), 665–680. DOI: 10.1111/ejed.12586

Bosch, E., & Spinath, B. (2023). Students' Motivation in an Online and a Face-To-Face Semester: A Comparison of Initial Level, Development, and Use of Learning Activities. *Zeitschrift für Psychologie*, 231(2), 93–102. DOI: 10.1027/2151-2604/a000519

Boschetti, F., Price, J., & Walker, I. (2016). Myths of the future and scenario archetypes. *Technological Forecasting and Social Change*, 111, 76–85. DOI: 10.1016/j.techfore.2016.06.009

Bowen, K., & Thomas, A. (2014). Badges: A Common Currency for Learning. *Change*, 46(1), 21–25. DOI: 10.1080/00091383.2014.867206

Bozkurt, A., & Brown, M. (2022). Microcredentials: Stackable, Combinable, or Transferable Qualifications. *EdTechnica: The Open Encyclopedia of Educational Technology*. DOI: 10.59668/371.8264

Brauer, S. (2023). *Case study Finland: Micro-credentials for labour market education and training. First look at mapping micro-credentials in European labour-market-related education, training, and learning: take-up, characteristics, and functions.* CEDEFOP.

Braxton, S. N. (2022). Competency frameworks, alternative credentials and the evolving relationship of higher education and employers in recognizing skills and achievements. *The International Journal of Information and Learning Technology*, 40(5), 373–387. https://doi-org.ezproxy.snhu.edu/10.1108/IJILT-10-2022-0206. DOI: 10.1108/IJILT-10-2022-0206

Brown, M. (2012). Learning Analytics: Moving from Concept to Practice. *EDUCAUSE Learning Initiative*. https://library.educause.edu/-/media/files/library/2012/7/elib1203-pdf.pdf

Brown, M., Nic Giolla Mhichíl, M., Beirne, E., & Mac Lochlainn, C. (2021). *The global micro-credential landscape: Charting a new credential ecology for lifelong learning.*

Brown, M., Nic Giolla Mhichíl, M., Beirne, E., & Mac Lochlainn, C. (2021). *The Global Micro-credential Landscape: Charting a New Credential Ecology for Lifelong Learning.* http://hdl.handle.net/11599/3894

Brown, M., Giolla Mhichil, M. N., Beirne, E., & Mac Lochlainn, C. (2021). The global micro-credential landscape: Charting a new credential ecology for lifelong learning. *Journal of Learning Development*, 8(2), 228–254. DOI: 10.56059/jl4d.v8i2.525

Brown, M., McGreal, R., & Peters, M. (2023). A strategic institutional response to micro-credentials: Key questions for educational leaders. *Journal of Interactive Media in Education*, 2023(1), 7. DOI: 10.5334/jime.801

Bruguera, C. (2023). *Exploring learners' motivations and preferences for micro-credentials: a mixed-method study*. Ubiquity Proceedings., DOI: 10.5334/uproc.67

Bryant, J., Heitz, C., Sanghvi, S., & Wagle, D. (2018). *How artificial intelligence will impact K-12 teachers.*

Buchanan, John vd., (2020) "The Futures of Work: What Education Can and Can't Do", s.2-4, erişim 13 Ekim, 2020. https://unesdoc.unesco.org/ark:/48223/pf0000374435

Burrell, D. N. & Mcandrew, I. (2023). Addressing Bio-Cybersecurity Workforce Employee Shortages in Biotechnology and Health Science Sectors in the US. Scientific Bulletin. sciendo.com

Burton, E., Goldsmith, J., Koenig, S., Kuipers, B., Mattei, N., & Walsh, T. (2017). Ethical considerations in artificial intelligence courses. *AI Magazine*, 38(2), 22–34. DOI: 10.1609/aimag.v38i2.2731

Caetano, F. J. P., Casanova, D. G., & Moreira, D. M. P. (2023). Microcredentials: an opportunity towards the digital transformation. *International Conference on Higher Education Advances*, 665–673. DOI: 10.4995/HEAd23.2023.16125

Cantor, P., Osher, D., Berg, J., Steyer, L., & Rose, T. (2021). Malleability, plasticity, and individuality: How children learn and develop in context 1. In The science of learning and development (pp. 3-54). Routledge. tandfonline.com

Carey, K. L., & Stefaniak, J. E. (2018). An exploration of the utility of digital badging in higher education settings. *Educational Technology Research and Development*, 66(5), 1211–1229. DOI: 10.1007/s11423-018-9602-1

Caspari-Sadeghi, S. (2023). Learning assessment in the age of big data: Learning analytics in higher education. *Cogent Education*, 10(1), 2162697. Advance online publication. DOI: 10.1080/2331186X.2022.2162697

Castillo-Segura, P., Fernández-Panadero, C., Alario-Hoyos, C., Muñoz-Merino, P. J., & Kloos, C. D. (2021). A cost-effective IoT learning environment for the training and assessment of surgical technical skills with visual learning analytics. [science-direct.com]. *Journal of Biomedical Informatics*, 124, 103952. DOI: 10.1016/j.jbi.2021.103952 PMID: 34798158

Cathexis Consulting. (2024). *Evaluation of Ontario's micro-credential strategy, 2020-23.* Minister of Colleges and Universities, Government of Ontario.

Cedefop (2024). *Microcredentials: Striving to combine creditability and agility.* European Centre for the Development of Vocational Training. (Briefing Note).

CEDEFOP. (2020). *Coronavirus Boosts Interest in Online Learning*. CEDEFOP.

Cedefop. (2022). *ARE MICROCREDENTIALS BECOMING A BIG DEAL?* Deterding, S., Dixon, D., Khaled, R., & Nacke, L. (2011). From Game Design Elements to Gamefulness: Defining Gamification. *Proceedings of the 15th International Academic MindTrek Conference: Envisioning Future Media Environments, MindTrek 2011, 11*, 9–15. DOI: 10.1145/2181037.2181040

Celik, I. (2023). Towards Intelligent-TPACK: An empirical study on teachers' professional knowledge to ethically integrate artificial intelligence (AI)-based tools into education. Computers in Human Behavior. sciencedirect.com

Chaka, C. (2022). Fourth industrial revolution—a review of applications, prospects, and challenges for artificial intelligence, robotics and blockchain in higher education. Research and Practice in Technology Enhanced Learning, 18, 002. https://doi.org/ DOI: 10.58459/rptel.2023.18002

Chakravorty, D. K., Lawrence, R., He, Z., Brashear, W., Liu, H., Palughi, A. J., & Palsole, S. V. (2023). Access to Computing Education Using Micro-Credentials for Cyberinfrastructure. *Journal of Computational Science*, 14(2).

Chakroun, B., & Keevy, J. (2018). *Digital credentialing: implications for the recognition of learning across borders.*

Chandler, K., & Perryman, L. A. (2023). 'People have started calling me an expert': The impact of Open University microcredential courses. *Journal of Interactive Media in Education*, 2023(1), 8. DOI: 10.5334/jime.804

Chang, J., & Liu, D. (2024). Optimising Learning Outcomes: A Comprehensive Approach to Virtual Simulation Experiment Teaching in Higher Education. [HTML]. *International Journal of Human-Computer Interaction*, •••, 1–21. DOI: 10.1080/10447318.2024.2314825

Chango, W., Cerezo, R., Sanchez-Santillan, M., Azevedo, R., & Romero, C. (2021). Improving prediction of students' performance in intelligent tutoring systems using attribute selection and ensembles of different multimodal data sources. *Journal of Computing in Higher Education*, 33(3), 614–634. DOI: 10.1007/s12528-021-09298-8

Chapman, T. (2022, October 13). Microcredentials: Practices for developing employer partnerships. *College Is Education.* https://collegiseducation.com/insights/microcredentials/micro-credentials-practices-for-developing-employer-partnerships/

Charles, R., & Charles, T. (2024). High School Students' Perceptions of Using AI for Learning. *Voice of the Publisher*, 10(3), 284–297. DOI: 10.4236/vp.2024.103024

Charles, T. (2021). The past, present and future of assessments in the higher education sector. In Hill, C., Lamie, J., & Gore, T. (Eds.), *The Evolution of Transnational Education* (pp. 126–136). Routledge. DOI: 10.4324/9781003225386-13

Charles, T., & Hill, C. (2023). Remaining steadfast in the face of overwhelming change: Ethics and practice in emergency remote teaching–A case study in Dubai. In Lamie, J., & Hill, C. (Eds.), *The evolving nature of universities* (pp. 89–98). Routledge. DOI: 10.4324/9781003389361-7

Chatoor, K., Pilla, N., Balata, L., & Kaufman, A. (2024). *Supporting student mental health in Ontario: Exploring best practices and identifying gaps.* Higher Education Quality Council of Ontario (mimeo). https://heqco.ca/pub/supporting-student-mental-health-in-ontario-exploring-best-practices-and-identifying-gaps/

Chen, L., Chen, P., & Lin, Z. (2020). Artificial Intelligence in Education: A Review. *IEEE Access, 8*, 75264–75278. IEEE Access. DOI: 10.1109/ACCESS.2020.2988510

Chen, A. M. H., Brown, S., Mark, K., & McBane, S. (2023). An overview of Instructional approaches and decision-making strategies to curtail curricular overload. *American Journal of Pharmaceutical Education*, 87(8), 100013. DOI: 10.1016/j.ajpe.2022.12.001 PMID: 37597910

Chengbin, W., Hongbin, W., Min, D., & Yongyan, F. (2022). Lean startup approaches (LSas): Convergence, integration and improvement. [HTML]. *Technological Forecasting and Social Change*, 179, 121640. DOI: 10.1016/j.techfore.2022.121640

Cheng, Z., Watson, S. L., & Newby, T. J. (2018). Goal Setting and Open Digital Badges in Higher Education. *TechTrends*, 62(2), 190–196. DOI: 10.1007/s11528-018-0249-x

Chen, X., Xie, H., Zou, D., & Hwang, G. J. (2020). Application and theory gaps during the rise of artificial intelligence in education. [sciencedirect.com]. *Computers and Education: Artificial Intelligence*, 1, 100002. DOI: 10.1016/j.caeai.2020.100002

Chetty, R., Friedman, J., & Rockoff, J. (2014). Measuring the impacts of teachers II: Teacher value-added and student outcomes in adulthood. *The American Economic Review*, 104(9), 2633–2679. DOI: 10.1257/aer.104.9.2633

Chiang, F. K., Shang, X., & Qiao, L. (2022). Augmented reality in vocational training: A systematic review of research and applications. [HTML]. *Computers in Human Behavior*, 129, 107125. DOI: 10.1016/j.chb.2021.107125

Chiles, R. M., Broad, G., Gagnon, M., Negowetti, N., Glenna, L., Griffin, M. A., Tami-Barrera, L., Baker, S., & Beck, K. (2021). Democratizing ownership and participation in the 4th Industrial Revolution: Challenges and opportunities in cellular agriculture. [springer.com]. *Agriculture and Human Values*, 38(4), 943–961. DOI: 10.1007/s10460-021-10237-7 PMID: 34456466

Chinta, S. V., Wang, Z., Yin, Z., Hoang, N., Gonzalez, M., Quy, T. L., & Zhang, W. (2024). *FairAIED: Navigating Fairness, Bias, and Ethics in Educational AI Applications* (arXiv:2407.18745). arXiv. https://doi.org//arXiv.2407.18745DOI: 10.48550

Chukowry, V., Nanuck, G., & Sungkur, R. K. (2021). The future of continuous learning–Digital badge and microcredential system using blockchain. Global Transitions Proceedings. sciencedirect.com

Chukwuemeka, O., & Endurance, G. W. (2022). Impact of Training and Development on Employees' Performance in Epenal Group Ltd. [HTML]. *International Journal on Integrated Education*, 5(5), 281–293.

Chung, E., Subramaniam, G., & Dass, L. C. (2020). Online learning readiness among university students in Malaysia amidst COVID-19. *Asian Journal of University Education*, 16(2), 46–58.

Cigdem, H., & Öncü, S. (2023). *Leveraging Learning Analytics to Improve Student Engagement*., DOI: 10.4018/978-1-6684-9527-8.ch004

Cividini-Motta, C., Livingston, C., & Efaw, H. (2024). Systematic review of differential reinforcement in skill acquisition. *Behavior Analysis in Practice*, 17(2), 401–416. DOI: 10.1007/s40617-023-00903-z PMID: 38966267

Clausen, J. (2021). Learning to fly: Development and design of a micro-credentialing system for an educator preparation program in the absence of a required educational technology course. *TechTrends*, 66(2), 276–286. DOI: 10.1007/s11528-021-00673-x PMID: 34664042

Clayton, T., Rosenberg, S., & Christman, E. (2023, January 3). Addressing skills gaps. *Educational Technology Insights*. https://distance-and-remote-learning.educationtechnologyinsights.com/cxoinsights/addressing-skills-gaps-nid-2190.html

Clayton, T., Rosenberg, S., Wyatt, J., VanOrsdale, B., & Bisaillon, D. (2024, February 6). Higher education and real-world training (HEaRT) – A new ecosystem for learning. *The Journal of Continuing Higher Education*, 72(3), 392–404. Advance online publication. DOI: 10.1080/07377363.2023.2291592

Clemens, J., Globerman, S., & Palacios, M. (2023). Four-day week? With Canada's low productivity, we may need six-day work weeks. *Globe and Mail, 17th May*. https://www.theglobeandmail.com/business/commentary/article-four-day-workweek-productivity-canada/

Clements, K., West, R. E., & Hunsaker, E. (2020). Getting started with open badges and open microcredentials. *International Review of Research in Open and Distance Learning*, 21(1), 134–152. DOI: 10.19173/irrodl.v21i1.4529

Coleman, J. D. (2018). Engaging undergraduate students in a co-curricular digital badging platform. *Education and Information Technologies*, 23(1), 211–224. DOI: 10.1007/s10639-017-9595-0

Conference Board of Canada. (2024). *State of skills – Quality of work*. https://fsc-ccf.ca/projects/state-of-skills-quality-of-work/

Corbeil, R., Khan, B. H., & Corbeil, M. E. (2021). *Micro-learning in the digital age: The design and delivery of learning in snippets*. Routledge. DOI: 10.4324/9780367821623

Corrin, L., Scheffel, M., & Gašević, D. (2020). Learning analytics: Pathways to impact. *Australasian Journal of Educational Technology*, 36(6), 1–6. DOI: 10.14742/ajet.6853

Council of the European Union. (2022). Council Recommendation on a European approach to micro-credentials for lifelong learning and employability. Official Journal of the European Union. C243:02. https://eur-lex.europa.eu/legal-content/EN/TXT/PDF/?uri=CELEX:32022H0627(02)

Coursera (2023). How industry micro-credentials are transforming higher education. Coursera Blog. https://blog.coursera.org/how-industry-micro-credentials-are-transforming-higher-education/

Coursera. (2024). *Explore-Goals*.https://www.coursera.org/

Cowie, N., & Sakui, K. (2022). Micro-credentials: Surveying the landscape. In T. D. Cooper & J. York, *Remote Teaching and Beyond: Selected papers from the JALTCALL2021 Conference*. https://jaltcall.org/wp-content/uploads/2022/02/Proceedings-2021.pdf

Creswell, J. W., & Clark, V. L. P. (2007). *Designing and conducting mixed methods research*. Sage Publications, Inc.

Cucchiara, S., Giglio, A., Persico, D., & Raffaghelli, J. E. (2014). *Supporting Self-regulated Learning Through Digital Badges: A Case Study*., DOI: 10.1007/978-3-319-13296-9_15

D'Agostino, S. (2023, March 2). Microcredentials confuse employers, colleges, and learners. *Inside Higher Ed*. https://www.insidehighered.com/news/2023/03/03/microcredentials-confuse-employers-colleges-and-learners

D'Mello, S. K., & Graesser, A. (2023). Intelligent tutoring systems: How computers achieve learning gains that rival human tutors. Handbook of educational psychology. [HTML]

Dai, J. J., Ding, D., Shi, D., Huang, S., Wang, J., Qiu, X., Huang, K., Song, G., Wang, Y., Gong, Q., Song, J., Yu, S., Zheng, L., Chen, Y., Deng, J., & Song, G. (2022). BigDL 2.0: Seamless Scaling of AI Pipelines from Laptops to Distributed Cluster. *2022 IEEE/CVF Conference on Computer Vision and Pattern Recognition (CVPR)*, 21407–21414. DOI: 10.1109/CVPR52688.2022.02076

Damron-Rodriguez, J., Frank, J. C., Abushakrah, J., Jukema, J., Maiden, R. J., Mcdonnell, A. E., Pianosi, B., Sterns, H., & Van Dussen, D. (2020). *Gerontology competencies in higher education*. The Gerontological Society of America. www.geron.org

Dao, T. T., Mai, X. T., Ngo, T., Le, T., & Ho, H. (2021). From efficiency analyses to policy implications: A multilevel hierarchical linear model approach. [HTML]. *International Journal of the Economics of Business*, 28(3), 457–470. DOI: 10.1080/13571516.2021.1981750

Darvishi, A., Khosravi, H., Sadiq, S., & Gašević, D. (2022). Incorporating <scp>AI</scp> and learning analytics to build trustworthy peer assessment systems. *British Journal of Educational Technology*, 53(4), 844–875. DOI: 10.1111/bjet.13233

Davidson, M., & Ruparell, S. (2020). *The future of Ontario workers*. June 24th (mimeo). https://cdn.agilitycms.com/colleges-ontario/documents-library/document-files/2020%20June%20-%20The%20Future%20of%20Ontarios%20Workers.pdf

Davidson, M. (2020). *The Future of Ontario's Workers: How Micro-Credentials Can be a Vital Part of the Post-pandemic Recovery*. WilsonCenter.

Davies, T. E., Li, H., Bessette, S., Gauvin, R., Patience, G. S., & Dummer, N. F. (2022). Experimental methods in chemical engineering: Scanning electron microscopy and X-ray ultra-microscopy—SEM and XuM. [wiley.com]. *Canadian Journal of Chemical Engineering*, 100(11), 3145–3159. DOI: 10.1002/cjce.24405

Dawson, A., Yeomans, E., & Brown, E. R. (2018). Methodological challenges in education RCTs: Reflections from England's Education Endowment Foundation. *Educational Research*, 60(3), 292–310. DOI: 10.1080/00131881.2018.1500079

de Carvalho, W. F., & Zárate, L. E. (2020). A new local causal learning algorithm applied in learning analytics. *The International Journal of Information and Learning Technology*, 38(1), 103–115. DOI: 10.1108/IJILT-04-2020-0046

De Rosa, M., Glumac, O., Bianco, V., & Pallonetto, F. (2024). A micro-credential approach for life-long learning in the urban renewable energy sector. Renewable Energy. sciencedirect.com

DeakinCo. (2017). *What are micro-credentials and how can they benefit both businesses and employees?* Deakin Co., https://deakinco.com/resource/what-are-micro-credentials-and-how-can-they-benefit-both-businesses-and-employees/#:~:text=Micro%2Dcredentialing%20offers%20you%20and,and%20learning%20on%20the%20job.&text=The%20flexibility%20and%20incremental%20nature,they%20accumulate%20in%20their%20role

Delgado Kloos, C., Muñoz-Merino, P. J., Alario-Hoyos, C., Estévez Ayres, I., & Fernández-Panadero, C. (2015). Mixing and blending MOOC technologies with face-to-face pedagogies. *2015 IEEE Global Engineering Education Conference (EDUCON)*, Tallinn, Estonia, 967–971. DOI: 10.1109/EDUCON.2015.7096090

Deloitte. (2023). *Strengthening Canada's labour market.* https://www2.deloitte.com/ca/en/pages/public-sector/blog/strengthening-canada-labour-market.html

Deming, D. J. (2017). The growing importance of social skills in the labor market. *The Quarterly Journal of Economics*, 132(4), 1593–1640. DOI: 10.1093/qje/qjx022

Deng, R., Benckendorff, P., & Gannaway, D. (2019). Learner engagement in moocs: Scale development and validation. *British Journal of Educational Technology*, 51(1), 245–262. DOI: 10.1111/bjet.12810

Dennen, V. P., & Burner, K. J. (2007). The Cognitive Apprenticeship Model in Educational Practice. In *Handbook of Research on Educational Communications and Technology* (3rd ed.). Routledge.

Denny, P., Khosravi, H., Hellas, A., Leinonen, J., & Sarsa, S. (2023). *Can We Trust AI-Generated Educational Content? Comparative Analysis of Human and AI-Generated Learning Resources* (arXiv:2306.10509). arXiv. http://arxiv.org/abs/2306.10509

Desmarchelier, R., & Cary, L. J. (2022). Toward just and equitable micro-credentials: An australian perspective. *International Journal of Educational Technology in Higher Education*, 19(1), 25. Advance online publication. DOI: 10.1186/s41239-022-00332-y PMID: 35669714

Devapitchai, J. J., Dheenadhayalan, K., Rajeshkumar, L., Meena, M. R., Soundarya, M., Sowmiya, M. S., & Manickam, T. (2024). Applications of Artificial Intelligence Techniques in Modern Banking Sectors. In *Blockchain Applications for Smart Contract Technologies* (pp. 279–298). IGI Global. DOI: 10.4018/979-8-3693-1511-8.ch014

Devapitchai, J. J., Krishnapriya, S. V., Karuppiah, S. P., & Saranya, S. (2024). Using AI-Driven Decision-Making Tools in Corporate Investment Planning. In *Generative AI for Transformational Management* (pp. 137–160). IGI Global. DOI: 10.4018/979-8-3693-5578-7.ch006

Digital Promise. (2024). Micro-credentials impact report 2024. Digital Promise. https://assets.ctfassets.net/2pudprfttvy6/6kCSgjxcL69gh4ziZnlBhr/ff912d112d1afbdf705a893b6e9f99ea/Micro-Credentials_Impact_Report_2024.pdf

Dirani, K. M., Abadi, M., Alizadeh, A., Barhate, B., Garza, R. C., Gunasekara, N., Ibrahim, G., & Majzun, Z. (2020). Leadership competencies and the essential role of human resource development in times of crisis: A response to Covid-19 pandemicm. *Human Resource Development International*, 23(4), 380–394. DOI: 10.1080/13678868.2020.1780078

Directorate for Education and Skills - Education Policy Directorate (2019). *Future of education and skills 2030: reflections on transformative competencies 2030.*

Dogan, M. E., Goru Dogan, T., & Bozkurt, A. (2023). The Use of Artificial Intelligence (AI) in Online Learning and Distance Education Processes: A Systematic Review of Empirical Studies. *Applied Sciences (Basel, Switzerland)*, 13(5), 3056. Advance online publication. DOI: 10.3390/app13053056

Donthu, N., Kumar, S., Mukherjee, D., Pandey, N., & Lim, W. M. (2021). How to conduct a bibliometric analysis: An overview and guidelines. *Journal of Business Research*, 133, 285–296. DOI: 10.1016/j.jbusres.2021.04.070

Downes, S. (2010). Learning networks and connective knowledge. Collective Intelligence and E-Learning 2.0, 1-26. https://doi.org/DOI: 10.4018/978-1-60566-729-4.ch001

Drewery, D., Woodside, J., & Eppel, K. (2022). Artificial intelligence and résumé critique experiences. *Canadian Journal of Career Development*, 21(2), 28–39. DOI: 10.53379/cjcd.2022.338

Duperrin, J. C., & Godet, M. (1973). Méthode de hiérarchisation des éléments d'un système: essai de prospective du système de l'énergie nucléaire dans son contexte sociétal, Centre national de l'entrepreneuriat (CNE); hal-02185432.

Durak, G. (2013). *The online teaching of programming languages: Examining learner's attitudes, satisfaction and success.* Unpublished doctoral dissertation. Anadolu University, Institude of Social Sciences.

Durak, G., & Çankaya, S. (2020). Undergraduate students ' views about emergency distance education during the COVID-19 pandemic. *European Journal of Open Education and E-Learning Studies*, 5(1), 122–147. https://doi.org/https://doi.org/10.46827/ejoe.v5i1.3441. DOI: 10.46827/ejoe.v5i1.3441

Durak, G., & Cankaya, S. (2023). *Introduction to Learning Analytics*., DOI: 10.4018/978-1-6684-9527-8.ch001

Durak, G., & Çankaya, S. (2024). Are alarm bells ringing in academia? Chatgpt as a sample of using chatbots in education. *Turkish Online Journal of Distance Education*, 25(3), 1–17. DOI: 10.17718/tojde.1353737

Durak, G., Çankaya, S., & İzmirli, S. (2020). COVID-19 pandemi döneminde türkiye'deki üniversitelerin uzaktan eğitim sistemlerinin incelenmesi. *Necatibey Eğitim Fakültesi Elektronik Fen Ve Matematik Eğitimi Dergisi*, 14(1), 787–809. DOI: 10.17522/balikesirnef.743080

Durak, G., Çankaya, S., Özdemir, D., & Can, S. (2024). Artificial intelligence in education: A bibliometric study on its role in transforming teaching and learning. *International Review of Research in Open and Distance Learning*, 25(3), 219–244. DOI: 10.19173/irrodl.v25i3.7757

Edovald, T., & Nevill, C. (2021). Working Out What Works: The Case of the Education Endowment Foundation in England. *ECNU Review of Education*, 4(1), 46–64. DOI: 10.1177/2096531120913039

Educause (2017, July 18). 7 things you should read about microcredentialing/digital badging. *Educause*. https://library.educause.edu/resources/2017/7/7-things-you-should-read-about-microcredentialing-digital-badging

EDUCAUSE. (2012). *7 Things You Should Know About Badges*. https://library.educause.edu/resources/2012/6/7-things-you-should-know-about-badges

edX (2024). *Enterprise-For Campus*.https://business.edx.org/campus

edX (n.d.). Professional certificate programs. *edX*. https://www.edx.org/certificates/professional-certificate

Egloffstein, M. (2018). Massive Open Online Courses in Digital Workplace Learning. In *Digital Workplace Learning* (pp. 149–166). Springer International Publishing., DOI: 10.1007/978-3-319-46215-8_9

Egloffstein, M., & Ifenthaler, D. (2017). Employee Perspectives on MOOCs for Workplace Learning. *TechTrends*, 61(1), 65–70. DOI: 10.1007/s11528-016-0127-3

Egloffstein, M., & Schwerer, F. (2019). Participation and Achievement in Enterprise MOOCs for Professional Development: Initial Findings from the openSAP University. In *Learning Technologies for Transforming Large-Scale Teaching, Learning, and Assessment*. Springer International Publishing., DOI: 10.1007/978-3-030-15130-0_6

Ehlers, U. D. (2018). Higher Creduation–Degree or Education? The Rise of Microcredentials and its Consequences for the University of the Future. In *European Distance and E-Learning Network* (EDEN) Conference Proceedings (No. 1, pp. 456-465). European Distance and E-Learning Network.

Eidesen, P., Bjune, A. E., & Lang, S. I. (2023). "show me how to use a microscope" – the development and evaluation of certification as direct assessment of practical lab skills. *Ecology and Evolution*, 13(10), e10592. Advance online publication. DOI: 10.1002/ece3.10592 PMID: 37841223

El Mawas, N., & Muntean, C. (2018). Supporting lifelong learning through development of 21 st century skills 10th International Conference on Education and New Learning Technologies, https://hal.archives-ouvertes.fr/hal-02250150

ELEARNING MARKET TRENDS AND FORECAST 2017-2021. (2016). www .docebo.com

Elhajji, M., Alsayyari, A. S., & Alblawi, A. (2020). Towards an artificial intelligence strategy for higher education in Saudi Arabia. *2020 3rd International Conference on Computer Applications & Information Security (ICCAIS)*, 1–7.

Elliott, A. (2021). Making sense of AI: Our algorithmic world. [HTML]

Ellis, L. E., Nunn, S. G., & Avella, J. T. (2016). Digital Badges and Micro-credentials: Historical Overview, Motivational Aspects, Issues, and Challenges. In *Foundation of Digital Badges and Micro-Credentials* (pp. 3–21). Springer International Publishing. DOI: 10.1007/978-3-319-15425-1_1

Emmert-Streib, F. (2021). From the digital data revolution toward a digital society: Pervasiveness of artificial intelligence. Machine Learning and Knowledge Extraction. mdpi.com

EMSI. (2021). A guide to market research for colleges and universities. *EMSI*. https://www.datocms-assets.com/62658/1643839553-emsi-market-research-guide.pdf

Ersozlu, Z., Taheri, S., & Koch, I. (2024). A review of machine learning methods used for educational data. *Education and Information Technologies*. Advance online publication. DOI: 10.1007/s10639-024-12704-0

Essel, H. B., Vlachopoulos, D., Tachie-Menson, A., Johnson, E. E., & Baah, P. K. (2022). The impact of a virtual teaching assistant (chatbot) on students' learning in Ghanaian higher education. *International Journal of Educational Technology in Higher Education*, 19(1), 57. DOI: 10.1186/s41239-022-00362-6

European Commission. (2015). ECTS users' guide 2015. https://op.europa.eu/en/publication-detail/-/publication/da7467e6-8450-11e5-b8b7-01aa75ed71a1

European Commission. (2020). A European approach to micro-credentials - output of the micro- credentials higher education consultation group - final report. *European Union*. Retrieved July 23, 2021, from

European Commission. (2020). *A European approach to micro-credentials: Background paper for the first meeting of the consultation group on micro-credentials*. https://education.ec.europa.eu/sites/default/files/document-library-docs/european-approach-micro-credentials-higher-education-consultation-group-output-annex-1.pdf

European Commission. (2020). A European approach to micro-credentials: Output of the micro-credentials higher education consultation group. https://education.ec.europa.eu/sites/default/files/document-library-docs/european-approach-micro-credentials-higher-education-consultation-group-output-final-report.pdf

European Commission. (2020). Achieving the European Education Area by 2025 - Communication. https://ec.europa.eu/education/resources-and-tools/document-library/eea-communication-sept2020_en

European Commission. (2021). *A European approach to micro-credentials*. https://education.ec.europa.eu/sites/default/files/2022-01/micro-credentials%20brochure%20updated.pdf Accessed on September 12, 2024.

European Commission. (2021). European Skills Agenda." Accessed December 6, 2022. https://ec.europa.eu/social/main.jsp?catId=1223

European Commission. (2022). Proposal for a Council Recommendation on a European Approach to Micro-Credentials for Lifelong Learning and Employability - Adoption. https://data.consilium.europa.eu/doc/document/ST-9237-2022-INIT/en/pdf

European MOOC Consortium (EMC). (2020). EMC common microcredential framework. *European MOOC Consortium*, 1–13. https://emc.eadtu.eu/images/EMC_Common_Microcredential_Framework_.pdf

European Training Foundation. (2022). *Guide to design, issue and recognise micro-credentials.*https://etf.europa.eu/sites/default/files/2023-05/Micro-Credential%20 Guidelines%20Final%20Delivery.pdf. Accessed: April 2024.

European Training Foundation. (2022). Guide to design, issue and recognize micro-credentionals. *European Training Foundation.* www.etf.europa.eu/sites/default/files/ 2023-05/Micro-Credential%20Guidelines%20Final%20%Delivery.pdf

European Union. (2021). *A European approach to micro-credentials.* https:// education.ec.europa.eu/sites/default/files/2022-01/micro-credentials%20brochure %20updated.pdf

Fadlelmula, , K. FQadhi, , S. M. (2024). Beyond the Classroom: Integrating the ORID Model for In-Depth Reflection and Assessment in Service-Learning. *Education Sciences, 14*(9), 987.

Fadzil, M., & Munira, T. A. (2008). Applications of Artificial Intelligence in an Open and Distance Learning institution. *2008 International Symposium on Information Technology, 1*, 1–7. DOI: 10.1109/ITSIM.2008.4631532

Familoni, B.Babajide Tolulope FamiloniNneamaka Chisom Onyebuchi. (2024). Advancements and challenges in ai integration for technical literacy: A systematic review. *Engineering Science & Technology Journal*, 5(4), 1415–1430. DOI: 10.51594/estj.v5i4.1042

Fan, X., Wei, X., Lewis, A., & Watts, J. (2024). Micro-credentialing as an approach to educator professional learning: Voices from developers, pursuers, and assessors. *Teaching and Teacher Education*, 148, 104700. DOI: 10.1016/j.tate.2024.104700

Farikah, F., Astuty, A., Mazid, S., & Mulyani, M. (2023). *Student Engagement in Virtual Learning: The Self-Determination Theory Perspective* (SSRN Scholarly Paper 4593589). Social Science Research Network. https://papers.ssrn.com/sol3/ papers.cfm?abstract_id=4593589

Farmer, T., & West, R. E. (2017). Opportunities and challenges with digital open badges. In *Foundations of learning and instructional design technology* (Vol. 56, pp. 45–48). https://lidtfoundations.pressbooks.com/chapter/open-badges/

Farmer, L. S. (2023). Technology use and its changing role in community education. In *Handbook of Research on Andragogical Leadership and Technology in a Modern World* (pp. 358–383). IGI Global. [HTML] DOI: 10.4018/978-1-6684-7832-5.ch019

Fastiggi, W. (2023). *The relationship between STEM education and environmental sustainability.* Technology for Learners. https://technologyforlearners.com/the -relationship-between-stem-education-and-environmental-sustainability/

Fazey, I., Schäpke, N., Caniglia, G., Hodgson, A., Kendrick, I., Lyon, C., & Saha, P. (2020). Transforming knowledge systems for life on Earth: Visions of future systems and how to get there. [sciencedirect.com]. *Energy Research & Social Science*, 70, 101724. DOI: 10.1016/j.erss.2020.101724

Fedock, B., Kebritchi, M., Sanders, R., & Holland, A. (2016). Digital badges and micro-credentials: Digital age classroom practices, design strategies, and issues. Foundation of Digital Badges and Micro-Credentials: Demonstrating and Recognizing Knowledge and Competencies, 273-286. https://doi.org/10.1007/978-3-319-15425-1_15

Fengchun, M., Wayne, H., Huang, R., Zhang, H., & UNESCO. (2021). *AI and education: A guidance for policymakers*. UNESCO Publishing.

Fergnani, A., & Jackson, M. (2019). Extracting scenario archetypes: A quantitative text analysis of documents about the future. *Futures & Foresight Science*, 1(2), e17. Advance online publication. DOI: 10.1002/ffo2.17

Ferman, B., Finamor, L., & Lima, L. (2019). A*re Public Schools Ready to Integrate Math Classes with Khan Academy?* Munich Personal RePEc Archive. https://mpra.ub.uni-muenchen.de/94736/

Ferrara, E. (2023). Fairness and Bias in Artificial Intelligence: A Brief Survey of Sources, Impacts, and Mitigation Strategies. *Sci*, 6(1), 1. Advance online publication. DOI: 10.3390/sci6010003

Ferri, F., Grifoni, P., & Guzzo, T. (2020). Online learning and emergency remote teaching: Opportunities and challenges in emergency situations. Societies. mdpi.com

Firat, M. (2023). Integrating AI Applications into Learning Management Systems to Enhance e-Learning. *Öğretim Teknolojisi ve Hayat Boyu Öğrenme Dergisi - Instructional Technology and Lifelong Learning*, 1–14. DOI: 10.52911/itall.1244453

Fischer, T., Oppl, S., & Stabauer, M. (2022). Micro-Credential Development: Tools, Methods and Concepts Supporting the European Approach. In the 17th *International Conference on Wirtschaftsinformatik*, Nuremberg, Germany, February 2022.

Fisher, R. M., & Leder, H. (2022). An assessment of micro-credentials in New Zealand vocational education. *International Journal of Training Research*, 20(3), 232–247. DOI: 10.1080/14480220.2021.2018018

Fitria, T. N. (2021, December). Artificial intelligence (AI) in education: Using AI tools for teaching and learning process. In Prosiding Seminar Nasional & Call for Paper STIE AAS (pp. 134-147). stie-aas.ac.id

Fitzgerald, R., & Huijser, H. (2023). The Opportunities and Challenges in the Portability and Authentication of Micro-credentials and Short Courses in a Post-COVID Landscape. Technology-Enhanced Learning and the Virtual University, 465-477. [HTML]

Fleming, P. (2021). *Dark academia – How universities die*. Pluto Press.

Flynn, S., Cullinane, E., Murphy, H., & Wylie, N. (2023). Micro-credentials and digital badges: Definitions, affordances, and design considerations for application in higher education institutions. *All Ireland Journal of Teaching and Learning in Higher Education*, 15(1), 1–19.

Flyverbom, M., & Garsten, C. (2021). Anticipation and organization: Seeing, knowing, and governing futures. *Organizational Theory*, 2(3), 1–25. DOI: 10.1177/26317877211020325

Fontela, E., & Hingel, A. (1993). Scenarios on economic and social cohesion in Europe. *Futures*, 25(2), 139–154. DOI: 10.1016/0016-3287(93)90160-U

Forero-Corba, W., & Bennasar, F. N. (2024). Techniques and applications of Machine Learning and Artificial Intelligence in education: A systematic review. *RIED-Revista Iberoamericana de Educación a Distancia*, 27(1), 111–127.

Foreshew, A., & Al-Jawad, M. (2022). An intersectional participatory action research approach to explore and address class elitism in medical education. [HTML]. *Medical Education*, 56(11), 1076–1085. DOI: 10.1111/medu.14857 PMID: 35718997

Forkan, A. R. M., Kang, Y.-B., Jayaraman, P. P., Du, H., Thomson, S., Kollias, E., & Wieland, N. (2023). VideoDL: Video-Based Digital Learning Framework Using AI Question Generation and Answer Assessment. [IJAC]. *International Journal of Advanced Corporate Learning*, 16(1), 19–27. DOI: 10.3991/ijac.v16i1.35207

Freeman-Green, S., Williamson, P., & Cornelius, E., K. (. (2023). Promoting Inclusive Practices in Education: Bridging Gaps and Fostering Independence. *Teaching Exceptional Children*, 56(2), 68–69. DOI: 10.1177/00400599231223785

Fuller, J. B., Langer, C., & Sigelman, M. (2022). Skills-based hiring is on the rise. Harvard Business Review Digital, February 11th. https://www.hbs.edu/faculty/Pages/item.aspx?num=62029

Fuller, J., Langer, C., & Sigelman, M. (2022). Skills-based hiring is on the rise. *Harvard Business Review*. Hbr.org/2022/02/skills-based-hiring-ison-the-rise

FutureLearn. (2020). FutureLearn launches microcredentials with six global partners. https://www.futurelearn.com/info/press-releases/futurelearn-launches-microcredentials-with-six-global-partners

FutureLearn. (2024). C*ourses.*https://www.futurelearn.com/?main-nav-submenu=main-nav-courses

Galetsi, P., Katsaliaki, K., & Kumar, S. (2019). Values, challenges and future directions of big data analytics in healthcare: A systematic review. In *Social Science and Medicine* (Vol. 241). Elsevier Ltd., DOI: 10.1016/j.socscimed.2019.112533

Galindo, M., Fennelly-Atkinson, R., Franklin, K., & Luna, C. (2024). The role of micro-credentials in lifelong learning and development: Empowering learners, empowering organizations. Digital Promise. https://digitalpromise.dspacedirect.org/bitstreams/a0742249-256a-479c-92dd-fd9d0784f4f5/download#:~:text=Micro%2Dcredentials%20disrupt%20postsecondary%20pathways,proving%20their%20competence%20through%20assessments

Galindo-Domínguez, H. (2021). Flipped classroom in the educational system: Trend or effective pedagogical model compared to other methodologies? *Journal of Educational Technology & Society*, 24(3), 44–60. .https://www.jstor.org/stable/27032855

Galindo-Domínguez, H., Delgado, N., Losada, D., & Etxabe, J. M. (2024). An analysis of the use of artificial intelligence in education in Spain: The in-service teacher's perspective. *Journal of Digital Learning in Teacher Education*, 40(1), 41–56. DOI: 10.1080/21532974.2023.2284726

Gallagher, S. R. (2018). *Educational Credentials Come of Age: A Survey on the Use and Value of Educational Credentials in Hiring*. Center for the Future of Higher Education & Talent Strategy.

Galvão, A., Cabeceiro, S. F., & Pinheiro, M. (2016). Impact of the Coaching Process on Business Productivity. *3º Congresso Da Ordem Dos Psicólogos Portugueses*, 969-985. https://www.ordemdospsicologos.pt/ficheiros/documentos/livro_de_actas_3ao_congresso_opp_final.pdf

Galvão, A. (2020a). *"Cover" of pedagogical innovation processes and resources applied to learning*. Self-published.

Galvão, A. (2020b). The Design Thinking process as an enabler of motivation for learning. In de Jesus, S. N. (Ed.), *Inovação e partilha pedagógica na UAlg* (pp. 23–26). University of Algarve Editora.

Galvão, A., Anes, E., & Chumbo, I. (2023). Design Thinking to Promote Mental Health Literacy for Higher Education Students. In Rodrigues, S., & Mourato, J. (Eds.), *The Impact of HEIs on Regional Development: Facts and Practices of Collaborative Work With SMEs* (pp. 130–143). IGI Global., DOI: 10.4018/978-1-6684-6701-5.ch008

Galvão, A., Anes, E., Pinheiro, M., & Gomes, M. J. (2019). Happiness: one of the determinants of occupational health. *V Congresso Ibero-Americano e Luso-Brasileiro de Psicologia Da Saúde - I Congresso Promoção Da Saúde e Do Bem-Estar No Ensino Superior*, 45-50.

Galvão, A., Pinheiro, M., Antão, C., & Gomes, M. J. (2019). Happiness and mental health in higher education students: a comparative study. *V Congresso Ibero-Americano e Luso-Brasileiro de Psicologia Da Saúde - I Congresso Promoção Da Saúde e Do Bem-Estar No Ensino Superior*, 39-45.

Gan, W., Sun, Y., & Sun, Y. (2022). Knowledge interaction enhanced sequential modeling for interpretable learner knowledge diagnosis in intelligent tutoring systems. [HTML]. *Neurocomputing*, 488, 36–53. DOI: 10.1016/j.neucom.2022.02.080

Garg, P., Raj, R., Kumar, V., Singh, S., Pahuja, S., & Sehrawat, N. (2023). Elucidating the role of consumer decision making style on consumers' purchase intention: The mediating role of emotional advertising using PLS-SEM. *Journal of Economy and Technology*, 1, 108–118. https://doi.org/10.1016/j.ject.2023.10.001

Garrido, A., Morales, L., & Serina, I. (2016). On the use of case-based planning for e-learning personalization. *Expert Systems with Applications*, 60, 1–15. https://doi.org/https://doi.org/10.1016/j.eswa.2016.04.030. DOI: 10.1016/j.eswa.2016.04.030

Garrison, D. R., Anderson, T., & Archer, W. (1999). Critical Inquiry in a Text-Based Environment: Computer Conferencing in Higher Education. *The Internet and Higher Education*, 2(2–3), 87–105. DOI: 10.1016/S1096-7516(00)00016-6

Gauthier, T. (2020). The value of microcredentials: The employer's perspective. *The Journal of Competency-Based Education*, 5(2), e01209. DOI: 10.1002/cbe2.1209

Geng, S., Niu, B., Feng, Y., & Huang, M. (2020). Understanding the focal points and sentiment of learners in mooc reviews: A machine learning and sc-liwc-based approach. *British Journal of Educational Technology*, 51(5), 1785–1803. DOI: 10.1111/bjet.12999

Ghafoor, S., & Abiodullah, M. (2024). Effect of flipped classroom approach on higher secondary students' academic performance. *Educational Research and Innovation, 4*(1). https://eri.com.pk/index.php/Journal/article/view/116/74

Gibson, D., Ostashewski, N., Flintoff, K., Grant, S., & Knight, E. (2013). Digital badges in education. *Education and Information Technologies*, 20(2), 1–8. DOI: 10.1007/s10639-013-9291-7

Gilboy, M. B., Heinerichs, S., & Pazzaglia, G. (2015). Enhancing student engagement using the flipped classroom. *Journal of Nutrition Education and Behavior*, 47(1), 109–114. DOI: 10.1016/j.jneb.2014.08.008 PMID: 25262529

Gish-Lieberman, J. J., Tawfik, A., & Gatewood, J. (2021). Micro-Credentials and Badges in Education: A Historical Overview. *TechTrends*, 65(1), 5–7. DOI: 10.1007/s11528-020-00567-4

Gligorea, I., Cioca, M., Oancea, R., Gorski, A.-T., Gorski, H., & Tudorache, P. (2023). Adaptive learning using artificial intelligence in e-learning: A literature review. *Education Sciences*, 13(12), 1216. DOI: 10.3390/educsci13121216

Göçen, A., & Aydemir, F. (2020). Artificial intelligence in education and schools. *Research on Education and Media*, 12(1), 13–21. DOI: 10.2478/rem-2020-0003

Godet, M. (1994). *From Anticipation to Action: A handbook of strategic prospective*. UNESCO Publishing.

Goel, P. K., Singhal, A., Bhadoria, S. S., Saraswat, B. K., & Patel, A. (2024). AI and Machine Learning in Smart Education: Enhancing Learning Experiences Through Intelligent Technologies. In *Infrastructure Possibilities and Human-Centered Approaches With Industry 5.0* (pp. 36-55). IGI Global.

Goglio, V., Bertolini, S., & Parigi, P. (2023). The perceived labour market value of massive open online courses (MOOCs) in Europe and the USA. *Journal of Education and Work*, 36(1), 37–51. DOI: 10.1080/13639080.2022.2162020

Goksel, N., & Bozkurt, A. (2019). *Artificial Intelligence in Education.*, DOI: 10.4018/978-1-5225-8431-5.ch014

Golden, G., Kato, S., & Weko, T. (2021, September 29). Promoting social inclusion through micro-credentials. *OECD Education and Skills Today*. https://oecdedutoday.com/promoting-social-inclusion-through-micro-credentials/

Gonzalez, D. P., & Villaire, M. (2021). Advancing Professional Development in Health Literacy: The Health Literacy Specialist Certificate Program and the Health Literacy Solutions Center. *American Journal of Health Education*, 52(6), 333–337. DOI: 10.1080/19325037.2021.1985020

Goopio, J., & Cheung, C. (2021). The MOOC dropout phenomenon and retention strategies. [HTML]. *Journal of Teaching in Travel & Tourism*, 21(2), 177–197. DOI: 10.1080/15313220.2020.1809050

Grangeat, M. (2016). Dimensions and Modalities of Inquiry-Based Teaching: Understanding the Variety of Practices. *Education Inquiry*, 7(4), 29863. Advance online publication. DOI: 10.3402/edui.v7.29863

Grant, S. (2016). History and Context of Open Digital Badges. In Mullenberg, L. Y., & Berge, Z. L. (Eds.), *Digital Badges in Education* (pp. 3–11). Routledge.

Greene, J. A., Oswald, C., & Pomerantz, J. (2015). Predictors of retention and achievement in a massive open online course. *American Educational Research Journal*, 52(5), 925–955. DOI: 10.3102/0002831215584621

Grek, S., & Russell, I. (2023). Beyond bologna? infrastructuring quality in european higher education. *European Educational Research Journal*, 23(2), 215–236. DOI: 10.1177/14749041231170518

Gribbins, M., & Bonk, C. J. (2023). An exploration of instructors' perceptions about online proctoring and its value in ensuring academic integrity. *British Journal of Educational Technology*, 54(6), 1693–1714. DOI: 10.1111/bjet.13389

Guan, C., Mou, J., & Jiang, Z. (2020). Artificial intelligence innovation in education: A twenty-year data-driven historical analysis. International Journal of Innovation Studies. sciencedirect.com

Güçlü Aydoğan, M., Draganović, S., & Elen, M. A. (2024). Online learning self-efficacy beliefs predict subjective well-being of college students during COVID-19 pandemic. *Journal of Educational Technology and Online Learning*, 7(3), 334–345. DOI: 10.31681/jetol.1513598

Guni, A., Normahani, P., Davies, A., & Jaffer, U. (2021). Harnessing machine learning to personalize web-based health care content. [jmir.org]. *Journal of Medical Internet Research*, 23(10), e25497. DOI: 10.2196/25497 PMID: 34665146

Guo, J., He, H., He, T., Lausen, L., Li, M., Lin, H., & Zhu, Y. (2020). Gluoncv and gluonnlp: Deep learning in computer vision and natural language processing. [jmlr.org]. *Journal of Machine Learning Research*, 21(23), 1–7.

Habiba, U.-E. -, Bogner, J., & Wagner, S. (2024). Towards Explainability as a Functional Requirement: A Vision to Integrate the Legal, End-User, and ML Engineer Perspectives. *Proceedings of the 2nd International Workshop on Responsible AI Engineering*, 16–19. DOI: 10.1145/3643691.3648590

Habib, M. (2023). Digital transformation strategy for developing higher education in conflict-affected societies. *Social Sciences & Humanities Open*, 8(1), 100627. https://doi.org/https://doi.org/10.1016/j.ssaho.2023.100627. DOI: 10.1016/j.ssaho.2023.100627

Halim, F. (2023). Development and validation of a questionnaire for microlearning requirements in micro-credentials: a pilot study. https://doi.org/DOI: 10.21203/rs.3.rs-3162218/v1

Hall, T. E., Meyer, A., & Rose, D. H. (2012). *Universal Design for Learning in the Classroom: Practical Applications*. Guilford Press.

Hamilton, N. (2023). From Dropout to Doctorate: A Phenomenology of the Self-Determination of Individuals who Persisted to Completion. *Doctoral Dissertations and Projects*. https://digitalcommons.liberty.edu/doctoral/4166

Hamutoğlu. Ünveren-Bilgiç, & Özden, (2023). *The Importance of Internal Quality Assurance Standards in Higher Education for Competitiveness and National Development. Proceeding*, 36th Asian Association of Open Universities Annual Conference (AAOU 2023), 28-30 September, İstanbul, Türkiye.

Ha, N. T. N., Spittle, M., Watt, A. P., & Dyke, N. V. (2022). A systematic literature review of micro-credentials in higher education: A non-zero-sum game. Higher Education Research &Amp. *Higher Education Research & Development*, 42(6), 1527–1548. DOI: 10.1080/07294360.2022.2146061

Hancock, B., Higgins, C., Law, J., Olson, S., Patel, N., & Dusen, K. V. (2022, November 15). Taking a skills-based approach to building the future workforce. *McKinsey & Company*. https://www.mckinsey.com/capabilities/people-and-organizational-performance/our-insights/taking-a-skills-based-approach-to-building-the-future-workforce

Hanne Shapiro Futures. Andersen, T., & Nedergaard Larsen, K. (2020). *[Title of the report, if available]* (Contract No. 1000245). Danish Technological Institute. Publications Office of the European Union. https://doi.org/DOI: 10.2766/30863

Hartnett, M. K. (2021). How and why are digital badges being used in higher education in New Zealand? *Australasian Journal of Educational Technology*, •••, 104–118. DOI: 10.14742/ajet.6098

Hase, A., Kahnbach, L., Kuhl, P., & Lehr, D. (2022). To use or not to use learning data: A survey study to explain german primary school teachers' usage of data from digital learning platforms for purposes of .... Frontiers in Education. frontiersin.org

Hassani, H., Silva, E. S., Unger, S., TajMazinani, M., & Mac Feely, S. (2020). Artificial intelligence (AI) or intelligence augmentation (IA): What is the future? [mdpi.com]. *AI*, 1(2), 8. DOI: 10.3390/ai1020008

Hatzi, O., Vrakas, D., Nikolaidou, M., Bassiliades, N., Anagnostopoulos, D., & Vlahavas, I. (2012). An Integrated Approach to Automated Semantic Web Service Composition through Planning. *IEEE Transactions on Services Computing*, 5(3), 319–332. DOI: 10.1109/TSC.2011.20

Healy, M. (2021). Microcredential learners need quality careers and employability support. *The Journal of Teaching and Learning for Graduate Employability*, 12(1), 21–23. DOI: 10.21153/jtlge2021vol12no1art1071

Hearn, G., Williams, P., Rodrigues, J. H. P., & Laundon, M. (2023). Education and training for industry 4.0: A case study of a manufacturing ecosystem. [HTML]. *Education + Training*, 65(8/9), 1070–1084. DOI: 10.1108/ET-10-2022-0407

Henderson, J., & Corry, M. (2021). Data literacy training and use for educational professionals. [emerald.com]. *Journal of Research in Innovative Teaching & Learning*, 14(2), 232–244. DOI: 10.1108/JRIT-11-2019-0074

Hendricks-Sturrup, R., Simmons, M., Anders, S., Aneni, K., Wright Clayton, E., Coco, J., Collins, B., Heitman, E., Hussain, S., Joshi, K., Lemieux, J., Lovett Novak, L., Rubin, D. J., Shanker, A., Washington, T., Waters, G., Webb Harris, J., Yin, R., Wagner, T., & Malin, B. (2023). Developing Ethics and Equity Principles, Terms, and Engagement Tools to Advance Health Equity and Researcher Diversity in AI and Machine Learning: Modified Delphi Approach. *JMIR AI*, 2, e52888. DOI: 10.2196/52888 PMID: 38875540

Hickmann, T., Bertram, C., Biermann, F., Brutschin, E., Kriegler, E., Livingston, J. E., Pianta, S., Riahi, K., Van Ruijven, B., & Van Vuuren, D. (2022). Exploring Global Climate Policy Futures and Their Representation in Integrated Assessment Models. *Politics and Governance*, 10(3), 171–185. DOI: 10.17645/pag.v10i3.5328

Higgs, L. (2020). Labour Rights, Artificial Intelligence and Automation in the context of the UK, Brexit, and Covid-19 with a comparative study of Singapore. gchumanrights.org

Higher Learning Commission. (2022). Evolving: Accreditation and the credential landscape. *Higher Learning Commission*. https://download.hlcommission.org/initiatives/2022StakeholdersRoundtablePapers.pdf

Hill, C., Abu-Ayyash, E., & Charles, T. (2023). By nature, a social animal: An exploration of perceptions of online group work. *Cambridge Journal of Education*, 53(5), 665–681. DOI: 10.1080/0305764X.2023.2206795

Holmes, W., & Anastopoulou, S. (2019). What do students at distance universities think about AI? *Proceedings of the Sixth (2019) ACM Conference on Learning @ Scale*. DOI: 10.1145/3330430.3333659

Holmes, W., Porayska-Pomsta, K., Holstein, K., Sutherland, E., Baker, T., Shum, S., & Koedinger, K. (2021). Ethics of ai in education: Towards a community-wide framework. *International Journal of Artificial Intelligence in Education*, 32(3), 504–526. DOI: 10.1007/s40593-021-00239-1

Ho, N., Pham, H., Sivapalan, S., & Dinh, V. (2022). The adoption of blended learning using coursera moocs: A case study in a vietnamese higher education institution. *Australasian Journal of Educational Technology*, 38(6), 121–138. DOI: 10.14742/ajet.7671

Hooda, M., Rana, C., Dahiya, O., Rizwan, A., & Hossain, M. S. (2022). Artificial Intelligence for Assessment and Feedback to Enhance Student Success in Higher Education. *Mathematical Problems in Engineering*, 2022, 1–19. Advance online publication. DOI: 10.1155/2022/5215722

House, K. M. (2020). Student perceptions of personalized learning in a rural school district.. louisville.edu

Hughes, E. M., Witzel, B. S., Myers, J., & Lin, T. H. (2023). Unpacking and Understanding Specific Learning Disabilities in Mathematics. *Teaching Exceptional Children*, 56(1), 26–32. DOI: 10.1177/00400599231175509

Humphrey, W.Jr, Laverie, D., & Muñoz, C. (2021). The use and value of badges: Leveraging salesforce trailhead badges for marketing technology education. *Journal of Marketing Education*, 43(1), 25–42. DOI: 10.1177/0273475320912319

Hunt, D. V. L., Lombardi, D. R., Atkinson, S., Barber, A. R. G., Barnes, M., Boyko, C. T., Brown, J., Bryson, J., Butler, D., Caputo, S., Caserio, M., Coles, R., Cooper, R. F. D., Farmani, R., Gaterell, M., Hale, J., Hales, C., Hewitt, C. N., Jankovic, L., & Rogers, C. D. F. (2012). Scenario archetypes: Converging rather than diverging themes. *Sustainability (Basel)*, 4(4), 740–772. DOI: 10.3390/su4040740

Hunt, T., Carter, R., Zhang, L., & Yang, S. (2020). Micro-credentials: The potential of personalized professional development. *Development and Learning in Organizations*, 34(2), 33–35. DOI: 10.1108/DLO-09-2019-0215

Hu, Y., Donald, C., & Giacaman, N. (2022). A revised application of cognitive presence automatic classifiers for moocs: A new set of indicators revealed? *International Journal of Educational Technology in Higher Education*, 19(1), 48. Advance online publication. DOI: 10.1186/s41239-022-00353-7 PMID: 36118283

Igami, M. Z., Bressiani, J., & Mugnaini, R. (2014). A new model to identify the productivity of theses in terms of articles using co-word analysis. *Journal of Scientometric Research*, 3(1), 3. DOI: 10.4103/2320-0057.143660

Inayatullah, S. (2020). Scenarios for Teaching and Training: From Being "Kodaked" to Futures Literacy and Futures-Proofing. CSPS Strategy and Policy Journal. metafuture.org

International Council of Distance Education (ICDE). (2019). *Report of the ICDE Working Group on the Present and Future of Alternative Digital Credentials* (ADCs). https://static1.squarespace.com/static/5b99664675f9eea7a3ecee82/t/5cc69fb771c10b798657bf2f/1556520905468/ICDE-ADC+report-January+2019+%28002%29.pdf

International Labour Organization. (2024). Micro-credentialing: Powerful new learning tool, or just "pouring old wine into new bottles"? ILO Employment Podcast Episode 38. https://www.ilo.org/media/543076/download

International Union for Health Promotion and Education. (2009). *Building health-promoting schools: "Guidelines for promoting health in the school environment."* https://www.dge.mec.pt/sites/default/files/ficheiros/iuhpe_hps_guidelinesii_2009_portuguese.pdf

Ionescu, C. A., Paschia, L., Gudanescu Nicolau, N. L., Stanescu, S. G., Neacsu Stancescu, V. M., Coman, M. D., & Uzlau, M. C. (2020). Sustainability analysis of the e-learning education system during pandemic period—Covid-19 in Romania. [mdpi.com]. *Sustainability (Basel)*, 12(21), 9030. DOI: 10.3390/su12219030

İpek, Z., Gözüm, A. I. C., Papadakis, S., & Kalogiannakis, M. (2023). Educational Applications of the ChatGPT AI System: A Systematic Review Research. *Educational Process International Journal*, 12(3), 26–55. DOI: 10.22521/edupij.2023.123.2

Iqbal, S., Naeem, M. A., & Nayyar, A. (2016, November). Status of MOOCs in Pakistan: optimism and concerns. In *2016 European Modelling Symposium (EMS)* (pp. 237-241). IEEE. DOI: 10.1109/EMS.2016.048

Iraj, H., Fudge, A., Khan, H., Faulkner, M., Pardo, A., & Kovanovic, V. (2021). ERIC - EJ1325384 - Narrowing the Feedback Gap: Examining Student Engagement with Personalized and Actionable Feedback Messages. *Journal of Learning Analytics*, 202, •••. https://eric.ed.gov/?id=EJ1325384

Jaakkola, H., & Thalheim, B. (2020). Sixty years–and more–of data modelling. In Information Modelling and Knowledge Bases XXXII (pp. 56-75). IOS Press. iospress.nl DOI: 10.3233/FAIA200820

Jackson, D., & Dean, B. A. (2023). Employability-related activities beyond the curriculum: How participation and impact vary across diverse student cohorts. *Higher Education*, 86(5), 1151–1172. DOI: 10.1007/s10734-022-00966-x

Jafari, F., & Keykha, A. (2024). Identifying the opportunities and challenges of artificial intelligence in higher education: A qualitative study. *Journal of Applied Research in Higher Education*, 16(4), 1228–1245. DOI: 10.1108/JARHE-09-2023-0426

Jayalath, J., & Esichaikul, V. (2022). Gamification to Enhance Motivation and Engagement in Blended eLearning for Technical and Vocational Education and Training. *Technology. Knowledge and Learning*, 27(1), 91–118. DOI: 10.1007/s10758-020-09466-2

Jdidou, Y., & Aammou, S. (2024). TRANSFORMING EDUCATION WITH AI: THE ROLE OF RECOMMENDATION SYSTEMS IN PERSONALIZED LEARNING. *EDULEARN24 Proceedings*, 7662–7669. DOI: 10.21125/edulearn.2024.1801

Jebadurai, D. J., Sheela, M. V., Rajeshkumar, L., Soundarya, M., Meena, R., Manickam, T., & Manikandan, M. (2024). AI-Driven Decision-Making and Optimization in Modern Agriculture Sectors. In *Using Traditional Design Methods to Enhance AI-Driven Decision Making* (pp. 269–288). IGI Global. DOI: 10.4018/979-8-3693-0639-0.ch012

Jemni, M., & Khribi, M. K. (2016). Toward empowering open and online education in the arab world through OER and MOOCs. *Lecture Notes in Educational Technology*, 9783662529232, 73–100. DOI: 10.1007/978-3-662-52925-6_4

Jeng, Y. L., & Huang, Y. M. (2019). Dynamic learning paths framework based on collective intelligence from learners. *Computers in Human Behavior*, 100, 242–251. Advance online publication. DOI: 10.1016/j.chb.2018.09.012

Jin, C. (2023). MOOC student dropout prediction model based on learning behavior features and parameter optimization. [HTML]. *Interactive Learning Environments*, 31(2), 714–732. DOI: 10.1080/10494820.2020.1802300

Johnson, L., Smith, R., Willis, H., Levine, A., & Haywood, K. (2011). *NMC Horizon Report: 2011 Higher Education Edition.*

Johnson, M. A. (2023, June 27). *Unlocking Student Success: Incorporating Micro-credentials into Academic Curricula.* Linkedin.

Jung, J. (2024). When massified higher education meets shrinking birth rates: the case of South Korea. Higher Education. springer.com

Kabita, N. D., & Ji, L. (2017). *The why, what and how of competency-based curriculum reforms: The Kenyan experience.*https://unesdoc.unesco.org/ark:/48223/pf0000250431

Kabugo, J. C., Jämsä-Jounela, S. L., Schiemann, R., & Binder, C. (2020). Industry 4.0 based process data analytics platform: A waste-to-energy plant case study. [sciencedirect.com]. *International Journal of Electrical Power & Energy Systems*, 115, 105508. DOI: 10.1016/j.ijepes.2019.105508

Kamenskih, A. (2022). The analysis of security and privacy risks in smart education environments. *Journal of Smart Cities and Society*, 1(1), 17–29. DOI: 10.3233/SCS-210114

Kapoor, S., & Kalia, G. (2024). Role of Virtual Reality in Education: Its Scope, Reach and Effect on Student Behavior. *Transforming Education with Virtual Reality*, 145-164.

Karachalios, G. & Papadakis, N. (2023). Micro-credentials and skills – Towards a paradigm shift in reskilling. Advanced in Social Sciences Journal, 10 (5), 95:102. DOI: 10.14738/assrj.105.14691

Kasriel, S. (2018). *The future of work won't be about college degrees; it will be about job skills. Consumer News and Business Channel.*https://www.cnbc.com/2018/10/31/the-future-of-work-wont-be-about-degrees-it-will-beabout-skills.html

Kaswan, K. S., Dhatterwal, J. S., & Ojha, R. P. (2024). AI in personalized learning. In *Advances in Technological Innovations in Higher Education.* CRC Press. DOI: 10.1201/9781003376699-9

Katiyar, P. (2024). Ai-driven personalized learning systems: enhancing educational effectiveness. eatp. https://doi.org/DOI: 10.53555/kuey.v30i5.4961

Kato, S., Galán-Muros, V., & Weko, T. (2020). The emergence of alternative credentials. OECD Education Working Papers, 216. https://doi.org/DOI: 10.1787/19939019

Kato, S., Galán-Muros, V., & Weko, T. (2020). The Emergence of Alternative Credentials. www.oecd.org/edu/workingpapers

Kazin, C. J., & Clerkin, K. M. (2018). *The potentials and limitations of microcredentials. Service Members opportunity Colleges.* https://supportsystem.livehelpnow.net/resources/23351/Potential%20and%20Limitations%20of%20Microcredentials%20FINAL_SEPT%202018.pdf

Keller, J. M. (1987). Development and use of the ARCS model of instructional design. *Journal of Instructional Development : JID*, 10(3), 2–10. DOI: 10.1007/BF02905780

Kember, D., Trimble, A., & Fan, S. (2023). An Investigation of the Forms of Support Needed to Promote the Retention and Success of Online Students. *American Journal of Distance Education*, 37(3), 169–184. DOI: 10.1080/08923647.2022.2061235

Keoy, K. H., Koh, Y. J., Iqbal, J., Anjum, S. S., Yeo, S. F., Cherukuri, A. K., Teoh, W. Y., & Piut, D. A. A. (2024). Streamlining micro-credentials implementation in higher education institutions: Considerations for effective implementation and policy development. [worldscientific.com]. *Journal of Information & Knowledge Management*, 23(01), 2350069. DOI: 10.1142/S0219649223500697

Keskin, S., & Yurdugül, H. (2022). E-learning experience: Modeling students' e-learning interactions using log data. *Journal of Educational Technology and Online Learning*, 5(1), 1–13. DOI: 10.31681/jetol.938363

Khan, S. (2011). *About Khan Academy.* http://www.khanacademy.org/about

Khan, A. H., Ejaz, N., Matthews, S., Snow, S., & Matthews, B. (2021, June). Speculative design for education: Using participatory methods to map design challenges and opportunities in Pakistan. In *Proceedings of the 2021 ACM Designing Interactive Systems Conference* (pp. 1748-1764). [HTML] DOI: 10.1145/3461778.3462117

Kharbat, F. F., Alshawabkeh, A., & Woolsey, M. L. (2021). Identifying gaps in using artificial intelligence to support students with intellectual disabilities from education and health perspectives. [HTML]. *Aslib Journal of Information Management*, 73(1), 101–128. DOI: 10.1108/AJIM-02-2020-0054

Kholbutaevich, T. O., & Anarbaevich, A. R. (2024). ELECTRONIC EDUCATION: TASKS, PROSPECTS, AND RESULTS. Global Book Publishing Services, 1-76. scientificpublication.org

Khosravi, H., Shum, S. B., Chen, G., Conati, C., Tsai, Y. S., Kay, J., & Gašević, D. (2022). Explainable artificial intelligence in education. [sciencedirect.com]. *Computers and Education: Artificial Intelligence*, 3, 100074.

Kifle, T. (2023, September 20). What makes an effective microcredential programme? *The Times Higher Education*. https://www.timeshighereducation.com/campus/what-makes-effective-microcredential-programme

Kiiskilä, P., Kukkonen, A., & Pirkkalainen, H. (2023). Are micro-credentials valuable for students? perspective on verifiable digital credentials. *SN Computer Science*, 4(4), 366. Advance online publication. DOI: 10.1007/s42979-023-01797-y

Kim, J., Lee, H., & Cho, Y. (2022). Learning design to support student-ai collaboration: Perspectives of leading teachers for ai in education. *Education and Information Technologies*, 27(5), 6069–6104. DOI: 10.1007/s10639-021-10831-6

Kır, Ş., & Bozkurt, A. (2022). Yükseköğretimde mikro-krediler üzerine kavramsal bir değerlendirme. *Uşak Üniversitesi Eğitim Araştırmaları Dergisi*, 8(1), 12–29. DOI: 10.29065/usakead.1037617

Kiyasseh, D., Laca, J., Haque, T., Miles, B., Wagner, C., Donoho, D., & Hung, A. (2023). A multi-institutional study using artificial intelligence to provide reliable and fair feedback to surgeons. *Communications Medicine*, 3(1), 42. Advance online publication. DOI: 10.1038/s43856-023-00263-3 PMID: 36997578

Kizito, O., & Kayi, O. Modest. (2024). *Global Perspectives on Micro-Learning and Micro-Credentials in Higher Education*. IGI Global.

Klímová, B., Pikhart, M., & Kacetl, J. (2023). Ethical issues of the use of ai-driven mobile apps for education. *Frontiers in Public Health*, 10, 1118116. Advance online publication. DOI: 10.3389/fpubh.2022.1118116 PMID: 36711343

Knox, J. (2014). Digital culture clash: "massive" education in thee-learning and digital culturesmooc. *Distance Education*, 35(2), 164–177. DOI: 10.1080/01587919.2014.917704

Kohler, M., Gamrat, C., Raish, V., & Gross, E. (2021). Microlearning and micro-credentials in higher education. In *Microlearning in the digital age* (pp. 109–128). Routledge. DOI: 10.4324/9780367821623-10

Köse, S., Karakurt, P., & Fırat, M. (2022). Relationship of Nursing Students' Anxiety Level in the Covid-19 Pandemic with E-Learning. *Turkish Journal of Science and Health*, 3(3), 168–175. DOI: 10.51972/tfsd.1085398

Krafft, M., Sajtos, L., & Haenlein, M. (2020). Challenges and opportunities for marketing scholars in times of the fourth industrial revolution. [sciencedirect.com]. *Journal of Interactive Marketing*, 51(1), 1–8. DOI: 10.1016/j.intmar.2020.06.001

Krathwohl, D. R. (2002). A revision of Bloom's taxonomy: An overview. *Theory into Practice*, 41(4), 212–218. DOI: 10.1207/s15430421tip4104_2

Kraus, S., Breier, M., Lim, W. M., Dabić, M., Kumar, S., Kanbach, D., Mukherjee, D., Corvello, V., Piñeiro-Chousa, J., Liguori, E., Palacios-Marqués, D., Schiavone, F., Ferraris, A., Fernandes, C., & Ferreira, J. J. (2022). Literature reviews as independent studies: Guidelines for academic practice. *Review of Managerial Science*, 16(8), 2577–2595. DOI: 10.1007/s11846-022-00588-8

Kuloglu, M. E., & Yıldız, S. (2022). UNDERGRADUATES' ATTITUDES TOWARDS DISTANCE EDUCATION AND PERCEPTIONS OF READINESS FOR E-LEARNING DURING THE COVID-19 PANDEMIC. *Turkish Online Journal of Distance Education*, 23(4), 121–130. DOI: 10.17718/tojde.1182767

Kumar, J. A., Richard, R. J., Osman, S., & Lowrence, K. (2022). Micro-credentials in leveraging emergency remote teaching: The relationship between novice users' insights and identity in malaysia. *International Journal of Educational Technology in Higher Education*, 19(1), 18. Advance online publication. DOI: 10.1186/s41239-022-00323-z PMID: 35382441

Kuo, B. C., Chang, F. T. Y., & Lee, Y. L. (2023). Trends and Issues of Digital Learning in Taiwan. Trends and Issues of Promoting Digital Learning in High-Digital-Competitiveness Countries: Country Reports and International Comparison. ed.gov

Kušić, S., Vrcelj, S., & Zovko, A. (2022). Micro-credentials – improvement or fragmentation in higher education? *Education and New Developments*, 152–156. Advance online publication. DOI: 10.36315/2022v2end033

Kusters, R., Misevic, D., Berry, H., Cully, A., Le Cunff, Y., Dandoy, L., Díaz-Rodríguez, N., Ficher, M., Grizou, J., Othmani, A., Palpanas, T., Komorowski, M., Loiseau, P., Moulin Frier, C., Nanini, S., Quercia, D., Sebag, M., Soulié Fogelman, F., Taleb, S., & Wehbi, F. (2020). Interdisciplinary research in artificial intelligence: Challenges and opportunities. *Frontiers in Big Data*, 3, 577974. DOI: 10.3389/fdata.2020.577974 PMID: 33693418

Kwak, Y., Ahn, J., & Seo, Y. (2022). Influence of ai ethics awareness, attitude, anxiety, and self-efficacy on nursing students' behavioral intentions. *BMC Nursing*, 21(1), 267. Advance online publication. DOI: 10.1186/s12912-022-01048-0 PMID: 36180902

Lameras, P. & Arnab, S. (2021). Power to the teachers: an exploratory review on artificial intelligence in education. Information. mdpi.com

Lampropoulos, G., & Kinshuk, . (2024). Virtual reality and gamification in education: A systematic review. *Educational Technology Research and Development*, 72(3), 1–95. DOI: 10.1007/s11423-024-10351-3

Lane, J., & Murgatroyd, S. (2021). *Micro-credentials – Small qualifications, big deal.* Canada West Foundation, September. Available at https://cwf.ca/research/publications/what-now-micro-credentials-small-qualifications-big-deal/

Lane, D. C., & Goode, C. (2021). Open For All: The OERu's Next Generation Digital Learning Ecosystem. *International Review of Research in Open and Distance Learning*, 22(4), 146–163. DOI: 10.19173/irrodl.v23i1.5763

Lang, J. (2023). Workforce upskilling: can universities meet the challenges of lifelong learning?. *International Journal of Information and Learning Technology, 40*(5), 388-400. https://doi.org/,Lo, C. K. (2023). What is the impact of ChatGPT on education? A rapid review of the literature. *Education Sciences, 13*(4), 410. https://doi.org/DOI: 10.1108/IJILT-01-2023-0001

Lanthier, S., Colyar, J., & Deakin, J. (2023). *Ontario college and university investments in digital learning during the pandemic.* Higher Education Quality Council of Ontario (mimeo). https://heqco.ca/pub/ontario-college-and-university-investments-in-digital-learning-during-the-pandemic/

Lauder, H. & Mayhew, K. (2020). Higher education and the labour market: an introduction. Oxford Review of Education. tandfonline.com

Laughlin, T. (2021). A vision for deeper agency and personalization in micro-credentials. Career ready education through experiential learning. [HTML]

Laughlin, T. (2021). A Vision for Deeper Agency and Personalization in Micro-Credentials. In Northrup, P., Rasmussen, K., & Colson, R. (Eds.), *Career Ready Education Through Experiential Learning* (pp. 19–45). IGI Global., DOI: 10.4018/978-1-7998-1928-8.ch002

LeBlanc, P. (2022). Microcredentials and skills-based hiring. In *Students first* (pp. 58–64). Harvard Press.

Lee-Chavarria, D., Loucks, T. L., Paranal, R., Sampson, R., & Feghali-Bostwick, C. (2024). Supporting clinical research professionals through educational innovations. *Frontiers in Pharmacology*, 14, 1304415. Advance online publication. DOI: 10.3389/fphar.2023.1304415 PMID: 38259267

Lee, J., & Hammer, J. (2011). Gamification in Education: What, How, Why Bother? *Academic Exchange Quarterly*, 15, 1–5.

Lee, S., & Geum, Y. (2021). How to determine a minimum viable product in app-based lean start-ups: Kano-based approach. [HTML]. *Total Quality Management & Business Excellence*, 32(15-16), 1751–1767. DOI: 10.1080/14783363.2020.1770588

Leivadeas, A., & Falkner, M. (2022). A survey on intent-based networking. [HTML]. *IEEE Communications Surveys and Tutorials*, 25(1), 625–655. DOI: 10.1109/COMST.2022.3215919

Leoste, J., Õun, T., Loogma, K., & San Martín López, J. (2021). Designing Training Programs to Introduce Emerging Technologies to Future Workers—A Pilot Study Based on the Example of Artificial Intelligence Enhanced .... Mathematics. mdpi.com

Lester, J., Bansal, M., Biswas, G., Hmelo-Silver, C., Roschelle, J., & Rowe, J. (2024). The AI Institute for Engaged Learning. *AI Magazine*, 45(1), 69–76. DOI: 10.1002/aaai.12161

Li, J. & Wei, Z. (2022). Intelligent Optimization Method of the Higher Vocational Education System for Labor Market Demand in Guangdong-Hong Kong-Macao Greater Bay Area. Mathematical Problems in Engineering. wiley.com

Li, K., Xirui, P., Song, J., Hong, B., & Wang, J. (2024). The application of augmented reality (ar) in remote work and education. *arXiv preprint arXiv:2404.10579.*

Li, X. (2024). Personalized learning path recommendation algorithm for english listening learning. jes, 20(6s), 2188-2199. https://doi.org/DOI: 10.52783/jes.3133

Li, K., Johnsen, J., & Canelas, D. A. (2021). Persistence, performance, and goal setting in massive open online courses. *British Journal of Educational Technology*, 52(3), 1215–1229. DOI: 10.1111/bjet.13068

Lim, W. M., & Kumar, S. (2023). Guidelines for interpreting the results of bibliometrics analysis: A sensemaking approach. *Global Business and Organizational Excellence*. https://api.semanticscholar.org/CorpusID:260600560

Lima, G. D. M., Ferreira, G. M. D. S., & Carvalho, J. D. S. (2024). Automation in education: Trending issues concerning Artificial Intelligence. *Educação e Pesquisa*, 50, e273857. DOI: 10.1590/s1678-4634202450273857por

Lim, S., Phan, T., Law, M., Goh, G., Lukies, M., Joseph, T., & Clements, W. (2022). Non-radiologist perception of the use of artificial intelligence (ai) in diagnostic medical imaging reports. *Journal of Medical Imaging and Radiation Oncology*, 66(8), 1029–1034. DOI: 10.1111/1754-9485.13388 PMID: 35191186

Ling, P., & Ling, L. (2023). Micro-credentials and Higher Education: The Bottom Line. In Introducing Multidisciplinary Micro-credentialing: Rethinking Learning and Development for Higher Education and Industry (pp. 149-167). Emerald Publishing Limited. [HTML]

Lin, J., Sha, L., Gašević, D., & Chen, G. (2022). Establishing trustworthy artificial intelligence in automated feedback. https://doi.org/DOI: 10.35542/osf.io/5efxn

Lin, Y., & Yu, Z. (2024). A bibliometric analysis of artificial intelligence chatbots in educational contexts. *Interactive Technology and Smart Education*, 21(2), 189–213. DOI: 10.1108/ITSE-12-2022-0165

Liu, B., Xing, W., Zeng, Y., & Wu, Y. (2022). Linking cognitive processes and learning outcomes: The influence of cognitive presence on learning performance in moocs. *British Journal of Educational Technology*, 53(5), 1459–1477. DOI: 10.1111/bjet.13193

Liu, Z. Q., Deryagin, A., & Glushkov, S. (2020). IT-architecture for corporate knowledge management systems. [iJET]. *International Journal of Emerging Technologies in Learning*, 15(14), 65–82. DOI: 10.3991/ijet.v15i14.14673

Li, Y., Zhang, M., Bonk, C. J., & Guo, N. (2015). Integrating MOOC and flipped classroom practice in a traditional undergraduate course: Students' experience and perceptions. [iJET]. *International Journal of Emerging Technologies in Learning*, 10(6), 4–10. DOI: 10.3991/ijet.v10i6.4708

Lizarelli, F. L., Torres, A. F., Antony, J., Ribeiro, R., Salentijn, W., Fernandes, M. M., & Campos, A. T. (2022). Critical success factors and challenges for Lean Startup: A systematic literature review. [HTML]. *The TQM Journal*, 34(3), 534–551.

Lo, C. K., & Hew, K. F. (2017). A critical review of flipped classroom challenges in K-12 education: Possible solutions and recommendations for future research. *Research and Practice in Technology Enhanced Learning*, 12(4), 4. DOI: 10.1186/s41039-016-0044-2 PMID: 30613253

Long, P. D., & Siemens, G. (2011). Penetrating the Fog: Analytics in Learning and Education. *Creative Education*, 13(9).

Lopes, C., Bernardes, Ó., Gonçalves, M. J. A., Terra, A. L., da Silva, M. M., Tavares, C., & Valente, I. (2022). E-learning enhancement through multidisciplinary teams in higher education: Students, teachers, and librarians. [mdpi.com]. *Education Sciences*, 12(9), 601. DOI: 10.3390/educsci12090601

Luckin, R., Holmes, W., & Forcier, L. B. (2016). *An argument for AI in Education.*

Mac Lochlainn, C., Nic Giolla Mhichil, M., Wessels, O., Kiiskilä, S., Pirkkalainen, H., & Palvalin, M. (2022). ECIU University Micro-Credentials: A Vision for European Learners, Values, and Priorities. *ECIU White Paper on Micro-Credentials.*

MacCallum, K., & Brown, C. (2022). Developing a micro-credential for learning designers: a delphi study. Ascilite Publications, e22198. DOI: 10.14742/apubs.2022.198

Mah, D.-K. (2016). Learning Analytics and Digital Badges: Potential Impact on Student Retention in Higher Education. *Technology. Knowledge and Learning*, 21(3), 285–305. DOI: 10.1007/s10758-016-9286-8

Mahmoud, M. H., & Abo El-Hamayed, S. H. (2016). An intelligent tutoring system for teaching the grammar of the Arabic language. *Journal of Electrical Systems and Information Technology*, 3(2), 282–294. https://doi.org/https://doi.org/10.1016/j.jesit.2016.04.001. DOI: 10.1016/j.jesit.2016.04.001

Maina, M. F., Ortiz, L. G., Mancini, F., & Melo, M. M. (2022). A micro-credentialing methodology for improved recognition of he employability skills. *International Journal of Educational Technology in Higher Education*, 19(1), 10. Advance online publication. DOI: 10.1186/s41239-021-00315-5 PMID: 35224180

Mandinach, E. B. & Schildkamp, K. (2021). Misconceptions about data-based decision making in education: An exploration of the literature. Studies in Educational Evaluation. sciencedirect.com

Mao, J., Chen, B., & Liu, J. C. (2024). Generative artificial intelligence in education and its implications for assessment. *TechTrends*, 68(1), 58–66. DOI: 10.1007/s11528-023-00911-4

Mardisentosa, B., Rahardja, U., Zelina, K., Oganda, F. P., & Hardini, M. (2021, November). Sustainable learning micro-credential using blockchain for student achievement records. In *2021 Sixth International Conference on Informatics and Computing (ICIC)* (pp. 1-6). IEEE. https://doi.org/10.1109/ICIC54025.2021.9632913

Marwan, S., Gao, G., Fisk, S., Price, T. W., & Barnes, T. (2020). Adaptive Immediate Feedback Can Improve Novice Programming Engagement and Intention to Persist in Computer Science. *Proceedings of the 2020 ACM Conference on International Computing Education Research*, 194–203. DOI: 10.1145/3372782.3406264

Mashford-Pringle, A., Tan, S., Stutz, S., & Tjong, G. (2023). Designing accountability measures for health professionals: results from a community-based micro-credential: case study on Indigenous cultural safety. *BMC Public Health*, 23(1), 879. https://doi.org/10.1186/s12889-023-15721-9

Masrek, M., Susantari, T., Mutia, F., Yuwinanto, H. P., & Atmi, R. T. (2024). Enabling education everywhere: How artificial intelligence empowers ubiquitous and lifelong learning. *Environment-Behaviour Proceedings Journal*, 9(SI18), 57–63. DOI: 10.21834/e-bpj.v9iSI18.5462

Matic, J. L. (2019). The internationalization of American higher education: A positional competition perspective. *Globalisation, Societies and Education*, 17(3), 274–284. DOI: 10.1080/14767724.2019.1584550

McGovern, T. (2020, June). Exploratory Study: Digital Badging. In InSITE 2020: Informing Science+ IT Education Conferences: Online (pp. 185-204). informing-science.org

McGovern, T. M. (2019). *Academic digital badges: Industry, employment, and prospects*. University of South Florida.

McGovern, T. M., & Gogan, J. L. (2022). Student, Interrupted: Can Digital Badging Improve Programmatic Agility and Help IS Students During Crises? *Communications of the Association for Information Systems*, 51(1), 51. DOI: 10.17705/1CAIS.05119

McGreal, R. (2024). Empowering Micro-Credentials Using Blockchain and Artificial Intelligence. In Omona, K., & O'dama, M. (Eds.), *Global Perspectives on Micro-Learning and Micro-Credentials in Higher Education* (pp. 75–90). IGI Global., DOI: 10.4018/979-8-3693-0343-6.ch006

McGreal, R., Mackintosh, W., Cox, G., & Olcott, D.Jr. (2022). Bridging the gap: Micro-credentials for development. *International Review of Research in Open and Distance Learning*, 23(3), 288–302. DOI: 10.19173/irrodl.v23i3.6696

McGreal, R., Mackintosh, W., Cox, G., & Olcott, D.Jr. (2022). Bridging the gap: micro-credentials for development: UNESCO chairs policy brief form-under the III world higher education conference (WHEC 2021) type: collective X. *International Review of Research in Open and Distributed Learning*, 23(3), 288–302.

McGreal, R., & Olcott, D.Jr. (2022). A strategic reset: Micro-credentials for higher education leaders. *Smart Learning Environments*, 9(1), 9. DOI: 10.1186/s40561-022-00190-1

Melai, T., van der Westen, S., Winkels, J., Antonaci, A., Henderikx, P., & Ubachs, G. (2020). *Concept and role of Short Learning Programmes in European higher education*. (Research Report No. 02.1). https://eslp.eadtu.eu/images/Concept_and_role_of_SLPs.pdf

Mellor, N. (2024). Using AI to Develop Capabilities in Arab Universities. In *Studies in Big Data* (Vol. 144, Issue March). Springer Nature Switzerland. DOI: 10.1007/978-3-031-52280-2_16

Mena-Guacas, A. F., Chacón, M. F., Munar, A. P., Ospina, M., & Agudelo, M. (2023). Evolution of teaching in short-term courses: A systematic review. *Heliyon*, 9(6), e16933. Advance online publication. DOI: 10.1016/j.heliyon.2023.e16933 PMID: 37332952

Meng, N., Dhimolea, T. K., & Ali, Z. (2022). AI-enhanced education: Teaching and learning reimagined. In *Bridging human intelligence and artificial intelligence* (pp. 107–124). Springer International Publishing. [HTML] DOI: 10.1007/978-3-030-84729-6_7

Miao, M., Ahmed, M., Ahsan, N., & Qamar, B. (2023). Intention to use technology for micro-credential programs: Evidence from technology acceptance and self-determination model. *International Journal of Educational Management*, 38(4), 948–977. DOI: 10.1108/IJEM-02-2023-0066

Micro, H. E. Consortium. (2019). *A briefing paper on the award, recognition, portability and accreditation of microcredentials: An investigation through interviews with key stakeholders & decision makers*. https://microcredentials.eu/wp-content/uploads/sites/20/2019/12/WP3-Interviews-with-Key-Stakeholders-Decision-Makers-Overall-Summary-Report.pdf. Accessed: April 2024.

MICROBOL. (2022). Common framework for micro-credentials in the EHEA. https://microcredentials.eu/wp-content/uploads/sites/20/2022/03/Micro-credentials_Framework_final-1.pdf

MicroHE Consortium. (2019). A briefing paper on the award, recognition, portability and accreditation of micro-credentials: An investigation through interviews with key stakeholders & decision makers. https://microcredentials.eu/wp- content/uploads/sites/20/2019/12/WP3-Interviews-with-Key-Stakeholders-Decision-Makers-Overall-Summary-Report.pdf (accessed 12 September 2024).

Miller, K. K., & Jorre, T. J. S. (2022). Digital micro-credentials in environmental science: An employer perspective on valued evidence of skills. *Teaching in Higher Education*, 29(4), 1058–1074. DOI: 10.1080/13562517.2022.2053953

Minton, M., & Bligh, B. (2021). Examining the use of Kahoot to support digital game-based formative assessments in UAE higher education. *Studies in Technology Enhanced Learning*, 1(2). Advance online publication. DOI: 10.21428/8c225f6e.32b8666f

Mir, U., Kar, A., & Gupta, M. (2021). Ai-enabled digital identity – inputs for stakeholders and policymakers. *Journal of Science and Technology Policy Management*, 13(3), 514–541. DOI: 10.1108/JSTPM-09-2020-0134

Moore, M. G. (1997). *Theory of transactional distance*. Routledge.

Moroder, K. (2014). *Micro-credentials: empowering lifelong learners.* Edutopia, https://www.edutopia.org/blog/micro-credentials-empowering-lifelong-learners-krista-moroder

Mouaheb, H., Fahli, A., Moussetad, M., & Eljamali, S. (2012). The Serious Game: What Educational Benefits? *Procedia: Social and Behavioral Sciences*, 46, 5502–5508. https://doi.org/https://doi.org/10.1016/j.sbspro.2012.06.465. DOI: 10.1016/j.sbspro.2012.06.465

Msweli, N. T., Twinomurinzi, H., & Ismail, M. (2022). The international case for micro-credentials for life-wide and life-long learning: A systematic literature review. *Interdisciplinary Journal of Information, Knowledge, and Management*, 17, 151–190. DOI: 10.28945/4954

Murgatroyd, S. (2022). The future is small – Micro-credentials and the skills agenda. *Revista Paraguaya de Education a Distancia, FACEN-UNA*, 3(1), 5–14.

Murgatroyd, S. (2024). *The future of higher education in an age of artificial intelligence*. Ethics Press.

Murtaza, D. A., Fadare, S. A., Mocsir, O. M., Fadare, C., Natividad, L. R., Rafique, T., Akhtar, N., Shaheen, D. J., & Taj, R. (2024). From Theory To Practice: Harnessing Ai For Enhanced Teaching-Learning Dynamics. *Educational Administration: Theory and Practice*, 30(4), 6331–6338.

Murtaza, M., Ahmed, Y., Shamsi, J., Sherwani, F., & Usman, M. (2022). Ai-based personalized e-learning systems: Issues, challenges, and solutions. *IEEE Access : Practical Innovations, Open Solutions*, 10, 81323–81342. DOI: 10.1109/ACCESS.2022.3193938

Musa, M., Ismail, M. N., & Md Fudzee, M. F. (2021). A Survey on Smart Campus Implementation in Malaysia. *JOIV : International Journal on Informatics Visualization*, 5(1), 51–56. DOI: 10.30630/joiv.5.1.434

Naidu, S. (2020). The mooc is dead—Long live mooc 2.0! *Distance Education*, 41(1), 1–5. DOI: 10.1080/01587919.2020.1727289

Naseer, F., Khalid, M. U., Ayub, N., Rasool, A., Abbas, T., & Afzal, M. W. (2024). Automated Assessment and Feedback in Higher Education Using Generative AI. In *Transforming Education With Generative AI: Prompt Engineering and Synthetic Content Creation* (pp. 433-461). IGI Global. DOI: 10.4018/979-8-3693-1351-0.ch021

National Education Association. (2024). Trauma informed pedagogy. *National Education Association*. https://nea.certificationbank.com/NEA/CandidatePortal/CategoryDetail.aspx?Stack=TRA

Nelson, N., Geltzer, A., & Hilgartner, S. (2008). Introduction: The anticipatory state: making policy-relevant knowledge about the future. *Science & Public Policy*, 35(8), 546–550. DOI: 10.3152/030234208X370648

Neo, M. (2022). The Merlin Project: Malaysian students' acceptance of an AI chatbot in their learning process. *Turkish Online Journal of Distance Education*, 23(3), 31–48. DOI: 10.17718/tojde.1137122

Networked, L. E. C. (2021). Networked learning in 2021: A community definition. [springer.com]. *Postdigital Science and Education*, 3(2), 326–369. DOI: 10.1007/s42438-021-00222-y

New Zealand Qualifications Authority (NZQA). (2024). *Guidelines for Applying for Approval of a Training Scheme or a Micro-credential*. https://www2.nzqa.govt.nz/assets/Tertiary/Approval-accreditation-and-registration/Micro-credentials/Guidelines-for-micro-credentials-January-2024.pdf

Newby, T. J., & Cheng, Z. (2020). Instructional digital badges: Effective learning tools. *Educational Technology Research and Development*, 68(3), 1053–1067. DOI: 10.1007/s11423-019-09719-7

Newby, T., Wright, C., Besser, E., & Beese, E. (2016). Passport to Designing, Developing and Issuing Digital Instructional Badges. In *Foundation of Digital Badges and Micro-Credentials* (pp. 179–201). Springer International Publishing., DOI: 10.1007/978-3-319-15425-1_10

Ng, D. W. L., & Keng, L. K. N. (2023). Innovative and Emerging Intersections Between Industry and Academia: Rationale for Micro-credentialing. In Introducing Multidisciplinary Micro-credentialing: Rethinking Learning and Development for Higher Education and Industry (pp. 49-77). Emerald Publishing Limited. [HTML]

Ng, D., Leung, J., Su, J., Ng, R., & Chu, S. (2023). Teachers' ai digital competencies and twenty-first century skills in the post-pandemic world. *Educational Technology Research and Development*, 71(1), 137–161. DOI: 10.1007/s11423-023-10203-6 PMID: 36844361

Nguyen, A., Kremantzis, M., Essien, A., Petrounias, I., & Hosseini, S. (2024). Enhancing Student Engagement Through Artificial Intelligence (AI): Understanding the Basics, Opportunities, and Challenges. In *Journal of University Teaching and Learning Practice* (Issue 6).

Ni, L. B. (2018). AI-Enhanced Digital Learning : Revolutionizing Middle East. *History of Education*, 1(1), 40–44.

North, K. (2021). Learning in the Year 2030. Managing Work in the Digital Economy: Challenges, Strategies and Practices for the Next Decade, 223-238. [HTML]

Nuthall, K. (2024, September). No Title. *University World News*. https://www.universityworldnews.com/post.php?story=20240920144632455

NZQA. (2023). Guidelines for micro-credential listing, approval and accreditation. Wellington: New Zealand Qualifications Authority. https://www2.nzqa.govt.nz/tertiary/approval-accreditation-and-registration/micro-credentials/guidelines/

O'Dea, X., & O'Dea, M. (2023). Is Artificial Intelligence Really the Next Big Thing in Learning and Teaching in Higher Education? A Conceptual Paper. *Journal of University Teaching & Learning Practice*, 20(5), 5. Advance online publication. DOI: 10.53761/1.20.5.06

Oberlack, C., Sietz, D., Bürgi Bonanomi, E., de Bremond, A., Dell'Angelo, J., Eisenack, K., Ellis, E. C., Epstein, G., Giger, M., Heinimann, A., Kimmich, C., Kok, M. T., Manuel-Navarrete, D., Messerli, P., Meyfroidt, P., Václavík, T., & Villamayor-Tomas, S. (2019). Archetype analysis in sustainability research: Meanings, motivations, and evidence-based policy making. *Ecology and Society*, 24(2), art26. Advance online publication. DOI: 10.5751/ES-10747-240226

Ocumpaugh, J., Roscoe, R. D., Baker, R. S., Hutt, S., & Aguilar, S. J. (2024). Toward asset-based instruction and assessment in artificial intelligence in education. *International Journal of Artificial Intelligence in Education*, •••, 1–40. DOI: 10.1007/s40593-023-00382-x

OECD (2018a). *Health at a Glance 2017: OECD Indicators*. OECD Publishing. DOI: 10.1787/health_glance-2015-en

OECD (2018b). *Skills strategy implementation guidance for Portugal* (OECD Skills Studies). OECD. DOI: 10.1787/9789264298705-en

OECD. (2018c). The Future of Education and Skills: Education 2030. In *OECD Education Working Papers*.http://www.oecd.org/education/2030/E2030 Position Paper (05.04.2018).pdf

OECD. (2019). *Learning compass 2030: Conceptual learning framework.* www.oecd.org/education/2030-project

OECD. (2021). Quality and value of micro-credentials in higher education: Preparing for the future. https://www.oecd.org/en/publications/quality-and-value-of-micro-credentials-in-higher-education_9c4ad26d-en.html

OECD. (2023). *Micro-credentials for lifelong learning and employability: Uses and possibilities. OECD Education Policy Perspectives, No. 66*. OECD Publishing., DOI: 10.1787/9c4b7b68-

OECD. (2024). *Education at a glance*. OECD. https://www.oecd.org/en/publications/education-at-a-glance-2024_c00cad36-en.html

Ofosu-Ampong, K. (2024). Beyond the hype: Exploring faculty perceptions and acceptability of AI in teaching practices. *Discover Education*, 3(1), 38. DOI: 10.1007/s44217-024-00128-4

Okunlaya, R. O., Syed Abdullah, N., & Alias, R. A. (2022). Artificial intelligence (AI) library services innovative conceptual framework for the digital transformation of university education. [HTML]. *Library Hi Tech*, 40(6), 1869–1892. DOI: 10.1108/LHT-07-2021-0242

Olakanmi, E. E. (2017). The Effects of a Flipped Classroom Model of Instruction on Students' Performance and Attitudes Towards Chemistry. *Journal of Science Education and Technology*, 26(1), 127–137. DOI: 10.1007/s10956-016-9657-x

Olcott, D.Jr. (2022). Micro-credentials: A catalyst for strategic reset and change in US higher education. *American Journal of Distance Education*, 36(1), 19–35. DOI: 10.1080/08923647.2021.1997537

Oliver, B. (2019). *Making micro-credentials work for learners, employers and providers* (pp. 1435129097-1637135585). Available at https://www.researchgate.net/publication/335109512_Making_micro-credentials_work_for_learners_employers_and_providers

Oliver, B. (2019). *Making micro-credentials work for learners, employers and providers. Deakin University.*https://dteach.deakin.edu.au/wp-content/uploads/sites/103/2019/08/Making-micro-credentials-work-Oliver-Deakin-2019-full-report.pdf

Oliver, B. (2019). *Making micro-credentials work for learners, employers and providers.* DTeach. https://dteach.deakin.edu.au/microcredentials/

Oliver, B. (2019). Making Micro-Credentials Work for Learners, Employers and Providers. https://dteach.deakin.edu.au/2019/08/02/microcredentials/

Oliver, B. (2019). Making micro-credentials work for learners, employers and providers. https://www.assuringgraduatecapabilities.com/uploads/4/5/0/5/45053363/making-micro-credentials-work-oliver-deakin-2019.pdf (accessed 10 May 2024).

Oliver, B. (2019). Making micro-credentials work for learners, employers and providers. *Research Gate*. https://www.researchgate.net/publication/335109512_Making_micro-credentials_work_for_learners_employers_and_providers

Oliver, B. (2019). *Making micro-credentials work for learners, employers, and providers*. Retrieved from https://www.researchgate.net/publication/335109512

Oliver, B. (2022). Towards a common definition of micro-credentials. *UNESCO*. https://unesdoc.unesco.org/ark:/48223/pf0000381668

Oliver, B. (2019). *Making micro-credentials work for learners, employers, and providers*. Deakin University., https://dteach.deakin.edu.au/wp-content/uploads/sites/103/2019/08/Making-micro-credentials-work-Oliver-Deakin-2019-full-report.pdf

Oliver, B. (2021). Micro-credentials: A learner value framework. *Journal of Teaching and Learning for Graduate Employability*, 12(1), 48–51. DOI: 10.21153/jtlge2021vol12no1art1456

Omona, K., & O'dama, M. K. (Eds.). (2024). *Global perspectives on micro-learning and micro-credentials in higher education*. IGI Global., DOI: 10.4018/979-8-3693-0343-6

Öncü, S., Çolakoğlu, M., & Colak, H. (2024). Engagement dynamics in information technology education: A comparative analysis of online vs. face-to-face instruction. *Journal of Educational Technology and Online Learning*, 7(3), 321–333. DOI: 10.31681/jetol.1508735

Onesi-Ozigagun, O., Ololade, Y. J., Eyo-Udo, N. L., & Ogundipe, D. O. (2024). Revolutionizing education through AI: A comprehensive review of enhancing learning experiences. *International Journal of Applied Research in Social Sciences*, 6(4), 589–607. DOI: 10.51594/ijarss.v6i4.1011

OpenUpEd. (2015). D*efinition Massive Open Online Courses (MOOCs)*. https://www.openuped.eu/images/docs/Definition_Massive_Open_Online_Courses.pdf

Orak, C., & Turan, Z. (2024). Using artificial intelligence in digital video production: A systematic review study. *Journal of Educational Technology and Online Learning*, 7(3), 286–307. DOI: 10.31681/jetol.1459434

Orman, R., Şimşek, E., & Çakır, M. A. K. (2023). Micro-credentials and reflections on higher education. *Higher Education Evaluation and Development*, 17(2), 96–112. DOI: 10.1108/HEED-08-2022-0028

Orr, D., Pupinis, M., & Kirdulyte, G. (2020). Towards a European Approach to Micro-credentials: A Study of Practices and Commonalities in Offering Micro -credentials in European Higher Education. Luxembourg: Publications of the European Union NESET report. https://www.voced.edu.au/content/ngv:89657

Orr, D., Pupinis, M., & Kirdulytė, G. (2020). Towards a European approach to micro-credentials: A study of practices and commonalities in offering micro-credentials in European higher education: Analytical report. Publications Office of the European Union. https://op.europa.eu/en/publication-detail/-/publication/033a7af4-40e3-11eb-b27b-01aa75ed71a1/language-en

Ortagus, J. C., Kelchen, R., Rosinger, K., & Voorhees, N. (2020). Performance-Based Funding in American Higher Education: A Systematic Synthesis of the Intended and Unintended Consequences. *Educational Evaluation and Policy Analysis*, 42(4), 520–550. DOI: 10.3102/0162373720953128

Osman, S. A., & Ahmed, Z. E. (2024). *Navigating AI Integration: Case Studies and Best Practices in Educational Transformation*. AI-Enhanced Teaching Methods. [HTML] DOI: 10.4018/979-8-3693-2728-9.ch011

Ossiannilsson, E. (2021). MOOCS for lifelong learning, equity, and liberation. *MOOC (massive open online courses)*.

Ossiannilsson, E. (2023). Open educational resources (OER) and some of the United Nations sustainable development goals. *International Journal of Information And Learning Technology*, 40(5), 548–561. DOI: 10.1108/IJILT-01-2023-0002

Ostashewski, N., & Reid, D. (2015). A History and Frameworks of Digital Badges in Education. In *Gamification in Education and Business* (pp. 187–200). Springer International Publishing., DOI: 10.1007/978-3-319-10208-5_10

Otani, K., Deng, Y., Herrmann, P. A., & Kurz, R. S. (2020). Patient satisfaction, quality attributes, and organizational characteristics: A hierarchical linear model approach. [sagepub.com]. *Journal of Patient Experience*, 7(5), 801–806. DOI: 10.1177/2374373519892410 PMID: 33294618

Ouyang, F., Wu, M., Zheng, L., Zhang, L., & Jiao, P. (2023). Integration of artificial intelligence performance prediction and learning analytics to improve student learning in online engineering course. *International Journal of Educational Technology in Higher Education*, 20(1), 4. DOI: 10.1186/s41239-022-00372-4 PMID: 36683653

Ozmen Garibay, O., Winslow, B., Andolina, S., Antona, M., Bodenschatz, A., Coursaris, C., Falco, G., Fiore, S. M., Garibay, I., Grieman, K., Havens, J. C., Jirotka, M., Kacorri, H., Karwowski, W., Kider, J., Konstan, J., Koon, S., Lopez-Gonzalez, M., Maifeld-Carucci, I., & Xu, W. (2023). Six human-centered artificial intelligence grand challenges. [tandfonline.com]. *International Journal of Human-Computer Interaction*, 39(3), 391–437. DOI: 10.1080/10447318.2022.2153320

Palmer, B. (2021). *An analysis ofmicro-credentials' in VET.* Available at https://www.ncver.edu.au/__data/assets/pdf_file/0041/9666257/An-analysis-of-micro-credentials-in-VET.pdf

Panagiotakis, S., Papadokostaki, K., Kostas, V., & Malamos, A. (2019). *Towards a novel and LMS-free Pervasive Learning System exploiting the Experience API.* 156383. DOI: 10.4108/eai.13-7-2018.156383

Pandita, A., & Kiran, R. (2023). The Technology Interface and Student Engagement Are Significant Stimuli in Sustainable Student Satisfaction. *Sustainability (Basel)*, 15(10), 10. Advance online publication. DOI: 10.3390/su15107923

Papadakis, S., Kalogiannakis, M., Sifaki, E., & Vidakis, N. (2018a). *Access Moodle Using Smart Mobile Phones. A Case Study in a Greek University* (pp. 376–385). DOI: 10.1007/978-3-319-76908-0_36

Papadakis, A., Barianos, K., Kalogiannakis, M., Papadakis, S., & Vidakis, N. (2022). ARION: A Digital eLearning Educational Tool Library for Synchronization Composition & Orchestration of Learning Session Data. *Applied Sciences (Basel, Switzerland)*, 12(17), 8722. DOI: 10.3390/app12178722

Papadakis, S., Kalogiannakis, M., Sifaki, E., & Vidakis, N. (2018b). Evaluating Moodle use via Smart Mobile Phones. A case study in a Greek University. *EAI Endorsed Transactions on Creative Technologies*, 5(16), 156382. DOI: 10.4108/eai.10-4-2018.156382

Parker, H. E. (2015). Digital Badges to Assess Bloom's Affective Domain. *The National Teaching & Learning Forum*, 24(4), 9–11. DOI: 10.1002/ntlf.30031

Paul, B. S., & Anuradha, A. (2024). Artificial Intelligence in Different Business Domains: Ethical Concerns. In *Exploring the Ethical Implications of Generative AI* (pp. 13-33). IGI Global.

Paul, J., Lim, W. M., O'Cass, A., Hao, A. W., & Bresciani, S. (2021). Scientific procedures and rationales for systematic literature reviews (SPAR-4-SLR). *International Journal of Consumer Studies*, 45(4). Advance online publication. DOI: 10.1111/ijcs.12695

Pawilen, G. T., Lubong, K. S., & Fausto, C. J. R. S. (2022). A proposed model in designing curriculum for microcredentials in the Philippines. *International Journal of Curriculum and Instruction*, 15(1), 508–520. https://files.eric.ed.gov/fulltext/EJ1382892.pdf

Peele-Eady, T. B., & Moje, E. B. (2020). Communities as contexts for learning. In Handbook of the cultural foundations of learning (pp. 230-246). Routledge. taylor-francis.com DOI: 10.4324/9780203774977-16

Pelletier, K., Brown, M., Brooks, D. C., McCormack, M., Reeves, J., Arbino, N., Bozkurt, A., Crawford, S., Czerniewicz, L., Gibson, R., Linder, K., Mason, J., & Mondelli, V. (2021). *2021 EDUCAUSE Horizon Report Teaching and Learning Edition*. EDUCAUSE. https://www.learntechlib.org/p/219489/

Pence, H. E. (2020). How Should Chemistry Educators Respond to the Next Generation of Technology Change? *Education Sciences*, 10(2), 34. Advance online publication. DOI: 10.3390/educsci10020034

Pendy, B. (2023). Artificial intelligence: The future of education. *Jurnal Indonesia Sosial Sains*, 2(11). Advance online publication. DOI: 10.59141/jiss.v2i11.801

PEQAB. (2024). *Ontario micro-credentials: Harnessing the potential (mimeo)*. Post Secondary Quality Assessment Board of Ontario. Available at https://www.peqab.ca/OMCReport.html

Pérez-Sanagustín, M., Hilliger, I., Alario-Hoyos, C., Delgado Kloos, C., & Rayyan, S. (2017). H-MOOC framework: Reusing MOOCs for hybrid education. *Journal of Computing in Higher Education*, 29(1), 47–64. DOI: 10.1007/s12528-017-9133-5

Pérez-Sanagustín, M., Hilliger, I., Schwarzenberg, P., & Parra, D. (2015). A framework of hybrid MOOC-based pedagogies. In Changee, W., & Wapla, M. (Eds.), *EC-TEL 2015 workshops* (pp. 6–10). https://educate.gast.it.uc3m.es/wp-content/uploads/2015/09/A-Framework-of-Hybrid-MOOC-based-pedagogies-HybridED-ECTEL2015.pdf

Perpetual (n.d.). Suny microcredentials case study: Microcredential website redesign and marketing solutions. *Perpetual*. https://www.perpetualny.com/case-study/suny-microcredentials

Pertuz, S., Reyes, O., Cristobal, E. S., Meier, R., & Castro, M. (2023). MOOC-based flipped classroom for on-campus teaching in undergraduate engineering courses. *IEEE Transactions on Education*, 66(5), 468–478. DOI: 10.1109/TE.2023.3282896

Peters, M. (2023). *Skills alignment for lifelong learners in higher education: smart catalogues for reskilling and upskilling pathways*. Ubiquity Proceedings., DOI: 10.5334/uproc.71

Pham, S. T., & Sampson, P. M. (2022). The development of artificial intelligence in education: A review in context. [HTML]. *Journal of Computer Assisted Learning*, 38(5), 1408–1421. DOI: 10.1111/jcal.12687

Pichette, J., Brumwell, S., Rizk, J., & Han, S. (2021). Making sense of microcredentials. Higher Education Quality Council of Ontario. https://heqco.ca/pub/making-sense-of-microcredentials

Pickard, L. (2018, 18th July). Analysis of 450 MOOC-Based Microcredentials Reveals any Options But Little Consistency. Class Central.

Pickard, L., Shah, D., & De Simone, J. J. (2018). Mapping microcredentials across MOOC platforms. *In 2018 Learning with MOOCs (LWMOOCS), Madrid, Spain.* (pp. 17-21). IEEE. DOI: 10.1109/LWMOOCS.2018.8534617

Piedra, D. (2021). Open digital badges: The future of skill validation and credentialing. In *Handbook of Research on Innovations in Non-Traditional Educational Practices* (pp. 1–14). IGI Global. [HTML] DOI: 10.4018/978-1-7998-4360-3.ch001

Pirkkalainen, H., Sood, I., Padron Napoles, C., Kukkonen, A., & Camilleri, A. (2023). How might micro-credentials influence institutions and empower learners in higher education? *Educational Research*, 65(1), 40–63. https://doi.org/10.1080/00131881.2022.2157302

Pohl, C., Klein, J. T., Hoffmann, S., Mitchell, C., & Fam, D. (2021). Conceptualising transdisciplinary integration as a multidimensional interactive process. [sciencedirect.com]. *Environmental Science & Policy*, 118, 18–26. DOI: 10.1016/j.envsci.2020.12.005

Pollard, V., & Vincent, A. (2022). Micro-credentials: A Postdigital Counternarrative. *Postdigital Science and Education*, 4(3), 843–859. DOI: 10.1007/s42438-022-00311-6

Ponte, F., & Saray, V. (2022). The evolution of a micro-credential. *ASCILITE Publications*, 546–551. DOI: 10.14742/apubs.2019.328

Popkhadze, N. (2021). The Good, The Bad and The Ugly: AI in the higher education. *Hallinnon Tutkimus*, 40(4), 254–263. DOI: 10.37450/ht.107896

Porter, D., & Beale, R. (2015). *A policy brief on MOOCs*. The Commonwealth of Learning. https://oasis.col.org/server/api/core/bitstreams/7365921f-bb0b-4a25-be44-fa7e25981fe2/content

Porter, D., & Perris, K. (2021). *Workforce Development in the Post-COVID World: Digital Micro-credentials as a Lever for Transformation*. https://www.col.org/news/col-blog/workforce-development-post-covid-world-digital-micro-credentials-lever-transformation

Portugal. (2021). Decree Law 27/2021, of 16th April. *Diário da República*, n.º 74/2021, Série I. https://dre.pt/web/guest/pesquisa/-/search/161894401/details/normal?l=1 Parte superior do formulário

Pregowska, A., Masztalerz, K., Garlińska, M., & Osial, M. (2021). A worldwide journey through distance education—from the post office to virtual, augmented and mixed realities, and education during the COVID-19 pandemic. Education Sciences. mdpi.com

Prince, M., Felder, R., & Brent, R. (2020). ACTIVE STUDENT ENGAGEMENT IN ONLINE STEM CLASSES: APPROACHES AND RECOMMENDATIONS. *Advances in Engineering Education*, •••, 8.

Proctor, C. (2021, October 5). Defining the role for high-quality microcredentials in higher education. *Evolllution*. https://evolllution.com/programming/credentials/defining-a-role-for-high-quality-microcredentials-in-higher-education

Prud'homme-Genereux, A. (n.d.). Marketing and launch. *BCcampus Micro-credential Toolkit for B.C.* https://opentextbc.ca/bcmicrocredential/chapter/marketing-and-launch/

Putnam, C. (2024). Upskilling, reskilling become increasingly popular strategies for employers. *Rochester Business Journal*, 39(48), 8–10.

Puustinen, M., & Pulkkinen, L. (2001). Models of Self-regulated Learning: A review. *Scandinavian Journal of Educational Research*, 45(3), 269–286. DOI: 10.1080/00313830120074206

Qi, X., Sun, G., & Yue, L. (2023). Applying Self-Optimised Feedback to a Learning Management System for Facilitating Personalised Learning Activities on Massive Open Online Courses. *Sustainability (Basel)*, 15(16), 12562. DOI: 10.3390/su151612562

Rad, P., Roopaei, M., Beebe, N., Shadaram, M., & Au, Y. A. (n.d.). *AI Thinking for Cloud Education Platform with Personalized Learning*. http://hdl.handle.net/10125/49890

Radanliev, P., Santos, O., Brandon-Jones, A., & Joinson, A. (2024). Ethics and responsible ai deployment. *Frontiers in Artificial Intelligence*, 7, 1377011. Advance online publication. DOI: 10.3389/frai.2024.1377011 PMID: 38601110

Rajabalee, Y. B. (2023). The Implementation of Micro-Credentials in Formal and Informal Learning: A Systematic. semanticscholar.org

Raja, S., Jebadurai, D. J., Ivan, L., Mykola, R. V., Ruslan, K., & Nadiia, P. R. (2024). Impact of Artificial Intelligence in Students' Learning Life. In *AI in Business: Opportunities and Limitations* (Vol. 2, pp. 3–17). Springer Nature Switzerland. DOI: 10.1007/978-3-031-49544-1_1

Rajendran, S., Mathivanan, S. K., Jayagopal, P., Janaki, K. P., Bernard, B., Pandy, S., & Somanathan, M. S. (2022). Emphasizing privacy and security of edge intelligence with machine learning for healthcare. *International Journal of Intelligent Computing And Cybernetics*, 15(1), 92–109. DOI: 10.1108/IJICC-05-2021-0099

Raj, R., Singh, A., Kumar, V., & Verma, P. (2024). Achieving professional qualifications using micro-credentials: A case of small packages and big challenges in higher education. *International Journal of Educational Management*, 38(4), 916–947. DOI: 10.1108/IJEM-01-2023-0028

Ralston, S. J. (2021). Higher education's microcredentialing craze: A postdigital-deweyan critique. *Postdigital Science and Education*, 3(1), 83–101. DOI: 10.1007/s42438-020-00121-8

Ralston, S. J. (2021). Higher education's microcredentialing craze: A postdigital-Deweyan critique. *Postdigital Science and Education*, 3(1), 83–101. https://doi.org/10.1007/s42438-020-00121-8

Ramírez-Montoya, M. S., Martínez-Pérez, S., Rodríguez-Abitia, G., & López-Caudana, E. (2022). Digital accreditations in mooc-based training on sustainability: Factors that influence terminal efficiency. *Australasian Journal of Educational Technology*, •••, 164–182. DOI: 10.14742/ajet.7082

Rane, N., Choudhary, S., & Rane, J. (2023). *Education 4.0 and 5.0: Integrating Artificial Intelligence (AI) for Personalized and Adaptive Learning* (SSRN Scholarly Paper 4638365). DOI: 10.2139/ssrn.4638365

Ranjan, J., & Foropon, C. (2021). Big data analytics in building the competitive intelligence of organizations. [HTML]. *International Journal of Information Management*, 56, 102231. DOI: 10.1016/j.ijinfomgt.2020.102231

Redden, E. (2020). 41% of recent grads work in jobs that do not require a degree. *Inside Higher Education, February 17th*. https://www.insidehighered.com/quicktakes/2020/02/18/41-recent-grads-work-jobs-not-requiring-degree

Reed, A. (2023). Micro-credentials and the role of evidence: Increasing the potential for learner-centeredness, inclusivity and an expansive model of assessment and credentialing. *International Journal of Information and Learning Technology*, 40(5), 401–412. DOI: 10.1108/IJILT-12-2022-0228

Reed, A., Kong, Y., & Abramovich, S. (2024). Assessment, credential, or both? Higher education faculty's design principles for micro-credentials. *Discover Education*, 3(1), 16. https://doi.org/10.1007/s44217-024-00100-2

Reedy, A., Pfitzner, D., Rook, L., & Ellis, L. (2021). Responding to the COVID-19 emergency: Student and academic staff perceptions of academic integrity in the transition to online exams at three Australian universities. *International Journal for Educational Integrity*, 17(9), 9. Advance online publication. DOI: 10.1007/s40979-021-00075-9

Reeves, T. C., & Hedberg, J. G. (2014). MOOCs: Let's get REAL. *Educational Technology*, 54(1), 3–8. https://www.jstor.org/stable/44430228

Renumol, V. (2021). A systematic literature review on adaptive content recommenders in personalized learning environments from 2015 to 2020. *Journal of Computers in Education*, 9(1), 113–148. DOI: 10.1007/s40692-021-00199-4

Resei, C., Friedl, C., Staubitz, T., & Rohloff, T. (2019). Micro-credentials in EU and Global. Corship Corporate Edupreneurship. https://openhpi-public.s3.openhpicloud.de/pages/research/27kLG703NBaxDgjuaNjOWe/Corship-R1.1c_micro-credentials.pdf

Resei, C., Friedl, C., Staubitz, T., & Rohloff, T. (2019). *Micro-credentials in EU and global.* Corship Corporate Edupreneurship. https://www.corship.eu/wp-content/uploads/2019/07/Corship-R1.1c_micro-credentials.pdf

Reynoldson, M. (2023). Marketing micro-credentials: An analysis of actors, voices and messages in educational innovation discourse. *Innovations in Education and Teaching International*, 60(6), 953–963. DOI: 10.1080/14703297.2022.2083657

Rieder, A. T. (2022). Using Micro-credentials and Digital Badges in Education and Training: A Literature Review. *Proceedings of Society for Information Technology & Teacher Education International Conference*, 246–251.

Rincón-Flores, E. G., Mena, J., Montoya, M. S. R., & Ramírez-Velarde, R. V. (2019). The use of gamification in xmoocs about energy: Effects and predictive models for participants' learning. *Australasian Journal of Educational Technology*, •••, 43–59. DOI: 10.14742/ajet.4818

Risquez, A., Cassidy, D., & O'Suilleabhain, G. (2020). Badge of honour? an exploration of the use of digital badges to support a partnership approach to faculty development. *Australasian Journal of Educational Technology*, 36(5), 18–29. DOI: 10.14742/ajet.6112

Rivera, E., & Revilla, M. L. (1984). A cross-impact simulation and analysis of events through time with a micro-computer. Microprocessing and microprogramming, 13(3), 189-198. https://doi.org/DOI: 10.1016/0165-6074(84)90030-9

Rodrigo Castañeda Valle. Simon Normandeau, & Gara Rojas González (2015). *Education at a glance interim report: update of employment and educational attainment indicators*. https://www.oecd.org/edu/eag.htm

Rodriguez, C. O. (2012). MOOCs and the AI-Stanford like courses: Two successful and distinct course formats for massive open online courses. *European Journal of Open, Distance and E-Learning*. https://files.eric.ed.gov/fulltext/EJ982976.pdf

Rodriguez, E., Burguillo, J. C., Rodriguez, D. A., Mikic, F. A., Gonzalez-Moreno, J. C., & Novegil, V. (2008). Developing virtual teaching assistants for open e-learning platforms. *2008 19th EAEEIE Annual Conference*, 193–198. DOI: 10.1109/EAEEIE.2008.4610185

Rof, A., Bikfalvi, A., & Marques, P. (2024). Exploring learner satisfaction and the effectiveness of microlearning in higher education. *The Internet and Higher Education*, 62, 100952. DOI: 10.1016/j.iheduc.2024.100952

Roll, I., McNamara, D., Sosnovsky, S., Luckin, R., & Dimitrova, V. (2021). *Artificial intelligence in education*. Springer International Publishing. [HTML]

Rosenberg, S. (2022, January 4). Lifelong learning in higher education: Diversifying credentials to engage learners. *Evolllution*. https://evolllution.com/programming/credentials/lifelong-learning-in-higher-education-diversifying-credentials-to-engage-learners/

Rossiter, D., & Tynan, B. (2019). Designing & Implementing Micro-Credentials: A Guide for Practitioners.http://hdl.handle.net/11599/3279

Rossiter, D., & Tynan, B. (2019). *Designing and implementing micro-credentials: A guide for practitioners*.

Rossiter, D., & Tynan, B. (2019). *Designing and Implementing Micro-Credentials: A Guide for Practitioners. Commonwealth of Learning*. https://oasis.col.org/server/api/core/bitstreams/770ff842-9a5e-424b-a253-0757fa539086/content

Rouf, N., Malik, M. B., Arif, T., Sharma, S., Singh, S., Aich, S., & Kim, H. C. (2021). Stock market prediction using machine learning techniques: A decade survey on methodologies, recent developments, and future directions. [mdpi.com]. *Electronics (Basel)*, 10(21), 2717. DOI: 10.3390/electronics10212717

Ruan, S., Jiang, L., Xu, Q., Liu, Z., Davis, G. M., Brunskill, E., & Landay, J. A. (2021). EnglishBot: An AI-Powered Conversational System for Second Language Learning. *26th International Conference on Intelligent User Interfaces*, 434–444. DOI: 10.1145/3397481.3450648

Ruddy, C., & Ponte, F. (2019). Preparing students for university studies and beyond: A micro-credential trial that delivers academic integrity awareness. *Journal of the Australian Library and Information Association*, 68(1), 56–67. DOI: 10.1080/24750158.2018.1562520

Rueda-Gómez, K. L., Rodríguez-Muñiz, L. J., & Muñiz-Rodríguez, L. (2024). Factors that mediate the success of the use of online platforms to support learning: The view of university teachers. *Education and Information Technologies*, 29(2), 2459–2482. DOI: 10.1007/s10639-023-11916-0

Ruiz-Rojas, L. I., Acosta-Vargas, P., De-Moreta-Llovet, J., & Gonzalez-Rodriguez, M. (2023). Empowering Education with Generative Artificial Intelligence Tools: Approach with an Instructional Design Matrix. *Sustainability (Basel)*, 15(15), 15. Advance online publication. DOI: 10.3390/su151511524

Rüütmann, T. (2023). Engineering Pedagogy and Engineering Educators' Competency Model For Effective Teaching And Learning Steam. *Problems Of Education In The 21st Century, 81*(4), 531–546. DOI: 10.33225/pec/23.81.531

Ryoo, J. & Winkelmann, K. (2021). Innovative learning environments in STEM higher education: Opportunities, challenges, and looking forward. oapen.org

Sabharwal, D., Kabha, R., & Srivastava, K. (2023). Artificial intelligence (ai)-powered virtual assistants and their effect on human productivity and laziness: Study on students of delhi-ncr (india) & fujairah (uae). *Journal of Content Community and Communication*, 17(9), 162–174. DOI: 10.31620/JCCC.06.23/12

Sadeq, N., & Stanback, B. (2021, December 17). Adapting the Environmental Scan for Gerontology Graduate Students' Career Exploration. *Innovation in Aging*, 5(Suppl 1), 757. DOI: 10.1093/geroni/igab046.2806

Saheb, T., & Saheb, T. (2023). Topical review of artificial intelligence national policies: A mixed method analysis. *Technology in Society*, 74, 102316. https://doi.org/ https://doi.org/10.1016/j.techsoc.2023.102316. DOI: 10.1016/j.techsoc.2023.102316

Sailer, M., & Homner, L. (2020). The Gamification of Learning: A Meta-analysis. *Educational Psychology Review*, 32(1), 77–112. DOI: 10.1007/s10648-019-09498-w

Sale, R. R. (2023). The Composition of Opportunity: Organizational Approaches to Developing Workforce Education Pathways Through Cross-Sector Partnerships. proquest.com

Salmon, M. (2023). Drivers of the global push for microcredentials in higher education: Flexibility and employability in contemporary university systems. *Perspectives*, 27(4), 179–187. DOI: 10.1080/13603108.2023.2229767

Sandhu, R., Channi, H. K., Ghai, D., Cheema, G. S., & Kaur, M. (2024). An Introduction to Generative AI Tools for Education 2030. Integrating Generative AI in Education to Achieve Sustainable Development Goals, 1-28. [HTML]

Santana-Dominguez, I., Ballesteros-Rodriguez, J. L., & Domínguez-Falcón, C. (2022). An application of training transfer literature to the analysis of training for entrepreneurship: A conceptual model. [sciencedirect.com]. *International Journal of Management Education*, 20(2), 100649. DOI: 10.1016/j.ijme.2022.100649

Sappaile, B. I., Vandika, A. Y., Deiniatur, M., Nuridayanti, N., & Arifudin, O. (2024). The Role of Artificial Intelligence in the Development of Digital Era Educational Progress. *Journal of Artificial Intelligence and Development*, 3(1), 1–8.

Sardabi, N., Kia, M., & Ghajarieh, A. (2023). *The Role of Motivational Strategies on Young EFL Learners' Basic Psychological Needs: A Self-Determination Theory Perspective*. DOI: 10.30479/jmrels.2022.17055.2042

Sargent, J., Rienties, B., Perryman, L. A., & Fitzgerald, E. (2023). Investigating the Views and Use of Stackable Microcredentials within a Postgraduate Certificate in Academic Practice. *Journal of Interactive Media in Education, 2023*(1). DOI: 10.5334/jime.805

Sarı, T., Nayir, F., & Bozkurt, A. (2024). Reimagining education: Bridging artificial intelligence, transhumanism, and critical pedagogy. *Journal of Educational Technology and Online Learning*, 7(1), 102–115. DOI: 10.31681/jetol.1308022

Scheffel, M., Drachsler, H., Stoyanov, S., & Specht, M. (2014). Quality Indicators for Learning Analytics. *Journal of Educational Technology & Society*, 17(4), 117–132.

Schmidt, S. M. P., & Ralph, D. L. (2016). The Flipped Classroom: A twist on teaching. *Contemporary Issues in Education Research (CIER), 9*(1), 1–6. https://files.eric.ed.gov/fulltext/EJ1087603.pdf

Schneider, G. F., Kontes, G. D., Qiu, H., Silva, F. J., Bucur, M., Malanik, J., Schindler, Z., Andriopolous, P., de Agustin-Camacho, P., Romero-Amorrortu, A., & Grün, G. (2020). Design of knowledge-based systems for automated deployment of building management services. [sciencedirect.com]. *Automation in Construction*, 119, 103402. DOI: 10.1016/j.autcon.2020.103402

Schoon, I., Nasim, B., Sehmi, R., & Cook, R. (2015). *The Impact of Early Life Skills on Later Outcomes.*

Schumacher, C., & Ifenthaler, D. (2018). Features students really expect from learning analytics. *Computers in Human Behavior*, 78, 397–407. DOI: 10.1016/j.chb.2017.06.030

Selvaratnam, R., & Sankey, M. (2020). Survey of micro-credentialing Practice in Australasian Universities 2020. ACODE Whitepaper. https://publications.ascilite.org/index.php/APUB/article/view/695/424

Selvaratnam, R. M., & Sankey, M. D. (2021). An integrative literature review of the implementation of micro-credentials in higher education: Implications for practice in Australasia. *Journal of Teaching and Learning for Graduate Employability*, 12(1), 1–17.

Selvaratnam, R. M., Warburton, S., Parrish, D., & Crew, S. (2024). A maturity model for micro-credentialing and shorter forms of learning practice in Australasian universities. *Journal of Higher Education Policy and Management*, 46(4), 1–16. DOI: 10.1080/1360080X.2023.2299150

Selvaratnam, R., & Sankey, M. (2021). The State of Micro-Credentials Implementation and Practice in Australasian Higher Education. *Open Praxis*, 13(2), 228–238. DOI: 10.5944/openpraxis.13.2.130

Seo, K., Tang, J., Roll, I., Fels, S., & Yoon, D. (2021). The impact of artificial intelligence on learner–instructor interaction in online learning. *International Journal of Educational Technology in Higher Education*, 18(1), 54. Advance online publication. DOI: 10.1186/s41239-021-00292-9 PMID: 34778540

Sepulveda, T. A. C. (2020). *Development of a System Architecture for the Prediction of Student Success using Machine Learning Techniques—ProQuest* [MISSOURI UNIVERSITY OF SCIENCE AND TECHNOLOGY]. https://www.proquest.com/openview/9f61bd7c4ab8f6b2c90abe399fb21fc3/1?pq-origsite=gscholar&cbl=18750&diss=y

Shah, D. (2021). By the numbers: MOOCs in 2021. *Class Central*. https://www.classcentral.com/report/mooc-stats-2021

Shapiro, H., Lee, C. H., Roth, N. E. W., & Li, K. (2017). Understanding the massive open online course (mooc) student experience: An examination of attitudes, motivations, and barriers. Computers &Amp. *Computers & Education*, 110, 35–50. DOI: 10.1016/j.compedu.2017.03.003

Sharma, H., Jain, V., Mogaji, E., & Babbilid, A. S. (2024). Blended learning and augmented employability: A multi-stakeholder perspective of the micro-credentialing ecosystem in higher education. *International Journal of Educational Management*. Advance online publication. https://doi.org/10.1108/IJEM-12-2022-0497

Shay, A. (2023). Micro-credentialing. *Clinical Nurse Specialist CNS*, 37(6), 299–300. DOI: 10.1097/NUR.0000000000000780 PMID: 37870516

Sheather, J., & Slattery, D. (2021, October 18). The great resignation: How do we support and retain staff already stretched to their limit? [BMJ]. *British Medical Journal*, 375, 2533. DOI: 10.1136/bmj.n2533 PMID: 34663568

Shehzad, N., & Charles, T. (2023). Exploring the impact of instructor social presence on student engagement in online higher education. *Contemporary Educational Technology*, 15(4), ep484. DOI: 10.30935/cedtech/13823

Shi, D., Zhou, J., Wang, D., & Wu, X. (2022). Research status, hotspots, and evolutionary trends of intelligent education from the perspective of knowledge graph. Sustainability. mdpi.com

Shoaib, M., Sayed, N., Singh, J., Shafi, J., Khan, S., & Ali, F. (2024). AI student success predictor: Enhancing personalized learning in campus management systems. *Computers in Human Behavior*, 158, 108301. DOI: 10.1016/j.chb.2024.108301

Shonfeld, M., Cotnam-Kappel, M., Judge, M., Ng, C. Y., Ntebutse, J. G., Williamson-Leadley, S., & Yildiz, M. N. (2021). Learning in digital environments: A model for cross-cultural alignment. [springer.com]. *Educational Technology Research and Development*, 69(4), 1–20. DOI: 10.1007/s11423-021-09967-6 PMID: 33654347

Shuibin, G., Benjamin, T., & Naam, Y. D. (2020). AN ASSESSMENT ON THE IMPACT OF TRAINING AND DEVELOPMENT ON EMPLOYEE PRODUCTIVITY IN GHANA EDUCATION SERVICE, WA. [HTML]. *International Journal of Information, Business and Management*, 12(1), 42–70.

Shwedeh, F., Salloum, S. A., Aburayya, A., Fatin, B., Elbadawi, M. A., Al Ghurabli, Z., & Al Dabbagh, T. (2024). AI Adoption and Educational Sustainability in Higher Education in the UAE. In *Artificial Intelligence in Education: The Power and Dangers of ChatGPT in the Classroom* (pp. 201–229). Springer Nature Switzerland., https://doi.org/10.1007/978-3-031-52280-2_14

Shwedeh, F., Salloum, S. A., Aburayya, A., Fatin, B., Elbadawi, M. A., Al Ghurabli, Z., & Al Dabbagh, T. (2024). AI Adoption and Educational Sustainability in Higher Education in the UAE. *Studies in Big Data*, 144(March), 201–229. DOI: 10.1007/978-3-031-52280-2_14

Sidhu, R. & Gage, W. H. (2021). Enhancing the odds of adopting e-learning or community-focused experiential learning as a teaching practice amongst university faculty. Heliyon. cell.com

Silcoff, J., & O'Kane, J. (2023). How the Liberals' multibillion tech plan created chaos instead of growth. *Globe and Mail, January 20th*. https://www.theglobeandmail.com/business/article-liberals-tech-plan-economic-growth/

Singh, A. D., Abuhamdeih, S., & Raghunathan, S. (2019). *Inspiring the Advancement of MOOCs in the Middle East. MOOCs and Open Education in the Global South: Challenges*. Successes, and Opportunities.

Singh, S. V., & Hiran, K. K. (2022). The Impact of AI on Teaching and Learning in Higher Education Technology. *Journal of Higher Education Theory and Practice*, 22(13), 13. https://articlearchives.co/index.php/JHETP/article/view/3553

Singla, J., Kaur, B., Prashar, D., Jha, S., Joshi, G. P., Park, K., Tariq, U., & Seo, C. (2020). A Novel Fuzzy Logic-Based Medical Expert System for Diagnosis of Chronic Kidney Disease. [wiley.com]. *Mobile Information Systems*, 2020(1), 8887627. DOI: 10.1155/2020/8887627

Siregar, T. (2024). *Differentiated Instruction from the Perspective of Cognitive Load Theory*.

Sitar-Tăut, D.-A., Mican, D., & Moisescu, O.-I. (2024). To be (online) or not to be? The antecedents of online study propensity and e-learning-dependent dropout intention in higher education. *Technological Forecasting and Social Change*, 207, 123566. DOI: 10.1016/j.techfore.2024.123566

Sitas, N., Harmáčková, Z. V., Anticamara, J. A., Arneth, A., Badola, R., Biggs, R., Blanchard, R., Brotons, L., Cantele, M., Coetzer, K., DasGupta, R., den Belder, E., Ghosh, S., Guisan, A., Gundimeda, H., Hamann, M., Harrison, P. A., Hashimoto, S., Hauck, J., & Valle, M. (2019). Exploring the usefulness of scenario archetypes in science-policy processes: Experience across IPBES assessments. *Ecology and Society*, 24(3), art35. Advance online publication. DOI: 10.5751/ES-11039-240335

Smolenski, N. (2021). Blockchain for Education: A New Credentialing Ecosystem. OECD Digital Education Outlook 2021 Pushing the Frontiers with Artificial Intelligence, Blockchain and Robots: Pushing the Frontiers with Artificial Intelligence, Blockchain and Robots, 209. google.com

Snyder, C., Paska, L. M., & Besozzi, D. (2014). Cast from the Past: Using Screencasting in the Social Studies Classroom. *Social Studies*, 105(6), 310–314. DOI: 10.1080/00377996.2014.951472

Somasundaram, M., Junaid, K. A. M., & Mangadu, S. (2020). Artificial intelligence (AI) enabled intelligent quality management system (IQMS) for personalized learning path. Procedia Computer Science. sciencedirect.com

Song, T., Choi, Y., Jeon, J. H., & Cho, Y. K. (2023). A machine learning approach to discover migration modes and transition dynamics of heterogeneous dendritic cells. Frontiers in Immunology. frontiersin.org

Soon, J. J., & Ismail, R. (2021). Professional Jobs and Structural Unemployment in the Post-Pandemic World: Is Micro-Credentialing the Missing Bridge. *The New Normal: Reinventing Professional Life and Familial Bonding in the Post COVID, 19*.

Sorin, V., Barash, Y., Konen, E., & Klang, E. (2020). Deep learning for natural language processing in radiology—Fundamentals and a systematic review. [HTML]. *Journal of the American College of Radiology*, 17(5), 639–648. DOI: 10.1016/j.jacr.2019.12.026 PMID: 32004480

Souto-Otero, M. (2021). Validation of non-formal and informal learning in formal education: Covert and overt. *European Journal of Education*, 56(3), 365–379. DOI: 10.1111/ejed.12464

Srinivasa, K. G., Kurni, M., & Saritha, K. (2022). Harnessing the Power of AI to Education. In *Learning, teaching, and assessment methods for contemporary learners: pedagogy for the digital generation* (pp. 311–342). Springer Nature Singapore. [HTML] DOI: 10.1007/978-981-19-6734-4_13

Stahl, B. C. (2021). Artificial intelligence for a better future: an ecosystem perspective on the ethics of AI and emerging digital technologies. oapen.org

Stamatakis, A., Trampas, A. M., Kontoulis, V., Barianos, A. K., Papadakis, A., & Vidakis, N. (2020). *AN OPEN SOURCE TRAINING MANAGEMENT SYSTEM TO SUPPORT THE PERSONAL PHYSICAL AND MENTAL TRAINING*. 5558–5566. DOI: 10.21125/edulearn.2020.1457

Statistics Canada. (2022). Postsecondary enrolments and graduates, 2017-2018. 19 February. https://www150.statcan.gc.ca/n1/daily-quotidien/200219/dq200219b-eng.htm

Strada (2021). Explore public viewpoint data: Covid-19 work and education survey. *Strada*. https://cci.stradaeducation.org/explore-public-viewpoint-data/

Subasinghe, C., & Giridharan, B. (2023). Introducing Multidisciplinary Micro-credentialing: Rethinking Learning and Development for Higher Education and Industry. In Introducing Multidisciplinary Micro-credentialing: Rethinking Learning and Development for Higher Education and Industry (pp. 3-16). Emerald Publishing Limited. [HTML]

Subasinghe, C., & Giridharan, B. (2023). Introducing multidisciplinary micro-credentialing: rethinking learning and development for higher education and industry. In *Introducing Multidisciplinary Micro-credentialing: Rethinking Learning and Development for Higher Education and Industry* (pp. 3–16). Emerald Publishing Limited. DOI: 10.1108/978-1-80382-459-820231002

Surono, S. (2023). Development of micro credential design for project management to improve the quality of engineering practices. *International Journal of Social Service and Research*, 3(11), 2910–2920. DOI: 10.46799/ijssr.v3i11.598

Sykes, J. (2023). A self-reflective design study of three visio and visio-haptic artifacts for use in mechanical engineering design education. umanitoba.ca

Taiar, T. A. and R. (2023). *Human Interaction & Emerging Technologies (IHIET-AI 2023): Artificial Intelligence & Future Applications*. AHFE Conference.

Tammeleht, A. (2023). Development and piloting of a micro-credential programme in research ethics and integrity leadership – an example from estonia., 733-740. https://doi.org/DOI: 10.4995/HEAd23.2023.16220

Tamoliune, G., Greenspon, R., Tereseviciene, M., Volungeviciene, A., Trepule, E., & Dauksiene, E. (2023). Exploring the potential of micro-credentials: A systematic literature review. *Frontiers in Education*, 7, 1006811. DOI: 10.3389/feduc.2022.1006811

Tang, H., & Qian, Y. (2022). Designing MOOCs with LITTLE. *Cogent Education*, 9(1), 2064411. Advance online publication. DOI: 10.1080/2331186X.2022.2064411

Tang, H., & Xing, W. (2021). Massive open online courses for professional certificate programs? perspectives on professional learners' longitudinal participation patterns. *Australasian Journal of Educational Technology*, •••, 136–147. DOI: 10.14742/ajet.5768

Tang, Y. Y., Hölzel, B. K., & Posner, M. I. (2015). The neuroscience of mindfulness meditation. *Nature Reviews. Neuroscience*, 16(4), 213–225. DOI: 10.1038/nrn3916 PMID: 25783612

Tan, K. T., Chan, J. I. L., Arumugam, P. V., & Lee, H. W. (2024). CLOSING THE TALENT GAP: A PROPOSED MICRO-CREDENTIAL MODEL IN MALAYSIAN FORMAL EDUCATION. *Turkish Online Journal of Distance Education*, 25(4), 67–80. DOI: 10.17718/tojde.1400152

Taye, D. & Getnet, B. (2020). The impact of employee turnover on organizational performance: A case study of Mada Walabu University, Bale Robe, Ethiopia. American journal of pure and applied biosciences. academia.edu

Tebepah, I. R., & Ikeremo, E. S. (2024). *Comparative Review of Selected Adaptive e-Learning Platforms. 10*(5).

Tee, P. K., Cham, T. H., Aw, E. C. X., Khudaykulov, A., & Zhang, X. (2024). Marketing micro-credentials: Understanding learners' engagement and willingness to pay more. *International Journal of Educational Management*, 38(4), 1001–1020. https://doi.org/10.1108/IJEM-03-2023-0096

Thakur, N., Singh, A., & Sangal, A. L. (2022). Cloud services selection: A systematic review and future research directions. [HTML]. *Computer Science Review*, 46, 100514. DOI: 10.1016/j.cosrev.2022.100514

The Council of the European Union. (2022). Council recommendation of 16 June 2022 on a European approach to micro-credentials for lifelong learning and employability. *Official Journal of the European Union.*https://eur-lex.europa.eu/legal-content/EN/TXT/PDF/?uri=CELEX:32022H0627(02)

The Council of the European Union. (2022). *Council recommendation of 16 June 2022 on a European approach to micro-credentials for lifelong learning and employability*. The Council of the European Union.

The Global Network for Age-friendly Cities and Communities. looking back over the last decade, looking forward to the next. Geneva, Switzerland: World Health Organization; 2018 (WHO/FWC/ALC/18.4). Licence: CC BY-NC-SA 3.0 IGO.

The State University of New York. (n.d.). Microcredentials. *The State University of New York*. https://www.suny.edu/microcredentials/

Tinsley, B., Cacicio, S., Shah, Z., Parker, D., Younge, O., & Luke Luna, C. (2022). Micro-credentials for social mobility in rural postsecondary communities: a landscape report. https://doi.org/DOI: 10.51388/20.500.12265/151

Tlili, A., Jemni, M., Khribi, M. K., Huang, R., Chang, T. W., & Liu, D. (2020). Current state of open educational resources in the Arab region: An investigation in 22 countries. *Smart Learning Environments*, 7(1), 11. Advance online publication. DOI: 10.1186/s40561-020-00120-z

Tooley, M., & Hood, J. (2021). Harnessing Micro-Credentials for Teacher Growth: A National Review of Early Best Practices. New America. https://www.newamerica.org/education-policy/reports/harnessing-micro-credentials-teacher-growth/ (accessed 10 May 2024).

Tschofen, C., & Mackness, J. (2012). Connectivism and dimensions of individual experience. *International Review of Research in Open and Distance Learning*, 13(1), 124–143. DOI: 10.19173/irrodl.v13i1.1143

Tulloch, J., Zamani, R., & Akrami, M. (2020). Machine learning in the prevention, diagnosis and management of diabetic foot ulcers: a systematic review. IEEE Access. ieee.org

Tuomi, I. (2022). Artificial intelligence, 21st century competences, and socio-emotional learning in education: More than high-risk? *European Journal of Education*, 57(4), 601–619. DOI: 10.1111/ejed.12531

Tzimas, D., & Demetriadis, S. (2021). Ethical issues in learning analytics: A review of the field. [HTML]. *Educational Technology Research and Development*, 69(2), 1101–1133. DOI: 10.1007/s11423-021-09977-4

Um, H., Kim, H., Choi, D., & Oh, H. (2023). An AI-based English education platform during the COVID-19 pandemic. Universal Access in the Information Society. springer.com

UNESCO. (2018). Digital credentialing: implications for the recognition of learning across borders. UNESCO Education Sector. https://unesdoc.unesco.org/ark:/48223/pf0000264428. (accessed 10 May 2024).

UNESCO. (2021). Understanding the impact of artificial intelligence on skills development. In *United Nations Educational*. Scientific and Cultural Organization.

United Nations (2015). *Transforming our world: The 2030 agenda for sustainable development.* DOI: 10.1201/b20466-7

United Nations, Department of Economic and Social Affairs. (n.d.). Goals 4: Ensure inclusive and equitable quality education and promote lifelong learning opportunities for all. Retrieved June 5, 2024, from https://sdgs.un.org/goals/goal4

United Nations. (2018). Transforming Our World: The 2030 Agenda for Sustainable Development. In *A New Era in Global Health*. United Nations., DOI: 10.1891/9780826190123.ap02

UPCEA. (2020). Hallmarks of excellence in credential innovation. *UPCEA*. https://upcea.edu/wp-content/uploads/2020/05/UPCEA-Hallmarks-of-Excellence-in-Credential-Innovation-May-20-2020.pdf

UPCEA. (2023). The effect of employer understanding and engagement on non-degree credentials. *UPCEA*. https://upcea.edu/wp-content/uploads/2023/05/The-Effect-of-Employer-Understanding-and-Engagement-on-Non-Degree-Credentials_UPCEA-and-Collegis_February-2023.pdf

Urfa, M., & Durak, G. (2017). Implementation of the flipped classroom model in the Scientific Ethics course. *Journal of Education and e-learning Research*, 4(3), 108–117. DOI: 10.20448/journal.509.2017.43.108.117

Usher, A. (2024a). Three developments on the international student file. Feb 20th. https://higheredstrategy.com/three-developments-on-the-international-students-file/

Usher, A. (2024b). Marc Miller strikes again. Sept 23rdhttps://higheredstrategy.com/marc-miller-strikes-again/

Usher, A. (2024c). The eighth wonder of the world: Ontario college finances to 2023-4. https://higheredstrategy.com/the-eighth-wonder-of-the-world-ontario-college-finances-to-2023-24

Usher, A., & Balfour, J. (2024). *The State of Postsecondary Education in Canada, 2024*. Higher Education Strategy Associates.

Uzwyshyn, R., Balnaves, E., Boffy, F. X., Chakarova, J., Kleinveldt, L., Sánchez Nogales, E., ... & IFLA Information Technology Standing Committee. (2022). Trends and Issues in Library Technology, June 2022. ifla.org

Valerio, A. (2024). Anticipating the Impact of Artificial Intelligence in Higher Education: Student Awareness and Ethical Concerns in Zamboanga City, Philippines. *Cognizance Journal of Multidisciplinary Studies*, 4(6), 10–47760. DOI: 10.47760/cognizance.2024.v04i06.024

van der Vorst, T., & Jelicic, N. (2019). *Artificial Intelligence in Education: Can AI bring the full potential of personalized learning to education?*https://www.econstor.eu/handle/10419/205222

Van Wart, M., Ni, A., Medina, P., Canelon, J., Kordrostami, M., Zhang, J., & Liu, Y. (2020). Integrating students' perspectives about online learning: A hierarchy of factors. *International Journal of Educational Technology in Higher Education*, 17(1), 1. Advance online publication. DOI: 10.1186/s41239-020-00229-8 PMID: 34778515

Varadarajan, S., Koh, J. H. L., & Daniel, B. K. (2023). A systematic review of the opportunities and challenges of micro-credentials for multiple stakeholders. *International Journal of Educational Technology in Higher Education*, 20(1), 13. DOI: 10.1186/s41239-023-00381-x PMID: 36874535

Vashishth, T. K., Sharma, V., Sharma, K. K., Kumar, B., Panwar, R., & Chaudhary, S. (2024). *AI-Driven Learning Analytics for Personalized Feedback and Assessment in Higher Education.*, DOI: 10.4018/979-8-3693-0639-0.ch009

Vega, J., Rodriguez, M., Check, E., Moran, H., & Loo, L. (2024). Duolingo evolution: From automation to Artificial Intelligence. *2024 IEEE Colombian Conference on Applications of Computational Intelligence (ColCACI)*, 1–6. DOI: 10.1109/ColCACI63187.2024.10666523

Venable, M. A. (2021). 2021 alternative education pathways report. *BestColleges.com*. https://www.bestcolleges.com/research/alternative-education-pathways/

Vidakis, N., Barianos, K., Trampas, A., Papadakis, S., Kalogiannakis, M., & Kostas, V. (2019, October). *Generating Education in-Game Data: The Case of an Ancient Theatre Serious Game*. DOI: 10.5220/0007810800360043

Vidakis, N., Barianos, K. A., Xanthopoulos, G., & Stamatakis, A. (2018). Cultural inheritance educational environment: The ancient theatre game thimeledu. *Proceedings of the European Conference on Games-Based Learning, 2018-Octob*.

Vijayalakshmi, S., Madhavi, B., Jayanthi, N., Bansode, G. S., Sharma, N., & Shanthi, K. G. (2024, March). Smart Education With Iot And Ai: Revolutionizing Learning In The Digital Age. In *2024 2nd International Conference on Disruptive Technologies (ICDT)* (pp. 1282-1286). IEEE.

Vilaça, T., Darlington, E., Velasco, M., Martinis, O., & Masson, J. (2019). *SHE Manual for schools 2.0.*www.schoolsforhealth.org/resources/materials-and-tools/

Villar-Aguilés, A., & Muñoz-Rodríguez, D. (2024). Complex trajectories in higher education students: Online and face-to-face universities. *Journal of New Approaches in Educational Research*, 13(1), 4. DOI: 10.1007/s44322-023-00006-1

Visser, M., van Eck, N. J., & Waltman, L. (2021). Large-scale comparison of bibliographic data sources: Scopus, web of science, dimensions, crossref, and microsoft academic. *Quantitative Science Studies*, 2(1), 20–41. DOI: 10.1162/qss_a_00112

Vodoukis, N., & Pagiatakis, G. (2022). Massive open online courses (MOOCs): Practices, trends, and challenges for the higher education. *European Journal of Education and Pedagogy*, 3(2), 288–295. https://www.ej-edu.org/index.php/ejedu/article/view/365. DOI: 10.24018/ejedu.2022.3.3.365

Vogel, K. M. & Ouagrham-Gormley, S. B. (2023). Scientists as spies?: Assessing US claims about the security threat posed by China's Thousand Talents Program for the US life sciences. Politics and the Life Sciences. cambridge.org

Walji, S., Deacon, A., Small, J., & Czerniewicz, L. (2016). Learning through engagement: Moocs as an emergent form of provision. *Distance Education*, 37(2), 208–223. DOI: 10.1080/01587919.2016.1184400

Walpola, R., & Lucas, C. (2021). Reflective practice: The essential competency for health systems and healthcare practitioners during the COVID-19 pandemic. *Reflective Practice*, 22(2), 143–146. DOI: 10.1080/14623943.2020.1860925

Wang, X., Li, L., Tan, S. C., Yang, L., & Lei, J. (2023). Preparing for AI-enhanced education: Conceptualizing and empirically examining teachers' AI readiness. Computers in Human Behavior. e-tarjome.com

Wang, K., & Zhu, C. (2019). MOOC-based flipped learning in higher education: Students' participation, experience and learning performance. *International Journal of Educational Technology in Higher Education*, 16(1), 33. DOI: 10.1186/s41239-019-0163-0

Wang, W., Zhao, Y., Wu, Y. J., & Goh, M. (2023). Factors of dropout from MOOCs: A bibliometric review. [HTML]. *Library Hi Tech*, 41(2), 432–453. DOI: 10.1108/LHT-06-2022-0306

Ward, R., Crick, T., Davenport, J. H., Hanna, P., Hayes, A., Irons, A., Miller, K., Moller, F., Prickett, T., & Walters, J. (2023). Using Skills Profiling to Enable Badges and Micro-Credentials to be Incorporated into Higher Education Courses. *Journal of Interactive Media in Education, 2023*(1). DOI: 10.5334/jime.807

Wardat, Y., Tashtoush, M., AlAli, R., & Saleh, S. (2024). Artificial intelligence in education: Mathematics teachers' perspectives, practices and challenges. *Iraqi Journal for Computer Science and Mathematics*, 5(1), 60–77. DOI: 10.52866/ijcsm.2024.05.01.004

Webster, W. (n.d.). What is psychogenic segmentation? A beginner's guide. *Qualtrics*. https://www.qualtrics.com/experience-management/brand/psychographic-segmentation/

Weeraratne, B., & Chin, B. (2018). Can Khan Academy e-learning video tutorials improve mathematics achievement in Sri Lanka? *International Journal of Education and Development using Information and Communication Technology (IJEDICT), 14(*3), 93-112. https://files.eric.ed.gov/fulltext/EJ1201489.pdf

Weinberg, B. H. (1974). Bibliographic coupling: A review. *Information Storage and Retrieval, 10*(5), 189–196. https://doi.org/https://doi.org/10.1016/0020-0271(74)90058-8

Wen, D., & Lin, F. (2008). Ways and Means of Employing AI Technology in E-Learning Systems. *2008 Eighth IEEE International Conference on Advanced Learning Technologies*, 1005–1006. DOI: 10.1109/ICALT.2008.304

West, R. E., Newby, T., Cheng, Z., Erickson, A., & Clements, K. (2020). Acknowledging All Learning: Alternative, Micro, and Open Credentials. In *Handbook of Research in Educational Communications and Technology: Learning Design: Fifth Edition*. Springer International Publishing. DOI: 10.1007/978-3-030-36119-8_27

Wheelahan, L. & Moodie, G. (2021). Analysing micro-credentials in higher education: a Bernsteinian analysis. Journal of Curriculum Studies. tandfonline.com

Wheelahan, L. & Moodie, G. (2022). Gig qualifications for the gig economy: micro-credentials and the 'hungry mile'. Higher Education. springer.com

Wheelahan, L., & Moodie, G. (2021). Analysing micro-credentials in higher education: A Bernsteinian analysis. *Journal of Curriculum Studies*, 53(2), 212–228. DOI: 10.1080/00220272.2021.1887358

Wheelahan, L., & Moodie, G. (2021). Gig qualifications for the gig economy: Micro-credentials and the 'hungry mile'. *Higher Education*, 83(6), 1279–1295. DOI: 10.1007/s10734-021-00742-3 PMID: 34366441

Wheelahan, L., & Moodie, G. (2024). Analysing micro-credentials in higher education: a Bernsteinian analysis. In *Towards Powerful Educational Knowledge* (pp. 70–86). Routledge. DOI: 10.4324/9781032712802-6

White, S. (2021). Developing credit based micro-credentials for the teaching profession: An Australian descriptive case study. *Teachers and Teaching*, 27(7), 696–711. DOI: 10.1080/13540602.2021.2003324

WHO. (2021). *UN Decade of Healthy Ageing: plan of action 2021-2030.* Retrieved from https://cdn.who.int/media/docs/default-source/decade-of-healthy-ageing/decade-proposal-final-apr2020-en.pdf

Willems, J., Farley, H., & Campbell, C. (2019). The increasing significance of digital equity in higher education. *Australasian Journal of Educational Technology*, 35(6), 1–8. DOI: 10.14742/ajet.5996

Williams, D., & Finlayson, J. (2023). Canada faces 40 years of stagnant incomes – government economic strategy is failing. *Globe and Mail, September 12th*. https://www.theglobeandmail.com/business/commentary/article-canada-economic-growth-strategy/

Williams, P. (2023). AI, Analytics and a New Assessment Model for Universities. Education Sciences. mdpi.com

Williamson, B., & Hogan, A. (2021). Pandemic privatisation in higher education: Edtech and university reform. qut.edu.au

Wolstenholme, E. F. (2003). Towards the definition and use of a core set of archetypal structures in system dynamics. *System Dynamics Review*, 19(1), 7–26. DOI: 10.1002/sdr.259

Wong, B. T. (2021). A survey on the pedagogical features of language massive open online courses. *Asian Association of Open Universities Journal*, 16(1), 116–128. DOI: 10.1108/AAOUJ-03-2021-0028

Wong, J., Baars, M., de Koning, B. B., & Paas, F. (2021). Examining the use of prompts to facilitate self-regulated learning in Massive Open Online Courses. *Computers in Human Behavior*, 115, 106596. DOI: 10.1016/j.chb.2020.106596

Woods, K., & Woods, J. A. (2023). Less Is More: Exploring the Value of Micro-Credentials Within a Graduate Program. *The Journal of Continuing Higher Education*, 71(2), 215–223. DOI: 10.1080/07377363.2021.1966923

World Economic Forum. (2020). *The Future of Jobs Report 2020.* Switzerland: World Economic Forum.

Wu, L., Hsieh, P. J., & Wu, S. M. (2022). Developing effective e-learning environments through e-learning use mediating technology affordance and constructivist learning aspects for performance impacts…. [HTML]. *The Internet and Higher Education*, 55, 100871. DOI: 10.1016/j.iheduc.2022.100871

Wu, X., Hall, A., & Wang, Q. (2019). Investigating the implementation of accredited massive online open courses (moocs) in higher education: The boon and the bane. *Australasian Journal of Educational Technology*, 35(3). Advance online publication. DOI: 10.14742/ajet.3896

Xie, B., Liu, H., Alghofaili, R., Zhang, Y., Jiang, Y., Lobo, F. D., Li, C., Li, W., Huang, H., Akdere, M., Mousas, C., & Yu, L. F. (2021). A review on virtual reality skill training applications. [frontiersin.org]. *Frontiers in Virtual Reality*, 2, 645153. DOI: 10.3389/frvir.2021.645153

Xin, X., Shu-Jiang, Y., Nan, P., ChenXu, D., & Dan, L. (2022). Review on A big data-based innovative knowledge teaching evaluation system in universities. Journal of innovation & knowledge, 7(3), 100197. sciencedirect.com

Xin, Y. & Corpuz, G. V. (2024). The challenge of labor education in higher vocational colleges. Frontiers in Educational Research. francis-press.com

Xu, Y., Liu, X., Cao, X., Huang, C., Liu, E., Qian, S., ... & Zhang, J. (2021). Artificial intelligence: A powerful paradigm for scientific research. The Innovation, 2(4). cell.com

Yanek, J. J. (2020). Digital Badges: A Study of K-12 Educators' Degree of Exposure to 21st Century Skills Developed through Micro-Credentials. [HTML]

Yang, B. (2022). An empirical study on the application of machine learning for higher education and social service. *Journal of Global Information Management*, 30(7), 1–16. DOI: 10.4018/JGIM.296723

Yılık, M. A. (2021). Micro-credentials, Higher Education and Career Development: Perspectives of University Students. *Higher Education Governance and Policy*, 2(2), 126–139.

Yilmaz, H., & Yanık, S. (2022). Prioritization of Factors Affecting Sustainability of Distance Education in Higher Education Institutions. International Graduate Research Symposium - IGRS'22, (1-3 June).

Yilmaz, H., Karadayi-Usta, S., & Yanık, S. (2022). A novel neutrosophic AHP-Copeland approach for distance education: Towards sustainability. *Interactive Learning Environments*, 1–23. DOI: 10.1080/10494820.2022.2141265

Yilmaz, H., Karadayi-Usta, S., Yanik, S., & Kahraman, C. (2024). Decision process: A stakeholder-oriented video conferencing software selection in sustainable distance education. In *Decision-Making Models* (pp. 19–46). Academic Press.

Yilmaz, R., Yurdugül, H., Yilmaz, F. G. K., Şahin, M., Sulak, S., Aydin, F., & Ömer, O. R. A. L. (2022). Smart MOOC integrated with intelligent tutoring: A system architecture and framework model proposal. [sciencedirect.com]. *Computers and Education: Artificial Intelligence*, 3, 100092. DOI: 10.1016/j.caeai.2022.100092

Yokutkhon, R. (2024). The use of virtual reality and augmented reality in education. *Journal of new century innovations, 48*(1), 157-161.

Young, D., West, R. E., & Nylin, T. A. (2019). Value of Open Microcredentials to Earners and Issuers: A Case Study of National Instruments Open Badges. *International Review of Research in Open and Distance Learning*, 20(5), 104–121. DOI: 10.19173/irrodl.v20i5.4345

Yu, H., Miao, C., Leung, C., & White, T. J. (2017). Towards AI-powered personalization in MOOC learning. In *npj Science of Learning* (Vol. 2, Issue 1). Springer Nature. DOI: 10.1038/s41539-017-0016-3

Yu, S. & Lu, Y. (2021). An introduction to artificial intelligence in education. [HTML]

Yuan, L. (2024). Where does AI-driven Education, in the Chinese Context and Beyond, go next? *International Journal of Artificial Intelligence in Education*, 34(1), 31–41. DOI: 10.1007/s40593-023-00341-6

Yu, D.-Y., Zhang, L., Li, Y.-L., Lan, T., Gu, L.-N., & Yang, S.-S. (2024). The implementation of a MOOC-based flipped classroom teaching method in the context of oncology radiotherapy residency training. *Journal of Cancer Education*. DOI: 10.1007/s13187-024-02513-x PMID: 39369377

Yu, L., & Yu, Z. (2023). Qualitative and quantitative analyses of artificial intelligence ethics in education using VOSviewer and CitNetExplorer. *Frontiers in Psychology*, 14, 1061778. DOI: 10.3389/fpsyg.2023.1061778 PMID: 36968737

Zainuddin, Z., & Halili, S. (2016). Flipped Classroom Research and Trends from Different Fields of Study. *International Review of Research in Open and Distance Learning*, 17(3), 313–340. DOI: 10.19173/irrodl.v17i3.2274

Zakharova, I., & Jarke, J. (2022). Educational technologies as matters of care. *Learning, Media and Technology*, 47(1), 95–108.

Zamiri, M., & Esmaeili, A. (2024). Strategies, methods, and supports for developing skills within learning communities: A systematic review of the literature. *Administrative Sciences*, 14(9), 231. Advance online publication. DOI: 10.3390/admsci14090231

Zawacki-Richter, O., Marín, V. I., Bond, M., & Gouverneur, F. (2019). Systematic review of research on artificial intelligence applications in higher education – where are the educators? *International Journal of Educational Technology in Higher Education*, 16(1), 39. DOI: 10.1186/s41239-019-0171-0

Zhai, X., Chu, X., Chai, C. S., Jong, M. S. Y., Istenic, A., Spector, M., Liu, J.-B., Yuan, J., & Li, Y. (2021). A Review of Artificial Intelligence (AI) in Education from 2010 to 2020. [wiley.com]. *Complexity*, 2021(1), 8812542. DOI: 10.1155/2021/8812542

Zhang, G. (2024). Optimization and application of english word memory algorithm based on reinforcement learning. jes, 20(6s), 1786-1799. https://doi.org/DOI: 10.52783/jes.3096

Zhang, X., & Tobias, T. C. R. (2023). Exploring the Efficacy of Adaptive Learning Technologies in Online Education: A Longitudinal Analysis of Student Engagement and Performance. *International Journal of Science and Engineering Applications*. DOI: 10.7753/IJSEA1212.1007

Zhang, H., Lee, I., & Moore, K. (2024). An Effectiveness Study of Teacher-Led AI Literacy Curriculum in K-12 Classrooms. *Proceedings of the AAAI Conference on Artificial Intelligence*, 38(21), 23318–23325. DOI: 10.1609/aaai.v38i21.30380

Zhang, J., & West, R. E. (2020). Designing microlearning instruction for professional development through a competency-based approach. *TechTrends*, 64(3), 310–318. DOI: 10.1007/s11528-019-00449-4

Zhang, K., & Aslan, A. B. (2021). AI technologies for education: Recent research & future directions. *Computers and Education: Artificial Intelligence*, 2, 100025. DOI: 10.1016/j.caeai.2021.100025

Zhang, L., Xuan, Y., & Zhang, H. (2020). Construction and application of SPOC-based flipped classroom teaching mode in Installation Engineering Cost curriculum based on OBE concept. *Computer Applications in Engineering Education*, 28(6), 1503–1519. DOI: 10.1002/cae.22320

Zhang, P., Ma, S., Zhao, Y., Ling, J., & Sun, Y. (2024). Analysing influencing factors and correlation paths of learning burnout among secondary vocational students in the context of social media: An integrated ISM–MICMAC approach. *Heliyon*, 10(7), e28696. Advance online publication. DOI: 10.1016/j.heliyon.2024.e28696 PMID: 38586410

Zhang, W. E., Sheng, Q. Z., Alhazmi, A., & Li, C. (2020). Adversarial attacks on deep-learning models in natural language processing: A survey. [TIST]. *ACM Transactions on Intelligent Systems and Technology*, 11(3), 1–41. DOI: 10.1145/3374217

Zhang, X., Liu, C., Chai, K., & Poslad, S. (2020). A challenge-response assisted authorisation scheme for data access in permissioned blockchains. *Sensors (Basel)*, 20(17), 4681. DOI: 10.3390/s20174681 PMID: 32825194

Zou, H., Ullah, A., Qazi, Z., Naeem, A., & Rehan, S. (2024). Impact of micro-credential learning on students' perceived employability: The mediating role of human capital. *International Journal of Educational Management*, 38(4), 897–915. https://doi.org/10.1108/IJEM-01-2023-0002

Zyda, M. (2005). From Visual Simulation to Virtual Reality to Games. *Computer*, 38(9), 25–32. DOI: 10.1109/MC.2005.297

About the Contributors

Gurhan Durak is a Professor of Instructional Technologies at Balikesir University. Dr. Durak gained his Ph.D. in Distance Education at Anadolu University. His academic interest areas are open and distance learning, Generative Artificial Intelligence, Learning analytics, virtual reality, Metaverse in education, social learning networks, support services in distance education, online learning, and administration of distance education. He has authored over 60 articles, book contributions, books, and editorials, and is a Chief Editor of the Journal of Educational Technology and Online Learning, as well as a member of the Editorial Boards of other international journals.

Serkan Çankaya is Associate Prof. Dr. in the Department of Management Information Systems at İzmir Democracy University. Dr. Çankaya received an M.S. degree in the Computer Education & Instructional Technology Department at Balıkesir University. He gained his Ph.D. in Computer Education & Instructional Technology Department at Anadolu University at June 2013. His academic interest areas are artificial intelligence(ai) in education, generative ai, open and distance learning, virtual reality, metaverse in education, social learning networks, support services in distance education, online learning, and administration of distance education. He has authored over 50 articles, book contributions, books, and editorials, and is a Chief Editor of the International Journal of Computers in Education, as well as a member of the Editorial Boards of other international journals.

* * *

Mohamed Ally is Professor of Online and Distance Education and Researcher in the Technology Enhanced Knowledge Research Institute (TEKRI) at Athabasca University in Canada. He is also a Commonwealth of Learning Research Chair. Dr. Ally was the Director of the School of Computing and Information Systems and the Centre for Distance Education at Athabasca University. He obtained his Ph.D. from the University of Alberta, Canada. His current areas of research include mobile learning, e-learning, distance education, augmented reality, virtual reality, mixed reality, and the use of emerging fourth industrial revolution technologies (4IR) in education and training. Dr. Ally was President of the International Federation of Training and Development Organizations (IFTDO) and is one of the Founding Directors of the International Association of Mobile Learning (IamLearn) and the International Association of Blended Learning (IABL). He recently edited 17 books on the use of emerging technologies in education. His book "Mobile Learning: Transforming the Delivery of Education and Training" won the Charles A. Wedemeyer Award in the United States for significant contribution to distance education. Dr. Ally has presented keynote speeches, papers, and workshops in many countries.

Ashar was born in Bune Village, Libureng District, Bone Regency, South Sulawesi, on August 15, 1983. He is the second of four children born to H. Arif and Hj. Dawiah. He completed his primary education at SD Negeri 180 Bune in 1995, his secondary education at SMP Negeri 1 Libureng in 1998, and graduated from Madrasah Aliyah Negeri 1 Kajuara Lappariaja in 2001. In 2002, Ashar pursued higher education at Universitas Negeri Makassar, where he enrolled in the Faculty of Engineering, majoring in Automotive Engineering Education, and earned a bachelor's degree in Education in 2007. He continued his academic journey by undertaking a Master's program in Educational Administration with a specialization in Early Childhood Education (PAUD) at Universitas Negeri Makassar in 2008. Currently, he is pursuing doctoral studies in Islamic Studies, with a concentration in Education and Teaching, at Universitas Islam Negeri (UIN) Alauddin Makassar, a program he commenced in 2021. Since 2014, Ashar has been serving as a permanent faculty member at the Early Childhood Education (PAUD) Program within the Faculty of Teacher Training, Education, and Literature (FKIPS) at Universitas Islam Makassar (UIM), Al-Gazali, where he continues his academic contributions to this day.

Andi Asrifan, S.Pd, M.Pd, a distinguished figure in the realm of education, particularly in English Language Education, has made significant contributions through his extensive research, teaching, and leadership roles. As the Head of the Institute for Cooperation and International Affairs at Universitas Muhammadiyah Sidenreng Rappang, Dr. Asrifan's academic journey is marked by a rich tapestry of achievements, including a Doctor of Education in English Language Education. His work spans various facets of education, language, and technology, reflecting the diverse topics covered in his publications and research endeavors. These include, but are not limited to, the impact of the COVID-19 pandemic on educational practices, methodologies in English as a Foreign Language (EFL) classrooms, and the integration of technology in teaching and learning processes. Dr. Asrifan's commitment to advancing educational standards and practices is further evidenced by his active participation in international conferences, webinars, and workshops across countries like India, the Philippines, and Pakistan. These events, organized by various institutions and associations, underscore his role as a global educator and thought leader. His dedication to professional development is also highlighted through his involvement in numerous courses and certifications in personal branding, public speaking, and literacy teaching. Moreover, Dr. Asrifan's leadership extends beyond academia into organizational and educational development, where he has served in various capacities, including as an external examiner for Ph.D. dissertations and a reviewer for scientific journals. His accolades, memberships in professional organizations, and roles as an ambassador for international associations speak volumes of his influence and commitment to fostering educational excellence and sustainable development goals globally.

Amine Hatun Ataş holds a Ph.D. in Computer Education and Instructional Technology, reflecting her expertise in leveraging technology for educational advancement. Currently, affiliated with Galatasaray University. She integrates her academic insights at the Center of Distance Education, Application and Research, contributing to both research and educational practices within the institution. Dr. Ataş's research interests revolve around learning, technology, and instructional design. Her current focus areas include Artificial Intelligence, Computer-Supported Collaborative Learning (CSCL), E-learning, and the impact of smartphone addiction on especially higher education settings. Through her work, she seeks to explore innovative ways of utilizing technology to enhance learning experiences.

Aras Bozkurt is a researcher and faculty member at Anadolu University, Türkiye. With MA and PhD degrees in distance education, Dr. Bozkurt's work focuses on empirical studies in areas such as distance education, online learning, networked learning, and educational technology. He applies critical theories like connectivism, rhizomatic learning, and heutagogy to his research. Dr. Bozkurt is also interested in emerging research paradigms, including social network analysis, sentiment analysis, and data mining. Dr. Bozkurt's studies also cover the integration of artificial intelligence technologies into educational processes in the axis of human-machine interaction. His dedication to advancing the field is reflected in his editorial roles as the Editor-in-Chief of Open Praxis and Asian Journal of Distance Education, as well as his roles as an associate editor for prestigious journals like

Higher Education Research and Development, Online Learning, eLearn Magazine, and Computer Applications in Engineering Education.

Isabel Chumbo is an assistant professor at the Polytechnic University of Bragança. She holds a PhD in Translation Studies and her research interests are in the field of translation and intercultural studies. She has been involved in several European projects related to the improvement of teaching in higher education through digital technologies.

Harun Cigdem, PhD, is currently an assistant professor at the Department of Computer Technology, National Defence University. His research interests involve e-learning applications, self-regulated learning, student engagement, the design and implementation of e-learning/blended learning environments along with effective and interactive use of ICT in educational settings.

Toni Clayton is the Executive Director at SNHU's Global Campus, Dr. Toni Clayton leads the efforts of Academic Programs and Health Professions with a focus on organizational effectiveness and efficiency, creating effective partnerships, leading strategic change & initiatives, and cultivating engaging learner experiences. She serves as Vice-Chair of Global Campus IRB, is a Certified Professional Coach, Healthcare Economist, and Lean Six Sigma Black Belt. Dr. Clayton embodies the principle that teamwork leads to results-oriented work groups that drive the organization to fulfill its mission of learner transformation. This work is reflected through the creation of the first healthcare microcredential developed in 2020 and the award-winning experiential-learning Higher Education and Real-World Training (HEaRT) model launched in 2018. Dr. Clayton earned her doctorate from Capella University, MBA from Indiana Wesleyan University, and bachelor's from Indiana University. In 2023, Clayton was presented the Leadership Award by the Association of Continuing Higher Education (ACHE) for extraordinary contributions in leadership, theory, and practice in continuing higher education on a national level. She also received the 2022 WCET Outstanding Work (WOW) Award, 2021 ACHE Distinguished Non-Credit Program Award, 2021 D2L Excellence Award, 2020 University Professional and Continuing Education Association's (UPCEA) Excellent in Engagement, and 2020 Online Learning Consortium (OLC) Effective Practice Award. Outside of her professional work, she enjoys building parade floats, kayaking, and volunteering with the local Veterans of Foreign War (VFW). Connect with her on..

Merve Çolakoğlu has a master's degree in Computer Education and Instructional Technology at Balıkesir University. Her research interests include STEM education, student engagement, artificial intelligence and learning analytics in education.

Clifford De Raffaele was conferred an electrical engineering degree from the University of Malta, a Masters in ICT from the department of Computer and Communications Engineering and a Ph.D. in Computer Science from Middlesex University. Dr. Ing. De Raffaele held senior management roles in Higher Education, whereby he served as the Associate Director for Academia and Research at Middlesex University Malta, and recently held the post of Director for Research and Innovation at the Malta College for Arts, Science and Technology, whereby he was responsible for leading all research and innovation initiatives stemming across the organization as well as setting the strategic direction of MCAST towards pursuing research opportunities. Following his management career, he undertook a more active role in academia and currently holds a senior lecturing position in computer science at Middlesex University. Dr. Ing. De Raffaele has participated in numerous national and EU funded research projects in the capacity of collaborating partner, lead researcher and principal investigator. He serves on various strategic boards at national level on academia and research and is currently an executive member of the IEEE Malta Section. His current research interests include Biomedical Devices, Innovative User Interfaces, Image/Video Processing and Emerging Technologies.

D.Joel Jebadurai working as Associate Professor in Department of MBA, St.Joseph's college of Engineering, OMR, Chennai, Tamil Nadu, India. He has published more than 50 research articles for his credit.

Erniati, S.Pd., M.Pd., is a dedicated lecturer with a strong background in Indonesian language and literature education. She earned her Bachelor's degree in Indonesian Language Education from Universitas Muhammadiyah Makassar in 2009 and completed her Master's degree at Universitas Negeri Makassar in 2012. Currently, Erniati serves as a permanent lecturer at Universitas Islam Makassar, where she teaches various subjects, including scientific writing, Indonesian language skills, and research methodology. Her extensive teaching experience also includes working as an external lecturer at multiple institutions, such as AKPER and ATEM Muhammadiyah Makassar. In addition to her teaching responsibilities, Erniati is actively involved in research, with studies focusing on enhancing students' skills in reading, writing, and speaking Indonesian, utilizing innovative techniques like media flipbooks and discovery learning. She has presented at numerous national seminars and contributed to community service projects aimed at improving literacy and language skills in schools across Makassar. Erniati's commitment to education extends beyond the classroom, as she regularly participates in professional development activities and contributes to curriculum development initiatives that integrate Islamic values with modern educational practices. Her dedication to fostering language proficiency and critical thinking skills in her students underscores her role as a pivotal figure in the academic community.

Ana Galvão is a senior full professor in the area of health sciences at the Polytechnic University of Bragança. She is also a health and clinical psychologist, labour and organizational psychologist, a specialist in psychological coaching by the Portuguese Order of Psychologysts. Apart from that she is a member of the LiveWell - *Research Center for Active Living and Wellbeing.*

Analisa Hamdan is an Award-winning innovative educator, and Scopus-indexed manuscript reviewer with a passion for teaching and learning, research, and publications. A highly motivated and results-oriented educator with a proven track record of success. I am skilled in designing and delivering engaging and effective instruction to a variety of learners, including those with special needs and young children. I am also experienced in learning experience design, e-learning, information technology, multimodal instruction, instructional design, pedagogy, and curriculum development. A member of the Pertubuhan Pembangunan Penyelidikan dan Dasar Pendidikan Tinggi Malaysia (PenDaPaT), the Qualitative Research Association of Malaysia, the International Association for Mobile Learning (IAMLearn), and the Mobile Learning Association of Malaysia.

Sehar un Nisa Hassan, Ph.D. currently working as an Associate Prof. at the College of Public Health and Health Informatics. I have over 18 years of experience in the higher education sector, conducting academic research and publications. My current level of professional competencies and experiences are useful for the adaptation, and improvement of the curriculum for graduate and post-graduate programs necessary to reduce the challenge of skills gaps in Saudi population. My recent trainings and preferences for use of AI tools in education and research align with the current trends in academia. Moreover, I am involved in delivery of higher education and thus keen in exploring and addressing psychological, social, and environmental factors that may impact student learning processes and performance. Few of my research projects focuses on investigating psychological, cognitive and emotional correlates of online educational experiences. The use of technology and online education is both current and future trends in the education sector. Currently, I am working on projects that focus upon leveraging artificial intelligence to enhance the creation, delivery, and assessment in the field of education.

Eugénia Maria Garcia Jorge Anes is an assistant professor at the Polytechnic University of Bragança. She lectures several subjects in the school of health sciences and is a member of the LiveWell - *Research Center for Active Living and Wellbeing.*

Michail Kalogiannakis is an Associate Professor in the Department of Special Education, at University of Thessaly in Greece and an Associate Tutor at School of Humanities at the Hellenic Open University. He graduated from the Physics Department of the University of Crete and continued his post-graduate studies at the University Paris 7-Denis Diderot (D.E.A. in Didactic of Physics), University Paris 5-René Descartes-Sorbonne (D.E.A. in Science Education) and received his Ph.D degree at the University Paris 5-René Descartes-Sorbonne (PhD in Science Education). His research interests include: science education in early childhood, science teaching and learning, e-learning, the use of ICT in science education, distant and adult education and mobile learning. He has published over 200 articles in international conferences and journals, and has served on the program committees of numerous international conferences. Google Scholar citations.

Şeyda Kır, is an instructor at Yozgat Bozok University and a PhD candidate in the Department of Distance Education at Anadolu University. She graduated from Anadolu University, Distance Education Department Master's Program in 2019. Her research interests are MOOCs, OERs, micro-credentials, open pedagogy, lifelong learning, adult education, and open and distance learning.

Jonathan JS Kovilpillai is a seasoned educator with over two decades of teaching experience, primarily associated with Asia Pacific University (APU), Kuala Lumpur, as the Program Manager for the Digital Leading Hub. He exhibits exceptional administrative acumen, proficiently managing projects and programmes. His innovative curriculum development strategies cater to various learning styles, ensuring enhanced student understanding. Known for conducting valuable workshops and training sessions, Jonathan's initiatives have significantly increased technology transformation among APU academic staff. Jonathan is currently pursuing his PhD in digital learning transformation.

M. Soundarya is an Assistant Professor, School of Management studies, Sathyabama Institute of Science and Technology, Chennai. She has Completed the Doctorate in Full time from the Department of Bank Management, Alagappa University, Karaikudi. She has done MBA, MBA (Marketing), M.Phil, B.Com.,CA, PGDVAT & Service Tax from Alagappa University. Her area of specialization is Banking, Insurance, Credit Management and Marketing. She has been Worked as Guest Lecture in the Department of Bank Management, Alagappa University. She has a five years research experience and one year teaching experience. She has published more than sixty Journals in various reputed journals in Scopus, UGC Care Listed, ABDC Category Journals and Peer reviewed Journals. She is strong in SPPS and AMOS. Honored with Best Faculty Award on December 2023 in

Knowledge Research Academy in Coimbatore. She acted as resource person for various institutions

Thirupathi Manickam, M.Com, M.Phil, B.Ed, TN-SET, KSET, Ph.D., works as an Assistant professor in the Department of Professional Studies at CHRIST (Deemed To Be University), Bangalore. It is one of the leading institutions in Bangalore, Karnataka, and the institution is Accredited by NIRF, NBA and NAAC Accredited university. He has more than seven years of teaching and Research experience. He has 67 citations and four h-Index. He has published 25 research papers in Scopus, Web of Science, UGC-CARE, and UGC-approved and leading international journals, and 14 presented papers at national and international conferences. He has also participated in over 40 seminars, conferences, FDP & workshops at the National and International Levels. His areas of expertise are Financial Accounting, Corporate Accounting, Financial Management, Management Accounting, Taxation, Digital Marketing and Technology Management.

Kelly McKenna is an associate professor in the Adult Education and Training graduate program in the School of Education at Colorado State University. She is a Fulbright Scholar, past Presidential Leadership Fellow, Faculty Institute for Inclusive Excellence Mentor, and repeat Global Teaching Scholar with Semester at Sea. She completed her Ph.D. in educational technology and earned a master's degree in education and human resource studies with a specialization in Adult Education and Training. Dr. McKenna has been the recipient of multiple teaching awards and has experience with face-to-face, blended, and online instruction. Her scholarship is within the field of adult and higher education, with research objectives aimed to support lifelong learners in their educational and occupational endeavors by creating optimal learning environments and facilitating successful experiences for all learners. She focuses on distance education with attention to technology enhanced teaching and learning and online learning communities.

Siti Haslina Md Harizan is a Senior Lecturer at the School of Distance Education, Universiti Sains Malaysia. She holds a PhD in Strategic Marketing and an MBA from Universiti Sains Malaysia, along with a B.Tech (Hons.) in Information System from Universiti Teknologi PETRONAS. With extensive experience in marketing, green marketing, and consumer behavior, Dr. Siti has contributed significantly to sustainable marketing and distance education. Her research has been published in various international journals, and she has presented at numerous conferences globally. Dr. Siti is also actively involved in professional organizations, including the Institute of Marketing Malaysia and the International

Islamic Marketing Association. She is dedicated to integrating sustainability in distance education and exploring the impact of technology on learning.

Stephen John Murgatroyd (born 31 October 1950, Bradford, Yorkshire, England) is a writer, broadcaster and consultant. Murgatroyd was educated at St. Bede's Grammar School and University College Cardiff, where in 1972 he graduated with honors with a bachelor of arts in research methodology. After graduating, he became a special needs teacher in Cwmbran, Wales. He also became a tutor with the Open University of the United Kingdom. A year later he became a full-time research fellow with the Open University, directing its first major longitudinal study of adult learners. He later became senior counsellor at the Open University in Wales. In 1983 he received a master's of philosophy from the Open University of the UK. It was around this time that Murgatroyd became associate editor of the British Journal of Guidance and Counselling and a founding board member of the British Psychological Society's Counseling Psychology section – all of which earned him a fellowship in the British Psychological Society in 1985. He earned his doctorate in 1987, also from the Open University. In 1986, Murgatroyd became a dean at Athabasca University. Later, he became the first executive director of the Centre for Innovative Management, home of the world's first on-line executive MBA – a programme he managed from 1993 to 1997. This work resulted in an honorary doctorate in "e-learning" from Athabasca University in 2000. In 1998 he left the Athabasca to join Axia NetMedia Corporation, where he helped develop a non-profit master's degree programme offered in association with Middlesex University, where he is a visiting professor. He returned to Athabasca University in 2003, where he served as executive director for external relations until May 2005. He is now Chief Scout of the Innovation Expedition and Principal of Murgatroyd Communications & Consulting Inc. He works extensively with governments, companies and not for profit organizations. He has written and published 25 books (including two bibliographies), three pamphlets, 30 chapters in edited works, 49 peer reviewed papers in academic journals, 44 contributions to journals and magazines (including reviews) and [twenty, fifty five] journalistic pieces in newspapers and magazines since 1972. He was elected a Fellow of the Royal Society for the encouragement of Arts, Manufactures and Commerce (RSA) (UK) in 2009. He has been active in the non-profit sector, as a former board member of the Galileo Educational Network, trustee of the Alberta Heritage Community Foundation, Chair of the Human Resources Committee of Alberta Ballet and one of the founders of the Alberta Council of Technologies. He currently serves as a Director of Energy Futures Network. He is married with two adult sons and currently lives in Edmonton, Alberta, Canada.

Jusmaniar Nonci is an experienced educator and academic leader with a strong background in English education and curriculum development. She earned her Bachelor's and Master's degrees in English Education from Universitas Negeri Makassar, Indonesia, and has held various academic roles, including Head of the English Education Study Program at Universitas Islam Makassar (UIM) and Secretary of the ASEAN and South East Study Centre at the same institution. Jusmaniar is also actively involved in research, focusing on innovative teaching methods and literacy improvement. Her published works include studies on teaching English literacy to students with disabilities and the use of technology to enhance student learning experiences. In addition to her academic roles, Jusmaniar serves as an assessor for the National Accreditation Board of Indonesian Schools and has facilitated numerous training programs for teachers and headmasters, aimed at improving education quality. She has been recognized with several awards for her contributions to curriculum development and research by the Indonesian Ministry of Education and Culture. With extensive experience in both teaching and leadership, Jusmaniar continues to impact the field of education through her dedication to improving learning outcomes and fostering educational innovation in Indonesia.

Semiral Öncü, PhD, is currently an assistant professor at the Department of Educational Sciences, Instructional Technologies Program, Balikesir University. His research interests involve student engagement, the design and implementation of e-learning/blended learning environments along with effective and interactive use of ICT in educational settings.

Fahd Raza is an established academic and researcher with worldwide exposure in diverse fields. He is passionately enthusiastic about Generative AI. Fahd also has extensive experience in academic organizations of all dimensions in diverse roles, with an established record of technological advisory and implementation follow through, teaching, editorial, and strategic management; and enriching policy and operational efficiency as synergistic tools for organizational excellence.

Stacey Rosenberg currently serves as the Associate Chief Nursing Administrator at Southern New Hampshire University (SNHU), and the Secondary Nurse Planner for the American Nurses Credentialing Center (ANCC) Nursing Continuing Professional Development Unit. Her nursing career began with an Associate Degree of Science-Nursing, followed by a Bachelor of Science Degree in Nursing. She later earned her Master of Science Degree in Nursing, specializing in Nurse Education and Adult Health Clinical Nurse Specialist and a Doctor of Nursing Practice. As a Board-Certified Adult Health Clinical Nurse Specialist (ACNS-BC) and a Certified Nurse Educator (CNE), Stacey brings extensive clinical experience in acute and skilled care, along with expertise in employee, community, and public health. With over two decades in academia, she has imparted her knowledge through online, hybrid, and face-to-face modalities across various educational levels. Dr. Rosenberg's contributions extend beyond the classroom, encompassing roles in administration, curriculum and program development, and accreditation. Her leadership in both higher education and continuing education reflects a commitment to addressing the evolving needs of learners. Her focus areas include emerging credentials, flexible learning models, and global health initiatives. Additionally, Dr. Rosenberg is a co-chair and co-creator of the acclaimed Higher Education and Real-World Training (HEaRT) experiential learning model and SNHU's first microcredential. Recognized for her excellence, she also serves as an international speaker, emphasizing Nursing Education in her presentations. Dr. Rosenberg remains dedicated to shaping the future of nursing education and healthcare through her multifaceted contributions. Connect with her on LinkedIn.

S.Krishnakumari is employed as an Assistant Professor in the School of Management Studies, Sathyabama Institute of Science and Technology, Chennai. She had completed MBA from MepcoSchlenk Engineering College specialized with HR and Systems during 2005 and M.H.R.M during 2007. Awarded Ph.D in Management from the Mother Teresa Women's University, Kodaikanal in 2017. She started her career in the field of HR and then switched towards teaching since 2006. She is passionate in teaching with 18 years of experience, administering education and classroom procedures by fostering academic development. she had also completed M.Sc. Psychology and professionally trained in the areas of Mentoring and Leadership. She effectively organizes several training programmes on Personality & Self Development for the students and faculty. She had won the prestigious Dr.Lilavathi Award from AICTE, India during March 2022, and also various awards such as Outstanding Mentor Award for the year 2020 and the Best Teacher Award from Cape Forum You Trust. She had published several research papers in both National and International Journals and also associated as editorial member in few publications. She had authored and published books on the titles such as Marketing Management and Customer Relationship Management and Managerial Economics. She is also associated with several professional bodies like CII, MMA, etc for supporting the academic activities.

Sadaruddin was born in Bone on June 15, 1980. He is a dedicated lecturer in the Early Childhood Education Teacher Training Program at the Faculty of Teacher Training and Education, Universitas Islam Makassar. He also serves as a tutor at the Open University (UPBJJT) and as an adjunct lecturer at Universitas Negeri Makassar and Universitas Islam Negeri Alauddin Makassar. Sadaruddin holds a Bachelor's degree in Automotive Engineering Education from Universitas Negeri Makassar, a Master's degree in Early Childhood Education Administration from the same university, and a Doctorate in Educational Sciences. His professional experience includes roles such as Head of Administration at the Regional Distribution Center of the Ministry of Trade and Industry, Business Development Manager at Kospermindo, and local consultant for various international projects. He has actively contributed to the academic community as an assessor for the National Accreditation Board for Early Childhood and Non-Formal Education, and as a member of the editorial boards for several journals. His research focuses on early childhood education, and he has published numerous articles and presented at national and international conferences. Sadaruddin's dedication to education and his extensive experience in teaching, research, and administration highlight his commitment to advancing the field of early childhood education.

Trisno Setiawan, M.Pd., is an accomplished educator with a strong background in physics education, holding both a Bachelor's and Master's degree in Physics Education from Universitas Mataram and Universitas Negeri Malang, respectively. He is currently serving as a lecturer at Universitas Negeri Makassar, contributing to the Physics Education program in the Faculty of Mathematics and Natural Sciences (MIPA). His extensive experience spans multiple teaching and leadership roles, including serving as a PPPK trainer for various institutions, including the Social Services Departments of Lombok Barat and Mataram, and as a coach for scholastic and psychological tests for candidates in governmental and police services. Beyond his teaching roles, Trisno has also worked in project coordination, having served as the Coordinator for Data and Reporting at the Lombok Barat Disaster Management Agency (BPBD) and the National Disaster Management Agency (BNPB), where he oversaw recovery efforts following natural disasters. Active in professional organizations and educational initiatives, he has participated in numerous national and international seminars, including the International Conference on Halal Tourism and the 26th International Conference on Teaching, Education, and Learning (ICTEL). His work reflects a deep commitment to advancing education and supporting community development in Indonesia.

Abtar Kaur Singh has more than 30 years of teaching and leadership experience at various learning institutions. She is an alumnus of University of Malaya (PhD), Syracuse University (MS Instructional Design) and Indiana University (Post-Doctoral Fulbright). She was attached to the Ministry of Education (Malaysia) before she joined the University of Malaya as a lecturer and Chief Instructional Designer, Open University Malaysia as Director for Centre of Instructional Design and Technology and later as Deputy Dean of Post Graduate Studies, and as Dean of School of E-Education, Hamdan Bin Mohammed Smart University (Dubai). She has provided consultancy and training under the auspices of World Bank, UNESCO, the UNDP, and the Commonwealth of Learning (COL) to educators worldwide. Her more recent e-learning project was for the Kingdom of Saudi Arabia. She is on several journals and advisory boards, and her recent appointments include the following: Asian Representative for the International Council of Badges and Credentials (ICoBC) and International Advisory Board member of the International Journal of Educational Technology in Higher Education (ETHE). Prof Abtar has published widely in international journals, books, and book chapters and has won numerous international awards related to e-learning. She was the winner of the coveted International Competition on Innovative University Practices in ICT in Education, a competition organized by the UNESCO Institute for Information Technologies in Education (UNESCO IITE) in St. Petersburg, Russia, in 2015. A Fulbright scholar, she has been closely involved in the research, teaching, and development of technological innovations in higher education in Malaysia and abroad. Her research is focused on amongst others, how learning design can be affected in online, e- and mobile learning. Prof Abtar is currently looking into Next Generation Digital Learning Environments (NGDLE) and AI Technologies related to disruptive learning environments. Since 2022, Prof Abtar has held the prestigious position of the UNESCO Chair on Harnessing Innovations in Technology to Support Teachers & Quality Learning and was the first academic from a private university in Malaysia to be appointed to the prestigious position. As the UNESCO Chair, Prof. Dr. Abtar drives research, training and knowledge sharing initiatives on harnessing innovations in technology to support teachers and quality in teaching and learning in Malaysia as well as developing economies in Asia and around the world. This also includes equipping teachers and professionals in education with state-of-the-art knowledge and tools to enhance hybrid learning. She foster's collaboration among stakeholders in education and leverage technological innovations to promote inclusive education for everyone including girls and children as an integral part of UNESCO's wider Medium-Term Strategy and Sustainable Development Goal (SDG) to leverage education programmes to reduce poverty. Prof Abtar also conducts research and innovation to capitalize on disruptive technologies in the areas of the Fourth Industrial Revolution (IR4.0) such as artificial intelligence (AI), Internet of Things (IoT), and Big Data & Analytics to promote inclusive and equitable education for people in developing economies.

Seda Yanik currently works at Istanbul Technical University as an associate professor in Industrial Engineering Department. Her research interests include data analytics and machine learning, transportation/logistics modeling and optimization, and decision support systems. Dr. Seda Yanik has also been a visiting researcher at the Logistics & Discrete Optimization Department at Karlsruhe Institute of Technology in Germany, analyzing health-care demand and designing locational health-care services. Prior to joining academia in 2007, she worked for international companies SAP and Adidas.

Hakan Yıldırım is a senior lecturer at Eskişehir Osmangazi University, Türkiye. He received his B.A. in Computer Education and Instructional Technology from Anadolu University. He received his M.A. and Ph.D. degrees in the Department of Distance Education at Anadolu University respectively in 2017 and 2023. His research interests include blockchain technology, human-computer interaction, and learning management systems.

Hulya Yilmaz is a lecturer at the Quality Coordination Office of Kirklareli University. She is also currently continuing her Ph.D. in Industrial Engineering at the Istanbul Technical University. She received a master's degree in Industrial Engineering from the Istanbul Technical University in 2017. Before joining academia in 2019, she worked for the textile industry for about four years as a planning and quality specialist. Her research interests include quality control and management, multi-criteria decision-making, fuzzy decision making, and sustainability.

Soha Zoelfakar is a dedicated educator and researcher with expertise in higher education, vocational training, and professional development, committed to fostering transformative learning experiences and advancing educational excellence.

Index

A

B

C

D

E

F

G

H

I

J

L

M

N

O

P

R

S

T

U

V

W

www.ingramcontent.com/pod-product-compliance
Lightning Source LLC
LaVergne TN
LVHW080615300926
849162LV00005B/1165